SOLZHENITSYN

200 Years Together
Volume 1
The Jews before the Revolution

Aleksandr Solzhenitsyn
(1918–2008)

Aleksandr Solzhenitsyn was a Russian novelist, historian, and outspoken critic of Soviet totalitarianism. He is remembered as one of the most important writers and dissidents of the 20th century. His works provided a powerful and damning account of the Soviet Union's repressive system and have had a lasting impact on both literature and political thought. He was awarded the Nobel Prize in Literature in 1970 for the ethical force with which he pursued the indispensable traditions of Russian literature.

Two Hundred Years Together
Volume 1 — The Jews before the Revolution

Двести лет вместе, *Dvesti let vmeste—2001–2002*

Translated and published by
Omnia Veritas Limited

www.omnia-veritas.com

© Omnia Veritas Ltd - 2024

All rights reserved. No part of this publication may be reproduced, distributed, or transmitted in any form or by any means, including photocopying, recording, or other electronic or mechanical methods, without the prior written permission of the publisher, except in the case of brief quotations embodied in critical reviews and certain other noncommercial uses permitted by copyright law.

INTRODUCTION TO THE MATERIAL 11
ON THE PERIMETER OF THIS STUDY. WHAT COULD BE THE LIMITS OF THIS BOOK? 13
ABRIDGED MENTIONS OF THE MAIN SOURCES CITED IN NOTES BY THE AUTHOR 15

CHAPTER 1 17
BEFORE THE 19TH CENTURY 17
From the Beginnings in Khazaria 17
The Judaizing Heresy 23
The Kahal And Civil Rights 35
Derzhavin And The Belarus Famine 44

CHAPTER 2 56
DURING THE REIGN OF ALEXANDER IST 56

CHAPTER 3 88
DURING THE REIGN OF NICHOLAS IST 88

CHAPTER 4 121
IN THE AGE OF REFORMS 121

CHAPTER 5 165
AFTER THE MURDER OF ALEXANDER II 165

CHAPTER 6 190
IN THE RUSSIAN REVOLUTIONARY MOVEMENT 190

CHAPTER 7 228
THE BIRTH OF ZIONISM 228

CHAPTER 8 243
AT THE TURN OF THE 20TH CENTURY 243

CHAPTER 9 304
DURING THE REVOLUTION OF 1905 304

CHAPTER 10 373
THE PERIOD OF THE DUMA 373

CHAPTER 11 405

JEWS AND RUSSIANS BEFORE THE FIRST WORLD WAR: THE GROWING AWARENESS 405
CHAPTER 12 .... **426**
DURING THE WAR (1914-1916) 426
OTHER TITLES **459**

"The meaning of earthly existence lies not, as we have grown used to thinking, in prospering but in the development of the soul."

Introduction to the Material

Having worked with the history of the Russian revolution for fifty years, I have encountered many times the problems between the Russians and the Jews. Again and again they worked themselves into the happenings, drove a wedge into the human psyche and whipped up passions.

I did not lose hope that an author would beat me to the punch and bring forth, with the necessary amplitude and equilibrium, this bright spear. But we are dealing more often with one-sided reproaches: either the Russians are guilty against the Jews, worse, guilty of perpetual depravity, and rightly so; or, on the other hand, the Russians who have treated this problem rationally have done so for the most part excessively harsh, without giving the other party even the slightest merit.

It cannot be said that there is a lack of publishers; notably among the Russian Jewry, there they are far more numerous than amongst the Russians.

Nevertheless, despite the abundance of brilliant minds and decorated pens, we still have not had a up-to-date analysis of our mutual history that can satisfy both parties. We must learn not to tighten the rope when it is already so tense. I would have liked to apply my efforts to a subject less thorny. But I believe this history – or at least the effort to penetrate it – should not remain 'forbidden'.

The history of the 'Jewish Problem' in Russia (and Russia only?) is above all else exceptionally rich. Talking about it means listening to new voices and passing them on to the reader. (In this book, the Jewish voices will be heard more often than those of the Russians.)

But the whirlwinds of the social climate force us towards the razor's edge. You can feel the weight of both sides, all the grievances and accusations, plausible as well as improbably, which grow as they go.

The purpose that guides me throughout this work on the life common the Russians and the Jews consists of looking for all the points necessary for a mutual understanding, all the possible voices which, once we get rid of the bitterness of the past, can lead us towards the future.

Like all other people, like all of us, the Jewish people is at the same time an active and passive element of History; more than once they have accomplished, be it unconsciously, important works that History has offered them. The 'Jewish Problem' has been observed from diverse angles, but always with passion and often in self-delusion. Yet the events which have affected this or that people in the course of History have not always, far from, been determined by this one people, but by all those who surrounded it.

An attitude that is too passionately for one party or the other is humiliating to them. Nevertheless, there cannot be problems that man can't approach with reason. Speaking openly, amply, is more honest, and, in our case precise, speaking about it is essential. Alas, mutual wounds have piled up in popular memory. But if we look at the past, when will the memory heal? As long as popular opinion does not find a pen to shed light thereupon, it will stay a vague rumour, worse: menacing.

We cannot cut ourselves off from the past centuries permanently. Our world has shrunk, and, whatever are the dividing lines, we find ourselves neighbours again. For many years I have delayed writing this book; I would've been glad not to take this burden upon me, but the delays of my life have neared exhaustion, and here I am.

I have never been able to acknowledge anyone's right to conceal any of what has been. Neither can I accept any agreement founded on bringing false light on the past. I call both parties – Russian and Jewish – to look for mutual understanding, to recognize each others' share of the sin, because it is easy to look away: surely this is not us... I sincerely strive to comprehend the two parties in the presence of this long historical conflict. I plunge myself into the events, not the polemics. I want to show. I won't enter into the discussions except for those extreme cases where fairness is covered by layers upon layers of lies. I dare hope that this book will not be received by the extremists and the fanatics, that, on the contrary, it will favour mutual understanding. I hope to find caring people amongst the Jews as well as the Russians.

Here is how the author envisaged his task and ultimate goal: to try and foresee, in the future of Russo-Jewish relations, accessible ways that could lead to the good of all.

I wrote this book by bending myself only on what the historical materials told and looking for charitable issues for the future. But let's face it: in recent years the situation in Russia has evolved in such a drastic fashion that the problems studied herein have found themselves relegated to the background and don't have the acuteness today of Russia's other problems.

On the perimeter of this study.
What could be the limits of this book?

I am fully aware of the complexity and breadth of the subject matter. I understand that it also has a metaphysical aspect. It is even said that the Jewish Problem can be rigorously understood only from a mystical and religious point of view. Of course I recognize the reality from this point of view, but, although many books have already touched the subject, I think it remains inaccessible to men, that it is by nature out of scope, even for the experts.

Yet all the important purposes of human history contain mystical influences, this does not prevent us from examining them on a concrete historical plane. I doubt whether we should necessarily call upon superiour considerations to analyze phenomena which our within our immediate reach.

Within the limits of our earthly existence, we can make judgments on the Russians, as well as on the Jews, starting from lowly criteria. As for those above, let's leave them to God!

I want to clarify this problem only in the categories of History, politics and everyday life and culture, and almost exclusively within the limits of the two centuries of Russians and Jews living together in one state. Never would I have dared to approach the depths of the Jewish History, tri- or quadri-millenniar, sufficiently represented in numerous works and in meticulous encyclopedias.

Neither do I intend to examine the History of the Jews in the countries nearest to us: Poland, Germany, Astria-Hungary. I concentrate myself on Russian-Jewish relations, insisting on the twentieth century, so crucial and so catastrophic in the destiny of our two peoples. Based on the hard experience of our coexistence, I try to dispel the misunderstandings, false accusations, while recalling the legitimate grievances. The works published in the first decades of the twentieth century have had little time to embrace this experience in its totality.

Of course, a contemporary author cannot overlook their existence, despite half a century and the state of Israel as well as it's enormous influence on the lives of the Jews and other peoples over the globe. He cannot, if only if he wants a extensive comprehension on the internal life of Israel and it's spiritual orientations — also through incidental reflections, this must shine through in this book. But it would be an outrageous claim on the part of the author not to introduce here an analysis of the problems inherent to Zionism and the life of Israel. I nevertheless give special attention to the writings published in our day by the learned Russian Jews who lived for decades in the Soviet Union before emigrating to Israel, and who have therefore had the opportunity to reflect, from their own experience, on a number Jewish Problems.

Abridged Mentions of the Main Sources Cited in Notes by the Author

• **"22"**: Social, political and literary review of the Jewish intelligentsia from the USSR in Israel, Tel Aviv. The bibliographic notes called by a number are from the author. Of these, those marked with an asterisk refer to a second-hand reference. The explanatory notes marked with an asterisk are translators.

• **ARR**: Archives of the Russian Revolution, edited by J. Guessen, Berlin, ed. Slovo, 1922–1937.

• **BJWR-1**: Kriga o rousskom cvreïstve: ot 1860 godov do Revolioutsii 1917 g. [Book on the Jewish World of Russia: from the 1860s to the Revolution of 1917], New York, ed. Of the Union of Russian Jews, 1960.

• **BJWR-2**: Kriza o rousskom evreïstve, 1917–1967 [The Book on the Jewish World of Russia, 1917–1967], New York, ed. Of the Union of Russian Jews, 1968.

• **JE**: Jewish Encyclopædia in 16 volumes, St. Petersburg, Society for the Promotion of Jewish Scientific Publishing and Ed. Brokhaus and Efron, 1906–1913.

• **JW**: Evreïskii mir [The Jewish World], Paris, Union of Russo-Jewish intellectuals.

• **RaJ**: Rossia i evrei [Russia and the Jews], Paris, YMCA Press, 1978 (original ed., Berlin, 1924).

• **RHC**: Istoriko-revolutsionnyi sbornik [Revolutionary Historical Collection], edited by V. I. Nevski, 3 vols., M. L., GIZ, 1924–1926.

• **RJE**: Rossiskaia Evreiskaya Entsiklopedia [Russian Jewish Encyclopedia], M. 1994, 2nd edition currently being published, corrected and expanded.

• **Izvestia**: News from the Soviet of Workers 'and Soldiers' Deputies of Petrograd.

• **SJE**: Small Jewish Encyclopedia, Jerusalem, 1976, ed. Of the Society for the Study of Jewish Communities.

• **TW**: Vremia i my [The Time and We], international review of literature and social problems, Tel Aviv.

Chapter 1

Before the 19th century

From the Beginnings in Khazaria

In this book the presence of the Jews prior to 1772 will not be discussed in detail. However, for a few pages, we will go over the older epochs.

One could say that the paths of Russians and Jews first crossed in the wars between the Kiev Rus and the Khazars [Ancient people of the Turkish race established in the region of the Low Volga since long. In the 6th century they founded a vast empire stretching from the Oural to Dniepr, which fell in the 10th century after their defeat by the prince of Kiev, Sviatoslav (966)], but that isn't completely right, since only the upper class of the Khazars were of Hebraic descent, the tribe itself consisted of Turcs who converted to Judaism.

If one follows the presentation of J.D. Bruzkus, respected Jewish author of the mid-20th century, a certain part of the Jews from Persia moved across the Derbent Pass to lower Volga where Atil on the west coast of Caspian on the Volga delta, the capital city of the Khazarian Khanate[1], rose up starting 724 AD.

The tribal princes of the Turkish Khazars (at the time still idol-worshippers), did not want to accept the Muslim faith, lest they should be subordinated to the caliph of Baghdad, nor Christianity, lest they come under vassalage to the Byzantine emperor; and so the clan went over to the Jewish faith in 732.

But there was also a Jewish colony in the Bosporan Kingdom[2] on the Taman Peninsula at east end of the Crimea, separating the Black Sea from the Sea of Azov, to which Hadrian had Jewish captives brought in 137, after the victory over Bar-Kokhba [Founded in 480BC by the greek,

---

[1] J. D. Brutskus, Istoki rousskogo evreïstva (Les origines des Juifs russes), in Annuaire du monde juif, 1939. Paris, éd. de l'Union des intellectuels russo-juifs, pp. 17-23.
[2] EJ, t. 15, p. 648.

conquered by Mithridate in 107BC, remained under Roman protectorate until the 4th century].

Later a Jewish settlement sustained itself without break under the Goths and Huns in the Crimea. Kaffa (Feodosia) especially remained Jewish. In 933 Prince Igor [Grand Prince of Kiev 912–945, successor of Oleg the wise] temporarily possessed Kerch, and his son Sviatoslav [Grand Prince 960–972] wrested the Don region from the Khazars.

The Kiev Rus already ruled the entire Volga region including Atil in 909, and Russian ships appeared at Samander, south of Atil on the west coast of the Caspian. The Kumyks [Turkish speaking people; independent state in the 15th century, annexed to Russia in 1784] in the Caucasus were descendants of the Khazars. In the Crimea, on the other hand, they combined with the Polovtsy [Turkish speaking people from Asia that occupied the southern steppes of Russia 11th century], a nomadic Turkish people from central Asia who had lived in the northern Black Sea area and the Caucasus since the 10th century, called Cuman by western historians. This admixture formed the Crimean Tatars.

But unlike the Tatars the Karaim [Turkish speaking people professing a belief similar to Judaism, but without recognizing the Talmud (11th to 12th century)], a Jewish sect that does not follow the Talmud, and Jewish residents of the Crimea did not go over to the Muslim faith. The Khazars were finally overrun much later by Tamerlane or Timur, the 14th century conqueror.

A few researchers, however hypothesize (exact proof is absent) that the Hebrews had wandered to some extent through the south Russian region in a westward and northwesterly direction. Thus the Orientalist and Semitist Abraham Harkavy, for example writes that the Jewish congregation in the future Russia "emerge from Jews that came from the Black Sea coast and from the Caucasus, where their ancestors had lived since the Assyrian and Babylonian captivity."[3] J. D. Bruzkus also leans to this perspective. Another opinion suggests these were the remnant of the Ten Lost Tribes of Israel [after the death of Salomon, under the rule of Roboam, ten of the twelve tribes of Israel separated from the House of David, formed the Kingdom of Israel and then were punished and dispersed].

This migration presumably ended after the conquest in 1097 of Timutarakans on the eastern shore of the Kerch straits, overlooking the eastern end of the Crimean Peninsula; the eastern flank of the old Bosporan Kingdom, by the Polovtsy. According to Harkavy's opinion the vernacular of these Jews at least since the ninth century was Slavic, and only in the

---

[3] PEI, I. 2, p. 40.

17th century, when the Ukrainian Jews fled from the pogroms of the Ukrainian Cossack warlord Bogdan Chmelnitzki [Hetman. Ukrainian leader (1593–1657), victoriously led the Ukrainian Cossacks against Poland with the aid of the Crimean Tatars. In 1654 he received the protection of Moscow and became the vasal of tsar Alexis Mikhaïlovitch], who led a successful Cossack rebellion against Poland with help from the Crimean Tatars, did Yiddish become the language of Jews in Poland.

In various manners the Jews also came to Kiev and settled there. Already under Igor, the lower part of the city was called Kosary; in 933 Igor brought in Jews that had been taken captive in Kerch. Then in 965 Jews taken captive in the Crimea were brought there; in 969 Kosaren from Atil and Samander, in 989 from Cherson and in 1017 from Timutarakan. In Kiev western or Ashkenazi Jews also emerged in connection with the caravan traffic from west to east, and starting at the end of the eleventh century, perhaps on account of the persecution in Europe during the first Crusade.[4]

Later researchers confirm likewise that in the 11th century, the Jewish element in Kiev was derived from the Khazars. Still earlier, at the turn of the 10th century the presence of "a Khazar force and a Khazar garrison" was chronicled in Kiev... And "already in the first half of the 11th century the Jewish-Khazar element in Kiev played a significant role."[5] In the 9th and 10th century, Kiev was multinational and tolerant towards different ethnicities.

At the end of the 10th century, in the time when Prince Vladimir I. Svyatoslavich [Saint Vladimir (956-1015), son of Sviatoslav, became sole sovereign of the Kievian Russia of which he's considered the founder.

Converted to Byzantine Christianity which he established in the whole country in 988AD] was choosing a new faith for the Russians, there were not a few Jews in Kiev, and among them were found educated men who suggested taking on the Jewish faith. The choice fell out otherwise than it had 250 hears earlier in the Khazar Kingdom. The Russian historian Karamsin relates it like this: "After he (Vladimir) had listened to the Jews, he asked where their homeland was. 'In Jerusalem,' answered the delegates, 'but God has chastised us in his anger and sent us into a foreign

---

[4] EJ, t. 9, p. 526.
[5] *V N. Toporov*, Sviatost i sviatye v russkoï doukhovnoï koultoure (La sainteté et les saints russes dans la culture russe spirituelle), t. 1, M. 1995, pp. 283-286. 340.

land.' 'And you, whom God has punished, dare to teach others?' said Vladimir. 'We do not want to lose our fatherland like you have.'"[6]

After the Christianization of the Rus, according to Bruzkus, a portion of the Khazar Jews in Kiev also went over to Christianity and afterwards in Novgorod perhaps one of them, Luka Zhidyata,[7] was even one of the first bishops and spiritual writers. Christianity and Judaism being side-by-side in Kiev inevitably led to the learned zealously contrasting them. From that emerged the work significant to Russian literature, *Sermon on Law and Grace* by Hilarion, first Russian Metropolitan in the middle 11th century, which contributed to the settling of a Christian consciousness for the Russians that lasted for centuries.

The polemic here is as fresh and lively as in the letters of the apostles.[8] In any case, it was the first century of Christianity in Russia. For the Russian neophytes of that time, the Jews were interesting, especially in connection to their religious presentation, and even in Kiev there were opportunities for contact with them. The interest was greater than later in the 18th century, when they again were physically close.

Then, for more than a century, the Jews took part in the expanded commerce of Kiev. "In the new city wall completed in 1037 there was the Jews' Gate, which closed in the Jewish quarter."[9] The Kiev Jews were not subjected to any limitations, and the princes did not handle themselves with hostility, but rather indeed vouchsafed to them protection, especially Sviatopluk Iziaslavich, Prince of Novgorod (r. 1078-1087) and Grand Prince of Kiev from 1093 until 1113, since the trade and enterprising spirit of the Jews brought the princes financial advantage.

In 1113 A.D., Vladimir Monomakh, out of qualms of conscience, even after the death of Sviatopluk, hesitated to ascend the Kiev throne prior to one of the Svyatoslaviches, and "rioters, exploiting the anarchy, plundered the house of the regimental commander Putiata and all Jews that had stood under the special protection of the greedy Sviatopluk in the capital city. One reason for the Kiev revolt was apparently the usury of the Jews. Exploiting the shortage of money of the time, they enslaved the debtors with exorbitant interest."[10] (For example there are indications in the statute of Vladimir Monomakh that Kiev moneylenders received interest up to 50

---

[6] *N. M. Karamzine*, Isloria gosoudarstva Rossiiskogo (Histoire de la nation russe), Saint-Pétersbourg. 1842-1844, t. 1, p. 127. Cf. également : S. M. Soloviev. Isloria Rossii s drevneichikh vremen (Histoire de la Russie depuis les origines) en 15 volumes, M. 1962-1966. t. 1. p. 181.
[7] *Brutskus*, pp. 21-22 ; EJ, t. 7, p. 588.
[8] *Toporov*, t. 1, p. 280.
[9] PEJ, t. 4, p. 253.
[10] *Karamzine*, t. 2. pp. 87-88.

percent per annum.) Karamsin therein appeals to the Chronicles and an extrapolation by Basil Tatistcheff (1686–1750), student of Peter the Great, and the first Russian historian. In Tatistcheff we find moreover:

"Afterwards they clubbed down many Jews and plundered their houses, because they had brought about many sicknesses to Christians and commerce with them had brought about great damage. Many of them, who had gathered in their synagogue seeking protection, defended themselves as well as they could, and gained time until Vladimir could arrive." But when he came, "the Kievites pleaded with him for retribution toward the Jews, because they had taken all the trades from Christians and under Sviatopluk had had much freedom and power... They had also brought many over to their faith."[11]

According to M. N. Pokrovski, the Kiev Pogrom of 1113 was of a social and not national character. However the leaning of this class-conscious historian toward social interpretations is well-known. After he ascended to the Kiev throne, Vladimir answered the complainants, "Since many Jews everywhere have received access to the various princely courts and have migrated there, it is not appropriate for me, without the advice of the princes, and moreover contrary to right, to permit killing and plundering them. Hence I will without delay call the princes to assemble, to give counsel."[12] In the Council a law limiting interest was established, which Vladimir attached to Yaroslav's statute. Karamsin reports, appealing to Tatistcheff, that Vladimir "banned all Jews" upon the conclusion of the Council, "and from that time forth there were none left in our fatherland." But at the same time he qualifies: "In the chronicles in contrast it says that in 1124 the Jews in Kiev died in a great fire; consequently, they had not been banned."[13] Bruzkus explains, that it "was a whole quarter in the best part of the city... at the Jew's Gate next to the Golden Gate."[14] At least one Jew enjoyed the trust of Andrei Bogoliubsky in Vladimir.

Among the confidants of Andrei was a certain Ephraim Moisich, whose patronymic Moisich or Moisievich indicates his Jewish derivation, and who according to the words of the Chronicle was among the instigators of the treason by which Andrei was murdered.[15] However there is also a notation that says that under Andrei Bogoliubsky "many Bulgarians and Jews from the Volga territory came and had themselves baptized" and that

---

[11] *V. N. Tatischev*, Histoire russe en 7 volumes, t. 2, M. 1963, p. 129.
[12] *Ibidem*, p. 129.
[13] *Kuramzine*, t. 2. Notes, p. 89.
[14] *Brutskus*, p. 23.
[15] *Suloviev*, livre I, p. 546.

after the murder of Andrei his son Georgi fled to a Jewish prince in Dagestan.[16]

In any case the information on the Jews in the time of the Suzdal Rus is scanty, as their numbers were obviously small. The *Jewish Encyclopedia* notes that in the Russian heroic songs (Bylinen) the "Jewish Czar" – e.g. the warrior Shidowin in the old Bylina about Ilya and Dobrinia – is "a favorite general moniker for an enemy of the Christian faith."[17]

At the same time it could also be a trace of memories of the struggle against the Khazars. Here, the religious basis of this hostility and exclusion is made clear. On this basis, the Jews were not permitted to settle in the Muscovy Rus.

The invasion of the Tatars portended the end of the lively commerce of the Kiev Rus, and many Jews apparently went to Poland. (Also the Jewish colonization into Volhynia and Galicia continued, where they had scarcely suffered from the Tatar invasion.) The Encyclopedia explains: "During the invasion of the Tatars (1239) which destroyed Kiev, the Jews also suffered, but in the second half of the 13th century they were invited by the Grand Princes to resettle in Kiev, which found itself under the domination of the Tatars. On account of the special rights, which were also granted the Jews in other possessions of the Tatars, envy was stirred up in the town residents against the Kiev Jews."[18]

Something similar happened not only in Kiev, but also in the cities of North Russia, which "under the Tatar rule, were accessible for many merchants from Khoresm or Khiva, who were long since experienced in trade and the tricks of profit-seeking. These people bought from the Tatars the principality's right to levy tribute, they demanded excessive interest from poor people and, in case of their failure to pay, declared the debtors to be their slaves, and took away their freedom. The residents of Vladimir, Suzdal, and Rostov finally lost their patience and rose up together at the pealing of the bells against these usurers; a few were killed and the rest chased off."[19] A punitive expedition of the Khan against the mutineers was threatened, which however was hindered via the mediation of Alexander Nevsky. Lastly, "in the documents of the 15th century, Kievite Jewish tax-leasers are mentioned, who possessed a significant fortune."[20]

---

[16] *Brutskus*, p. 26.
[17] EJ, t. 9, p. 5.
[18] *Ibidem*, p. 517.
[19] *Karamzine*, t. 4, pp. 54-55.
[20] PEJ. t. 4, p. 254.

The Judaizing Heresy

A migration of Jews from Poland to the East, including White Russia [Belarus], should also be noted in the 15th century: there were leasers of tolls and other assessments in Minsk, Polotsk, and in Smolensk, although no settled congregations were formed there. After the short-lived banishment of Jews from Lithuania (1496) the "eastward movement went forth with particular energy at the beginning of the 16th century."[21]

The number of Jews that migrated into the Muscovy Rus was insignificant although "influential Jews at that time had no difficulties going to Moscow."[22]

Toward the end of the 15th century in the very center of the spiritual and administrative power of the Rus, a change took place that, though barely noticed, could have drawn an ominous unrest in its wake, and had far-reaching consequences in the spiritual domain. It had to do with the "Judaizing Heresy."

Saint Joseph of Volokolamsk (1439–1515) who resisted it, observed: "Since the time of Olga [Saint Olga (?-969), princess of Kiev, wife of prince Igor of whom she became widow in 945; exercised rule until her son Sviatoslav became of age. Converted in 954, she did however not succeed in spreading Christianity throughout the whole country] and Vladimir, the God-fearing Russian world has never experienced such a seduction."[23]

According to Kramsin it began thus: the Jew Zechariah, who in 1470 had arrived in Novgorod from Kiev, "figured out how to lead astray two spirituals, Dionis and Aleksei; he assured them that only the Law of Moses was divine; the history of the Redeemer was invented; the Messiah was not yet born; one should not pray to icons, etc. Thus began the Judaizing heresy."[24] The renowned Russian historian Sergey Solovyov (1820–79) expands on this, that Zechariah accomplished it "with the aid of five accomplices, who also were Jewish," and that this heresy "obviously was a mixture of Judaism and Christian rationalism that denied the mystery of the holy Trinity and the divinity of Jesus Christ."[25]

"The Orthodox Priest Aleksei called himself Abraham, his wife he called Sarah and along with Dionis corrupted many spirituals and laymen. But it is hard to understand how Zechariah was able so easily to increase the

---

[21] EJ, t. 5, p. 165.
[22] *Ibidem*, 1.13. p. 610.
[23] *Karamzine*, t. 6. p. 121.
[24] *Ibidem*, p. 121.
[25] *Soloviev*, livre III, p. 185.

number of his Novgorod pupils, since his wisdom consisted entirely and only in the rejection of Christianity and the glorification of Judaism. Probably, Zechariah seduced the Russians with the Jewish cabbala, a teaching that captured curious ignoramuses and in the 15th century was well-known, when many educated men sought in it the solution to all important riddles of the human spirit. The cabbalists extolled themselves..., they were able... to discern all secrets of nature, explain dreams, prophecy the future, and conjure spirits."[26]

J. Gessen, a Jewish historian of the 20th century, presents in contrast the opinion: "It is certain that Jews participated neither in the introduction of the heresy... nor its spread."[27] (But with no indication of his sources). The encyclopedia of Brockhaus and Efron [1890–1906, Czarist Russian equivalent to the Encyclopedia Britannica] explains: "Apparently the genuinely Jewish element played no outstanding role, limiting its contribution to a few rituals."[28]

The Jewish Encyclopedia, which appeared about the same time, writes on the other hand: "today, since the publication of the 'Psalter of the Judaizers' and other memorials, the contested question of the Jewish influence on the sects must... be seen as settled in a positive sense."[29]

"The Novgorod heretics presented an orderly exterior, appeared to fast humbly and zealously fulfilled all the duties of piety."[30] They made themselves noticed by the people and contributed to the rapid spreading of the heresy.[31]

When after the fall of Novgorod Ivan Vasilievich III (1440–1505) Grand Prince of Moscovy, united the greater Russian territory under Moscow's rule visited the city, he was impressed by their piety and took both of the first heretics, Aleksei and Dionis, to Moscow in 1480 and promoted them as high priests of the Assumption of Mary and the Archangel cathedrals of the Kremlin. With them also the schism was brought over, the roots of which remained in Novgorod. Aleksei found special favor with the ruler and had free access to him, and with his secret teaching enticed not only several high spirituals and officials, but moved the Grand Prince to appoint the archimandrite (head abbot in Eastern Orthodoxy) Zossima as Metropolitan, that is, the head of the entire Russian church — a man from

---

[26] *Karamzine*, t. 6, pp. 121-122.
[27] *J. Hessen,* Istoria evreïskogo naroda v Rossii (Histoire du peuple juif en Russie), en 2 vol., 1.1, Leningrad, 1925, p. 8.
[28] Dictionnaire encyclopédique en 82 volumes, Saint-Pétersbourg, 1890-1904, t. 22, 1904, p. 943.
[29] EJ, t. 7, p. 577.
[30] *Karamzine*, t. 6, p. 122.
[31] 31 *Sotoviev*, livre III, p. 185.

the very circle of the those he had enticed with the heresy. In addition, he enticed Helena to the heresy — daughter-in-law of the Grand Prince, widow of Ivan the Younger and mother of the heir to the throne, the "blessed nephew Dimitri."[32]

The rapid success of this movement and the ease with which it spread is astonishing. This is obviously to be explained through mutual interests. When the 'Psalter of the Judaizing' and other works — which could mislead the inexperienced Russian reader and were sometimes unambiguously anti-Christian – were translated from Hebrew into Russian, one could have assumed that only Jews and Judaism would have been interested in them. But also the Russian reader was interested in the translations of Jewish religious texts. This explains the success which the propaganda of the 'Judaizing' had in various classes of society.[33] The sharpness and liveliness of this contact is reminiscent of that which had emerged in Kiev in the 11th century.

The Novgorod Archbishop Gennadi uncovered the heresy in 1487, sent irrefutable proofs of it to Moscow, hunted the heresy out and unmasked it, until in 1490 a church Council assembled to discuss the matter under leadership of the just-promoted Metropolitan Sossima. "With horror they heard the complaint of Gennadi,... that these apostates insult Christ and the mother of God, spit on the cross, call the icons idolatrous images, bite on them with their teeth and throw them into impure places, believe in neither the kingdom of Heaven nor the resurrection of the dead, and entice the weak, while remaining quiet in the presence of zealous Christians."[34] From the judgment of the Council it is apparent, that the Judaizers did not recognize Jesus Christ as the Son of God, that they taught the Messiah had not yet appeared, that they observed the Old Testament Sabbath day rather then the Christian Sunday.[35] It was suggested to the Council to execute the heretics but, in accordance with the will of Ivan III, they were sentenced instead to imprisonment and the heresy was anathematized.

> "In view of the coarseness of the time and the seriousness of the moral corruption, such a punishment was extraordinarily mild."[36]

The historians unanimously explain this hesitation of Ivan in that the heresy had already spread widely under his own roof and was practiced by well-known, influential people, among whom was Feodor Kuritsyn, Ivan's plenipotentiary Secretary, "famous on account of his education and his

---

[32] *Karamzine*, t. 6, pp. 120-123.
[33] *Toporov*, t. 1, p. 357.
[34] *Karamzine*, t. 6. p. 123.
[35] EJ, t. 7, p. 580.
[36] *Karamzine*, t. 6, p. 123.

capabilities".[37] The noteworthy liberalism of Moscow flowed from the temporary 'Dictator of the Heart' F. Kuritsyn. The magic of his secret salon was enjoyed even by the Grand Prince and his daughter-in-law. The heresy was by no means in abatement, but rather prospered magnificently and spread itself out. At the Moscow court astrology and magic along with the attractions of a pseudo-scientific revision of the entire medieval worldview were solidly propagated, which was "free-thinking and carried by the appeal of enlightenment, and the power of fashion."[38]

The *Jewish Encyclopedia* sets forth moreover that Ivan III "out of political motivations did not stand against the heresy. With Zechariah's help, he hoped to strengthen his influence in Lithuania," and besides that he wanted to secure the favor of influential Jews from the Crimea: "of the princes and rulers of Taman Peninsula, Zacharias de Ghisolfi," and of the Jew Chozi Kokos, a confidant of the Khan Mengli Giray or Girai.[39]

After the Council of 1490 Sossima continued to sponsor a secret society for several years, but then was himself discovered, and in 1494 the Grand Prince commanded him to depose himself without process and to withdraw into a cloister, without throwing up dust and to all appearances willingly. "The heresy however did not abate. For a time (1498) its votaries in Moscow seized almost all the power, and their charge Dmitri, the son of the Princess Helena, was coronated as Czar."[40] Soon Ivan III reconciled himself with his wife Sophia Paleologos, and in 1502 his son Vassili inherited the throne. (Kurizyn by this time was dead.) Of the heretics, after the Council of 1504, one part was burned, a second part thrown in prison, and a third fled to Lithuania, "where they formally adopted the Mosaic faith".[41]

It must be added that the overcoming of the Judaizing heresy gave the spiritual life of the Muscovy Rus at turn of the 16th century a new impetus, and contributed to recognizing the need for spiritual education, for schools for the spiritual; and the name of Archbishop Gennadi is associated with the collecting and publication of the first church-Slavic Bible, of which there had not to that point been a consolidated text corpus in the Christian East. The printing press was invented, and "after 80 years this Gennadi Bible was printed in Ostrog (1580-82); with its appearance, it took over the entire orthodox East".[42] Even academy member S. F. Platonov gives a

---

[37] *Soloviev*, livre III. p. 168.
[38] A.V. Kariachev, Olchcrki po istorii Russkoï Tserkvi (Essais sur l'histoire de l'Église russe) en 2 vol., Paris. 1959, t. 1, pp. 495, 497.
[39] EJ. t. 13, p. 610.
[40] *Ibidem*, t. 7, p. 579.
[41] PEJ, t. 2, p. 509.
[42] *Kartachev*, t. 1, p. 505.

generalizing judgment about the phenomenon: "The movement of Judaizing no doubt contained elements of the West European rationalism... The heresy was condemned; its advocates had to suffer, but the attitude of critique and skepticism produced by them over against dogma and church order remained."[43]

Today's *Jewish Encyclopedia* remembers "the thesis that an extremely negative posture toward Judaism and the Jews was unknown in the Muskovy Rus up to the beginning of the 16th century," and derives it from this struggle against the "Judaizers".[44] Judging by the spiritual and civil measures of the circumstances, that is thoroughly probable. J. Gessen however contends: "it is significant, that such a specific coloring of the heresy as Judaizing did not lessen the success of the sects and in no way led to the development of a hostile stance toward the Jews."[45]

Judging by its stable manner of life, it was in neighboring Poland that the biggest Jewish community emerged, expanded and became strong from the 13th to the 18th century. It formed the basis of the future Russian Jewry, which became the most important part of world Jewry until the 20th century. Starting in the 16th century a significant number of Polish and Czech Jews emigrated into the Ukraine, White Russia and Lithuania.[46] In the 15th century Jewish merchants traveled still unhindered from the Polish-Lithuanian Kingdom to Moscow. But that changed under Ivan IV the Terrible: Jewish merchants were forbidden entry.

When in 1550 the Polish King Sigismund August desired to permit them free entry into Russia, this was denied by Ivan with these words: "We absolutely do not permit the entry of the Jew into my lands, because we do not wish to see evil in our lands, but rather may God grant that the people in my land may have rest from that irritation. And you, our brother, should not write us on account of the Jews again,"[47] for they had "alienated the Russians from Christianity, brought poisonous plants into our lands and done much evil to our lands."[48]

According to a legend Ivan the Terrible, upon the annexation of Polotsk in 1563, ordered all Jews to be baptized in response to complaints of Russian residents "against evil things and bullying" by Jews, leasers and others empowered by Polish magnates. Those that refused, apparently about 300 persons, are supposed to have been drowned in his presence in the Dvina.

---

[43] *S. F. Platonov,* Moskva i Zapad (Moscou et l'Occident), Berlin, 1926, pp. 37-38.
[44] PEJ, t. 2, p. 509.
[45] *Hessen,* t. 1, p. 8.
[46] *Brutskus*; CM, t. 1, p 28.
[47] EI, t. 8, p. 749.
[48] Hessen, t. 1. pp. 8-9.

But careful historians, as e.g. J. I. Gessen, do not confirm this version even in moderated form and do not mention it once.

Instead of that, Gessen writes that under the False Dimitri I (1605-06) both Jews and other foreigners "in relatively large number" were baptized in Moscow. The story goes according to In the Time of Troubles by Sergey Ivanov, regarding the 15-year period of confusion following the failed Rurik Dynasty in 1598–1613 that the False Dimitri II, aka the "Thief of Tushino", was "born a Jew."[49] The sources give contradictory information regarding the ancestry of the Thief of Tushino. Some assert that he was born Matthieu Vercvkinc, the son of an Ukrainian priest; "or a Jew, as is said in the official documents; if one believes a foreign historian, he knew Hebrew, read the Talmud, the books of the rabbis… Sigismond sent a Jew who passed himself for the Tsarevitch Dimitri." [50] The *Jewish Encyclopedia* says: "Jews made up part of the imposters following and suffered after his fall. According to some sources … the False Dimitri II was a baptised Jew who had served under False Dimitri I."[51]

Polish-Lithuanians, who had arrived in numerously in Russia during the Time of Troubles, were, at the start of this period, limited in their rights and "the Jews who came from those countries partook in the fate of their compatriots" for whom it had been forbidden to take their merchandise to Moscow and the neighbouring cities.[52] The Moscow-Polish agreement on the accession to the throne of Vladislav [Polish king (1595–1648)] stipulated: "one must not be forced to embrace the Roman belief, nor other confessions, and the Jews should not be allowed to enter the state of Moscow to trade."[53] But others sources point out that the Jewish merchants had access to Moscow, even after the Time of Troubles. [54] "The contradictory decrees show that the government of Michel Feodorovitch [First Czar of the Romanov dynasty (1596–1645), elected by the Assembly of the people in 1613] was not pursuing any specific policy concerning the Jews… but he was rather tolerant towards them."[55]

"Under the rule of Alexis Mikhaïlovitch [Son of the previous, Czar of Russia from 1645 to 1676], signs can be found of Jewish presence in Russia — the Code does not contain any restriction when it comes to the Jews…

---

[49] Ibidem, p. 9.
[50] Karamzine, t. 12, p. 35-36 ; notes, p. 33.
[51] PEJ. t. 7, p. 290.
[52] Hessen, t. I, p. 9.
[53] Karamzine, t. 12, p. 141.
[54] M. Dijour. Evrci v ckonomitcheskoï jizni Rossii (Les Juifs dans la vie économique de la Russie), in LMJR, p. 156.
[55] EJ, t. 13, p. 611.

they had then access to all Russian cities, including Moscow."[56] Hessen asserts that the population taken during the Russian offensive in Lithuania in the 30's of the 17th century contained a fair number of Jews, and "their arrangements were the same as that of the others." Following the military actions of the 1650–1660's, "the Jewish prisoners found themselves in the state of Moscow again, and their treatment was not worse than that of the other prisoners."

After the signing of the treaty of Androussiv in 1667 in which Smolensk, Kiev and the whole eastern bank of the Dniper River remained Russian, "it was proposed that the Jews should stay in the country. Many of them profited from the situation, some embraced Christianity and amongst the prisoners were some of the founders of the later Russian nobility."[57] (Certain baptised Jews settled in the the 17th century along the Don, in the Cossack village of Starotcherkassk, and about a dozen Cossack families are descended from them.) Around the same year of 1667, the Englishman Samuel Collins, residing in Moscow at the time, wrote that "in a short time, the Jews have spread remarkably through the city and in the court," apparently under the protection of a Jewish surgeon of the court.[58]

Under Czar Feodor III, a decree was tried that "if Jews clandestinely arrive in Moscow with merchandise," they are not to be assessed toll, because "with or without wares, they are forbidden entry to Smolensk."[59] But "the practice did not correspond to the theory."[60]

In the first year of Peter the Great (1702), doors were opened to talented foreigners, but not Jews: "I would rather see Mohammedans and pagans than Jews come here. They are rogues and deceivers. I root out evil, I do not spread it; there is no place, nor work for them in Russia, in spite of all of their efforts to bribe my entourage."[61]

Yet there is no evidence of limitations imposed on them under Peter the Great, nor special laws. To the contrary, due to the general benevolence given to all foreigners, they became involved in a wide range of activities, and even positions close to the Emperor:

> • Vice-chancellor Baron Peter Shafirov, he was later found guilty of embezzlement and disordedly conduct, for which received capital punishment, later commuted to banishment. After the death of Peter

---

[56] Ibidem.
[57] J. Guessen, t. 1, pp. 9-10.
[58] EJ, 1.11, p. 330.
[59] Ibidem.
[60] EJ, 1.13, p. 612.
[61] *Soloviev*, livre VJH, p. 76.

his punishments were lifted and he was commissioned write down the life of his late master.[62]

- His cousins Abram Veselovsky, and
- Isaac Veselovsky, close confidants of Peter
- Anton de Vieira, general police master of Petersburg
- Vivière, head of secret police
- Acosta, the jester

and others. To A. Veselovsky, Peter wrote that "what matters is competence and honesty, not baptism or circumcision."[63] Jewish mercantile houses in Germany inquired whether Russia would guarantee their commerce with Persia, but never received an answer.[64]

At start of the 18th century there was increased Jewish trade activity in Little Russia and Ukraine, a year before Russian merchants got the right to engage in such commerce. The Ukrainian Hetman Skoropadski gave order several times for their expulsion, but this was not obeyed and Jewish presence actually increased.[65] In 1727, Catherine I, giving in to Menchikov shortly before her death, decreed the removal of Jews from Ukraine and Russian cities (in this case, "the large share taken by the Jews in the productionn and trading of brandy may have played a part"), but this only lasted one year.[66]

In 1728, Peter II "permitted Jews into Little Russia," first as "temporary visitors" on the ground of their usefulness for trade, then "more and more reasons were found to make it permanent." Under Anna this right was extended to Smolensk in 1731 and Slobodsky in 1734. Permission was given to Jews to lease land and to distil brandy, and, after 1736, to supply Polish vodka to any public drinking places, including those in Greater Russia.[67]

It is important to mention Baltic financier Levy Lipman. While czarina Anna Iwanowna was still living in Courland she was in dire need of money "and it is probable that Lipman was on occasions of use to her." Under Peter I, he had already settled in St Petersburg. Under Peter II, he "became a financial agent or Juweler at the Russian court." After Anna Iwanowna ascended to the throne, he "accrued important relations at the court," and

---

[62] *Ibidem*, livre X, p. 477.
[63] EI, t. 5, p. 519.
[64] EJ, 1.11, p. 330.
[65] *Hessen*, t. 1, pp. 11-12.
[66] *Ibidem*, p. 13 ; EJ, t. 2, p. 592.
[67] *Hessen*, t. 1, pp. 13-15 ; EJ, t. 2, p. 592.

achieved the rank of High Commissar. "Due to his direct contact with the czarina, he also had close ties to her favourite, Biron... His contemporaries assert that... Biron came to him for council on the vital problems of the Russian state. One of the ambassadors at the court wrote: "... One could say that it is Lipman who is truly ruling Russia." Through time these accusations became milder.[68] Nevertheless, Biron "had transferred nearly all of the financial administration and several commercial monopolies."[69] ("Lipman retained his functions at the court, even after Anna Leopoldowna ... had exiled Biron."[70])

Anna Iwanownas had also been influenced by Lipman in her general attitude towards the Jews. Even if, around the time of her ascension to the throne in 1730, she expressed in a letter to her ambassador to the Ukrainian Hetman, her concerns that "only a tiny part of the Small Russians engage in commerce, and that it is mainly the Greek, the Turks and the Jews who are involved in trading,"[71] (from which we can conclude that the alleged expulsion from 1727 never occurred, and that the aforementioned decrees had never gone beyond letters on a page). In 1739, Jews were banned from leasing land in Small Russia; and in 1740 about 600 Jews were expelled from the country.[72] (In opposition to which stood also the interests of the landlords.) One year after her ascension to the throne, Elisabeth III signed a *Ukase* [an imperial Russian decree] (December 1742): "It is forbidden for a Jew to live anywhere within our empire; now it has been made known to us, that these Jews still find themselves in our realm and, under various pretexts, especially in Little Russia. They prolong their stay, which is in no way beneficial; but as we must expect only great injuries to our loyal subjects from such haters of the name of our Savior Jesus Christ, we order all Jews, male and female, along with their entire possession, to be sent without delay from our realm, over the border, and in the future not allowed back in, unless it should be that one of them should confess our Christian religion."[73]

This was the same religious intolerance that shook Europe for centuries. The way of thinking of that time was not unique in any special Russian way, nor was it an exclusively Jew-hostile attitude. Among Christians the religious intolerance was not practiced with any less cruelty. Thus, the Old Believers, i.e. men of the same orthodox faith, were persecuted with fire and sword.

---

[68] EJ, t. 10, pp. 224-225.
[69] Ibidem, t. 4, p. 591.
[70] Ibidem, t. 10, p. 225.
[71] Soloviev, livre X. pp. 256-257.
[72] Hessen, t. 1. p. 15.
[73] Soloviev, livre XI, pp. 155-156.

This *ukase* of Elisabeth was made known throughout the realm, but immediately attempts were made to move the ruler to relent. The military chancellor reported to the Senate from the Ukraine that already 140 people were evicted, but that "the prohibition against Jews to bring goods in would lead to a reduction in state income."[74] The Senate reported to the Czarina that "trade had suffered great damage in Little Russia as well as the Baltic provinces by the ukase of the previous year to not allow Jews into the realm, and also the state purse would suffer by the reduction of income from tolls." The Czarina answered with the resolution: "I desire no profit from the enemies of Christ."[75]

Gessen concluded that "Russia remained, under Elisabeth, without Jews."[76] The Jewish historian S. Doubnov proposes that under Elisabeth "according to contemporary historians..., towards 1753 ... 35,000 Jews had been chased from the country."[77] But this figure is in stark contrast to the arrangement made three years earlier by Anna Iwanow — and which had not been followed, namely to expel 600 Jews from the whole of Ukraine, too far as well from the 142 expelled Jews mentioned in the report from the Senate to Elisabeth.[78] V.I. Telnikov suggests[79] that the "contemporary historian", from whom these numbers stem, never existed. That this "contemporary historian" of whom Doubnov cites neither the name, nor the title of the work, is no other than E. Herrmann, who published this number, not at that time, but exactly one century later, in 1853, and also with no reference as to the source... but with a strange extension,[80] namely that the Jews "were commanded to leave the land under penalty of death," which shows that this historian was ignorant of the fact that Elisabeth had been the one who abolished capital punishment in Russia (for religious reasons) at the time of her ascension to the throne. Telnikov remarks that one of the great Jewish historians, Heinrich Graertz, does not speak a word on the execution of these decrees by Elizabeth. For comparison, let's state

---

[74] Hessen, 1. 1, p. 16.
[75] Soloviev, livre XI, p. 204.
[76] Hessen, t. I, p. 18.
[77] S. M Doubnov, History of the Jews in Russia and Poland, from the earliest times until the présent day, Philadelphie, the Jewish Publication Society of America, 1916, vol. 1, p. 258. Trad. française diffusée par les éd. du Cerf, Paris, 1992.
[78] EJ, t. 7, p. 513.
[79] Dans son livre inachevé et resté inédit sur la politique du régime tsariste à l'égard des Juifs, Telnikov fait état de nombreuses et importantes sources que nous avons utilisées avec reconnaissance dans la première partie de cet ouvrage.
[80] E. Herrmann, Geschichte des russischen Staats. Fünfter band: Von der Thronbesteigung der Kaiserin Elisabeth bis zur Feier des Friedens von kainardsche (1742-1775), Hambourg, 1853, p. 171.

here that according to G. Sliosberg "attempts were made to chase the Jews from Ukraine."[81]

It is more likely that, having encountered strong resistance, not just from the Jews, but also the landowners and the state apparatus, the decree of Elisabeth was not put into practice, much like the numerous preceding similars.

Under Elisabeth, Jews occupied important positions. The diplomat Isaak Wesselowskij was entrusted with governance responsibilities and overwhelmed "with favours from the empress"; he also pressed chancellor A. Bestushew-Ryumin to block the expulsion of the Jews. (Later he gave Russian language classes to the heir, later Peter III. And his brother Feodor was curator of Moscow University.[82]) Of note also is the rise of the Saxon merchant Grunstein, a Lutheran, who converted to the Orthodox faith, after an unsuccessful trade with Persia ended with him being taken captive. He enlisted in the Preobrashensker Regiment, was among the active participants in the coup which brought Elizabeth to the throne, received the rank of adjutant as a reward, was inducted into the hereditary and was presented 927 serfs, no more and no less.

(How generously they handed out these serfs, our Orthodox czars!) But after that, "the success of his career clouded his mind." Sometimes he threatened to murder the Prosecutor General. One time, on the nocturnal streets, without knowing who it was, he beat up a relative of the Empress' favoured Alexej Rasumowskij. The "Brawl on the Road" "did not go unpunished, and he was exiled to Ustyug."[83]

Peter III, who ruled for no more than six months, had barely had time to take a position on the Jewish Problem. (Although he probably carried with him a scar, due to a certain "Jew Mussafi who, during Peter's youth in Holstein," had been an intermediary for the lending of money, which had ruined the treasury of Holstein; "Mussafi went into hiding as soon as it was announced that the Grand Prince had come of age."[84])

But the latter figure having questionable origins; strong resistance to the edict by Jews, land proprietors and the state apparati meant it was enforced almost as little as previous attempts had been. Catherine II, who became Czarina 1762 in consequence of a coup, also being a neophyte to Eastern Orthodoxy herself, was unwilling to start her reign opening things up for Jews, though the Senate advised it. Jews pressed for it and had spokesmen

---

[81] *G. B. Sliosberg*, Dorevolioutsionnyi stroï Rossii (Le régime prérévolutionnaire de Russie), Paris, 1933, p. 264.
[82] EJ, t. 5. pp. 519-520.
[83] *Soloviev*, livre XI, pp. 134, 319-322.
[84] *Ibidem*, p. 383.

in Petersburg, Riga, and Ukraine. She found a way around her own law in permitting their entry for colonization into "New Russia," the area between Crimea and Moldavia, which was still a wasteland. This was organized secretly from Riga, and the nationality of the Jews was kept more or less secret. Jews went there from Poland and Lithuania. In the first Partition of Poland, 1772, Russia reacquired White Russia (Belarus) along with her 100,000 Jews.

After the 11th century more and more Jews came into Poland because princes and later kings encouraged "all active, industrious people" from western Europe to settle there. Jews actually received special rights, e.g. in the 13th century from Boleslav the Pious; in the 14th century, from Kasimir the Great; in the 16th century from Sigismund I and Stephan Bathory; though this sometimes alternated with repression, e.g. in the 15th century by Vladislav Yagiello and Alexander, son of Kasimir. Tthere were two pogroms in Krakow. In the 16th century several ghettos were constructed partly to protect the Jews. The Roman Catholic spirituals were the most continuous source of hostility to the Jewish presence. Nevertheless, on balance it must have been a favorable environment, since in first half of the 16th century the Jewish population increased substantially. There was a big role for Jews in the business activity of landlords, in that they became leasers of brandy-distilling operations.

After the Tatar devastation, Kiev in the 14th century came under Lithuania and/or Poland, and with this arrangement more and more Jews wandered from Podolia and Volhynia into the Ukraine, in the regions of Kiev, Poltava, and Chernigov. This process accelerated when a large part of Ukraine came directly under Poland in the Union of Lublin, 1569. The main population consisted of Orthodox peasants, who for a long time had had special rights and were free of tolls. Now began an intensive colonization of the Ukraine by the Szlachta (Polish nobility) with conjoint action by the Jews. The Cossacks were forced into immobility, and obligated to perform drudgery and pay taxes. The Catholic lords burdened the Orthodox peasants with various taxes and service duties, and in this exploitation the Jews also partly played a sad role. They leased from the lords the "propination," i.e. the right to distil vodka and sell it, as well as other trades. The Jewish leaser, who represented the Polish lord, received – of course only to a certain degree – the power that the landholder had over the peasants; and since the Jewish leasers strove to wring from the peasants a maximum profit, the rage of the peasants rose not only against the Catholic landlords but also against the Jewish leasers. When from this situation a bloody uprising of the Cossacks arose in 1648 under leadership of Chmelnitsky, Jews as well as Poles were the victims. An estimated 10,000 Jews died.

The Jews were lured in by the natural riches of the Ukraine and by Polish magnates that were colonizing the land, and thus assumed an important economic role. Since they served the interests of the landlords and the régime the Jews brought on themselves the hatred of the residents. N. I. Kostomarov adds that the Jews leased not only various branches of the privileged industries but even the Orthodox churches, gaining the right to levy a fee for baptisms.

After the uprising, the Jews, on the basis of the Treaty of Belaia Tserkov (1651) were again given the right to resettle in the Ukraine. As before, the Jews were residents and leasers of the royal industries and the industries of the Szlachta, and so it was to remain. Going into the 18th century, brandy distilling was practically the main profession of Jews. This trade often led to conflicts with the peasants, who sometimes were drawn into the taverns not so much because they were well-to-do, but on account of their poverty and misery.

Included among the restrictions placed on the Polish Jews in response to demands of the Catholic Church was the prohibition against Jews having Christian house-servants. Because of the recruitment coupled with the state tax increases in neighboring Russia, not a few refugees came to Poland, where they had no rights. In the debates of Catherine's commission for reworking a new Law code (1767/68), one could hear that in Poland "already a number of Russian refugees are servants to Jews."

The Kahal And Civil Rights

The Jews of Poland maintained a vigorous economic relation to the surrounding population, yet in the five centuries that they lived there, did not permit any influence from outside themselves. One century after another rolled by in post-medieval European development, while the Polish Jews remained confined to themselves and became increasingly anachronistic in appearance. They had a fixed order within themselves. Here it is granted, that these conditions, which later remained intact also in Russia until the middle of the 19th century, were favorable for the religious and national preservation of the Jews from the very beginning of their Diaspora. The whole of Jewish life was guided by the Kahal, which had developed from the communal life of the Jews. The Kahal, pl. *Kehilot* was the autonomous organization of the leadership of the Jewish congregations in Poland.

The Kahal was a buffer between Polish authorities and the Jewish people; it collected taxes, for example. It took care of the needy and also regulated Jewish commerce, approved resales, purchases, and leases. It adjudicated disputes between Jews, which could not be appealed to the secular legal system without incurring the ban (herem). What may have started as a democratic institution took on the qualities of an oligarchy bent on maintaining its own power. In turn, the rabbis and Kahal had a mutually exploitative relationship, in that the rabbis were the executive enforcement arm of the Kahal, and owed their position to appointment by the Kahal. Likewise, the Kahal owed the maintenance of its power more to the secular régime than to its own people.

Toward end of 17th century and through 18th century, the country was torn by strife; the magnates' arbitrariness increased further. Jews became poor and demoralized, and hardened in early medieval forms of life. They became child-like, or better childish oldsters. 16th century Jewish spiritual rulers were concentrated in German and Polish Jewry. They put barriers up against contact with outsiders. The rabbinate held the Jews in firm bondage to the past.

The fact that the Jewish people have held themselves together in their diaspora for 2,000 years inspires wonder and admiration. But when one examines certain periods more closely, as e.g. the Polish/Russian one in the 16th and into the middle of the 17th century, and how this unity was only won by means of methods of suppression exercised by the Kehilot, then one no longer knows if it can be evaluated merely as an aspect of religious tradition. If the slightest trace of such isolationism were detected amongst us Russians, we would be severely faulted.

When Jewry came under the rule of the Russian state, this indigenous system remained, in which the hierarchy of the Kahal had a self-interest. According to J. I. Gessen, all the anger that enlightened Jews felt against the ossifying Talmudic tradition became stronger in the middle of the 19th century:

"The representatives of the ruling class of Jewry staked everything on persuading the [Russian] administration of the necessity to maintain this centuries-old institution, which reflected the interests both of the Russian power and of the ruling Jewish class; the Kahal in connection with the rabbis held all the power and not seldom abused it: it misappropriated public funds, trampled the rights of the poor, arbitrarily increased taxes and wreaked vengeance on personal enemies." At the end of the 18th century the governor of one the administrative regions attached to Russia wrote in his report: "The rabbis, the spiritual Council and the Kahal, which are knitted closely together, hold all things in their hand and lord it over the conscience of the Jews, and in complete isolation rule over them, without any relation to the civil order."

In 18th century Eastern European Jewry two movements developed: the religious one of the Hassidim [or Hasidim, or Chasidim] and the enlightening one favoring secular culture, spearheaded by Moses Mendelsohn; but the Kehiloth suppressed both with all its might. In 1781 the Rabbinate of [Lithuanian] Vilna placed the ban over the Hasidim and in 1784 the Assembly of Rabbis in [White Russian] Mogilev declared them as "outlaws and their property as without owner." hereafter mobs laid waste to the houses of Hasidim in several cities, it was an intra-Jewish pogrom. The Hasidim were persecuted in the most cruel and unfair manner; their rivals did not even feel embarrassed to denounce them before the Russian authorities with false political charges. In turn, in 1799 the officials arrested members of the Kehilot of Vilna for embezzlement of tax money, based on the complaints of Hasidics.

The Hasidim movement expanded, being especially successful in certain provinces. The rabbis had Hasidic books publicly burned and the Hasidim emerged as defenders of the people against abuses of the Kehilot. It is apparent that in those times the religious war between Jews overshadowed other questions of religious life.

The part of White Russia that fell to Russia in 1772 consisted of the Provinces of Polotsk (later Vitebsk) and Mogilev. In a communiqué to those governments in the name of Catherine it was explained that their residents "of whichever sex and standing they might be" would from now on have the right to public exercise of faith and to own property in addition to "all rights, freedoms and privileges which their subjects previously enjoyed." The Jews were thus legally set as equals to Christians, which had not been the case in Poland. As to the Jews, it was added that their businesses "stay and remain intact with all those rights that they today…enjoy" — i.e. nothing would be taken away from Polish rights either. Through this, the previous power of the Kehilot survived: the Jews with their Kahal system remained isolated from the rest of the population and were not immediately taken into the class of traders and businessmen that corresponded to their predominant occupations.

In the beginning, Catherine was on her guard not only against any hostile reaction of the Polish nobility, from whom power threatened to slip away, but also against giving an unfavorable impression to her Orthodox subjects. But she did extend wider rights to the Jews, whom she wished well and promised herself of their economic utility to the nation. Already in 1778 the most recent general Russian regulation was extended to White Russia: those holding up to 500 rubles belonged to the class of trade-plying townsmen; those with more capital, to the class of merchant, endowed into one of three guilds according to possession: both classes were free of the poll tax and paid 1% of their capital which was "declared according to conscience."

This regulation was of particularly great significance: it set aside the national isolation of Jews up to that time — Catherine wanted to end that.

Further, she subverted the traditional Polish perspective on Jews as an element standing outside the state. Moreover, she weakened the Kahal system, the capability of the Kahal to compel. The process began of pressing Jews into the civil organism. The Jews availed themselves to a great extent of the right to be registered as merchants — so that e.g. 10% of the Jewish population in the Mogilev Province declared themselves as merchants (but only 5.5% of the Christians.) The Jewish merchants were now freed from the tax obligation to the Kahal and did not have to apply to the Kahal any more for permission to be temporarily absent — they had only to deal with the cognizant magistrate. In 1780 the Jews in Mogilev and Shklov greeted Catherine upon her arrival with odes.

With this advance of Jewish merchants the civil category "Jew" ceased to exist. All other Jews had now likewise to be assigned to a status, and obviously the only one left for them was "townsmen." But at first, few wanted to be reclassified as such, since the annual poll tax for townsmen at that time was 60 kopecks but only 50 kopecks for "Jews." However, there was no other option. From 1783, neither the Jewish townsmen nor merchants needed to pay their taxes to the Kahal, but instead, to the magistrate, each according to his class, and from him they also received their travel passes.

The new order had consequences for the cities, which only took status into consideration, not nationality. According to this arrangement, all townsmen and thus also all Jews had the right to participate in the local class governance and occupy official posts. Corresponding to the conditions of that time this meant that the Jews became citizens with equal rights.

The entry of Jews as citizens with equal right into the merchant guilds and townsmen class was an event of great social significance. It was supposed to transform the Jews into an economic power that would have to be reckoned with, and raise their morale. It also made the practical protection of their life-interests easier. At that time the classes of traders and tradesmen just like the municipal commonwealth had a broad self-determination. Thus, a certain administrative and judicial power was placed into the hands of Jews just like Christians, through which the Jewish population held a commercial and civil influence and significance. Jews could now not only become mayors but also advisory delegates and judges.

At first limitations were enacted in the larger cities to ensure that no more Jews occupied electable positions than Christians. In 1786 however Catherine sent to the Governor General of White Russia a command written by her own hand: to actualize the equality of Jews "in the municipal-class self-governance unconditionally and without any hesitation" and to "impose an appropriate penalty upon anyone that should hinder this equality." It should be pointed out that the Jews thus were given equal rights not only in contrast to Poland, but also earlier than in France or the German states. (Under Frederick the Great the Jews suffered great limitations.) Indeed: the Jews in Russia had from the beginning the personal freedom that the Russian peasants were only granted 80 years later. Paradoxically, the Jews gained greater freedom than even the Russian merchants and tradesmen. The latter had to live exclusively in the cities, while in contrast the Jewish population could live in colonies in the country and distill liquor.

Although the Jews dwelled in clusters not only in the city but also in the villages, they were accounted as part of the city contingent inclusive of merchant and townsmen classes. According to the manner of their activity and surrounded by unfree peasantry they played an important economic roll. Rural trade was concentrated in their hands, and they leased various posts belonging to the landowners' privilege – specifically, the sale of vodka in taverns – and therewith fostered the expansion of drunkenness. The White-Russian powers reported: "The presence of Jews in the villages acts with harm upon the economic and moral condition of the rural population, because the Jews encourage drunkenness among the local population." In the stance taken by the powers-that-be, it was indicated among other things that the Jews led the peasants astray with drunkenness, idleness and poverty, that they had given them vodka on credit, received pledges in pawn for vodka, etc. But the brandy operations were an attractive source of income for both the Polish landowners and the Jewish commissioners.

Granted, the gift of citizenship that the Jews received brought a danger with it: obviously the Jews were also supposed to acquiesce to the general rule to cease the brandy business in the villages and move out. In 1783 the following decree was published: "The general rule requires every citizen to apply himself in a respectable trade and business, but not the distilling of schnapps as that is not a fitting business," and whenever the proprietor "permits the merchant, townsman or Jew to distill vodka, he will be held as a law-breaker." And thus it happened: they began to transfer the Jews from the villages to the cities to deflect them from their centuries-old occupation, the leasing of distilleries and taverns."

To the Jews the threat of a complete removal from the villages naturally appeared not as a uniform civil measure, but rather as one that was set up specially to oppose their national religion. The Jewish townsmen that were supposed to be resettled into the city and unambiguously were to be robbed of a very lucrative business in the country, fell into an inner-city and inner-Jewish competition. Indignation grew among the Jews, and in 1784 a commission of the Kehilot traveled to St Petersburg to seek the cancellation of these measures. (At the same time the Kehilot reasoned that they should, with the help of the administration, regain their lost power in its full extent over the Jewish population.) But the answer of the Czarina read: "As soon as the people yoked to the Jewish law have arrived at the condition of equality, the Order must be upheld in every case, so that each according to his rank and status enjoys the benefits and rights, without distinction of belief or national origin."

But the clenched power of the Polish proprietors also had to be reckoned with. Although the administration of White Russia forbad them in 1783 to lease the schnapps distilling to unauthorized person, especially Jews, the landlords continued to lease this industry to Jews. That was their right, an inheritance of centuries-old Polish custom. The Senate did not venture to apply force against the landholders and in 1786 removed their jurisdiction to relocate Jews into cities. For this a compromise was found: The Jews would be regarded as people that had relocated to the cities, but would retain the right to temporary visits to the villages. That meant that those that were living in the villages continued to live there. The Senate permission of 1786 permitted the Jews to live in villages and Jews were allowed to lease from the landholders the right to produce and sell alcoholic beverages, while Christian merchants and townsmen did not obtain these rights.

Even the efforts of the delegation of Kehilot in St Petersburg was not wholly without success. They did not get what they came for – the establishment of a separate Jewish court for all contentions between Jews – but in 1786 a significant part of their supervisory right was given back: the supervision of Jewish townsmen i.e. the majority of the Jewish population. This included not only the division of public benefits but also the levying of poll tax and adjudicating the right to separate from the congregation. Thus, the administration recognized its interest in not weakening the power of the Kahal.

In all Russia, the status of traders and businessmen (merchants and townsmen) did not have the right to choose their residences. Their members were bound to that locality in which they were registered, in order that the financial position of their localities would not be weakened. However, the Senate made an exception in 1782 for White Russia: the merchants could move "as the case might be, as it was propitious for commerce" from one city to another. The ruling favored especially the Jewish merchants.

However, they began to exploit this right in a greater extent than had been foreseen: Jewish merchants began to be registered in Moscow and Smolensk.

Jews began soon after the annexation of White Russia in 1782 to settle in Moscow. By the end of the 18th century the number of Jews in Moscow was considerable. Some Jews that had entered the ranks of the Moscow merchant class began to practice wholesaling. Other Jews in contrast sold foreign goods from their apartments or in the courts, or began peddling, though this was at the time forbidden. In 1790 the Moscow merchants submitted a complaint to the government: "In Moscow has emerged a not insignificant number of Jews from foreign countries and from White Russia who as opportunity afforded joined the Moscow merchant guilds and then utilized forbidden methods of business, which brought about very hurtful damage, and the cheapness of their goods indicates that it involves smuggling, but moreover as is well-known they cut coins: it is possible, that they will also do this in Moscow." As a response to their thoroughly cagey findings, the Moscow merchants demanded their removal from Moscow. The Jewish merchants appealed with a counter-complaint that they were not accepted into the Smolensk and Moscow merchant guilds.

The Council of Her Majesty heard the complaints. In accordance with the Unified Russian Order, she firmly established that the Jews did not have the right to be registered in the Russian trading towns and harbors, but only in White Russia. "By no means is usefulness to be expected" from the migration of Jews into Moscow. In December 1791 she promulgated a highest-order ukase, which prohibited Jews from joining the merchant guilds of the inner provinces, but permitted them for a limited time for trade reasons to enter Moscow. Jews were allowed to utilize the rights of the merchant guild and townsman class only in White Russia. The right to permanent residency and membership in the townsman class, Catherine continued, was granted in New Russia, now accessible in the viceregencies of Yekaterinoslav ("Glory of Catherine the Great", later changed to Dnepropetrovsk) and Taurida; that is, Catherine allowed Jews to migrate into the new, expansive territories, into which Christian merchants and townsmen from the provinces of interior Russia generally were not permitted to emigrate.

When in 1796 it was made known that groups of Jews had already immigrated into the Kiev, Chernigov and Novgorod-Syeversk Provinces, it was likewise granted there to utilize the right of the merchant guild and the townsman class. The pre-Revolution Jewish Encyclopedia writes: "The ukase of 1791 laid the groundwork for setting up the Pale of Settlement," even if it wasn't so intended. Under the conditions of the then-obtaining social and civic order in general, and of Jewish life in particular, the administration could not consider bringing about a particularly onerous situation and conclude for them exceptional laws, which among other things would restrict the right of residency. In the context of its time, this ukase did not contain that which in this respect would have brought the Jews into a less favorable condition than the Christians. The ukase of 1791 in no way limited the rights of Jews in the choice of residency, created no special borders, and for Jews the way was opened into new regions, into which in general people could not emigrate. The main point of the decree was not concerned with their Jewishness, but that they were traders; the question was not considered from the national or religious point of view, but only from the viewpoint of usefulness.

This *ukase* of 1791, which actually granted privileges to Jewish merchants in comparison to Christian ones, was in the course of time the basis for the future Pale of Settlement, which almost until the Revolution cast as it were a dark shadow over Russia. By itself, however, the *ukase* of 1791 was not so oppressive as to prevent a small Jewish colony from emerging in St Petersburg by the end of the reign of Catherine II. Here lived the famous tax-leaser Abram Peretz and some of the merchants close to him, and also, while the religious struggle was in full swing, the rabbi Avigdor Chaimovitch and his opponent, the famous hassidic Tzadik Zalman Boruchovitch.

In 1793 and 1795 the second and third Partition of Poland took place, and the Jewish population from Lithuania, Poldolia, and Volhynia, numbering almost a million, came under Russia's jurisdiction. This increase in population was a very significant event, though for a long time not recognized as such. It later influenced the fate of both Russia and the Jewry of East Europe. After centuries-long wandering Jewry came under one roof, in a single great congregation.

In the now vastly-expanded region of Jewish settlement, the same questions came up as before. The Jews obtained rights of merchant guilds and townsmen, which they had not possessed in Poland, and they got the right to equal participation in the class-municipal self-government, then had to accept the restrictions of this status: they could not migrate into the cities of the inner-Russian provinces, and were liable to be moved out of the villages.

With the now huge extent of the Jewish population, the Russian regime no longer had a way to veil the fact that the Jews continued to live in the villages simply by modeling it as a "temporary visit." A burning question was whether the economic condition could tolerate so many tradesmen and traders living amongst the peasants. In order to defuse the problem, many *shtetl* were made equal to cities. Thus, the legal possibility came about for

Jews to continue living there. But with the large number of Jews in the country and the high population density in the cities, that was no solution.

It seemed to be a natural way out that the Jews would take advantage of the possibility offered by Catherine to settle in the huge, scarcely-occupied New Russia. The new settlers were offered inducements, but this did not succeed in setting a colonization movement into motion. Even the freedom of the new settlers from taxes appeared not to be attractive enough to induce such a migration. Thus Catherine decided in 1794 to induce the Jews to emigrate with contrary measures: the Jews were relocated out of the villages. At the same time, she decided to assess the entire Jewish population with a tax that was double that paid by the Christians. Such a tax had already been paid for a long time by the Old Believers, but applied to the Jews, this law proved to be neither effective nor of long duration.

Those were the last regulations of Catherine. From the end of 1796 Paul I reigned. The *Jewish Encyclopedia* evaluates him in this way: "The time of the angry rule of Paul I passed well for the Jews… All edicts of Paul I concerning the Jews indicate that the monarch was tolerant and benevolent toward the Jewish population." When the interest of Jews conflicted with Christians, Paul I by no means automatically sided with the Christian. Even when in 1797 he ordered measures to reduce the power of the Jews and the spirituals over the peasants, that was actually directed against the Jews: the point was the protection of the peasants. Paul recognized also the right of the Hasidim not to have to live in secrecy. He extended the right of Jews to belong to the merchant-and townsmen-class even to the Courland Province which was no Polish inheritance, and later, it also did not belong to the Pale of Settlement. Consistent with that policy, he denied the respective petitions of the parishes of Kovno, Kamenez-Podolsk, Kiev and Vilna, to be permitted to move the Jews out of their cities.

Paul had inherited the stubborn resistance of the Polish landholders against any changing of their rights; among these was the right over the Jews and the right to hold court over them. They misused these rights often. Thus the Complaint of the Jews of Berdychiv [Ukraine] against the princes of Radziwill stated: "in order to hold our religious services, we must first pay gold to those to whom the prince has leased our faith," and against Catherine's former favorite Simon Zorich: "one ought not to have to pay him for the air one breathes." In Poland many shtetl and cities were the possession of nobles, and the landowners assessed arbitrary and opportunistic levies that the residents had to pay.

Derzhavin And The Belarus Famine

Since the start of the reign of Paul I there was a great famine in White Russia, especially in the province of Minsk. The poet Gavrila Romanovich Derzhavin, then serving as Senator, was commissioned to go there and determine its cause and seek a solution — for which task he received no money to buy grain, but instead had the right to confiscate possessions of negligent landowners, sell their stockpile and distribute them.

Derzhavin was not just a great poet, but also an outstanding statesman who left behind unique proofs of his effectiveness which merits examination. The famine, as Derzhavin confirmed, was unimaginable. He writes "when I arrived in White Russia, I personally convinced myself of the great scarcity of grain among the villagers. Due to the very serious hunger — virtually all nourished themselves from fermented grass, mixed with a tiny portion of meal or pearl barley. The peasants were malnourished and sallow like dead people. In order to remedy this, I found out which of the rich landowners had grain in their storehouses, took it to the town center and distributed it to the poor; and I commanded the goods of a Polish Count in view of such pitiless greed to be yielded to a trustee. After the nobleman was made aware of the dire situation he awoke from his slumber or better, from his shocking indifference toward humanity: he used every means to feed the peasants by acquiring grain from neighboring provinces and when after two months the harvest time arrived and the famine ended." When Derzhavin visited the provincial government, he so pursued the noble rulers and district police captains that the nobility banded together and sent the Czar a scurrilous complaint against him.

Derzhavin discovered that the Jewish schnapps distillers exploited the alcoholism of the peasants: "After I had discovered that the Jews from profit-seeking use the lure of drink to beguile grain from the peasants, convert it into brandy and therewith cause a famine. I commanded that they should close their distilleries in the village Liosno. I informed myself from sensible inhabitants as well as nobles, merchants, and villagers about the manner of life of the Jews, their occupations, their deceptions and all their pettifogging with which they afflict the poor dumb villages with hunger; and on the other hand, by what means one could protect them from the common pack and how to facilitate for them an honorable and respectable way out to enable them to become useful citizens."

Afterwards, in the autumn months, Derzhavin described many evil practices of the Polish landlords and Jewish leasers in his "Memorandum on the mitigation of famine in White Russia and on the lifestyles of the Jews, which he also made known to the czar and the highest officials of state. This *Memorandum* is a very comprehensive document that evaluates the conditions inherited from the Poles as well as the possibilities for overcoming the poverty of the peasants, describing the peculiarities of the Jewish way of life of that time and includes a proposal for reform in comparison to Prussia and Austria.

The very explicit practical presentation of the recommended measures makes this the first work of an enlightened Russian citizen concerning Jewish life in Russia, in those first years in which Russia acquired Jews in a large mass.

That makes it a work of special interest. The *Memorandum* consists of two parts: (1) on the residence of White Russian in general (in reviews of the Memorandum we usually find no mention of this important part) and (2) on the Jews.

In part one, Derzhavin begins by establishing that the agricultural economy was in shambles. The peasants there were "lazy on the job, not clever, they procrastinate every small task and are sluggish in field work." Year in, year out "they eat unwinnowed corn: in the spring, Kolotucha or Bolotucha from eggs and rye meal. In summer they content themselves with a mixture of a small amount of some grain or other with chopped and cooked grass. They are so weakened, that they stagger around."

The local Polish landlords "are not good proprietors. They do not manage the property themselves, but lease it out, a Polish custom. But for the lease there are no universal rules protecting the peasants from overbearing or to keep the business aspect from falling apart. Many greedy leasers, by imposing hard work and oppressive taxes bring the people into a bad way and transform the into poor, homeless peasants.' This lease is all the worst for being short-term, made for 1–3 years at a time so that the leaser hastens to get his advantage from it without regard to the exhausting of the estate."

The emaciation of the peasants was sometimes even worse: "several landlords that lease the traffic in spirits in their villages to the Jews, sign stipulations that the peasants may only buy their necessities from these leasers [at triple price]; likewise the peasants may not sell their product to anyone except the Jewish lease holder, cheaper than the market price." Thus "they plunge the villagers into misery, and especially when they distribute again their hoarded grain they must finally give a double portion; whoever does not do it is punished. The villagers are robbed of every possibility to prosper and be full."

Then he develops in more detail the problem of the liquor distilling.

Schnapps was distilled by the landlords, the landed nobility [Szlachta] of the region, the priests, monks, and Jews. Of the almost million Jews, two to three thousand lived in the villages and lived mainly from the liquor traffic. The peasants, "after bringing in the harvest, are sweaty and careless in what they spend; they drink, eat, enjoy themselves, pay the Jews for their old debts and then, whatever they ask for drinks. For this reason the shortage is already manifest by winter... In every settlement there is at least one, and in several settlements quite a few taverns built by the landlords, where for their advantage and that of the Jewish lease-holders, liquor is sold day and night... There the Jews trick them out of not only the life-sustaining grain, but that which is sown in the field, field implements, household items, health and even their life." And all that is sharpened by the mores of the koleda "... Jews travel especially during the harvest in autumn through the villages, and after they have made the farmer along with his whole family drunk, drive them into debt and take from them every last thing needed to survive... In that they box the drunkard's ears and plunder him, the villager is plunged into the deepest misery." He lists also other reasons for the impoverishing of the peasants.

Doubtless behind these fateful distilleries stand the Polish landlords. Proprietor and leaser acted in behalf of the owner and attend to making a profit:

"To this class" Gessen asserts "belonged not just Jews but also Christians" especially priests. But the Jews were an irreplaceable, active and very inventive link in the chain of exploitation of these illiterate emaciated peasants that had no rights of their own. If the White Russian settlement had not been injected with Jewish tavern managers and leasers, then the wide-spread system of exploitation would not have functioned, and removing the Jewish links in the chain would have ended it.

After this Derzhavin recommended energetic measures, as for example for the expurgation of these burdens of peasant life. The landlords would need to attend to this problem. Only they alone who are responsible for the peasants should be allowed to distill liquor "under their own... supervision and not from far-removed places," and to see to it, that "every year a supply of grain for themselves and the peasants" would be on hand, and indeed as much as would be needed for good nutrition. "If the danger arises that this is not done, then the property is to be confiscated for the state coffers. The schnapps distilling is to begin no sooner than the middle of September and end middle of April, i.e. the whole time of land cultivation is to be free of liquor consumption. In addition, liquor is not to be sold during worship services or at night. Liquor stores should only be permitted in the main streets, near the markets, mills and establishments where foreigners gather."

But all the superfluous and newly-built liquor stores, "whose number has greatly increased since the annexation of White Russia are immediately to cease use for that purpose: the sale of liquor in them to be forbidden. In villages and out-of-the-way places there should not be any, that the peasant not sink into drunkenness." Jews however should "not be permitted to sell liquor either by the glass or the keg... nor should they be the brew masters in the distilleries," and "they should not be allowed to lease the liquor stores." Koledas are also to be forbidden; as well as the short-term leasing of operations. By means of exacting stipulations "the leaser is to be prevented from working an operation into the ground." Market abuse to be forbidden under threat of punishment, by which the landlords do not permit their peasants to buy what they need somewhere else, or to sell their surplus somewhere other than to their proprietor. There were still other economic proposals: "in this manner the scarcity of food can in the future be prevented in the White Russian Province."

In the second part of the *Memorandum*, Derzhavin, going out from the task given by the Senate, submitted a suggestion for the transformation of the life of the Jews in the Russian Kingdom— not in isolation, but rather in the context of the misery of White Russia and with the goal to improve the situation. But here he set himself the assignment to give a brief overview of Jewish history, especially the Polish period in order to explain the current customs of the Jews.

Among others, he used his conversations with the Berlin-educated enlightened Jew, physician Ilya Frank, who put his thoughts down in writing.

> "The Jewish popular teachers mingle mystic-Talmudic pseudo-exegesis of the Bible with the true spirit of the teachings... They expound strict laws with the goal of isolating the Jews from other peoples and to instill a deep hatred against every other religion... Instead of cultivating a universal virtue, they contrive... an empty ceremony of honoring God... The moral character of the Jews has changed in the last century to their disadvantage, and in consequence they have become pernicious subjects... In order to renew the Jews morally and politically, they have to be brought to the point of returning to the original purity of their religion... The Jewish reform in Russia must begin with the foundation of public schools, in which the Russian, German and Jewish languages would be taught."

What kind of prejudice is it to believe that the assimilation of secular knowledge is tantamount to a betrayal of religion and folk and that working the land is not suitable for a Jew? Derzhavin declined in his *Memorandum* a suggestion by Nota Chaimovitsh Notkin, a major merchant from Shklov, whom he had also met. Although Notkin demurred from the most important conclusions and suggestions of Derzhavin that had to do with Jews, he was at the same time in favor, if possible, of excluding the Jews from the production of liquor; and saw it as needful for them to get an education and pursue a productive career, preferably working with their hands, whereby he also held out the possibility of emigration "into the fruitful steppe for the purpose of raising sheep and crops."

Following the explanation of Frank who rejected the power of the Kehilot, Derzhavin proceeded from the same general consequences: "The original principles of pure worship and ethics" of the Jews had been transformed into "false concepts," by which the simple Jewish people "is misled, and constantly is so led, so much so that between them and those of other faiths a wall has been built that cannot be broken through, which has been made firm, a wall that firmly binds the Jews together and, surrounded by darkness, separates them from their fellow citizens." Thus in raising their children "they pay plenty for Talmud instruction — and that without time limit... As long as the students continue in their current conditions, there is no prospect for a change in their ways... They believe themselves to be the true worshippers of God, and despise everyone of a different faith... There the people are brought to a constant expectation of the Messiah... They believe their Messiah, by overthrowing all earthly things will rule over them in flesh and blood and restore to them their former kingdom, fame and glory."

Of the youths he wrote: "they marry all too young, sometimes before they reach ten years old, and though nubile, they are not strong enough." Regarding the Kahal system: the inner-Jewish collection of levies provides "to the Kehilot every year an enviable sum of income that is incomparably higher than the state taxes that are raised from individuals in the census lists. The Kahal elders do not excuse anyone from the accounting. As a result, their poor masses find themselves in the condition of severe emaciation and great poverty, and there are many of them... In contrast, the members of the kahal are rich, and live in superfluity; by ruling over both levers of power, the spiritual and secular,... they have a great power over the people. In this way they hold them... in great poverty and fear." The Kehilot "issues to the people every possible command... which must be performed with such exactitude and speed, that one can only wonder."

Derzhavin identified the nub of the problem thusly: "the Jews' great number in White Russia... is itself a heavy burden for the land on account of the disproportion to that of the crop farmers... This disproportion is the outstanding one of several important reasons that produces here a shortage of grain and other edible stores... Not one of them was a crop farmer at that time, yet each possessed and gobbled up more grain than the peasant with his large family, who had harvested it by the sweat of his brow... Above all, in the villages they... are occupied in giving the peasant all their necessities on credit, at an extraordinary rate of interest; and thus the peasant, who at some time or other became a debtor to them, can no longer get free of it." Arching over this are the "frivolous landlords that put their villages into Jewish hands, not just temporarily but permanently." The landowners however are happy to be able to shift everything on to the Jews: "according to their own words, they regard the Jews as the sole reason for the wasting of the peasants" and the landlord only rarely acknowledges "that he, if they were removed from his holdings, would suffer no small loss, since he receives from them no small income from the lease."

Thus Derzhavin did not neglect to examine the matter from a variety of angles: "In fairness to the Jews we must point out also that during this grain shortage they have taken care to feed not a few hungry villagers—though everyone also knows that that came with a bill: upon the harvest being brought in, they will get it back 100-fold." In a private report to the Attorney General, Derzhavin wrote, "It is hard not to err by putting all the blame on one side. The peasants booze away their grain with the Jews and suffer under its shortage. The landholders cannot forbid drunkenness, for they owe almost all their income to the distilling of liquor. And all the blame cannot be placed even on the Jews, that they take the last morsel of bread away from the peasant to earn their own life sustenance."

To Ilya Frank, Derzhavin once said, "since the providence of this tiny scattered people has preserved them until the present, we too must take care for their protection." And in his report he wrote with the uprightness of that time, "if the Most High Providence, to the end of some unknown purpose, leaves on account of His purposes this dangerous people to live on the earth, then governments under whose scepter they have sought protection must bear it...

They are thus obligated extend their protection to the Jews, so that they may be useful both to themselves and to the society in which they dwell."

Because of all his observations in White Russia, and of his conclusion, and of all he wrote in the Memorandum, and especially because of all these lines, and probably also because he "praised the keen vision of the great Russian monarchs which forbade the immigration and travel of these clever robbers into their realm," Derzhavin is spoken of as a fanatical enemy of Jews, a great AntiSemite. He is accused – though unjustly, as we have seen – of imputing the drunkenness and poverty of the White Russian peasant exclusively to the Jews, and his positive measures were characterized as given without evidence, to serve his personal ambition. But that he was in no wise prejudiced against the Jews, is indicated in that (1) his whole Memorandum emerged in 1800 in response to the actual misery and hunger of the peasants, (2) the goal was to do well by both the White Russian peasant and the Jews, (3) he distinguished them economically and (4) his desire was to orient the Jews toward a real productive activity, of whom, as Catherine planned, a part first and foremost was supposed to have been relocated in territories that were not closed.

As a critical difficulty Derzhavin saw the instability and transientness of the Jewish population, of which scarcely 1/6 was included in the census. "Without a special, extraordinary effort it is difficult to count them accurately, because, being in cities, shtetl, manor courts, villages, and taverns, they constantly move back and forth, they do not identify themselves as local residents, but as guests that are here from another district or colony." Moreover, "they all look alike… and have the same name," and have no surname; and "not only that, all wear the same black garments: one cannot distinguish them and misidentifies them when they are registered or identified, especially in connection with judicial complaints and investigations." Therein the Kehilot takes care not "to disclose the real number, in order not unduly to burden their wealthy with taxes for the number registered."

Derzhavin sought however a comprehensive solution "to reduce the number of Jews in the White Russian villages… without causing damage to anyone and thus to ease the feeding of the original residents; yet at the same time, for those that should remain, to provide better and less degrading possibilities for earning their sustenance." In addition, he probed how to "reduce their fanaticism and, without retreating in the slightest from the rule of toleration toward different religions, to lead them by a barely-noticed way to enlightenment; and after expunging their hatred of people of other faiths, above all to bring them to give up their besetting intention of stealing foreign goods."

The goal was to find a way to separate the *freedom of religious conscience from freedom from punishment of evil deeds.*

Thereafter he laid out by layers and explicitly the measures to be recommended, and in doing so gave proof of his economic and statesmanlike competence. First, "that the Jews should have no occasion for any kind of irritation, to send them into flight or even to murmur quietly," they are to be reassured of protection and favor by a manifest of the Czar, in which should be strengthened the principle of tolerance toward their faith and the maintenance of the privileges granted by Catherine, "only with one small change to the previous principles." (But those "that will not submit to these principles shall be given the freedom to emigrate" — a demand that far exceeded in point of freedom the 20th century Soviet Union).

Immediately thereafter it states: after a specific time interval, after which all new credit is temporarily forbidden, all claims of debt between Jews and Christians to be ordered, documented, and cleared "in order to restore the earlier relation of trust so that in the future not the slightest obstruction should be found for the transformation of the Jews to a different way of life... for the relocation into other districts" or in the old places, "for the assignment of a new life conditions."

Free of debt, the Jews are thus to be made as soon as possible into freemen. All reforms "for the equalization of debt of poor people" is to be applied to poor Jews, to deflect the payment of Kahal debts or for the furnishings for migrants.

From the one group, no tax is to be levied for three years — from the other, for six years. Instead, that money is to be dedicated to the setting up of factories and work places for these Jews. Landowners must abandon obligating Jews in their shtetls to set up various factories, and instead begin on their estates to cultivate grain, "in order that they may earn their bread with their own hands," but "under no circumstance is liquor to be sold anywhere, secretly or openly," or these landholders would themselves lose their rights to the production of liquor.

It was also non-negotiable to carry out a universal, exact census of the population under responsibility of the Kahal elders. For those that had no property to declare as merchant or townsman, two new classes were to be created with smaller income Jews: village burgher and "colonist" (where the denotation "krestyanin" or farmer would not be used because of its similarity to the word 'Christian'.) The Jewish settlers would have to be regarded as free and not as serfs, but "under no condition or pretext may they dare to take Christian man-or maid-servants, they may not own a single Christian peasant, nor to expand themselves into the domain of magistrates and town fathers, so that they not gain any special rights over Christians. After they have declared their wish to be enrolled in a particular status, then must "the necessary number of young men" be sent to Petersburg, Moscow, or Riga — one group "to learn the keeping of merchant books," second to learn a trade, the third to attend schools for agriculture and land management.

Meanwhile "some energetic and precise Jews should be selected as deputies... for all these areas where land is designated for colonization." (There follows minutiae on the arrangements of plans, surveying the land, housing construction, the order to release different groups of settlers, their rights in transit, the grace-period in which they would remain tax-free — all these details that Derzhavin laid out so carefully we pass by.) On the inner ordering of the Jewish congregation: "in order to place the Jews...under the secular authorities... just the same as everyone else, the Kehilot may not continue in any form." Together with the abolishment of the Kehilot is "likewise abolished all previous profiteering assessments, which the Kehilot raised from the Jewish people... and at the same time, the secular taxes are to be assessed... as with the other subjects" (i.e. not doubled), and the schools and synagogues must be protected by law. "The males may not marry younger than 17 nor the females than 15 years."

Then there is a section on education and enlightenment of the Jews. The Jewish schools to the 12th year, and thereafter the general schools, are to become more like those of other religions; "those however that have achieved distinction in the high sciences are to be received in the academies and universities as honorary associates, doctors, professors" — but "they are not... to be taken into the rank of officers and staff officers," because "although they may also be taken into the military service, they will not take up arms against the enemy on Saturday, which in fact often does happen." Presses for Jewish books are to be constructed. Along with synagogues are to be constructed Jewish hospitals, poor houses, and orphanages.

Thus Derzhavin concluded quite self-consciously: "thus, this cross-grained [scattered] people known as Jews... in this its sad condition will observe an example of order." Especially regarding enlightenment: "This first point will bear fruit — if not today and immediately, definitely in the coming times, or at worst after several generations, in unnoticed way," and then the Jews would become "genuine subjects of the Russian throne." While Derzhavin was composing his *Memorandum*, he also made it known what the Kehilot thought about it, and made it clear that he was by no means making himself their friend.

In the official answers their rejection was formulated cautiously. It stated, "the Jews are not competent for cultivating grain nor accustomed to it, and their faith is an obstacle... They see no other possibilities than their current occupations, which serve their sustenance, and they do not need such, but would like to remain in their current condition." The Kehilot saw moreover, that the report entailed their own obsolescence, the end of their source of income, and so began, quietly, but stubbornly and tenaciously, to work against Derzhavin's whole proposal.

This opposition expressed itself, according to Derzhavin, by means of a complaint filed by a Jewess from Liosno to the Czar, in which she alleged that, in a liquor distillery, Derzhavin "horrifically beat her with a club, until she, being pregnant, gave birth to a dead infant." The Senate launched an investigation. Derzhavin answered: "As I was a quarter hour long in this factory, I not only did not strike any Jewess, but indeed did not even see one." He sought a personal reception by the Czar. "Let me be imprisoned, but I will reveal the idiocy of the man that has made such claims... How can your Highness... believe such a foolish and untrue complaint?" (The Jew that had taken the lying complaint was condemned to one year in the penitentiary, but after 2 or 3 months Derzhavin "accomplished" his being set free, this being now under the reign of Alexander I.)

The Czar Paul I was murdered in May 1801 and was unable to come to any resolution in connection with Derzhavin's *Memorandum*. It led at the time to small practical results, as one could have expected, since Derzhavin lost his position in the change of court.

Not until the end of 1802 was the "Committee for the Assimilation of the Jews" established to examine Derzhavin's detailed *Memorandum* and prepare corresponding recommendations. The committee consisted of two Polish magnates close to Alexander I: Prince Adam [Jerzy] Czartoryski and Count (Graf) Severin Potocki as well as Count Valerian Subov. Derzhavin observed regarding all three, that they too had great holdings in Poland, and would notice a significant loss of income if the Jews were to be removed, and that "the private interests of the above-mentioned Worthies would outweigh those of the state.")

Also on the committee were Interior Minister Count Kotshubey and the already-mentioned Justice Minister, the first in Russian history— Derzhavin himself. Michael Speransky also worked with the committee. The committee was charged to invite Jewish delegates from the Kehiloth of every province and these – mostly merchants of the First Guild – did come. Besides that the committee members had the right to call enlightened and well-meaning Jews of their acquaintance. The already-known Nota Notkin, who had moved from White Russia to Moscow and then St Petersburg; the Petersburg tax-leaser Abram Perets, who was a close friend of Speransky; Yehuda Leib Nevachovich and Mendel Satanaver, — both friends of Perets – and others. Not all took part in the hearings, but they exercised a significant influence on the committee members. Worthy of mention: Abram Perets' son Gregory was condemned in the Decembrist trial and exiled – probably only because he had discussed the Jewish Question with Pavel Pestel, but without suspecting anything of the Decembrist conspiracy – and because his grandson was the Russian Secretary of State, a very high position. Nevachovich, a humanist (but no cosmopolitan) who was deeply tied to Russian cultural life – then a rarity among Jews – published in Russian *The Crying Voice of the Daughter of Judah* (1803) in which he urged Russian society to reflect on the restrictions of Jewish rights, and admonished the Russians to regard Jews as their countrymen, and take the Jews among them into Russian society.

The committee came to an overwhelmingly-supported resolution: "The Jews are to be guided into the general civil life and education... To steer them toward productive work" it should be made easier for them to become employed in trades and commerce, the constriction of the right of free mobility should be lessened; they must become accustomed to wearing ordinary apparel, for "the custom of wearing clothes that are despised strengthens the custom to be despised." But the most acute problem was the fact that Jews, on account of the liquor trade, dwelled in the villages at all. Notkin strove to win the committee to the view of letting the Jews continue to live there, and only to take measures against possible abuses on their part.

"The charter of the committee led to tumult in the Kehiloth," Gessen wrote. A special convocation of their deputies in 1803 in Minsk resolved "to petition our Czar, may his fame become still greater, that they (the Worthies) assume no innovations for us." They decided to send certain delegates to Petersburg, explained, that an assembly had been held for that purpose, and even called for a three-day Jewish fast. Unrest gripped the whole Pale of Settlement. Quite apart from the threatened expulsion of Jews from the villages, the Kehiloth took a negative stance toward the cultural question out of concern to preserve their own way of life. As answer to the main points of the Recommendation the Kehiloth explained that the Reform must in any case be postponed 15–20 years.

Derzhavin wrote "there were from their side various rebuttals aimed to leave everything as it was." In addition, Gurko, a White Russian landowner sent Derzhavin a letter he had received: a Jew in White Russia had written him regarding one of his plenipotentiaries in Petersburg. It said that they had, in the name of all Kehilot of the world, put the cherem or herem, (i.e. the ban) on Derzhavin as a Persecutor, and had gathered a million to be used as gifts (bribes) for this situation and had forwarded it to St Petersburg. They appealed for all efforts to be applied to the removal of Derzhavin as Attorney General, and if that were not possible to seek his life. However the thing they wanted to achieve was not to be forbidden to sell liquor in the village tavern, and in order to make it easier to advance this business, they would put together opinions from foreign regions, from different places and peoples, on how the situation of the Jews could be improved. In fact such opinions, sometimes in French, sometimes, in German, began to be sent to the Committee.

Besides this, Nota Notkin became the central figure that organized the little Jewish congregation of Petersburg. In 1803 he submitted a brief to the Committee in which he sought to paralyze the effect of the proposal submitted by Derzhavin. Derzhavin writes that Notkin came to him one day and asked, with "feigned well-wishing," that he, Derzhavin, should not take a stand all alone against his colleagues on the Committee, who all are on the side of the Jews; whether he would not accept 100,000 or, if that was too little, 200,000 rubles, "only so that he could be of one mind with all his colleagues on the committee." Derzhavin decided to disclose this attempt at bribery to the Czar and prove it to him with Gurko's letter. He thought such strong proofs prove effective and the Czar would start to be wary of the people that surrounded him and protected the Jews. Speransky also informed the Czar of it, but Speransky was fully committed to the Jews, and from the first meeting of the Jewish Committee it became apparent that all members represented the view that the liquor distilling should continue in the hands of Jews as before.

Derzhavin opposed it. Alexander bore himself ever more coldly toward him and dismissed his Justice Minister shortly thereafter (1803). Beside this, Derzhavin's papers indicate that whether in military or civil service he had come into disfavor. He retired from public life in 1805.

Derzhavin foresaw much that developed in the problematic Russo-Judaic relationship throughout the entire 19th century, even if not in the exact and unexpected form that it took in the event. He expressed himself coarsely, as was customary then, but he did not intend to oppress the Jews; on the contrary, he wanted to open to the Jews paths to a more free and productive life.

Chapter 2

During the Reign of Alexander Ist

At the end of 1804, the Committee in charge of the Organisation of the Jews concluded its work by drafting a "Regulation on Jews" (known as the "Regulation of 1804"), the first collection of laws in Russia concerning Jews.

The Committee explained that its aim was to improve the condition of the Jews, to direct them towards a useful activity "by opening this path exclusively for their own good... and by discarding anything that might divert them from it, without calling for coercive measures." [85] The Regulation established the principle of equal civil rights for Jews (Article 42): "All Jews who live in Russia, who have recently settled there, or who have come from foreign countries for their commercial affairs, are free and are under the strict protection of the laws in the same way other Russian subjects are." (In the eyes of Professor Gradovsky, "We can not but see in this article the desire to assimilate this people to the whole population of Russia."[86])

The Regulation gave the Jews greater opportunities than Derzhavin's original proposals; thus, in order to create textile or leather factories, or to move to agricultural economy on virgin lands, it proposed that a government subsidy be directly paid. Jews were given the right to acquire land without serfs, but with the possibility of hiring Christian workers. Jews who owned factories, merchants, and craftsmen had the right to leave the Pale of Settlement "for a time, for business purposes," thus easing the borders of this newly established area. (All that was promised for the current of the coming year was the abrogation of double royalties[87], but it soon disappeared.) All the rights of the Jews were reaffirmed: the

---

[85] *Hessen*, Istoria evreïskogo naroda v Rossii (History of the Jewish People in Russia), in 2 volumes, t. 1, Leningrad, 1925, p. 149.

[86] *M. Kovalevsky*, Ravnopravie evreev i ego vragi (The Equality of the Rights of Jews and their Adversaries), in Schit, literary collection edited by L. Andréev, M. Gorky and F. Sologoub, 3rd edition completed, Russian Society for the Study of the lives of Jews, Moscow, 1916, p. 117.

[87] Double tax instituted for the Jews by Catherine (to whom the "old believers" had long been subjected), but which was hardly applied.

inviolability of their property, individual liberty, the profession of their religion, their community organisation — in other words, the *Kehalim* system was left without significant changes (which, in fact, undermined the idea of a fusion of the Jewish world within the Russian state): the *Kehalim* retained their old right to collect royalties, which conferred on them a great authority, but without the ability of increasing them; Religious punishments and anathemas (*Herem*) were forbidden, which assured liberty to the *Hassidim*. In accordance with the wishes of the *Kehalim*, the project of establishing Jewish schools of general education was abandoned, but "all Jewish children are allowed to study with other children without discrimination in all schools, colleges, and all Russian universities," and in these establishments no child "shall be under any pretext deviated from his religion or forced to study what might be contrary or opposed to him." Jews "who, through their abilities, will attain a meritorious level in universities in medicine, surgery, physics, mathematics, and other disciplines, will be recognised as such and promoted to university degrees." It was considered essential that the Jews learn the language of their region, change their external appearance and adopt family names. In conclusion, the Committee pointed out that in other countries "nowhere were used means so liberal, so measured, and so appropriate to the needs of the Jews." J. Hessen agrees that the Regulation of 1804 imposed fewer restrictions on Jews than the Prussian Regulations of 1797. Especially since the Jews possessed and retained their individual liberty, which a mass of several million Russian peasants subjected to serfdom did not enjoy.[88] "The Regulation of 1804 belongs to the number of acts imbued with the spirit of tolerance."[89]

The Messenger of Europe, one of the most read journals of the times wrote: "Alexander knows that the vices we attribute to the Jewish nation are the inevitable consequences of oppression that has burdened it for many centuries. The goal of the new law is to give the State useful citizens, and to Jews a homeland."[90]

However, the Regulation did not resolve the most acute problem in accordance with the wishes of all Jews, namely the Jewish population, the *Kehalim* deputies, and the Jewish collaborators of the Committee. The Regulation stipulated that: "No one among the Jews... in any village or town, can own any form of stewardship of inns or cabarets, under their name nor under the name of a third party, nor are they allowed to sell alcohol or live in such places"[91] and proposed that the entire Jewish population leave the countryside within three years, by the beginning of

---

[88] *Hessen*, t. 1, pp. 148–158; JE, t. 1, pp. 799-800.
[89] JE, t. 13, pp. 158-159.
[90] *Hessen*, t. 1, p. 158–159.
[91] JE, t. 3, p. 79.

1808. (We recall that such a measure had already been advocated under Paul in 1797, even before the Derzhavin project appeared: not that all Jews without exception were to be distanced from the villages, but in order that "by its mass, the Jewish population in the villages would not exceed the economic possibilities of the peasants as a productive class, it is proposed to reduce the number of them in the agglomerations of the districts."[92] This time it was proposed to direct the majority of the Jews to agricultural labour in the virgin lands of the Pale of Settlement, New Russia, but also the provinces of Astrakhan and the Caucasus, exonerating them for ten years of the royalties they up to then had to pay, "with the right to receive a loan from the Treasury for their enterprises" to be reimbursed progressively after ten years of franchise; to the most fortunate, it was proposed to acquire land in personal and hereditary ownership with the possibility of having them exploited by agricultural workers."[93]

In its refusal to allow distillation, the Committee explained: "As long as this profession remains accessible to them... which, in the end, exposes them to the recriminations, contempt, and even hatred of inhabitants, the general outcry towards them will not cease." [94] Moreover, "Can we consider this measure [of removing the Jews from villages] as repressive when they are offered so many other means not only to live in ease, but also to enrich themselves in agriculture, industry, crafts; and that they are also given the possibility of possessing land in full ownership? How could this people be regarded as oppressed by the abolition of a single branch of activity in a State in which they are offered a thousand other activities in fertile, uninhabited areas suitable for the cultivation of cereals and other agricultural production...?"[95]

These are compelling arguments. However, Hessen finds that the text of the Committee testifies to "a naive look... on the nature of the economic life of a people [consisting in] believing that economic phenomena can be changed in a purely mechanical way, by decree."[96] From the Jewish side, the projected relocation of the Jews from villages and the ban imposed on them on making alcohol, the "secular occupation" of the Jews[97], was

---

[92] *Hessen*, t. 1, p. 128.
[93] *V. N. Nikitin*, Evrei i zemledeltsy: Istoritcheskoe. zakonodatelnoe. administra-tivnoc i bylovoc polojenie kolonii so vremeni ikh vozniknivenia do nachikh dneï (The Jews in Agriculture: Historical, legal, administrative, practice of the colonies from their origin to the present day), 1807-1887, Saint Petersburg, 1887, pp. 6-7.
[94] *Prince N. N. Golitsyn*, Istoria rousskogo zakonodatelstva o evreiakh (History of Russian Legislation for the Jews), Saint Petersburg, t. 1, 1649-1825, p. 430.
[95] *Ibidem*, t. 1, pp. 439-440.
[96] Ibidem.
[97] JE, t. 3. p. 79.

perceived as a terribly cruel decision. (And it was in these terms that it was condemned by Jewish historiography fifty and even a hundred years later.)

Given the liberal opinions of Alexander I, his benevolence towards the Jews, his perturbed character, his weak will (without a doubt forever broken by his accession to the throne at the cost of his father's violent death), it is unlikely that the announced deportation of the Jews would have been energetically conducted; even if the reign had followed a peaceful course, it would have undoubtedly been spread out over time.

But soon after the adoption of the 1804 Regulations, the threat of war in Europe was outlined, followed by the application of measures favouring the Jews by Napoleon, who united a Sanhedrin of Jewish deputies in Paris. "The whole Jewish problem then took an unexpected turn. Bonaparte organised in Paris a meeting of the Jews whose main aim was to offer the Jewish nation various advantages and to create a link between the Jews scattered throughout Europe. Thus, in 1806, Alexander I ordered a new committee to be convened to "examine whether special steps should be taken, and postpone the relocation of the Jews."[98]

As announced in 1804, the Jews were supposed to abandon the villages by 1808. But practical difficulties arose, and as early as 1807 Alexander I received several reports highlighting the necessity of postponing the relocation. An imperial decree was then made public, "requiring all Jewish societies… to elect deputies and to propose through them the means which they consider most suitable for successfully putting into practice the measures contained in the Regulation of December 9th, 1804." The election of these Jewish deputies took place in the western provinces, and their views were transmitted to St. Petersburg. "Of course, these deputies expressed the opinion that the departure of the Jews residing in the villages had to be postponed to a much later time.

(One of the reasons given was that, in the villages, the innkeepers had free housing, whereas in towns and cities, they would have to pay for them). The Minister of Internal Affairs wrote in his report that "the relocation of Jews currently residing in villages to land belonging to the State will take several decades, given their overwhelming number."[99] Towards the end of 1808, the Emperor gave orders to suspend the article prohibiting the Jews from renting and producing alcohol, and to leave the Jews where they lived, "until a subsequent ruling." [100] Immediately afterwards (1809) a new committee, said "of the Senator Popov", was instituted for the study of all

---

[98] *G. R. Derzhavin*, works in 9 vol., 2nd ed., Saint Petersburg, 1864–1883, t. 6, 1876, pp. 761–762.
[99] *Hessen*, t. 1, pp. 163-165.
[100] JE, t. 1. p. 801.

problems and the examination of the petitions formulated by the Jewish deputies. This Committee "considered it indispensable" to put an "energetic" end to the relocation of the Jews and to retain the right to the production and trade of vodka.[101] The Committee worked for three years and presented its report to the Emperor in 1812. Alexander I did not endorse this report: he did not wish to undermine the importance of the previous decision and had in no way lost his desire to act in favour of the peasants: "He was ready to soften the measure of expulsion, but not to renounce it."[102] Thereupon the Great War broke out with Napoleon, followed by the European war, and Alexander's concerns changed purpose.

Since then, displacement out of the villages never was initiated as a comprehensive measure in the entire Pale of Settlement, but at most in the form of specific decisions in certain places.[103]

During the war, according to a certain source, the Jews were the only inhabitants not to flee before the French army, neither in the forests nor inland; in the neighbourhood of Vilnius, they refused to obey Napoleon's order to join his army, but supplied him forage and provisions without a murmur; nevertheless, in certain places it was necessary to resort to requisitions.[104]

Another source reports that "the Jewish population suffered greatly from the abuses committed by Napoleon's soldiers," and that "many synagogues were set on fire," but goes even further by stating that "Russian troops were greatly helped by what was called the "Jewish post," set up by Jewish merchants, which transmitted the information with a celerity unknown at the time (inns serving as 'relay')"; they even "used Jews as couriers for the connections between the various detachments of the Russian army." When the Russian army reassumed possession of the land, "the Jews welcomed the Russian troops with admiration, bringing bread and alcohol to the soldiers." The future Nicholas I, Grand Duke at that time, noted in his diary: "It is astonishing that they [Jews] remained surprisingly faithful to us in 1812 and even helped us where they could, at the risk of their lives."[105] At the most critical point of the retreat of the French at the passage of Berezina, the local Jews communicated to the Russian command the presumed crossing point; this episode is well known. But it was in fact a successful ruse of General Laurançay: he was persuaded that the Jews

---

[101] *Ibidem.*
[102] *Hessen*, 1.1, p. 163-167.
[103] JE, t. 5, p. 859.
[104] *S. Pozner*, Evrei Litvy i Beloroussii 125 let lomou nazad (The Jews of Lithuania and Belarus 125 Years Ago), in M.J., Directory, 1939, pp. 60, 65–66.
[105] PJE, t. 7. pp. 309–311.

would communicate this information to the Russians, and the French, of course, chose another crossing point.[106]

After 1814, the reunification of central Poland brought together more than 400,000 Jews. The Jewish problem was then presented to the Russian government with more acuteness and complexity. In 1816, the Government Council of the Kingdom of Poland, which in many areas enjoyed a separate state existence, ordered the Jews to be expelled from their villages—they could also remain there, but only to work the land, and this without the help of Christian workers. But at the request of the *Kahal* of Warsaw, as soon as it was transmitted to the Emperor, Alexander gave orders to leave the Jews in place by allowing them to engage in the trade of vodka, on the sole condition that they should not sell it *on credit*.[107]

It is true that in the Regulations published by the Senate in 1818, the following provisions are again found: "To put an end to the coercive measures of proprietors, which are ruinous for the peasants, for non-repayment of their debts to the Jews, which forces them to sell their last possessions... Regarding the Jews who run inns, it is necessary to forbid them to lend money at interest, to serve vodka on credit, to then deprive the peasants of their livestock or any other things that are indispensable to them."[108] Characteristic trait of the entirety of Alexander's reign: no spirit of continuation in the measures taken; the regulations were promulgated but there was no effective control to monitor their implementation. Same goes with the statute of 1817 with regard to the tax on alcohol: in the provinces of Great Russia, distillation was prohibited to the Jews; however, as early as 1819, this prohibition was lifted "until Russian artisans have sufficiently perfected themselves in this trade."[109]

Of course, Polish owners who were too concerned by their profits opposed the eradication of Jewish distilleries in the rural areas of the western provinces; and, at that time, the Russian Government did not dare act against them.

However, in the Chernigov province where their establishment was still recent, the successful removal of the distilleries in the hands of owners and Jews was undertaken in 1821, after the governor reported following a bad harvest that "the Jews hold in hard bondage the peasants of the Crown and Cossacks."[110] A similar measure was taken in 1822 in the province of Poltava; in 1823 it was partially extended to the provinces of Mogilev and

---

[106] *Cf*, Rousskaïa Volia (The Russian Will), Petrograd, 1917, 22 April, p. 3.
[107] *Hessen*, t. 1, pp. 222-223.
[108] JE*, t. 3, pp. 80-81.
[109] *Ibidem*, t. 5, pp. 609, 621.
[110] *Ibidem*, p. 612.

Vitebsk. But its expansion was halted by the pressing efforts of the *Kehalim*.

Thus, the struggle led over the twenty-five year reign of Alexander against the production of alcohol by the transplantation of the Jews out of villages gave little results. But distilling was not the only type of production in the Pale of Settlement.

Owners leased out various assets in different sectors of the economy, here a mill, there fishing, elsewhere bridges, sometimes a whole property, and in this way not only peasant serfs were leased (such cases multiplied from the end of the eighteenth century onwards[111]), but also the "serfs" churches, that is to say orthodox churches, as several authors point out: N. I. Kostomarov, M. N. Katkov, V. V. Choulguine. These churches, being an integral part of an estate, were considered as belonging to the Catholic proprietor, and in their capacity as operators, the Jews considered themselves entitled to levy money on those who frequented these churches and on those who celebrated private offices. For baptism, marriage, or funeral, it was necessary to receive the authorisation of "a Jew for a fee"; "the epic songs of Little Russia bursts with bitter complaints against the 'Jewish farmers' who oppress the inhabitants."[112]

The Russian governments had long perceived this danger: the rights of the farmers were likely to extend to the peasant himself and directly to his work, and "the Jews should not dispose of the personal labour of the peasants, and by means of a lease, although not being Christians, become owners of peasant serfs"—which was prohibited on several occasions both by the decree of 1784 and by the ordinances of the Senate of 1801 and 1813: "the Jews cannot possess villages or peasants, nor dispose of them under any name whatsoever."[113]

However, the ingenuity of the Jews and the owners managed to circumvent what was forbidden. In 1816, the Senate discovered that "the Jews had found a means of exercising the rights of owners under the name of *krestentsia*, that is to say, after agreement with the owners, they harvest the wheat and barley sown by the peasants, these same peasants must first thresh and then deliver to the distilleries leased to these same Jews; they must also watch over the oxen that are brought to graze in their fields, provide the Jews with workers and wagons… Thus the Jews dispose of all these areas… while the landlords, receiving from them substantial rent referred to as *krestentsia*, sell to the Jews all the harvest to come that are

---

[111] JE, t. 11, p. 492.
[112] *V. V. Choulguine,* Tchto nam v nikh ne nravitsia…: Ob antisemitism v Rossii (What we do not like about them: Anti-Semitism in Russia). Paris, 1929, p. 129.
[113] JE*, t. 3, p. 81.

sown on their lands: one can conclude from this that they condemn their peasants to famine."[114]

It is not the peasants who are, so to speak, claimed as such, but only the *krestentsia*, which does not prevent the result from being the same.

Despite all the prohibitions, the practice of the *krestentsia* continued its crooked ways. Its extreme intricacy resulted from the fact that many landowners fell into debt with their Jewish farmers, receiving money from them on their estate, which enabled the Jews to dispose of the estate and the labour of the serfs. But when, in 1816, the Senate decreed that it was appropriate "to take the domains back from the Jews," he charged them to recover on their own the sums they had lent. The deputies of the *Kehalim* immediately sent a humble petition to his Majesty, asking him to annul this decree: the general administrator in charge of foreign faith affairs, the Prince N.N. Golitsyn, convinced the Emperor that "inflicting punishment on only one category of offenders with the exception" of owners and officials. The landlords "could still gain if they refuse to return the capital received for the *krestentsia* and furthermore keep the *krestentsia* for their profit"; if they have abandoned their lands to the Jews in spite of the law, they must now return the money to them.[115]

The future Decembrist P. I. Pestel, at that time an officer in the western provinces, was by no means a defender of the autocracy, but an ardent republican; he recorded some of his observations on the Jews of this region, which were partially included in the preamble to his government programme ("Recommendations for the Provisional Supreme Government"): "Awaiting the Messiah, the Jews consider themselves temporary inhabitants of the country in which they find themselves, and so they never, on any account, want to take care of agriculture, they tend to despise even the craftsmen, and only practice commerce." "The spiritual leaders of the Jews, who are called rabbis, keep the people in an incredible dependence by forbidding them, in the name of faith, any reading other than that of the Talmud... A people that does not seek to educate itself will always remain a prisoner of prejudice"; "the dependence of the Jews in relation to the rabbis goes so far that any order given by the latter is executed piously, without a murmur." "The close ties between the Jews give them the means to raise large sums of money... for their common needs, in particular to incite different authorities to concession and to all sorts of embezzlements which are useful to them, the Jews." That they readily accede to the condition of possessors, "one can see it ostensibly in the provinces where they have elected domicile. All commerce is in their

---

[114] *Ibidem**.
[115] *Ibidem**, p. 82; cf. equally *Hessen*, t. 1. pp. 185, 187.

hands, and few peasants are not, by means of debts, in their power; this is why they terribly ruin the regions where they reside." "The previous government [that of Catherine] has given them outstanding rights and privileges which accentuate the evil they are doing," for example the right not to provide recruits, the right not to announce deaths, the right to distinct judicial proceedings subject to the decisions of the rabbis, and "they also enjoy all the other rights accorded to other Christian ethnic groups"; "Thus, it can be clearly seen that the Jews form within the State, a separate State, and enjoy more extensive rights than Christians themselves."

"Such a situation cannot be perpetuated further, for it has led the Jews to show a hostile attitude towards Christians and has placed them in a situation" contrary to the public order that must prevail in the State.[116]"

In the final years of Alexander I's reign, economic and other type of prohibitions against Jewish activities were reinforced. In 1818, a Senate decree now forbade that "never may Christians be placed in the service of Jews for debts."[117] In 1819, another decree called for an end to "the works and services that peasants and servants perform on behalf of Jews."[118] Golitsyn, always him, told the Council of Ministers "those who dwell in the houses of the Jews not only forget and no longer fulfil the obligations of the Christian faith, but adopt Jewish customs and rites."[119] It was then decided that "Jews should no longer employ Christians for their domestic service."[120] It was believed that "this would also benefit the needy Jews who could very well replace Christian servants."[121] But this decision was not applied. (This is not surprising: among the urban Jewish masses there was poverty and misery, "for the most part, they were wretched people who could scarcely feed themselves,"[122] but the opposite phenomenon has never been observed: the Jews would hardly work in the service of Christians. Undoubtedly some factors opposed it, but they also apparently had means of subsistence coming from communities between which solidarity reigned.)

However, as early as 1823, Jewish farmers were allowed to hire Christians. In fact, "the strict observance of the decision prohibiting" Christians from working on Jewish lands "was too difficult to put into practice."[123]

---

[116] *P. I. Pestel*, Rousskaïa pravda (Russian Truth), Saint Petersburg, 1906, chap. 2, § 14, pp. 50-52.
[117] *Ibidem**, t. 11, p. 493.
[118] *Ibidem**, 1.1, p. 804.
[119] *Ibidem**, 1.11, p. 493.
[120] *Ibidem**, t. 1, p. 804.
[121] *Ibidem*, t. 11, p. 493.
[122] *Hessen**. t. 1, pp. 206–207.
[123] JE, t. 11, p. 493.

During these same years, to respond to the rapid development of the sect of the *soubbotniki*[124] in the provinces of Voronezh, Samara, Tula, and others, measures were taken for the Pale of Settlement to be more severely respected.

Thus, "in 1821, Jews accused of 'heavily exploiting' the peasants and Cossacks were expelled from the rural areas of the Chernigov province and in 1822 from the villages of Poltava province."[125]

In 1824, during his journey in the Ural Mountains, Alexander I noticed that a large number of Jews in factories, "by clandestinely buying quantities of precious metals, bribed the inhabitants to the detriment of the Treasury and the manufacturers", and ordered "that the Jews be no longer tolerated in the private or public factories of the mining industry."[126]

The Treasury also suffered from smuggling all along the western frontier of Russia, goods and commodities being transported and sold in both capitals without passing through customs. The governors reported that smuggling was mainly practised by Jews, particularly numerous in the border area. In 1816, the order was given to expel all the Jews from a strip sixty kilometres wide from the frontier and that it be done in the space of three weeks. The expulsion lasted five years, was only partial and, as early as 1821, the new government authorised the Jews to return to their former place of residence. In 1825 a more comprehensive but much more moderate decision was taken: The only Jews liable to deportation were those not attached to the local *Kehalim* or who did not have property in the border area.[127] In other words, it was proposed to expel only intruders. Moreover, this measure was not systematically applied.

The Regulation of 1804 and its article stipulating the expulsion of the Jews from the villages of the western provinces naturally posed a serious problem to the government: where were they to be transferred? Towns and villages were densely populated, and this density was accentuated by the competition prevailing in small businesses, given the very low development of productive labour. However, in southern Ukraine stretched New Russia, vast, fertile, and sparsely populated.

Obviously, the interest of the state was to incite the mass of non-productive Jews expelled from the villages to go work the land in New Russia. Ten years earlier, Catherine had tried to ensure the success of this incentive by striking the Jews with a double royalty, while totally exempting those who

---

[124] Sabbatarians: sect whose existence is attested from the late seventeenth century, which was characterised by pronounced Judaising tendencies.
[125] PJE, t. 7, p. 313; Kovalevski, in Schit [The Butcher], p. 17.
[126] JE, 1.1, p. 805.
[127] JE, t. 12, p. 599.

would accept to be grafted to New Russia. But this double taxation (Jewish historians mention it often) was not real, as the Jewish population was not censused, and only the *Kahal* knew the manpower, while concealing the numbers to the authorities in a proportion that possibly reached a good half. (As early as 1808, the royalty ceased to be demanded, and the exemption granted by Catherine no longer encouraged any Jews to migrate).

This time, and for Jews alone, more than 30,000 hectares of hereditary (but non-private) land was allocated in New Russia, with 40 hectares of State land per family (in Russia the average lot of the peasants was a few hectares, rarely more than ten), cash loans for the transfer and settlement (purchase of livestock, equipment, etc, which had to be repaid after a period of six years, within the following ten years); the prior construction of an izba log house was offered to the settlers (in this region, not only the peasants but even some owners lived in mud houses), to exempt them of royalties for ten years with maintenance of individual freedom (in these times of serfdom) and the protection of the authorities.[128] (The 1804 Regulations having exempted Jews from military service, the cash compensation was included in the royalty fee.) The enlightened Jews, few at the time (Notkine, Levinson), supported the governmental initiative—"but this result must be achieved through incentives, in no way coercive"—and understood very well the need for their people to move on to productive work.

The eighty years of the difficult saga of Jewish agriculture in Russia are described in the voluminous and meticulous work of the Jew V. N. Nikitin (as a child, he had been entrusted to the cantonists, where he had received his name), who devoted many years to the study of the archives of the enormous unpublished official correspondence between St. Petersburg and New Russia.

An abundant presentation interspersed with documents and statistical tables, with tireless repetitions, possible contradictions in the reports made at sometimes very distant times by inspectors of divergent opinions, all accompanied by detailed and yet incomplete tables—none of this has been put in order, and it offers, for our brief exposition, much too dense material. Let us try, however, by condensing the citations, to draw a panorama that is simultaneously broad and clear.

The government's objective, Nikitin admits, in addition to the colonisation programme of unoccupied lands, was to give the Jews more space than they had, to accustom them to productive physical labour, to help guard them from "harmful occupations" by which, "whether they liked it or not, many of them made the life of the peasant serfs even more difficult than it already

---

[128] *Nikitin*, pp. 6-7.

was." "The government... bearing in mind the improvement of their living conditions, proposed to them to turn to agriculture...; The government... did not seek to attract Jews by promises; on the contrary, it endeavoured that there should be no more than three hundred families transferred each year"[129]; it deferred the transfer so long as the houses were not built on the spot, and invited the Jews, meanwhile, to send some of their men as scouts. Initially, the idea was not bad, but it had not sufficiently taken into account the mentality of the Jewish settlers nor the weak capacities of the Russian administration. The project was doomed in advance by the fact that the work of the earth is an art that demands generations to learn: one cannot attach successfully to the earth people who do not wish it or who are indifferent to it.

The 30,000 hectares allocated to Jews in New Russia remained inalienable for decades. *A posteriori*, the journalist I.G. Orchansky considered that Jewish agriculture could have been a success, but only if Jews had been transferred to the nearby Crown lands of Belarus where the peasant way of life was under their control, before their eyes.[130] Unfortunately, there was scarcely any land there (for example, in the province of Grodno there were only 200 hectares, marginal and infertile lands "where the entire population suffered from poor harvests."[131] At first there were only three dozen families willing to emigrate.

The Jews hoped that the expulsion measures from the western provinces would be reported; it had been foreseen in 1804 that its application would extend on three years, but it was slow to begin. The fateful deadline of January 1st, 1808 approaching, they began to leave the villages under escort; from 1806 onwards, there was also a movement in favour of emigration among the Jews, the more so as the rumour indicated the advantages which were connected with it. The demands for emigration then flooded *en masse*: "They rushed there... as it were the Promised Land...; like their ancestors who left Chaldea in Canaan, entire groups left surreptitiously, without authorisation, and some even without a passport. Some resold the passport they had obtained from other departing groups, and then demanded that they be replaced under the pretext that they had lost it. The candidates for departure "were day by day more numerous," and all "insistently demanded land, housing and subsistence."[132]

The influx exceeded the possibilities of reception of the Support Office of the Jews created in the province of Kherson: time was lacking to build

---

[129] *Ibidem*, pp. 7, 58, 154.
[130] *I. Orchansky*, Evrei v Rossii (Jews in Russia), Essays and Studies, fasc. 1, Saint Petersburg, 1872, pp. 174-175.
[131] *Nikitin*, pp. 3, 128.
[132] *Ibidem**, pp. 7, 13, 16, 19, 58.

houses, dig wells, and the organisation suffered from the great distances in this region of the steppes, the lack of craftsmen, doctors, and veterinarians. The government was indiscriminate of the money, the good provisions, and sympathy towards the migrants, but the Governor Richelieu demanded in 1807 that the entrances be limited to 200, 300 families per year, while receiving without limitation those who wished to settle on their own account. "In case of a bad harvest, all these people will have to be fed for several years in a row." (The poorest settlers were paid daily allowances.) However, the governors of the provinces allowed those over-quota who wished to leave—without knowing the exact number of those who were leaving; hence many vicissitudes along the way, due to misery, sickness, death.[133] Some quite simply disappeared during the trip.

Distances across the steppe (between one hundred and three hundred kilometres between a colony and the Office), the inability of the administration to keep an accurate count and establish a fair distribution, meant that some of the migrants were more helped than others; some complained that they did not receive any compensation or loans. The colony inspectors, too few in numbers, did not have time to take a closer look (they received a miserable wage, had no horses, and walked on foot). After a period of two years of stay, some settlers still had no farm, no seeds, nor bread. The poorest were allowed to leave wherever they pleased, and "those who renounced their condition as farmers recovered their former status as *bourgeois*." But only a fifth of them returned to their country of origin, and the others wandered (the loans granted to those who had been scratched off the list of settlers were to be considered definitively lost). Some reappeared for a time in the colonies, others disappeared "without looking back or leaving a trace," the others pounded the pavement in the neighbouring towns "by trading, according to their old habit."[134]

The many reports of the Office and inspectors provide insight into how the new settlers were operating. To train the settlers who did not know where to start or how to finish, the services of peasants of the Crown were requested; the first ploughing is done for the most part through hired Russians. The habit is taken of "correcting defects by a hired labour." They sow only a negligible portion of the plot allocated to them, and use poor-quality seeds; one has received specific seeds but does not plough or sow; another, when sowing, loses a lot of seeds, and same goes during harvest. Due to lack of experience, they break tools, or simply resell them. They do not know how to keep the livestock.

---

[133] *Ibidem**, pp. 14, 15, 17, 19, 24, 50.
[134] *Ibidem*, pp. 26, 28, 41, 43-44, 47, 50, 52, 62-63, 142.

"They kill cattle for food, then complain that they no longer have any"; they sell cattle to buy cereals; they do not make provision for dried dung, so their izbas, insufficiently heated, become damp; they do not fix their houses, so they fall apart; they do not cultivate vegetable gardens; they heat the houses with straw stored to feed the cattle. Not knowing how to harvest, neither to mow nor to thresh, the colonists cannot be hired in the neighbouring hamlets: no one wants them. They do not maintain the good hygiene of their homes, which favours diseases. They "absolutely did not expect to be personally occupied with agricultural labour, doubtlessly they thought that the cultivation of the land would be assured by other hands; that once in possession of great herds, they would go and sell them at the fairs." The settlers "hope to continue receiving public aid." They complain "of being reduced to a pitiable condition," and it is really so; of having "worn their clothes up to the rope," and that is the case; but the inspection administration replies: "If they have no more clothes, it is out of idleness, for they do not raise sheep, and sow neither linen nor hemp," and their wives "neither spin nor weave." Of course, an inspector concluded in his report, if the Jews cannot handle their operations, it is "by habit of a relaxed life, because of their reluctance to engage in agricultural work and their inexperience," but he thought it fair to add: "agriculture must be prepared from earliest youth, and the Jews, having lived indolently until 45 to 50 years, are not in a position of transforming themselves into farmers in such a short time."[135]

The Treasury was obliged to spend two to three times more on the settlers than expected, and extensions kept on being demanded. Richelieu maintained that "the complaints come from the lazy Jews, not from the good farmers"; However, another report notes that "unluckily for them, since their arrival, they have never been comforted by an even remotely substantial harvest."[136]

"In response to the many fragments communicated to St. Petersburg to signal how the Jews deliberately renounced all agricultural work," the ministry responded in the following way: "The government has given them public aid in the hope that they will become farmers not only in name, but in fact. Many immigrants are at risk, if not incited to work, to remain debtors to the state for a long time."[137] The arrival of Jewish settlers in New Russia at the expense of the state, uncontrolled and ill-supported by an equipment programme, was suspended in 1810. In 1811 the Senate gave the Jews the right to lease the production of alcohol in the localities belonging to the Crown, but within the limits of the Pale of Settlement. As

---

[135] *Ibidem**, p. 72.
[136] *Ibidem*, pp. 24, 37-40, 47-50, 61, 65, 72-73, 93.
[137] *Ibidem*, pp. 29, 37-38.

soon as the news was known in New Russia, the will to remain in agriculture was shaken for many settlers: although they were forbidden to leave the country, some left without any identity papers to become innkeepers in villages dependent on the Crown, as well as in those belonging to landowners. In 1812, it appeared that of the 848 families settled there were in fact only 538; 88 were considered to be on leave (parties earning their living in Kherson, Nikolayev, Odessa, or even Poland); as for the others, they had simply disappeared. This entire programme—"the authoritative installation of families on land"—was something *unprecedented* not only in Russia but in the whole of Europe."[138]

The Government now considered that "in view of the Jews' now proven disgust for the work of the land, seeing that they do not know how to go about it, given the negligence of the inspectors", it appears that the migration has given rise to major disturbances; therefore "the Jews should *be judged indulgently*." On the other hand, "how can we guarantee the repayment of public loans by those who will be allowed to leave their status as farmers, how to palliate, without injuring the Treasury, the inadequacies of those who will remain to cultivate the land, how to alleviate the fate of those people who endured so many misfortunes and are living on the edge?[139] As for the inspectors, they suffered not only from understaffing, a lack of means, and various other shortcomings, but also from their negligence, absenteeism, and delays in the delivery of grain and funds; they saw with indifference the Jews selling their property; there were also abuses: in exchange of payment, they granted permits for long-term absences, including for the most reliable workers in a family, which could quickly lead to the ruin of the farm.

Even after 1810–1812, the situation of the Jewish colonies showed no sign of improvement: "tools lost, broken, or mortgaged by the Jews"; "Oxen, again, slaughtered, stolen, or resold"; "Fields sown too late while awaiting warmth"; use of "bad seeds" and in too close proximity to houses, always on the one and same plot; no groundwork, "sowing for five consecutive years on fields that had only been ploughed once," without alternating the sowing of wheat and potatoes; insufficient harvest from one year to another, "yet again, without harvesting seeds." (But the bad harvests also benefit the immigrants: they are then entitled to time off.) Livestock left uncared for, oxen given for hire or "assigned as carriages… they wore them down, did not nourish them, bartered or slaughtered them to feed themselves, only to say later that they had died of disease." The authorities either provided them with others or let them leave in search of a livelihood.

---

[138] *Ibidem*, pp. 29, 49, 67, 73, 89, 189.
[139] *Ibidem**, pp. 87–88.

"They did not care to build safe pens to prevent livestock from being stolen during the night; they themselves spent their nights sound asleep; for shepherds, they took children or idlers who did not care for the integrity of the herds"; on feast days or on Saturdays, they left them out to graze without any supervision (moreover, on Saturday, it is forbidden to catch the thieves!). They resented their rare co-religionists, who, with the sweat of their brow, obtained remarkable harvests. The latter incurred the Old Testament curse, the *Herem*, "for if they show the authorities that the Jews are capable of working the land, they will eventually force them to do so." "Few were assiduous in working the land… they had the intent, while pretending to work, to prove to the authorities, by their continual needs, their overall incapacity."

They wanted "first and foremost to return to the trade of alcohol, which was re-authorised to their co-religionists." Livestock, instruments, seeds, were supplied to them several times, and new loans for their subsistence were relentlessly granted to them. "Many, after receiving a loan to establish themselves, came to the colonies only at the time of the distribution of funds, only to leave again… with this money to neighbouring towns and localities, in search for other work"; "they resold the plot that had been allocated to them, roamed, lived several months in Russian agglomerations at the most intense moments of agricultural labour, and earned their living… by deceiving the peasants." The inspectors' tables show that half of the families were absent with or without authorisation, and that some had disappeared forever. (An example was the disorder prevailing in the village of Izrae-levka in the province of Kherson, where "the inhabitants, who had come to their own account, considered themselves entitled to practice other trades: they were there only to take advantage of the privileges; only 13 of the 32 families were permanent residents, and again they only sowed to make it seem legitimate, while the others worked as tavern-keepers in neighbouring districts."[140]

The numerous reports of the inspectors note in particular and on several occasions that "the disgust of Jewish women for agriculture… was a major impediment to the success of the settlers." The Jewish women who seemed to have put themselves to work in the fields subsequently diverted from it. "At the occasion of marriages, the parents of Jewish women agreed with their future sons-in-law for them not to compel their wives to carry out difficult agricultural labour, but rather hire workers"; "They agreed to prepare ornaments, fox and hare furs, bracelets, head-dresses, and even pearls, for days of celebrations."

---

[140] *Ibidem**, pp. 64, 78-81, 85, 92-97, 112, 116-117, 142-145.

These conditions led young men to satisfy the whims of their wives "to the point of ruining their farming"; they go so far as "to indulge in possessing luxurious effects, silks, objects of silver or gold," while other immigrants do not even have clothing for the wintertime. Excessively early marriages make "the Jews multiply significantly faster than the other inhabitants." Then, by the exodus of the young, the families become too little provided for and are incapable of ensuring the work. The overcrowding of several families in houses too scarce generates uncleanliness and favours scurvy. (Some women take *bourgeois* husbands and then leave colonies forever.[141])

Judging from the reports of the Control Office, the Jews of the various colonies continually complained about the land of the steppes, "so hard it must be ploughed with four pairs of oxen." Complaints included bad harvests, water scarcity, lack of fuel, bad weather, disease generation, hail, grasshoppers. They also complained about the inspectors, but unduly, seeing that upon examination the complaints were deemed unfounded. Immigrants "complain shamelessly of their slightest annoyances," They "ceaselessly increase their demands"—"when it is justified, they are provided for via the Office." On the other hand, they had little reason to complain about limitations to the exercise of their piety or of the number of schools open in the agglomerations (in 1829, for eight colonies, there were forty teachers[142]).

However, as pointed out by Nikitin, in the same steppe, during the same period, in the same virgin lands, threatened by the same locusts, cultivations by German colonists, Mennonites, and Bulgarians had been established. They also suffered from the same bad harvests, the same diseases, but however, most of them always had enough bread and livestock, and they lived in beautiful houses with outbuildings, their vegetable gardens were abundant, and their dwellings surrounded by greenery. (The difference was obvious, especially when the German settlers, at the request of the authorities, came to live in the Jewish settlements to convey their experience and set an example: even from a distance, their properties could be distinguished.)

In the Russian colonies the houses were also better than those of the Jews. (However, Russians had managed to get into debt with some Jews who were richer than them and paid their debts while working in their fields.) The Russian peasants, Nikitin explains, "under the oppression of serfdom, were accustomed to everything… and stoically endured all misfortunes." That is how the Jewish settlers who had suffered losses following various

---

[141] *Ibidem*, pp. 79, 92, 131, 142, 146-149.
[142] *Ibidem**, pp. 36, 106, 145.

indignities were assisted "by the vast spaces of the steppe that attracted fugitives serfs from all regions…

Chased by sedentary settlers, the latter replied by the looting, the theft of cattle, the burning of houses; well received, however, they offered their work and know-how. As reflective and practical men, and by instinct of self-preservation, the Jewish cultivators preferred receiving these fugitives with kindness and eagerness; in return, the latter willingly helped them in ploughing, sowing, and harvesting"; Some of them, to hide better, embraced the Jewish religion. "These cases came to light," in 1820 the government forbade Jews to use Christian labour.[143]

Meanwhile, in 1817, the ten years during which the Jewish settlers were exempt from royalties had passed, and they were now to pay, like the peasants of the Crown. Collective petitions emanating not only from the colonists, but also from public officials, demanded that the privilege should be extended for a further fifteen years.

A personal friend of Alexander I, Prince Golitsyn, Minister of Education and Religious Affairs, also responsible for all problems concerning the Jews, took the decision to exempt them from paying royalties for another five years and to postpone the full repayment of loans up to thirty years. "It is important to note, on the honour of the authorities of St. Petersburg, that no request of the Jews, before and now, has ever been ignored."[144]

Among the demands of the Jewish settlers, Nikitin found one which seemed to him to be particularly characteristic: "Experience has proven, in as much as agriculture is indispensable to humanity, it is considered the most basic of occupations, which demands more physical exertion than ingenuity and intelligence; and, all over the world, those affected to this occupation are those incapable of more serious professions, such as industrialists and merchants; it is the latter category, inasmuch as it demands more talent and education, which contributes more than all others the prosperity of nations, and in all periods it has been accorded far more esteem and respect than that of agricultors. The slanderous representations of the Jews to the government resulted in depriving the Jews of the freedom to exercise their favourite trade—that of commerce—and to force them to change their status by becoming farmers, *the so-called plebs*. Between 1807 and 1809, more than 120,000 people were driven out of villages [where most lived on the alcohol trade], and were forced to settle in uninhabited places." Hence their claim to: "return to them the status of bourgeois with the right, attested in the passport, to be able to leave without

---

[143] *Ibidem*, pp. 13, 95, 109, 144, 505.
[144] *Ibidem*, pp. 99-102, 105, 146.

hindrances, according to the wishes of each individual."[145] These are well-weighed and unambiguous formulas. From 1814 to 1823, the farming of Jews did not prosper. The statistical tables show that each registered individual cultivated less than two-thirds of a hectare. As "they tried to cut off the harshest work" (in the eyes of the inspectors), they found compensation in commerce and other miscellaneous trades.[146]

Half a century later, the Jewish journalist I.G. Orchansky proposed the following interpretation: "What could be more natural for the Jews transplanted here to devote themselves to agriculture to have seen a vast field of virgin economic activity, and to have precipitated themselves there with their customary and favourite occupations, which promised in the towns a harvest more abundant than that which they could expect as farmers. Why, then, demand of them that they should necessarily occupy themselves with agricultural labour, which undoubtedly, would not turn out well for them," considering "the bubbling activity that attracts the Jews in the cities in formation."[147]

The Russian authorities at that time saw things differently: in time, the Jews "could become useful cultivators," if they resumed "their status as *bourgeois*, they would only increase the number of parasites in the cities."[148] On record: 300,000 rubles spent on nine Jewish settlements, a colossal sum considering the value of the currency at the time.

In 1822 the additional five years of royalty exemption had elapsed, but the condition of the Jewish farms still required new franchises and new subsidies: *"the state of extreme poverty of the settlers"* was noted, linked "to their inveterate laziness, disease, mortality, crop failures, and ignorance of agricultural work."[149]

Nevertheless, the young Jewish generation was gradually gaining experience in agriculture. Recognising that good regular harvests were not in the realm of the impossible, the settlers invited their compatriots from Belarus and Lithuania to join them, all the more since there had been bad harvests there; the Jewish families flocked *en masse*, with or without authorisation, as in 1824, they feared the threat of general expulsion in the western part of the country; In 1821, as we have already mentioned, measures had been taken to put an end to the Jewish distilleries in the province of Chernigov, followed by two or three other regions. The

---

[145] *Ibidem*, pp. 99-102, 105, 146.
[146] *Ibidem**, pp. 103-104.
[147] *Orchansky*, pp. 170, 173-174.
[148] *Nikitin*, p. 114.
[149] *Ibidem**, p. 135.

governors of the western provinces let all the volunteers go without much inquiry as to how much land was left in New Russia for the Jews.

From there, it was announced that the possibilities of reception did not exceed 200 families per year, but 1,800 families had already started the journey (some strayed in nature, others settled along the way). From then on, the colonists were refused all state aid (but with ten years exemption of royalties); however, the *Kehalim* were interested in getting the poorest to leave in order to have less royalties to pay, and to a certain extent, they provided those who left with funds from the community. (They encouraged the departure of the elderly, the sick, and large families with few able-bodied adults useful to agriculture; and when the authorities demanded a written agreement from the leavers, they were provided with a list of signatures devoid of any meaning.[150] Of the 453 families who arrived in the neighbourhood of Ekaterinoslav in 1823, only two were able to settle at their own expense. What had pushed them there was the mad hope of receiving public aid, which might have dispensed the newcomers from work. In 1822, 1,016 families flocked to New Russia from Belarus: the colonies were rapidly filled with immigrants to whom provisional hospitality was offered; confinement and uncleanliness engendered diseases.[151]

Also, in 1825, Alexander I prohibited the relocation of the Jews. In 1824 and 1825, following further bad harvests, the Jews were supported by loans (but, in order not to give them too much hope, their origin was concealed: they supposedly came from the personal decision of an inspector, or as a reward for some work). Passports were again issued so that the Jews could settle in towns.

As for paying royalties, even for those settled there for eighteen years, it was no longer discussed.[152]

At the same time, in 1823, "a decree of His Majesty orders... that in the provinces of Byelorussia the Jews shall cease all their distillery activities in 1824, abandon farmhouses and relay stations" and settle permanently "in the towns and agglomerations." The transfer was implemented. By January 1824, some 20,000 people had already been displaced. The Emperor demanded to see to it that the Jews were "provided with activities and subsistence" during this displacement, "so that, without home base, they would not suffer, under these conditions, of more pressing needs such as that of food."[153] The creation of a committee composed of four ministers

---

[150] *Ibidem*, p. 118.
[151] *Ibidem**, pp. 110, 120-129, 132, 144, 471.
[152] *Ibidem*, pp. 138, 156.
[153] *Hessen*, 1.1. pp. 205-206.

(the fourth "ministerial cabinet" created for Jewish affairs) produced no tangible results either in terms of funding, nor in administrative capacities, nor in the social structure of the Jewish community, which was impossible to rebuild from the outside.

In this, as before in many other domains, the emperor Alexander I appears to us to be weak-willed in his impulses, inconstant and inconsistent with his resolves (as we can see him passive in the face of strengthening secret societies which were preparing to overthrow the throne). But in no case should his decisions be attributed to a lack of respect for the Jews. On the contrary, he was listening to their needs and, even during the war of 1812-14, he had kept at Headquarters the Jewish delegates Zindel Sonnenberg and Leisen Dillon who "defended the interests of the Jews." (Dillon, it is true, was soon to be judged for having appropriated 250,000 rubles of public money and for having extorted funds from landowners.) Sonnenberg, on the other hand, remained for a long time one of Alexander's close friends. On the orders of the Tsar, (1814) a permanent Jewish deputation functioned for a number of years in St. Petersburg, for which the Jews had themselves raised funds, "for there were plans for major secret expenditures within government departments." These deputies demanded that "throughout Russia, the Jews should have the right to engage in the trade, farming, and distillation of spirits", that they be granted "privileges in matters of taxation," that "the backlogs be handed over," that "the number of Jews admitted to be members of the magistrate no longer be limited." The Emperor benevolently listened to them, made promises, but no concrete measures were taken.[154]

In 1817 the English Missionary Society sent the lawyer Louis Weil, an equal rights activist for the Jews, to Russia for the specific purpose of acquainting himself with the situation of the Jews of Russia: he had an interview with Alexander I to whom he handed a note. "Deeply convinced that the Jews represented a sovereign nation, Weil affirmed that all Christian peoples, since they had received salvation of the Jews, were to render to them the highest homage and to show them their gratitude by benefits." In this last period of his life, marked by mystical dispositions, Alexander had to be sensitive to such arguments. Both he and his government were afraid of "touching with an imprudent hand the religious rules" of the Jews. Alexander had great respect for the venerable people of the Old Covenant and was sympathetic to their present situation. Hence his utopian quest to make this people access the New Testament. To this end, in 1817, with the help of the Emperor, the Society of Christians of Israel was created, meaning Jews who converted to Christianity (not necessarily orthodoxy), and because of this enjoyed considerable privileges: they had

---

[154] *Ibidem*, pp. 176-181; JE, t. 7, pp. 103-104.

the right, everywhere in Russia, "to trade and to carry on various trades without belonging to guilds or workshops," and they were "freed, they and their descendants, forever, of any civil and military service." Nevertheless, this society experienced no influx of converted Jews and soon ceased to exist.[155]

The good dispositions of Alexander I in regards to the Jews made him express his conviction to put an end to the accusations of ritual murders which arose against them. (These accusations were unknown in Russia until the division of Poland, from where they came. In Poland they appeared in the sixteenth century, transmitted from Europe where they were born in England in 1144 before resurfacing in the twelfth-thirteenth century in Spain, France, Germany, and Great Britain. Popes and Monarchs fought off these accusations without them disappearing in the fourteenth nor fifteenth century. The first trial in Russia took place in Senno, near Vitebsk, in 1816, was not only stopped "by Her Majesty's decision", but incited the Minister of Religious Affairs, Golitsyn, to send the authorities of all provinces the following injunction: henceforth, not to accuse the Jews "of having put to death Christian children, solely supported by prejudices and without proof."[156] In 1822–1823 another affair of this kind broke out in Velije, also in the province of Vitebsk. However, the court decreed in 1824: "The Jews accused in many uncertain Christian testimonies of having killed this boy, supposedly to collect his blood, must be exonerated of all suspicion."[157]

Nevertheless, in the twenty-five years of his reign, Alexander I did not sufficiently study the question to conceive and put into practice a methodical solution satisfactory to all, regarding the Jewish problem as it was in Russia at the time.

How to act, what to do with this separated people who has not yet grafted onto Russia, and which continues to grow in number, is also the question to which the Decembrist Pestel who opposed the Emperor, sought an answer for the Russia of the future, which he proposed to direct. In *The Truth of Russia* he proposed two solutions. Either make the Jews merge for good in the Christian population of Russia: "Above all, it is necessary to deflect the effect, harmful to Christians, of the close link that unites the Jews amongst themselves or which is directed against Christians, which completely isolates the Jews from all other citizens... Convene the most knowledgeable rabbis and Jewish personalities, listen to their proposals

---

[155] *Hessen*, 1.1, pp. 180, 192-194.
[156] PJE, t. 4, pp. 582-586; Hessen, 1.1, p 183.
[157] *Hessen**, t. 1, pp. 211-212.

and then take action… If Russia does not expel the Jews, all the more they shouldn't adopt unfriendly attitudes towards Christians."

The second solution "would consist in helping the Jews create a separate state in one of the regions of Asia Minor. To this end, it is necessary to establish a gathering point for the Jewish people and to send several armies to support it" (we are not very far from the future Zionist idea). The Russian and Polish Jews together will form a people of more than two million souls. "Such a mass of men in search of a country will have no difficulty in overcoming obstacles such as the opposition of the Turks. Crossing Turkey from Europe, they will pass into Asiatic Turkey and occupy there enough place and land to create a specifically Jewish state. However, Pestel acknowledges that "such an enormous undertaking requires special circumstances and an entrepreneurial spirit of genius."[158]

Nikita Muravyov, another Decembrist, stipulated in his proposed Constitution that "Jews can enjoy civil rights in the places where they live, but that the freedom to settle in other places will depend on the particular decisions of the People's Supreme Assembly."[159]

Nevertheless, the instances proper to the Jewish population, the *Kehalim*, opposed with all their might the interference of state power and all external influence. On this subject, opinions differ. From the religious point of view, as many Jewish writers explain, living in the diaspora is a historical punishment that weighs on Israel for its former sins. Scattering must be assumed to merit God's forgiveness and the return to Palestine. For this it is necessary to live without failing according to the Law and not to mingle with the surrounding peoples: that is the ordeal. But for a liberal Jewish historian of the early twentieth century, "the dominant class, incapable of any creative work, deaf to the influences of its time, devoted all its energies to preserving from the attacks of time, both external and internal, a petrified national and religious life." The *Kahal* drastically stifled the protests of the weakest. "The cultural and educational reform of 1804 confined itself to illusorily blurring the distinctive and foreign character of the Jews, without having recourse to coercion," or even "taking mercy on prejudices"; "these decisions sowed a great disturbance within the *Kahal*… in that they harboured a threat to the power it exercised over the population"; in the Regulation, the most sensitive point for the *Kahal* "was the prohibition of delivering the unruly to the *Herem*," or, even more severe, the observation that "to keep the population in servile submission to a social order, as it had been for centuries, it was forbidden to change garb."[160] But it can not

---

[158] *Pestel*, pp. 52-53.
[159] *Hessen**, t. 2, p. 18.
[160] *Hessen*, I. 1. pp. 169-170.

be denied that the *Kehalim* also had reasonable regulatory requirements for the life of the Jews, such as the *Khasaki* rule allowing or forbidding the members of the community from taking on a particular type of farming or occupation, which put an end to excessive competition between Jews.[161] "Thou shalt not move the bounds of thy neighbour" (Deuteronomy, XIX, 14).

In 1808, an unidentified Jew transmitted an anonymous note (fearing reprisals from the *Kahal*) to the Minister of Internal Affairs, entitled "Some remarks concerning the management of the life of the Jews." He wrote: "Many do not regard as sacred the innumerable rites and rules... which divert attention from all that is useful, enslave the people to prejudices, take by their multiplication an enormous amount of time, and deprive the Jews of 'the advantage of being good citizens'." He noted that "the rabbis, pursuing only their interest, have enclosed life in an intertwining of rules", have concentrated in their hands all the police, legal, and spiritual authority; "more precisely, the study of the Talmud and the observance of rites as a unique means of distinguishing oneself and acquiring affluence have become 'the first dream and aspiration of the Jews'"; And although the governmental Regulation "limits the prerogatives of the rabbis and *Kelahim*, "the spirit of the people remained the same." The author of this note considered "the rabbis and the *Kahal* as the main culprits of the ignorance and misery of the people."[162]

Another Jewish public man, Guiller Markevich, a native of Prussia, wrote that the members of the Vilnius *Kahal*, with the help of the local administration, exerted a severe repression against all those who denounced their illegal acts; now deprived of the right to the *Herem*, they kept their accusers for long years in prison, and if one of them succeeded in getting a message from his cell to the higher authorities, "they sent him without any other form of trials to the next world." When this kind of crime was revealed, "the *Kahal* spent large sums to stifle the affair."[163] Other Jewish historians give examples of assassinations directly commissioned by the Jewish *Kahal*.

In their opposition to governmental measures, the *Kehalim* relied essentially on the religious sense of their action; thus "the union of the *Kahal* and the rabbis, desirous of maintaining their power over the masses, made the government believe that every act of a Jew was subject to such and such a religious prescription; the role of religion was thereby increased. As a result, the people of the administration saw in the Jews not members

---

[161] *Ibidem*, p. 51; JE, t. 14, p. 491.
[162] *Hessen*, t. 1, pp. 171-173.
[163] *Hessen**, t. 2, pp. 11-13.

of different social groups, but a single entity closely knit together; the vices and infractions of the Jews were explained not by individual motives, but by 'the alleged land amorality of the Jewish religion'."[164]

"The union of *Kehalim* and rabbis did not want to see or hear anything. It extended its leaden cover over the masses. The power of the *Kahal* only increased while the rights of the elders and rabbis were limited by the Regulation of 1804. "This loss is offset by the fact that the *Kahal* acquired—it is true, only in a certain measure—the role of a representative administration which it had enjoyed in Poland. The *Kahal* owed this strengthening of its authority to the institution of deputies." This deputation of the Jewish communities established in the western provinces, in charge of debating at leisure with the government the problems of Jewish life, was elected in 1807 and sat intermittently for eighteen years. These deputies endeavoured, above all, to restore to the rabbis the right to the *Herem*; They declared that to deprive the rabbis of the right to chastise the disobedient is contrary to the religious respect which the Jews are obliged by law to have for the rabbis." These deputies succeeded in persuading the members of the Committee (of Senator Popov, 1809) that the authority of the rabbis was a support for the Russian governmental power. "The members of the Committee did not resist in front of the threat that the Jews would escape the authority of the rabbis to delve into depravity"; the Committee was "prepared to maintain in its integrity all this archaic structure to avoid the terrible consequences evoked by the deputies... Its members did not seek to know who the deputies considered to be 'violators of the spiritual law'; they did not suspect that they were those who aspired to education"; the deputies "exerted all their efforts to strengthen the authority of the *Kahal* and to dry at the source the movement towards culture."[165] They succeeded in deferring the limitations previously taken to the wearing of traditional Jewish garb, which dated back to the Middle Ages and so blatantly separated the Jews from the surrounding world. Even in Riga, "the law that ordered the Jews to wear another garment was not applied anywhere", and it was reported by the Emperor himself—while awaiting new legislation[166]...

All requests of the deputies were not satisfied, far from it. They needed money and "to get it, the deputies frightened their communities by ominously announcing the intentions of the government and by amplifying the rumours of the capital." In 1820, Markevitch accused the deputies "of

---

[164] *Ibidem*, t. 1, p. 195.
[165] *Ibidem*, pp. 173-175.
[166] *Ibidem**, pp. 191-192.

intentionally spreading false news... to force the population to pay to the *Kahal* the sums demanded."[167]

In 1825, the institution of the Jewish deputies was suppressed. One of the sources of tension between the authorities and *Kehalim* resided in the fact that the latter, the only ones authorised to levy the capitation on the Jewish population, "hid the 'souls' during the censuses" and concealed a large quantity of them. "The government thought that it knew the exact numbers of the Jewish population in order to demand the corresponding amount of the capitation," but it was very difficult to establish it.[168] For example, in Berdichev, "the unrecorded Jewish population... regularly accounted for nearly half the actual number of Jewish inhabitants."[169] (According to the official data that the Government had succeeded in establishing for 1818, the Jews were 677,000, an already important number, for example, by comparison with the data of 1812, the number of male individuals had suddenly doubled...—but it was still an undervalued figure, for there were about 40,000 Jews from the kingdom of Poland to add.) Even with reduced figures of the *Kehalim*, there were unrecovered taxes every year; and not only were they not recuperated but they augmented from year to year. Alexander I personally told the Jewish representatives of his discontent at seeing so many concealments and arrears (not to mention the smuggling industry). In 1817 the remission of all fines and surcharges, penalties, and arrears was decreed, and a pardon was granted to all those who had been punished for not correctly recording 'souls', but on the condition that the *Kehalim* provide honest data from then on."[170] But "no improvement ensued. In 1820, the Minister of Finance announced that all measures aimed at improving the economic situation of the Jews were unsuccessful... Many Jews were wandering without identity papers; a new census reported a number of souls two to three times greater (if not more) than those previously provided by Jewish societies."[171]

However, the Jewish population was constantly increasing. Most researchers see one of the main reasons for this growth as being the custom of early marriages prevalent at that time among the Jews: as early as 13 years old for boys, and from 12 years old onwards for girls. In the anonymous note of 1808 quoted above, the unknown Jewish author writes that this custom of early unions "is at the root of innumerable evils" and prevents the Jews from getting rid "of inveterate customs and activities that draw upon them the general public's indignation, and harms them as well

---

[167] *Ibidem*, p. 209.
[168] *Ibidem*, p. 178.
[169] *Orchansky*, p. 32.
[170] *Hessen*, t. 1, pp. 178-179, 184, 186.
[171] *Ibidem*, I. 2, pp. 62-63.

as others." Tradition among the Jews is that "those who are not married at a young age are held in contempt and even the most destitute draw on their last resources to marry their children as soon as possible, even though these newlyweds incur the vicissitudes of a miserable existence. Early marriages were introduced by the rabbis who took advantage of them. And one will be better able to contract a profitable marriage by devoting himself to the study of the Talmud and the strict observance of the rites. Those who married early were indeed only occupied with studying the Talmud, and when finally came the time to lead an autonomous existence, these fathers, ill-prepared for labour, ignorant of the working life, turn to the manufacture of alcohol and petty trading." The same goes for crafts: "By marrying, the fifteen-year-old apprentice no longer learns his trade, but becomes his own boss and only ruins the work."[172] In the mid-1920s, "in the provinces of Grodno and Vilnius, there was a rumour that it would be forbidden to enter into marriage before reaching the age of majority", which is why "there was a hasty conclusion of marriages between children who were little more than 9 years old."[173]

These early marriages debilitated the life of the Jews. How could such a swarming, such a densification of the population, such competition in similar occupations, lead to any thing else than misery? The policy of the *Kehalim* contributed to "the worsening of the material conditions of the Jews."[174]

Menashe Ilier, a distinguished Talmudist but also a supporter of the rationalism of the age of Enlightenment, published in 1807 a book, which he sent to the rabbis (it was quickly withdrawn from circulation by the rabbinate, and his second book was to be destined to a massive book burning). He addressed "the dark aspects of Jewish life." He stated: "Misery is inhumanly great, but can it be otherwise when the Jews have more mouths to feed than hands to work? It is important to make the masses understand that it is necessary to earn a living by the sweat of their brow… Young people, who have no income, contract marriage by counting on the mercy of God and on the purse of their father, and when this support is lacking, laden with family, they throw themselves on the first occupation come, even if it is dishonest. In droves they devote themselves to commerce, but as the latter cannot feed them all, they are obliged to resort to deceit. This is why it is desirable that the Jews turn to agriculture. An army of idlers, under the appearance of 'educated people', live by charity and at the expense of the community. No one cures the people: the rich only think of enriching themselves, the rabbis think only of the disputes

---

[172] *Ibidem**, t. 1, pp. 171-172.
[173] *Ibidem*, t. 2, p. 56.
[174] *Ibidem*, t. 1, p. 210.

between *Hassidim* and *Minagdes* (Jewish Orthodox), and the only concern of the Jewish activists is to short-circuit 'the misfortune presented in the form of governmental decrees, even if they contribute to the good of the people'."[175]

Thus "the great majority of the Jews in Russia lived on small trade, crafts, and small industries, or served as intermediaries"; "they have inundated the cities of factories and retail shops."[176] How could the economic life of the Jewish people be healthy under these conditions?

However, a much later Jewish author of the mid-twentieth century was able to write, recalling this time: "It is true that the Jewish mass lived cheaply and poorly. But the Jewish community as a whole was not miserable."[177]

There is no lack of interest in the rather unexpected testimonies of the life of the Jews in the western provinces, seen by the participants in the Napoleonic expedition of 1812 who passed through this region. On the outskirts of Dochitsa, the Jews "are rich and wealthy, they trade intensively with Russian Poland and even go to the Leipzig fair." At Gloubokie, "the Jews had the right to distil alcohol and make vodka and mead," they "established or owned cabarets, inns, and relays located on highways." The Jews of Mogilev are well-off, undertake large-scale trading (although "a terrible misery reigns around that area"). "Almost all the Jews in those places had a license to sell spirits.

Financial transactions were largely developed there." Here again is the testimony of an impartial observer: "In Kiev, the Jews are no longer counted. The general characteristic of Jewish life is ease, although it is not the lot of all."[178]

On the level of psychology and everyday life, the Russian Jews have the following 'specific traits': "a constant concern about... their fate, their identity... how to fight, defend themselves..." "*cohesion* stems from established customs: the existence of an authoritarian and powerful social structure charged with preserving... the uniqueness of the way of life"; "adaptation to new conditions is to a very large extent collective" and not individual.[179]

We must do justice to this organic unity of land, which in the first half of the nineteenth century "gave the Jewish people of Russia its original aspect.

---

[175] *Ibidem*, pp. 170 171; -JE, t. 10, pp. 855-857.
[176] *Hessen*, t. 1, pp. 190, 208.
[177] B. C. Dinour, Religiozno-natsionalnyj oblik rousskoo cvreïstva (The Religious and National Physionomy of Russian Jews), in BJWR-1, p. 318.
[178] *Pozner*, in JW-1, pp. 61, 63–64.
[179] *Dinour*, BJWR-1, pp. 61, 63–64.

This world was compact, organic, subject to vexations, not spared of suffering and deprivation, but it was a world in itself. Man was not stifled within it. In this world, one could experience *joie de vivre*, one could find one's food... one could build one's life to one's taste and in one's own way, both materially and spiritually... Central fact: the spiritual dimension of the community was linked to traditional knowledge and the Hebrew language."[180]

But in the same book devoted to the Russian Jewish world, another writer notes that "the lack of rights, material misery, and social humiliation hardly allowed self-respect to develop among the people."[181]

The picture we have presented of these years is complex, as is almost any problem related to the Jewish world. Henceforth, throughout our development, we must not lose sight of this complexity, but must constantly bear it in mind, without being disturbed by the apparent contradictions between various authors.

"Long ago, before being expelled from Spain, the Jews [of Eastern Europe] marched at the head of other nations; today [in the first half of the seventeenth century], their cultural impoverishment is total. Deprived of rights, cut off from the surrounding world, they retreated into themselves. The Renaissance passed by without concern for them, as did the intellectual movement of the eighteenth century in Europe. But this Jewish world was strong in itself. Hindered by countless religious commandments and prohibitions, the Jew not only did not suffer from them, but rather saw in them the source of infinite joys. In them, the intellect found satisfaction in the subtle dialectic of the Talmud, the feeling in the mysticism of the Kabbalah. Even the study of the Bible was sidelined, and knowledge of grammar was considered almost a crime."[182]

The strong attraction of the Jews to the Enlightenment began in Prussia during the second half of the eighteenth century and received the name of *Haskala* (Age of Enlightenment). This intellectual awakening translated their desire to initiate themselves in European culture, to enhance the prestige of Judaism, which had been humiliated by other peoples. In parallel with the critical study of the Jewish past, *Haskala* militants (the *Maskilim*; the "enlightened", "educated") wanted to harmoniously unite Jewish culture with European knowledge.[183] At first, "they intended to remain faithful to traditional Judaism, but in their tracks they began to

---

[180] *Ibidem*, p. 318.
[181] J. Mark, Literatoura na idich v Rossii (Yiddish Language Literature in Russia), in BJWR-1, p. 520.
[182] JE, t. 6, p. 92.
[183] *Ibidem*, pp. 191-192.

sacrifice the Jewish tradition and take the side of assimilation by showing increasing contempt... for the language of their people"[184] (Yiddish, that is). In Prussia this movement lasted the time of a generation, but it quickly reached the Slavic provinces of the empire, Bohemia, and Galicia. In Galicia, supporters of *Haskala*, who were even more inclined to assimilation, were already ready to introduce the Enlightenment by force, and even "often enough had recourse to it"[185] with the help of authorities. The border between Galicia and the western provinces of Russia was permeable to individuals as well as to influences. With a delay of a century, the movement eventually penetrated into Russia.

At the beginning of the nineteenth century in Russia, the government "endeavoured precisely to overcome Jewish 'particularism' outside of religion and worship", as a Jewish author euphemistically specifies[186], confirming that this government did not interfere with the religion or religious life of the Jews.

We have already seen that the Regulation of 1804 opened the doors of primary schools, secondary schools, and universities to all Jewish children, without any limitations or reservations. However,—"the aim of all the efforts of the Jewish ruling class was to nip in the bud this educational and cultural reform"[187]; "The *Kahal* endeavoured to extinguish the slightest light of the Enlightenment."[188] To "preserve in its integrity the established religious and social order... the rabbinate and Hasidism were endeavouring to eradicate the seedlings of secular education."[189]

Thus, "the great masses of the Pale of Settlement felt horror and suspicion for Russian schooling and did not want to hear about it."[190] In 1817, and again in 1821, in various provinces, there were cases where the *Kehalim* prevented Jewish children from learning the Russian language in any school, whichever it was. The Jewish deputies in St. Petersburg repeated insistently that "they did not consider it necessary to open Jewish schools" where languages other than Hebrew would be taught.[191] They recognised only the *Heder* (elementary school of Jewish language) and the *Yeshiva*

---

[184] J. Kissine, Rasmychlenia o ousskom evreïstve i ego lileraloure (Thoughts on Russian Judaism and its literature), in Evreïskii mir. 2, New York, ed. Of the Jewish Russian Union, 1944, p. 171.
[185] JE, t. 6, pp. 192-193.
[186] *Dinour*, LVJR-1, p. 314.
[187] *Hessen*, p. 160.
[188] *Ibidem*, p. 160.
[189] *Ibidem*, t. 2, p. 1.
[190] M. Troitsky, Evrei v rousskoï chkole (The Jews in Russian Schools), in LVJR-1, p. 350.
[191] *Hessen**, t. 1, pp. 188–189.

(graduate school intended to deepen the knowledge of the Talmud); "almost every important community" had its *Yeshiva*.[192]

The Jewish body in Russia was thus hindered and could not free itself on its own.

But the first cultural protagonists also emerged from it, unable to move things without the help of Russian authorities. In the first place Isaac-Ber Levinson, a scholar who had lived in Galicia, where he had been in contact with the militants of *Haskala*, regarded not only the rabbinate but also the *Hasidim* as responsible for many popular misfortunes. Basing himself on the Talmud itself and on rabbinical literature, he demonstrated in his book *Instructions to Israel* that Jews were not forbidden to know foreign languages, especially not the official language of the country where they lived, if necessary in private as well as in public life; that knowledge of the secular sciences does not pose a threat to national and religious sentiment; finally, that the predominance of commercial occupations is in contradiction with the Torah as with reason, and that it is important to develop productive work. But to publish his book, Levinson had to use a subsidy from the Ministry of Education; he himself was convinced that cultural reform within Judaism could only be achieved with the support of the higher authorities.[193]

Later, it was Guesanovsky, a teacher in Warsaw, who, in a note to the authorities, without relying on the Talmud, but on the contrary, by opposing it, imputed to the *Kahal* and the rabbinate "the spiritual stagnation which had petrified the people"; he stated that solely the weakening of their power would make it possible to introduce secular schooling; that it was necessary to control the *Melamed* (primary school teachers) and to admit as teachers only those deemed pedagogically and morally suitable; that the *Kahal* had to be dismissed from the financial administration; and that the age of nuptial contracts had to be raised. Long before them, in his note to the Minister of Finance, Guiller Markevitch, already quoted, wrote that in order to save the Jewish people from spiritual and economic decline, it was necessary to abolish the *Kehalim*, to teach the Jews languages, to organise work for them in factories, but also to allow them to freely engage in commerce throughout the country and use the services of Christians.

Later, in the 1930s, Litman Feiguine, a Chernigov merchant and a major supplier, took up most of these arguments with even greater insistence, and through Benkendorff[194] his note ended up in the hands of Nicolas I

---

[192] *Dinour*, LVJR-1, p. 315.
[193] *Hessen*, t. 2, pp. 4–7.
[194] Count Alexander Benkendorff (1783–1844), named in 1814 by Nicholas I Commander of the gendarmes and of the 3rd Section (the intelligence service).

(Feiguine benefited from the support of bureaucratic circles). He defended the Talmud but reproached the *Melamed* for being "the lowest of the incompetents"... who taught a theology "founded on fanaticism", inculcated in children "the contempt of other disciplines as well as the hatred of the Heterodox." He also considered it essential to suppress the *Kehalim*. (Hessen, the sworn enemy of the *Kahal* system, affirms that the latter, "by its despotism", aroused among the Jews "an obscure resentment.")[195]

Long, very long, was the path that enabled secular education to penetrate into Jewish circles. Meanwhile, the only exceptions were in Vilnius, where, under the influence of relations with Germany, the *Maksilim* intellectual group had gained strength, and in Odessa, the new capital of New Russia, home to many Jews from Galicia (due to the permeability of frontiers), populated by various nationalities and in the throes of intense commercial activity,—hence the *Kahal* did not feel itself powerful there. The intelligentsia, on the contrary, had the feeling of its independence and blended culturally (by the way of dressing, by all external aspects) in the surrounding population.[196] Even though "the majority of the Odessite Jews were opposed to the establishment of a general educational establishment"[197] principally due to the efforts of the local administration, in the 30s, in Odessa as in Kishinev were created secular schools of the private type which were successful."[198]

Then, in the course of the nineteenth century, this breakthrough of the Russian Jews towards education irresistibly intensified and would have historical consequences for Russia as for all mankind during the twentieth century. Thanks to a great effort of will, Russian Judaism managed to free itself from the state of threatening stagnation in which it found itself and to fully accede to a rich and diversified life. By the middle of the nineteenth century, there was a clear discernment of the signs of a revival and development in Russian Judaism, a movement of high historical significance, which no one had yet foreseen.

---

[195] *Hessen*, t. 2, pp. 8–10; JE, 1.15, p. 198.
[196] *Hessen*, t. 2, pp. 2–3.
[197] JE, t. 11, p. 713.
[198] *Troitsky*, in BJWR-1, p. 351.

Chapter 3

During the Reign of Nicholas I[st]

With regard to the Jews, Nicholas I was very resolute. It was during his reign, according to sources, that more than half of all legal acts relating to Jews, from Alexis Mikhailovich to the death of Alexander II[199], were published, and the Emperor personally examined this legislative work to direct it.[200]

Jewish historiography has judged that his policy was exceptionally cruel and gloomy. However, the personal interventions of Nicholas I did not necessarily prejudice the Jews, far from it. For example, one of the first files he received as an inheritance from Alexander I was the reopening, on the eve of his death (while on his way to Taganrog), of the "Velije affair"—the accusation against the Jews for having perpetrated a ritual murder on the person of a child.

The Jewish Encyclopedia writes that "to a large extent, the Jews are indebted to the verdict of acquittal to the Emperor who sought to know the truth despite the obstruction on the part of the people he trusted." In another well-known case, linked to accusations against the Jews (the "assassination of Mstislavl"), the Emperor willingly turned to the truth: after having, in a moment of anger, inflicted sanctions against the local Jewish population, he did not refuse to acknowledge his error.[201] By signing the verdict of acquittal in the Velije case, Nicolas wrote that "the vagueness of the requisitions had not made it possible to take another decision", adding nevertheless: "I do not have the moral certainty that Jews could have committed such a crime, or that they could not have done it." "Repeated examples of this kind of assassination, with the same clues," but always without sufficient evidence, suggest to him that there might be a fanatical sect among the Jews, but "unfortunately, even among us Christians, there

---

[199] (1818-1881), The "liberator" tsar whose name is associated with the "great reforms" of the 1860s (abolition of serfdom, justice, the press, zemstvos, etc.) and the rise of the revolutionary movement; assassinated on March 13, 1881 by a commando of *the Will of the People*.
[200] JE, t. 11, p. 709.
[201] *Ibidem*, pp. 709–710.

also exists sects just as terrifying and incomprehensible."[202] "Nicholas I and his close collaborators continued to believe that certain Jewish groups practised ritual murders."[203] For several years, the Emperor was under the severe grip of a calumny that smelled of blood... therefore his prejudice that Jewish religious doctrine was supposed to present a danger to the Christian population was reinforced."[204]

This danger was understood by Nicolas in the fact that the Jews could convert Christians to Judaism. Since the eighteenth century, the high profile conversion to the Judaism of Voznitsyn, a captain of the Imperial army, had been kept in mind. "In Russia, from the second half of the seventeenth century onwards, groups of 'Judaisers' multiplied. In 1823, the Minister of Internal Affairs announced in a report "the wide-spread of the heresy of 'Judaisers' in Russia, and estimated the number of its followers at 20,000 people."

Persecutions began, after which "many members of the sect pretended to return to the bosom of the Orthodox Church while continuing to observe in secret the rites of their sect."[205]

"A consequence of all this was that the legislation on the Jews took, at the time of Nicholas I... a religious spin."[206] The decisions and actions of Nicholas I with regard to the Jews were affected, such as his insistence on prohibiting them from having recourse to Christian servants, especially Christian nurses, for "work among the Jews undermines and weakens the Christian faith in women."

In fact, notwithstanding repeated prohibitions, this provision "never was fully applied... and Christians continued to serve" amongst the Jews.[207]

The first measure against the Jews, which Nicolas considered from the very beginning of his reign, was to put them on an equal footing with the Russian population with regard to the subjugation to compulsory service to the State, and in particular, requiring them to participate physically in conscription, which they had not been subjected to since their attachment to Russia. The *bourgeois* Jews did not supply recruits, but acquitted 500

---

[202] *Hessen*, Istoria evreïskogo naroda v Rossii (History of the Jewish People in Russia), in 2 vol., t. 2, Leningrad, 1927, p. 27.
[203] LJE, t. 7, p. 322.
[204] JE, t. 11, pp. 709 710.
[205] LJE, t. 2, p. 509.
[206] JE, 1.11, p. 710.
[207] *Hessen*, t. 2, pp. 30 31.

rubles per head.[208] This measure was not dictated solely by governmental considerations to standardise the obligations of the population (the Jewish communities were in any case very slow to pay the royalties, and moreover, Russia received many Jews from Galicia where they were already required to perform military service); nor by the fact that the obligation to provide recruits "would reduce the number of Jews not engaged in productive work"—rather, the idea was that the Jewish recruit, isolated from his closed environment, would be better placed to join the lifestyle of the nation as a whole, and perhaps even orthodoxy. [209] Taken into account, these considerations considerably tightened the conditions of the conscription applied to the Jews, leading to a gradual increase in the number of recruits and the lowering of the age of the conscripts.

It cannot be said that Nicolas succeeded in enforcing the decree on the military service of the Jews without encountering resistance. On the contrary, all instances of execution proceeded slowly. The Council of Ministers discussed at length whether it was ethically defensible to take such a measure "in order to limit Jewish overcrowding"; as stated by Minister of Finance Georg von Cancrin, "all recognise that it is inappropriate to collect humans rather than money." The *Kehalim* did not spare their efforts to remove this threat from the Jews or to postpone it. When, exasperated by such slow progress, Nicholas ordered a final report to be presented to him in the shortest delays, "this order, it seems, only incited the *Kehalim* to intensify their action behind the scenes to delay the advancement of the matter. And they apparently succeeded in winning over to their cause one of the high officials," whereby "the report never reached its destination"! At the very top of the Imperial apparatus, "this mysterious episode," concludes J. Hessen, "could not have occurred without the participation of the *Kahal*." A subsequent retrieval of the report was also unfulfilled, and Nicolas, without waiting any longer, introduced the conscription for the Jews by decree in 1827[210] (then, in 1836, equality in obtaining medals for the Jewish soldiers who had distinguished themselves[211]).

Totally exempted from recruitment were "the merchants of all guilds, inhabitants of the agricultural colonies, workshop leaders, mechanics in

---

[208] V. N. *Nikitin*, Evrei zemlevladeltsy: Istoritcheskoe. zakonodatelnoe, administrativnoe i bytovoe polojenie kolonij so vremeni ikh vozniknovenia do nachikh dneï [Jewish farmers: historical, legislative, administrative and concrete situation of the colonies from their creation to the present day], 1807 1887, Saint Petersburg, 1887, p. 263.
[209] JE, t. 13, p. 371.
[210] *Hessen**, t. 2, pp. 32 34.
[211] JE, t. 11, pp. 468 469.

factories, rabbis and all Jews having a secondary or higher education."[212] Hence the desire of many Jewish *bourgeois* to try to make it into the class of merchants, *bourgeois* society railing to see its members required to be drafted for military service, "undermining the forces of the community, be it under the effect of taxation or recruitment." The merchants, on the other hand, sought to reduce their visible "exposure" to leave the payment of taxes to the *bourgeois*.

Relations between Jewish merchants and *bourgeois* were strained, for "at that time, the Jewish merchants, who had become more numerous and wealthier, had established strong relations in governmental spheres." The *Kahal* of Grodno appealed to Saint Petersburg to demand that the Jewish population be divided into four "classes"—merchants, *bourgeois*, artisans, and cultivators—and that each should not have to answer for the others.[213] (In this idea proposed in the early 30s by the *Kehalim* themselves, one can see the first step towards the future "categorisation" carried out by Nicolas in 1840, which was so badly received by the Jews.)

The *Kehalim* were also charged with the task of recruiting among the Jewish mass, of which the government had neither recorded numbers nor profiles. The *Kahal* "put all the weight of this levy on the backs of the poor", for "it seemed preferable for the most deprived to leave the community, whereas a reduction in the number of its wealthy members could lead to general ruin." The *Kehalim* asked the provincial authorities (but they were denied) the right to disregard the turnover "in order to be able to deliver to recruitment the 'tramps', those who did not pay taxes, the insufferable troublemakers", so that "the owners... who assume all the obligations of society should not have to provide recruits belonging to their families"; and in this way the *Kehalim* were given the opportunity to act against certain members of the community.[214]

However, with the introduction of military service among the Jews, the men who were subject to it began to shirk and the full count was never reached.

The cash taxation on Jewish communities had been considerably diminished, but it was noticed that this did by no means prevent it from continuing to be refunded only very partially. Thus, in 1829, Nicholas I granted Grodno's request that in certain provinces Jewish recruits should be levied in addition to the tariff imposed in order to cover tax arrears. "In 1830 a Senate decree stipulated that the appeal of an additional recruit reduced the sums owed by the *Kahal* of 1,000 rubles in the case of an adult,

---

[212] LJE, t. n7, p. 318.
[213] *Hessen*, t. 2, pp. 68 71.
[214] *Ibidem*, pp. 59-61.

500 rubles in the case of a minor."[215] It is true that following the untimely zeal of the governors this measure was soon reported, while "Jewish communities themselves asked the government to enlist recruits to cover their arrears." In government circles "this proposal was welcomed coldly, for it was easy to foresee that it would open new possibilities of abuse for the *Kehalim*."[216] However, as we can see, the idea matured on one side as well as on the other. Evoking these increased stringencies in the recruitment of Jews by comparison with the rest of the population, Hessen writes that this was a "glaring anomaly" in Russian law, for in general, in Russia, "the legislation applicable to the Jews did not tend to impose more obligations than that of other citizens."[217]

Nicholas I's keen intelligence, inclined to draw clearly legible perspectives (legend has it that the Saint Petersburg - Moscow railway was, as a result, mapped out with a ruler!), in his tenacious determination to transform the particularist Jews into ordinary Russian subjects, and, if possible, into Orthodox Christians, went from the idea of military recruitment to that of Jewish cantonists. The cantonists (the name goes back to 1805) was an institution sheltering the children of the soldiers (lightening in favour of the fathers the burden of a service which lasted... twenty-five years!); it was supposed to extend the "sections for military orphans" created under Peter the Great, a kind of school for the government which provided the students with technical knowledge useful for their subsequent service in the army (which, in the eyes of civil servants, now seems quite appropriate for young Jewish children, or even highly desirable to keep them from a young age and for long years cut off from their environment. In preparation to the cantonist institution, an 1827 decree granted "Jewish communities the right to recruit a minor instead of an adult", from the age of 12 (that is, before the age of nuptiality among the Jews). The *New Jewish Encyclopedia* believes that this measure was "a very hard blow."

But this faculty in no way meant the obligation to call a soldier at the age of 12[218], it had nothing to do with "the introduction of compulsory conscription for Jewish children," [219] as wrote erroneously the Encyclopedia, and as it ended up being accredited in the literature devoted to the Jews of Russia, then in the collective memory. The *Kehalim* even found this a profitable substitution and used it by recruiting "the orphans, the children of widows (sometimes bypassing the law protecting only

---

[215] LJE, t. 7, p. 317.
[216] *Hessen*, t. 2, pp. 64 65.
[217] *Ibidem*, p. 141.
[218] *Ibidem*, p. 34.
[219] LJE, t. 7, p. 317.

children)", often "for the benefit of the progeny of a rich man."[220] Then, from the age of 18, the cantonists performed the usual military service, so long at the time—but let us not forget that it was not limited to barracks life; the soldiers married, lived with their families, learned to practice other trades; they received the right to establish themselves in the interior provinces of the empire, where they completed their service. But, unquestionably, the Jewish soldiers who remained faithful to the Jewish religion and its ritual suffered from being unable to observe the Sabbath or contravene the rules on food.

Minors placed with cantonists, separated from their family environment, naturally found it difficult to resist the pressure of their educators (who were encouraged by rewards to successfully convert their pupils) during lessons of Russian, arithmetic, but above all, of catechism; they were also rewarded for their conversion, moreover, it was facilitated by their resentment towards a community that had given them up to recruitment. But, conversely, the tenacity of the Jewish character, the faithfulness to the religion inculcated at an early age, made many of them hold their grounds. Needless to say, these methods of conversion to Christianity were not Christian and did not achieve their purpose.

On the other hand, the accounts of conversions obtained by cruelty, or by death threats against the cantonists, supposedly collective drownings in the rivers for those who refused baptism (such stories received public attention in the decades that followed), fall within the domain of pure fiction. As the *Jewish Encyclopedia* published before the Revolution the "popular legend" of the few hundred cantonists allegedly killed by drowning was born from the information published in a German newspaper, according to which "eight hundred cantonists were taken away one fine day to be baptised in the water of a river, two of them perished by drowning..."[221]

The statistical data from the Military Inspection Archives to the General Staff[222] for the years 1847 1854, when the recruitment of Jewish cantonists was particularly high, showed that they represented on average only 2.4% of the many cantonists in Russia, in other words, that their proportion did not exceed that of the Jewish population in the country, even taking into account the undervalued data provided by the *Kehalim* during the censuses.

Doubtlessly the baptised had an interest in exculpating themselves from their compatriots in exaggerating the degree of coercion they had to

---

[220] LJE. t. 4, pp. 75 76.
[221] JE, t. 9 (which covers the years 1847 1854), p. 243.
[222] *K. Korobkov*, Evreïskaïa rekroutchina v tsarstvovanie Nikolaia 1 (The Recruitment of Jews under the Reign of Nicolas I), in Evreïskaia starina, Saint Petersburg, 1913, t. 6, pp. 79 80.

undergo in their conversion to Christianity, especially since as part of this conversion they enjoyed certain advantages in the accomplishment of their service. Moreover, "many converted cantonists remained secretly faithful to their original religion, and some of them later returned to Judaism."[223]

In the last years of the reign of Alexander I, after a new wave of famine in Belarus (1822), a new senator had been sent on mission: he had come back with the same conclusions as Derzhavin a quarter of a century before. The "Jewish Committee" established in 1823, composed of four ministers, had proposed to study "on what grounds it would be expedient and profitable to organise the participation of the Jews in the State" and to "put down in writing all that could contribute to the improvement of the civil situation of this people." They soon realised that the problem thus posed was beyond their strength, and in 1825 this "Jewish Committee" at the ministerial level had been replaced by a "Directors Committee" (the fifth), composed of the directors of their ministries, who devoted themselves to studying the problem for another eight years.[224]

In his eagerness, Nicholas preceded the work of this committee with his decisions. Thus, as we have seen, he introduced conscription for the Jews. This is how he set a deadline of three years to expel the Jews from all the villages of the western provinces and put an end to their activity of alcohol manufacturing, but, as under his predecessors, this measure experienced slowdowns, stoppages, and was ultimately reported. Subsequently, he prohibited Jews from holding taverns and diners, from living in such places, and ensuring the retail sale of alcohol in person, but this measure was not applied either.[225]

Another attempt was made to deny the Jews one of their favourite jobs: the maintenance of post houses (with their inns and taverns), but again in vain because, apart from the Jews, there was not enough candidates to occupy them.[226]

In 1827, a leasing system of the distilling activities was introduced throughout the empire, but there was a considerable fall in the prices obtained at the auctions when the Jews were discarded and "it happened that there was no other candidate to take these operations," so that they had to be allowed to the Jews, whether in the towns or in the countryside, even beyond the area of residence. The government was, in fact, relieving the Jews of the responsibility of organising the collection of taxes on liquor

---

[223] JE, t. 9, pp. 242 243.
[224] *Ibidem*, t. 7, pp. 443 444.
[225] *Hessen*, t. 2. p. 39.
[226] JE, i. 12, p. 787 ; Hessen, t. 2, p. 39.

and thus receiving a regular return.²²⁷ "Long before the merchants of the first guild were allowed to reside in any part of the empire, all farmers enjoyed the freedom to move and resided in capitals and other cities outside the Pale of Settlement... From the midst of the farmers came prominent Jewish public men" like Litman Feiguine, already mentioned, and Evsel Günzburg ("he had held an alcohol manufacturing tenancy in a besieged Sevastopol"); "In 1859 he founded in Saint Petersburg a banking establishment... one of the most important in Russia"; later, "he participated in the placement of Russian Treasury bonds in Europe"; he was the founder of the dynasty of the Günzburg barons²²⁸). Beginning in 1848, all "Jewish merchants of the first guild were allowed to lease drinking places even where Jews had no right to reside permanently."²²⁹

The Jews also received a more extensive right with respect to the distillation of alcohol. As we remember, in 1819, they were allowed to distil it in the provinces of Great Russia "until Russian artisans acquire sufficient competence." In 1826 Nicolas decided to repatriate them to the Pale of Settlement, but in 1827 he conceded to several specific requests to keep distillers in place, for example in the state factories in Irkutsk.²³⁰

Vladimir Solvoyov quotes the following thoughts from Mr. Katkov: "In the western provinces it is the Jew who deals with alcohol, but is the situation better in the other provinces of Russia? ... The Jewish innkeepers who get the people drunk, ruin the peasants and cause their doom, are they present throughout Russia? What is happening elsewhere in Russia, where Jews are not admitted and where the flow of liquor is held by an Orthodox bartender or a kulak?"²³¹

Let us listen to Leskov, the great connoisseur of Russian popular life: "In the provinces of Greater Russia where Jews do not reside, the number of those accused of drunkenness, or crimes committed under the influence, are regularly and significantly higher than within the Pale of Settlement. The same applies to the number of deaths due to alcoholism... And this is not a new phenomenon: it has been so since ancient times."²³²

---

[227] *Ibidem*, t. 5, p. 613.
[228] Russian Jewish Encyclopedia, 2ⁿᵈ ed. Reviewed, corrected and augmented, t. 1, Moscow, 1994, p. 317.
[229] JE, t. 12. p. 163.
[230] *Ibidem**, t. 11, p. 710.
[231] Letter from V. I. Soloviev to T. Gertz, in *V. Soloviev*, Evrcïskij vopros - khristianskij vopros (The Jewish Problem is a Christian Problem), collection of articles, Warsaw, 1906, p. 25.
[232] *Nicolas Leskov*, Evrei v Rossii: neskolko zametchanij po evreïskomou voprosou. (The Jews in Russia: A few remarks on the Jewish Problem). Petrograd, 1919 (reproduction of the ed. of 1884). p. 31.

However, it is true, statistics tell us that in the western and southern provinces of the empire there was one drinking place per 297 inhabitants, whereas in the eastern provinces there was only one for 585. The newspaper *The Voice*, which was not without influence at the time, was able to say that the trade of alcohol of the Jews was "the wound of this area"—namely the western region—"and an intractable wound" at that. In his theoretical considerations, I.G. Orchansky tries to show that the stronger the density in drinking places, the less alcoholism there was (we must understand that, according to him, the peasant will succumb less to temptation if the flow of drinks is found under his nose and solicits him 24 hours a day—remember Derzhavin: the bartenders trade night and day; but will the peasant be tempted by a distant cabaret, when he will have to cross several muddy fields to reach it? No, we know only too well that alcoholism is sustained not only by demand, but also by the supply of vodka. Orchansky nevertheless pursues his demonstration: when the Jew is interposed between the distiller and the drunken peasant, he acts objectively in favour of the peasant because he sells vodka at a lower price, but it is true that he does so by pawning the effects of the peasant. Certainly, he writes, some believe nevertheless that Jewish tenants have "a poor influence on the condition of the peasants", but it is because, "in the trade of bartending, as in all the other occupations, they differ by their know-how, skill and dynamism."[233] It is true that elsewhere, in another essay of the same collection, he recognises the existence of "fraudulent transactions with the peasants"; "it is right to point out that the Jewish trade is grossly deceitful and that the Jewish dealer, tavern-keeper and usurer exploit a miserable population, especially in the countryside"; "faced with an owner, the peasant holds on firmly to his prices, but he is amazingly supple and confident when dealing with a Jew, especially if the latter holds a bottle of vodka in reserve... the peasant is often brought to sell his wheat dirt cheap to the Jew." [234] Nevertheless, to this crude, glaring, arresting truth, Orchansky seeks attenuating circumstances. But this evil that eats away the will of the peasants, how to justify it?...

Due to his insistent energy, Nicholas I, throughout his reign, did not only face failures in his efforts to transform Jewish life in its different aspects. This was the case with Jewish agriculture.

The "Regulation on the obligations of recruitment and military service of the Jews", dated 1827, stipulated that Jewish farmers "transferred..." on private plots were released, as well as their children, from the obligation to provide recruits for a period of fifty years (exemption incurring from the

---

[233] *I. Orchansky*, Evrei v Rossii (Jews in Russia, essays and studies), fasc. 1, Saint Petersburg, 1872, pp. 192,195, 200,207.
[234] *Ibidem*, pp. 114,116, 124,125.

moment they actually began to "engage in agricultural work"). As soon as this regulation was made public, more Jews returned to the colonies than those who had absented themselves on their own initiative, that had been signalled absent.[235]

In 1829 a more elaborate and detailed regulation concerning Jewish cultivators was published: it envisaged their access to the *bourgeois* class provided that all their debts were paid; authorisation to absent themselves for up to three months to seek a livelihood during periods when the land did not require their physical work; sanctions against those who absent themselves without authorisation, and rewards for distinguished agricultural leaders. V. Nikitin admits: "To compare the severe constraints imposed on Jewish farmers, 'but with rights and privileges exclusively granted to the Jews', with those of the other taxable classes, it must be observed that the government treated the Jews with great benevolence."[236]

And, from 1829 to 1833, "the Jews labour the land with zeal, fate rewards them with good harvests, they are satisfied with the authorities, and vice versa, and general prosperity is tainted only by fortuitous incidents, without great importance." After the war with Turkey—1829—"the arrears of taxes are entirely handed over to the Jewish residents as to all the settlers... for 'having suffered from the passage of years'." But according to the report of the supervisory committee, "the bad harvest of 1833 made it impossible to retain [the Jews] in the colonies, it allowed many who had neither the desire nor the courage to devote themselves to the agricultural work of sowing nothing, or almost nothing, of getting rid of the cattle, going away from here and there, of demanding subsidies and not paying royalties." In 1834, more than once, they saw "the sale of the grain which they had received, and the slaughter of the cattle", which was also done by those who were not driven to do so by necessity; The Jews received bad harvests more often than other peasants, for, with the exception of insufficient seedlings, they worked the land haphazardly, at the wrong time, which was due to the "the habit, transmitted from generation to generation, of practising easy trades, of mismanaging, and neglecting the surveillance of livestock."[237]

One might have thought that three decades of unfortunate experiences in the implementation of Jewish agriculture (compared to universal experience) would suffice for the government to renounce these vain and expensive attempts. But no! Did the reiterative reports not reach Nicholas I? Or were they embellished by the ministers? Or did the inexhaustible

---

[235] *Nikitin**, pp. 168-169, 171.
[236] *Ibidem*, pp. 179,181.
[237] *Ibidem**, pp. 185-186. 190 191.

energy and irrefragable hope of the sovereign impel him to renew these incessant attempts?

In any case, Jewish agriculture, in the new Jewish Regulation dated 1835 and approved by the Emperor (the result of the work of the "Directors Committee"), is not at all excluded, but on the contrary, enhanced: "to organise the lives of the Jews according to rules which would enable them to earn a decent living by practising agriculture and industry, gradually dispensing instruction to their youth, which would prevent them from engaging in idleness or unlawful occupations." If the Jewish community were previously required to pay 400 rubles per household, now "every Jew was allowed to become a farmer at any time, all tax arrears were immediately handed over to him, and to his community"; They were given the right to receive land from the state in usufruct without time limit (but within the Pale of Settlement), to acquire plots of land, to sell them, to rent them. Those who became farmers were exempt from taxation for twenty-five years, property tax for ten years, recruitment for fifty years. In reverse, no Jew "could be forced to become a farmer". "The industries and trades practised in the context of village life were also allowed to them."[238] (One hundred and fifty years have passed. Forgetful of the past, an eminent and most enlightened Jewish physicist formulates his vision of Jewish life in those days: "A Pale of Settlement coupled with the prohibition (!) of practicing agriculture."[239] "The historian and thinker M. Guerchenson uses a more general formulation: "Agriculture is forbidden to the Jew by the spirit of his people because, by attaching to the land, man takes root more easily in a given place."[240])

The influential Minister of Finance, Cancrin, proposed to place the deserted lands of Siberia at the disposal of Jewish agriculture; Nicolas gave his approval to this project at the end of the same year 1835. It was proposed to attribute to Jewish settlers "up to 15 hectares of good land per male individual", with tools and workhorses billed to the Treasury, and paid transportation costs, including food. It seems that poor Jews, laden with large families, were tempted to undertake this journey to Siberia. But this time the *Kehalim* were divided in their calculations: these poor Jews were indeed necessary to satisfy the needs of recruitment (instead of wealthy families); it was concealed from them that the arrears were all handed over

---

[238] *Nikitin**, pp. 193-197.
[239] *E. Gliner*, Stikhia s tchelovctchcskim lilsom? (The element with a human face?), in "Vremia i my" (International Review of Literature and Social Problems). New York, 1993, n° 122, p. 133.
[240] *M. Guerchenson*, Soudby evreïskogo naroda (The Destinies of the Jewish People), in 22, Literary and political review of the Jewish intelligentsia emigrated from the USSR to Israel, Tel-Aviv, n° 19, 1981, p. 111.

to them and they were required to carry them out beforehand. But the government changed its mind, fearing the difficulties of a transfer so far away, and that the Jews, on the spot, lacking examples of know-how and love of work, and would resume their "sterile trade, which rested essentially on dishonest operations that have already done so much harm in the western provinces of the empire", their "innkeeper occupations of ruining inhabitants by satisfying their inclination for drinking," and so on. In 1837, therefore, the transfer to Siberia was stopped without the reasons being publicised.[241] In the same year, the Inspectorate estimated that in New Russia "the plots of land reserved for Jewish settlers contained a black potting soil of the highest quality, that they were 'perfectly suited to the cultivation of cereals, that the steppes were excellent for the production of hay and livestock farming'." (local authorities, however, disputed this assessment).[242]

Also in the same year of 1837, a Ministry of Public Goods was established, headed by Count P. Kiselyov, who was entrusted with the transition measure intended to prepare the abolition of serfdom, the task of "protecting the free cultivators" (the peasants of the Crown)—there were seven and a half million of them registered—including the Jewish farmers—but they were only 3,000 to 5,000 families, or "a drop of water in the sea, relative to the number of peasants of the Crown." Nevertheless, as soon as it was created, this ministry received numerous petitions and recriminations of all kinds coming from Jews. "Six months later it became clear that it would be necessary to give the Jews so much attention that the main tasks of the ministry would suffer."[243] In 1840, however, Kiselyov was also appointed president of a newly created committee (the sixth one[244]) "to determine the measures to be taken to reorganise the lives of the Jews in Russia", meaning he also was to tackle the Jewish problem.

In 1839, Kiselyov had a law passed by the State Council authorising the Jews on the waiting lists for recruitment to become cultivators (provided that they were doing so with their whole family), which signified that they would benefit from the major advantage of being dispensed with military service. In 1844, "a still more detailed settlement concerning Jewish farmers" gave them—even in the Pale of Settlement—the right to employ for three years Christians who were supposed to teach them how to properly manage a farm. In 1840, "many Jews came to New Russia supposedly at their own expense (they produced on the spot 'attestations' that they had the means to do so), in fact, they had nothing and made it

---

[241] *Nikitin*, pp. 197-199. 202,205, 209, 216.
[242] *Ibidem*, pp. 229,230.
[243] *Ibidem*, pp. 232,234.
[244] JE, t. 9, pp. 488 489.

known from their very first days that their resources were exhausted"; "there were up to 1,800 families of which several hundred possessed neither papers nor any proof whatsoever of where they came from and how they found themselves in New Russia"; and "they never ceased to come running, begging not to be left to rot in their misery." Kiselyov ordered to receive them by levying the spendings to the "settlers in general, without distinction of ethnic group." In other words, he assisted them well beyond the amounts provided for. In 1847, "additional ordinances" were enacted to make it easier for Jews to become farmers.[245]

Through his ministry, Kiselyov had the ambition to establish model colonies and then "to eventually settle this people on a large scale": for this purpose, he set up one after the other colonies in the province of Ekaterinoslav, on fertile soils, well irrigated by rivers and streams, with excellent pastures and hay fields, hoping very much that the new settlers would benefit from the remarkable experience already gained by the German settlers, (but as it was difficult to find volunteers among them to settle in the midst of the Jewish settlements, it was decided to employ them as wage earners). New credits were constantly granted to these future model colonies; all arrears were remitted to them. In the second year of their settlement, Jewish families were required to have at least one vegetable garden and one seeded hectare, and to ensure a slow increase in the area sown over the years. Insofar as they had no experience in the selection of livestock, this task was entrusted to the curators. Kiselyov sought to facilitate the travelling conditions of families (accompanied by a small number of day labourers) and to find ways to provide specialised agricultural training to a certain contingent of settlers. But in some families there was still very little to worry about agronomy: in extreme cold, people did not even go out to feed the beasts—so they had to equip them with long hooded coats![246]

In the meantime, the flow of Jews migrating to agriculture did not dry up, especially since the western provinces suffered from bad harvests. Families that did not include the necessary number of able-bodied men were often dispatched, "the *Kehalim* sent by force the destitute and invalid, retaining the rich and healthy to have the possibility of better responding to collections, to pay royalties and thereby maintain their institutions." "In order to prevent the influx of a large number of needy destitutes," the ministry had to demand that the governors of the western provinces have strict control over the departures—but, on site, departures of contingents were hastened without even waiting to know whether lodging was ready; moreover, the credits allocated to the starters were retained, which

---

[245] *Nikitin*, pp. 239, 260, 263, 267, 355, 358.
[246] *Ibidem*, pp. 269, 277, 282, 300, 309, 329, 330, 346, 358, 367, 389, 391, 436, 443, 467.

sometimes compromised a whole year of agricultural work. In the province of Ekaterinoslav, there was not even time to distribute the land to the volunteers: 250 families left on their own to settle in Odessa.[247]

However, the reports of various inspectors from different places blended as one: "By submitting to this end, [the Jews] could make good, or even excellent, farmers, but they take advantage of the first occasion to abandon the plough, to sacrifice their farms, and to return to horse-trading and their favourite occupations." "For the Jew, the number one job is the industry, even the most humble, of total insignificance, but on condition that it provides the greatest profit margin... Their fundamentally industrious mindset found no satisfaction in the peaceful life of the cultivator", "did not create in them the slightest desire to devote themselves to agriculture; what attracted them there was first and foremost the abundance of land, the scarcity of the Jewish population, the proximity of borders, trade and lucrative industry, not to mention the franchises which exempted them from royalties and conscription." They thought they would only be compelled to organise their houses; as to lands, they hoped to "lease them at an appreciable rate, in order to occupy themselves, as in the past, with commerce and industry." (This is what they declared naively to the inspectors.) And "it was with total disgust that they tackled the work of the earth." Moreover, "religious rules... did not favour the Jewish cultivators", they forced them to long periods of inactivity, as, for example, during the spring plantings, the long Passover holiday; In September, that of the Tabernacles lasted fourteen days "at the time when intensive agricultural work, such as soil preparation and sowing, is needed, although, according to the opinion of Jews who deserve all trust, Scripture requires strict observance during the first and last two days of the celebrations." On the other hand, the spiritual leaders of Jewish settlements (there were sometimes as many as two prayer houses, one for the Orthodox—or *Mitnagdes*—, another for the *Hasidim*) entertained the idea that as a chosen people they were not destined for the hard work of the farmer, which is the bitter lot of the *goyim*." "They rose late, devoted an entire hour to prayer, and went away to work when the sun was already high in the sky"—to which was added the Sabbath, resting from Friday night until Sunday morning.[248]

From a Jewish point of view, I. Orchansky actually arrives at conclusions similar to those of the inspectors: "Leasing a farm and employing wage-earners... encounters more sympathy among the Jews than the passage, in all regards difficult, to agricultural labour... We note a growing tendency for Jews engaged in rural activity to exercise it first and foremost by leasing

---

[247] *Ibidem*, pp. 309, 314, 354,359, 364,369.
[248] *Nikitin**, pp. 280-285, 307, 420,421, 434, 451, 548.

land and using it through the assistance of wage-earners. In New Russia, the failures of Jewish agriculture stem from "their lack of accustomed to physical labour and the profits they derive from urban trades in southern Russia." But also to emphasise the fact that in a given colony the Jews "had built a synagogue *with their own hands*," and that in others maintained vegetable gardens "with their own hands."[249]

Nevertheless, the numerous reports of the inspectors agreed that in the 40s and in these "model" colonies, as in the past, "the standard of living of the settlers, their activities and their enterprises were well behind those of the peasants of the Crown or landowners." In the province of Kherson, in 1845, among the Jewish settlers, "The farms are in a very unsatisfactory state, most of these settlers are very poor: they dread the work of the land, and few cultivate it properly; also, even in years of good harvest, they obtain only low yields"; "In the plots, the soil is hardly stirred," women and children hardly work the land and "a lot of 30 hectares is barely enough for their daily subsistence." "The example of the German settlers is followed only by a very small number of Jewish residents; most of them 'show a clear aversion' to agriculture and they 'comply with the demands of the authorities only to receive a passport that allows them to go...' They leave a lot of land in fallow, work the land only in certain places, according to the goodwill of each one... they treat the cattle with too much negligence... harass the horses until they die, nourish them little, especially on the days of the Sabbath"; they milk delicate cows of the German race at any hour of the day, so that they no longer give milk. "Jews were provided free fruit trees, 'but they did not plant orchards.' Houses had been built in advance for them—some were 'elegant, very dry and warm, solid'; in other places, they had been poorly constructed and expensive, but even where they had been built reliably, with good quality materials... the negligence of the Jews, their inability to keep their lodgings in good condition... had led them to such a state of degradation that they could no longer be inhabited without urgent repairs"; they were invaded by humidity which led to their decay and favoured diseases; many houses were abandoned, others were occupied by several families at the same time 'without there being any kinship between them, and, in view of the impetuous character of these people and their propensity to quarrels', such cohabitation gave rise to endless complaints."[250]

Responsibility for unpreparedness for this large migration is evident to both parties: poor coordination and delays in the administration's actions; here and there, the development of the houses, poorly guarded, left much to be desired, giving rise to many abuses and waste. (This led to the transfer

---

[249] Orchansky, pp. 176, 182, 185, 191,192.
[250] *Nikitin*, pp. 259, 280, 283, 286. 301. 304,305, 321, 402,403. 416,419, 610.

of several officials and trials for some of them.) But in the Jewish villages, the elders also reluctantly controlled the careless ones whose farm and equipment deteriorated; hence the appointment of supervisors chosen among retired non-commissioned officers whom the Jews got drunk and coaxed with bribes. Hence also the impossibility of levying royalties on the settlers, either on account of indigence—"in every community there were only about ten farmers who were barely capable of paying for themselves"— or because of the "natural inclination of the Jews to evade their payment"; over the years, arrears only increased and they were given again and again without requiring any reimbursement. For each day of absence without authorisation, the settler paid only 1 kopeck, which hardly weighed on him, and he easily compensated for it with the gains he made in the city. (By way of comparison: in the villages the *Melamed* received from 3,000 to 10,000 rubles per year, and in parallel to the *Melamed* there had been an attempt to introduce into the colonies, in addition to the use of the Jewish language, a general education based on Russian and arithmetic, but "simple people" had little "confidence in the educational institutions founded by the government."[251])

"It became more and more indisputable that the 'model colonies' so ardently desired by Kiselyov were just a dream"; but, while curbing (1849) the sending of new families, he did not lose hope and affirmed again in 1852 in one of his resolutions: "The more arduous an affair, the more one must be firm and not to be discouraged by the first lack of successes." Until then, the curator was not the true leader of the colony, "he sometimes has to put up with the mockery and insolence of the settlers who understood very well that he had no power over them"; he was entitled only to advise them. More than once, due to the exasperation provoked by failures, projects had been proposed which would have consisted in giving the settlers compulsory lessons in such a way that they would have to put them into practice within a period of two or three days, with a verification of results; to deprive them of the free disposal of their land; to radically eliminate leave of absence; and even to introduce punishments: up to thirty lashes the first time, double in case of recidivism, then prison, and, depending on the seriousness of the offense, enlistment in the army. (Nikitin asserts that this project of instruction, as soon as it was known, "exerted such terror upon the Jewish cultivators, that they redoubled their efforts, and hastened to procure cattle, to furnish themselves with agricultural tools... and showed an astonishing zeal in the work of the fields and the care taken to their house." But Kiselyov gave his approval to a watered-down project (1853): "The lessons must correspond perfectly to the capacities and experience of those for whom they are intended", the

---

[251] *Ibidem**, pp. 290, 301, 321,325, 349, 399, 408, 420,421, 475, 596.

instructor responsible for organising agricultural work can deviate from it only in the sense of a reduction in tasks, and for the first offense, no punishment, for the second and third, ten to twenty lashes, no more. (Enlistment in the army was never applied, "no one... has ever been made a soldier for his failings at work," and in 1860, the act was definitively repealed.[252])

Let us not forget that we were still in the age of serfdom. But half a century after the conscientious attempts of the government to entice the Jews to provide productive labour on virgin lands, the outlines of the villages of Arakcheyev[253] began to appear.

It is astonishing that the imperial power did not understand, at this stage, the sterility of the measures taken, the desperate character of this whole enterprise of returning to the land.

Furthermore, the process was not over...

After the introduction of compulsory military service, alarming rumours spread among the Jewish population, announcing a new and terrible legislation prepared especially by the "Jewish Committee". But in 1835, a General Regulation concerning the Jews was finally promulgated (intended to replace that of 1804), and, as the *Jewish Encyclopædia* discreetly notes, "it imposed no new limitations on the Jews."[254] If we want to know more: this new regulation "preserved for Jews the right to acquire all kinds of immovable property excluding inhabited areas, to conduct all kinds of commerce on an equal footing with other subjects, but only within the Pale of Settlement."[255] These Regulations of 1835 confirmed the protection of all the rights recognised to the Jewish faith, introduced distinctions for the rabbis, conferring on them the rights granted to the merchants of the first guild; established a reasonable age to marry (18 and 16 years old); adopted measures to ensure that the Jewish attire did not differ too much and did not cut off the Jews from the surrounding population; oriented the Jews towards means of earning their livelihood through productive labour (which prohibited only the sale of spirits on credit or secured on domestic effects), authorised all kinds of industrial activities (including the renting of distilleries). To have Christians in their service was forbidden only for

---

[252] *Ibidem**, p. 350-351, 382,385, 390, 425, 547, 679.
[253] Count Alexis Araktchev (1769 1834), a favourite of Alexander I, creator of the "military colonies" which were to house the soldiers with their families and replace the garrisons.
[254] JE, 1.12, p. 695.
[255] M. *Kovalevsky*, Ravnopravie evreev i ego vragui (The Equal Rights of Jews and their Enemies), in Schit: literatournyj sbornik (Literary collection), under the dir. of L. Andreyev, M. Gorky and F. Sologub, 3rd ed. increased, Moscow, Russian Society for the Study of Jewish Life, 1916, p. 117.

regular employment but authorised "for short-term work" (without the time limits being specified) and "for work in factories and factories", as well as "as an aide in the work of the fields, gardens and vegetable gardens"[256] which sounded like a mockery of the very idea of "Jewish agriculture". The Regulations of 1835 called upon Jewish youth to educate itself; it did not restrict Jewish enrolment to secondary schools or university.[257] Jews who had received the rank of doctor in any discipline, once recognised (not without formalities) of their distinguished qualities, were entitled to enter in the service of the State. (Jewish doctors already enjoyed this right.) With regard to local government, the Regulation abrogated the previous limitations: from now on, Jews could hold office in local councils, magistrates and municipalities "under the same conditions as if members of other faiths had been elected to office." (It is true that some local authorities, particularly in Lithuania, objected to this provision: in certain circumstances, the mayor has to lead his citizens to church—how could a Jew do it? Also, can a Jew sit among the judges when the oath is sworn on the cross? In the face of these strong reservations, a decree in 1836 stipulated that in the western provinces the Jews could occupy in the magistracy and the municipalities only one third of the positions.[258]) Finally, with regard to the thorny economic problem inherent in cross-border smuggling, which was so detrimental to the interests of the State, the Regulation permitted the Jews already residing there to remain there, but prohibited any new installations.[259]

For a State that still maintained millions of its subjects in serfdom, all that has just been mentioned might not appear as a system of cruel constraints.

During the examination of the Regulation before the Council of State, the discussions concerned the possibility of allowing the Jews free access to the internal provinces of Great Russia, and the opinions expressed on this subject were as numerous as they were varied. Some argued that "to admit the Jews to settle in the central provinces, they had to be able to justify certain moral qualities and a sufficient level of education"; others replied that "Jews can be of great use because of their commercial and industrial activity, and that competition cannot be prevented by prohibiting anybody from residing and practising commerce"; "it is necessary to raise the problem... plainly put: can the Jews be tolerated in this country? If one considers that they cannot be so, then all must be cast out," rather than "leave this category in the midst of the nation in a situation likely to engender in them continuous discontent and grumbles." And "if it is

---

[256] JE, t. 11, p. 494.
[257] *Kovalevsky*, in Schit, p. 117.
[258] *Hessen**, t. 2, pp. 50 52, 105,106.
[259] JE, t. 12, p. 599.

necessary to tolerate their presence in this country, then it is important to free them from any limitations placed on their rights."[260]

Moreover, the "archaic Polish privileges (abandoned by the Russian State since the reign of Catherine) which granted urban communities the power to introduce restrictions on the right of residence for the Jews" reappeared with further acuteness in Vilnius first, then in Kiev. In Vilnius, the Jews were forbidden to settle in certain parts of the city. In Kiev, the local merchants were indignant that "the Jews, to the great displeasure of every one, engage in commerce and business between the walls of the monasteries of Pechersk [261] ... that they take over all commercial establishments in Pechersk" and exclude "trade Christians"; they urged the Governor-General to obtain a ban (1827) "on the Jews to live permanently in Kiev... Only a few categories of individuals would be able to go there for a determined period of time." "As always in such circumstances, the Government was obliged to postpone on several occasions the deadline set for their expulsion." The discussions went back to the "Directorial Committee", divided the Council of State into two equal camps, but under the terms of the Regulation of 1835 Nicolas confirmed the expulsion of the Jews from Kiev. However, shortly after, "certain categories of Jews were again allowed to reside temporarily in Kiev." (But why were Jews so lucky in commercial competition? Often, they sold at lower prices than Christians, contenting themselves with a "lesser profit" than the Christians demanded; but in some cases, their merchandise was deemed to have come from smuggling, and the governor of Kiev, who had taken the defense of the Jews, remarked that "if the Christians were willing to take the trouble, they could oust the Jews without these coercive measures."[262]) Thus, "in Belarus, the Jews had the right to reside only in the towns; In Little Russia, they could live everywhere, with the exception of Kiev and certain villages; In New Russia, in all inhabited places with the exception of Nikolayev and Sevastopol,"[263] military ports from which the Jews had been banned for reasons related with the security of the State.

"The 1835 Regulations allowed merchants and [Jewish] manufacturers to participate in the main fairs of the interior provinces in order to temporarily trade there, and granted them the right to sell certain goods outside the Pale of Settlement."[264] In the same way, artisans were not entirely deprived of access to the central provinces, even if only temporarily. According to the

---

[260] *Hessen*, t. 2. pp. 47, 48.
[261] Or "the Grottoes": a group of monasteries whose origins go back to the middle of the eleventh century and which still exist today.
[262] *Ibidem*, pp. 40-42.
[263] LJE, t. 7, p. 318.
[264] JE, t. 14, p. 944.

Regulation of 1827, "the authorities of the provinces outside the Pale of Settlement had the right to authorise the Jews to remain there for six months."[265] Hessen points out that the 1835 Regulations "and subsequent laws extended somewhat for the Jews the possibility of temporarily living outside the Pale of Settlement", especially since the local authorities turned a blind eye "when the Jews bypassed the prohibitions."[266] Leskov confirms in a note he wrote at the request of the governmental committee: "In the 40s", the Jews "appeared in the villages of Great Russia belonging to the great landowners in order to offer their services... Throughout the year, they rendered timely visits 'to the lords of their acquaintance'" in the neighbouring provinces of Great Russia, and everywhere they traded and tackled work. "Not only were the Jews not driven out, they were retained." "Usually, people welcomed and gave refuge to Jewish artisans...; everywhere the local authorities treated them with kindness, for, as for the other inhabitants, the Jews provided important advantages."[267] "With the help of interested Christians, the Jews violated the limiting decrees. And the authorities were in their turn incited to derogate from the laws... In the provinces of Central Russia, it was decided to fix fines to be imposed on the owners who let the Jews settle in their home."[268]

This is how, led by conservative (more specifically religious) considerations of not wanting fusion between Christians and Jews, the authorities of the Russian state, faced with the economic push that attracted Jews beyond the Pale of Settlement, were unable either to make a clear decision or to clearly apply it in practice. As for the dynamic and enterprising character of the Jews, it suffered from too much territorial concentration and too strong internal competition; it was natural for them to overflow as widely as possible.

As I. Orchansky observed: "The more the Jews are scattered among the Christian population, the higher is their standard of living."[269]

But it would be hard to deny that, even in its official perimeter, the Pale of Settlement for Jews in Russia was very large: in addition to what had been inherited from the dense Jewish grouping in Poland, the provinces of Vilnius, Grodno, Kaunas, Vitebsk, Minsk, Mogilev, Volhynia, Podolsk and Kiev (in addition to Poland and Courland) were added the vast and fertile provinces of Poltava, Ikaterinoslav, Chernigov, Tauride, Kherson and Bessarabia, all together larger than any state, or even group of European states. (A short time later, from 1804 to the mid-30s, the rich provinces of

---

[265] *Ibidem*, t. 11, p. 332.
[266] *Hessen*, t. 2, pp. 46, 48.
[267] *Leskov*, pp. 45-48.
[268] *Hessen*, t. 2, p. 49.
[269] *Orchansky*, p. 30.

Astrakhan and the Caucasus were added, but the Jews hardly settled there; again in 1824, in Astrakhan, "no Jew was registered as taxable."[270] This made fifteen provinces within the Pale of Settlement, compared with thirty-one for "Deep Russia". And few were more populous than the provinces of central Russia. As for the Jews' share of the population, it did not exceed that of the Moslems in the provinces of the Urals or the Volga. Thus the density of Jews in the Pale of Settlement did not result from their number, but rather from the uniformity of their occupations. It was only in the immensity of Russia that such an area might seem cramped.

It is objected that the extent of this area was illusory: it excluded all zones outside cities and other agglomerations. But these spaces were agricultural areas or intended for agriculture, and it was understood that this domain, accessible to the Jews, did not attract them; their whole problem was rather how to use these spaces for alcohol trade. Which was a deviation.

And if the large Jewish mass had not moved from narrow Poland to vast Russia, the very concept of the Pale of Settlement would never have been born.

In narrow Poland, the Jews would have lived densely piled up, with greater poverty, growing rapidly without carrying out any productive work, 80% of the population practising petty trade and the dealing of intermediaries.

In any case, nowhere in Russian cities were implemented obligatory ghettos for the Jews, as was still known here and there in Europe. (If not the suburb of Glebovo, in Moscow, for those who went there as visitors.)

Let us remember once more that this Pale of Settlement coexisted for three quarters of a century with the serfdom of the majority of the Russian rural population, and so, by comparison, the weight of these limitations to the freedom of coming and going was somewhat lifted. In the Russian Empire, many peoples lived by millions in high density areas within their respective regions. Within the borders of a multinational state, peoples often lived compactly more or less as separate entities. So it was with the example of the Karaites and the Jews "of the mountains", the latter having the freedom to choose their place of residence but which they hardly used. No comparison is possible with the territorial limits, the "reserves" imposed on the native populations of conquered countries by colonisers (Anglo-Saxons or Spanish) who came from elsewhere.

It is precisely the absence of a national territory among the Jews, given the dynamism they displayed in their movements, their highly practical sense, their zeal in the economic sphere, which promised to become imminently an important factor influencing the life of the country as a whole. We can

---

[270] JE. t. 3, p. 359.

say that it is on the one hand, the Jewish Diaspora's need to access all the existing functions, and on the other, the fear of an overflow of their activity which fuelled the limiting measures taken by the Russian government.

Yes, as a whole, the Jews of Russia turned away from agriculture. In crafts, they were preferably tailors, shoemakers, watchmakers, jewellers. However, despite the constraints imposed by the Pale, their productive activity was not limited to these small trades.

The *Jewish Encyclopædia* published before the Revolution writes that for the Jews, before the development of heavy industry, "what was most important was the trade of money; irrespective of whether the Jew intervened as a pawnbroker or money changer, as a farmer of public or private income, as tenant or tenant—he was primarily involved in financial transactions." For even in the period of rural economy in Russia, "the demand for money was already felt in ever-increasing proportions."[271] Thence, the transfer of Jewish capital into this industry for them to participate in it. Already, under Alexander I, energetic arrangements had been made to encourage the participation of Jews in industry, especially in drapery. "It subsequently played an important part in the accumulation of capital in the hands of the Jews," and then "they did not fail to use this capital successively in factories and plants, mining, transportation and banking. Thus began the formation of a lower and upper Jewish *bourgeoisie*.[272] The Regulations of 1835 "also provided privileges for Jewish manufacturers."[273]

By the 40s of the nineteenth century, the sugar industry had grown considerably in the south-western provinces. First, The Jewish capitalists began by granting subsidies to the refineries belonging to the landowners, then by assuming their administration, followed by becoming owners, and finally building their own factories. In Ukraine and New Russia, powerful "sugar kings", among others Lazare and Lev Brodski. "Most of these Jewish sugar producers had begun in the distillery of alcohol... or as tenants of cabarets." This situation also took place in flour-milling.[274]

At the time, no contemporary understood or bothered to foresee what power was being accumulated there, material first, then spiritual. Of course, Nicholas I was the first not to see, nor understand. He had too high

---

[271] JE, t. 13. p. 646.
[272] *J.M. Dijour*, Evrei v ekonomitcheskoï jizni Rossii (The Jews in Russian Economic life), in BJWR-1, pp. 164,165.
[273] JE, t. 15, p. 153.
[274] *Dijour*, in LJE-1, pp. 165,168.

an opinion of the omnipotence of the imperial power and of the efficiency of military-type administrative methods.

But he obstinately desired success in the education of the Jews so that the Jews could overcome their extraneousness in relation to the rest of the population, situation in which he saw a major danger. As early as 1831, he pointed out to the "Directors Committee" that "among the measures likely to improve the situation of the Jews, special attention should be given to raising them via education… by the creation of factories, the prohibition of precocious marriages, a better organisation of the *Kehalim*…, a change in clothing customs."[275] And in 1840, when the "Committee in charge of identifying measures for a radical transformation of the life of Jews in Russia" was founded, one of the first aims envisaged by this committee was "to promote the moral development of the new generation by the creation of Jewish schools in a spirit contrary to the Talmudic teaching currently in force."[276]

All the progressive Jews of that time also wanted general education (they were only divided on whether to totally exclude the Talmud from the program or to study it in the upper grades, "with the illumination of a scientific approach, thus relieved from undesirable additions"[277]). A newly established general education school in Riga was headed by a young graduate of the University of Munich, Max Lilienthal, who aspired to invest himself in the "spread of education among Russian Jews." In 1840, he was cordially received in Saint Petersburg by the ministers of the interior and education, and wrote to the "Committee for the Transformation of the Life of the Jews" proposing the project of a consistory and theology seminary with the aim of training rabbis and teachers "according to pure ethical foundations", as opposed to "calcified talmudists"; However, "before acquiring the essential principles of faith, it would not be permissible to study profane matters." Thus the ministerial project was modified: the number of hours devoted to the teaching of Jewish matters was increased.[278] Lilienthal also sought to persuade the government to take preventive measures against the *Hasidim*, but without success: government power "wanted a front unifying the various Jewish social milieux who waged war."[279] Lilienthal, who had developed his school in Riga "with amazing success", was invited by the Ministry to visit the provinces of the Pale of Settlement in order to contribute to the work of education, through public meetings and conferences with Jewish personalities. His journey, at

---

[275] *Hessen**, t. 2, p. 77.
[276] *Ibidem*, p. 84; JE, t. 13. p. 47.
[277] *Hessen*, t. 2, p. 83.
[278] *Ibidem*, p. 84; JE, t. 13. p. 47.
[279] *Hessen*, t. 2. pp. 85, 86.

least externally, was a great success; as a general rule, he met with little open hostility and seemed to have succeeded in convincing the influential circles of the Jewish world. "The enemies... of the reform... had to express their approval outwardly." But the hidden opposition was, of course, very important. And when school reform was finally applied, Lilienthal renounced his mission. In 1844, he left unexpectedly for the United States, never to return. "His departure from Russia—perhaps a way of escape—remains shrouded in mystery."[280]

Thus, under Nicholas I, not only did the authorities not oppose the assimilation of the Jews, but rather they called for it; however, the Jewish masses who remained under the influence of the *Kahal*, feared constraining measures in the religious sphere, and so did not lend themselves to it.

Nevertheless, school reform did begin in 1844, despite the extreme resistance of the leaders of the *Kehalim*. (And although "in creating these Jewish schools there was no attempt to reduce the number of Jews in general schools, on the contrary, it was pointed out that they should, as before, be open to the Jews."[281]) Two kinds of Jewish public schools were created ("modelled on Jewish elementary schools in Austria"[282]): two years, corresponding to Russian parish schools, and four years, corresponding to district schools. Only Jewish disciplines were taught by Jewish (and Hebrew) teachers; the others were given by Russian teachers. (As Lev Deitch, a frenzied revolutionary, admits, "The crowned monster ordered them [Jewish children] to learn Russian."[283]) For many years, these schools were led by Christians, and were only led by Jews much later.

"Faithful to traditional Judaism, having learned or overshadowed the secret objective of Uvarov [Minister of Education], the majority of the Jewish population saw in these government measures of education a means of persecution like the others."[284] (Said Uvarov, who, for his part, sought to bring the Jews closer to the Christian population by eradicating "prejudices inspired by the precepts of the Talmud", wanted to exclude the latter entirely from the education system, considering it as an anti-Christian compendium[285]).

Continuing for many years to distrust the Russian authorities, the Jewish population turned away from these schools and fuelling a real phobia of

---

[280] *Ibidem*, pp. 84, 86 87.
[281] JE, 1.13, pp. 47, 48.
[282] *Ibidem*, t. 3, p. 334.
[283] *L Deitch*, Roi evreev v rousskom revolioutsionnom dvïjenii, (The Role of Jews in the Russian Revolutionary Movement), t. 1, 2nd ed., Moscow-Leningrad, GIZ, 1925, p. 11.
[284] JE, t. 9, p. 111.
[285] *Hessen*, t. 2, p. 85.

them: "Just as the population sought to escape conscription, it distrusted these schools, fearing to leave their children in these homes of "free-thinking". Well-off Jewish families often sent to public schools not their own offspring, but those of the poor.[286] Thus was entrusted to a public school P. B. Axelrod[287]; He then went on to college, and then obtained broad political notoriety as Plekhanov and Deitch's companion in the struggle within the Liberation of Labour[288]). If in 1855 only the duly registered *Heder* had 70,000 Jewish children, the public schools of both types received only 3,200.[289]

This fear of public education was perpetuated for a long time in Jewish circles. In this way, Deitch remembers the 60s, not the middle of nowhere, but in Kiev: "I remember the time when my countrymen considered it a sin to learn Russian" and only tolerated its use "in relations with the *goyim*."[290] A. G. Sliozberg remembers that, until the 70s, entering college was regarded as a betrayal of the essence of Jewishness, the college uniform being a sign of apostasy. "Between Jews and Christians there was an abyss which only a few Jews could cross, and only in the great cities where Jewish public opinion did not paralyse the will of all."[291] Young people attached to Jewish traditions did not aspire to study in Russian universities, although the final diploma, according to the Recruitment Law of 1827, dispensed one of military service for life. However, Hessen points out that among Russian Jews belonging to "the most affluent circles", "the spontaneous desire to integrate… the public schools was growing."[292]

He adds that in Jewish public schools "not only the Christian superintendents but the majority of Jewish teachers who taught the Jewish disciplines in the German language were far from the required level." Thus, "in parallel with the establishment of these public schools, it was decided to organise a graduate school intended for the training of teachers, to form better educated rabbis capable of acting progressively on the Jewish masses. Rabbinic schools of this type were founded in Vilnius and Zhytomir (1847)." "Despite their shortcomings, these schools were of some use," according to the testimony of the liberal J. Hessen, "the rising generation was familiarising itself with the Russian language and its grammar."[293] The revolutionary Mr. Krol was of the same opinion, but he

---

[286] *Ibidem*, p. 120.
[287] Paul Axelrod (1850–1928), founder in Geneva of the very small group "Liberation of Labour" embryo of the future Russian Social Democratic Party, founded in 1898.
[288] *Deitch*, p. 12-13.
[289] I. M. Trotsky, The Jews in Russian Schools, in BJWR-1, pp. 351, 354.
[290] *Deitch*, p. 10.
[291] JE, 1.11, p. 713.
[292] *Hessen*, t. 11, p. 112.
[293] *Ibidem*, p. 121.

also condemned the government unreservedly: "The laws of Nicholas I instituting primary public schools and rabbinic schools were reactionary and hostile to the Jews; schools, willingly or unwillingly, allowed a small number of Jewish children to learn secular education. As for the "enlightened" intellectuals (the *Maskilim*) and those who now despised the "superstitions of the masses", they "had no place to go", according to Krol, and remained strangers amongst their own. "Nevertheless, this evolution played an enormous role in the spiritual awakening of Russian Jews during the second half of the nineteenth century," even if the *Maskilim*, who wanted to enlighten the Jewish masses, met with "the fierce opposition of fanatical Jewish believers who saw in profane science an alienation of the devil."[294]

In 1850 a kind of superstructure was created: an institute of "Jewish scholars", as well as a consulting inspectorate among the heads of academies.

Those who came from the newly created rabbinical schools occupied in 1857 the functions of "public rabbis"; Elected unwillingly by their community, their designation was subject to the approval of the authorities of their province.

But their responsibility remained purely administrative: the Jewish communities regarded them as ignoramuses in the Hebrew sciences, and the traditional rabbis were maintained as genuine "spiritual rabbis."[295] (Numerous graduates of rabbinic schools, "found no positions, neither as rabbis nor teachers", pursued their studies at university[296], then became doctors or lawyers.) Nicholas I did not release his pressure to regulate the internal life of the Jewish community. The *Kahal*, who already possessed an immense power over the community, grew even stronger from the moment conscription was introduced: it was given the right to "give for recruitment at any moment every Jew who did not pay his royalties, who had no fixed abode or committed intolerable misdemeanors in Jewish society," and it used this right for the benefit of the rich. "All this nourished the indignation of the masses towards the rulers of the *Kehalim* and became one of the causes of the irremediable decline of the *Kahal*." Thus, in 1844, the *Kehalim* "were dissolved everywhere, and their functions were transmitted to municipalities and town halls"[297]; In other words, urban Jewish communities found themselves subject to the uniform legislation of

---

[294] M. Krol, Natsionalism i assimiliatsia v evreïskoï islorii (Nationalism and Assimilation in Jewish History), in JW, p. 188.
[295] LJE, t. 4, p. 34; B. C. Dinour. Religiosno-natsionalnyj oblik rousskogo evreïstva (The Religious and National Profile of the Russian Jews) in BJWR-1. p. 314.
[296] *Hessen*, t. 2, p. 179.
[297] LJE*, 1.4, pp. 20 21.

the state. But this reform was not completed either: the collection of the arduous and evanescent arrears and the lifting of the recruits were again entrusted to the Jewish community, whose "recruiters" and tax collectors were substituted for the ancients of the *Kehalim*. As for the registry of births, and thus the counting of the population, they remained in the hands of the rabbis.

The government of Nicolas also took a position on the inextricable problem of the internal tax collection of Jewish communities, first of all on the so-called "casket" (indirect tax on the consumption of kosher meat). A provision of 1844 specified that part of the proceeds should be used to cover public arrears in the community, to finance the organisation of Jewish schools and to distribute subsidies to Jews who devoted themselves to agriculture.[298] But there was also an unexpected imbroglio: although the Jews "were subject to the capitation on the same basis as the Christian *bourgeois*", that is, to a direct tax, "the Jewish population, thanks to the amount of the "casket", were, it is to say, in a privileged position to pay the royalty"; in fact, from then on "Jews, including the wealthiest, covered by personal payments only an insignificant part of the taxes owed to the tax authorities, turning the balance into arrears," and these never ceased to accumulate: by the mid-50s, they exceeded 8 million rubles.

There followed a new imperial decree dictated by exasperation: "for every 2,000 rubles" of new arrears, "an adult had to be provided as recruit."[299] In 1844 a new and energetic attempt was made—again aborted—to expel the Jews from the villages.

Hessen pictorially writes that "in Russian laws designed to normalise the lives of Jews, one hears as a cry of despair: in spite of all its authority, the government fails to extirpate the existence of the Jews from the depths of Russian life."[300]

No, the leaders of Russia had not yet realised the full weight and even the "unassimilability" of the immense Jewish legacy received as a gift under the successive divisions of Poland: what to do with this intrinsically resistant and rapidly expanding group in the Russian national body? They could not find reliable rulings and were all the more incapable of foreseeing the future. The energetic measures of Nicholas I surged one after the other, but the situation was apparently only getting more complicated.

A similar failure, which was escalating, followed Nicholas I in his struggle against the Jewish contrabands at the frontiers. In 1843 he categorically

---

[298] *Hessen*, t. 2, pp. 89 90.
[299] JE, t. 12, p. 640.
[300] *Hessen*, t. 2, p. 19.

ordered the expulsion of all Jews from a buffer zone of fifty kilometres deep adjacent to Austria and Prussia, in spite of the fact that "at some frontier customs the merchants who traded were practically all Jews."[301] The measure was immediately corrected by numerous exemptions: first, a two-year period was allowed for the sale of the goods, and then the duration was extended, and material assistance was offered to the expellees for their new settlement; furthermore, they were exempted for five years from all royalties. For several years the transfer was not even initiated, and soon "the government of Nicholas I stopped insisting on the expulsion of the Jews from this border strip of fifty kilometres, which allowed some of them to stay where they lived."[302]

It was on this occasion that Nicolas received a new warning of which he did not measure the extent and the consequences for the whole of Russia: this formidable but very partially enforced measure, intended to expel the Jews from the frontier zone, motivated by a contraband which had assumed an extension dangerous to the State, had aroused in Europe such indignation that it may be asked whether it was not this measure that drastically confused European public opinion with Russia. It may be said that this particular decree of 1843 must date from the very beginning of the era when the Western Jewish world, in the defense of its co-religionists in Russia, began to exert a decisive influence, which, from then on, would never fall again.

One of the manifestations of this new attention was the arrival in Russia in 1846 of Sir Moses Montefiore, the bearer of a letter of recommendation from Queen Victoria instructing him to obtain the "improvement of the fate of the Jewish population" of Russia. He went to several cities of high Jewish density; then, from England, sent a long letter to the emperor recommending the emancipation of the Jews from all limiting legislation, to grant them "equal rights with all other subjects" (with the exception, of course, of the serfs), "in the short term: to abolish all constraints in the exercise of the right to settle and to circulate between the boundaries of the Pale of Settlement", to allow merchants and craftsmen to visit the provinces, "to allow Christians to be employed in the service of the Jews..., to restore the *Kahal*..."[303]

But, on the contrary, Nicolas did not relinquish his determination to bring order to the lives of the Jews of Russia. He resembled Peter the Great in his resolution to structure by decree the whole State and the whole of society according to his plan, and to reduce the complexity of society to

---

[301] *Hessen*, 1.1, p. 203.
[302] LJE, t. 7. p. 321.
[303] *Hessen*, I. 2, pp. 107 108.

simple, easily understood categories, as Peter had formerly "trimmed" all that disturbed the clear configuration of the taxable classes.

This time it was a question of differentiating the Jewish population from the towns—the *bourgeois*. This project began in 1840; when the intention was to go beyond the national and religious singularity of the Jews (the opinions of Levinson, Feiguine, and Gueseanovsky were then examined), they endeavoured to "study the root of their obstinate isolation" in relation to "the absence of any productive work in them", their "harmful practice of small trades, accompanied by all sorts of frauds and tricks." Regarding the "idleness" of many Jews, the government circles blamed it on "inveterate habits"; they considered that "the Jewish mass might have been able to find livelihoods, but traditionally refused to exercise certain types of employment."[304]

Count Kiselyov proposed to the Emperor the following measure: without affecting the Jewish merchants, perfectly well-settled, to worry about the so-called *bourgeois* Jews, more precisely to divide them into two categories: to count in the first those who benefit from goods and a solid sedentary lifestyle, and include in the second those who are devoid of these factors and set a period of five years for them to be made craftsmen in workshops, or farmers. (One regarded as an artisan the one who enrolled forever in a workshop: as a sedentary *bourgeois*, one who had enrolled in a workshop for a certain time.[305])

As for those who did not fulfil these conditions at the end of the period of five years and remained confined to their former state, they would be considered "useless" and subjected to military service and a period of work of a particular type: they would be enrolled in the army (those 20 years old and onwards) in number three times higher than the standard required, not for the usual twenty-five years of military service, but for only ten. And, meanwhile, "they would be used in the army or the navy by instilling in them, above all, different trades and then, with their consent, they would make craftsmen or farmers". In other words, they would be forcibly given vocational education. But the government did not have the funds to do so and was considering using the "casket" tax, as Jewish society could only be interested in this effort to rehabilitate its members through labour.[306]

In 1840, Nicholas I gave his approval to the project. (The phrase "unnecessary Jews" was replaced by "not performing productive work.") All measures to transform the lives of the Jews were reduced to a single decree providing for the following steps: 1) "regularisation of the collection

---

[304] *Ibidem**, pp. 79-80.
[305] JE, t. 13, p. 439.
[306] *Hessen**, t. 2. pp. 81, 82.

of the 'casket' and suppression of the *Kahal*"; 2) creation of general education schools for Jews; 3) institution of "parochial rabbis"; 4) "establishment of the Jews on land belonging to the State" for agricultural purposes; 5) categorisation; 6) prohibition to wear the long garment. Kiselyov thought of introducing social categorisation in a fairly distant future; Nicholas placed it before agriculture, which, for a quarter of a century, had not ceased to be a failure.[307]

However, the categorisation provided for a period of five years for the choice of occupations, and the measure itself was not announced until 1846, meaning it could not turn into a reality until January 1852. (In 1843 the Governor-General of New Russia, Count Vorontsov, rose up against this measure: he wrote that the occupations "of this numerous class of merchants and intermediaries were 'vilified' and that [80%] of the Jewish population was counted as 'useless' elements," which meant that 80% of the Jews were mainly engaged in trade, and Vorontsov hoped that, given the vast economic potential of New Russia, "any form of constraint could be limited", he did not think it necessary to expel the Jews from the villages, but thought that it was enough to intensify their education. He warned that the categorisation would probably arouse indignation in Europe.[308])

Scalded by the way Europe had reacted to the attempt to expel the Jews from the border area, the Russian government drew up a detailed statement on the new measure in 1846: in Poland, Jews had neither citizenship nor the right to own immovable property, and was therefore restricted to petty trading and the sale of alcohol; incorporated in Russia, they saw the limits of their residence extended, they received civil rights, access to the class of merchants in the cities, the right to own real estate, to enter the category of farmers, the right to education, including access to universities and academies.[309]

It must be admitted that the Jews did receive all these rights from the first decades of their presence in the famous "prison of the peoples". Nevertheless, a century later, in a collection written by Jewish authors, one finds the following assessment: "When the annexation to Russia of the Polish provinces with their Jewish population, *promises* were made concerning Rights, and *attempts* to realise them [italics are mine, A. S.; said promises were kept, and the attempts were not without success]. But at the same time, mass expulsions outside villages had begun (indeed, they had been outlined, but were never effective), double taxation was

---

[307] *Ibidem*, pp. 82-83.
[308] *Ibidem*, pp. 100 103.
[309] *Ibidem*, p.103.

implemented [which was not levied in a systematic way, and eventually abandoned] and to the institution of the Pale of Settlement was undertaken"³¹⁰ [we have seen that the borders of this area were originally a geographical heritage]. If one thinks that this way of exposing history is objective, then one will never reach the truth.

Unfortunately, however, the government communiqué of 1846 pointed out that the Jews did not take advantage of many of these measures: "Constantly defying integration with the civil society in which they live, most kept their old way of life, taking advantage of the work of others, which, on all sides, legitimately entails the complaints of the inhabitants." "For the purpose [of raising the standard of living of the Jews], it is important to free them from their dependence on the elders of the community, the heirs of the former leaders of the *Kahal*, to spread education and practical knowledge in the Jewish population, to create Jewish schools of general education, to provide means for their passage to agriculture, to blur the differences of clothing which are unfair to many Jews. As for the government, "it esteems itself entitled to hope that the Jews will abandon all their reprehensible ways of living and turn to a truly productive and useful work." Only those who refuse to do so will be subject to "incentivised measures for parasitic members affecting society and harming it."³¹¹

In his reply to this text, Montefiore condemned the categorisation by insisting that all the misfortune came from the limitations imposed on the free circulation of the Jews and their trade. Nicolas retorted that if the passage of the Jews to productive work was successful, time, "of itself, would gradually mitigate these limitations."³¹² He was counting on the possibility of re-education through work... Being held in check here and there, and elsewhere in his efforts to transform the way of life of the Jews, he had the ambition to break the Jews' tendency to close in on themselves and to solve the problem of their integration with the surrounding population through labour, and the problem of labour by drastically reinforced conscription. The reduction of the length of military service for the Jews (from 25 to ten years) and the intention of providing them with vocational training was scarcely clear; what was perceived concretely was the levying of recruits, now proportionately three times more numerous than among Christians: "Ten recruits per year per thousand male

---

³¹⁰ *Dinour*, in BJWR-1. p. 319.
³¹¹ *Hessen**. t. 2. pp. 103 104.
³¹² *Ibidem*, pp. 107 110.

inhabitants, and for Christians seven recruits per thousand once every two years."[313]

Faced with this increase in recruitment, more people sought to escape. Those who were designated for conscription went into hiding. In retaliation, at the end of 1850, a decree stipulated that all recruits not delivered on time should be compensated by three additional recruits in addition to the defaulter! Now Jewish communities were interested in *capturing* the fugitives or replacing them with innocent people. (In 1853 a decree was issued enabling Jewish communities and private individuals to present as a recruit any person taken without papers.) The Jewish communities were seen to have paid "takers" or "snatchers" who captured their "catch"[314]; they received from the community a receipt attesting that the community had used their services when handing over those who did not respond to the call, or who carried expired passports—even if they were from another province—or teenagers without a family.

But that was not enough to compensate for the missing recruits. In 1852 two new decrees were added: the first provided for each recruit provided in excess of the quota imposed, to relieve the community of 300 rubles of arrears[315]; the second "prohibited the concealment of Jews who evaded military service and demanded severe punishment for those who had fled conscription, imposed fines on the communities that had hidden them, and, instead of the missing recruits, to enlist their relatives or the community leaders responsible for the delivery of the recruits within the prescribed time limits. Seeking by all means to escape recruitment, many Jews fled abroad or went to other provinces."[316]

From then on, the recruitment gave rise to a real bacchanale: the "snatchers" became more and more fierce; on the contrary, men in good health and capable of working scurried off, went into hiding, and the backlogs of the communities grew. The sedentary and productive part uttered protests and demands: if recruitment began to strike to an equal extent the "useful elements" and those which do not exercise productive work, then the vagabonds will always find means of hiding and all the weight of the recruitment would fall on the "useful", which would spread among them disorder and the ruin."[317]

The administrative overflows made the absurdity of the situation clear because of the difficulties that ensued; questions were raised, for example,

---

[313] LJE. t. 4. p. 75.
[314] JE, t. 9. p. 243.
[315] *Hessen*, 1.2. p. 115.
[316] LJE, t. 7, p. 323.
[317] *Hessen*, t. 2, pp. 114-118.

about the different types of activity: are they "useful" or not? This fired up the Saint Petersburg ministries.[318] The Council of State demanded that the social categorisation be delayed so long as the regulations of the workshops were not elaborated. The Emperor, however, did not want to wait. In 1851, the "Provisional Rules for the Categorisation of Jews", and "Special Rules for Jewish Workshops" were published. The Jewish population was deeply concerned, but according to the testimony of the Governor General of the South-West, it no longer believed that this categorisation would enter into force."[319]

And, in fact, "… it did not take place; the Jewish population was not divided into categories." [320] In 1855, Nicholas I died suddenly, and categorisation was abandoned forever.

Throughout the years 1850 1855, the sovereign had, on the whole, displayed a limitless sense of pride and self-confidence, accumulating gross blunders which stupidly led us into the Crimean war against a coalition of States, before suddenly dying while the conflict was raging.

The sudden death of the Emperor saved the Jews from a difficult situation, just as they were to be saved a century later by the death of Stalin.

Thus ended the first six decades of massive presence of Jews in Russia. It must be acknowledged that neither their level nor their lack of clarity prepared the Russian authorities at that time to face such an ingrained, gnarled and complex problem. But to put on these Russian leaders the stamp "persecutors of the Jews" amounts to distorting their intentions and compounding their abilities.

---

[318] *Ibidem*, p. 112.
[319] JE, 1.13, p. 274.
[320] *Hessen*, t. 2, p. 118.

Chapter 4

In the Age of Reforms

At the moment of the ascension of Alexander II to the throne, the Peasant Question in Russia had been overripe for a century and demanded immediate resolution. Then suddenly, the Jewish Question surfaced and demanded a no less urgent solution as well. In Russia, the Jewish Question was not as ancient as the deep-rooted and barbaric institution of serfdom and up to this time it did not seem to loom so large in the country. Yet henceforth, for the rest of 19th century, and right to the very year of 1917 in the State Duma, the Jewish and the Peasant questions would cross over and over again; they would contend with each other and thus become intertwined in their competing destiny.

Alexander II had taken the throne during the difficult impasse of the Crimean War against a united Europe. This situation demanded a difficult decision, whether to hold out or to surrender.

Upon his ascension, "voices were immediately raised in defense of the Jewish population."— After several weeks, His Majesty gave orders "to make the Jews equal with the rest of population in respect to military duty, and to end acceptance of underage recruits." (Soon after, the "skill-category" draft of Jewish philistines was cancelled; this meant that "all classes of the Jewish population were made equal with respect to compulsory military service."[321])

This decision was confirmed in the Coronation Manifesto of 1856: "Jewish recruits of the same age and qualities which are defined for recruits from other population groups are to be admitted while acceptance of underage Jewish recruits was to be abolished."[322] Right then the institution of military cantonists was also completely abolished; Jewish cantonists who were younger than 20 years of age were returned to their parents even if they already had been turned into soldiers. [Cantonists were the sons of

---

[321] *Evreyskaya Entsiklopediya* [The Jewish Encyclopedia] (henceforth—EE [JE]): V 16 T. Sankt-St.Petersburg.: Obshchestvo dlya Nauchnikh Evreyskikh Izdaniy I Izd-vo Brokrauz-Efron [Society for Scientific Jewish Publications and Brokrauz-Efron Publishing House], 1906–1913. T 13, p. 373–374.
[322] *EE** [JE], T 3, p. 163.

Russian conscripts who, from 1721, were educated in special "canton (garrison) schools" for future military service].

The lower ranks who had served out their full term (and their descendents) received the right to live anywhere on the territory of the Russian Empire. (They usually settled where they terminated their service. They could settle permanently and had often become the founders of new Jewish communities.[323]

In a twist of fate and as a historical punishment, Russia and the Romanov Dynasty got Yakov Sverdlov from the descendents of one such cantonist settler.[324])

By the same manifesto the Jewish population "was forgiven all [considerable] back taxes" from previous years. ("Yet already in the course of the next five years new tax liabilities accumulated amounting to 22% of the total expected tax sum.[325])

More broadly, Alexander II expressed his intention to resolve the Jewish Question — and in the most favorable manner. For this, the approach to the question was changed drastically. If during the reign of Nicholas I the government saw its task as first reforming the Jewish inner life, gradually clearing it out through productive work and education with consequent removal of administrative restrictions, then during the reign of Alexander II the policy was the opposite: to begin "with the intention of integrating this population with the native inhabitants of the country" as stated in the Imperial Decree of 1856.[326]

So the government had began quick removal of external constraints and restrictions not looking for possible inner causes of Jewish seclusion and morbidity; it thereby hoped that all the remaining problems would then solve themselves.

To this end, still another Committee for Arranging the Jewish Way of Life was established in 1856. (This was already the seventh committee on Jewish affairs, but by no means the last). Its chairman, the above-mentioned Count Kiselyov, reported to His Majesty that "the goal of

---

[323] Ibid. T 11, p. 698; *Yu Gessen*. Istoriya evreyskogo naroda v Rossii* [History of the Jewish People in Russia] (henceforth— *Yu. Gessen*): V 2 T. L., 1925–1927. T 2, p. 160.
[324] *Kratkaya Evreyskaya Entsiklopedia* [The Short Jewish Encyclopedia] (henceforth *KEE* [SJE]): [V 10 T.] Jerusalem, 1976–2001. T 4, p. 79.
[325] *Yu. Gessen*. T 2, p. 183.
[326] M. Kovalevskiy*. *Ravnopravie evreyev i ego vragi* [Jewish Equal Rights and its Opponents]// *Shchit: Literaturniy sbornik* [Shchit: A Literary Anthology]/Under the Editorship of L. Andreyev, M Gor'kiy, and F. Sologub. 3rd Edition., dop. M.: *Russkoe Obshchestvo dly izucheniya evreyskoy zhizni* [Russian Society for the Study of Jewish Life], 1916, p. 117-118.

integrating Jews with the general population" "is hindered by various temporary restrictions, which, when considered in the context of general laws, contain many contradictions and beget bewilderment." In response, His Majesty ordered "a revision of all existing statutes on Jews to harmonize them with the general strategy directed toward integration of this people with the native inhabitants, to the extent afforded by the moral condition of Jews"; that is, "the fanaticism and economic harmfulness ascribed to them."[327]

No, not for nothing had Herzen struggled with his *Kolokol*, or Belinsky and Granovsky, or Gogol! (For although not having such goals, the latter acted in the same direction as the former three did.) Under the shell of the austere reign of Nicholas I, the demand for decisive reforms and the will for them and the people to implement them were building up, and, astonishingly, new projects were taken by the educated high governmental dignitaries more enthusiastically than by educated public in general. And this immediately impacted the Jewish Question. Time after time, the ministers of Internal Affairs (first Lanskoi and then Valuev) and the Governors General of the Western and Southwestern Krais [administrative divisions of Tsarist Russia] shared their suggestions with His Majesty who was quite interested in them. "Partial improvements in the legal situation of the Jews were enacted by the government on its own initiative, yet under direct supervision by His Majesty."[328] These changes went along with the general liberating reforms which affected Jews as well as the rest of population.

In 1858, Novorossiysk Governor General Stroganov suggested immediate, instant, and complete equalization of the Jews in all rights — but the Committee, now under the chairmanship of Bludov, stopped short, finding itself unprepared for such a measure. In 1859 it pointed out, for comparison, that "while the Western-European Jews began sending their children to public schools at the first invitation of the government, more or less turning themselves to useful occupations, the Russian government has to wrestle with Jewish prejudices and fanaticism"; therefore, "making Jews equal in rights with the native inhabitants cannot happen in any other way than a gradual change, following the spread of true enlightenment among them, changes in their inner life, and turning their activity toward useful occupations."[329]

The Committee also developed arguments against equal rights. It suggested that the question being considered was not so much a Jewish question, as it was a Russian one; that it would be precipitous to grant equal rights to

---

[327] *EE* [JE], T 1, p. 812-813.
[328] Ibid. p. 808.
[329] Ibid. p. 814–815; *Yu Gessen**, T 2, p. 147–148.

Jews before raising the educational and cultural level of Russian population whose dark masses would not be able to defend themselves in the face of the economic pressure of Jewish solidarity; that the Jews hardly aspire toward integration with the rest of the citizens of the country, that they strive toward achieving all civil rights while retaining their isolation and cohesion which Russians do not possess among themselves.

However, these voices did not attain influence. One after another, restrictions had been removed. In 1859 the Prohibition of 1835 was removed: it had forbidden the Jews to take a lease or manage populated landowner's lands. (And thus, the right to rule over the peasants; though that prohibition was "in some cases ... secretly violated." Although after 1861 lands remaining in the property of landowners were not formally "populated.") The new changes were aimed "to make it easier for landowners to turn for help to Jews if necessary" in case of deterioration of in the manorial economy, but also "in order to somewhat widen the restricted field of economic activity of the Jews." Now the Jews could lease these lands and settle on them though they could not buy them.[330]

Meanwhile in the Southwestern Krai "capital that could be turned to the purchase of land was concentrated in the hands of some Jews ... yet the Jews refused to credit landowners against security of the estate because estates could not be purchased by Jews." Soon afterwards Jews were granted the right to buy land from landowners inside the Pale of Settlement.[331]

With development of railroads and steamships, Jewish businesses such as keeping of inns and postal stations had declined. In addition, because of new liberal customs tariffs introduced in1857 and 1868, which lowered customs duties on goods imported into Russia, "profits on contraband trade" had immediately and sharply decreased.[332]

In 1861 the prohibition on Jews to acquire exclusive rights to some sources of revenue from estates was abolished. In the same year the systems of tax farming and 'wine farming' [translator's note: concessions from the state to private entrepreneurs to sell vodka to the populace in particular regions] were abolished. This was a huge blow to a major Jewish enterprise. "Among Jews, 'tax collector' and 'contractor' were synonyms for wealth"; now Orshansky writes, they could just dream about "the time of the Crimean War, when contractors made millions, thanks to the flexible conscience and peculiar view of the Treasury in certain circles"; "thousands of Jews lived and got rich under the beneficial wing of tax

---

[330] *Yu Gessen*, T 2, p. 163.
[331] *Yu Gessen*, T 2, p. 164.
[332] Ibid. p. 161–162.

farming." Now the interests of the state had begun to be enforced and contracts had become much less profitable. And "trading in spirits" had become "far less profitable than ... under ... the tax farming system."[333] However, as the excise was introduced in the wine industry in place of the wine farming system, no special restrictions were laid on Jews and so now they could sell and rent distillation factories on a common basis in the Pale of Settlement provinces.[334] And they had so successfully exercised this right to rent and purchase over next two decades that by the 1880s between 32% and 76% of all distillation factories in the Jewish Pale of Settlement belonged to Jews, and almost all of them fell under category of a 'major enterprise'.[335] By 1872, 89% of distillation factories in the Southwestern Krai were rented by Jews.[336] From 1863 Jews were permitted to run distillation in Western and Eastern Siberia (for "the most remarkable specialists in the distillation industry almost exclusively came from among the Jews"), and from 1865 the Jewish distillers were permitted to reside everywhere.[337]

Regarding the spirits trade in the villages, about one-third of the whole Jewish population of the Pale lived in villages at the start of 1880s, with two or three families in each village,[338] as remnants of the *korchemstvo* [from "tavern" — the state-regulated business of retail spirits sale]. An official government report of 1870 stated that "the drinking business in the Western Krai is almost exclusively concentrated in the hands of Jews, and the abuses encountered in these institutions exceed any bounds of tolerance."[339] Thus it was demanded of Jews to carry on the drinking business only from their own homes. The logic of this demand was explained by G. B. Sliozberg: in the villages of Little Russia [Ukraine], that is, outside of the legal limits of the Polish autonomy, the landowners did not have the right to carry on trade in spirits — and this meant that the Jews could not buy spirits from landowners for resale. Yet at the same time the

---

[333] I. Orshanskiy. *Evrei v Rossii: Ocherki i issledovaniya* [The Jews in Russia: Essays and Research]. Vip. 1 (henceforth— *I. Orshanskiy*). Sankt-St. Petersburg., 1872, p. 10–11.

[334] V.N. Nikitin. *Evrei zemledel'tsi: Istoricheskoe, zakonodatel'noe, administrativnoe i bitovoe polozhenie kolonii co vremeni ikh vozniknoveniya do nashikh dney 1807-1887* [Jewish Farmers: the Historical, Legal, Administrative, and Everyday Condition of the Colonies, from the Time of Their Origin to Our Days. 1807-1887]. (henceforth—*V.N. Nikitin*). Sankt-St. Petersburg, 1887, p. 557.

[335] *EE* [JE], T 5, p. 610-611.

[336] Ibid. T 13, p. 663.

[337] Ibid*, T 5, p. 622.

[338] Yu. Larin. *Evrei i antisemitizm v SSSR* [The Jews and Anti-Semitism in the USSR]. Moscow; Leningrad: GIZ, 1929, p. 49.

[339] *I. Orshanskiy*, p. 193.

Jews might not buy even a small plot of peasant land; therefore, the Jews rented peasant homes and conducted the drinking business from them.

When such trade was also prohibited — the prohibition was often evaded by using a 'front' business: a dummy patent on a spirits business was issued to a Christian to which a Jew supposedly only served as an 'attendant.'[340]

Also, the 'punitive clause' (as it is worded in the *Jewish Encyclopedia*), that is, a punishment accompanying the prohibition against Jews hiring a Christian as a personal servant, was repealed in 1865 as "incompatible with the general spirit of the official policy of tolerance." And so "from the end of the 1860s many Jewish families began to hire Christian servants."[341]

Unfortunately, it is so typical for many scholars studying the history of Jewry in Russia to disregard hard-won victories: if yesterday all strength and attention were focused on the fight for some civil right and today that right is attained — then very quickly afterwards that victory is considered a trifle. There was so much said about the "double tax" on the Jews as though it existed for centuries and not for very few short years, and even then it was never really enforced in practice. The law of 1835, which was at the time greeted by Jews with a sense of relief, was, at the threshold of 20th century dubbed by S. Dubnov as a 'Charter of Arbitrariness.' To the future revolutionary Leo Deutsch, who in the 1860s was a young and still faithful subject, it looked like the administration "did not strictly [enforce] some essential ... restrictions on ... the rights" of Jews, "they turned a blind eye to ... violations"; "in general, the life of Jews in Russia in the sixties was not bad.... Among my Jewish peers I did not see anyone suffering from depression, despondence, or estrangement as a result of oppression" by their Christian mates.[342] But then he suddenly recollects his revolutionary duty and calls everything given to the Jews during the reign of Alexander I as, "in essence, insignificant alleviations" and, without losing a beat, mentions "the crimes of Alexander II"— although, in his opinion, the Tsar shouldn't have been killed.[343] And from the middle of the 20th century it already looks like for the whole of 19th century that various committees and commissions were being created for review of Jewish legal restrictions "and they came to the conclusion that the existing legal restrictions did not achieve their aims and should be ... abolished.... Yet

---

[340] G.B. Sliozberg. *Dela minuvshikh dney: Zapiski russkogo evreya* [Affairs of the Past: the Notes of a Russian Jew] (henceforth— *G.B. Sliozberg*): V 3 T. Paris, 1933–1934. T 1, p. 95.
[341] *EE**, T 11, p. 495.
[342] L. Deych. *Rol' evreyev v russkom revolyutsionnom dvizhenii* [The Role of the Jews in the Russian Revolutionary Movement]. T 1. Second Edition. Moscow,; Leningrad.: GIZ, 1925, p. 14, 21–22.
[343] Ibid. p. 28.

not a single one of the projects worked out by the Committees ... was implemented."[344] It's rid of, forgotten, and no toasts made.

After the first Jewish reforms by Alexander II, the existence of the Pale of Settlement had become the most painful issue. "Once a hope about a possibility of future state reforms had emerged, and first harbingers of expected renewal of public life had barely appeared, the Jewish intelligentsia began contemplating the daring step of raising the question of abolishing the Jewish Pale of Settlement altogether."[345] Yet still fresh in the Jewish memory was the idea of 'selectivity': to impose additional obligations on not-permanently-settled and unproductive Jews. And so in 1856 an idea to petition His Majesty appeared in the social strata of "Jewish merchants, citizens of St. Petersburg, and out-of-towners," who "by their social standing and by the nature of their activity, more closely interacted with the central authorities."[346] The petition asked His Majesty "not to give privileges to the whole Jewish population, but only to certain categories," to the young generation "raised in the spirit and under the supervision of the government," "to the upper merchant class," and "to the good craftsmen, who earn their bread by sweat of their brow"; so that they would be "distinguished by the government with more rights than those who still exhibited nothing special about their good intentions, usefulness, and industriousness.... Our petition is so that the Merciful Monarch, distinguishing wheat from chaff, would be kindly disposed to grant several, however modest privileges to the worthy and cultivated among us, thus encouraging good and praiseworthy actions."[347] (Even in all their excited hopes they could not even imagine how quickly the changes in the position of the Jews would be implemented in practice —already in 1862 some of the authors of this petition would ask "about extending equal rights to all who graduate from secondary educational institutions," for the grammar school graduates "of course, must be considered people with a European education."[348]

And yes, "in principle, the Tsar did not mind violations of the laws concerning the Jewish Pale of Settlement in favor of individual groups of the Jewish population." In 1859 Jewish merchants of the 1st Guild were granted the right of residency in all of Russia (and the 2nd Guild in Kiev

---

[344] A.A. Gal'denveyzer. *Pravovoe polozhenie evreyev v Rossii* // [Sb.] *Kniga o russkom evreystve: Ot 1860-kh godov do Revolyutsii 1917g* [The Legal Position of the Jews in Russia//[Anthology] The Book of Russian Jewry: from the 1860s to the Revolution of 1917]. (henceforth—KRE-1). New York: *Soyuz Russkikh Evreyev* [Union of Russian Jews], 1960, p. 119.
[345] *Yu Gessen*. T 2, p. 143.
[346] *EE* [JE], T 1, p. 813.
[347] *Yu. Gessen**, T 2, p. 144-145; *EE* [JE] T 1, p. 813.
[348] *Yu Gessen*, T 2, p. 158.

from 1861; and also for all three guilds in Nikolayev, Sevastopol, and Yalta)[349] with the right of arranging manufacturing businesses, contracts, and acquiring real estate. Earlier, doctors and holders of masters degrees in science had already enjoyed the right of universal residency (including the right to occupy posts in government service; here we should note a professor of medicine G.A. Zakharyin, who in the future would pronounce the fatal judgment about the illness of Alexander III). From 1861 this right was granted to "candidates of universities," that is, simply to university graduates,[350] and also "to persons of free professions."[351]

The Pale of Settlement restrictions were now lifted even from the "persons, desiring to obtain higher education ... namely to persons, entering medical academies, universities, and technical institutes."[352] Then, as a result of petitions from individual ministers, governors, and influential Jewish merchants (e.g., Evzel Ginzburg), from 1865 the whole territory of Russia including St. Petersburg was opened to Jewish artisans, though only for the period of actual professional activity. (The notion of artisans was then widened to include all kinds of technicians such as typesetters and typographic workers.)[353]

Here it is worth keeping in mind that merchants relocated with their clerks, office workers, various assistants, and Jewish service personnel, craftsmen, and also with apprentices and pupils. Taken altogether, this already made up a notable stream. Thus, a Jew with a right of residency outside of the Pale was free to move from the Pale, and not only with his family.

Yet new relaxations were outpaced by new petitions. In 1861, immediately after granting privileges for the "candidates of universities," the Governor General of the Southwestern Krai had asked to allow exit from the Pale to those who completed state professional schools for the Jews, that is, incomplete high school-level establishments. He had vividly described the condition of such graduates: "Young people graduating from such schools find themselves completely cut off from Jewish society.... If they do not find occupations according to their qualifications within their own circles, they get accustomed to idleness and thus, by being unworthy representatives of their profession, they often discredit the prestige of education in the eyes of people they live among."[354]

---

[349] *Yu Gessen*, T 2, p. 144, 154–155.
[350] *EE* [JE], T 1, p. 817.
[351] *KEE* [SJE], T 4, p. 255.
[352] Sm.: *M. Kovalevskiy* // Shchit, p. 118.
[353] *EE* [JE], T 1, p. 818; T 11, p. 458-459; T 14, p. 841.
[354] *Yu Gessen*, T 2, p. 150.

In that same year, the Ministers of Internal Affairs and Education declared in unison "that a paramount cause of the disastrous condition of Jews is hidden in the abnormal share of Jews occupied in commerce and industry versus the rest engaged in agriculture"; and because of this "the peasant is unavoidably preyed upon by Jews as if he is obligated to surrender a part of his income to their maintenance." Yet the internal competition between the Jews creates a "nearly impossible situation of providing for themselves by legal means." And therefore, it is necessary to "grant the right of universal residence to merchants" of the 2nd and 3rd Guilds, and also to graduates of high or equivalent schools.[355]

In 1862 the Novorossiysk Governor General again called for "complete abolition of the Jewish Pale of Settlement" by asking "to grant the right of universal residency to the *entire* [Jewish] people."[356]

Targeted permissions for universal residency of certain Jewish groups were being issued at a slower but constant rate. From 1865 acceptance of Jews as military doctors was permitted, and right after that (1866–1867), Jewish doctors were allowed to work in the ministries of Education and Interior.[357] From 1879 they were permitted to serve as pharmacists and veterinarians; permission was also granted "to those preparing for the corresponding type of activity,"[358] and also to midwives and feldshers, and "those desiring to study medical assistant arts."[359]

Finally, a decree by the Minister of Internal Affairs Makov was issued allowing residence outside the Pale to all those Jews who had already illegally settled there.[360]

Here it is appropriate to add that in the 1860s "Jewish lawyers ... in the absence of the official Bar College during that period were able to get jobs in government service without any difficulties."[361]

Relaxations had also affected the Jews living in border regions. In 1856, when, according to the Treaty of Paris, the Russian state boundary retreated close to Kishinev and Akkerman, the Jews were not forced out of this newly-formed frontier zone. And in 1858 "the decrees of Nicholas I, which directed Jews to abandon the fifty versts [an obsolete Russian measure, a

---

[355] Ibid*, p. 148.
[356] Ibid, p. 150.
[357] Ibid. p. 169.
[358] *Yu Gessen*, T 2, p. 208.
[359] *EE* [JE], T 15, p. 209; T 1, p. 824.
[360] Perezhitoe: Sbornik, posvyashchenniy obshchestvennoy i kul'turnoy istorii evreyev v Rossii [Past Experiences: An Anthology Dedicated to the Social and Cultural History of the Jews in Russia]. T 2, Sankt-St. Petersburg, 1910, p. 102.
[361] *G.B. Sliozberg*, T 1, p. 137.

verst is slightly more than a kilometer] boundary zone, were conclusively repealed."[362] And from 1868 movement of Jews between the western provinces of Russia and Polish Kingdom was allowed (where previously it was formally prohibited).[363]

Alongside official relaxations to the legal restrictions, there were also exceptions and loopholes in regulations. For example, in the capital city of St. Petersburg "despite ... prohibitions, the Jews all the same settled in for extended times"; and "with the ascension of Alexander II ... the number of Jews in St. Petersburg began to grow quickly. Jewish capitalists emerged who began dedicating significant attention to the organization of the Jewish community" there; "Baron Goratsy Ginzburg, for example... L. Rozental, A Varshavsky, and others."[364] Toward the end of Alexander II's reign, E. A. Peretz (the son of the tax farmer Abram Peretz) became the Russian Secretary of State. In the 1860s "St. Petersburg started to attract quite a few members of the commercial, industrial and intellectual [circles] of Jewry."[365]

According to the data of the Commission for Arranging the Jewish Way of Life, in 1880-81, 6,290 Jews were officially registered in St. Petersburg,[366] while according to other official figures, 8,993; and according to a local census from 1881, there were 16,826 Jews in St. Petersburg, i.e., around 2% of the total city population.[367]

In Moscow in 1856 the obligation of arriving Jewish merchants to exclusively reside in the Glebovsky Quarter was repealed; "the Jews were allowed to stay in any part of the city. During the reign of Alexander II ... the Jewish population of Moscow grew quickly"; by 1880 it was around 16,000."[368]

It was a similar situation in Kiev. After 1861, "a quick growth of the Jewish population of Kiev had began" (from 1,500 in 1862, to 81,000 by 1913). From the 1880s there was an influx of Jews to Kiev. "Despite frequent police roundups, which Kiev was famous for, the numbers of Jews there

---

[362] *KEE* [SJE], T 7, p. 327.
[363] *EE* [JE], T 1, p. 819.
[364] Also, T 13, p. 943–944.
[365] I.M. Trotskiy. *Samodeyatel'nost i samopomoshch' evreyev v Rossii* [The Individual Initiative and Self-Help of the Jews in Russia] (OPE, ORT, EKO, OZE, EKOPO) // KRE-1, p. 471.
[366] *Yu. Gessen*. T 2, p. 210.
[367] *EE* [JE], T 13, p. 947; *KEE* [SJE], T 4, p. 770.
[368] *KEE* [SJE], T 5, p. 473.

considerably exceeded the official figures.... By the end of the 19th century, the Jews accounted for 44% of Kiev merchants."[369]

Yu. I. Hessen calls "the granting of the right of universal residency (1865) to artisans" most important. Yet Jews apparently did not hurry to move out of the Pale. Well, if it was so overcrowded in there, so constraining, and so deprived with respect to markets and earnings, why then did they make "almost no use of the right to leave the Pale of Settlement?" By 1881, in thirty-one of the interior provinces, Jewish artisans numbered 28,000 altogether (and Jews in general numbered 34,000). Hessen explains this paradox in the following way: prosperous artisans did not need to seek new places while the destitute did not have the means for the move, and the middle group, "which somehow managed from day to day without enduring any particular poverty," feared that after their departure the elders of their community would refuse to extend an annual passport to them for tax considerations, or even "demand that the outgoing parties return home."[370]

But one can strongly doubt all this statistics. We have just read that in St. Petersburg alone there were at least twice as many Jews than according to official data. Could the slow Russian state apparatus really account for the mercury-quick Jewish population within a definite time and in all places?

And the growth of Jewish population of Russia was rapid and confident. In 1864 it amounted to 1,500,000 without counting Jews in Poland.[371] And together with Poland in 1850 it was 2,350,000; and in 1860 it was already 3,980,000. From the initial population of around 1,000,000 at the time of the first partitions of Poland, to 5,175,000 by the census of 1897 — that is, after a century, it grew more than *five* times. (At the start of the 19th century Russian Jewry amounted to 30% of the world's Jewish population, while in 1880 it was already 51%).[372]

This was a major historical event. At the time, its significance was grasped neither by Russian society, nor by Russian administration. This fast numerical growth alone, without all other peculiarities of the Jewish Question, had already put a huge state problem for Russia. And here it is necessary, as always in any question, to try to understand both points of view.

With such an enormous growth of Russian Jewry, two national needs were clashing ever more strongly. On one hand was the need of Jews (and a

---

[369] Also, T 4, p. 255.
[370] *Yu Gessen*. T 2, p. 159–160, 210.
[371] Also, p. 159.
[372] *B.Ts. Dinur. Religiozno-natsional'niy oblik russkogo evreystva* [The Religious-National Look of Russian Jewry] // KRE-1, p. 311-312.

distinct feature of their dynamic 3,000-year existence) to spread and settle as wide as possible among non-Jews, so that a greater number of Jews would be able to engage in manufacturing, commerce, and serve as intermediaries (and to get involved into the culture of the surrounding population). On the other was the need of Russians, as the government understood it, to have control over their economic (and then cultural) life, and develop it themselves at their own pace.

Let's not forget that simultaneously with all these relief measures for the Jews, the universal liberating reforms of Alexander II were implemented one after another, and so benefiting Jews as well as all other peoples of Russia. For example, in 1863 the capitation [i.e., poll or head] tax from the urban population was repealed, which meant the tax relief for the main part of Jewish masses; only land taxes remained after that, which were paid from the collected kosher tax.[373]

Yet precisely the most important of these Alexandrian reforms, the most historically significant turning point in the Russian history — the liberation of peasants and the abolition of the Serfdom in 1861 — turned out to be highly unprofitable for Russian Jews, and indeed ruinous for many. "The general social and economic changes resulting from the abolition of peasant servitude ... had significantly worsened the material situation of broad Jewish masses during that transitional period."[374] The *social* change was such that the multi-million disenfranchised and immobile peasant class ceased to exist, reducing the relative advantage of Jewish personal freedom. And the *economic* change was such that "the peasant, liberated from the servitude, ... was less in the need of services by the Jew"; that is, the peasant was now at liberty from the strict prohibition against trading his products and purchasing goods himself — that is, through anyone other than a pre-assigned middleman (in the western provinces, almost always a Jew). And now, as the landowners were deprived of free serf labor, in order not to be ruined, "they were compelled to get personally engaged in the economy of their estates — an occupation where earlier Jews played a conspicuous role as renters and middlemen in all kinds of commercial and manufacturing deals."[375]

It's noteworthy that the land credit introduced in those years was displacing the Jew "as the financial manager of the manorial economy."[376] The

---

[373] *EE* [JE], T 12, p. 640.
[374] *Yu Gessen*, T 2, p. 161.
[375] Also.
[376] Also.

development of consumer and credit associations led to "the liberation of people from the tyranny of usury."[377]

An intelligent contemporary conveys to us the Jewish mood of the time. Although access to government service and free professions was open to the Jews and although "the industrial rights of the Jews were broadened" and there were "more opportunities for education" and "on every ... corner" the "rapprochement between the Jewish and Christian populations was visible" and although the remaining "restrictions ... were far from being strictly enforced" and "the officials now treated the Jewish population with far more respect than before," yet the situation of Jews in Russia "at the present time ... is very dismal." "Not without reason," Jews "express regret ... for good old times."

Everywhere in the Pale of Settlement one could hear "the Jewish lamentations about the past." For under serfdom an "extraordinary development of mediation" took place; the lazy landowner could not take a step without the "Jewish trader or agent," and the browbeaten peasant also could not manage without him; he could only sell the harvest through him, and borrowed from him also. Before, the Jewish business class "derived enormous benefit from the helplessness, wastefulness, and impracticality of landowners," but now the landowner had to do everything himself. Also, the peasant became "less pliant and timid"; now he often establishes contacts with wholesale traders himself and he drinks less; and this "naturally has a harmful effect on the trade in spirits, which an enormous number of Jews lives on." The author concludes with the wish that the Jews, as happened in Europe, "would side with the productive classes and would not become redundant in the national economy."[378]

Now Jews had begun renting and purchasing land. The Novorossiysk Governor General (1869) requested in a staff report to forbid Jews in his region to buy land as was already prohibited in nine western provinces. Then in 1872 there was a memorandum by the Governor General of the Southwestern Krai stating that "Jews rent land not for agricultural occupations but only for industrial aims; they hand over the rented land to peasants, not for money but for a certain amount of work, which exceeds the value of the usual rent on that land, and thereby they "establish a sort of their own form of servitude." And though "they undoubtedly reinvigorate the countryside with their capital and commerce," the Governor General "considered concentration of manufacture and agriculture in the same hands un-conducive, since only under free competition can peasant farms and businesses avoid the "burdensome

---

[377] Yu. Orshanskiy, *p. 12.*
[378] *I. Orshanskiy*, p. 1-15.

subordination of their work and land to Jewish capital, which is tantamount to their inevitable and impending material and moral perdition." However, thinking to limit the renting of land to Jews in his Krai, he proposed to "give the Jews an opportunity to settle in all of the Greater Russian provinces."[379]

The memorandum was put forward to the just-created Commission for Arranging the Jewish Way of Life (the eighth of the 'Jewish Commissions', according to count), which was then highly sympathetic to the situation of the Jews. It received a negative review which was later confirmed by the government: to forbid the Jewish rent of land would be "a complete violation of rights" of ... landowners. Moreover, the interests of the major Jewish renter "merge completely with those of other landowners.... Well, it is true, that the Jewish proletarians group around the major [Jewish] renters and live off the work and means of the rural population. But the same also happens in the estates managed by the landowners themselves who to this time cannot manage without the help of the Jews."[380]

However, in the areas inhabited by the Don Cossacks, the energetic economic advancement of the Jews was restricted by the prohibition of 1880 to own or rent the real estate. The provincial government found that "in view of the exclusive situation of the Don Province, the Cossack population which is obligated to military service to a man, [this] is the only reliable way to save the Cossack economy from ruin, to secure the nascent manufacturing and commerce in the area." For "a too hasty exploitation of a region's wealth and quick development of industry ... are usually accompanied by an extremely uneven distribution of capital, and the swift enrichment of some and the impoverishment of others. Meanwhile, the Cossacks must prosper, since they carry out their military service on their own horses and with their own equipment."[381] And thus they had prevented a possible Cossack explosion.

So what happened with the conscription of Jews into military service after all those Alexandrian relief measures of 1856? For the 1860s, this was the picture: "When Jews manage to find out about the impending Imperial Manifest about recruit enrollment before it is officially published ... all members of Jewish families fit for military service flee from their homes in all directions...." Because of the peculiarities of their faith and "lack of comradeship and the perpetual isolation of the Jewish soldier ... the military service for the Jews was the most threatening, the most ruinous,

---

[379] *Yu. Gessen*, T 2, p. 224-225.
[380] *EE* [JE], T 3, p. 83-84.
[381] *EE** [JE], T 7, p. 301-302.

and the most burdensome of duties."³⁸² Although from 1860 the Jewish service in the Guards was permitted, and from 1861promotions to petty officer ranks and service as clerks,³⁸³ there was still no access to officer ranks.

I. G. Orshansky, a witness to the 1860s, certifies: "It is true, there is much data supporting the opinion that in the recent years the Jews in fact had not fulfilled their conscription obligations number-wise. They purchase old recruit discharges and present them to the authorities"; peasants sometimes keep them without knowing their value as far back as from 1812; so now Jewish resourcefulness puts them to use. Or, they "hire volunteers" in place of themselves and "pay a certain sum to the treasury." "Also they try to divide their families into smaller units," and by this each family claims the privilege of "the only son," (the only son was exempt from the military service). Yet, he notes "all the tricks for avoiding recruitment ... are similarly encountered among the 'pure-blooded' Russians" and provides comparative figures for Ekaterinoslav Guberniya. I. G. Orshansky had even expressed surprise that Russian peasants prefer "to return to the favorite occupation of the Russian people, farming," instead of wanting to remain in the highly-paid military service.³⁸⁴

In 1874 a unified regulation about universal military service had replaced the old recruit conscription obligation giving the Jews a "significant relief."

"The text of the regulation did not contain any articles that discriminated against Jews."³⁸⁵ However, now Jews were not permitted to remain in residence in the interior provinces after completion of military service. Also, special regulations aimed "to specify the figure of male Jewish population" were introduced, for to that day it largely remained undetermined and unaccounted."

The governors received "information about abuses of law by Jews wishing to evade military service"³⁸⁶. In 1876 the first "measures for ensuring the proper fulfillment of military duty by Jews"³⁸⁷ were adopted. The *Jewish Encyclopedia* saw "a heavy net of repressive measures" in them. "Regulations were issued about the registration of Jews at conscription districts and about the replacement of Jews not fit for service by Jews who were fit"; and about verification of the validity of exemptions for family

---

³⁸² *G.B. Sliozberg*, T 2, p. 155-156.
³⁸³ *EE* [JE], T 3, p. 164.
³⁸⁴ *I. Orshanskiy*, p. 65-68.
³⁸⁵ *KEE* [SJE], T 7, p. 332.
³⁸⁶ *EE* [JE], T 1, p. 824.
³⁸⁷ Also*, T 3, p. 164.

conditions: for violation of these regulations "conscription ... of only sons was permitted."[388]

A contemporary and then influential St. Petersburg newspaper, *Golos* [*The Voice*] cites quite amazing figures from the official governmental "Report on the Results of Conscription in 1880.... For all [of the Russian Empire] the shortfall of recruits was 3,309; out of this, the shortfall of Jews was 3,054, which amounts to 92%."[389]

Shmakov, a prominent attorney, not well-disposed toward Jews, cites such statistics from the reference, *Pravitelstvenniy Vestnik* [The Government Bulletin]: for the period 1876–1883: "out of 282,466 *Jews* subject to conscription, 89,105 — that is, 31.6% — did not show up." (The general shortfall for the whole Empire was 0.19%.) The Administration could not help but notice this, and a number of "steps toward the elimination of such abuse" were introduced. This had an effect, but only short-term. In 1889 46,190 Jews were subjected to call-up, and 4,255 did not appear, that is 9.2%. But in 1891 "from a general number of 51,248 Jews recorded on the draft list, 7,658, or 14.94%, failed to report; at that time the percentage of Christians not reporting was barely 2.67%. In 1892, 16.38% of Jews failed to report as compared with 3.18% of Christians. In 1894 6,289 Jews did not report for the draft, that is, 13.6%. Compare this to the Russian average of 2.6%.[390]

However, the same document on the 1894 draft states that "in total, 873,143 Christians, 45,801 Jews, 27,424 Mohammedans, and 1,311 Pagans" were to be drafted. These are striking figures — in Russia, there were 8.7% Muslims (according to the 1870 count) but their share in the draft was only 2.9%! The Jews were in an unfavorable position not only in comparison with the Mohammedans but with the general population too: their share of the draft was assigned 4.8% though they constituted only 3.2% of Russian population (in 1870). (The Christian share in the draft was 92% (87% of Russian population).[391]

From everything said here one should not conclude that at the time of the Russo-Turkish War of 1877–1878, Jewish soldiers did not display courage and resourcefulness during combat. In the journal *Russkiy Evrei* [*The Russian Jew*] we can find convincing examples of both virtues.[392] Yet during that war much irritation against Jews arose in the army, mainly

---

[388] Also, T 1, p. 824; *KEE* [SJE], T 7, p. 332.
[389] *Golos* [The Voice], 1881, No46, 15 (27) February, p. 1.
[390] A. Shmakov. *"Evreyskie" rechi* ["Jewish" Questions]. Moscow, 1897, p. 101–103.
[391] *Entsiklopedicheskiy slovar'* [Encyclopedic Dictionary]: V 82 T. Sankt-St. Petersburg.: Brokgauz i Efron, 1890-1904. T 54, p. 86.
[392] *EE* [JE], T 3, p. 164-167.

because of dishonest contractor-quartermasters — and "such were almost exclusively Jews, starting with the main contractors of the Horovits, Greger, and Kagan Company." [393] The quartermasters supplied (undoubtedly under protection of higher circles) overpriced poor-quality equipment including the famous "cardboard soles", due to which the feet of Russian soldiers fighting in the Shipka Pass were frostbitten.

In the Age of Alexander II, the half-century-old official drive to accustom the Jews to agriculture was ending in failure.

After the repeal of disproportionate Jewish recruitment, farming had "immediately lost all its appeal" for Jews, or, in words of one government official, a "false interpretation of the Manifest by them" had occurred, "according to which they now considered themselves free of the obligation to engage in farming," and that they could now migrate freely. "The petitions from the Jews about resettling with the intent to work in agriculture had ended almost completely."[394]

Conditions in the existing colonies remained the same if not worse: "fields… were plowed and sowed pathetically, just for a laugh, or for appearance's sake only." For instance, in 1859 "the grain yield in several colonies was even smaller than the amount sown." In the new 'paradigmatic' colonies, not only barns were lacking, there was even no overhangs or pens for livestock. The Jewish colonists leased most of their land to others, to local peasants or German colonists. Many asked permission to hire Christians as workers, otherwise threatening to cut back on sowing even further — and they were granted such a right, regardless of the size of the actual crop.[395]

Of course, there were affluent Jewish farmers among the colonists. Arrival of German colonists was very helpful too as their experience could now be adopted by Jews. And the young generation born there was already more accepting toward agriculture and German experience; they were more "convinced in the advantageousness of farming in comparison to their previous life in the congestion and exasperating competition of shtetls and towns."[396]

Yet the incomparably larger majority was trying to get away from agriculture. Gradually, inspectors' reports became invariably monotonic: "What strikes most is the general Jewish dislike for farm work and their regrets about their former artisan occupations, trade, and business"; they displayed "tireless zeal in any business opportunity," for example, "at the

---

[393] *G.B. Sliozberg*, T 1, p. 116.
[394] *V.N. Nikitin**, p. 448, 483, 529.
[395] Also*, p 473, 490, 501, 506–507, 530–531, 537–538, 547–548, 667.
[396] Also, p. 474–475, 502, 547.

very high point of field work ... they could leave the fields if they discovered that they could profitably buy or sell a horse, an ox, or something else, in the vicinity." [They had] a predilection for penny-wise trade," demanding, according to their "conviction, less work and giving more means for living." "Making money was easier for Jews in nearby German, Russian, or Greek villages, where the Jewish colonist would engage in tavern-keeping and small trade." Yet more damaging for the arable land were long absences of the workers who left the area for distant places, leaving only one or two family members at home in the colonies, while the rest went to earn money in brokerages. In the 1860s (a half-century after the founding of colonies) such departure was permitted for the entire families or many family members simultaneously; in the colonies quite a few people were listed who had never lived there. After leaving the colonies, they often evaded registering with their trade guild in the new place, and "many stayed there for several consecutive years, with family, unregistered to any guild, and thus not subject to any kind of tax or obligation." And in the colonies, the houses built for them stood empty, and fell into disrepair. In 1861, Jews were permitted to maintain drinking houses in the colonies.[397]

Finally, the situation regarding Jewish agriculture had dawned on the St. Petersburg authorities in all its stark and dismal reality. Back taxes (forgiven on numerous occasions, such as an imperial marriage) grew, and each amnesty had encouraged Jews not to pay taxes or repay loans from now on. (In 1857, when the ten years granted to collect past due taxes had expired, five additional years were added. But even in 1863 the debt was still not collected.) So what was all that resettling, privileges and loans for? On the one hand, the whole 60-year epic project had temporarily provided Jews with means "of avoiding their duties before the state" while at the same time failing to instill love for agriculture among the colonists." "The ends were not worthy of the means." On the other hand, "simply a permission to live outside of the Pale, even without any privileges, attracted a huge number of Jewish farmers" who stopped at nothing to get there.[398]

If in 1858 there were officially 64,000 Jewish colonists, that is, eight to ten thousand families, then by 1880 the Ministry had found only 14,000, that is, less than two thousand families.[399] For example, in the whole Southwestern Krai in 1872 the commission responsible for verifying

---

[397] *V.N. Nikitin**, p. 502-505, 519, 542, 558, 632, 656, 667.
[398] Also*, p. 473, 510, 514, 529–533, 550, 572.
[399] Also, p. 447, 647.

whether or not the land is in use or lay unattended had found fewer than 800 families of Jewish colonists.[400]

Russian authorities had clearly seen now that the entire affair of turning Jews into farmers had failed. They no longer believed that "their cherished hope for the prosperity of colonies could be realized." It was particularly difficult for the Minister Kiselyov to part with this dream, but he retired in 1856. Official documents admitted failure, one after another: "resettlement of the Jews for agricultural occupation 'has not been accompanied by favorable results'."

Meanwhile "enormous areas of rich productive black topsoil remain in the hands of the Jews unexploited." After all, the best soil was selected and reserved for Jewish colonization. That portion, which was temporarily rented to those willing, gave a large income (Jewish colonies lived off it) as the population in the South grew and everyone asked for land. And now even the worst land from the reserve, beyond that allotted for Jewish colonization, had also quickly risen in value.[401] The Novorossiysk Krai had already absorbed many active settlers and "no longer needed any state-promoted colonization."[402]

So the Jewish colonization had become irrelevant for state purposes. And in 1866 Alexander II had ordered and end to the enforcement of several laws aimed at turning Jews into farmers. Now the task was to equalize Jewish farmers with the rest of the farmers of the Empire. Everywhere, Jewish colonies turned out to be incapable of independent existence in the new free situation. So now it was necessary to provide legal means for Jews to abandon agriculture, even individually and not in whole families (1868), so they could become artisans and merchants. They had been permitted to redeem their parcels of land; and so they redeemed and resold their land at a profit.[403]

However, in the dispute over various projects in the Ministry of State Property, the question about the reform of Jewish colonies dragged out and even stopped altogether by 1880. In the meantime with a new recruit statute of 1874, Jews were stripped of their recruiting privileges, and with that any vestiges of their interest in farming were conclusively lost. By 1881 "in the colonies 'there was a preponderance of farmsteads with only one apartment house, around which there were no signs of settlement; that is, no fence, no

---

[400] *EE* [JE], T 7, p. 756.
[401] *V.N. Nikitin**, p. 478–479, 524, 529–533, 550–551.
[402] *EE* [JE], T 7, p. 756.
[403] *V.N. Nikitin*, p. 534, 540, 555, 571, 611–616, 659.

housing for livestock, no farm buildings, no beds for vegetables, nor even a single tree or shrub; there were very few exceptions.'"[404]

The state councilor Ivashintsev, an official with 40 years experience in agriculture, was sent in 1880 to investigate the situation with the colonies. He had reported that in all of Russia "no other peasant community enjoyed such generous benefits as had been given [to Jews]" and "these benefits were not a secret from other peasants, and could not help but arouse hostile feelings in them." Peasants adjacent to the Jewish colonies "'were indignant ... because due to a shortage of land they had to rent the land from Jews for an expensive price, the land which was given cheaply to the Jews by the state in amounts in fact exceeding the actual Jewish needs.' It was namely this circumstance which in part explained ... 'the hostility of peasants toward Jewish farmers, which manifested itself in the destruction of several Jewish settlements'" (in 1881-82).[405]

In those years, there were commissions allotting land to peasants from the excess land of the Jewish settlements. Unused or neglected sectors were taken back by the government. "In Volynsk, Podolsk, and Kiev guberniyas, out of 39,000 desyatins [one desyatin = 2.7 acres] only 4,082 remained [under Jewish cultivation]."[406] Yet several quite extensive Jewish farming settlements remained: Yakshitsa in the Minsk Guberniya, not known for its rich land, had 740 desyatins for 46 [Jewish] families;[407] that is, an average of 16 desyatins per family, something you will rarely find among peasants in Central Russia; in 1848 in Annengof of Mogilyov Guberniya, also not vast in land, twenty Jewish families received 20 desyatins of state land each, but by 1872 it was discovered that there were only ten families remaining, and a large part of the land was not cultivated and was choked with weeds.[408] In Vishenki of Mogilyov Guberniya, they had 16 desyatins per family;[409] and in Ordynovshchina of Grodno Guberniya 12 desyatins per [Jewish] family. In the more spacious southern guberniyas in the original settlements there remained: 17 desyatins per [Jewish] family in Bolshoi Nagartav; 16 desyatins per [Jewish] family in Seidemenukh; and 17 desyatins per family in Novo-Berislav. In the settlement of Roskoshnaya in Ekaterinoslav Guberniya they had 15 desyatins per family, but if total colony land is considered, then 42 desyatins per family.[410] In Veselaya (by 1897) there were 28 desyatins per family. In Sagaidak, there

---

[404] *V.N. Nikitin*, p. 635, 660–666.
[405] Also*, p. 658–661.
[406] *EE* [JE], T 7, p. 756.
[407] Also, T 16, p. 399.
[408] Also, T 2, p. 596.
[409] Also, T 5, p. 650.
[410] Also, T 13, p. 606.

were 9 desyatins, which was considered a small allotment.[411] And in Kiev Province's Elyuvka, there were 6 Jewish families with 400 desyatins among them, or 67 desyatins per family! And land was rented to the Germans."[412]

Yet from a Soviet author of the 1920s we read a categorical statement that "Tsarism had almost completely forbidden the Jews to engage in agriculture."[413]

On the pages which summarize his painstaking work, the researcher of Jewish agriculture V. N. Nikitin concludes: "The reproaches against the Jews for having poor diligence in farming, for leaving without official permission for the cities to engage in commercial and artisan occupations, are entirely justified... We by no means deny the Jewish responsibility for such a small number of them actually working in agriculture after the last 80 years." Yet he puts forward several excuses for them: "[The authorities] had no faith in Jews; the rules of the colonization were changed repeatedly"; sometimes "officials who knew nothing about agriculture or who were completely indifferent to Jews were sent to regulate their lives.... Jews who used to be independent city dwellers were transformed into villagers without any preparation for life in the country."[414]

At around the same time, in 1884, N. S. Leskov, in a memorandum intended for yet another governmental commission on Jewish affairs headed by Palen, had suggested that the Jewish "lack of habituation to agricultural living had developed over generations" and that it is "so strong, that it is equal to the loss of ability in farming," and that the Jew would not become a plowman again unless the habit is revived gradually.[415]

(Lev Tolstoy had allegedly pondered: who are those "confining the entire nation to the squeeze of city life, and not giving it a chance to settle on the land and begin to do the only natural man's occupation, farming. After all, it's the same as not to give the people air to breathe. ... What's wrong with Jews settling in villages and starting to live a pure working life, which, probably, this ancient, intelligent, and wonderful people has already

---

[411] Also, T 5, p. 518; T 13, p. 808.
[412] Also, T 16, p. 251.
[413] *Yu Larin. Evrei i antisemitizm v SSSR* [The Jews and Antisemitism in the USSR], p. 36.
[414] *V.N. Nikitin*, p. xii-xiii.
[415] *N.S. Leskov. Evrei v Rossii: Neskol'ko zamechaniy po evreyskomu voprosu* [The Jews in Russia: Several Observations on the Jewish Question]. Pg., 1919 [reprint s izd. 1884], p. 61, 63.

yearned for? ..."⁴¹⁶ — On what planet was he living? What did he know about the 80 years of practical experience with [Jewish] agricultural colonization?)

And yet the experience of the development of Palestine where the Jewish settlers felt themselves at home had showed their excellent ability to work the land; moreover, they did it in conditions much more unfavorable than in Novorossiya. Still, all the attempts to persuade or compel the Jews toward arable farming in Russia (and afterwards in the USSR) had failed (and from that came the degrading legend that the Jews in general are incapable of farming).

And thus, after 80 years of effort by the Russian government it turned out that all that agricultural colonization was a grandiose but empty affair; all the effort, all the massive expenditures, the delay of the development of Novorossiya — all were for nothing. The resulting experience shows that it shouldn't have been undertaken at all.

Generally examining Jewish commercial and industrial entrepreneurship, I. G. Orshansky justly wrote at the start of the 1870s that the question about Jewish business activity is "the essence of the Jewish Question," on which "fate of Jewish people in any country depends." "[An entrepreneur] from the quick, mercantile, resourceful Jewish tribe" turns over a ruble five times "while a Russian turns it two times." There is stagnation, drowsiness, and monopoly among the Russian merchants. (For example, after the expulsion of the Jews from Kiev, life there had become more expensive). The strong side of Jewish participation in commercial life lies in the acceleration of capital turnover, even of the most insignificant working capital. Debunking the opinion, that so-called Jewish corporate spirit gives them a crucial advantage in any competition, that "Jewish [merchants] always support each other, having their bankers, contractors, and carriers," Orshansky attributed the Jewish corporate spirit only to social and religious matters, and not to commerce, where, he claimed, Jews fiercely compete against each other (which is in contradiction with the Hazaka prescribing separation of spheres of activity, which, according to him, "had gradually disappeared following the change in legal standing of Jews"⁴¹⁷). He had also contested the opinion that any Jewish trade does not enrich the country, that "it exclusively consists of exploitation of the productive and working classes," and that "the profit of the Jews is a pure loss for the nation." He disagreed, suggesting that Jews constantly look for and find

---

⁴¹⁶ *L.N. Tolstoy o evreyakh/Predisl. O.Ya. Pergamenta* [L.N. Tolstoy on the Jews/Foreword O.Ya. Pergamenta], Sankt-PeterburgSt. Petersburg.: *Vremya* [Time], 1908, p. 15.
⁴¹⁷ *EE* [JE], T 15, p. 492.

new sales markets and thereby "open new sources of earnings for the poor Christian population as well."[418]

Jewish commercial and industrial entrepreneurship in Russia had quickly recovered from the two noticeable blows of 1861, the abolition of serfdom and the abolition of wine farming. "The financial role of Jews had become particularly significant by the 1860s, when previous activities amassed capital in their hands, while liberation of peasants and the associated impoverishment of landowners created a huge demand for money on the part of landowners statewide. Jewish capitalists played a prominent role in organization of land banks."[419] The whole economic life of the country quickly changed in many directions and the invariable Jewish determination, inventiveness, and capital were keeping pace with the changes and were even ahead of them. Jewish capital flowed, for example, to the sugar industry of the Southwest (so that in 1872 one fourth of all sugar factories had a Jewish owner, as well as one third of joint-stock sugar companies),[420] and to the flour-milling and other factory industries both in the Pale of Settlement and outside. After the Crimean War "an intensive construction of railroads" was underway; "all kinds of industrial and commercial enterprises, joint stock companies and banks arose" and "many Jews ... found wide application for their strengths and talents in those undertakings ... with a few of them getting very rich incredibly fast."[421]

"Jews were involved in the grain business for a long time but their role had become particularly significant after the peasant liberation and from the beginning of large-scale railroad construction." "Already in 1878, 60% of grain export was in the hands of Jews and afterwards it was almost completely controlled by Jews." And "thanks to Jewish industrialists, lumber had become the second most important article of Russian export (after grain)." Woodcutting contracts and the acquisition of forest estates by Jews were not prohibited since 1835. "The lumber industry and timber trade were developed by Jews. Also, Jews had established timber export." "The timber trade is a major aspect of Jewish commerce, and, at the same time, a major area of concentration of capital.... Intensive growth of the Jewish timber trade began in the 1860–1870s, when as a result of the abolition of serfdom, landowners unloaded a great number of estates and forests on the market." "The 1870s were the years of the first massive surge of Jews into industries" such as manufacturing, flax, foodstuff, leather,

---

[418] *I. Orshanskiy*, p. 71-72, 95-98, 106-107, 158-160.
[419] *EE* [JE], T 13, p. 646.
[420] *I.M. Dizhur. Evrei v ekonomicheskoy zhizni Rossii* [The Jews in the Economic Life of Russia] // KRE-1, p. 168; *EE* [JE], T 13, p.662.
[421] *L. Deych. Rol' evreyev...*[The Role of the Jews..], T 1, p. 14–15.

cabinetry, and furniture industries, while "tobacco industry had long since been concentrated in the hands of Jews."[422]

In the words of Jewish authors: "In the epoch of Alexander II, the wealthy Jewish bourgeoisie was ... completely loyal ... to the monarchy. The great wealth of the Gintsburgs, the Polyakovs, the Brodskys, the Zaitsevs, the Balakhovskys, and the Ashkenazis was amassed exactly at that time." As already mentioned, "the tax-farmer Evzel Gintsburg had founded his own bank in St. Petersburg." Samuil Polyakov had built six railroad lines; the three Polyakov brothers were granted hereditary nobility titles.[423] "Thanks to railroad construction, which was guaranteed and to a large extent subsidized by the government, the prominent capital of the Polyakovs, I. Bliokh, A. Varshavsky and others were created." Needless to say, many more smaller fortunes were made as well, such as that of A. I. Zaks, the former assistant to E. Gintsburg in tax-farming, who had moved to St. Petersburg and created the Savings and Loan Bank there; "he arranged jobs for his and his wife's many relatives at the enterprises he was in charge of."[424]

Not just the economy, the entire public life had been transformed in the course of Alexandrian reforms, opening new opportunities for mercurial Jewry.

"In the government resolutions permitting certain groups of Jews with higher education to enter government service, there was no restriction in regard to movement up the job ladder. With the attainment of the Full State Advisor rank, a Jew could be elevated to the status of hereditary nobility on common grounds."[425]

In 1864 the land reform began. It "affected all social classes and strata. Its statute ... did not in any way restrict the eligibility of Jews to vote in country administrative elections or occupy elected country offices. In the course of twenty-six years of the statute being in effect, Jews could be seen in many places among town councilors and in the municipal executive councils."[426]

Similarly, the judicial statutes of 1864 stipulated no restrictions for Jews. As a result of the judicial reform, an independent judicial authority was created, and in place of private mediators the legal bar guild was

---

[422] *EE* [JE], T 13, p. 647, 656–658, 663–664; *G.B. Sliozberg*, T 3, p. 93; *KEE* [SJE], T 7, p. 337.
[423] M.A. Aldanov. *Russkie evrei v 70-80-kh godakh: Istoricheskiy etyud* [The Russian Jews in the 1870–1880s: An Historical Essay] // KRE-1, p. 45-46.
[424] *G.B. Sliozberg*, T 1, p. 141-142.
[425] *KEE* [SJE], T 7, p. 328, 331.
[426] *EE* [JE], T 7, p. 762.

established as an independent class with a special corporate structure (and notably, even with the un-appealable right to refuse legal assistance to an applicant "on the basis of moral evaluation of his person," including evaluation of his political views).

And there were no restrictions on Jews entering this class. Gessen wrote: "Apart from the legal profession, in which Jews had come to prominence, we begin noticing them in court registries among investigative officials and in the ranks of public prosecutors; in some places we already see Jews in the magistrate and district court offices"; they also served as jurors"[427] without any quota restrictions (during the first decades after the reform). (Remarkably, during civil trials the Jews were taking conventional juror's oath without any provision made for the Jewish religion).

At the same time municipal reform was being implemented. Initially it was proposed to restrict Jewish representation among town councilors and in the municipal executive councils by fifty percent, but because of objections by the Minister of Internal Affairs, the City Statute of 1870 had reduced the maximal share to one third; further, Jews were forbidden from occupying the post of mayor.[428] It was feared "that otherwise Jewish internal cohesion and self-segregation would allow them to obtain a leading role in town institutions and give them an advantage in resolution of public issues."[429] On the other hand, Jews were equalized in electoral rights (earlier they could vote only as a faction), which led to "the increased influence of Jews in all city governing matters (though in the free city of Odessa these rules were in place from the very beginning; later, it was adopted in Kishinev too. "Generally speaking, in the south of Russia the social atmosphere was not permeated by contempt toward Jews, unlike in Poland where it was diligently cultivated."[430])

Thus "perhaps ... the best period in Russian history for Jews" went on. "An access to civil service was opened for Jews.... The easing of legal restrictions and the general atmosphere of 'the Age of Great Reforms' had affected the spirit of the Jewish people beneficially."[431] It appeared that under the influence of the Age of Great Reforms "the traditional daily life of the Jewish populace had turned toward the surrounding world" and that Jewry "had begun participating as far as possible in the struggle for rights and liberty.... There was not a single area in the economic, public and

---

[427] *Yu. Gessen*, T 2, p. 168.
[428] Also, p. 168.
[429] Also, p. 206.
[430] *EE* [JE], T 6, p. 712, 715-716.
[431] Also, T 13, p. 618.

spiritual life of Russia unaffected by the creative energies of Russian Jews."[432]

And remember that from the beginning of the century the doors of Russian general education were opened wide for Jews, though it took a long time for the unwilling Jews to enter.

Later, a well-known lawyer and public figure, Ya. L. Teytel thus recalled the Mozyr grammar school of the 1860s: "The director of the school ... often ... appealed to the Jews of Mozyr, telling them about the benefits of education and about the desire of government to see more Jews in grammar schools.

Unfortunately, such pleas had fallen on deaf ears."[433] So they were not enthusiastic to enroll during the first years after the reform, even when they were offered free education paid for by state and when school charters (1864) declared that schools are open to everyone regardless confession.[434] "The Ministry of National Education ... tried to make admission of Jews into general education institutions easier"; it exhibited "benevolence toward young Jewish students." [435] (Here L. Deutsch had particularly distinguished the famous surgeon N. I. Pirogov, then a trustee of the Novorossiysk school district, suggesting that he had "strongly contributed to the alleviation of hostility among my tribesmen toward 'goyish' schools and sciences."[436]) Soon after the ascension of Alexander II, the Minister of Education thus formulated the government plan: "It is necessary to spread, by any means, the teaching of subjects of general education, while avoiding interference with the religious education of children, allowing parents to take care of it without any restrictions or hindrances on the part of government."[437] Education in state public schools was made mandatory for children of Jewish merchants and honorary citizens.[438]

Yet all these measures, privileges and invitations, did not lead to a drastic increase in Jewish admissions. By 1863 the share of Jewish students in Russian schools reached 3.2%,[439] that is, equal to their percentage in the population of the empire. Apart from the rejection of Russian education by the Jewry, there was a certain influence from Jewish public leaders who now saw their task differently: "With the advent of the Age of Great

---

[432] KRE-1, *Predislovie* [Foreword], p. iii-iv.
[433] Y.L. Teytel'. *Iz moey zhizni za 40 let* [From My Life of 40 Years]. Paris: Y. Povolotskiy and Company, 1925, p. 15.
[434] I.M. Trotskiy. *Evrei v russkoy shkole* [The Jews in Russian School] // KRE-1, p. 354.
[435] *Yu. Gessen.* T 2, p. 179.
[436] L. Deych. Rol' evreyev..., *T 1, p.* 14.
[437] *EE* [JE]*, T 13, p. 48.
[438] Also, p. 49.
[439] *Yu. Gessen*, T 2, p. 179.

Reforms, 'the friends of enlightenment' had merged the question of mass education with the question of the legal situation of Jews,"[440] that is, they began struggling for the immediate removal of all remaining restrictions. After the shock of the Crimean War, such a liberal possibility seemed quite realistic.

But after 1874, following enactment of the new military statute which "granted military service privileges to educated individuals," almost a magical change happened with Jewish education. Jews began entering public schools in mass.[441] "After the military reform of 1874, even Orthodox Jewish families started sending their sons into high schools and institutions of higher learning to reduce their term of military service."[442] Among these privileges were not only draft deferral and easement of service but also, according to the recollections of Mark Aldanov, the possibility of taking the officer's examination "and receiving officer rank." "Sometimes they attained titles of nobility."[443]

In the 1870s "an enormous increase in the number of Jewish students in public education institutions" occurred, leading to creation of numerous degreed Jewish intelligentsia." In 1881 Jews composed around 9% of all university students; by 1887, their share increased to 13.5%, i.e., one out of every seven students. In some universities Jewish representation was much higher: in the Department of Medicine of Kharkov University Jews comprised 42% of student body; in the Department of Medicine of Odessa University — 31%, and in the School of Law — 41%.[444] In all schools of the country, the percentage of Jews doubled to 12% from 1870 to 1880 (and compared to 1865, it had quadrupled).

In the Odessa school district it reached 32% by 1886, and in some schools it was 75% and even more.[445] (When D. A. Tolstoy, the Minister of Education from 1866, had begun school reforms in 1871 by introducing the Classical education standard with emphasis on antiquity, the ethnic Russian intelligentsia boiled over, while Jews did not mind).

However, for a while, these educational developments affected only "the Jewish bourgeoisie and intelligentsia. The wide masses remained faithful ... to their cheders and yeshivas," as the Russian elementary school offered

---

[440] *EE* [JE], T 13, p. 48.
[441] *Yu. Gessen*, T 2, p. 208.
[442] *KEE* [SJE], T 7, p. 333.
[443] *M.A. Aldanov* // KRE-1, p. 45.
[444] *I.M. Trotskiy. Evrei v russkoy shkole* [The Jews in Russian Schools] // KRE-1, p. 355-356.
[445] *EE* [JE], T 13, p. 50.

nothing in the way of privileges."⁴⁴⁶ "The Jewish masses remained in isolation as before due to specific conditions of their internal and outside life."⁴⁴⁷ Propagation of modern universal culture was extremely slow and new things took root with great difficulty among the masses of people living in shtetls and towns of the Pale of Settlement in the atmosphere of very strict religious traditions and discipline."⁴⁴⁸ "Concentrated within the Pale of Settlement, the Jewish masses felt no need for the Russian language in their daily lives.... As before, the masses were still confined to the familiar hold of the primitive cheder education."⁴⁴⁹ And whoever had just learned how to read had to immediately proceed to reading the Bible in Hebrew.⁴⁵⁰

From the government's point of view, opening up general education to Jews rendered state Jewish schools unnecessary. From 1862 Jews were permitted to take posts of senior supervisors in such schools and so "the personnel in these schools was being gradually replenished with committed Jewish pedagogues, who, acting in the spirit of the time, worked to improve mastery of Russian language and reduce teaching of specifically Jewish subjects."⁴⁵¹ In 1873 these specialized schools were partially abolished and partially transformed, some into primary specialized Jewish schools of general standard, with 3 or 6 years study courses, and two specialized rabbinical schools in Vilna and Zhitomir were transformed into teacher training colleges.⁴⁵² The government ... sought to overcome Jewish alienation through integrated education; however, the Commission for Arranging the Jewish Way of Life was receiving reports both from Jewish advocates, often high-ranked, and from the opponents of reform who insisted that "Jews must never be treated ... in the same way as other ethnic groups of the Empire, that they should not be permitted unrestricted residence all over the country; it might be allowed only after all possible measures were tried to turn Jews into useful productive citizens in the

---

⁴⁴⁶ *I.M. Trotskiy. Evrei v russkoy shkole* [The Jews in Russian Schools] // KRE-1, p. 355-356.
⁴⁴⁷ *EE* [JE], T 13, p. 618.
⁴⁴⁸ *G.Ya. Aronson. V bor'be za grazhdanskie i natsional'nie prava: Obshchestvennie techeniya v russkom evreystve* [In the Struggle for Civil and National Rights: Social Currents in Russian Jewry] // KRE-1, p. 207.
⁴⁴⁹ *Yu. Gessen.* T 2, p. 178, 180.
⁴⁵⁰ *Ya.G. Frumkin. Iz istorii russkogo evreystva: Vospominaniya, materiali, dokumenti* [From the History of Russian Jewry: Memoirs, Materials, and Documents] // KRE-1, p. 51.
⁴⁵¹ *Yu. Gessen,* T 2, p. 180.
⁴⁵² *EE* [JE], T 1, p. 823.

places where they live now and when these measures would prove their success beyond any doubt."[453]

Meanwhile, through the shock of ongoing reforms, especially of the abolition of the burdensome recruiting obligation in 1856 (and through it the negation of the corresponding power of Jewish leaders over their communities), and then of the repeal of the associated special taxation in 1863, "the administrative power of the community leaders was significantly weakened in comparison to their almost unrestricted authority in the past" inherited from the Qahal (abolished in 1844), that omnipotent arbiter of the Jewish life.[454]

It was then, at the end of 1850s and during the 1860s, when the baptized Jew, Yakov Brafman, appeared before the government and later came out publicly in an energetic attempt at radical reformation of the Jewish way of life.

He had petitioned the Tsar with a memorandum and was summoned to St. Petersburg for consultations in the Synod. He set about exposing and explaining the Qahal system (though a little bit late, since the Qahal had already been abolished). For that purpose he had translated into Russian the resolutions of the Minsk Qahal issued in the period between the end of the 18th and the beginning of the 19th centuries. Initially he published the documents in parts and later (in 1869 and 1875) as a compilation, *The Book of Qahal*, which revealed the all-encompassing absoluteness of the personal and material powerlessness of the community member. The book "had acquired exceptional weight in the eyes of the authorities and was accepted as an official guidebook; it won recognition (often by hearsay) in wide circles of Russian society"; it was referred to as the "Brafman's triumph" and lauded as an "extraordinary success."[455] (Later the book was translated into French, German, and Polish.)[456] *The Book of Qahal* managed to instill in a great number of individuals a fanatical hatred toward Jews as the 'worldwide enemy of Christians'; it had succeeded in spreading misconceptions about Jewish way of life."[457]

The 'mission' of Brafman, the collection and translation of the acts issued by the Qahal had "alarmed the Jewish community"; At their demand, a government commission which included the participation of Jewish community representatives was created to verify Brafman's work. Some "Jewish writers were quick to come forward with evidence that Brafman

---

[453] *Yu Gessen**, T 2, p. 205.
[454] Also, p. 170.
[455] Also, p. 200–201.
[456] *KEE* [JEE], T 1, p. 532.
[457] Yu. Gessen, T 2, p. 200–201.

distorted some of the Qahal documents and wrongly interpreted others"; one detractor had even had doubts about their authenticity."[458] (A century later in 1976, *The Short Jewish Encyclopedia* confirmed the authenticity of Brafman's documents and the good quality of his translation but blamed him for false interpretation.[459] *The Russian Jewish Encyclopedia* (1994) pointed out that "the documents published by Brafman are a valuable source for studying the history of Jews in Russia at the end of the 18th and the beginning of the 19th centuries."[460] (Apropos, the poet Khodasevich was the grand-nephew of Brafman).

Brafman claimed "that governmental laws cannot destroy the malicious force lurking in the Jewish self-administration... According to him, Jewish self-rule is not limited to Qahals ... but allegedly involves the entire Jewish people all over the world ... and because of that the Christian peoples cannot get rid of Jewish exploitation until everything that enables Jewish self-segregation is eliminated." Further, Brafman "view[ed] the Talmud not as a national and religious code but as a 'civil and political code' going 'against the political and moral development of Christian nations'"[461] and creating a 'Talmudic republic'. He insisted that "Jews form a nation within a nation"; that they "do not consider themselves subject to national laws";[462] that one of the main goals of the Jewish community is to confuse the Christians to turn the latter into no more than fictitious owners of their property." [463] On a larger scale, he "accused the Society for the Advancement of Enlightenment among the Jews of Russia and the Alliance Israélite Universelle for their role in the 'Jewish world conspiracy'."[464] According to Yu. Gessen's opinion, "the only demand of *The Book of Qahal* ... was the radical extermination of Jewish self-governance" regardless of all their civil powerlessness.[465]

The State Council, "having mitigated the uncompromised style of *The Book of Qahal*, declared that even if administrative measures would succeed in erasing the outward differences between Jews and the rest of population, "it will not in the least eliminate the attitudes of seclusion and nearly the outright hostility toward Christians which thrive in Jewish communities. This Jewish separation, harmful for the country, can be destroyed, on one hand, through the weakening of social connections

---

[458] *EE* [JE], T 4, p. 918.
[459] *KEE* [SJE], T 1, p. 532.
[460] *Rossiyskaya Evreyskaya Entsiklopediya* [The Russian Jewish Encyclopedia] (henceforth REE). Moscow, 1994—...T 1, p. 164.
[461] *Yu. Gessen*. T 2, p. 200–201.
[462] *EE* [JE], T 4, p. 918, 920.
[463] *KEE* [SJE], T 1, p. 532.
[464] *REE* [RJE], T 1, p. 164.
[465] *Yu. Gessen*, T 2, p. 202.

between the Jews and reduction of the abusive power of Jewish elders to the extent possible, and, on the other hand, through spreading of education among Jews, which is actually more important."[466]

And precisely the latter process — education — was already underway in the Jewish community. A previous Jewish Enlightenment, the *Haskalah* Movement of the 1840s, was predominantly based on German culture; they were completely ignorant of Russian culture (they were familiar with Goethe and Schiller but did not know Pushkin and Lermontov)[467] "Until the mid-19th century, even educated Jews, with rare exceptions, having mastered the German language, at the same time did not know the Russian language and literature."[468]

However, as those Maskilim sought self-enlightenment and not the mass education of the Jewish people, the movement died out by the 1860s.[469] "In the 1860s, Russian influences burst into the Jewish society. Until then Jews were not living but rather residing in Russia,[470] perceiving their problems as completely unconnected to the surrounding Russian life. Before the Crimean War the Jewish intelligentsia in Russia acknowledged German culture exclusively but after the reforms it began gravitating toward Russian culture.

Mastery of the Russian language "increases ... self-esteem."[471] From now on the Jewish Enlightenment developed under the strong influence of the Russian culture. "The best... Russian Jewish intellectuals abandoned their people no longer"; they did not depart into the "area of exclusively personal interests", but cared "about making their people's lot easier." Well, after all, Russian literature taught that the strong should devote themselves to the weak.[472]

However, this new enlightenment of the Jewish masses was greatly complicated by the strong religiosity of said masses, which in the eyes of

---

[466] Also*, p. 202–203.
[467] S.M. Sliozberg. O russko-evreyskoy intelligentsia *[On the Russo-Jewish Intelligentsia]* // Evreyskiy mir: Ezhegodnik na 1939g. [Jewish World: Yearbook for 1939] (henceforth—*EM-1* [JW-1]). Paris: Ob'edinenie russko-evreyskoy intelligentsia [Association of the Russo-Jewish Intelligentsia], p. 34.
[468] *EE* [JE], T 3, p. 334.
[469] Yudl. Mark. *Literatura na idish v Rossii* [Literature in Yiddish in Russia] // KRE-1, p. 521; G.Ya. Aronson. *Russko-Evreyskaya pechat'* [Russo-Jewish Press] // Also, p. 548.
[470] B. Orlov. Ne te vi uchili alfaviti // Vremya i mi: Mezhdunarodniy zhurnal literature i obshchestvennikh problem *(henceforth-VM)*. Tel'—Aviv, 1975, No1, p. 130.
[471] M. Osherovich. *Russkie evrei v Soedinennikh Shtatakh Ameriki* [Russian Jews in the United States of America] // KRE-1, p. 289-290.
[472] S.M. Sliozberg//EM-1, p. 35.

progressives was doubtlessly a regressive factor,[473] whereas the emerging Jewish Enlightenment movement was quite secular for that time. Secularization of the Jewish public consciousness "was particularly difficult because of the exceptional role religion played in the Diaspora as the foundation of Jewish national consciousness over the course of the many centuries." And so "the wide development of secular Jewish national consciousness" began, in essence, only at the end of the century.[474] "It was not because of inertia but due to a completely deliberate stance as the Jew did not want risking separation from his God."[475]

So the Russian Jewish intelligentsia met the Russian culture at the moment of birth. Moreover, it happened at the time when the Russian intelligentsia was also developing expansively and at the time when Western culture gushed into Russian life (Buckle, Hegel, Heine, Hugo, Comte, and Spencer). It was pointed out that several prominent figures of the first generation of Russian Jewish intelligentsia (S. Dubnov, M. Krol, G. Sliozberg, O. Gruzenberg, and Saul Ginzburg) were born in that period, 1860–1866[476] (though their equally distinguished Jewish revolutionary peers — M. Gots, G. Gershuni, F. Dan, Azef, and L. Akselrod — were also born during those years and many other Jewish revolutionaries, such as P. Akselrod and L. Deych, were born still earlier, in the 1850s).

In St. Petersburg in 1863 the authorities permitted establishment of the Society for the Spreading of Enlightenment among the Jews in Russia (SSE) supported by the wealthy Evzel Gintsburg and A. M. Brodsky. Initially, during the first decade of its existence, its membership and activities were limited; the Society was preoccupied with publishing activities and not with school education; yet still its activities caused a violent reaction on the part of Jewish conservatives[477] (who also protested against publication of the Pentateuch in Russian as a blasphemous encroachment on the holiness of the Torah). From the 1870s, the SSE provided financial support to Jewish schools. Their cultural work was conducted in Russian, with a concession for Hebrew, but not Yiddish,

---

[473] G.Ya. Aronson*. V bor'be za...[In the Struggle for...] // KRE-1, p 210.
[474] S. Shvarts. Evrei v Sovetskom Soyuze c nachala Vtoroy mirovoy voyni. 1939-1965 [The Jews in the Soviet Union from the Start of the Second World War. 1939-1965]. New York: Amerikanskiy evreyskiy rabochiy komitet [American Jewish Workers Committee], 1966, p. 290.
[475] I.M. Bikerman. K samopoznaniyu evreya: Chem mi bili, chem mi stali, chem mi dolzhni bit'. [What We Were, What We Became, and What We Should Be]. Paris, 1939, p. 48.
[476] K. Leytes. Pamyati M.A. Krolya [The Memoirs of M.A. Krol'] // Evreyskiy mir [Jewish World]: Anthology 2 (henceforth EM-2 [JW-2]). New York: Soyuz russkikh evreyev v N'yu Yorke [Union of Russian Jews in New York], 1944, p. 408-411.
[477] EE [JE], T 13, p. 59.

which was then universally recognized as a 'jargon'.[478] In the opinion of Osip Rabinovich, a belletrist, the "'spoiled jargon' used by Jews in Russia cannot 'facilitate enlightenment, because it is not only impossible to express abstract notions in it, but one cannot even express a decent thought with it'."[479] "Instead of mastering the wonderful Russian language, we Jews in Russia stick to our spoiled, cacophonous, erratic, and poor jargon."[480] (In their day, the German Maskilim ridiculed the *jargon* even more sharply.)

And so "a new social force arose in Russian Jewry, which did not hesitate entering the struggle against the union ... of capital and synagogue", as expressed by the liberal Yu. I. Gessen. That force, nascent and for the time being weak, was the Jewish periodical press in the Russian language.[481]

Its first-born was the Odessa magazine *Rassvet* [Dawn], published for two years from 1859 to 1861 by the above-mentioned O. Rabinovich. The magazine was positioned to serve "as a medium for dissemination of 'useful knowledge, true religiousness, rules of communal life and morality'; it was supposed to predispose Jews to learn the Russian language and to 'become friends with the national scholarship'"[482] *Rassvet* also reported on politics, expressing "love for the Fatherland" and the intention to promote "the government's views"[483] with the goal "of communal living with other peoples, participating in their education and sharing their successes, while at the same time preserving, developing, and perfecting our distinct national heritage."[484] The leading *Rassvet* publicist, L. Levanda, defined the goal of the magazine as twofold: "to act defensively and offensively: defensively against attacks from the outside, when our human rights and confessional (religious) interests must be defended, and offensively against our internal enemy: obscurantism, everydayness, social life troubles, and our tribal vices and weaknesses."[485]

This last direction, "to reveal the ill places of the inner Jewish life," aroused a fear in Jewish circles that it "might lead to new legislative repressions." So the existing Jewish newspapers (in Yiddish) "saw the *Rassvet's* direction as extremely radical." Yet these same moderate newspapers by their mere appearance had already shaken "'the patriarchal structure' of

---

[478] *I.M. Trotskiy. Samodeyatel'nost'...*[Individual Initiative...] // KRE-1, p. 471-474.
[479] *Yu. Gessen*, T 2, p. 172.
[480] *EE* [JE]*, T 3, p. 335.
[481] *Yu. Gessen*, T 2, p. 170.
[482] Also, p. 171.
[483] *G.Ya. Aronson*. Russko-Evreyskaya pechat'* [Russo-Jewish Press] // KRE-1, p. 562.
[484] *S.M. Ginzburg** // *EM-1* [JW-1], p. 36.
[485] *Yu. Gessen**, T 2, p. 173.

[Jewish] community life maintained by the silence of the people."[486] Needless to say, the struggle between the rabbinate and Hasidic Judaism went on unabated during that period and this new 1860s' struggle of the leading publicists against the stagnant foundations of daily life had added to it. Gessen noted that "in the 1860s, the system of repressive measures against ideological opponents did not seem offensive even for the conscience of intelligent people." For example, publicist A. Kovner, 'the Jewish Pisarev' [a radical Russian writer and social critic], could not refrain from tipping off a Jewish newspaper to the Governor General of Novorossiysk.[487] (In the 1870s Pisarev "was extremely popular among Jewish intellectuals.")[488]

M. Aldanov thinks that Jewish participation in Russian cultural and political life had effectively begun at the end of the 1870s (and possibly a decade earlier in the revolutionary movement).[489]

In the 1870s new Jewish publicists (L. Levanda, the critic S. Vengerov, the poet N. Minsky) began working with the general Russian press. (According to G. Aronson, Minsky expressed his desire to go to the Russo-Turkish War to fight for his brothers Slavs). The Minister of Education Count Ignatiev then expressed his faith in Jewish loyalty to Russia. After the Russo-Turkish War of 1877–1878, rumors about major auspicious reforms began circulating among the Jews. In the meantime, the center of Jewish intellectual life shifted from Odessa to St. Petersburg, where new writers and attorneys gained prominence as leaders of public opinion. In that hopeful atmosphere, publication of *Rassvet* was resumed in St. Petersburg in 1879. In the opening editorial, M. I. Kulisher wrote: "Our mission is to be an organ of expression of the necessities of Russian Jews ... for promoting the awakening of the huge mass of Russian Jews from mental hibernation ... it is also in the interests of Russia.... In that goal the Russian Jewish intelligentsia does not separate itself from the rest of Russian citizens."[490]

Alongside the development of the Jewish press, Jewish literature could not help but advance —first in Hebrew, then in Yiddish, and then in Russian, inspired by the best of Russian literature.[491] Under Alexander II, "there

---

[486] Also*, p. 174.
[487] Also, p. 174–175.
[488] *EE* [JE], T 3, p. 480.
[489] *M.A. Aldanov*//KRE-1, p. 44.
[490] *G.Ya. Aronson*. Russko-evreyskaya pechat'* [Russo-Jewish Press] // KRE-1, p. 558-561.
[491] *M. Krol'. Natsionalizm i assimilyatsiya v evreyskoy istorii* [Nationalism and Assimilation in Jewish History] // EM-1 [JW-1], p. 188-189.

were quite a few Jewish authors who persuaded their co-religionists to study the Russian language and look at Russia as their homeland."[492]

Naturally, in the conditions of the 1860s–1870s, the Jewish educators, still few in numbers and immersed in Russian culture, could not avoid moving toward assimilation, in the same direction "which under analogous conditions led the intelligent Jews of Western Europe to unilateral assimilation with the dominant people." [493] However, there was a difference: in Europe the general cultural level of the native peoples was consistently higher and so in Russia these Jews could not assimilate with the Russian people, still weakly touched by culture, nor with the Russian ruling class (who rejected them); they could only assimilate with the Russian intelligentsia, which was then very small in number but already completely secular, rejecting, among other things, their God. Now Jewish educators also tore away from Jewish religiosity and, "being unable to find an alternative bond with their people, they were becoming completely estranged from them and spiritually considered themselves solely as Russian citizens."[494]

"A worldly rapprochement between the Russian and Jewish intelligentsias" was developing.[495] It was facilitated by the general revitalization of Jewish life with several categories of Jews now allowed to live outside the Pale of Settlement. Development of railroad communications and possibilities of travel abroad — "all this contributed to a closer contact of the Jewish ghetto with the surrounding world."[496] Moreover, by the 1860s "up to one-third ... of Odessa's Jews could speak Russian."[497] The population there grew quickly, "because of massive resettlement to Odessa of both Russian and foreign Jews, the latter primarily from Germany and Galicia." [498] The blossoming of Odessa by the middle of the 19th century presaged the prosperity of all Russian Jewry toward the end of the 19th — to the beginning of 20th century. Free Odessa developed according to its own special laws, differing from the All-Russian statutes since the beginning of the 19th century. It used to be a free port and was even open to Turkish ships during the war with Turkey. "The main occupation of Odessa's Jews in this period was the grain trade. Many Jews were small traders and middlemen (mainly between the landowners and the exporters), as well as

---

[492] *James Parkes*. The Jew and his Neighbor: a Study of the Causes of anti-Semitism. Paris: YMCA-Press, 1932, p. 41.
[493] *Yu Gessen*, T 2, p. 198.
[494] Also.
[495] Also, p. 177.
[496] *EE* [JE], T 13, p. 638.
[497] *G.Ya. Aronson. Russko-Evreyskaya pechat'* [Russo-Jewish Press]//KRE-1, p. 551.
[498] *KEE* [SJE], T 6, p. 117.

agents of prominent foreign and local (mainly Greek) wheat trading companies.

At the grain exchange, Jews worked as stockbrokers, appraisers, cashiers, scalers, and loaders"; "the Jews were in a dominant position in grain commerce: by 1870 most of grain export was in their hands. In 1910 ... 89.2% of grain exports was under their control."[499] In comparison with other cities in the Pale of Settlement, more Jews of the independent professions lived in Odessa and they had better relations with educated Russian circles, and were favorably looked upon and protected by the high administration of the city.... N. Pirogov [a prominent Russian scientist and surgeon], the Trustee of the Odessa School District from 1856–1858, particularly patronized the Jews."[500] A contemporary observer had vividly described this Odessa's clutter with fierce competition between Jewish and Greek merchants, where "in some years half the city, from the major bread bigwigs, to the thrift store owners, lived off the sale of grain products." In Odessa, with her non-stop business commotion bonded by the Russian language, "it was impossible to draw a line, to separate clearly a 'wheat' merchant or a banker from a man of an intellectual profession."[501]

Thus in general "among the educated Jews ... the process of adopting all things Russian ... had accelerated." [502] "European education and knowledge of the Russian language had become necessities"; "everyone hurried to learn the Russian language and Russian literature; they thought only about hastening integration and complete blending with their social surroundings"; they aspired not only for the mastery of the Russian language but for "for the complete Russification and adoption of 'the Russian spirit', so that "the Jew would not differ from the rest of citizens in anything but religion." The contemporary observer M. G. Morgulis wrote: "Everybody had begun thinking of themselves as citizens of their homeland; everybody now had a new Fatherland."[503]

"Members of the Jewish intelligentsia believed that 'for the state and public good they had to get rid of their ethnic traits and ... to merge with the dominant nationality.' A contemporary Jewish progressive wrote, that 'Jews, as a nation, do not exist', that they 'consider themselves Russians of

---

[499] Also, p. 117–118.
[500] Also, p. 118.
[501] K. Itskovich. Odessa-khlebniy gorod [Odessa—City of Bread]//Novoe russkoe slovo [The New Russian Word], New York, 1984, 21 March, p. 6.
[502] EE [JE], T 3, p. 334-335.
[503] Also*, T 13, p. 638.

the Mosaic faith...' 'Jews recognize that their salvation lies in the merging with the Russian people'."[504]

It is perhaps worth naming here Veniamin Portugalov, a doctor and publicist. In his youth he harbored revolutionary sentiments and because of that he even spent some time as a prisoner in the Peter and Paul Fortress. From 1871 he lived in Samara. He "played a prominent role in development of rural health service and public health science. He was one of the pioneers of therapy for alcoholism and the struggle against alcohol abuse in Russia." He also organized public lectures. "From a young age he shared the ideas of *Narodniks* [a segment of the Ruslsian *intelligentsia*, who left the cities and went to the people ('narod') in the villages, preaching on the moral right to revolt against the established order] about the pernicious role of Jews in the economic life of the Russian peasantry. These ideas laid the foundation for the dogmas of the Judeo-Christian movement of the 1880s" (The Spiritual Biblical Brotherhood).

Portugalov deemed it necessary to free Jewish life from ritualism, and believed that "Jewry could exist and develop a culture and civilization only after being dissolved in European peoples" (he had meant the Russian [people]).[505]

A substantial reduction in the number of Jewish conversions to Christianity was observed during the reign of Alexander II as it became unnecessary after the abolishment of the institution of military cantonists and the widening of Jewish rights.[506] And from now on the sect of Skhariya the Jew began to be professed openly too.[507]

Such an attitude on the part of affluent Jews, especially those living outside the Pale of Settlement and those with Russian education, toward Russia as undeniably a homeland is noteworthy. And so it had to be noticed and was. "In view of the great reforms, all responsible Russian Jews were, without exaggeration, patriots and monarchists and adored Alexander II. M. N. Muravyov, then Governor General of the Northwest Krai famous for his ruthlessness toward the Poles [who rebelled in 1863], patronized Jews in the pursuit of the sound objective of winning the loyalty of a significant portion of the Jewish population to the Russian state."[508] Though during

---

[504] G.Ya. Aronson. *V bor'be za*...[In the Struggle for...]//KRE-1, p. 207.
[505] *KEE* [SJE], T 6, p. 692–693.
[506] *EE*, T 11, p. 894.
[507] *KEE* [SJE], T 2, p. 510.
[508] V.S. Mandel'. *Konservativnie i razrushitel'nie elemente v evreystve* [Conservative and Destructive Elements in Jewry] // *Rossiya i evrei: Sb. 1* [Russia and the Jews: Anthology 1 (henceforth— *RiE* [RandJ])/*Otechestvennoe obedinenie russkikh evreyev za granitsey* [The Patriotic Union of Russian Jews Abroad]. Paris: YMCA-Press, 1978 [1st Publication—Berlin: Osnova, 1924], p. 195.

the Polish uprising of 1863 Polish Jewry was mainly on the side of the Poles;[509] "a healthy national instinct prompted" the Jews of the Vilnius, Kaunas, and Grodno Guberniyas "to side with Russia because they expected more justice and humane treatment from Russians than from the Poles, who, though historically tolerating the Jews, had always treated them as a lower race."[510] (This is how Ya. Teitel described it: "The Polish Jews were always detached from the Russian Jews"; they looked at Russian Jews from the Polish perspective. On the other hand, the Poles in private shared their opinion on the Russian Jews in Poland: "The best of these Jews are our real enemy. Russian Jews, who had infested Warsaw, Lodz, and other major centers of Poland, brought with them Russian culture, which we do not like.")[511]

In those years, the Russification of Jews on its territory was "highly desirable" for the Tsarist government.[512] Russian authorities recognized "socialization with Russian youth ... as a sure method of re-education of the Jewish youth to eradicate their 'hostility toward Christians'."[513]

Still, this newborn Russian patriotism among Jews had clear limits. The lawyer and publicist I. G. Orshansky specified that to accelerate the process "it was necessary to create conditions for the Jews such that they could consider themselves as free citizens of a free civilized country."[514] The above-mentioned Lev Levanda, 'a Jewish scholar' living under the jurisdiction of the Governor of Vilnius, then wrote: "I will become a Russian patriot only when the Jewish Question is resolved conclusively and satisfactory." A modern Jewish author who experienced the long and bitter 20th century and then had finally emigrated to Israel, replied to him looking back across the chasm of a century: "Levanda does not notice that one cannot lay down conditions to Motherland. She must be loved unconditionally, without conditions or pre-conditions; she is loved simply because she is the Mother. This stipulation — love under conditions — was extremely consistently maintained by the Russian-Jewish intelligentsia for one hundred years, though in all other respects they were ideal Russians."[515]

And yet in the described period "only small and isolated groups of Jewry became integrated into 'Russian civil society; moreover, it was happening

---

[509] *I.M. Trotskiy. Evrei v russkoy shkole* [The Jews in Russian Schools] // KRE-1, p. 356.
[510] *V.S. Mandel'* // *RiE* [RandJ], p. 195.
[511] *Ya. Teytel'. Iz moey zhizni...*[From My Life...], p. 239.
[512] See.: *EE* [JE], T 3, p. 335; and others.
[513] *Yu. Gessen*, T 2, p. 208.
[514] *EE* [JE], T 3, p. 335.
[515] *B. Orlov* // VM, 1975, No1, p. 132.

in the larger commercial and industrial centers ... leading to the appearance of an exaggerated notion about victorious advance of the Russian language deep into Jewish life," all the while "the wide Jewish masses were untouched by the new trends ... isolated not only from the Russian society but from the Jewish intelligentsia as well."[516] In the 1860s and 1870s, the Jewish people *en masse* were still unaffected by assimilation, and the danger of the Jewish intelligentsia breaking away from the Jewish masses was real. (In Germany, Jewish assimilation went smoother as there were no "Jewish popular masses" there — the Jews were better off socially and did not historically live in such crowded enclaves).[517]

However, as early as the end of the 1860s, some members of the Jewish intelligentsia began voicing opposition to such a conversion of Jewish intellectuals into simple Russian patriots. Perets Smolensky was the first to speak of this in 1868: that assimilation with the Russian character is fraught with 'national danger' for the Jews; that although education should not be feared, it is necessary to hold on to the Jewish historical past; that acceptance of the surrounding national culture still requires preservation of the Jewish national character[518]; and that the Jews are not a religious sect, but a nation."[519]

So if the Jewish intelligentsia withdraws from its people, the latter would never liberate itself from administrative oppression and spiritual stupor. (The poet I. Gordon had put it this way: "Be a man on the street and a Jew at home.") The St. Petersburg journals *Rassvet* (1879–1882) and *Russkiy Evrei* [Russian Jew] had already followed this direction.[520] They successfully promoted the study of Jewish history and contemporary life among Jewish youth. At the end of the 1870s and the beginning of the 1880s, cosmopolitan and national directions in Russian Jewry became distinct.[521] "In essence, the owners of *Rassvet* had already abandoned the belief in the truth of assimilation.... *Rassvet* unconsciously went by the path ... of the awakening of ethnic identity ... it was clearly expressing a Jewish national bias.... The illusions of Russification ... were disappearing."[522]

---

[516] *Yu. Gessen*, T 2, p. 181.
[517] *G.Ya. Aronson. V bor'be za...*[In the Struggle for...] // KRE-1, p. 208-209.
[518] *Yu. Gessen*, T 2, p. 198-199.
[519] *EE* [JE], T 3, p. 336.
[520] *Yu. Gessen*, T 2, p. 232-233.
[521] S.M. Ginzburg. Nastroeniya evreyskoy molodezhi v 80-kh godakh proshlogo stoletiya. //EM-2, p. 380.
[522] *G.Ya. Aronson. Russko-evreyskaya pechat'* [Russo-Jewish Press] // KRE-1, p. 561-562.

The general European situation of the latter half of the 19th century facilitated development of national identity. There was a violent Polish uprising, the war for the unification of Italy, and then of Germany, and later of the Balkan Slavs. The national idea blazed and triumphed everywhere. Obviously, these developments would continue among the Jewish intelligentsia even without the events of 1881–1882.

Meanwhile, in the 1870s, the generally favorable attitudes of Russians toward Jews, which had developed during the Alexandrian reforms, began to change. Russian society was concerned with Brafman's publications, which were taken quite seriously.

All this coincided with the loud creation of the Alliance Israélite Universelle in Paris in 1860; its goal was "to defend the interests of Jewry" all over the world; its Central Committee was headed by Adolphe Cremieux.[523]

"Insufficiently well-informed ... about the situation of Jews in Russia," the Alliance "took interest in Russian Jewry" and soon "began consistently working on behalf of Russian Jews." The Alliance did not have Russian branches and did not function within Russia. Apart from charitable and educational work, the Alliance, in defending Russian Jews, several times addressed Russian government directly, though often inappropriately. (For example, in 1866 the Alliance appealed to prevent the execution of Itska Borodai who was convicted of politically motivated arson. However, he was not sentenced to death at all, and other Jews implicated in the affair were acquitted even without the petition.

In another case, Cremieux protested against the resettlement of Jews to the Caucasus and the Amur region — although there was no such Russian government plan whatsoever. In 1869 he again protested, this time against the nonexistent persecution of Jews in St. Petersburg.[524] Cremieux had also complained to the President of the United States about similarly nonexistent persecutions against the Jewish religion by the Russian government).

Nevertheless, according to the report of the Russian ambassador in Paris, the newly-formed Alliance (with the Mosaic Tablets over the Earth on its emblem) had already enjoyed "extraordinary influence on Jewish societies in all countries." All this alarmed the Russian government as well as Russian public.

Yakov Brafman actively campaigned against the Universal Jewish Alliance. He claimed that the Alliance, "like all Jewish societies, is double-

---

[523] *EE* [JE], T 1, p. 932; *KEE* [SJE], T 1, p. 103.
[524] *EE* [JE], T 1, p. 945-950.

faced (its official documents proclaim one thing while the secret ones say another)" and that the task of the Alliance is "to shield the Jewry from the perilous influence of Christian civilization."[525] As a result, the Society for the Spreading of Enlightenment among the Jews in Russia was also accused of having a mission "to achieve and foster universal Jewish solidarity and caste-like seclusion."[526])

Fears of the Alliance were also nurtured by the very emotional opening proclamation of its founders "to the Jews of all nations" and by the dissemination of false Alliance documents. Regarding Jewish unity the proclamation contained the following wording: "Jews! ... If you believe that the Alliance is good for you, that while being the parts of different nations you nevertheless can have common feelings, desires, and hopes ... if you think that your disparate efforts, good aspirations and individual ambitions could become a major force when united and moving in one direction and toward one goal ... then please support us with your sympathy and assistance."[527]

Later in France a document surfaced containing an alleged proclamation "To Jews of the Universe" by Aldolphe Cremieux himself. It was very likely a forgery. Perhaps it was one of the drafts of the opening proclamation not accepted by the Alliance founders. However it had resonated well with Brafman's accusations of the Alliance having hidden goals: "We live in alien lands and we cannot take an interest in the variable concerns of those nations until our own moral and material interests are endangered ... the Jewish teachings must fill the entire world...." Heated arguments were exchanged in this regard in Russian press. I. S. Aksakov concluded in his newspaper *Rus* that "the question of the document under discussion being ... a falsehood is rather irrelevant in this case because of veracity of the expressed herein Jewish views and aspirations."[528]

The pre-revolutionary *Jewish Encyclopedia* writes that from the 1870s "fewer voices were heard in defense of Jews" in the Russian press. "The notion of Jews allegedly united under the aegis of a powerful political organization administered by the Alliance Israélite Universelle was taking root in Russian society."[529] Thus the foundation of the Alliance produced in Russia (and possibly not only in Russia) a reaction counterproductive to the goals that the Alliance had specified.

---

[525] Also, p. 948–950.
[526] Also*, T 2, p. 742.
[527] Also, T 1, p. 933–936.
[528] *EE* [JE], T 1, p. 950-951; *I.S. Aksakov. Soch.* [Essays].: V7 T Moscow., 1886–1887. T 3, p. 843–844.
[529] *EE* [JE], T 2, p. 738.

If the founders of the Alliance could have foreseen the sheer scale of condemnations against the idea of worldwide Jewish solidarity and even the accusations of conspiracy which had erupted after the creation of the organization, they might have refrained from following that route, especially considering that the Alliance did not alter the course of Jewish history.

After 1874, when a new military charter introducing the universal military service obligation in Russia came into force, "numerous news article on draft evasion by Jews began fueling resentment against the Jews in the Russian society."[530] The Alliance Israélite Universelle was accused of intending "to care about young Jews leaving Russia to escape conscription enforced by the new law" so that "using support from abroad, the Jews would have more opportunities than other subjects to move out of the country." (This question would arise once again precisely a century later in the 1970s.) Cremieux replied that the mission of the Alliance was "the struggle against religious persecution" and that the Alliance had decided "henceforth not to assist Jews trying to evade military obligation in Russia." Rather it would issue "an appeal to our coreligionists in Russia in order to motivate them to comply with all the requirements of the new law."[531]

Besides crossing the border, another way to evade military service was self-mutilation. General Denikin (who was quite a liberal before and even during the revolution) described hundreds of bitter cases of the self-mutilation he personally saw during several years of service at the military medical examination board in Volyn Guberniya. Such numerous and desperate self-injuries are all the more striking considering that it was already the beginning of the 20th century.[532]

As previously mentioned, the influx of Jews into public schools, professional schools and institutions of higher learning had sharply increased after 1874 when a new military charter stipulating educational privileges came into force. This increase was dramatic. While calls to restrict Jewish enrollment in public education institutions were heard from the Northwestern Krai even before, in 1875, the Ministry of Public Education informed the government that it was impossible to admit all Jews trying to enter public educational institutions without constraining the Christian population."[533]

---

[530] Also, p. 738–739.
[531] Also, T 1, p. 948–949.
[532] *A.I. Denikin. Put' russkogo ofitsera* [The Path of a Russian Officer]. New York: Publisher-named-Chekov, 1953, p. 284.
[533] *EE* [JE], T 13, p. 50–51.

It is worth mentioning here the G. Aronson's regretful note that even D. Mendeleev of St. Petersburg University "showed anti-Semitism."[534] The *Jewish Encyclopedia* summarizes all of the 1870s period as "a turnaround in the attitudes of a part of Russian intelligentsia ... which rejected the ideals of the previous decade especially in regard to ... the Jewish Question."[535]

An interesting feature of that time was that it was the press (the rightist one, of course) and not governmental circles that was highly skeptical (and in no way hostile) towards the project of full legal emancipation of the Jews. The following quotes are typical. How can "all the citizenship rights be granted to this ... stubbornly fanatical tribe, allowing them to occupy the highest administrative posts? ... Only education ... and social progress can truly bring together Jews and Christians.... Introduce them into the universal family of civilization, and we will be the first to say words of love and reconciliation to them." "Civilization will generally benefit from such a rapprochement as the intelligent and energetic tribe will contribute much to it. The Jews ... will realize that time is ripe to throw off the yoke of intolerance which originates in the overly strict interpretations of the Talmud." "Until education brings the Jews to the thought that it is necessary to live not only at the expense of Russian society but also for the good of this society, no discussion could be held about granting them more rights than those they have now." "Even if it is possible to grant the Jews all civil rights, then in any case they cannot be allowed into any official positions 'where Christians would be subject to their authority and where they could have influence on the administration and legislation of a Christian country.'"[536]

The attitude of the Russian press of that time is well reflected in the words of the prominent St. Petersburg newspaper *Golos*: "Russian Jews have no right to complain that the Russian press is biased against their interests. Most Russian periodicals favor equal civil rights for Jews;" it is understandable "that Jews strive to expand their rights toward equality with the rest of Russian citizens"; yet... "some dark forces drive Jewish youth into the craziness of political agitation. Why is that only a few political trials do not list Jews among defendants, and, importantly, among the most prominent defendants? ... That and the common Jewish practice of evading military service are counterproductive for the cause of expanding the civil rights of Jews"; "one aspiring to achieve rights must prove beforehand his ability to fulfill the duties which come with those rights" and "avoid putting

---

[534] G.Ya. Aronson. *Russko-evreyskaya pechet'* [Russo-Jewish Press] // KRE-1, p. 558.
[535] *EE* [JE], T 12, p. 525-526.
[536] *EE* [JE]*, T 2, p. 736, 740.

himself into an extremely unfavorable and dismal position with respect to the interests of state and society."[537]

Yet, the *Encyclopedia* notes, "despite all this propaganda, bureaucratic circles were dominated by the idea that the Jewish Question could only be resolved through emancipation. For instance, in March 1881 a majority of the members of the Commission for Arranging the Jewish Way of Life tended to think that it was necessary to equalize the Jews in rights with the rest of the population."[538] Raised during the two decades of Alexandrian reforms, the bureaucrats of that period were in many respects taken by the reforms' triumphant advances. And so proposals quite radical and favorable to Jews were put forward on several occasions by Governors General of the regions constituting the Pale of Settlement.

Let's not overlook the new initiatives of the influential Sir Moses Montefiore, who paid another visit to Russia in 1872; and the pressure of both Benjamin Disraeli and Bismarck on Russian State Chancellor Gorchakov at the Berlin Congress of 1878. Gorchakov had to uneasily explain that Russia was not in the least against religious freedom and did grant it fully, but "religious freedom should not be confused with Jews having equal political and civil rights."[539]

Yet the situation in Russia developed toward emancipation. And when in 1880 the Count Loris-Melikov was made the Minister of the Interior with exceptional powers, the hopes of Russian Jews for emancipation had become really great and well-founded. Emancipation seemed impending and inevitable.

And at this very moment the members of Narodnaya Volya assassinated Alexander II, thus destroying in the bud many liberal developments in Russia, among them the hopes for full Jewish civil equality.

Sliozberg noted that the Tsar was killed on the eve of Purim. After a series of attempts, the Jews were not surprised at this coincidence, but they became restless about the future.[540]

---

[537] *Golos* [The Voice], 1881, No46, 15 (27) February, p. 1.
[538] *EE* [JE], T 2, p. 740.
[539] Also, T 4, p. 246, 594.
[540] *G.B. Sliozberg*, T 1, p. 99.

Chapter 5
After the Murder of Alexander II

The murder of the Tsar-Liberator, Alexander II, shocked the people's consciousness — something the *Narodovol'tsi* intended, but that has been intentionally or unintentionally ignored by historians with the passing of decades. The deaths of heirs or tsars of the previous century – Aleksei Petrovich, Ivan Antonovich, Peter III, and Paul – were violent, but that was unknown to the people. The murder of March 1st, 1881, caused a panic in minds nationwide. For the common people, and particularly for the peasant masses it was as if the very foundations of their lives were shaken. Again, as the Narodovol'tsi calculated, this could not help but invite some explosion. And an explosion did occur, but an unpredictable one: Jewish pogroms in Novorossiya and Ukraine.

Six weeks after the regicide, the pogroms of Jewish shops, institutions, and homes "suddenly engulfed a vast territory, with tremendous, epidemic force."[541]

"Indeed, it was rather spontaneous. ... Local people, who, for the most different reasons desired to get even with the Jews, posted incendiary posters and organized basic cadres of pogromists, which were quickly joined by hundreds of volunteers, who joined without any exhortation, caught up in the generally wild atmosphere and promise of easy money. In this there was something spontaneous. However, ... even the crowds, fueled by alcohol, while committing theft and violence, directed their blows in one direction only: in the direction of the Jews — the unruliness only stopping at the thresholds of Christian homes."[542]

The first pogrom occurred in Elizavetgrad, on 15 April. "Disorder intensified, when peasants from the neighboring settlements arrived, in

---

[541] *Evreyskaya Entsiklopediya* (dalee — EE). [The Jewish Encyclopedia (from here — JE)]. V 16 T. Sankt-Peterburg.: *Obshchestvo dlya Nauchnikh Evreyskikh Izdaniy i Izdatel'stvo Brokgauz-Efron*, 1906-1913. T. 12, s. 611. Society for Scientific Jewish Publications and Publisher Brokgauz-Efron.

[542] Yu. Gessen. Istoriya evreyskogo naroda v Rossii *(dalee – Yu. Gessen): V2 T. L., 1925–1927.* T2., s. 215–216. History of the Jewish People of Russia (from here — Yu. Gessen).

order to profit off the goods of the Jews." At first the military did not act, because of uncertainty; finally "significant cavalry forces succeeded in ending the pogrom."[543] "The arrival of fresh forces put an end to the pogrom."[544] "There was no rape and murder in this pogrom."[545] According to other sources: "one Jew was killed. The pogrom was put down on 17 April by troops, who fired into the crowd of thugs."[546] However, "from Elizavetgrad the stirring spread to neighboring settlements; in the majority of cases, the disorders were confined to plundering of taverns." And after a week, a pogrom occurred in the Anan'evskiy Uezd [district] of Odessa Guberniya [province], then in Anan'ev itself, "where it was caused by some petty bourgeois, who spread a rumor that the Tsar was killed by Jews, and that there was an official order for the massacre of Jews, but the authorities were hiding this."[547] On 23 April there was a brief pogrom in Kiev, but it was soon stopped with military forces. However, in Kiev on 26 April a new pogrom broke out, and by the following day it had spread to the Kiev suburbs — and this was the largest pogrom in the whole chain of them; but they ended without human fatalities."[548] (Another tome of the same *Encyclopedia* reports the opposite, that "several Jews were killed."[549])

After Kiev, pogroms took place again in approximately fifty settlements in the Kiev Guberniya, during which "property of the Jews was subjected to plunder, and in isolated cases battery occurred." At the end of the same April a pogrom took place in Konotop, "caused mainly by workers and railroad hands, accompanied by one human fatality; in Konotop there were instances of self-defense from the Jewish side." There was still an echo of the Kiev Pogrom in Zhmerinka, in "several settlements of Chernigov Guberniya;" at the start of May, in the small town of Smel, where "it was suppressed with arriving troops the next day" ("an apparel store was plundered"). With echoes in the course of May, at the start of summer pogroms still broke out in separate areas in Ekaterinoslav and Poltava guberniyas (Aleksandrovsk, Romni, Nezhin, Pereyaslavl, and Borisov). Insignificant disorders took place somewhere in Melitopol Uezd. There

---

[543] Ibid. Pages 216–217.
[544] EE, T 12, page 612.
[545] L. Praysman [Priceman]. *Pogromi i samooborona.* [Pogroms and Self-defense] //"22": Obshchestvenno-politicheskiy i literaturniy zhurnal evreyskoy intelligentsii iz SSSR v Izraile [Public-Political and Literary Journal of the Jewish Intelligentsia from the USSR in Israel]. Tel-Aviv, 1986/87, No51, p. 174.
[546] *Kratkaya Evreyskaya Entsiklopediya (dale — KEE)* [The Short Jewish Encyclopedia (from here — SJE)]: [V10 T.] Jerusalem, 1976–2001. T 6, p. 562.
[547] *EE* [JE], T 12, p. 612.
[548] *KEE* [SJE], T 4, p.256.
[549] Ibid. T 6, p. 562.

were cases, when peasants immediately compensated Jews for their losses."[550]

"The pogrom movement in Kishinev, which began on 20 April, was nipped in the bud."[551] There were no pogroms in all of Byelorussia – not in that year, nor in the following years,[552] although in Minsk a panic started among the Jews during rumors about pogroms in the Southwestern Krai – on account of a completely unexpected occurrence.[553] And next in Odessa. Only Odessa already knew Jewish pogroms in the 19th Century — in 1821, 1859, and 1871. "Those were sporadic events, caused mainly by unfriendliness toward Jews on the part of the local Greek population,"[554] that is, on account of the commercial competition of the Jews and Greeks; in 1871 there was a three-day pogrom of hundreds of Jewish taverns, shops, and homes, but without human fatalities.

I.G. Orshanskiy writes in more detail about this pogrom, and states, that Jewish property was being intentionally destroyed: heaps of watches from the jewelers — they did not steal them, but carried them out to the roadway and smashed them. He agrees that the "nerve center" of the pogrom was hostility toward the Jews on the part of the Greek merchants, particularly owing to the fact, that after the Crimean War the Odessa Jews took the grocery trade and colonial commodities from the Greeks. But there was "a general dislike toward the Jews on the part of the Christian population of Odessa. ... This hostility manifested far more consciously and prominently among the intelligent and affluent class than among the common working people." You see, however, that different peoples get along in Odessa; "why then did only Jews arouse general dislike toward themselves, which sometimes turns into severe hatred?" One high school teacher explained to his class: "The Jews are engaged in incorrect economic relations with the rest of population." Orshanskiy objects that such an explanation removes "the heavy burden of moral responsibility." He sees the same reason in the psychological influence of Russian legislation, which singles out the Jews, namely and only to place restrictions on them. And in the attempt of Jews

---

[550] *EE* [JE], T 12, p 612-613.
[551] Ibid., p. 612.
[552] *KEE* [SJE], T 1, p. 325.
[553] S. Ginzburg. *Nastroeniya evreyskoy molodezhi v 80-kh godakh proshlogo stoletiya.* [The attitudes of Jewish Youth in the 80s Years of the Previous Century] // *Evreyskiy mir* [Jewish World]: Sb 2 [Anthology 2] (*dalee – EM-2*) [from here — JW-2]. New York: *Soyuz russkikh evreyev v N'yu Yorke* [Union of Russian Jews in New York], 1944, p. 383.
[554] *EE* [EJ], T 12, p 611.

to break free from restrictions, people see "impudence, insatiableness, and grabbing."[555]

As a result, in 1881 the Odessa administration, already having experience with pogroms – which other local authorities did not have – immediately put down disorders which were reignited several times, and "the masses of thugs were placed in vessels and dragged away from the shore"[556] — a highly resourceful method. (In contradiction to the pre-revolutionary, the modern *Encyclopedia* writes, that this time the pogrom in Odessa continued for three days).[557]

The pre-revolutionary *Encyclopedia* recognizes, that "the government considered it necessary to decisively put down violent attempts against the Jews";[558] so it was the new Minister of Interior Affairs, Count N.P. Ignatiev, (who replaced Loris-Melikov in May, 1881), who firmly suppressed the pogroms; although it was not easy to cope with rising disturbances of "epidemic strength" — in view of the complete unexpectedness of events, the extremely small number of Russian police at that time (Russia's police force was then incomparably smaller than the police forces in the West European states, much less than those in the Soviet Union), and the rare stationing of military garrisons in those areas. "Firearms were used for defense of the Jews against pogromists."[559] There was firing in the crowd, and [people] were shot dead. For example, in Borisov "soldiers shot and killed several peasants."[560] Also, in Nezhin "troops stopped a pogrom, by opening fire at the crowd of peasant pogromists; several people were killed and wounded."[561] In Kiev 1,400 people were arrested.[562]

All this together indicates a highly energetic picture of enforcement. But the government acknowledged its insufficient preparedness. An official statement said that during the Kiev pogrom "the measures to restrain the crowds were not taken with sufficient timeliness and energy."[563] In a report to His Majesty in June 1881 the Director of the Police Department, V.K. Plehve, named the fact that courts martial "treated the accused extremely

---

[555] I. Orshanskiy. *Evrei v Rossii: Ocherki i issledovaniya* [The Jews in Russia: Essays and Research]. Vip. 1. Sankt-Peterburg, 1872, p 212-222.
[556] *EE* [EJ] T 12, p.613.
[557] *KEE* [SJE], T 6, p. 562.
[558] *EE* [JE] T 1, p. 826.
[559] *Yu. Gessen*, T 12, p. 222.
[560] *EE* [JE], T 12, p. 613.
[561] *KEE* [SJE], T 6, p 562–563.
[562] S.M. Dubnov. *Noveyshaya Istoriya: Ot frantsuzkoy revolutsii 1789 goda do mirovoy voyni 1914 goda* [A New History: from the French Revolution of 1789 to the First World War of 1914]: V3 T. Berlin: Grani, 1923. T3 (1881–1914), p. 107.
[563] *EE* [JE], T 6, p. 612.

leniently and in general dealt with the matter quite superficially" as "one of the reasons for the development and insufficiently quick suppression of the disorders'"

Alexander III made a note in the report: "This is inexcusable."[564] But forthwith and later it did not end without accusations, that the pogroms were arranged by the government itself — a completely unsubstantiated accusation, much less absurd, since in April 1881 the same liberal reformer Loris Melikov headed the government, and all his people were in power in the upper administration. After 1917, a group of researchers – S. Dubnov, G. Krasniy-Admoni, and S. Lozinskiy — thoroughly searched for the proof in all the opened government archives – and only found the opposite, beginning with the fact that, Alexander III himself demanded an energetic investigation. (But to utterly ruin Tsar Alexander III's reputation a nameless someone invented the malicious slander: that the Tsar – unknown to anyone, when, and under what circumstances – said: "And I admit, that I myself am happy, when they beat Jews!" And this was accepted and printed in émigré liberation brochures, it went into liberal folklore, and even until now, after 100 years, it has turned up in publications as historically reliable.[565] And even in the *Short Jewish Encyclopedia*: "The authorities acted in close contact with the arrivals,"[566] that is, with outsiders. And it was 'clear' to Tolstoy in Yasnaya Polyana that it was "obvious": all matters were in the hands of the authorities. If "they wanted one — they could bring on a pogrom; if they didn't want one — there would be no pogrom.")[567]

As a matter of fact, not only was there no incitement on the part of the government, but as Gessen points out: "the rise of numerous pogrom brigades in a short time in a vast area and the very character of their actions, eliminates the thought of the presence of a single organizational center."[568]

And here is another contemporary, living testimony from a pretty much unexpected quarter — from The Black Repartition's *Worker's Leaflet*; that is, a proclamation to the people, in June 1881. The revolutionary leaflet thus described the picture: "Not only all the governors, but all other officials, police, troops, priests, zemstvo [elected district councils], and

---

[564] R. Kantor*. *Aleksandr III o evreyskikh pogromakh 1881-1883 gg.* [Aleksandr III on the Jewish Pogroms, 1881–1883]// *Evreyskaya letopis'* [The Jewish Chronicle]: Sb. [Anthology] 1. M.; Pg.: Paduga, 1923, p. 154.
[565] A. L'vov//*Novaya gazeta* [New Gazette], New York, 1981, No70, 5–11 September, p. 26.
[566] *KEE* [SJE], T 6, p. 563.
[567] *Mezhdunarodnaya evreyskaya gazeta* [International Jewish Gazette], 1992, March, No6 (70), p. 7.
[568] *Yu. Gessen*, T 2, p. 215.

journalists — stood up for the Kulak-Jews...The government protects the person and property of the Jews"; threats are announced by the governors "that the perpetrators of the riots will be dealt with according to the full extent of the law...The police looked for people who were in the crowd [of pogromists], arrested them, dragged them to the police station...Soldiers and Cossacks used the rifle butt and the whip... they beat the people with rifles and whips...some were prosecuted and locked up in jail or sent to do hard labor, and others were thrashed with birches on the spot by the police."[569]

Next year, in the spring of 1881, "pogroms renewed but already not in the same numbers and not in the same scale as in the previous year."[570] "The Jews of the city of Balta experienced a particularly heavy pogrom," riots also occurred in the Baltskiy Uezd and still in a few others. "However, according to the number of incidents, and according to their character, the riots of 1882 were significantly inferior to the movement of 1881 — the destruction of the property of Jews was not so frequent a phenomenon."[571] The pre-revolutionary *Jewish Encyclopedia* reports, that at the time of the pogrom in Balta, one Jew was killed.[572]

A famous Jewish contemporary wrote: in the pogroms of the 1880s, "they robbed unlucky Jews, and they beat them, but they did not kill them."[573] (According to other sources, 6–7 deaths were recorded.) At the time of the 1880–1890s, no one remembered mass killings and rapes. However, more than a half-century passed — and many publicists, not having the need to delve into the ancient [official] Russian facts, but then having an extensive and credulous audience, now began to write about massive and premeditated atrocities. For example, we read in Max Raisin's frequently published book: that the pogroms of 1881 led to the "rape of women, murder, and maiming of thousands of men, women, and children. It was later revealed, that these riots were inspired and thought out by the very government, which had incited the pogromists and hindered the Jews in their self-defense."[574]

---

[569] *Zerno: Rabochiy listok* [The Truth, (Grain of)]: Worker's Leaflet, June 1881, No3//*Istoriko-Revolyutsioniy Sbornik* (dalee – IPC) [Historical-Revolutionary Anthology (from here — HRA)]/Under the Editorship of V.I. Nevskiy: V 3 T.M.; L.: GIZ, 1924–1926. T 2, p. 360–361.
[570] *Yu. Gessen*, T 2, p. 217.
[571] *EE* [JE], T 12, p. 614.
[572] Ibid. T 3, p. 723.
[573] *M. Krol'. Kishinevskiy pogrom 1903 goda i Kishinevskiy pogromniy protsess* [The Kishinev Pogrom of 1903 and the Kishinev Pogrom Process] // EM-2, p. 370.
[574] *Max Raisin*. A History of the Jews in Modern Times. 2nd ed., New York: Hebrew Publishing Company, 1923, p. 163.

A G.B. Sliozberg, so rationally familiar with the workings of the Russian state apparatus — suddenly declared out-of-country in 1933, that the pogroms of 1881 originated not from below, but from above, with Minister Ignatiev (who at that time was still not Minister — the old man's memory failed him), and "there was no...doubt, that threads of the work of the pogrom could be found in the Department of Police"[575] — thus the experienced jurist afforded himself dangerous and ugly groundlessness.

And yes, here in a serious present-day Jewish journal — from a modern Jewish author we find that, contrary to all the facts and without bringing in new documents: that in Odessa in 1881 a "three-day pogrom" took place; and that in the Balta pogrom there was "direct participation of soldiers and police"; "40 Jews were killed and seriously wounded, 170 lightly wounded."[576] (We just read in the old Jewish Encyclopedia: in Balta *one* Jew was killed, and wounded — several. But in the new *Jewish Encyclopedia*, after a century from the events, we read: in Balta "soldiers joined the pogromists...Several Jews were killed, hundreds wounded, many women were raped."[577]) Pogroms are too savage and horrible a form of reprisal, for one to so lightly manipulate casualty figures.

There – spattered, basted – is it necessary to begin excavations again?

The causes of those first pogroms were persistently examined and discussed by contemporaries. As early as 1872, after the Odessa pogrom, the General-Governor of the Southwestern Krai warned in a report, that similar events could happen in his Krai also, for "here the hatred and hostility toward Jews has an historical basis, and only the material dependence of the peasants upon Jews together with the measures of the administration currently holds back an indignant explosion of the Russian population against the Jewish tribe." The General-Governor reduced the essence of the matter to economics, as he "reckoned and evaluated the business and manufacturing property in Jewish hands in the Southwestern Krai, and pointed to the fact, that, being increasingly engaged in the rent of landed estates, the Jews have re-rented and shifted this land to the peasants on very difficult terms." And such a causation "received wide recognition in 1881 which was full of pogroms."[578]

In the spring of 1881, Loris-Melikov also reported to His Majesty: "The deep hatred of the local population toward the Jews who enslave it lies at

---

[575] G.B. Sliozberg. *Dela minuvshikh dney: Zapiski russkogo evreya* [Things of Days Bygone: Notes of a Russian Jew]: V 3 T. Paris, 1933–1934. T 1, p. 118; T 3, p.53.
[576] *L. Praysman*//"22," 1986, No51, p. 175.
[577] *KEE* [SJE] T 6, p. 562–563.
[578] *Yu. Gessen*. T 2, p. 216, 220.

the foundation of the present disorders, but ill-intentioned people have undoubtedly exploited this opportunity."[579]

And thus explained the newspapers of the time: "Examining the causes which provoked the pogroms, only a few organs of the periodical press refer to the tribal and religious hatred; the rest think that the pogrom movement arose on economic grounds; in so doing, some see a protest in the unruly behaviors directed specially against the Jews, in light of their economic dominance over the Russian population". Yet others maintained that the mass of the people, in general squeezed economically, "looked for someone to vent their anger out on" and the Jews fit this purpose because of their having little rights.[580] A contemporary of these pogroms, the cited educator, V. Portugalov, also said "In the Jewish pogroms of the 1880s, I saw an expression of protest by the peasants and the urban poor against social injustice."[581]

Ten years later, Yu. I. Gessen emphasized, that "the Jewish population of the southern Guberniyas" in general was able to "find sources of livelihood among the Jewish capitalists, while the local peasantry went through extremely difficult times" as it did not have enough land, "to which the wealthy Jews contributed in part, by re-renting the landowner's lands and raising the rental fee beyond the ability of the peasants."[582]

Let us not leave out still another witness, known for his impartiality and thoughtfulness, whom no one accused of being "reactionary" or of "antiSemitism" – Gleb Uspenskiy. At the beginning of the 1980s, he wrote: "The Jews were beaten up, namely because they amassed a fortune on other people's needs, other people's work, and did not make bread with their own hands"; "under canes and lashes…you see, the people endured the rule of the Tatar and the German but when the Yid began to harass the people for a ruble — they did not take it!"[583]

But we should note that when soon after the pogroms a deputation of prominent Jews from the capital, headed by Baron G. Gintsburg, came to Alexander III at the beginning of May 1881, His Majesty confidently estimated that "in the criminal disorders in the south of Russia, the Jews served only as a pretext, that this business was the hand of the anarchists."[584] And in those same days, the brother of the Tsar, the Grand

---

[579] *R. Kantor** // Evreyskaya letopis' [The Jewish Chonicle]: Sb. [Anthology] 1, M.; Pg.: Raduga, 1923, p. 152.
[580] *Yu. Gessen*. T 2, p 218.
[581] *KEE* [SJE], T 6, p. 692.
[582] *Yu. Gessen*, T 2, p 219-220.
[583] *Gleb Uspenskiy*. Vlast' zemli [The Authority of the Land]. L.: Khudozh. Lit., 1967, p. 67, 88.
[584] *EE** [JE], T 1, p. 826.

Prince Vladimir Alexandrovich, announced to the same Gintsburg, that: "the disorders, as is now known by the government, have their sources not exclusively agitation against the Jews, but an aspiration to the work of sedition in general." And the General-Governor of the Southwestern Krai also reported, that "the general excited condition of the population is the responsibility of propagandists."[585] And in this the authorities turned out to be well-informed. Such quick statements from them reveal that the authorities did not waste time in the investigation. But because of the usual misunderstanding of the Russian administration of that time, and its incomprehension of the role of publicity, they did not report the results of the investigation to the public. Sliozberg blames that on the central authority in that it did not even make "attempts to vindicate itself of accusations of permitting the pogroms."[586] (True, but after all, it accused the government, as we saw, of deliberate instigation and guidance of the pogroms. It is absurd to start with proof that you are not a criminal.)

Yet not everyone wanted to believe that the incitements came from the revolutionaries. Here a Jewish memoirist from Minsk recalls: for Jews, Alexander II was not a "Liberator" — he did not do away with the Jewish Pale of Settlement, and although the Jews sincerely mourned his death, they did not say a single bad word against the revolutionaries; they spoke with respect about them, that they were driven by heroism and purity of thought. And during the spring and summer pogroms of 1881, they did not in any way believe that the socialists incited toward them: it was all because of the new Tsar and his government. "The government wished for the pogroms, it had to have a scapegoat." And now, when reliable witnesses from the South later indeed confirmed that the socialists engineered them, they continued to believe that it was the fault of the government.[587]

However, toward the start of the 20th Century, thorough authors admitted: "In the press there is information about the participation of separate members of the party, *Narodnaya Vol'ya* [People's Will] in the pogroms; but the extent of this participation is still not clear. ... Judging by the party organ, members of the party considered the pogroms as a sort of revolutionary activity, suggesting that the pogroms were training the people for revolutionary action",[588] "that the action which was easiest of all to direct against the Jews now, could, in its further development, come down on the nobles and officials. Accordingly, proclamations calling for an attack on the Jews were prepared."[589] Today, it is only superficially

---

[585] Ibid*, T 12, p. 614.
[586] G.B. Sliozberg. *Dela minuvshikh dney...* [Things of Days Bygone], T 1, p. 106.
[587] A. Lesin. *Epizodi iz moey zhizni* [Episodes from My Life] // EM-2, p. 385-387.
[588] *EE* [JE], T 12, p. 617-618.
[589] *Yu. Gessen*, T 2, p. 218.

talked about, like something generally known: "the active propaganda of the *Narodniks* (both members of Narodnaya Vol'ya and the Black Repartition was prepared to stir rebellion to any fertile soil, including antiSemitism."[590] From emigration, Tkachev, irrepressible predecessor of Lenin in conspiratorial tactics, welcomed the broadening pogrom movement.

Indeed, the Narodovol'tsi (and the weaker Chernoperedel'tsi [members of Black Repartition) could not wait much longer after the murder of the Tsar which did not cause instantaneous mass revolution which had been predicted and expected by them. With such a state of general bewilderment of minds after the murder of the Tsar-Liberator, only a slight push was needed for the reeling minds to re-incline into any direction.

In that generally unenlightened time, that re-inclination could probably have happened in different ways. (For example, there was then such a popular conception, that the Tsar was killed by nobles, in revenge for the liberation of the peasants.) In Ukraine, anti-Jewish motives existed. Still, it is possible the first movements of spring 1881 anticipated the plot of the Narodovol'tsi — but right then and there they suggested which way the wind would blow: it went against the Jews — never lose touch with the people! A movement from the heart of the masses — Of course! Why not use it? Beat the Jews, and later we will get to the landowners! And now the unsuccessful pogroms in Odessa and Ekaterinoslav were most likely exaggerated by the Narodniks. And the movement of the pogromists along the railroads, and participation of the railroad workers in the pogroms — everything points to the instigation of pogroms by easily mobile agitators, especially with that particularly inciting rumor that "they are hiding the order of the Tsar," namely to beat the Jews for the murder of his father. (The public prosecutor of the Odessa Judicial Bureau thus emphasized, "that, in perpetrating the Jewish pogroms, the people were completely convinced of the legality of their actions, firmly believing in the existence of a Tsar's decree, allowing and even authorizing the destruction of Jewish property."[591] And according to Gessen, "the realization that had taken root in the people, that the Jews stood outside of the law, and that the authorities defending the Jews could not come out against the people"[592]— had now taken effect. The Narodovol'tsi wanted to use this imaginary notion.) A few such revolutionary leaflets are preserved for history. Such a leaflet from 30 August 1881 is signed by the Executive Committee of the Narodnaya Vol'ya and reads straight away in Ukrainian: "Who seized the land, forests, and taverns? — The Yid — From whom, muzhik [peasant],

---

[590] *L. Praisman*//"22," 1986, No51, p. 173.
[591] *EE* [JE]*, T 1, p. 826.
[592] *Yu. Gessen*, T 2, p. 215.

do you have to ask for access to your land, at times hiding tears?...From Yids. — Wherever you look, wherever you ask — the Yids are everywhere. The Yid insults people and cheats them; drinks their blood"...and it concludes with the appeal: "Honest working people! Free yourselves!..."[593] And later, in the newspaper, Narodnaya Vol'ya, No. 6: "All attention of the defending people is now concentrated, hastily and passionately, on the merchants, tavern keepers, and moneylenders; in a word, on the Jews, on this local "bourgeoisie," who avariciously rob working people like nowhere else." And after, in a forward to a leaflet of the Narodnaya Vol'ya (already in 1883), some "corrections": "the pogroms began as a nationwide movement, 'but not against the Jews as Jews, but against *Yids*; that is, exploiter peoples.'"[594] And in the said leaflet, *Zerno*, the Chernoperedel'tsi: "The working people cannot withstand the Jewish robbery anymore. Wherever one goes, almost everywhere he runs into the Jew-Kulak. The Jew owns the taverns and pubs; the Jew rents land from the landowners, and then re-rents it at three times higher to the peasant; he buys the wholesale yields of crop and engages in usury, and in the process charges such interest rates, that the people outright call them "Yiddish [rates]"..."This is our blood!" said the peasants to the police officials, who came to seize the Jewish property back from them." But the same "correction" is in *Zerno*: "...and far from all among the Jews are wealthy...not all of them are kulaks...Discard with the hostility toward differing peoples and differing faiths" — and unite with them "against the common enemy": the Tsar, the police, the landowners, and the capitalists.[595]

However these "corrections" already came late. Such leaflets were later reproduced in Elizavetgrad and other cities of the South; and in the "South Russian Worker's Soviet" in Kiev, where the pogroms were already over, the Narodniks tried to stir them up again in 1883, hoping to renew, and through them — to spread the Russian-wide revolution.

Of course, the pogrom wave in the South was extensively covered in the contemporary press in the capital. In the "reactionary" *Moskovskiye Vedomosti*, M.N. Katkov, who always defended the Jews, branded the pogroms as originating with "malicious intriguers," "who intentionally darkened the popular consciousness, forcing people to solve the Jewish

---

[593] *Katorga i ssilka: Istoriko-revolyutsioniy vestnik* [Hard Labor and Exile: The Historical-Revolutionary Bulletin] Book 48, Moscow, 1928, p. 50-52.
[594] D. Shub. *Evrei v russkoy revolyutsii* [Jews in the Russian Revolution] // EM-2, p. 129-130.
[595] *IPC* [IRS], T 2, p. 360-361.

Question, albeit not by a path of thorough study, but with the help of "raised fists."[596]

The articles by prominent writers stand out. I.S. Aksakov, a steadfast opponent of complete civil liberty for the Jews, attempted to warn the government "against too daring steps" on this path, as early as the end of the 1850s. When a law came out allowing Jews with higher degrees to be employed in the administration, he objected (1862) saying that the Jews are "a bunch of people, who completely reject Christian teachings, the Christian ideal and code of morality (and, therefore, the entire foundation of Russian society), and practice a hostile and antagonistic faith." He was against political emancipation of the Jews, though he did not reject their equalization in purely civil rights, in order that the Jewish people could be provided complete freedom in daily life, self-management, development, enlightenment, commerce, and even allowing them to reside in all of Russia." In 1867 he wrote, that economically speaking "we should talk not about emancipation for Jews, but rather about the emancipation of Russians from Jews." He noted the blank indifference of the liberal press to the conditions of peasant's life and their needs. And now Aksakov explained the wave of pogroms in 1881 as a manifestation of the popular anger against "Jewish yoke over the Russian local people"; that's why during the pogroms, there was "an absence of theft," only the destruction of property and "a kind of simple-hearted conviction in the justness of their actions"; and he repeated, that it was worth putting the question "not about Jews enjoying equal rights with Christians, but about the equal rights of Christians with Jews, about abolishing factual inequality of the Russian population in the face of the Jews."[597]

On the other hand, an article by M.E. Saltykov-Shchedrin was full of indignation: "The history has never drawn on its pages a question more difficult, more devoid of humanity, and more tortuous, than the Jewish Question…There is not a more inhumane and mad legend than that coming out from the dark ravines of the distant past…carrying the mark of disgrace, alienation, and hatred…Whatever the Jew undertakes, he always remains stigmatized."[598] Shchedrin did not deny, "that a significant contingent of moneylenders and exploiters of various kinds are enlisted from the Jews," but he asked, can we really place blame on the whole Jewish tribe, on account of one type?[599]

---

[596] *EE* [JE], T 9, p. 381.
[597] I.S. Aksakov. *Sochineniya* [Essays]: V 7 T. Moscow, 1886–1887. T 3, p. 690, 693, 708, 716, 717, 719, 722.
[598] M.E. Saltykov-Shchedrin. *Iyul'skoe veyanie* [The July's Spirit]//Otechestvennie zapiski [Homeland Notes], 1882, No 8.
[599] *EE* [JE], T 16, p. 142.

Examining the whole discussion of that time, a present-day Jewish author writes: "the liberal, and conditionally speaking, progressive press was defending the thugs."[600] And the pre-revolutionary Jewish Encyclopedia comes to a similar conclusion: "Yet in the progressive circles, sympathies toward the woes of the Jewish people were not displayed sufficiently ...they looked at this catastrophe from the viewpoint of the aggressor, presenting him as destitute peasant, and completely ignoring the moral sufferings and material situation of the mobbed Jewish people." And even the radical *Patriotic Notes* evaluated it thus: the people rose up against the Jews because "they took upon themselves the role of pioneers of Capitalism, because they live according to the new *truth* and confidently draw their own comfortable prosperity from that new source at the expense of the surrounding community," and therefore, "it was necessary that 'the people are protected from the Jew, and the Jew from the people', and for this the condition of the peasant needs to be improved."[601]

In *A Letter from a Christian on the Jewish Question*, published in the Jewish magazine *Rassvet*, D. Mordovtsev, a writer sympathetic to the Jews, pessimistically urged the Jews "to emigrate to Palestine and America, seeing only in this a solution to the Jewish Question in Russia."[602]

Jewish social-political journalism and the memoirs of this period expressed grievance because the printed publications *against* the Jews, both from the right and from the revolutionary left, followed immediately after the pogroms. Soon (and all the more energetically because of the pogroms) the government would strengthen restrictive measures *against* the Jews. It is necessary to take note of and understand this insult.

It is necessary to thoroughly examine the position of the government. The general solutions to the problem were being sought in discussions in government and administrative spheres. In a report to His Majesty, N.P. Ignatiev, the new Minister of Internal Affairs, outlined the scope of the problem for the entire previous reign: "Recognizing the harm to the Christian population from the Jewish economic activity, their tribal exclusivity and religious fanaticism, in the last 20 years the government has tried to blend the Jews with the rest of the population using a whole row of initiatives, and has almost made the Jews equal in rights with the native inhabitants." However, the present anti-Jewish movement "incontrovertibly proves, that despite all the efforts of the government, the relations between the Jews and the native population of these regions

---

[600] Sh. Markish. *O evreyskoy nenavisti k Rossii* [About Jewish Hatred toward Russia]//"22," 1984, No38, p. 216.
[601] *EE* [JE], T 2, p. 741.
[602] *KEE* [SJE], T 5, p. 463.

remain abnormal as in the past," because of the economic issues: after the easing of civil restrictions, the Jews have not only seized commerce and trade, but they have acquired significant landed property. "Moreover, because of their cohesion and solidarity, they have, with few exceptions, directed all their efforts not toward the increase of the productive strength of the state, but primarily toward the exploitation of the poorest classes of the surrounding population." And now, after we have crushed the disorders and defended the Jews from violence, "it seems 'just and urgent to adopt no less energetic measures for the elimination of these abnormal conditions...between the native inhabitants and the Jews, and to protect the population from that harmful activity of the Jews.'"[603]

And in accordance with that, in November 1881, the governmental commissions, comprised of "representatives of all social strata and groups (including Jewish), were established in 15 guberniyas of the Jewish Pale of Settlement, and also in Kharkov Guberniya.[604] The commissions ought to examine the Jewish Question and propose their ideas on its resolution."[605] It was expected that the commissions will provide answers on many factual questions, such as: "In general, which aspects of Jewish economic activity are most harmful for the way of life of the native population in the region?" Which difficulties hinder the enforcement of laws regulating the purchase and rental of land, trade in spirits, and usury by Jews? Which changes are necessary to eliminate evasion of these laws by Jews? "Which legislative and administrative measures in general are necessary to negate the harmful influence of the Jews"

in various kinds of economic activity?[606] The liberal "Palenskaya" inter-ministerial "High Commission" established two years later for the revision of laws on the Jews, noted that "the harm from the Jews, their bad qualities, and traits" were somewhat recognized a priori in the program that was given to the provincial commissions.[607]

Yet many administrators in those commissions were pretty much liberal as they were brought up in the stormy epoch of Tsar Alexander II's reforms, and moreover, public delegates participated also. And Ignatiev's ministry received rather inconsistent answers. Several commissions were in favor of abolishing the Jewish Pale of Settlement. "Individual members [of the commissions] — and they were not few" — declared that the only just solution to the Jewish Question was the general repeal of all restrictions.[608]

---

[603] *Yu. Gessen**, T 2, p. 220-221.
[604] *EE* [JE], T 1, p. 827.
[605] *Yu. Gessen*, T 2, p. 221.
[606] *EE* [JE], T 1, p. 827.
[607] *Yu. Gessen*, T 2, p. 221.
[608] *EE* [JE], T 1, p. 827-828.

On the other hand, the Vilnius Commission stated that "because of mistakenly understood notion of universal human equality wrongly applied to Judaism to the detriment of the native people, the Jews managed to "seize economic supremacy"; that the Jewish law permits [them] "to profit from any weakness and gullibility of gentile." "Let the Jews renounce their seclusion and isolation, let them reveal the secrets of their social organization allowing light where only darkness appeared to outsiders; and only then can one think about opening new spheres of activity to the Jews, without fear that Jews wish to use the benefits of the nation, [while] not being members of the nation, and not taking upon themselves a share of the national burden."[609]

"Regarding residence in the villages and hamlets, the commissions found it necessary to restrict the rights of the Jews": to forbid them to live there altogether or to make it conditional upon the agreement of the village communities. Some commissions recommended completely depriving the Jews of the right to possess real estate outside of the cities and small towns, and others proposed establishing restrictions. The commissions showed the most unanimity in prohibiting any Jewish monopoly on alcohol sales in villages. The Ministry gathered the opinions of the governors, and "with rare exceptions, comments from the regional authorities were not favorable to the Jews": to protect the Christian population "from so haughty a tribe as the Jews"; "one can never expect the Jewish tribe to dedicate its talents…to the benefit of the homeland"; "Talmudic morals do not place any obstacles before the Jews if it is a question of making money at the expense of someone outside of the tribe."

Yet the Kharkov General-Governor did not consider it possible to take restrictive measures against the whole Jewish population, "without distinguishing the lawful from the guilty"; he proposed to "expand the right of movement for Jews and spread enlightenment among them."[610]

That same autumn, by Ignatiev's initiative, a special "Committee on the Jews" was established (the ninth by count already, with three permanent members, two of them professors), with the task of analyzing the materials of the provincial commissions and in order to draft a legislative bill.[611] (The previous "Commission for the Organization of the Life of the Jews" – that is, the eighth committee on Jews, which existed since 1872 – was soon abolished, "due to mismatch between its purpose and the present state of the Jewish Question.") The new Committee proceeded with the conviction that the goal of integrating the Jews with the rest of the population, toward

---

[609] Ibid*. T 2, p. 742-743.
[610] Ibid*, T 1, p. 827-828.
[611] Ibid, T 9, p. 690-691.

which the government had striven for the last 25 years, had turned out to be unattainable.[612] Therefore, "the difficulty of resolving the complicated Jewish Question compels [us] to turn for the instruction to the old times, when various novelties did not yet penetrate neither ours, nor foreign legislations, and did not bring with them the regrettable consequences, which usually appear upon adoption of new things that are contrary to the national spirit of the country."

From time immemorial the Jews were considered aliens, and should be considered as such.[613] Gessen comments: "the reactionary could not go further". And if you were so concerned about the national foundations then why you didn't worry about genuine emancipation of the peasantry during the past 20 years? And it was also true that Tsar Alexander II's emancipation of the peasants proceeded in a confused, unwholesome and corrupt environment.

However: "in government circles there were still people, who did not consider it possible, in general, to change the policy of the preceding reign"[614] — and they were in important posts and strong. And some ministers opposed Ignatiev's proposals. Seeing resistance, he divided the proposed measures into *fundamental* (for which passing in the regular way required moving through the government and the State Council) and *provisional*, which could by law be adopted through an accelerated and simplified process. "To convince the rural population that the government protects them from the exploitation by Jews, the permanent residence of Jews outside of their towns and shtetls (and the "government was powerless to protect them from pogroms in the scattered villages"), and buying and renting real estate there, and also trading in spirits was prohibited. And regarding the Jews already living there: it granted to the rural communities the right "to evict the Jews from the villages, based upon a verdict of the village meeting." But other ministers — particularly the Minister of Finance, N. Kh. Bunge, and the Minister of Justice, D.N. Nabokov, did not let Ignatiev implement these measures: they rejected the bill, claiming that it was impossible to adopt such extensive prohibitive measures, "without debating them within the usual legislative process."[615] So much for the boundless and malicious arbitrariness of the Russian autocracy.

Ignatiev's fundamental measures did not pass, and the provisional ones passed only in a greatly truncated form. Rejected were the provisions to

---

[612] *EE* [JE], T 2, p. 744.
[613] *Yu. Gessen**, T 2, p. 222.
[614] *EE* [JE] T 2, p. 744.
[615] Ibid. T 1, p. 829-830.

evict the Jews already living in the villages, to forbid their trade in alcohol or their renting and buying land in villages. And only because of the fear that the pogroms might happen again around Easter of 1882, a temporary measure (until passing of comprehensive legislation about the Jews) was passed which prohibited the Jews *again, henceforth* to take residence and enter into ownership, or make use of real estate property outside of their towns and shtetls (that is, in the villages), and also forbade them "to trade on Sundays and Christian holidays."[616] Concerning the Jewish ownership of local real estate, the government acted "to suspend temporarily the completion of sales and purchase agreements and loans in the name of the Jews...the notarization...of real estate rental agreements ... and the proxy management and disposal of property by them".[617] This mere relic of Ignatiev's proposed measures was approved on 3 May 1882, under title of *Temporary Regulations* (known as the *May Regulations*). And Ignatiev himself went into retirement after a month and his "Committee on the Jews" ceased its brief existence, and a new Minister of Internal Affairs, Count D.A. Tolstoy, issued a stern directive against possible new pogroms, placing full responsibility on the provincial authorities for the timely prevention of disorders.[618]

Thus, according to the *Temporary Regulations* of 1882, the Jews who had settled in rural regions before the 3rd of May, were not evicted; their economic activity there was essentially unrestricted. Moreover, these regulations only applied to the "guberniyas of permanent Jewish settlement," not to the guberniyas of the Russian interior. And these restrictions did not extend to doctors, attorneys, and engineers — i.e., individuals with "the right of universal residence according to educational requirement." These restrictions also did not affect any "existing Jewish colonies engaged in agriculture"; and there was still a considerable (and later growing) list of rural settlements, according to which, "in exception" to the *Temporary Regulations,* Jews were permitted to settle.[619]

After issuance of the "Regulations," inquiries began flowing from the regions and Senate explanations were issued in response. For example: that "journeys through rural regions, temporary stops and even temporary stays of individuals without the right of permanent residence are not prohibited by the Law of 3 May 1882"; that "only the rent of real estates and agrarian lands is prohibited, while rent of all other types of real estate property, such as distillation plants, ... buildings for trade and industry, and living quarters is not prohibited." Also, "the Senate deems permissible the notarization of

---

[616] *Yu. Gessen,* T 2, p. 226-227; *KEE* [SJE], T 7, p. 341.
[617] *EE* [JE], T 5, p. 815-817.
[618] Ibid. T 12, p. 616.
[619] *EE** [JE], T 5, p 815-817.

lumbering agreements with the Jews, even if the clearing of a forest was scheduled for a prolonged period, and even if the buyer of the forest was allowed use of the underbrush land"; and finally, that violations of the Law of 3rd May would not be subjected to criminal prosecution.[620]

It is necessary to recognize these Senate clarifications as mitigating, and in many respects, good-natured; "in the 1880s the Senate wrestled with ... the arbitrary interpretation of the laws." [621] However, the regulations forbidding the Jews to settle "outside the towns and shtetls" and/or to own "real estate"... "extremely restricted alcohol distillation business by Jews," as "Jewish participation in distillation before the 3rd May Regulations was very significant."[622]

It was exactly this measure to restrict the Jews in the rural wine trade (first proposed as early as 1804) that stirred universal indignation at the "extraordinary severity" "of the *May Regulations*," even though it was only implemented, and incompletely at that, in 1882. The government stood before a difficult choice: to expand the wine industry in the face of peasant proneness [to drunkenness] and thus to deepen the peasant poverty, or to restrict the free growth of this trade by letting the Jews already living in the villages to remain while stopping others from coming. And that choice – restriction – was deemed cruel.

Yet how many Jews lived in rural regions in 1882? We have already come across post-revolutionary estimates from the state archives: one *third* of the entire Jewish population of "the Pale" lived in villages, another third lived in shtetls, 29% lived in mid-size cities, and 5% in the major cities.[623] So the *Regulations* now prevented the "village" third from further growth?

Today these *May Regulations* are portrayed as a decisive and irrevocably repressive boundary of Russian history. A Jewish author writes: this was the first push toward emigration! — first "internal" migration, then massive overseas migration.[624] —The first cause of Jewish emigration was the "Ignatiev *Temporary Regulations*, which violently threw around one

---

[620] Ibid. p. 816–819.
[621] *KEE* [SJE], T 7, p. 342.
[622] *EE* [JE], T 5, p. 610-611.
[623] *Yu. Larin. Evrei i antisemitizm v SSSR* [Jews and Anti-Semitism in the USSR]. M.; L.: GIZ, 1929, p. 49-50.
[624] I.M. Dizhur. Evrei v ekonomicheskoy zhizni Rossii *[Jews in the Economic Life of Russia]* // *[Sankt-Peterburg.]* Kniga o russkom evreystve: Ot 1860-kh godov do Revolyutsii 1917 g. [The Book of Russian Jewry: from the 1860s to the Revolution of 1917]. (*dalee – KRE-1*) [henceforth — KRE-1]. New York: *Soyuz Russkikh Evreyev* [Union of Russian Jews], 1960, p. 160.

million Jews out of the hamlets and villages, and into the towns and shtetls of the Jewish Pale."[625]

Wait a second, how did they *throw the Jews out* and an entire million at that? Didn't they apparently only *prevent* new arrivals? No, no! It was already picked up and sent rolling: that from 1882 the Jews were not only *forbidden to live in the villages everywhere,* but in all the *cities,* too, except in the 13 guberniyas; that they *were moved back* to the shtetls of "the Pale" — that is why the mass emigration of Jews from Russia began![626]

Well, set the record straight. The first time the idea about Jewish emigration from Russia to America voiced was as early as in 1869 at the Conference of the Alliance (of the World Jewish Union) — with the thought that the first who settled there with the help of the Alliance and local Jews "would become a magnet for their Russian co-religionists."[627] Moreover, "the beginning of the emigration [of Jews from Russia] dates back to the mid-19th Century and gains significant momentum... after the pogroms of 1881. But only since the mid-1890s does emigration become a major phenomenon of Jewish economic life, assuming a massive scale"[628] — note that it says *economic* life, not political life.

From a global viewpoint Jewish immigration into the United States in the 19th Century was part of an enormous century-long and worldwide historical process. There were three successive waves of Jewish emigration to America: first the Spanish-Portuguese (Sephardic) wave, then the German wave (from Germany and Austria-Hungary), and only then from Eastern Europe and Russia (Ashkenazik).[629] For reasons not addressed here, a major historical movement of Jewish emigration to the U.S. took place in the 19th Century, and not only from Russia. In light of the very lengthy Jewish history, it is difficult to overestimate the significance of this emigration.

And from the Russian Empire "a river of Jewish emigration went from all the guberniyas that made up the Jewish Pale of Settlement; but Poland, Lithuania, and Byelorussia gave the greatest number of emigrants";[630] meaning they did not come from Ukraine, which was just experiencing the pogroms. The reason for this was this emigration was the same throughout

---

[625] *I.M. Dizhur. Itogi i perspektivi evreyskoy emigratsii* [Outcomes and Perspectives of Jewish Emigration] // EM-2, p. 34.
[626] *Yu. Larin.* The Jews and Anti-Semitism in the USSR, p. 52–53.
[627] *EE* [JE] T 1, p. 947.
[628] Ibid. T 16, p. 264.
[629] *M. Osherovich. Russkie evrei v Soedinenikh Shtatakh Ameriki* [Russian Jews in the United Statees of America] // KRE-1, p. 287.
[630] *Ya. D. Leshchinskiy. Evreyskoe naselenie Rossii i evreyskii trud.* The Jewish Population of Russia and Jewish Trouble]//KRE-1, p. 190.

— overcrowding, which created inter-Jewish economic competition. Moreover, relying on Russian state statistics, V. Tel'nikov turns our attention to the last two decades of the 19th Century; just after the pogroms of 1881–1882, comparing the resettlement of Jews from the Western Krai, where there were no pogroms, to the Southwest, where they were. The latter was numerically not less and was possibly more than the Jewish departure out of Russia.[631] In addition, in 1880, according to official data, 34,000 Jews lived in the internal guberniyas, while seventeen years later (according to the census of 1897) there were already 315,000 — a ninefold increase.[632]

Of course, the pogroms of 1881–1882 caused a shock but was it really a shock for the whole of Ukraine? For example, Sliozberg writes: "The 1881 pogroms did not alarm the Jews in Poltava, and soon they forgot about them."

In the 1880s in Poltava "the Jewish youth did not know about the existence of the Jewish Question, and in general, did not feel isolated from the Russian youth." [633] The pogroms of 1881 – 82, in their complete suddenness, could have seemed unrepeatable, and the unchanging Jewish economic pull was prevailing: go settle hither, where less Jews live. But undoubtedly and inarguably, a decisive turn of progressive and educated Jewry away from the hopes of a complete integration with the nation of "Russia" and the Russian population began in 1881. G. Aronson even concluded hastily, that "the 1871 Odessa Pogrom" "shattered the illusions of assimilation."[634] No, it wasn't that way yet! But if, for example, we follow the biographies of prominent and educated Russian Jews, then around 1881–1882 we will note in many of them a drastic change in their attitudes toward Russia and about possibilities of complete assimilation. By then it was already clear and not contested that the pogrom wave was indubitably spontaneous without any evidence for the complicity of the authorities. On the contrary, the involvement of the revolutionary *narodniks* was proven. However, the Jews did not forgive the Russian Government for these pogroms — and never have since.

---

[631] *Sbornik materialov ob ekonomicheskom polozheniya evreyev v Rossii* [An Anthology of Materials about the Economic Condition of the Jews in Russia]. Sankt-Peterburg.: *Evreyskoe Kolonizatsionnoe Obshchestvo* [Jewish Colonization Society], 1904. T 1. p. xxxiii-xxxv, xiv-xivi.
[632] *Yu. Gessen*, T 2, p. 210; *EE* [JE], T 11, p. 534-539.
[633] G.B. Sliozberg. Dela minuvshikh dney… *T 1, p. 98, 105.*
[634] *G.Ya. Aronson. V bor'be za grazhdanskie i natsional'nie prava: Obshchestvennie techeniya v russkom evreystve* [In the Struggle for the Civil and National Rights: Social Currents in Russian Jewry] // KRE-1, p. 208.

And although the pogroms originated mainly with the Ukrainian population, the Russians have not been forgiven and the pogroms have always been tied with the name of Russia.

"The pogroms of the 1880s ... sobered many [of the advocates] of assimilation" (but not all: the idea of assimilation still remained alive). And here, other Jewish publicists moved to the other extreme: in general it was impossible for Jews to live among other peoples, [for] they will always be looked upon as alien. And the "Palestinian Movement... began...'to grow quickly.'"[635]

It was under the influence of the 1881 pogroms that the Odessa doctor, Lev Pinsker, published his brochure, *Auto-Emancipation. The Appeal of a Russian Jew to his Fellow Tribesmen* (in Berlin in 1882, and anonymously). "It made a huge impression on Russian and West European Jewry." It was an appeal about the ineradicable foreignness of Jews in eyes of surrounding peoples.[636] We will discuss this further in Chapter 7. P. Aksel'rod claims that it was then that radical Jewish youths discovered that Russian society would not accept them as their own and thus they began to depart from the revolutionary movement. However, this assertion appears to be too far-fetched. In the revolutionary circles, except the Narodnaya Vol'ya, they did always thnik of the Jews as their own.

However, despite the cooling of attitudes of the Jewish intelligentsia toward assimilation, the government, as a result of inertia from Alexander II's reign, for a while maintained a sympathetic attitude toward the Jewish problem and did not yet fully replace it by a harshly-restrictive approach. After the year-long ministerial activities of Count Ignatiev, who experienced such persistent opposition on the Jewish Question from liberal forces in the upper governmental spheres, an Imperial "High Commission for Revision of the Active Laws about the Jews in the Empire" was established in the beginning of 1883 – or as it was named for its chairman, Count Palen – "The Palenskaya Commission" (so that by then, it became the tenth such 'Jewish Committee'). It consisted of fifteen to twenty individuals from the upper administration, members of ministerial councils, department directors (some were members of great families, such as Bestuzhev-Ryumin, Golytsin, and Speranskiy), and it also included seven "Jewish experts" — influential financiers, including Baron Goratsiy Gintsburg and Samuil Polyakov, and prominent public figures, such as Ya. Gal'pern, physiologist and publicist N. Bakst ("it is highly likely that the favorable attitude of the majority of the members of the Commission

---

[635] *Gershon Svet. Russkie evrei v sionizme i v stroitel'stve Palestini i Izrailya* [Russian Jews in Zionism and in the Building of Palestine and Israel] // KRE-1, p. 241-242.
[636] *EE* [JE], T 12, p. 526.

toward resolution of the Jewish Question was caused, to certain degree, by the influence" of Bakst), and Rabbi A. Drabkin.[637] In large part, it was these Jewish experts who prepared the materials for the Commission's consideration.

The majority of the Palenskaya Commission expressed the conviction, that "the final goal of legislation concerning the Jews [should be] nothing other than its abolition," that "there is only one outcome and only one path: the path of liberation and unification of the Jews with the whole population, under the protection of the same laws."[638] (Indeed, rarely in Russian legislation did such complicated and contradictory laws pile up as the laws about Jews that accumulated over the decades: 626 statutes by 1885! And they were still added later and in the Senate they constantly researched and interpreted their wording…). And even if the Jews did not perform their duties as citizens in equal measure with others, nevertheless it was impossible to "deprive the Jew of those fundamentals, on which his existence was based — his equal rights as a subject." Agreeing "that several aspects of internal Jewish life require reforming and that certain Jewish activities constituted exploitation of the surrounding population," the majority of the Commission condemned the system of "repressive and exclusionary measures." The Commission set as the legislative goal "to equalize the rights of Jews, with those of all other subjects," although it recommended "the utmost caution and gradualness" with this.[639]

Practically, however, the Commission only succeeded in carrying out a partial mitigation of the restrictive laws. Its greatest efforts were directed of the *Temporary Regulations* of 1882, particularly in regard to the renting of land by Jews. The Commission made the argument as if in the defense of the landowners, not the Jews: prohibiting Jews to rent manorial lands not only impedes the development of agriculture, but also leads to a situation when certain types of agriculture remain in complete idleness in the Western Krai — to the loss of the landowners as there is nobody to whom they could lease them. However, the Minister of Interior Affairs, D.A. Tolstoy, agreed with the minority of the Commission: the prohibition against new land-leasing transactions would not be repealed.[640]

The Palenskaya Commission lasted for five years, until 1888, and in its work the liberal majority always clashed with the conservative minority. From the beginning, "Count Tolstoy certainly had no intention to revise the laws to increase the repressive measures," and the 5-year existence of the

---

[637] Ibid. T 5, p. 862, T 3, p. 700.
[638] Ibid*, T 1, p. 832-833.
[639] *Yu. Gessen**, T2, p. 227-228.
[640] *EE* [JE], T 3, p. 85.

Palenskaya Commission confirms this. At that moment "His Majesty [also] did not wish to influence the decisions of his government on the matter of the increase of repressions against Jews." Ascending to the throne at such a dramatic moment, Alexander III did not hasten either to replace liberal officials, nor to choose a harsh political course: for long time he carefully examined things. "In the course of the entire reign of Alexander III, the question about a general revision of the legislation about the Jews remained open."[641] But by 1886-87, His Majesty's view already leaned toward hardening of the partial restrictions on the Jews and so the work of the Commission did not produce any visible result.

One of the first motivations for stricter control or more constraint on the Jews than during his father's reign was the constant shortfall of Jewish conscripts for military service; it was particularly noticeable when compared to conscription of Christians. According to the Charter of 1874, which abolished recruiting, compulsory military service was now laid on all citizens, without any difference in social standing, but with the stipulation that those unfit for service would be replaced: Christians with Christians, and Jews with Jews. In the case of Jews there were difficulties in implementation of that rule as there were both straightforward emigration of conscripts and their evasion which all benefited from great confusion and negligence in the official records on Jewish population, in the keeping of vital statistics, in the reliability of information about the family situation and exact place of residence of conscripts. (The tradition of all these uncertainties stretched back to the times of the *Qahals* (a theocratic organizational structure that originated in ancient Israelite society), and was consciously maintained for easing the tax burden.) "In 1883 and 1884, there were many occasions when Jewish recruits, contrary to the law, were arrested simply upon suspicion that they might disappear."[642] (This method was first applied to Christian recruits, but sporadically). In some places they began to demand photographs from the Jewish recruits — a very unusual requirement for that time. And in 1886 a "highly constraining" law was issued, "about several measures for providing for regular fulfillment of military conscription by Jews," which established a "300-ruble fine from the relatives of each Jew who evaded military call-up."[643] "From 1887 they stopped allowing Jews to apply for the examination for officer rank [educated soldiers had privileges in choosing military specialty in the course of service]."[644] (During the reign

---

[641] Ibid. T 1, p. 832-834.
[642] Ibid, T 3, p. 167.
[643] Ibid. T 1, p. 836.
[644] Ibid. T 3, p. 167.

of Alexander II, the Jews could serve in the officers' ranks.) But officer positions in military medicine always remained open to Jews.

Yet if we consider that in the same period up to 20 million other "aliens" of the Empire were completely freed from compulsory military service, then wouldn't it be better to free the Jews of it altogether, thus offsetting their other constraints with such a privilege? ... Or was it the legacy of the idea of Nicholas I continuing here — to graft the Jews into Russian society through military service? To occupy the idle?"

At the same time, Jews on the whole flocked into institutions of learning. From 1876 to 1883, the number of Jews in gymnasiums and gymnasium preparatory schools almost doubled, and from 1878 to 1886 – for an 8-year period – the number of Jewish students in the universities increased six times and reached 14.5%.[645] By the end of the reign of Alexander II they were receiving alarming complaints from the regional authorities about this. Thus, in 1878 the Governor of the Minsk Guberniya reported, "that being wealthier, the Jews can bring up their children better than the Russians; that the material condition of the Jewish pupils is better than that of Christians, and therefore in order that the Jewish element does not overwhelm the remaining population, it is necessary to introduce a quota system for the admission of Jews into secondary schools."[646] Next, after disturbances in several southern gymnasiums in 1880, the Trustee of the Odessa School District publicly came out with a similar idea. And in 1883 and 1885 two successive Novorossiysk (Odessa) General-Governors stated that an "over-filling of learning institutions with Jews" was taking place there, and it is either necessary "to limit the number of Jews in the gymnasiums and gymnasium preparatory schools" to 15% "of the general number of pupils," or "to a fairer norm, equal to the proportion of the Jewish population to the whole."[647] (By 1881, Jews made up 75% of the general number of pupils in several gymnasiums of the Odessa District.[648]) In 1886, a report was made by the Governor of Kharkov Guberniya, "complaining about the influx of Jews to the common schools."[649] In all these instances, the ministers did not deem it possible to adopt general restrictive solutions, and only directed the reports for consideration to the Palenskaya Commission, where they did not receive support.

From the 1870s students become primary participants in the revolutionary excitement. After the assassination of Alexander II, the general intention to put down the revolutionary movement could not avoid student

---

[645] *Yu. Gessen*, T 2, p. 230.
[646] *Yu. Gessen*, T 2, p. 229.
[647] *EE* [JE], T 13, p. 51; T 1, p. 834–835.
[648] *Yu. Gessen*, T 2, p. 231.
[649] *EE* [JE], T 1, p. 835.

"revolutionary nests" (and the senior classes of the gymnasiums were already supplying them). Within the government there arose the alarming connection that together with the increase of Jews among the students, the participation of students in the revolutionary movement noticeably increased. Among the higher institutions of learning, the Medical-Surgical Academy (later the Military-Medical Academy) was particularly revolutionized. Jews were very eager to enter it and the names of Jewish students of this academy began already appearing in the court trials of the 1870s.

And so the first special restrictive measure of 1882 restricted Jewish admissions to the Military-Medical Academy to an upper limit of 5%. In 1883, a similar order followed with respect to the Mining Institute; and in 1884 a similar quota was established at the Institute of Communications.[650] In 1885, the admission of Jews to the Kharkov Technological Institute was limited to 10%, and in 1886 their admission to the Kharkov Veterinary Institute was completely discontinued, since "the city of Kharkov was always a center of political agitation, and the residence of Jews there in more or less significant numbers is generally undesirable and even dangerous." [651] Thus, they thought to weaken the crescendo of revolutionary waves.

---

[650] Ibid. p. 834.
[651] Ibid*, T 13, p. 51.

Chapter 6

In the Russian Revolutionary Movement

In the Russia of the 60–70s of the nineteenth century, when reforms moved rapidly, there were no economic or social motives for a far-reaching revolutionary movement. Yet it was indeed under Alexander II, from the beginning of his reforming work, that this movement was born, as the prematurely-ripened fruit of ideology: in 1861 there were student demonstrations in Saint Petersburg; in 1862, violent fires of criminal origin in Saint Petersburg as well, and the sanguinary proclamation of Young Russia [652] (*Molodaia Rossiia*); in 1866, Karakozov's [653] gunshot, the prodromes of the terrorist era, half a century in advance.

And it was also under Alexander II, when the restrictions on the rights of the Jews were so relaxed, that Jewish names appeared among the revolutionaries. Neither in the circles of Stankyevich[654], Herzen[655] and Ogariov[656] nor in that of Petrachevsky, there had been only one Jew. (We do not speak here of Poland.) But at the student demonstrations of 1861

---

[652] *Molodaia Rossiia*: Revolutionary proclamation of the Russian Jacobins dated May 1862, written by P. G. Zaychnevsky.

[653] Dmitri Vladimirovich Karakozov (1840 1866) fired a shot at Alexander II on 4/16 April 1866: the first in a long series of attacks. Condemned to death and executed.

[654] Nikolai Vladimirovich Stankevich (1813 1840): philosopher and poet, humanist. Founded in 1831 the "Stankevich circle" where great intellectuals such as Bielinsky, Aksakov, Granovsky, Katkov, etc. meet. Emigrated in 1837.

[655] Alexander Ivanovich Herzen (1812-1870): writer, philosopher and "Occidentalist" Russian revolutionary. Spent six years in exile. Emigrated in 1847 and founded the first anti-war newspaper published abroad, *Kolokol* (The Bell). Author of Memoirs on his time, *Past and Thoughts*.

[656] Nikolai Platonovich Ogariov (1813 1877): poet, Russian revolutionary publicist. Friend and companion in arms of Herzen. Emigrated in 1856. Participated in the foundation of Land and Liberty.

Mikhoels, Outine[657] and Guen will participate. And we shall find Outine in the circle of Nechayev[658].

The participation of the Jews in the Russian revolutionary movement must get our attention; indeed, radical revolutionary action became a more and more widespread form of activity among Jewish youth. The Jewish revolutionary movement is a qualitatively important component of the Russian revolutionary movement in general. As for the ratio of Jewish and Russian revolutionaries over the years, it surprises us. Of course, if in the following pages we speak mainly of Jews, this in no way implies that there was not a large number of influential revolutionaries among the Russians: our focus is warranted by the subject of our study.

In fact, until the early 70s, only a very small number of Jews had joined the revolutionary movement, and in secondary roles at that. (In part, no doubt, because there were still very few Jews among the students.) One learns, for example, that Leon Deutsch at the age of ten was outraged about Karakozov's gunshot because he felt "patriotic". Similarly, few Jews adhered to the Russian nihilism of the 60s that, nevertheless, by their rationalism, they assimilated easily. "Nihilism has played an even more beneficial role in Jewish student youth than in Christian youth."[659]

However, as early as the early 70s, the circle of young Jews of the rabbinical school in Vilnius began to play an important role. (Among them, V. Yokhelson, whom we mention later, and the well-known terrorist A. Zundelevich—both brilliant pupils, destined to be excellent rabbis, A. Liebermann, future editor of *La Pravda* of Vienna, and Anna Einstein, Maxim Romm, Finkelstein.) This circle was influential because it was in close contact with the "smugglers"[660] and permitted clandestine literature, as well as illegal immigrants themselves, to cross the border.[661]

---

[657] Nikolai Isaakovich Outine (1841 1883): revolutionary, leading member of Earth and Freedom. Condemned to death *in absentia*. Emigrated in 1863, returned to Russia in 1878.

[658] Sergei Gennadyevich Nechayev (1847 1882): revolutionary and Russian conspirator, author of the famous *Catechism of the Revolutionary*. Organised in 1869 the murder of the student Ivanov, supposedly a traitor to the Cause (which inspired Dostoevsky's *The Demons*). Leaves abroad. Delivered by Switzerland to Russia, sentenced to twenty years of imprisonment. Dies in prison.

[659] L. Deutsch, King evreiev v rousskom revolioutsionnom dvijenii (The role of the Jews in the Russian revolutionary movement), vol. 1, 2nd ed., M.L., GIZ, 1925, pp. 20 22.

[660] People who succeed in passing, illegally through the borders, revolutionary writings banned in Russia.

[661] D. Schub, Evro vrousskoï revolyutsii (The Jews in the Russian Revolution). JW-2; Hessen, t. 2, p. 213.

It was in 1868, after high school, that Mark Natanson entered the Academy of Medicine and Surgery (which would become the Academy of Military Medicine). He will be an organiser and a leading figure in the revolutionary movement. Soon, with the young student Olga Schleisner, his future wife (whom Tikhomirov calls "the second Sophia Perovskaya", although at the time she was rather the first **), he laid the foundations of a system of so-called "pedagogical" circles, that is to say of propaganda ("*preparatory*, cultural and revolutionary work with intellectual youth"[662]) in several large cities. (These circles were wrongly dubbed "Tchaikovskyists", named after one of their less influential members, N.V. Tchaikovsky.) Natanson distinguished himself very quickly and resolutely from the circle of Nechayev (and he did not hesitate, subsequently, to present his views to the examining magistrate). In 1872 he went to Zurich with Pierre Lavrov, the principal representative of the "current of pacific propaganda"[663], which rejected the rebellion; Natanson wanted to establish a permanent revolutionary organ there. In the same year he was sent to Shenkursk in close exile and, through the intercession of his father-in-law, the father of Olga Schleiser, he was transferred to Voronezh, then Finland, and finally released to Saint Petersburg. He found there nothing but discouragement, dilapidation, inertia. He endeavoured to visit the disunited groups, to connect them, to weld them, and thus founded the first Land and Freedom organisation and spending hundreds of thousands of Rubles.

Among the principal organisers of Russian populism, Natanson is the most eminent revolutionary. It was in his wake that the famous Leon Deutsch appeared; As for the ironclad populist Alexander Mikhailov, he was a disciple of "Mark the Wise". Natanson knew many revolutionaries personally. Neither an orator nor a writer, he was a born organiser, endowed with an astonishing quality: he did not regard opinions and ideology, he did not enter into any theoretical discussions with anyone, he was in accord with all tendencies (with the exception of the extremist positions of Tkachev, Lenin's predecessor), placed each and everyone where they could be useful. In those years when Bakunin supporters and Lavrov supporters were irreconcilable, Natanson proposed to put an end to "discussions about the music of the future" and to focus instead on the real needs of the cause. It was he who, in the summer of 1876, organised the sensational escape of Piotr Kropotkin * on the "Barbarian", that half-blood who would often be spoken of. In December of the same year, he conceived and set up the first public meeting in front of the Cathedral of Our Lady of

---

[662] *O. V. Aptekman*, Dvc doroguiie teni (Two Dear Shadows); Byloie: newspaper Posviaschionnyi istorii osvoboditclnogo dvijeniia (Past: a review of the history of the liberation movement), M. 1921, No. 16, p. 9.

[663] Piotr Lavrovich Lavrov (1823-1900): famous theorist of populism. Emigrated in 1870. Published the magazine *Vperiod* (Forward).

Kazan, at the end of the Mass, on the day of Saint Nicholas: all the revolutionaries gathered there and for the first time, the red flag of Land and Liberty was displayed. Natanson was arrested in 1877, sentenced to three years' detention, then relegated to Yakutia and dismissed from revolutionary action until 1890.[664]

There were a number of Jews in the circle of "Tchaikovskyists" in Saint Petersburg as well as in its branches in Moscow, Kiev, Odessa. (In Kiev, notably, P.B. Axelrod, whom we have already mentioned, the future Danish publisher and diplomat Grigori Gurevitch, future teachers Semion Lourie and Leiser Lœwenthal, his brother Nahman Lœwenthal, and the two Kaminer sisters.) As for the first Nihilist circle of Leon Deutsch in Kiev, it was "constituted exclusively of young Jewish students"[665]. After the demonstration in front of the Cathedral of Our Lady of Kazan, three Jews were tried, but not Natanson himself. At the trial of the "fifty"[666] which took place in the summer of 1877 in Moscow, several Jews were charged for spreading propaganda among factory workers. At the trial of the "one hundred and ninety-three[667]", there were thirteen Jews accused. Among the early populists, we can also cite Lossif Aptekman and Alexander Khotinsky, who were highly influential.[668]

Natanson's idea was that revolutionaries should involve the people (peasants) and be for them like lay spiritual guides. This "march to the people", which has become so famous since then, began in 1873 in the "dolgushinian" circle (Dolgushin, Dmokhovsky, Gamov, etc.) where no Jews were counted.

Later, the Jews also "went to the people." (The opposite also happened: in Odessa, P. Axelrod tried to attract Jeliabov[669] in a secret revolutionary organisation, but he refused: at the time, he was still a Kulturtrasser.) In the mid-70s, there were only about twenty of these "populists", all or almost all Lavrov and not Bakunin. (Only the most extreme were listening to calls for the insurrection of Bakunin, such as Deutsch, who, with the help of Stefanovitch, had raised the "Tchiguirine revolt[670]" by having pushed the

---

[664] *L. Deutsch*, pp. 97, 108, 164, 169, 174, 196.
[665] *Ibidem*, pp. 20, 130, 139.
[666] Held in March 1877, also said trial of "Muscovites", of which sixteen women.
[667] Held from October 1877 to February 1878: the most important political trial of Russia before 1917 (there were four thousand arrests among the populists of the "march to the people").
[668] *Ibidem*, pp. 33, 86 88, 185.
[669] Andrei Ivanovich Jeliabov (1851 1881): one of the founders of The Will of the People. Named the "Russian Robespierre". Organiser of the attacks against Alexander II. Executed in April 1881.
[670] In 1876-77. A group of revolutionary populists tried to raise a peasant insurrection in the district of Tchiguirine in Ukraine.

peasants into thinking that the tsar, surrounded by the enemy, had the people saying: turn back all these authorities, seize the land, and establish a regime of freedom!) It is interesting to note that almost no Jewish revolutionary launched into the revolution because of poverty, but most of them came from wealthy families. (In the three volumes of the *Russian Jewish Encyclopædia* there is no shortage of examples.) Only Paul Axelrod came from a very poor family, and, as we have already said, he had been sent by the *Kahal* to an institution solely to supplement the established quota. (From there, very naturally, he entered the gymnasium of Mogilev, then the high school of Nejine.) Came from wealthy merchant environments: Natanson, Deutsch, Aptekman (whose family had many Talmudists, doctors of the law—including all his uncles. Khotinsky, Gurevitch, Semion Lourie (whose family, even in this milieu, was considered "aristocratic", "little Simon was also destined to be a rabbi", but under the influence of the Enlightenment, his father, Gerts Lourie, had entrusted his son to college to become a professor); the first Italian Marxist, Anne Rosenstein (surrounded from childhood by governesses speaking several languages), the tragic figures of Moses Rabinovitch and Betty Kaminskaya, Felicie Cheftel, Joseph Guetsov, member of the Black Repartition, among many others. And then again Khrystyna (Khasia) Grinberg, "of a wealthy traditionalist merchant family", who in 1880 joined the Will of the People: her dwelling housed clandestine meetings, she was an accomplice in the attacks on Alexander II, and even became in 1882 the owner of a clandestine dynamite factory—then was condemned to deportation.[671] Neither did Fanny Moreinis come from a poor family; she also "participated in the preparations of attacks against the Emperor Alexander II", and spent two years in the prison of Kara.[672] Some came from families of rabbis, such as the future doctor of philosophy Lioubov Axelrod or Ida Axelrod. There were also families of the petty *bourgeoisie*, but wealthy enough to put their children through college, such as Aizik Aronchik (after college, he entered the School of Engineers of Saint Petersburg, which he soon abandoned to embark in revolutionary activities), Alexander Bibergal, Vladimir Bogoraz, Lazarus Goldenberg, the Lœwenthal brothers. Often, mention is made in the biographies of the aforementioned, of the Academy of Military Medicine, notably in those of Natanson, Bibergal, Isaac Pavlovsky (future counterrevolutionary[673]), M.

---

[671] RJE, t. 1, M. 1994, p. 377.
[672] RJE, t. 2, p. 309.
[673] Isaac Yakovlevich Pavlovsky, known as I. Yakovlev: journalist, one of the accused of the trial of the one hundred and ninety-three. Emigre, protected by Turgenev, became the correspondent in Paris of the *New Times*.

Rabinovitch, A. Khotinsky, Solomon Chudnovsky, Solomon Aronson (who happened to be involved in these circles), among others.[674]

Therefore it was not material need that drove them, but the strength of their convictions. It is not without interest to note that in these Jewish families the adhesion of young people to the revolution has rarely—or not at all—provoked a break between "fathers and sons", between parents and their children. "The 'fathers' did not go after the 'sons' very much, as was then the case in Christian families.

(Although Gesya Gelfman had to leave her family, a traditional Old Alliance family, in secret.) The "fathers" were often very far from opposing their children. Thus Guerz Lourie, as well as Isaac Kaminer, a doctor from Kiev: the whole family participated in the revolutionary movement of the 70s, and himself, as a "sympathiser..., rendered great service"[675] to the revolutionaries; three of them became the husbands of his daughters. (In the 1990s, he joined the Zionist movement and became the friend of Achad-Haam.[676])

Neither can we attribute anti-Russian motivations to these early Jewish revolutionaries, as some do in Russia today. In no way!

It all began with the same "nihilism" of the 60s. "Having initiated itself to Russian education and to 'goy' culture", having been imbued with Russian literature, "Jewish youth was quick to join the most progressive movement of the time", nihilism, and with an ease all the greater as it broke with the prescriptions of the past. Even "the most fanatical of the students of a *yeshiva*, immersed in the study of the Talmud," after "two or three minutes of conversation with a nihilist", broke with the "patriarchal mode of thought". "He [the Jew, even pious] had only barely grazed the surface of 'goy' culture, he had only carried out a breach in his vision of the traditional world, but already he was able to go far, very far, to the extremes." These young men were suddenly gripped by the great universal ideals, dreaming of seeing all men become brothers and all enjoying the same prosperity. The task was sublime: to liberate mankind from misery and slavery![677]

And there played the role of Russian literature. Pavel Axelrod, in high school, had as his teachers Turgenev, Bielinsky, Dobrolyubov (and later

---

[674] *Deutsch*, pp. 77-79, 85, 89,112, 140, 21X: V. I. Iohelsohn, Daliokoie prochloie (A distant Past); Byloie, 1918, No. 13, pp. 54 55.
[675] *Deutsch*, pp. 18, 149, 151, 154.
[676] Ahad-Haam (ie "One of his people"), says Asher Finzberg: Yiddish writer very involved in the Zionist movement.
[677] *Ibidem*, pp. 17-18.

Lassalle[678] who would make him turn to the revolution). Aptekman was fond of Chernyshevsky, Dobrolyubov, Pissarev (and also Bukle). Lazare Goldenberg, too, had read and re-read Dobrolyubov, Chernyshevsky, Pissarev, Nekrasov—and Rudin[679], who died on the barricades, was his hero. Solomon Tchudnovsky, a great admirer of Pissarev, wept when he died. The nihilism of Semion Lourie was born of Russian literature, he had fed on it. This was the case for a very large number—the list would be too long.

But today, a century later, there are few who remember the atmosphere of those years. No serious political action was taking place in the "street of the Jews", as it was then called, while, in the "Street of the Russians", populism was rising. It was quite simple: it was enough to "sink, and merge into the movement of Russian liberation"[680]! Now this fusion was more easily facilitated, accelerated by Russian literature and the writings of radical publicists.

By turning to the Russian world, these young people turned away from the Jewish world. "Many of them conceived hostility and disdain to the Judaism of their fathers, just like towards a parasitic anomaly."[681] In the 70s "there were small groups of radical Jewish youths who, in the name of the ideals of populism, moved more and more away from their people..., began to assimilate vigorously and to appropriate the Russian national spirit."[682] Until the mid-70s, the socialist Jews did not consider it necessary to do political work with their fellow men, because, they thought, the Jews have never possessed land and thus cannot assimilate socialist ideas. The Jews never had peasants of their own.

"None of the Jewish revolutionaries of the 70s could conceive of the idea of acting for one's own nation alone." It was clear that one only acted in the dominant language and only for the Russian peasants. "For us... there were no Jewish workers. We looked at them with the eyes of russifiers: the Jew must assimilate completely with the native population"; even artisans were regarded as potential exploiters, since they had apprentices and

---

[678] Ferdinand Lassalle (1825 1864): philosopher, economist, jurist and famous German socialist.
[679] Rudin, the hero of Turgenev's novel, *Rudin* (1856), whom the author put to death on the barricades in Paris in 1848.
[680] K. *Leites*, Pamiati M. A. Krolia (The memory of M. A. Krol), JW-2, p. 410.
[681] B. *Frumkin*. Iz istorii revolioutsionnogo dvijeniia sredi evreiev v 1870-x godakh (Pages of the history of the revolutionary movement among the Jews in the 70s) Sb. Soblazn Sotsializma: Revolutionsiia v Rossii i evrei (Rec. The Temptation of Socialism Revolution in Russia and the Jews), composed by A. Serebrennikov, Paris, YMCA Press; Rousskii Put (The Russian Way), 1995. p. 49.
[682] JE, L 3, p. 336.

employees. In fact, Russian workers and craftsmen were not accorded any importance as an autonomous class: they existed only as future socialists who would facilitate work in the peasant world.[683]

Assimilation once accepted, these young people, by their situation, naturally tended towards radicalism, having lost on this new soil the solid conservative roots of their former environment.

"We were preparing to go to the people and, of course, to the Russian people. We deny the Jewish religion, like any other religion; we considered our jargon an artificial language, and Hebrew a dead language... We were sincere assimilators and we saw in the Russian education and culture salvation for the Jews... Why then did we seek to act among the Russian people, not the Jewish people? It comes from the fact that we had become strangers to the spiritual culture of the Jews of Russia and that we rejected their thinkers who belonged to a traditionalist *bourgeoisie*... from the ranks of which we had left ourselves... We thought that, when the Russian people would be freed from the despotism and yoke of the ruling classes, the economic and political freedom of all the peoples of Russia, including the Jewish people, would arise. And it must be admitted that Russian literature has also somewhat inculcated the idea that the Jewish people were not a people but a parasitic class."[684]

Also came into play the feeling of *debt* owed to the people of Great Russia, as well as "the faith of the populist rebels in the imminence of a popular insurrection."[685] In the 70s, "the Jewish intellectual youth... 'went to the people' in the hope of launching, with its feeble hands, the peasant revolution in Russia."[686] As Aptekman writes, Natanson, "like the hero of the *Mtsyri* of Lermontov,

Knew the hold of only one thought, lived *only one*, but burning passion.

This thought was the happiness of the people; this passion, the struggle for liberation."[687] Aptekman himself, as depicted by Deutsch, was "emaciated, of small stature, pale complexion," "with very pronounced national features"; having become a village nurse, he announced socialism to the peasants through the Gospel.[688]

---

[683] *Deutsch*, pp. 56, 67-68.
[684] *Iohelson*, Byloie, 1918, No. 13, pp. 56 57.
[685] *Ibidem*, pp. 61, 66.
[686] G. J. Aronson, V. borbe za grajdanskiie i nalsionalnyie prava: obschcstvcnnyie tetcheniia v rousskom evreistve (In the struggle for national civil rights: the social currents among the Jews of Russia), UR-1, p. 210.
[687] *Aptekman*. Byloie, 1921, No. 16, pp. 11 12.
[688] *Deutsch*, pp. 183-185.

It was a little under the influence of their predecessors, the members of the Dolgouchin circle, whom inscribed on the branches of the crucifix: "In the name of Christ, Liberty, Equality, Fraternity," and almost all preached the Gospel, that the first Jewish populists turned to Christianity, which they used as a support point and as an instrument. Aptekman writes about himself: "I have converted to Christianity by a movement from the heart and love for Christ."[689]

(Not to be confused with the motives of Tan Bogoraz, who in the 80s had converted to Christianity "to escape the vexations of his Jewish origin."[690] Nor with the feint of Deutsch who went to preach the molokanes[691] by presenting himself as a 'good orthodox'.") But, adds Aptekman, "in order to give oneself to the people, there is no need to repent": with regard to the Russian people, "I had no trace of repentance. Moreover, where could it have come from? Is it not rather for me, the descendant of an oppressed nation, to demand the settlement of this dealing, instead of paying the repayment of some, I am not sure which, fantastic loan? Nor have I observed this feeling of repentance among my comrades of the nobility who were walking with me on the same path."[692]

Let us note in this connection that the idea of a rapprochement between the desired socialism and historical Christianity was not unconnected with many Russian revolutionaries at the time, and as justification for their action, and as a convenient tactical procedure. V. V. Flerovsky[693] wrote: "I always had in mind the comparison between this youth who was preparing for action and the first Christians." And, immediately after, the next step: "By constantly turning this idea into my head, I have come to the conviction that we will reach our goal only by one means— *by creating a new religion*... It is necessary to teach the people to devote all their forces to oneself exclusively... I wanted to create *the religion of brotherhood*"— and the young disciples of Flerovsky tried to "lead the experiment by wondering how a religion that would have neither God nor saints would be received by the people."

---

[689] *O. V. Aptekman*, Flerovski-Bervi i kroujok Dolgouchina (Bervi-Flerovsky and the circle of Dolgouchine), Byloie, 1922, No. 18, p. 63.
[690] JE, t. 4, p. 714.
[691] Molokanes or "milk drinkers" (they consume milk during Lent) are a Russian sect that goes back to the eighteenth century. They were persecuted, exiled in 1800 north of the Sea of Azov, and some immigrated to the United States.
[692] *Aptekman*, Byloie, 1922, No. 18, p. 63.
[693] Vassili Vasilievich Bervi-Flerovsky (1829 1918): Russian publicist, sociologist, economist. Participated in the populism of the 60s. In exile from 1862 to 1887. Wrote the *Notes of a Revolutionary Utopian*.

His disciple Gamov, from the circle of Dolgouchine, wrote even more crudely: "We must invent a religion that would be against the tsar and the government... We must write a catechism and prayers in this spirit."[694]

The revolutionary action of the Jews in Russia is also explained in another way. We find it exposed and then refuted by A. Srebrennikov: "There is a view that if, through the reforms of the years 1860–1863, the 'Pale of Settlement' had been abolished, our whole history would have unfolded otherwise... If Alexander II had abolished the 'Pale of Settlement', there would have been neither the Bund[695] nor Trotskyism!" Then he mentioned the internationalist and socialist ideas that flowed from the West, and wrote: "If the suppression of the Pale of Settlement had been of capital importance to them, all their struggle would have stretched towards it. Now they were occupied with everything else: they dreamed of overthrowing tsarism!"[696]

And, one after the other, driven by the same passion, they abandoned their studies (notably the Academy of Military Medicine) to "go to the people". Every diploma was marked with the seal of infamy as a means of exploitation of the people. They renounced any career, and some broke with their families. For them, "every day not put to good use [constitutes] an irreparable loss, criminal for the realisation of the well-being and happiness of the disinherited masses."[697]

But in order to "go to the people", it was necessary to "make oneself simple", both internally, for oneself, and practically, "to inspire confidence to the masses of the people, one had to infiltrate it under the guise of a workman or a *moujik*."[698] However, writes Deutsch, how can you go to the people, be heard and be believed, when you are betrayed by your language, your appearance and your manners? And still, to seduce the listeners, you must throw jokes and good words in popular language! And we must also be skilful in the work of the fields, so painful to townspeople. For this reason, Khotinsky worked on the farm with his brother, and worked there as a ploughman. The Lœwenthal brothers learned shoemaking and carpentry. Betty Kamenskaya entered as a worker in a spinning mill to a very hard position. Many became caregivers. (Deutsch writes that, on the whole, other activities were better suited to these revolutionary Jews: work

---

[694] *Ibidem*.
[695] *The Bund* (in Yiddish: the Union): the "General Union of Jewish Workers of Lithuania, Poland and Russia", founded in Vilnius in 1897, related to the SD party in 1898 1903; then again in 1906-1918 close to the Mensheviks. Dissolved in 1921.
[696] Obschaia gazela (*General Gazette*), No. 35, 31 August 6 Sept. 1995, p. 11.
[697] *Deutsch*, pp. 106, 205 206.
[698] *Iohelson*, Byloie, 1918, No. 13, p. 74.

within factions, conspiracy, communications, typography, border-crossing.)[699]

The "march to the people" began with short visits, stays of a few months—a "fluid" march. At first, they relied only on the work of agitation. It was imagined that it would suffice to convince the peasants to open their eyes to the regime in power and the exploitation of the masses, and to promise that the land and the instruments of production would become the property of all.

In fact, this whole "march to the people" of the populists ended in failure. And not only because of some inadvertent gunshot directed against the Tsar (Solovyov, 1879), which obliged them all to flee the country and to hide very far from the cities. But above all because the peasants, perfectly deaf to their preaching, were even sometimes ready to hand them over to the authorities. The populists, the Russians (hardly more fortunate) like the Jews, lost "the faith... in a spontaneous revolutionary will and in the socialist instincts of the peasantry", and "transformed into impenitent pessimists."[700]

Clandestine action, however, worked better. Three residents of Minsk, Lossif Guetsov, Saul Levkov, and Saul Grinfest, succeeded in setting up a clandestine press in their city that would serve the country as a whole. It survived until 1881. It was there that was printed in gold letters the leaflet on "the execution of Alexander II". It printed the newspaper *The Black Repartition*[701], and then the proclamations of The Will of the People. Deutsche referred to them as "peaceful propagandists". Apparently, the term "peaceful" embraced everything that was not bombing—smuggling, illegal border-crossing, and even the call to avoid paying taxes (appeal to the peasants of Lazare Goldenberg).

Many of these Jewish revolutionaries were heavily condemned (heavily, even by the measures of our time). Some benefited from a reduction of their punishment—like Semion Lourie, thanks to his father who obtained for him a less severe regime in prison. There was also public opinion, which leaned towards indulgence. Aptekman tells us that in 1881—after the assassination of Alexander II—"they lived relatively freely in the prison of Krasnoyarsk" where "the director of the prison, a real wild beast, was suddenly tamed and gave us all kinds of permissions to contact the deportees and our friends." Then "we were received in transit prisons not as detainees, but as noble captives"; "the prison director came in,

---

[699] *Deutsch*, pp. 34-37, 183.
[700] *Ibidem*, pp. 194 et suiv. ; *Iohelson*, Byloie, 1918, No. 13, p. 69.
[701] *The Black Repartition*, a clandestine newspaper bearing the same name as the organisation, which knew five issues in 1880 1881 Minsk-Geneva.

accompanied by soldiers carrying trays with tea, biscuits, jam for everyone, and, as a bonus, a small glass of vodka. Was it not idyllic? We were touched."[702]

The biographies of these early populists reveal a certain exaltation, a certain lack of mental equilibrium. Leo Deutsch testifies: Leon Zlatopolsky, a terrorist, "was not a mentally balanced person". Aptekman himself, in his cell, after his arrest, "was not far from madness, as his nerves were shaken." Betty Kamenskaya, "... from the second month of detention... lost her mind"; she was transferred to the hospital, then her father, a merchant, took her back on bail. Having read in the indictment that she would not be brought before the court, she wanted to tell the prosecutor that she was in good health and could appear, but soon after, she swallowed poison and died.[703] Moses Rabinovitch, in his cell, "had hallucinations... his nerves were exhausted"; he resolved to feign repentance, to *name* those whom the instruction was surely already acquainted with, in order to be liberated. He drew up a declaration promising to say everything he knew and even, upon his release from prison, to seek and transmit information. The result was that he confessed everything without being released and that he was sent to the province of Irkutsk where he went mad and died "barely over the age of 20." Examples of this kind are not lacking. Leiser Tsukerman, immigrated to New York, and put an end to his life. Nahman Lœwenthal, after having immigrated to Berlin, "was sent into the dizzying downward spiral of a nervous breakdown," to which was added an unhappy love; "he swallowed sulphuric acid and threw himself into the river"—at the age of about 19.[704] These young individuals had thrown themselves away by overestimating their strength and the resistance of their nerves.

And even Grigori Goldenberg, who, in cold blood, had defeated the governor of Kharkov and asked his comrades, as a supreme honor, to kill by his own hand the Tsar (but his comrades, fearing popular anger, had apparently dismissed him as a Jew; apparently, this argument often prompted populists to designate most often Russians, to perpetrate attacks): after being arrested while carrying a charge of dynamite, he was seized by unbearable anguish in his cell of the Troubetskoy bastion, his spirit was broken, he made a full confession that affected the whole movement, petitioned that Aaron Zundelevich come share his cell (who showed more

---

[702] *Aptekman*, Byloie. 1922, No. 18. pp. 73, 75.
[703] *Deutsch*, pp. 38, 41, 94, 189.
[704] *Ibidem*, pp. 78-79, 156,157.

indulgence than others towards his actions). When it was refused, he committed suicide.[705]

Others, who were not directly involved, suffered, such as Moses Edelstein, who was by no means an ideologist, who had "slipped", for a price, clandestine literature; he suffered much in prison, prayed to Yahweh for himself and his family: he repented during the judgment: "I did not imagine that there could be such bad books." Or S. Aronson who, after the trial of the "one hundred and ninety-three", disappeared completely from the revolutionary scene.[706]

Another point is worthy of noting; it was the facility with which many of them left that Russia which they had long ago intended to save. In fact, in the 70s emigration was regarded as desertion in revolutionary circles: even if the police seek you, go underground, but do not run away![707]—Tan Bogoraz left to live twenty years in New York.—Lazar Goldenberg-Getroitman also "left to New York in 1885, where he gave classes on the history of the revolutionary movement in Russia"; he returned to Russia in 1906, after the amnesty, to leave again rather quickly to Britain, where he remained until his death."[708]—In London, one of the Vayner brothers became the owner of a furniture workshop and Mr. Aronson and Mr. Romm became Clinical Doctors in New York.—After a few years in Switzerland, I. Guetsov went to live in America, having radically broken with the Socialist movement.—Leiser Lœwenthal, emigrated to Switzerland, completed his medical studies in Geneva, became the assistant of a great physiologist before obtaining a chair of histology in Lausanne.—Semion Lourie also finished his studies in a faculty of medicine in Italy, but died shortly after.—Liubov Axelrod ("the Orthodox"[709]) remained for a long time in immigration, where she received the degree of Doctor of Philosophy from the University of Berlin (later he inculcated dialectical materialism to students of Soviet graduate schools.) A. Khotinsky also entered the Faculty of Medicine of Bern (but died the following year from a galloping consumption). Grigory Gurayev made a

---

[705] Grigori Goldenberg v Petropavolvskoi kreposti (Grigori Goldenberg in prison Saint-Pierre-el-Saint-Paul); Krasnyi arkhiv: istorilcheskii journal Tsentrarkhiva RSFSR (The Red Archives: Historical Review of the FSSR Archives Center), M., 1922 1941, t. 10; 1925, pp. 328-331.
[706] *Deutsch**, pp. 85-86.
[707] *Ibidem*, p.132.
[708] RJE, t. 1. p. 344.
[709] Liubov Issaakovna Axelrod: philosopher, writer, member of the Menshevik party. His pen name is "the Orthodox" (in the non-confessional sense of the word).

fine career in Denmark; he returned to Russia as the country's ambassador in Kiev, where he stayed until 1918.[710]

All this also shows how many talented men there were among these revolutionaries. Men such as these, endowed with such lively intelligence, when they found themselves in Siberia, far from wasting or losing their reason, they opened their eyes to the tribes which surrounded them, studied their languages and their customs, and wrote ethnographic studies about them: Leon Sternberg on the Ghiliaks,[711] Tan-Bogoraz on the Tchouktches,[712] Vladimir Yokhelson on the Yukaghirs,[713] and Naoum Guekker on the physical type of the Iakuts.[714] [715]

Some studies on the Buryats[716] are due to Moses Krohl. Some of these Jewish revolutionaries willingly joined the socialist movement in the West. Thus V. Yokhelson and A. Zundelevich, during the Reichstag elections in Germany, campaigned on the side of the Social Democrats. Zundelevich was even arrested for having used fraudulent methods.

Anne Rosenstein, in France, was convicted for organising a street demonstration in defiance of the regulations governing traffic on the street; Turgenev intervened for her and she was expelled to Italy where she was twice condemned for anarchist agitation (she later married F. Turati,[717] converted him to socialism and became herself the first Marxist of Italy). Abram Valt-Lessine, a native of Minsk, published articles for seventeen years in New York in the socialist organ of America *Vorwarts* and exerted a great influence on the formation of the American labour movement.[718] (That road was going to be taken by many others of our Socialists...)

It sometimes happened that revolutionary emigrants were disappointed by the revolution. Thus Moses Veller, having distanced himself from the movement, succeeded, thanks to Turgenev's intervention with Loris-Melikov, to return to Russia. More extravagant was the journey of Isaac

---

[710] *Deutsch*, pp. 61-62, 198 201, 203 216.
[711] The Ghiliaks are a tribe of the north of the island of Sakhalin and the valley of the lower Amur.
[712] The Tchouktches, a tribe of eastern Siberia occupying a territory ranging from the Sea of Behring to the Kolyma. Nomads and sedentary. Opposed the Russian conquest.
[713] The Yukaghirs are a tribe of the north-east of Siberia, very small in number.
[714] JE, t. 6, p. 284.
[715] The Iakuts are a people of northeastern Siberia, occupying both banks of the Lena, extending east to the Kolyma River, north to the Arctic Ocean, south to the Yablovoi mountains.
[716] The Buryats, people of Siberia around Lake Baikal, partly repressed towards Mongolia.
[717] Filippo Turati (1857 1932): one of the founders of the Italian Socialist Party. Emigrated in 1926.
[718] RJE, t. 2, p. 166; t. l, p. 205.

Pavlovsky: living in Paris, as "illustrious revolutionary", he had connections with Turgenev, who made him know Emile Zola and Alphonse Daudet; he wrote a novel about the Russian nihilists that Turgenev published in the *Vestnik Evropy*[719] (The Messenger of Europe), and then he became the correspondent in Paris of *Novoye Vremia*[720] "the New Times" under the pseudonym of I. Iakovlev—and even, as Deutsch writes, he portrayed himself as "anti-Semite", sent a petition in high places, was pardoned and returned to Russia.[721]

That said, the majority of the Jewish revolutionaries blended in, just like the Russians, and their track was lost. "With the exception of two or three prominent figures... all my other compatriots were minor players," writes Deutsch.[722] A Soviet collection, published the day after the revolution under the title of "Historical and Revolutionary Collection",[723] quotes many names of humble soldiers unknown to the revolution. We find there dozens, even hundreds of Jewish names. Who remembers them now? However, all have taken action, all have brought their contribution, all have shaken more or less strongly the edifice of the State.

Let us add: this very first contingent of Jewish revolutionaries did not fully join the ranks of the Russian revolution, all did not deny their Judaism. A. Liebermann, a great connoisseur of the Talmud, a little older than his populist fellow students, proposed in 1875 to carry out a specific campaign in favour of socialism among the Jewish population. With the help of G. Gurevich, he published a socialist magazine in Yiddish called *Emes* (*Pravda* = Truth) in Vienna in 1877. Shortly before, in the 70s, A. Zundelevich "undertook a publication in the Hebrew language", also entitled *Truth*. (L. Shapiro hypothesises that this publication was "the distant ancestor of Trotsky's *The Pravda*.[724] The tradition of this appellation was durable.) Some, like Valt-Lessine, insisted on the convergence of internationalism with Judaic nationalism. "In his improvised conferences and sermons, the prophet Isaiah and Karl Marx

---

[719] The Messenger of Europe: 1) a journal founded by Karamzin and published from 1802 to 1830; 2) a monthly magazine with a liberal orientation, which appeared from 1866 to 1918 in Saint Petersburg.

[720] *The New Times*: ultra-conservative Petersburg daily founded by the publicist Suvorin. Which appeared from 1868 to 1917.

[721] *Deutsch*, pp. 84-85; Lohelsohn. Byloe, 1918, no. 13, pp. 53 75; L. Goumtch. Pervyie evreiskiie rabotchiie kroujki (The first Jewish workers' circles), Byloie, 1907, n. 6/18, p. 68.

[722] *Deutsch*, p. 231.

[723] RHC, t. 1, 2.

[724] Leonard Schapiro, The Role of the Jews in the Russian Revolutionary Movement, The Slavonic and East European Review, Vol. 40, London, Athlone Press, 1961 62, p. 157.

figured as authorities of equal importance."⁷²⁵ In Geneva was founded the Jewish Free Typography,⁷²⁶ intended to print leaflets addressed to the Jewish working-class population.

Specifically Jewish circles were formed in some cities. A "Statute for the Organisation of a Social-Revolutionary Union of the Jews of Russia", formulated at the beginning of 1876, showed the need for propaganda in the Hebrew language and even to organise between Jews of the western region "a network of social-revolutionary sections, federated with each other and with other sections of the same type found abroad". "The Socialists of the whole world formed a single brotherhood," and this organisation was to be called the Jewish Section of the Russian Social-Revolutionary Party.⁷²⁷

Hessen comments: the action of this Union among the Jewish masses "has not met with sufficient sympathies", and that is why these Jewish socialists, in their majority, "lent a hand to the common cause", that is to say, to the Russian cause.⁷²⁸ In fact, circles were created in Vilnius, Grodno, Minsk, Dvinsk, Odessa, but also, for example, in Elts, Saratov, Rostov-on-Don.

In the very detailed founding act of this "Social-Revolutionary Union of all Jews in Russia", one can read surprising ideas, statements such as: "*Nothing ordinary has the right to exist* if it has no rational justification"⁷²⁹ (!) By the end of the 70s, the Russian revolutionary movement was already sliding towards terrorism. The appeal to the revolt of Bakunin had definitely prevailed over the concern for instruction of the masses of Lavrov. Beginning in 1879, the idea of populist presence among the peasants had no effect—the idea that dominated in The Will of the People—gained the upper hand over the rejection of terror by The Black Repartition. Terror, nothing but terror!!—much more: a systematic terror! (That the people did not have a voice in the matter, that the ranks of the intelligentsia were so sparse, did not disturb them.) Terrorist acts— including against the Tsar in person!—thus succeeded one another.

According to Leo Deutsch's assessment, only ten to twelve Jews took part in this growing terror, beginning with Aron Gobst (executed), Solomon Wittenberg (prepared an attack on Alexander II in 1878, executed in 1879), Aizik Aronchik (was involved in the explosion of the imperial train, condemned to a penal colony for life) and Gregory Goldenberg, already named. Like Goldenberg, A. Zundelevich—brilliant organiser of terror, but

---

⁷²⁵ JW.-2, p. 392.
⁷²⁶ JE, t. 13, p. 644.
⁷²⁷ *Hessen*, t. 2, pp. 213 214.
⁷²⁸ *Ibidem*, p. 214.
⁷²⁹ RHC, 1.1, p. 45.

who was not given the time to participate in the assassination of the Tsar—was arrested very early. There was also another quite active terrorist: Mlodetsky. As for Rosa Grossman, Krystyna Grinberg and the brothers Leo and Saveli Zlatopolsky, they played a secondary role. (In fact, Saveli, as of March 1st, 1881[730], was a member of the Executive Committee); As for Gesya Gelfman, she was part of the basic group of the "actors of March 1st."[731]

Then it was the 80s that saw the decline and dissolution of populism. Government power took over; belonging to a revolutionary organisation cost a firm eight to ten years of imprisonment. But if the revolutionary movement was caught by inertia, its members continued to exist. One can quote here Sofia Ginzburg: she did not engage in revolutionary action until 1877; she tried to restore the Will of the People, which had been decimated by arrests; she prepared, just after the Ulyanov group[732], an attack on Alexander III.[733] So—and so was forgotten in deportation, another was coming back from it, a third was only leaving for it—but they continued the battle.

Thusly was a famous deflagration described by the memorialists: the rebellion in the prison of Yakutsk in 1889. An important contingent of political prisoners had been told that they were going to be transferred to Verkhoyansk and, from there, even further, to Srednie-Kolymsk, which they wanted to avoid at all costs. The majority of the group were Jewish inmates. In addition, they were informed that the amount of baggage allowed was reduced: instead of five poods[734] of books, clothes, linen, five poods also of bread and flour, two poods of meat, plus oil, sugar and tea (the whole, of course, loaded on horses or reindeer), a reduction of five poods in all. The deportees decided to resist. In fact, it had already been six months that they had been walking freely in the city of Yakutsk, and some had obtained weapons from the inhabitants. "While you're at it, might as well perish like this, and may the people discover all the abomination of the Russian government—perishing so that the spirit of combat is revived among the living!" When they were picked up to be taken to the police station, they first opened fire on the officers, and the soldiers answered with

---

[730] March 1st, 1881: day of the assassination of Alexander II.

[731] *Deutsch*, pp. 38-39, Protses dvadtsati narodovoltsev v 1882 g. (The trial of the members of The Will of the People in 1882), Byloie, 1906, no. 1, pp. 227 234.

[732] The "Ulyanov group", named after Alexander Ilyich Ulyanov, Lenin's elder brother. Faction of the Will of the People. Alexander Ulyanov prepared an attack on Alexander III in 1887. He was condemned to death and executed.

[733] RJE, t. 1, p. 314.

[734] One pood is equivalent to 16.38 kilos.

a salvo. Condemned to death, together with N. Zotov, were those who fired the first shots at the vice-governor: L. Kogan-Bernstein and A. Gausman.

Condemned to forced labour in perpetuity were: the memorialist himself, O. Minor, the celebrated M. Gotz[735], and also "A. Gurevitch and M. Orlov, Mr. Bramson, Mr. Braguinsky, Mr. Fundaminsky, Mr. Ufland, S. Ratine, O. Estrovitch, Sofia Gurevitch, Vera Gotz, Pauline Perly, A. Bolotina, N. Kogan-Bernstein." The *Jewish Encyclopædia* informs us that for this mutiny twenty-six Jews and six Russians were tried.[736]

That same year, 1889, Mark Natanson returned from exile and undertook to forge, in place of the old dismantled populist organisations, a new organisation called The Right of the People (*Narodnoie Pravo*). Natanson had already witnessed the emergence of Marxism in Russia, imported from Europe, and its competition with populism. He made every effort to save the revolutionary movement from decadence and to maintain ties with the Liberals ('the best liberals are also semi-socialists"). Not more than before did he look at nuances of convictions: what mattered to him was that all should unite to overthrow the autocracy, and when Russia was democratic, then it would be figured out. But the organisation he set up this time proved to be amorphous, apathetic and ephemeral. Besides, respecting the rules of the conspiracy was no longer necessary. As Isaac Gurvitch very eloquently pointed out, "because of the absence of conspiracy, a mass of people fall into the clutches of the police, but the revolutionaries are now so numerous that these losses do not count—trees are knocked down, and chips go flying!"[737]

The fracture that had occurred in the Jewish consciousness after 1881-1882 could not but be reflected somewhat in the consciousness of Jewish revolutionaries in Russia. These young men had begun by drifting away from Judaism, and many had returned to it. They had "left the 'street of the Jews' and then returned to their people": "Our entire historical destiny is linked to the Jewish ghetto, it is from it that our national essence is forged."[738] Until the pogroms of 1881 1882, - "absolutely none of us revolutionaries thought for a moment" that we should publicly explain the participation of the Jews in the revolutionary movement. But then came the pogroms, which caused "among... the majority of our countrymen an explosion of indignation." And now "it was not only the cultivated Jews,

---

[735] Mikhail Rafaelovich Gotz (1866 1906): member of the S.-R. party. Emigrated in 1900.
[736] *O. S. Minor*, Iakutskaia drama 22 marta 1889 goda (The drama of Yakutia of 22 March 1889), Byloie, 1906, no. 9, pp. 138,141, 144; JE, t. 5, p. 599.
[737] *Gounitch*, Byloie. 1907, no. 6/18, p. 68.
[738] *I. Mark*, Pamiati I. M. Tcherikover (In memory of I. M. Tcherikover), JW-2, pp. 424, 425.

but some Jewish revolutionaries who had no affinity with their nation, who suddenly felt obliged to devote their strength and talents to their unjustly persecuted brothers."[739] "The pogroms have awakened sleeping feelings, they have made young people more susceptible to the sufferings of their people, and the people more receptive to revolutionary ideas.

Let this serve as a basis for an autonomous action of the Jewish mass": "We are obstinately pursuing our goal: the destruction of the current political regime."[740]

But behold, the unexpected support to the anti-Jewish pogroms brought by the leaflets of The Will of the People! Leo Deutsch expresses his perplexity in a letter to Axelrod, who also wonders: "The Jewish question is now, in practice, really insoluble for a revolutionary. What would one do, for example, in Balta, where the Jews are being attacked? To defend them is tantamount to "arousing hatred against the revolutionaries who not only killed the Tsar, but also support the Jews"… Reconciliation propaganda is now extremely difficult for the party."[741]

This perplexity, P. L. Lavrov himself, the venerated chief, expresses it in his turn: "I recognise that the Jewish question is extremely complex, and for the party, which intends to draw itself closer to the people and raise it against the government, it is difficult in the highest degree… because of the passionate state in which the people find themselves and the need to have it *on our side*."[742]

He was not the only one of the Russian revolutionaries to reason this way. In the 80s, a current reappeared among the socialists, advocating directing attention and propaganda to specifically Jewish circles, and preferably the ones of workers. But, as proletariat, there were not many people among the Jews—some carpenters, binders, shoemakers. The easiest was certainly to act among the most educated printers. Isaac Gurvitch recounts: with Moses Khourguine, Leon Rogaller, Joseph Reznik, "in Minsk we had set ourselves the task of creating a nucleus of educated workers." But if we take, for example, Belostok or Grodno, "we found no working class": the recruitment was too weak.

The creation of these circles was not done openly; it was necessary to conspire either to organise the meeting outside the city, or to hold it in a private apartment in the city, but then systematically beginning with lessons of Russian grammar or natural sciences… and then only by

---

[739] *Deutsch*, pp. 3-4.
[740] *I. Iliacheviich* (I. Rubinovilch), Chto delay evreiam v Rossii? (What can the Jews do in Russia?), Soblazn Sotsializma (The Temptation of Socialism), pp. 185,186.
[741] *Schub*, JW-2*, p. 134.
[742] *Ibidem*, pp. 133,134.

recruiting volunteers to preach socialism to them. As I. Martar explains: it was these preliminary lessons that attracted people to the revolutionary circles. "Skilled and wise," capable of becoming their own masters, "those who had attended our meetings had received instruction there, and especially mastery of Russian, for language is a precious weapon in the competitive struggle of petty commerce and industry"; After that, our "lucky guys", freed from the role of hired labourers and swearing to their great gods that they themselves would never employ hired labour, had to have recourse to it, due to the requirements of the market."[743] Or, once formed in these circles, "the worker abandoned his trade and went away to take examinations 'externally'."[744]

The local Jewish *bourgeoisie* disliked the participation of young people in the revolutionary circles, for it had understood—faster and better than the police—where all of this would lead.[745]

Here and there, however, things advanced; with the aid of socialist pamphlets and proclamations provided by the printing press in London, the young revolutionaries themselves drafted "social-democrat formulations on all programmatic questions". Thus, for ten years, a slow propaganda led little by little to the creation of the Bund.

But, "even more than police persecution, it was the emerging immigration to America that hampered our work. In fact, we trained socialist workers for America." The concise recollections of Isaac Gurvitch on the first Jewish workers' circles are enamelled by obiter dicta such as: Schwartz, a student who participated in revolutionary agitation, "subsequently immigrated to America; he lives in New York".—as well, at a meeting in Joseph Reznik's apartment: "There were two workers present, a carpenter and a joiner: both are now in America." And, two pages later, we learn that Reznik himself, after his return from exile, "went to live in America." Conversely, a young man named Guirchfeld, who came from America to do revolutionary work, "is currently a doctor in Minneapolis" and was a Socialist candidate for the post of governor.

—"One of the most active members of the first Abramovich circle, a certain Jacob Zvirine…, after serving his twelve months in the Kresty prison… immigrated to America and now lives in New York."— "Shmulevich ("Kivel") … in 1889… was forced to flee from Russia; he lived until 1896 in Switzerland where he was an active member of the

---

[743] *I. Martov*, Zapiski sotsial-demokrata (Notebooks of a Social-Democrat), Berlin, ed. Grjebine, 1922, pp. 187, 189.
[744] *N. A. Buchbinder*, Rabotchiie o propagandistskikh kroujkakh (Workers in regard to circles of propagandists), Soblazn sotsializma (The temptation of socialism), p. 230.
[745] *Gurvitch*, Byloie, op. cit., pp. 65 68, 74.

social democratic organisations", then "he moved to America... and lives in Chicago". Finally, the narrator himself:

"In 1890 I myself left Russia," although a few years earlier "we were considering things differently. To lead a socialist propaganda among the workers is *the obligation* of every honest educated man: it is our way of paying our "historical debt" to the people. And since I have the obligation to make propaganda, it follows very obviously that I have the right to demand that I be given the opportunity to fulfil this obligation." Arriving in New York in 1890, Gurvich found there a "Russian workers' association of self-development," consisting almost exclusively of artisans from Minsk, and in order to celebrate the Russian New Year they organised in New York "The Ball of the Socialists of Minsk."[746] In New York, "the local socialist movement... predominantly was Jewish."[747]

As we can see, from that time the ocean did not constitute a major obstacle to the cohesion and the pursuit of the revolutionary action carried out by the Jews. This living link would have oh so striking effects in Russia.

Yet all Jewish young people had not abandoned the Russian revolutionary tradition, far from it; many even stood there in the 80s and 90s. As D. Schub shows, the pogroms and the restrictive measures of Alexander III only excited them even more strongly for combat.

Then it became necessary to explain as well as possible to the little Russian people why so many Jews participated in the revolutionary movement.

Addressing uneducated people, the popular pamphlets gradually forged a whole phraseology that had its effects until 1917—including 1917. It is a booklet of this kind that allows us to reconstruct their arguments.

Hard is the fate of the Russian, the subject of the Tsar; the government holds him in his iron fist. But "still more bitter is the lot of the indigent Jew": "the government makes fun of him, pressures him to death. His existence is only a life of famine, a long agony", and "his brothers of misery and toil, the peasants and the Russian workers..., as long as they are in ignorance, treat him as a foreigner." There followed, one after the other, didactic questions: "Are Jewish capitalists enemies of the working people of Russia?" The enemies are all capitalists without distinction, and it is of little importance to the working people to be plundered by such and such: one should not concentrate their anger on those who are Jews.—"The Jew has no land... he has no means to prosper. If the Jews do not devote themselves to the labour of the land, it is because "the Russian government

---

[746] Ibidem, pp. 66-68, 72-77.
[747] J. Krepliak, Poslesloviie k statie Lessina (Postface to the article by Lessine), JW-2, p. 392.

has not allowed them to reside in the countryside"; but in their colonies they are "excellent cultivators." The fields are superbly enhanced... by the work of their arms. They do not use any outside labour, and do not practice any extra trade... they like the hard work of the land."—"Are destitute Jews harming the economic interests of Russian workers? If the Jews do business, "it is out of necessity, not out of taste; all other ways are closed to them, and one has to live"; "they would cease with joy to trade if they were allowed to leave their cage." And if there are thieves among them, we must accuse the Tsarist government. "The Jewish workers began the struggle for the improvement of their condition at the time when the Russian working people were subjected. The Jewish workers "before all the others have lost patience"; "And even now tens of thousands of Jews are members of Russian Socialist parties. They spread the hatred of the capitalist system and the tsarist government through the country"; they have rendered "a proud service to the Russian working people", and that is why Russian capitalists hate them. The government, through the police, assisted in the preparation of the pogroms; it sent the police and the army to lend a helping hand to the looters"; "Fortunately, very few workers and peasants were among them."—"Yes, the Jewish masses hate this irresponsible tsarist government", because "it was the will of the government that the skull of Jewish children be smashed against walls... that Jewish women, elderly and children alike, be raped in the streets. And yet, "He lies boldly, the one who treats the Jews as enemies of the Russian people... And besides, how could they hate Russia? Could they have another country?"[748]

There are amazing resurgences in the revolutionary tradition. In 1876, A. Biebergal had been convicted for taking part in the demonstration on the square in front of Our Lady of Kazan. And it was there that his eldest daughter, a student of graduate studies of Saint Petersburg, was apprehended on the same spot in Kazan on the anniversary of this demonstration, twenty-five years later, in 1901. (In 1908, Member of a group S. -R.[749], she was condemned to the penal colonies for the attack on the Grand Duke Vladimir Alexandrovich.[750])

In fact, over the years, Russian revolutionaries increasingly needed the input of the Jews; they understood more and more what advantage they

---

[748] *Abramova*, Vragi li trudovomou narodou evrei? (Are the Jews enemies of the working people?), Tiflis, Izdatelskaia Komissiia Kraicvogo Soveta Kavkazskoi armii (Editorial Commission of the Regional Soviet of the Caucasian Army), 1917, pp. 331.
[749] S.-R.: Social-Revolutionary party. Born in 1901, it preached terror. Subjected to splits after the revolution of 1905. Remained powerful among the intelligentsia.
[750] Grand Duke Vladimir Alexandrovich (1847 1909): brother of Alexander III, father of the Grand Duke Cyril.

derived from them—of their dual struggle: against the vexations on the plane of nationality, and against those of an economic order—as a detonator for the revolution.

In 1883, in Geneva, appears what can be considered as the head of the emerging social democracy: the "Liberation of Labour" group. Its founders were, along with Plekhanov and Vera Zasulich, L. Deutsch and P. Axelrod.[751] (When Ignatov died in 1885, he was replaced by Ingerman.)

In Russia comes to life a current that supports them. Constituted of former members of the dismantled Black Repartition (they considerably exceeded those of the Will of the People), they will be called "liberationists" (*osvobojdentsy*).

Among them are a number of young Jews, among whom we can name the two best known: Israel Guelfand (the future and famous Parvus) and Raphael Soloveitchik. In 1889 Soloveitchik, who had travelled through Russia to set up revolutionary action in several cities, was arrested and tried with other members of the Liberation of Labour group, which included several Jewish names.[752]

Others who belonged to this social revolutionary trend were David Goldendach, the future, well-known Bolshevik "Riazanov" (who had fled Odessa in 1889 and had taken refuge abroad to escape military service[753]).

Nevertheless, what remained of the Will of the People after its collapse was a fairly large group. Among them were Dembo, Rudevitch, Mandelstam, Boris Reinchtein, Ludwig Nagel, Bek, Sofia Chentsis, Filippeo, Leventis, Cheftel, Barnekhovsky, etc.[754]

Thus a certain amount of energy had been preserved to fuel the rivalries between small groups—The Will of the People, The Black Repartition, Liberation of Labour—and theoretical debates. The three volumes of the "Historical and Revolutionary Collection" published in the (Soviet) 20s, which we use here, offer us, in an interminable and tedious logorrhea, an account of the cut and thrust, allegedly much more important and sublime than all the questions of universal thought and history. The detail of these debates constitute a deadly material on the spiritual fabric of the Russian revolutionaries of the years 80 90, and it still awaits its historian.

But from the thirties of the Soviet era onwards, it was no longer possible to enumerate with pride and detail all those who had had their share in the revolution; a sort of taboo settled in historical and political publications,

---

[751] *Deutsch*, p. 136.
[752] RHC, t. 2, pp. 36, 38 40.
[753] *Ibidem*, t. 2, pp. 198, 199.
[754] *Ibidem*, p. 36.

the role and name of the Jews in the Russian revolutionary movement ceased to be evoked—and even now, this kind of evocation creates uneasiness. Now, nothing is more immoral and dangerous than to silence anything when History is being written: it only creates a distortion of opposite meaning.

If, as can be read in the *Jewish Encyclopædia*, "to account for the genuine importance of the Jewish component in the Russian liberation movement, to express it in precise figures, does not seem possible," [755] one can nevertheless, based on various sources, give an approximate picture.

Hessen informs us that "of the 376 defendants, accused of crimes against the State in the first half of 1879, there were only 4% Jews," and "out of the 1,054 persons tried before the Senate during the year 1880…, there were 6.5% of Jews."[756] Similar estimates are found among other authors.

However, from decade to decade, the number of Jews participating in the revolutionary movement increases, their role becomes more influential, more recognised. In the early years of Soviet rule, when it was still a matter of pride, a prominent communist, Lourie-Larine, said: "In tsarist prisons and in exile, Jews usually constituted nearly a quarter of all prisoners and exiles." [757] Marxist historian M. N. Pokrovsky, basing himself on the workforce of the various congresses, concludes that "the Jews represent between a quarter and a third of the organisations of all the revolutionary parties."[758] (*The modern Jewish Encyclopædia* has some reservations about this estimate).

In 1903, in a meeting with Herzl, Witte endeavoured to show that, while representing only 5% of the population of Russia, i.e. 6 million out of 136 million, the Jews had in their midst no less than 50% of revolutionaries.[759]

General N. Sukhotin, commander-in-chief of the Siberian region, compiled statistics on January 1st, 1905 of political prisoners under surveillance for all of Siberia and by nationality. This resulted in 1,898 Russians (42%), 1,678 Jews (37%), 624 Poles (14%), 167 Caucasians, 85 Baltic and 94 of other nationalities. (Only the exiles are counted there, prisons and penal colony convicts are not taken into account, and the figures are only valid for the year 1904, but this, however, gives a certain overview.) There is,

---

[755] JE, t. 13, p. 645.
[756] *Hessen*, t. 2, p. 212.
[757] *I. Larme*, Evrei i Anti-Semitism v SSSR (The Jews and Anti-Semitism in the USSR), ML, 1929, p. 31.
[758] SJE, t. 7*, 1994, p. 258.
[759] *G. Svet*, Rousskiie evrei v sionizme i v stroitelstve Palestiny i Izrailia (The Russian Jews in Zionism and the Edification of Israel), p. 258.

moreover, an interesting precision in connection with those who "went into hiding": 17% of Russians, 64% of Jews, 19% of other nationalities.[760]

Here is the testimony of V. Choulguine: in 1889, the news relating to the student demonstrations of Saint Petersburg reached Kiev. "The long corridors of the university were teeming with a crowd of young people in effervescence. I was struck by the predominance of the Jews. Were they more or less numerous than the Russians, I could not say, but they 'predominated' incontestably, for it was they who were in charge of this tumultuous melee in jackets. Some time later, the professors and the non-striking students began to be chased out of lecture halls. Then this 'pure and holy youth' took false photographs of the Cossacks beating the students; these photographs were said to have been taken 'on the fly' when they were made from drawings: "Not all Jewish students are left-wingers, some were on our side, but those ones suffered a lot afterwards, they were harassed by society." Choulguine adds: "The role of the Jews in the revolutionary effervescence within universities was notorious and unrelated to their number across the country."[761]

Milyukov described all this as "legends about the revolutionary spirit of the Jews… They [government officials] need legends, just like the primitive man needs rhymed prose."[762] Conversely, G. P. Fedotov wrote: "The Jewish nation, morally liberated from the 80s onwards, like the Russian intelligentsia under Peter the Great, is in the highest degree uprooted, internationalist and active… It immediately assumed the leading role in the Russian revolution… It marked the moral profile of the Russian revolutionary with its incisive and sombre character."[763] From the 80s onwards, the Russian and Jewish elites merged not only in a common revolutionary action, but also in all spiritual fads, and especially in the passion for non-rootedness.

In the eyes of a contemporary, simple witness to the facts (Zinaida Altanskaya, who corresponded from the town of Orel with Fyodor Kryukov[764]), this Jewish youth of the beginning of the century appeared as

---

[760] Iz islorii borby s revolioutsici v 1905 g. (Fragments of the History of the Fight with the Revolution of 1905), Krasnyi arkhiv (Red Archives), 1929, vol. 32, p. 229.
[761] V. V. Choulguine, "Chto nam v nikh ne nravitsa…": Ob antisemitizme v Rossii. ("What we do not like about them": anti-Semitism in Russia), Paris, 1929, pp. 53 54, 191.
[762] Duma State, 4th Legislature, Transcripts of Meetings, Session 5, Meeting 18, 16 Dec. 1916, p. 1174.
[763] G. P. Fedotov, Litso Rossii; Sbornik stratei (The Face of Russia, collection of articles) (1918-1931), Paris, YMCA Press, 1967, pp. 113, 114.
[764] Fyodor Dmitrievich Kryukov (1870 1920): writer of the Gift, populist, died of typhus during the civil war. He has been attributed the true paternity of the *Peaceful Gift* of the Cholokov Nobel prize.

follows: "... with them, there is the art and the love of fighting. And what projects!—vast, bold!

They have something of their own, a halo of suffering, something precious. We envy them, we are vexed" (that the Russian youth is not the same).

M. Agursky states the following hypothesis: "Participation in the revolutionary movement was, so to speak, a form of assimilation [more] 'suitable' than the common assimilation through baptism"; and it appears all the more worthy because it also meant a sort of revolt against one's own Jewish *bourgeoisie*[765]—and against one's own religion, which counted for nothing for the revolutionaries.

However, this "proper" assimilation was neither complete nor even real: many of these young men, in their haste, tore themselves from their own soil without really taking root in Russian soil, and remained outside these two nations and two cultures, to be nothing more than this material of which *internationalism* is so fond of.

But as the equal rights of the Jews remained one of the major demands of the Russian revolutionary movement, these young people, by embarking in the revolution, kept in their hearts and minds, the idea they were still serving the interests of their people. This was the thesis that Parvus had adopted as a course of action during his entire life, which he had formulated, defended and inculcated to the young people: the liberation of the Jews from Russia can only be done by overthrowing the Tsarist regime.

This thesis found significant support for a particular layer of Jewish society—middle-aged people, well-off, set, incredibly estranged from the spirit of adventure, but who, since the end of the nineteenth century, fed a permanent irritation against the Russian mode of government. It was in this ideological field that their children grew up before they even received the sap of Judaism to subsist from. An influential member of the Bund, Mr. Raies, points out that at the turn of the nineteenth and twentieth centuries "the Jewish *bourgeoisie* did not hide the hopes and expectations it placed in the progress of the revolutionary movement... it, which it once rejected, now had the *bourgeoisie's* favours."[766]

---

[765] *M. Agursky*, Sovmcslimy li sionizm i sotsializm? (Are Zionism and socialism compatible?), "22", Obschestvenno-polititchcskii i literaturnyi journal evreiskoi intellignntsii iz SSSR V Izrail ("22": social and political review of Jewish intellectuals emigrated from the USSR in Israel), Tel-Aviv, 1984, No. 36. p. 130.

[766] *M. Rafes*, Natsionalstitcheskii "ouklon" Bunda (The nationalist "tendency" of the Bund), Soblazn Sotsializma (The temptation of socialism), p. 276.

G. Gershuni explained to his judges: "It is *your* persecutions that have driven us to the revolution." In fact, the explanation is to be found both in Jewish history and in Russian history—at their intersection.

Let us listen to G. A. Landau, a renowned Jewish publicist. He wrote after 1917: "There were many Jewish families, both small and middle-class, in which the parents, *bourgeois* themselves, saw with their benevolent eyes, sometimes proud, always quiet, their offspring being marked by the seal in fashion of one of the social-revolutionary ideologies in vogue." They also, in fact, "leaned vaguely in favour of this ideology which protested against the persecutors, but without asking what was the nature of this protest or what were these persecutions." And it was thus that "little by little, the hegemony of socialism took root in Jewish society..."—the negation of civil society and of the State, contempt for *bourgeois* culture, and of the inheritance of past centuries, an inheritance from which the Jews had less difficulty to tear themselves away from since they already had, by Europeanising themselves, renounced their own inheritance." The revolutionary ideas "in the Jewish milieu... were... doubly destructive," and for Russia and for themselves. But they penetrated the Jewish milieu much more deeply than the Russian milieu."[767]

A jeweller from Kiev, Marchak (who even created some pieces to decorate the churches of the city), testifies that "while I was frequenting the *bourgeoisie*, I was contaminated [by the revolutionary spirit]." [768] Moreover, this is what we see with the young Bogrov[769]: that energy, that passion which grows in him during his youth spent in the bosom of a very rich family. His father, a wealthy liberal, gave full liberty to his young terrorist son.—And the Gotz brothers, also terrorists, had for grandfathers two Muscovites rich as Croesus, Gotz on the one hand, and on the other, Vyssotsky, a multi-millionaire tea maker, and these, far from retaining their grandchildren, paid to the S.-R. hundreds of thousands of rubles.

"Many Jews have come to swell the ranks of the Socialists," continues Landau.[770] In one of his speeches in the Duma (1909), A. I. Guchkov quotes the testimony of a young S.-R.: among other causes of her

---

[767] *G. A. Landau*, Rcvolioutsionnyie idei v evreiskoi obschestvennosti (Revolutionary ideas in Jewish public opinion), Rossiia i evrei: Sb. 1 (Russia and the Jews, Collection 1). Otetchestvennoie obiedineniii ruskikh evreiev zagranitsei (Patriotic Union of Russian Jews Abroad), Paris, YMCA Press, 1978 (Berlin, Osnova, 1924), pp. 106 109.
[768] *A. O. Marchak*, Inlerviou radiostanlsii "Svoboda" (Interview at "Radio Liberty"), Vospominaniia o revolioutsii 1917 goda (Memories on the Revolution of 1917), Int. No. 17, Munich, 1965, p. 9.
[769] Dmitry Grigoryevich Bogrov: young secret service agent. Shot and killed the minister A. Stolypine in Kiev (1911). Condemned to death and executed.
[770] Landau, op. cit., p. 109.

disenchantment, "she said that the revolutionary movement was entirely monopolised by the Jews and that they saw in the triumph of the revolution their own triumph."[771]

The enthusiasm for the revolution has seized Jewish society from the bottom to the top, says I. O. Levin: "It is not only the lower strata of the Jewish population of Russia that have devoted themselves to the revolutionary passion," but this movement "could not fail to catch a large part of the intellectuals and semi-intellectuals of the Jewish people" (semi-intellectuals who, in the 20s, constituted the active executives of the Soviet regime). "They were even more numerous among the liberal professions, from dentists to university teachers—those who could settle outside the Pale of Settlement.

Having lost the cultural heritage of traditional Judaism, these people were nonetheless foreign to Russian culture and any other national culture. This spiritual vacuum, hidden under a superficially assimilated European culture, made the Jews, already inclined to materialism, by their trades as tradesmen or craftsmen, very receptive to materialistic political theories... The rationalist mode of thought peculiar to the Jews... predisposes them to adhere to doctrines such as that of revolutionary Marxism."[772]

The co-author of this collection, V. S. Mandel, remarks: "Russian Marxism in its purest state, copied from the original German, was never a Russian national movement, and Jews in Russia, who were animated by a revolutionary spirit, for which nothing could be easier than assimilating a doctrine exhibited in books in German, were naturally led to take an important part in the work of transplanting this foreign fruit on Russian soil." [773] F. A. Stepun expressed it thus: "The Jewish youth boldly discussed, quoting Marx in support, the question of the form in which the Russian *moujik* should possess the land. The Marxist movement began in Russia with the Jewish youth inside the Pale of Settlement."

Developing this idea, V. S. Mandel recalls "The Protocols of the Elders of Zion"..., this stupid and hateful falsity." Well, "these Jews see in the delusions of the 'Protocols' the malicious intention of the anti-Semites to eradicate Judaism," but they themselves are "ready, in varying degrees, to

---

[771] A. Guchkov, Retch v Gosoudarstvennoi Doume 16 dek. 1909; Po zaprosou o vzryvc na Astrakhanskoi oulitse (Speech to the State Duma of 16 Dec. 1909, enquiry into the explosion of Astrakhan Street), A. I. Goutchkov v Tretei Gosoudarstvennoi Doume (1907-1912 Gg.): Cb. Retchei (A. I. Guchkov to the third State Duma) (1907 1912), Collection of speeches, Saint Petersburg, 1912, pp. 143,144.

[772] I. O. Levin, Evrei u revolioutsi (*The Jews and the Revolution*), Rossia i evrei (*Russia and the Jews*), op. Cit., pp. 130,132.

[773] V. S. Mandel, Konservativnyiee i razrouchitelnyie idei v evreistve (Conservative ideas and destructive ideas in Jewish society), *ibidem*, p 199.

organise the world on new principles, and believe that the revolution marks a step forward towards the establishment of the heavenly Kingdom on earth, and attribute to the Jewish people, for its greatest glory, the role of leader of the popular movements for freedom, equality and justice—a leader who, of course, does not hesitate to break down the existing political and social regime." And he gives as an example a quotation from the book of Fritz Kahn, *The Hebrews as a Race and People of Culture*: "Moses, one thousand two hundred and fifty years before Jesus Christ, proclaimed the rights of man... Christ paid with his life the preaching of *Communist manifestos* in a capitalist state", then "in 1848, the star of Bethlehem rose for the second time... and it rose again above the roofs of Judea: Marx."[774]

Thus, "of this common veneration for the revolution emerge and distinguish certain currents of opinion in Jewish society—all desperately unrealistic, childishly pretentious, thereby irresistibly aspiring to a troubled era, and not in Russia alone, but encompassing the entire century."[775]

With what casualness and what gravity at the same time, with what beautiful promises Marxism penetrates into the consciousness of cultivated Russia! Finally, the revolution has found its scientific foundation with its cortège of infallible deductions and inevitable predictions!

Among the young Marxists, there is Julius Tsederbaum; Martov, the future great leader of the Mensheviks, who, together with his best friend Lenin, will first found the "Union for the Struggle for the Liberation of the Working Class" (of all Russia)—only he will not enjoy the same protection as Lenin, exiled in the merciful country of Minousine: he will have to serve his three years in the tough region of Tourukhan. It was he, too, who, together with Lenin, designed the *Iskra*[776] and set up a whole network for its dissemination.

But even before collaborating with Lenin to found the All-Russian Social-Democratic Party, Martov, then exiled to Vilnius, had set up the ideological and organisational foundations of a "Jewish Joint Labour Union for Lithuania, Poland and Russia". Martov's idea was that, from now on, propaganda within the masses should be favoured as work within the circles, and, for this, make it "more specifically Jewish", and, in particular, translate it into Yiddish. In his lecture, Martov described the principles of the new Union: "We expected everything from the movement of the

---

[774] *Mandel, ibidem*, pp. 172-173.
[775] *I. M. Biekerman*, Rossiya i rouskoie evreistvo (Russia and the Jews of Russia), *ibidem*, p. 34.
[776] *The Iskra* (The Spark) is the first Marxist newspaper created by Lenin abroad. Was published from 1900 to 1903. Was resumed by the Mensheviks and was published until 1905.

Russian working class and considered ourselves as an appendix of the pan-Russian workers' movement... we had forgotten to maintain the link with the Jewish mass who does not know Russian. But at the same time, "without suspecting it, we hoisted the Jewish movement to a height unmatched by the Russians." Now is the time to free the Jewish movement "from the mental oppression to which the [Jewish] *bourgeoisie* has subjected it," which is "the lowest and lowest *bourgeoisie* in the world", "to create a specifically Jewish workers' organisation, which will serve as guide and instructor for the Jewish proletariat." In the "national character of the movement," Martov saw a victory over the *bourgeoisie*, and with this "we are perfectly safe... from nationalism."[777] In the following year, Plekhanov, at the Congress of the International Socialist, described the Jewish Social-Democratic movement as "the vanguard of the working-class army in Russia."[778] It was the latter which became the Bund (Vilnius, 1897), six months before the creation of the Social-Democratic Party of Russia. The next stage is the First Congress of the Russian Social-Democratic Party, which takes place in Minsk (where the Central Committee of the Bund was located) in 1898. The *Jewish Encyclopædia* tells us that "out of eight delegates, five were Jewish: the envoys of a Kiev newspaper, *The Workers' Gazette*, B. Eidelman, N. Vigdorchik, and those of the Bund: A. Kremer, A. Mutnik, S. Katz [were also present Radchenko, Petruyvitch and Vannovsky]. Within the Central Committee of the party (of three members) which was constituted at this Congress entered A. Kremer and B. Eidelman."[779] Thus was born the Social-Democratic Labour Party of Russia, in a close relationship with the Bund. (Let us add: even before the creation of *Iskra*, it was to Lenin that the direction of the newspaper of the Bund had been proposed.[780])

The fact that the Bund was created in Vilnius is not surprising: Vilnius was "the Lithuanian Jerusalem", a city inhabited by a whole cultivated Jewish elite, and through which transited, in provenance of the West, all the illegal literature heading to Saint Petersburg and Moscow.[781]

But the Bund, despite its internationalist ideology, "became a factor of national unity of Jewish life," even though "its leaders were guarding

---

[777] I. *Martov*, Povorotnyi punkt v istorii evreiskogo rabotchego dvijeniia (A turning point in the history of the workers' movement Soblazn Sotsializma (The temptation of socialism), pp. 249, 259-264, JE, t. 5, p. 94.
[778] G. V. Plekhanov o sotsialistitcheskom dvijenii sredi evreiev (G. V. Plekhanov on the socialist movement among the Jews), Soblazn Sotsializma (The temptation of socialism), p. 266.
[779] SJE, t. 7, p. 396.
[780] V. I. *Lenin*, Sotchincniia (Works in 45 vols., 4th ed.), Gospolitizdat, 1941 1967, vol. 5, pp. 463-464, 518.
[781] *Schub*, JW-2, p. 137.

against nationalism as if it were the plague" (like the Russian Social-Democrats who succeeded in watching out for it until the end). While subsidies flowed from abroad, consented by the wealthy Jewish milieus, the Bund advocated the principle that there is not a single Jewish people, and rejected the idea of a "universal Jewish nation,"[782] claiming on the contrary, that there are exist two antagonistic classes within the Jewish people (the Bund feared that nationalistic dispositions might "obscure the class consciousness of the proletariat").

However, there was hardly any Jewish proletariat in the strict sense of the term: the Jews seldom entered factories, as F. Kohn explains, "they considered it disgraceful not to be their own master", albeit very modestly—as an artisan or even an apprentice, when one can nurture the hope of opening one's own workshop. "To be hired in a factory was to lose all illusions as to the possibility of becoming one day one's own master, and that is why working in a factory was a humiliation, a disgrace."[783] (Another obstacle was the reluctance of employers to hire workers whose day of rest was Saturday and not Sunday.) As a result, the Bund declared "Jewish proletariat" both the artisans, and small traders, and clerks (was not every employed worker a proletarian, according to Marx?), and even commercial intermediaries. To all these individuals the revolutionary spirit could be inculcated, and they had be joined to the struggle against the autocracy. The Bund even declared that the Jews "are the best proletariat in the world."[784] (The Bund never renounced the idea of "strengthening its work among Christian workers.")

Not suspected of sympathy for socialism, G. B. Sliosberg writes in this regard that the enormous propaganda deployed by the Bund and some of its interventions "have done harm, and in particular an immediate damage to Jewish trade and their start-up industries." The Bund was turning against the employing instructors the very young apprentices, kids of 14–15 years old; its members broke the tiles of "more or less opulent Jewish houses." In addition, "on Yom-Kippur, young people from the Bund went into the

---

[782] *Aronson*, V borbe za… (In the fight for…), BJWR-1, p. 222.
[783] Revolioutsionnoie dvijeniie sredi evreiev (The revolutionary movement among the Jews) Sb. 1, M.; Vsesoiouznoie Obschestvo Politkatorjan i Ssylno-poselentsev (Collection 1, M., Association for the Soviet Union of Prisoners and Political Exiles), 1930, p. 25.
[784] S. *Dimanstein*, Revolioutsionnoie dvijeniie sredi evreiev (The Revolutionary Movement Among the Jews), Sb. 1905: Istoriia rcvolioutsionnogo dvijeniia v otdelnykh otcherkakh (Collection 1905: History of the Revolutionary Movement, some separate studies), directed by N. Pokrovsky, T. 3, Book 1, M-L., 1927, pp. 127, 138, 156.

great synagogue [in Vilnius], interrupted the prayer and started an incredible party, with beer flowing abundantly..."[785]

But, in spite of its class fanaticism, the Bund was increasingly based on a universal current equally characteristic of *bourgeois* liberalism: "It was increasingly understood in the cultivated world that the national idea plays an essential role in the awakening of self-consciousness in every man, which obliged the theoreticians of the proletarian circles themselves to raise more broadly the national question"; thus, in the Bund, "assimilationist tendencies were gradually supplanted by national tendencies." [786] —This, Jabotinsky confirms: "As it grows, the Bund replaces a national ideology with cosmopolitanism." [787] Abram Amsterdam, "one of the first important leaders of the Bund", who died prematurely, "tried to reconcile the Marxist doctrine with the ideas of nationalism."[788]—In 1901, at a congress of the Bund, one of the future leaders of the year Seventeen, Mark Lieber (M. I. Goldman), who was then a young man of 20, declared: "so far we have been cosmopolitan believers.

We must become national. Do not be afraid of the word. National does not mean nationalist." (May we understand it, even if it is ninety years late!) And, although this congress had endorsed a resolution against "the exaltation of the national sentiment which leads to chauvinism", he also pronounced himself for the national autonomy of the Jews "regardless of the territory inhabited by them."[789]

This slogan of national autonomy, the Bund developed it for a few years, both in its propaganda and its campaign of political banquets of 1904... although nobody knew exactly what could mean autonomy without territory.

Thus, every Jewish person was given the right to use only his own language in his dealings with the local administration and the organs of the State... but how? (For should not this right also be granted to the nationals of other nations?)

It should also be noted that, in spite of its socialist tendencies, the Bund, "in its social-democratic programme", pronounced itself "against the

---

[785] G. B. *Sliosberg*, Dela minouvehikh dnei: Zapiski ruskogo evreia (Things of the Past: Notes of a Russian Jew), 3 vols., Paris, 1933 1934, vol. 3, pp. 136 137.
[786] JE, t. 3, p. 337.
[787] V. *Jabotinski*, Vvdeniie (Preface) to Kh. N. Bialik, Pesni i poemy (Songs and poems), Saint Petersburg, ed. Zaltsman, 1914, p. 36.
[788] JE, t. 2, p. 354.
[789] Aronson, V borbe za... (In the fight for...), BJWR-1*, pp. 220-222.

demand for the restoration of Poland... and against constituent assemblies for the marches of Russia."[790] Nationalism, yes—but for oneself alone?

Thus, the Bund admitted only Jews in its midst. And once this orientation was taken, and although it was radically anticlerical, it did not accept the Jews who had denied their religion. The parallel Russian Social-Democratic organisations, the Bund, call them "Christian"—and, moreover, how could they be represented differently? But what a cruel offence for Lenin[791] to be so catalogued among the "Christians"!

The Bund thus embodies the attempt to defend Jewish interests, in particular against Russian interests. Here too, Sliosberg acknowledges: "The Bund's action has resulted in a sense of dignity and awareness of the rights of Jewish workers."[792]

Subsequently, the Bund's relations with the Russian Social-Democratic Party were not easy. As with the Polish Socialist Party, which at the time of the birth of the Bund had an "extremely suspicious" attitude towards it and declared that "the isolationism of the Bund places it in an adversarial position in relation to us." [793] Given its increasingly nationalistic tendencies, the Bund could only have conflicting relations with the other branches of Russian Social-Democracy.

Lenin thus describes the discussion he and Martov had with Plekhanov in Geneva in September 1900: "G. V.[794] shows a phenomenal intolerance by declaring that [i.e. the Bund] is in no way a social-democratic organisation, but that it is simply an exploiting organisation that takes advantage of the Russians; he says that our aim is to drive this Bund out of the Party, that the Jews are all without exception chauvinists and nationalists, that the Russian party must be Russian and not turn itself in "bound hand and foot" to the tribe of Gad[795]... G. V. has stuck to his positions without wanting to reconsider them, saying that we simply lack knowledge of the Jewish world and experience in dealing with it."[796] (From what ear Martov, the first initiator of the Bund, must have heard this diatribe?!)

In 1898 the Bund, despite its greater seniority, agreed to join the Russian Social-Democratic Party, but as *a whole*, with full autonomy over Jewish

---

[790] JE, t. 5, p. 99.
[791] *Lenin*, 4th ed., Vol. 6, p. 298.
[792] *Sliosberg*, t. 2, p. 258.
[793] JE*, t. 5, p. 95.
[794] G. V.: Georgiy Valentinovich Plekhanov (1856 1918). Social-democrat, Marxist, leading member of The Will of the People. Emigrated in 1880. Leader of the Menshevik party.
[795] Gad. One of the twelve sons of Jacob. One of the twelve tribes of Israel.
[796] *Lenin*, 4th ed., Vol. 4, p. 311.

affairs. It therefore agreed to be a member of the Russian party, but on condition that it did not interfere in its affairs. Such was the agreement between them.

However, at the beginning of 1902, the Bund considered that autonomy, so easily obtained at the 1st Congress of the Social Democratic Party, was no longer enough for it and that it now wanted to join the party on a *federal* basis, benefiting of full independence, even in programme matters. Regarding this it published a pamphlet against the *Iskra*.[797] The central argument, Lenin explains, was that the Jewish proletariat "is a part of the Jewish people, which occupies a special place among the nations."[798]

At this stage, Lenin sees red and feels obliged to clash with the Bund himself. He no longer calls only "to maintain pressure [against autocracy] by avoiding a fragmentation of the party into several independent formations,"[799] but he embarks on a passionate argument to prove (following, admittedly, Kautsky) that Jews are by no means a nation: they have neither common language nor territory (a flatly materialistic judgement: the Jews are one of the most authentic nations, the most united found on earth. United, it is in spirit. In his superficial and vulgar internationalism, Lenin could not understand the depth or historical roots of the Jewish question.) "The idea of a separate Jewish people is politically reactionary,"[800] it justifies Jewish particularism. (And all the more "reactionary" were Zionists to him!) Lenin saw a solution for the Jews only in their total assimilation—which amounts to saying, in fact, to cease outright being Jewish.

In the summer of 1903, at the 2nd Congress of the Social-Democratic Party of Russia in Brussels, out of 43 delegates, there were only five of the Bund (however, "many Jews participated"). And Martov, "supported by twelve Jews" (among them Trotsky, Deutsch, Martynov, Liadov, to name but a few), spoke on behalf of the party against the "federal" principle demanded by the Bund. The members of the Bund then left the Congress (which permitted Lenin's proposed statutes in paragraph 1 to prevail), and then also left the party.[801] (After the split of the Social Democratic Party into Bolsheviks and Mensheviks, "the leaders of the Mensheviks were A. Axelrod, A. Deutsch, L. Martov, M. Lieber, L. Trotsky,"[802] as well as F. Dan, R. Abramovich—Plekhanov remaining on the sidelines.)

---

[797] JE, t. 5, pp. 96, 97.
[798] *Lenin*, 4th ed., t.7, p.77.
[799] *Ibidem*, t. 6, p. 300.
[800] *Ibidem*, t. 7, pp. 83 84.
[801] JE, t. 5, p. 97; SJE, I. 7, p. 397.
[802] SJE, t. 7, p. 397.

On the "Street of the Jews," as it was then called, the Bund quickly became a powerful and active organisation. "Until the eve of the events of 1905, the Bund was the most powerful social-democratic organisation in Russia, with a well-established apparatus, good discipline, united members, flexibility and great experience in conspiring." Nowhere else is there a discipline like in the Bund. The "bastion" of the Bund was the North-West region.[803]

However, formidable competition arose with the "Independent Jewish Workers' Party" which was created in 1901 under the influence and the exhortations of Zubatov[804]: it persuaded the Jewish workers and all who would listen that it was not the social democratic ideology they needed but struggle against the *bourgeoisie* defending their economic interests to them—the government was interested in their success, they could act legally, their authority would a benevolent referee. The head of this movement was the daughter of a miller, the intrepid Maria Vilbouchevitch. "The supporters of Zubatov… enjoyed great success in Minsk with the (Jewish) workers"; they were passionately opposed to the members of the Bund and obtained much by organising economic strikes. They also acted, not without success, in Odessa (Khuna Shayevich). But just as, throughout the country, the frightened government (and Plehve[805]) foiled Zubatov's project, likewise with the "independents": Shayevich was arrested in 1903, sentenced to a fairly short sentence—but then came the news of the Kishinev pogrom, and the "independents" had their hands tied.[806]

Meanwhile, "the Bund was receiving help from foreign groups" from Switzerland first and then from Paris, London, the United States where "action groups… had reached sizeable proportions." Organised "clubs, Rotarian action groups, associations of aid to the work of the Bund in Russia. This aid was mainly financial."[807]

From 1901, the Bund renounced "economic terror" (lashing out on employers, monitoring factories), because it "obscured the social-democratic consciousness of the workers", and they pretended equally of condemning political terror."[808] This did not prevent Guirsh Lekkert, a

---

[803] *Dimanstein*, "1905", vol. 3, Book I, pp. 127, 138, 156.
[804] Sergei Vasilyevich Zubatov (1864 1917): Chief of the Moscow Police and Special Police Department (1902–1905).
[805] Viatcheslav Konstantinovich Plehve (1846 1904): cunning Minister of the Interior, killed by the terrorist S. R. Sozonov.
[806] *N. A. Buchbinder*, Nezavissimaia evreiskaia rabolchaia partiia (The Independent Jewish Workers' Party). Krasnaia letopis: lstoritcheskii journal (Red Chronicle: Historical Review), 1922, no. 2-3, pp. 208,241.
[807] JE, t. 5, p. 101; SJE, t. 1, pp. 559,560.
[808] JE, t.5, p.96.

cobbler who was a member of the Bund, from shooting at the governor of Vilnius—and to be hanged for it. The young Mendel Deutsch, still a minor, also fired shots whose significance marked "the apogee of the movement of the Jewish masses."[809] And already the Bund was wondering if it should not go back to terror. In 1902, the Berdichev Conference endorsed a resolution on "organised revenge". But a debate broke out in the Bund, and the following year the Congress formally annulled this decision of the Conference.[810] According to Lenin, the Bund, in 1903, went through "terrorist temptations, which it then got over."[811]

Terror, which had already manifested itself more than once in Russia, enjoyed a general indulgence, an indulgence which was in the air of the time, and which, with the increasingly widespread custom of holding, "just in case," a firearm (and it was easy to obtain one via smuggling) could not fail to arouse, in the minds of the youth of the Pale of Settlement, the idea of forming their own combat regiments.

But the Bund had active and dangerous competitors. Is it a historical coincidence, or the time had simply come for the Jewish national consciousness to be reborn, in any case, it is in 1897, the year of the creation of the Bund, just a month prior, the First Universal Congress of Zionism took place. And it was in the early 1900s that young Jews pioneered a new path, "a public service path… at the crossroads between *Iskra* and Bne Moshe" ("the sons of Moses"), some turning right, the others heading left."[812] "In the programmes of all our groupings which appeared between 1904 and 1906, the national theme held its proper place."[813] We have seen that the Socialist Bund had not cut it off, and it now only had to condemn Zionism all the more firmly in order to excite national sentiment to the detriment of class consciousness.

It is true that "the numbers of the Zionist circles among the youth gave way to the number of young people adhering to the revolutionary socialist parties."[814]

(Although there were counter-examples: thus the publisher of the Jewish Socialist *La Pravda* of Geneva, G. Gurevitch, had re-converted to devote himself entirely to the issue of the Jews' settlement in Palestine.) The ditch dug between Zionism and the Bund was gradually filled by such and such

---

[809] *Dimanstein*, "1905", T. 3, Book I, pp. 149,150.
[810] JE*, t. 5, p. 97.
[811] *Lenin*, 4th ed. 6, p. 288.
[812] I. Ben-Tsvi.
[813] S. M. Ginzburg, O roussko-evreiskoi intelligentsii (From the Russo-Jewish Intelligence), Sb. Evreiski mir; Ejegodnik na 1939 g. (Rcc. The Jewish World, Annual for the year 1939), Paris, Association of the Russo-Jewish Intelligence, p. 39.
[814] *Sliosberg*, t. 3, p. 133.

a new party, then another, then a third—Poalei-Tsion, Zeirei-Tsion, the "Zionist-Socialists", the *serpovtsy* (*seimovtsy*)—, each combining in its own way Zionism and socialism.

It is understandable that between parties so close to one other a fierce struggle developed, and this did not facilitate the task of the Bund. Nor did the emigration of the Jews from Russia into Israel, which gained momentum in those years: why emigrate? What sense does this have when the Jewish proletariat must fight for socialism side by side with the working class of all countries..., which would automatically solve the Jewish question everywhere?

The Jews have often been criticised in the course of history for the fact that many of them were usurers, bankers, merchants. Yes, the Jews formed a significant detachment, creator of the world of capital—and mainly in its financial forms. This, the great political economist Werner Sombart described it with a vigorous and convincing pen. In the first years of the Revolution this circumstance was, on the contrary, attributed to the Jews, as an inevitable *formation* on the road to socialism. And in one of his indictments, in 1919, Krylenko found it necessary to emphasise that "the Jewish people, since the Middle Ages, has taken out of their ranks the holders of a new influence, that of capital... they precipitated... the dissolution of economic forms of another age."[815] Yes, of course, the capitalist system in the economic and commercial field, the democratic system in the political field are largely indebted to the constructive contribution of the Jews, and these systems in turn are the most favourable to the development of Jewish life and culture.

But—and this is an unfathomable historical enigma—these systems were not the only ones that the Jews favoured. As V. S. Mandel reminds us, if we refer to the Bible, we discover that "the very idea of a monarchy was invented by no other people but the Hebrews, and they transmitted it to the Christian world. The monarch is not chosen by the people, he is the chosen by God. Hence the rite which the Christian peoples have inherited from the coronation and anointing of the kings."[816] (One might rectify by recalling that the Pharaohs long ago were also anointed, and also bearers of the divine will.) For his part, the former Russian revolutionary A. Valt-Lessine remembers: "The Jews did not accord great importance to the revolutionary movement. They put all their hopes in the petitions addressed to Saint Petersburg, or even in the bribes paid to the officials of the ministries—but

---

[815] *N. V. Krylenko*, Za piat lct. 1918–1922: Obvinitelnyie retchi po naibolee kroupnym protsessam, zaslouchannym v Moskovskom i Verkhovnom Revolioutsionnykh Tribounalakh (Over five years, 1918 1922: Submissions made in the highest trials before the Supreme Court and the Moscow Revolutionary Tribunal), 1923, p. 353.

[816] *Mandel*, Rossia i evrei (Russia and the Jews), op. Cit., p. 177.

not at all in the revolution."[817] This kind of approach to the influential spheres received, on the part of the impatient Jewish youth, the sobriquet, known since the Middle Ages and now infamous, of *chtadlan*. Someone like G. B. Sliosberg, who worked for many years in the Senate and the Ministry of the Interior, and who patiently had to solve Jewish problems of a private nature, thought that this avenue was the safest, with the richest future for the Jews, and he was ulcerated to note the impatience of these young people.

Yes, it was perfectly unreasonable, on the part of the Jews, to join the revolutionary movement, which had ruined the course of normal life in Russia and, consequently, that of the Jews of Russia. Yet, in the destruction of the monarchy and in the destruction of the *bourgeois* order—as, some time before, in the reinforcement of it—the Jews found themselves in the vanguard. Such is the innate mobility of the Jewish character, its extreme sensitivity to social trends and the advancement of the future.

It will not be the first time in the history of mankind that the most natural impulses of men will suddenly lead to monstrosities most contrary to their nature.

---

[817] A. *Lessine*, Epizody iz moei jizni (Episodes of My Life), JW-2, p. 388.

Chapter 7

The Birth of Zionism

How did the Jewish conscience evolve in Russia during the second half of the nineteenth century? Towards 1910, Vladimir Jabotinsky describes this evolution in his somewhat passionate manner: at first, the mass of Jews opposed the Enlightenment, "the fanatic prejudice of an overvalued specificity." But time did its work, and "as much Jews, historically, fled humanist culture, as much they aspire to it now... and this thirst for knowledge is so widespread that it perhaps makes us, Jews of Russia, the first nation in the world." However, "running towards the goal, we passed it. Our goal was to form a Jew who, by staying Jewish, could live a life that would be that of the universal man", and "now we have totally forgotten that we must remain Jewish", "we stopped attaching a price to our Jewish essence, and it began to weigh on us." We must "extirpate this mentality from self-contempt and revive the mentality of self-respect... We complain that we are despised, but we are not far from despising ourselves."[818]

This description reflects the general trend towards assimilation, but not all aspects of the picture. As we have already seen (chapter 4), in the late sixties of the nineteenth century, the publicist and man of letters Smolenskin had spoken out vigorously against the tendency to assimilate Jewish intellectuals, as he had observed it in Odessa or as it had spread in Germany. And he at once declared war on both "bigots and false devotees who want to drive out all knowledge of the house of Israel." No! One must not be ashamed of their origins, one must cherish their national language and dignity; however, national culture can only be preserved through language, the ancient Hebrew. This is all the more important because "Judaism deprived of territory" is a particular phenomenon, "a spiritual

---

[818] V. *Jabotinsky*, O natsionalnom vospitanii (From the Education of National Sentiment), Sb. Felietony (Collection of Serials). Saint Petersburg. Typography "Herold", 1913, pp. 57.

nation".⁸¹⁹ The Jews are indeed a nation, not a religious congregation. Smolenskin advanced the doctrine of "progressive Jewish nationalism."⁸²⁰

Throughout the 70s, Smolenskin's voice remained practically unheard of. At the end of this period, however, the liberation of the Slavs from the Balkans contributed to the national awakening of the Jews of Russia themselves. But the pogroms of 1881 1882 caused the ideals of *Haskala* to collapse; "The conviction that civilisation was going to put an end to the persecutions of another age against the Jews and that these, thanks to the Enlightenment, would be able to approach the European peoples, this conviction was considerably shaken."⁸²¹ (The experience of the pogroms in the south of Ukraine is thus extrapolated to all the Jews of Europe?) Among the Jews of Russia "there appeared the type of the 'repentant intellectual', of those who aspired to return to traditional Judaism."⁸²²

It was then that Lev Pinsker, a well-known doctor and publicist, already sixty years of age, gave the Jews of Russia and Germany a vigorous appeal to *self-emancipation*.⁸²³ Pinsker wrote that faith in emancipation had collapsed, that it was now necessary to stifle every ounce of hope in brotherhood among peoples. Today, "the Jews do not constitute a living nation; they are strangers everywhere; they endure oppression and contempt on the part of the peoples who surround them." The Jewish people is "the spectre of a dead wandering among the living". "One must be blind not to see that the Jews are the 'chosen people' of universal hatred. The Jews cannot "assimilate to any nation and consequently cannot be tolerated by any nation." "By wanting to mingle with other peoples, they have frivolously sacrificed their own nationality," but "nowhere have they obtained that the others recognise them as native-born inhabitants equal to them." The destiny of the Jewish people cannot depend on the benevolence of other peoples. The practical conclusion thus lies in the creation of "a people on its own territory". What is needed, therefore, is to find an appropriate territory, "no matter where, in what part of the world,"⁸²⁴ and that the Jews come to populate it.

Moreover, the creation in 1860 of the Alliance [Israelite Universal] was nothing but the first sign of Jewish refusal of a single option—assimilation.

---

⁸¹⁹ JE*, t. 14, pp. 403 404.
⁸²⁰ *I.L. Klauzner*, Literatura na ivril v Rossii (Literature in Modern Hebrew in Russia). BJWR, p. 506.
⁸²¹ JE, 1.12, p. 259.
⁸²² *Ibidem*, t. 13, p. 639.
⁸²³ Title of his famous work.
⁸²⁴ *Ibidem*, t. 12, pp. 526,527; *Hessen**, t. 2, pp. 233 234; G. Svet, Rousskiie evrei v sionizme i v stroilelstve Palestiny i Izrailia (*The Jews of Russia in Zionism and the Edification of Palestine and Israel*). BJWR-1 *, pp. 244 245.

There already existed among the Jews of Russia a movement of *Palestinophilia*, the aspiration to return to Palestine. (Conforming, in essence, to traditional religious salutation: "Next year in Jerusalem.") This movement gained momentum after 1881 1882.

"Stretching out its efforts to colonise Palestine... so that within a century the Jews can finally leave the inhospitable land of Europe"... The slogans that the Enlightenment had previously broadcasted, inciting to fight "traditionalism, Hasidism and religious prejudices, gave way to a call for reconciliation and the union of all layers of Jewish society for the realisation of the ideals" of Palestine, "for the return to the Judaism of our fathers." "In many cities of Russia, circles were formed, called circles of the 'Lovers of Zion'—Khovevei-Tsion.[825] [826]

And it was thus that an idea joined another to rectify it. Going to settle elsewhere, yes, but not anywhere: in Palestine. But what had happened in Palestine? "The first crusade resulted in the virtual disappearance of the few Hebrews who remained in Palestine."

Nevertheless, "a tiny Jewish religious community had succeeded in surviving and the collapse of the Crusader State, and the conquest of the country by the Mamelukes, and the invasion by the Mongol hordes." Over the following centuries, the Jewish population was somewhat replenished by a modest migratory flow of "believers from different countries". At the end of the eighteenth century a certain number of Hasidim emigrated from Russia. "In the middle of the nineteenth century, there were twelve thousand Jews in Palestine," whereas at the end of the eleventh century there were twenty-five thousand.

"These Jewish towns in the land of Israel constituted what was called the *Yishuv*. All their inhabitants (men) were only studying Judaism, and nothing else. They lived on *Haluka*—subsidies sent by Jewish communities in Europe.

These funds were distributed by the rabbis, hence the absolute authority of the rabbis. The leaders of the *Yishuv* "rejected any attempt to create in the country even an embryo of productive work of Jewish origin." They were studying exclusively the Talmud, nothing else, and on a fairly elementary level. "The great Jewish historian G. Gretz, who visited Palestine in 1872," found that "only a minority studied for real, the others preferred to stroll the streets, remained idle, engaged in gossip and slander." He believed that "this system favours obscurantism, poverty and degeneration of the Jewish

---

[825] JE*, t. 12, pp. 259 260.
[826] A pioneering Zionist movement founded before Herzl.

population of Palestine"—and for this he himself "had to undergo *Herem*[827]."[828]

In 1882, in Kharkov, Palestinophile students founded the Biluim circle. They proposed to "create in Palestine a model agricultural colony", to set "the tone to the general colonisation of Palestine by the Jews"; they undertook to found circles in several cities of Russia. (Later they created a first settlement in Palestine, but were confronted to the hostility and opposition of the traditional *Yishuv*: the rabbis demanded that, according to ancient custom, the cultivation of the earth be suspended one year out of seven.[829])

Pinsker supported the advocates of the return to Palestine: in 1887 he summoned the first Congress of Palestinophiles in Katovice, then in Druskeniki, and the second in 1887. Propagandists began to cover the Pale of Settlement, speaking in synagogues and public meetings. (Deutsch testifies that after 1882 P. Axelrod himself contributed to palestinophilia...[830])

Of course, Smolenskin is one of the passionate apostles of the return to Palestine: bubbling and lively, he connects with Anglo-Jewish political actors, but he comes up against the opposition of the Alliance, who does not want to promote the colonisation of Palestine, but rather to direct the migratory wave towards America. He then describes the tactics of the Alliance as "betrayal of the cause of the people." His premature death cut his efforts short.[831]

We note, however, that this movement towards Palestine was rather weakly received by the Jews of Russia; it was even thwarted. "The idea of a political revival of the Jewish people brought a small handful of intellectuals behind it at the time, and it soon came up against fierce adversaries." [832] The conservative circles, the rabbinate and the *Tzadikim*[833] saw in this current towards Palestine an attack on the divine

---

[827] Herem (Hebrew word): the status of one who is cut off from the community due to impurity or consecration. The individual in state of Herem is an outlaw. A kind of excommunication.
[828] *M. Wartburg*, Plata za sionism (The Wage of Zionism), in "22": Obschestvenno-politicianski i liieratournyi journal evreiskoi intelligenlsii iz SSSR V Izraile ("22": politico-social and literary review of the Jewish intelligentsia emigrated from USSR to Israel), Tel Aviv, 1987, No. 56, pp. 112,114; Svet, SJE-1, pp. 235,243.
[829] JE, t. 4, pp. 577, 579; *Warthurg*, in "22", 1987, no. 56, p. 115.
[830] *L. Deulsch*, King evreiev v rousskom revolioutsionnom dvijenii (The role of the Jews in The Russian revolutionary movement), t. 1, 2nd ed., ML., 1925, pp. 5, 161.
[831] JE, t. 14, pp. 406 407.
[832] *Hessen*, t. 2, p. 234.
[833] Tzadikim (Hebrew word): the righteous.

will, "an attack on faith in the Messiah who alone must bring the Jews back to Palestine. As for the progressive assimilationists, they saw in this current a reactionary desire to isolate the Jews from the rest of enlightened humanity."[834]

The Jews of Europe did not support the movement either. Meanwhile, on site, the success of the return was revealed to be "too mitigated": "many colonists discovered their incompetence in the work of the land"; "the ideal of rebirth of the ancient country was crumbling into petty acts of pure benevolence"; "The colonies survived only because of the subsidies sent by Baron Rothschild." And in the early 1990s, "colonisation went through... a serious crisis due to an anarchic system of land purchase" and a decision by Turkey (the owner of Palestine) to ban the Jews of Russia from disembarking in Palestinian ports.[835]

It was at this time that the publicist, thinker and organiser Asher Ginzberg became known, under the eloquent pseudonym of Ahad Haam ("One of His People"). He strongly criticised practical palestinophilia as it had been constituted; what he advocated was, "before striving for a renaissance on a territory", to worry about "a 'rebirth of hearts', an intellectual and moral improvement of the people": "to install at the centre of Jewish life, a living and spiritual aspiration, a desire for national cohesion, revival and free development in a national spirit, but on the basis of all men."[836] This will later be called "spiritual Zionism" (but not "religious", and this is important).

That same year, 1889, in order to unite among them those who were dear to the idea of a rebirth of national feeling, Ahad Haam founded a league—or, as it is called—an *order*: Bne-Moshe[837] ("The sons of Moses"), whose status "resembled strongly those of the Masonic lodges; the applicant made the solemn promise of strictly executing all the demands of order; the new members were initiated by a master, the "big brother"; the neophyte undertook to serve without reserve the ideal of national rebirth, even if there was little hope that this ideal would be realised any time soon."[838] It was stipulated in the manifesto of order that "national consciousness takes precedence over religious consciousness, personal interests are subject to national interests," and it was recommended that a feeling of unreserved love for Judaism, placed above all other objectives of the movement. Thus

---

[834] JE, t. 12, p. 261.
[835] *Ibidem*, pp. 261,262.
[836] JE*, t. 3, pp. 480, 482.
[837] Association founded by Ahad Haam in Odessa.
[838] *Ibidem*, t. 4, pp. 683, 684.

was prepared "the ground for the reception of political Zionism" of Herzl[839]... of which Ahad Haam absolutely did not want.

He made several trips to Palestine: in 1891, 1893, and 1900. Regarding colonisation, he denounced an anarchic character and an insufficient rootedness in tradition.[840] He "severely criticised the dictatorial conduct of Baron Rothschild's emissaries."[841]

This is how Zionism was born in Europe, a decade behind Russia. The first leader of Zionism, Theodor Herzl, had been, until the age of thirty-six (he only lived to forty-four), a writer, a playwright, a journalist. He had never been interested in Jewish history or, *a fortiori*, in the Hebrew language, and, characteristically, as a good Austrian liberal, he considered the aspirations of the various "ethnic minorities" of the Austro-Hungarian Empire to self-determination and national existence to be *reactionary*, and found it normal to stifle them.[842] As Stefan Zweig writes, Herzl cherished the dream of seeing the Jews of Vienna enter the cathedral in order to be baptised and seeing the Jewish question resolved once and for all by the fusion of Judaism and Christianity. But anti-Jewish sentiments developed in Austria-Hungary in parallel with the rise of Pan-Germanism, while in Paris, where Herzl resided at the time, the Dreyfus affair broke out. Herzl had the opportunity to witness the "public degradation of Captain Dreyfus"; convinced of his innocence, he was deeply shaken and changed his course. "If separation is inevitable," he said, "well, let it be radical!

... If we suffer from being without a country, let us build ourselves a homeland!"[843] Herzl then had a revelation: it was necessary to create a Jewish state! "As if struck by lightning, Herzl was enlightened by this new idea: antiSemitism is not a fortuitous phenomenon subject to particular conditions, it is a permanent evil, it is the eternal companion of the eternal errant," and "'the only possible solution to the Jewish question', is a sovereign Jewish state."[844] (To conceive such a project after nearly two thousand years of diaspora, what imaginative power one needed, what exceptional audacity!) However, according to S. Zweig, Herzl's pamphlet entitled *A Jewish State* received from the Viennese *bourgeoisie* a welcome "perplexed and irritated... What's gotten into this writer, so intelligent, so cultivated and spiritual? Our language is German and not Hebrew, our homeland—beautiful Austria", Herzl, "does he not give our worst enemies

---

[839] *Svet*, op. cit., pp. 250 251.
[840] JE, t. 3, p. 481.
[841] SJE, t. 1, pp. 248,249.
[842] JE, t. 6, pp. 407 409.
[843] *Stefan Zweig*, Vtchrachnii mir. Vospominaniia evropeitsa (*The world of yesterday: Memories of a European*), in "22", 1994, No. 92, pp. 215,216.
[844] JE, t. 6, p. 409.

arguments against us: he wants to isolate us?" Consequently, "Vienna... abandoned him and laughed at him. But the answer came to him from elsewhere; it burst forth like a thunderbolt, so sudden, charged with such a weight of passion and such ecstasy that he was almost frightened to have awakened, around the world, a movement with his dozens of pages, a movement so powerful and through which he found himself overwhelmed. His answer did not come to him, it is true, from the Jews of the West... but from the formidable masses of the East. Herzl, with his pamphlet, had inflamed this nucleus of Judaism, which was smouldering under the ashes of the stranger."[845]

Henceforth, Herzl gives himself body and soul to his new idea. He "breaks off with those closest to him, he only frequents the Jewish people... He who, even recently, despised politics, now founds a political movement; he introduces to it a spirit and a party discipline, forms the framework of a future army and transforms the [Zionist] congresses into a true parliament of the Jewish people." At the first Congress of Basel in 1897 he produced a very strong impression "on the Jews who were meeting for the first time in a parliamentary role," and "during his very first speech, he was unanimously and enthusiastically proclaimed... leader and chief of the Zionist movement." He shows "a consummate art to find the formulas of conciliation", and, conversely, "the one who criticises his objective... or merely blames certain measures taken by him..., that one is the enemy not only of Zionism, but of the entire Jewish people."[846]

The energetic writer Max Nordau (Suedfeld) supported him by expressing the idea that emancipation is fallacious, since it has introduced seeds of discord into the Jewish world: the emancipated Jew believes that he really has found a homeland, when "all that is living and vital in Judaism, which represents the Jewish ideal, the courage and the ability to advance, all this is none other than Zionism."[847]

At this 1st Congress, the delegates of Russian Zionism "constituted one third of the participants... 66 out of 197." In the eyes of some, their presence could be regarded as a gesture of opposition to the Russian government. To Zionism had adhered all of the Russian Khovevei-Tsion, "thus contributing to the establishment of global Zionism." [848] Thus "Zionism drew its strength from the communities of oppressed Jews in the East, having found only limited support among the Jews of Western

---

[845] *Zweig*, in "22", op. cil., pp. 216,217.
[846] JE, t. 6, pp. 410 411.
[847] JE, 1.11, pp. 788 792.
[848] SJE, t. 7, p. 940.

Europe."[849] But it also followed that the Russian Zionists represented for Herzl a most serious opposition. Ahad Haam waged a fierce struggle against Herzl's political Zionism (alongside the majority of the palestinophiles), strongly criticising the pragmatism of Herzl and Nordau, and denouncing what he called "their indifference to the spiritual values of Judaic culture and tradition."[850] He found chimeric the hope of political Zionism to found an autonomous Jewish *state in the near future*; he regarded all this movement as extremely detrimental to the cause of the spiritual rebirth of the nation... "They do not care about the salvation of Judaism in perdition because they care nothing about spiritual and cultural heritage; they aspire not to the *rebirth* of the ancient nation, but to the *creation* of a new people from the dispersed particles of ancient matter."[851] (If he uses and even emphasises the word "Judaism," it is almost evident that it is not in the sense of the Judaic religion, but in the sense of the spiritual system inherited from ancestors. The *Jewish Encyclopædia* tells us about Ahad Haam that in the 70s, "he was more and more imbued with rationalism and deviated from religion."[852] If the only vocation for Palestine is to "become the spiritual centre that could unite, by national and spiritual ties, the dispersed nations,"[853] a centre which "would pour out its 'light' on the Jews of the whole world", would create "a new spiritual bond between the scattered members of the people", it would be less a "State of the Jews" than "an elite spiritual community."[854]

Discussions agitated the Zionists. Ahad Haam strongly criticised Herzl whom Nordau supported by accusing Ahad Haam of "covert Zionist". World Zionist congresses were held every year; in 1902 took place the one of the Russian Zionists in Minsk, and the discussions resumed. This is where Ahad Haam read his famous exposition: A spiritual rebirth.[855]

Zionism no longer met with amenity from the outside. Herzl expected this: as soon as the program of the Zionists would take a concrete form and as soon as the real departure to Palestine began, anti-Semitism everywhere would end.

But long before this result was reached, "stronger than others, the voice of those who... feared that the taking of a public position in the nationalist

---

[849] J. Parks, Evrei sredi narodov: Obzor pritchin anti-semitima (*The Jews among Peoples: An Overview of the Causes of Anti-Semitism*), Paris, YMCA Press, 1932, p. 45.
[850] SJE, t. 1, p. 249.
[851] JE, t. 3, p. 482.
[852] SJE, I. 1, p. 248.
[853] JE, 1.12, p. 262.
[854] *Wartburg*, in "22", 1987, no. 56, pp. 116, 117.
[855] JE, t. 3, p. 482.

sense of an assimilated Jew would give antisemites the opportunity to say that every assimilated Jew hides under his mask an authentic Jew... incapable of blending into the local population."[856] And as soon as an independent state was created, the Jews went everywhere to be suspected and accused of civic disloyalty, ideological isolationism—which their enemies had always suspected and accused them of.

In reply, at the Second Zionist Congress (1898), Nordau declared: "We reject with disdain the name of 'party'; the Zionists are not a party, they are the Jewish people themselves... Those who, on the contrary, are at ease in servitude and contempt, they keep themselves carefully apart, unless they fight us fiercely."[857]

As one English historian observes: Yes, "Zionism has done a great service to the Jews by restoring them a sense of dignity," and yet "it leaves unresolved the question of their attitude towards the countries in which they live."[858]

In Austria, a compatriot of Herzl, Otto Weininger, argued with him: "Zionism and Judaism are incompatible with the fact that Zionism intends to force the Jews to take upon themselves the responsibility of a state of their own, which contradicts the very essence of every Jew."[859] And he predicted the failure of Zionism.

In Russia in 1899, I. M. Biekerman argued strongly against Zionism, as an idea deemed "quacky, inspired by anti-Semitism, of reactionary inspiration and harmful by nature"; it is necessary "to reject the illusions of the Zionists and, without in any way renouncing the spiritual particularism of the Jews, struggle hand in hand with the cultural and progressive forces of Russia in the name of the regeneration of the common fatherland."[860]

At the beginning of the century, the poet N. Minsky had issued this criticism: Zionism marks the loss of the notion of universal man, it lowers the cosmopolitan dimensions, the universal vocation of Judaism to the level of an ordinary nationalism. "The Zionists, speaking tirelessly of nationalism, turn away from the genuinely national face of Judaism and in fact seek only to be like everyone else, not worse than others."[861]

---

[856] *Ibidem*, t. 6, p. 409.
[857] *Ibidem**, t. 11, p. 792.
[858] *Parks*, p. 186.
[859] *N. Goulina*, Kto boilsa Otto Veiningcra? (Who's afraid of Otto Weininger?). In "22"*, 1983, No. 31, p. 206.
[860] JE, t. 4, p. 556.
[861] *N. Minsky*, Natsionalnyi lik i patriotism (The National Face and Patriotism), Slovo, Saint Petersburg, 1909, 28 March (10 April), p. 2.

It is interesting to compare these sentences with the remark made before the revolution by the orthodox thinker S. Bulgakov: "The biggest difficulty for Zionism is that it is not able to recover the lost faith of the fathers, and it is obliged to rely on a principle that is either national, cultural or ethnic, a principle on which no genuine great nation can rely exclusively."[862]

But the first Russian Zionists—now, "it is from Russia that most of the founders of the State of Israel and the pioneers of the State of Israel came out,"[863] and it was in Russian that "were written the best pages of Zionist journalism"[864]—were filled with an irrepressible enthusiasm for the idea of returning to their people the lost homeland, the ancient land of the Bible and their ancestors, to create a State of unparalleled quality and to have men of exceptional quality grow there.

And this impulse, this call addressed to all to turn to physical work, the work of the earth!—Does not this appeal echo the exhortations of a Tolstoy, the doctrine of *asceticism*?[865] All streams lead to the sea. But, in the final analysis, how can a Zionist behave towards the country in which he resides for the time being?

For the Russian Zionists who devoted all their strength to the Palestinian dream, it was necessary to exclude themselves from the affairs that agitated Russia as such. Their statutes stipulated: "Do not engage in politics, neither internal nor external." They could only weakly, without conviction, take part in the struggle for equal rights in Russia. As for participating in the national liberation movement?—but that would be pulling the chestnuts out of the fire for the others![866]

Such tactics drew Jabotinsky's fiery reproaches: "Even passing travellers have an interest in the inn being clean and tidy."[867] And then, in *what language* should the Zionists display their propaganda? They did not know Hebrew, and, anyway, who would have understood it? Consequently:

---

[862] *Prou S. Bulgakov*, Khristianstvo i evreiskij vopros (Christianity and the Jewish Question), Paris. YMCA Press, 1991, p. 11.
[863] *F. Kolker*, Novyj plan pomoschi sovietskomou cvrcistvou (*A new plan for aid to the Jews of Russia*), in "22", 1983, No. 31, p. 149.
[864] *N. Goulina*, V poiskakh outratchennoi samoidenlilikatsii (*In Search of the Lost Self-Identity*), in "22", 1983, No. 29, p. 216.
[865] *Amos Oz*, Spischaia krasaviisa: griozy i pruboujdeniia (*Sleeping Beauty: dreams and awakening*), in "22", 1985, No. 42. p. 117.
[866] *G. J. Iaronson*, V borbe za granjdanskiie i nalsionalnyie prava: Obschestvennyie tetcheniia v rousskom evreistve (In the fight for civil and national rights: the social currents among the Jews of Russia), BJWR-1, pp. 218, 219.
[867] *Ibidem**, p. 219.

either in Russian or in Yiddish. And this brought closer once more the radicals of Russia[868] and the Jewish revolutionaries.

Evidently, the Jewish revolutionary youth jousted with the Zionists: no and no! The solution of the Jewish question does not lie in the departure out of Russia, it is in the political fight for equal rights here! Instead of going to settle far beyond the seas, we must make use of the possibility of affirming ourselves here in this country. And their arguments could not avoid shaking more than one by their clarity.

In the Bolshevik circles, the Zionists were denounced as "reactionary"; they were treated as "the party of the darkest, most desperate pessimism."[869]

Inevitably, intermediate currents were to emerge. Thus the Zionist party of the left Poalei-Tsion ("Workers of Zion"). It was in Russia that it was founded in 1899; it combined "socialist ideology with political Zionism." It was an attempt to find a median line between those concerned exclusively with class problems and those concerned only with national problems. "Profound disagreements existed within Poalei-Tsion on the question of participation in revolutionary action in Russia."[870] (And the revolutionaries themselves were divided, some leaning towards the Social-Democrats, others towards the Social Revolutionaries.)

"Other Tseirei-Tsion groups, ideologically close to non-Marxist socialist Zionism, began to form from 1905 onwards."[871] In 1904, a split within Poalei-Tsion gave birth to a new party, the "Socialist Zionists", breaking with the ideal of Palestine: the extension of Yiddish as a spoken language to all Jewish masses, that is quite sufficient, and we scorn the idea of national autonomy!

Zionism begins to take on a *bourgeois* and reactionary tint. What is needed is to create from it a socialist movement, to awaken revolutionary political instincts in the Jewish masses. The party "strongly supported" the "social and economic content" of Zionism, but denied the need to "revive the land of Judea, culture, Hebrew traditions." Granted, Jewish emigration is too chaotic, it must be oriented towards a specific territory, but "there is no essential link between Zionism and Palestine." The Hebrew state must be based on socialist and non-capitalist foundations. Such an emigration is a

---

[868] *Ibidem* pp. 219-220.
[869] S. Dimanstein. Revolioulsionnyie dvijeniia sredi evreiev (The revolution among the Jews), Sb. 1905: Istoriia revolioutsionnogo dvijeniia v otdclnykh otcherkakh (Collection 1905: History of the revolutionary movement in separate essays), directed by N. Pokrovsky, vol. 3, book 1, M.L., 1927, pp. 107, 116.
[870] SJE, t. 6, p. 551.
[871] *Ibidem*, t. 7, p. 941.

long-term historical process; the bulk of the Jewish masses will remain well into the future in their current places of residence. "The party has approved the participation of the Jews in the political struggle in Russia"[872]—that is to say, in the struggle for their rights in this country. As for Judaism and faith, they despised them.

All this mishmash had to generate a "socialist Jewish" group called "Renaissance", which "believed that the national factor is progressive by nature", and in 1906 the members of this group who had broken with the Zionists Socialist Party constituted the Soviet Socialist Workers' Party, the SERP. (They were called *serpoviys* or *seymovtsy*, for they demanded the election of a Jewish national Sejm— *Seim*—intended to be the "supreme organ of Jewish national self-government."[873]) For them, Russian and Hebrew were, in their capacity of languages of use, equal. And by advocating "autonomism" within the Russian state, the SERP, socialist, was distinguished from the Bund, also socialist.[874]

In spite of the disagreements that divided the Zionists among themselves, a general shift of Zionism towards socialism took place in Russia, which attracted the attention of the Russian government. Until then, it had not interfered with Zionist propaganda, but in 1903 Interior Minister Plehve addressed the governors of the provinces and to the mayors of the big cities a bulletin stating that the Zionists had relegated to the background the idea of leaving Palestine and had concentrated on the organisation of Jewish life in their places of residence, that such direction could not be tolerated and that consequently any public propaganda in favour of Zionism would now be prohibited, as well as meetings, conferences, etc.[875]

Made aware of this, Herzl (who had already solicited an audience with Nicholas II in 1899) went immediately to Saint Petersburg to ask to be received by Plehve. (It was just after the Kichinev pogrom, which occurred in the spring, of which Plehve had been strongly accused—and which had therefore attracted him the blame and invectives of the Russian Zionists...)

Plehve made Herzl understand (according to the latter's notes) that the Jewish question for Russia is grave, if not vital, and "we endeavour to solve it correctly... the Russian State wishes to have a homogeneous population", and it demands a patriotic attitude from all... "We want to assimilate [the Jews], but assimilation... is slow... I am not the enemy of

---

[872] *Ibidem**, pp. 1021-1022.
[873] *Aronson*, SJE-1, pp. 226, 229.
[874] SJE, 1.1, p. 705, t. 7, p. 1021.
[875] S. Ginzburg, Poezdka Teodora Gertzla v Petersburg (*Theodor Herzl's trip to Saint Petersburg*), JW, New York, Union of Russian Jews in New York, 1944, p. 199.

the Jews. I know them well, I spent my youth in Warsaw and, as a child, I always played with Jewish children.

I would very much like to do something for them. I do not want to deny that the situation of the Jews of Russia is not a happy one. If I were a Jew, I, too, would probably be an opponent of the government." "The formation of a Jewish State [accommodating] several million immigrants would be extremely desirable for us. That does not mean, however, that we want to lose all our Jewish citizens.

Educated and wealthy people, we would gladly keep them. The destitute without education, we would gladly let them go. We had nothing against Zionism as long as it preached emigration, but now "we note great changes"[876]

in its goals. The Russian government sees with a kindly eye the immigration of Zionists to Palestine, and if the Zionists return to their initial plans, they are ready to support them in the face of the Ottoman Empire. But it cannot tolerate the propagation of Zionism, which advocates a separatism of national inspiration within Russia itself[877]: this would entail the formation of a group of citizens to whom patriotism, which is the very foundation of the State, would be foreign. (According to N. D. Lyubimov, who was then director of the minister's cabinet, Plehve told him that Herzl, during the interview, had recognised that Western bankers were helping the revolutionary parties of Russia. Sliosberg, however, thinks this is unlikely.[878])

Plehve made his report to the Emperor, the report was approved, and Herzl received a letter of confirmation in the same vein. He felt that his visit to Plehve had been a success. Neither of them suspected that they had only eleven months left to live… Turkey had no intention of making any concessions to the Zionists, and the British Government, in that same year of 1905, proposed that not Palestine, but Uganda, be colonised.

In August 1903, at the Sixth Congress of the Zionists in Basel, Herzl was the spokesperson for this variant "which, of course, is not Zion", but which could be accepted on a provisional basis, in order for a Jewish state to be created as quickly as possible.[879]

This project provoked stormy debates. It seems that it met with some support, in the *Yishuv*, for new immigrants, discouraged by the harsh living

---

[876] *Ibidem**, pp. 202-203.
[877] SJE, t. 6, p. 533.
[878] G. B. Sliosberg, Dela minouvehikh dnei: Zapiski ruskogo evreia (Notes of a Jew of Russia) in 3 vols., Paris, 1933, 1934, t. 2, p. 301
[879] JE*, t. 6, p. 412.

conditions in Palestine. The Russian Zionists—who claimed to have more than all the need to quickly find a refuge—fiercely opposed the project. Headed by M. M. Oussychkine (founder of the Biluim group and, later, the right-hand man of Ahad Haam in the Bne-Moshe League), they recalled that Zionism was inseparable from Zion and that nothing could replace it![880]

Congress nevertheless constituted a commission to travel to Uganda to study the land.[881] The Seventh Congress, in 1905, heard its report, and the Ugandan variant was rejected.[882] Overcome by all these obstacles, Herzl succumbed to a heart attack before he knew the final decision.[883]

But this new dilemma provoked a new rupture in Zionism: they split the so-called "territorialists", led by Israel Zangwill, to which joined the English delegates. They established their International Council; the latter held its meetings, receiving subsidies from Jacob Schiff and Baron Rothschild. They had given up demanding "Palestine and nothing else". Yes, it was necessary to carry out a mass colonisation by the Jews, but wherever it was. Year after year, in their research, they reviewed a dozen countries. They almost selected Angola, but "Portugal is too weak, it will not be able to defend the Jews", and therefore "the Jews risk becoming the victims of the neighbouring tribes."[884] They were even ready to accept territory within Russia even if they could create an autonomous entity with an independent administration.

This argument: a strong country must be able to defend immigrants on the premises of their new residence, reinforced those who insisted on the need to *quickly* establish an independent state capable of hosting mass immigration.

This was suggested—and would suggest later—Max Nordau when he said that he was not afraid of the "economic unpreparedness of the country [that is, of Palestine] for the reception of newcomers."[885] However, for this, it was necessary to be get the better of Turkey, and also find a solution to the Arab problem. The adherents of this program understood that, in order to implement it, it was necessary to have recourse to the assistance of powerful allies. Now this assistance, no country, for the moment, proposed it. To arrive at the creation of the State of Israel, we must go through two more world wars.

---

[880] *Ibidem*, t. 15, p. 135.
[881] *Ibidem*, t. 3, p. 679.
[882] *Ibidem*, pp. 680, 681.
[883] JE, t. 6, p. 407.
[884] *Ibidem*, t. 14, pp. 827, 829.
[885] SJE, t. 7, pp. 861, 892.

Chapter 8

At the Turn of the 20th Century

It appears that after six years of reflection and hesitation, the Tsar Alexander III irrevocably chose, as of 1887, to contain the Jews of Russia by restrictions of a civil and political nature, and he held this position until his death.

The reasons were probably, on the one hand, the evident part played by the Jews in the revolutionary movement, on the other, the no less evident fact that many Jewish youths shunned military service: "only three quarters of those who should have been enrolled served in the army."[886] One noticed "the ever-increasing number of Jews who did not respond to the appeal", as well as the increasing amount of unpaid fines related to these absences: only 3 million rubles out of 30 million were returned annually to the funds of the State. (In fact, the government still had no accurate statistics on the Jewish population, its birth rate, its mortality rate before the age of 21. Let us remind that in 1876 [see Chapter 4], because of this absenteeism, there had been a restriction of the "favour accorded to certain persons by virtue of their family situation"—which meant that the only sons of Jewish families were now subjected, like the others, to general conscription, and as a result the proportion of Jewish conscripts had become greater than that of non-Jews. This situation was not corrected until the early 1900s under Nicolas II.[887])

As far as public education was concerned, the tsar's wish, which he had formulated in 1885, was that the number of Jews admitted to institutions outside the Pale of Settlement was in the same ratio as the number of Jews in the total population. But the authorities pursued two aims simultaneously: not only to slow down the growing flow of Jews towards education, but also to fight against the revolution, to make the school, as it was called, "not a pool of revolutionaries, but a breeding ground for

---

[886] J. *Larine*, Evrei i antisemitizm v SSSR (The Jews and anti-Semitism in the USSR), M.L., 1929, p. 140.

[887] G.V. *Sliosberg*, Diela minouvchikh dniei: Zapiski ruskogo evreia (Notes of a Jew of Russia), 3 vols., Paris, 1933, 1934, vol. 2, pp. 206 209.

science."[888] In the chancelleries, they were preparing a more radical measure which consisted of prohibiting access to education to elements likely to serve the revolution—a measure contrary to the spirit of Lomonosov[889] and profoundly vicious, prejudicial to the State itself: it was to deny the children of disadvantaged strata of the general population (the "sons of cooks") admission to colleges. The formulation, falsely reasonable, falsely decent, was: "Leave the school principals free to accept only children who are in the care of persons who can guarantee them good supervision at home and provide them with all that is necessary for the pursuit of their studies"—furthermore, in higher education establishments, it was planned to increase the right of access to classes.[890]

This measure provoked a strong outrage in liberal circles, but less violent and less lasting than the one that was instigated in 1887 by a new measure: the reduction of the number of Jews admitted to high schools and universities. It was originally planned to publish these two provisions within the framework of the same law. But the Council of Ministers opposed it, arguing that "the publication of a general decision accompanied by restrictions for the Jews could be misinterpreted." In June 1887, therefore, only a part was promulgated, the one that concerned non-Jews: "Measures aiming to regulate the contingent of pupils in secondary and higher education"—measures directed in fact against the common people... As for the reduction of the quota of the Jews, it was entrusted to the Minister of Education, Delianov, who implemented it in July 1887 by a bulletin addressed to the rectors of school boards. He fixed for the secondary and higher schools the *numerus clausus* of the Jews at 10% for the Pale of Settlement, 5% outside it, and 3% in the two capitals.

"Following the example of the Ministry of Public Instruction", other organisations began to introduce "quotas of admission into their institutions, and some were closed down to the Jews." (Such as the Higher School of Electricity, the Saint Petersburg School of Communication, and, most strikingly, the Academy of Military Medicine which temporarily prohibited, but "for many years", its access to Jews.[891])

This *numerus clausus* law, which had not been established during the ninety-three years of massive presence of Jews in Russia and which was to continue for twenty-nine years (practically until 1916) struck the Jewish society of Russia all the more painfully because in the years 1870–1880

---

[888] *Hessen*, t. 2, p. 231.
[889] Mikhail Vasilyevich Lomonosov (1711–1765): great scholar and Russian poet, representative of the Enlightenment in Russia. Of modest origin, he is the prototype of the genius born into the people. The University of Moscow bears his name.
[890] JE*, t. 13, p. 52.
[891] *Ibidem*, t. 13, pp. 52, 53.

there had been a "remarkable impulse of the Jews to enter schools and colleges", a phenomenon which Sliosberg in particular explains is "not due to the realisation of the masses of the necessity of education... but rather due to the fact that, for a Jew without capital, figuring out how to deploy one's forces in the economic field was very difficult, and due to the fact that conscription became compulsory for all, but that there were dispensations for the students." Thus, if only well-to-do Jewish youth had studied before, a "Jewish student proletariat" was now being created; if among the Russians, now as in the past, it was the favoured social classes that received higher education, among the Jews, in addition to the wealthy, young people from the underprivileged classes began to study.[892]

We would like to add that in those years there had been a turning-point in the whole world and in all fields of culture, towards a no longer elitist but generalised education—and the Jews, particularly intuitive and receptive, had been the first to feel it, at least instinctively. But how can we find a way to satisfy, without causing friction, without clashes, the constant and increasing aspiration of the Jews to education? In view of the fact that the indigenous population, in its mass, remained fairly asleep and backward, how to avoid prejudice to the development of either side?

Of course, the objective of the Russian government was the struggle against the revolution, for among the student youth many Jews had been noticed by their activism and their total rejection of the regime in place. However, when we know the enormous influence exerted by Pobedonostsev[893] during the reign of Alexander III, it must be admitted that the aim was also to defend the Russian nation against the imbalance that was to occur in the field of education. This is what testifies the Baron Morits von Hirsch, a big Jewish banker who visited Russia and to whom Pobedonostsev expressed his point of view: the policy of the government is inspired not by the idea that the Jews are a "threat", but by the fact that, rich in their multi-millennial culture, they are more spiritually and intellectually powerful than the still ignorant and unpolished Russian people—that is why measures had to be taken to balance the "low capacity of the local population to resist." (And Pobedonostsev asked Hirsch, known for his philanthropy, to promote the education of the Russian people in order to realise the equal rights of the Jews of Russia. According to Sliosberg, Baron Hirsch allocated one million rubles to private schools.[894])

---

[892] *Sliosberg*, t. 1, p. 92; t. 2, p. 89.
[893] Konstantin Petrovich Pobedonostsev (1827–1907) Statesman, member of the Council of the Empire since 1872, attorney general of the Holy Synod, preceptor of Nicholas II. Exercised great influence over Alexander III.
[894] *Ibidem*, t. 2, p. 33.

Like any historical phenomenon, this measure can be viewed from various angles, particularly from the two different angles that follow. For a young Jewish student, the most elementary fairness seemed flouted: he had shown capacities, application, he had to be admitted... But he was not!

Obviously, for these gifted and dynamic young people, to encounter such a barrier was more than mortifying; the brutality of such a measure made them indignant. Those who had hitherto been confined to the trades of commerce and handicrafts were now prevented from accessing ardently desired studies that would lead to a better life.

Conversely, the "native population" did not see in these quotas a breach of the principle of equality, on the contrary, even. The institutions in question were financed by the public treasury, and therefore by the whole population, and if the Jews were more numerous, it meant that it was at the expense of all; and it was known that, later on, educated people would enjoy a privileged position in society. And the other ethnic groups, did they also have to have a proportional representation within the "educated layer"? Unlike all the other peoples of the empire, the Jews now aspired almost *exclusively* to education, and in some places this could mean that the Jewish contingent in schools exceeded 50%. The *numerus clausus* was unquestionably instituted to protect the interests of Russians and ethnic minorities, certainly not to bully the Jews. (In the 20s of the twentieth century, a similar approach was sought in the United States to limit the Jewish contingent in universities, and immigration quotas were also established—but we shall come back to this. Moreover, the matter of quotas, put today in terms of "no less than"[895], has become a burning issue in America.) In practice, there have been many exceptions to the application of the *numerus clausus* in Russia. The first to avoid it were *girls'* high schools: "In most high schools for young girls, the quotas were not current, nor in several public higher education establishments: the conservatories of Saint Petersburg and Moscow, the School of Painting, Sculpture and Architecture of Moscow, the Kiev School of Commerce, etc."[896] *A fortiori* quotas were not applied in any private establishment; and these were numerous and of high quality.[897] (For example, at the Kirpitchnikova High School, one of the best high schools in Moscow, a quarter of the students were Jewish.[898] They were numerous at the famous

---

[895] An allusion to the *affirmative action* setting minimum allowances for the admission of ethnic minorities to the United States.
[896] SJE, t. 6, p. 854.
[897] *I. M. Troitsky*, Evrei v rousskoi chkole (The Jews in the Russian School), BJWR-1, p. 359.
[898] *P. D. Ilinsky*, Vospominaniya (Memoires), Biblioteka-fund "Ruskie Zarubejnie" (Library and Archives), "Russian Emigration" (BFER), collection 1, A-90, p. 2.

Polivanovskaya high school in Moscow, and the Androyeva girls' school in Rostov, where my mother was a pupil, there were in her class more than half of Jewish girls.) Business schools (under the Ministry of Finance), to which Jewish children were eager to register, were initially opened to them without any restrictions, and those which took place after 1895 were relatively light (for example: in commercial schools in the Pale of Settlement, financed out of private funds, the number of Jews admitted depended on the amount of money allocated by Jewish merchants for the maintenance of these schools, and in many of them the percentage of Jewish students was 50% or more).

If the official standard was strictly observed at the time of admission to the secondary classes, it was often largely overstepped in the larger classes.

Sliosberg explains this notably by the fact that the Jewish children who entered high school pursued it to the end, whereas the non-Jews often gave up their studies before completion. This is why, in large classes, there were often much more than 10% Jewish pupils.[899] He confirmed that they were numerous, for example, at the Poltava high school. Out of 80 boys, eight were Jewish.[900] In the boys 'schools of Mariupol, at the time when there was already a local Duma, about 14 to 15% of the pupils were Jewish, and in girls' high schools, the proportion was even higher.[901] In Odessa, where Jews constituted one-third of the population,[902] they were in 1894, 14% in the prestigious Richelieu high school, more than 10% in the gymnasium No. 2, 37% in gymnasium No. 3; in girls' high schools the proportion was of 40%; in business schools, 72%, and in university, 19%.[903]

To the extent that financial means permitted it, no obstacle prevented this thirst for education. "In a number of secondary schools in the central Russian provinces there were few Jewish pupils at that time, and parents took the opportunity to send their children there… The wealthiest parents had their children home schooled: they prepared for examinations to enter the next grade and thus reached this way the senior year."[904] In the period between 1887 and 1909, Jewish children were free to pass the school-leaving examinations, and "they graduated as equals those who had followed the curriculum." [905] The majority of "external" pupils were Jewish. A family like that of Jacob Marchak (a jeweller with no great

---

[899] *Sliosberg*, t. 2, p. 90.
[900] *N. V. Volkov-Mouromtsev*, Iounost. Ot Viazmy do Feodosii (Youth, From Viazma to Feodosiia), 2nd ed., M., Rousski Pout, Graal, 1997, p. 101.
[901] *I. E. Temirov*, Vospominaniia (Memoires). BFER, collection 1, A-29, p. 24.
[902] JE, t. 12, p. 58.
[903] *A. Lvov*, Novaia gazeta, New York, 5–11 Sept. 1981, No. 70, p. 26.
[904] JE, t. 13, pp. 54 55.
[905] *Ibidem*, t. 16, p. 205.

fortune, the father of the poet⁹⁰⁶), whose five children had a higher education, was not uncommon before the revolution.

Moreover, "private establishments were opened everywhere, whether mixed for the Jews and Christians, or for the Jews only... Some of these establishments enjoyed the same rights as public establishments; the others were authorised to issue certificates entitling them to enrol in higher educational establishments."⁹⁰⁷ "A network of private Jewish settlements was established, which formed the basis of a national-type education,"⁹⁰⁸ "The Jews were also oriented towards higher education establishments abroad: a large part of them, on their return to Russia, passed examinations before the State Commissions."⁹⁰⁹ Sliosberg himself observed that in the 80s, at the University of Heidelberg that "the majority of Russian listeners were Jews" and that some, among them, did not have their bachelor's degree.⁹¹⁰

One can rightly wonder whether the restrictions, dictated by fear in front of the revolutionary moods of the students, did not contribute to feeding said moods. If these were not aggravated by indignation at the *numerus clausus*, and by contacts maintained abroad with political emigrants.

What happened in Russian universities after the publication of the bulletin? There was no sharp fall, but the number of Jews decreased almost every year, from 13.8% in 1893 to 7% in 1902. The proportion of Jews studying at the universities of Saint Petersburg and Moscow remained no less than the imposed 3% norm throughout the period of validity of the said standard.⁹¹¹

Minister Delianov acceded more than once to the requests submitted to him, and authorised admission to university beyond the *numerus clausus*.⁹¹²

This was how "hundreds of students" were admitted. (Delianov's flexibility will succeed later the rigidity of Minister Bogolepov—and it is not excluded that this may have contributed to making him the target of

---

⁹⁰⁶ Samufi Yakovlevich Marchak (1887–1964) Russian man of letters of the Soviet era.
⁹⁰⁷ *Ibidem*, t. 13, p. 55.
⁹⁰⁸ SJE, t. 6, p. 854.
⁹⁰⁹ JE, t. 13, p. 55.
⁹¹⁰ *Sliosberg*, t. 1, p. 161.
⁹¹¹ S. V. Pozner, Evrei v obschei chkole K istorii zakonodatelstva i pravitelstvennoi politiki v oblasti evreiskogo voprosa (*The Jews in the Common School. For the History of the Legislation and State Policy in the Field of the Jewish Question*), Saint Petersburg, Razum, 1914, pp. 54-55.
⁹¹² *Cf. Sliosberg*, t. 2, p. 93.

terrorists[913].[914]) Sliosberg gives this overview: the percentage in the superior courts of medicine for women outweighed that of the Academy of Military Medicine and that of the university, and "all the Jewish girls of the empire poured in." Several hundred Jews were enrolled at the School of Psycho-neuropathology in Saint Petersburg, where they could enter without a baccalaureate, and so they were thousands over the years. It was called the School of Neuropathology, but it also housed a faculty of law. The Imperial Conservatory of Saint Petersburg was "filled with Jewish students of both sexes." In 1911, a private mining school opened in Ekaterinoslav.[915]

Admission to specialised schools, such as that of health officers, was done with great freedom. J. Teitel says that at the Saratov school of nurses (of high quality, very well equipped) Jews from the Pale of Settlement were admitted without any limitation—and without prior authorisation issued by the police for the displacement. Those who were admitted thus received full rights. This practice was confirmed by the governor of Saratov at that time, Stolypin. Thus the proportion of Jewish students could rise to 70%. In the other technical colleges of Saratov, Jews from the Pale of Settlement were admitted without any norm, and many of them continued their studies in higher education…

From the Pale of Settlement also came "a mass of external pupils that did not find their place in university, and for whom the Jewish community of the city struggled to find work."[916]

To all this it should be added that the number of establishments where the teaching was delivered in Hebrew was not limited. In the last quarter of the nineteenth century there were 25,000 primary schools (*Heder*) with 363,000 pupils in the Pale of Settlement (64% of all Jewish children).[917] It is true that in 1883 the old "Jewish establishments of the State" were closed due to having no use: no one went there any more. (But note: the opening of these institutions was once interpreted by the Jewish publicists as an act and a ruse of the "adverse reaction", and today their closure was also the "act of adverse reaction"!)

---

[913] Nikolai Pavlovich Bogolepov (1847–1901) lawyer, Minister of National Education. Mortally wounded in the attack perpetrated by P. Karpovitch.
[914] A. Goldenweiser, Pravovoie polojeniie evreiev v rossii (The legal situation of Jews in Russia), LMJR-1, p. 149.
[915] *Sliosberg*, t. 1, pp. 127, 128; t. 3, pp. 290, 292, 301.
[916] J. L. Teitel, Iz moiei jizni za 40 let (Stories of my life over forty years), Paris, J. Povolotsky and Co, 1925, pp. 170–176.
[917] J. M. Troitsky, Evrei v rousskoi chkole (The Jews in the Russian School), *op. cit.*, p. 358.

In summary: the admission quotas did not hinder the Jews' aspiration to education. Nor did they contribute to raising the educational level of the non-Jewish peoples of the empire; they only aroused bitterness and rage among the Jewish youth. But this, in spite of the prohibitions, was going to constitute an intelligentsia of vanguard. It was the immigrants from Russia who formed the nucleus of the first intellectual elite of the future State of Israel. (How many times do we read in the *Russian Jewish Encyclopædia* the notices "son of small craftsman", "son of small trader", "son of merchant", and, further on, "completed university"?)

The university diploma initially conferred the right to reside throughout the empire and to serve in the administration (later, access to education in academies, universities and public schools was once again limited). Graduates of the Faculty of Medicine—doctors and pharmacists—were allowed to "reside anywhere, whether they practised their profession or not," and like all those who had completed a higher degree, they could even "devote themselves to commerce or other trades", "be members of the merchant corps without having previously spent five years in the first guild in the Pale of Settlement" as was required of other merchants. "The Jews holding the title of Doctor of Medicine" could practice their profession in any district of the empire, hire a medical secretary and two aides among their co-religionists by bringing them from the Pale of Settlement. The right to reside in any place, as well as the right to trade, was attributed to all those who practised paramedical professions without having completed a higher education—dentists, nurses, midwives. As from 1903, a requirement was added: that these persons should mandatorily practise their field of specialisation.[918]

Restrictions also affected the bar, the independent body of lawyers set up in 1864. This profession paved the way for a successful career, both financially and personally, and to convey one's ideas: advocacy by lawyers in court were not subject to any censorship, they were published in the press, so that the speakers enjoyed greater freedom of expression than the newspapers themselves. They exploited it widely for social criticism and for the "edification" of society. The class of solicitors had transformed themselves in a quarter of a century into a powerful force of opposition: one should remember the triumphal acquittal of Vera Zasulich in 1878.[919] (The moral laxity of the lawyers' argumentation at the time strongly worried Dostoevsky: he explained it in his writings.[920]) Within this

---

[918] JE, t. 10, pp. 780-781.
[919] Vera Ivanovna Zasulich (1849-1919): revolutionary populist linked to Netchayev. Shot at the commander of the Saint Petersburg plaza (1873). Acquitted. Having become a Marxist, she was one of the leaders of the Menshevik party.
[920] In the *Journal of a writer* for the month of February 1876.

influential brotherhood, the Jews quickly occupied a preponderant place, revealing themselves to be the most gifted of all.

When, in 1889, the Council of the Sworn Attorneys of Saint Petersburg published "for the first time in its report the data concerning the number of Jews in this trade," the great Saint Petersburg lawyer A. J. Passover "renounced the title of member of the Council and was no longer a candidate for election."[921]

In the same year 1889, the Minister of Justice, Manasseine, presented a report to Tsar Alexander III; it was stated that "the bar is invaded by the Jews, who supplant the Russians; they apply their own methods and violate the code of ethics to which sworn-in attorneys must obey." (The document does not provide any clarification.[922]) In November 1889, on the orders of the tsar, a provision was made, supposedly provisionally (and consequently able to escape the legal procedure), requiring that "the admission to the numbers of those avowed and delegated authorities of non-Christian confession... will be henceforth, and until promulgation of a special law on the subject, possible only with the authorisation of the Minister of Justice."[923] But as apparently neither the Moslems nor the Buddhists availed themselves in large numbers of the title of lawyer, this provision proved to be *de facto* directed against the Jews.

From that year onwards, and for another fifteen years, practically no unbaptised Jew received this authorisation from the minister, not even such brilliant personalities—and future great advocates—as M. M. Winaver[924] or O. O. Gruzenberg: they remained confined for a decade and a half in the role of "law clerks". (Winaver even pleaded more than once in the Senate, and was very much listened to.) The "clerks" in fact pleaded with the same freedom and success as the attorneys themselves: here, there were no restrictions.[925]

In 1894, the new Minister of Justice, N. V. Muraviev, wanted to give this temporary prohibition the value of permanent law. His argument was as follows:

"The real danger is not the presence in the body of lawyers of a certain number of people of Jewish faith who have rejected to a large extent the

---

[921] JE, t. 6, p. 118.
[922] S. L. Kutcherov, Evrei v rousskoi advokatoure (*The Jews in the Russian Bar*), BJWR-1, p. 402.
[923] JE*, t. 1, pp. 469, 470.
[924] Maxime Moiseyevich Winaver (1862–1926): a lawyer born in Warsaw, one of the founders of the Constitutional-Democratic Party, of the Cadet party (1905), deputy in the Duma (1906). Immigrated to France in 1919.
[925] *Goldenweizer*, BJWR-1, p. 131.

notions contrary to the Christian norms which pertain to their nation, but it is in the fact that the number of such persons becomes so great that they are likely to acquire a preponderant importance and to exert an adverse influence on the general level of morality and on the activities of that corporation."[926] In the bill, it was advocated that the proportion of non-Christian solicitors be limited in each jurisdiction to 10%. The tsar's government rejected this project—but, as Mr. Krohl said, "this idea… did not meet the condemnation it deserved in the Russian public opinion", and within the Society of Jurists of Saint Petersburg, "only a few people protested vigorously…; the rest, the vast majority, were clearly in favour of the draft at the time of its discussion."[927] This gives an unexpected insight into the state of mind of the capital's intelligentsia in the mid-90s. (In the Saint Petersburg jurisdiction, 13.5% of the attorneys were Jews, while in Moscow, less than 5%.[928])

The prohibition for the clerks of solicitors to become themselves avowed was felt all the more painfully because it followed limitations in the scientific careers and the service of the State.[929] It would not be lifted before 1904.

In the 80s, a limitation on the number of Jewish jurors was introduced in the provinces of the Pale of Settlement, so that they did not have a majority within the juries.

It was also from the 80s that the hiring of Jews in the judicial administration ceased. There were, however, exceptions to this: thus J. Teitel, who had been appointed shortly after his university studies, remained there twenty-five years. He finished his career ennobled with the civil rank of general.

(It must be added that, later, Cheglovitov[930] forced him to retire "of his own free will.") In the exercise of his duties, he often had, he, the Israelite, to administer oaths to Orthodox witnesses, and he never met any objection from the clergy. J. M. Halpern, also an official in the judicial administration, had acceded to the high-ranking position of Deputy Director of the Ministry of Justice and to the rank of Secret Advisor.[931] Halpern sat on the Pahlen Commission in the capacity of expert. (Before that, the first prosecutor of the Senate had been G. I. Trahtenberg, and his deputy G. B. Sliosberg had initiated himself to defend the rights of the

---

[926] *Kurcherov*, BJWR-1*, p. 404.
[927] JE, t. 1, pp. 471-472.
[928] *Kurcherov, Ibidem, p. 405.*
[929] Ibidem.
[930] Ivan Grigorievich Cheglovitov (1861–1918) Minister of Justice in 1906–1915, President of the Council of the Empire. Shot without judgement by the Bolsheviks in retaliation for the failed assassination of Fanny Kaplan against Lenin.
[931] JE, t. 6, p. 118.

Jews.) He was also first prosecutor of the Senate S. J. Outine—but he was baptised and consequently, was not taken into account.

The religious criterion has never been a false pretence for the tsarist government, but has always been a real motive. It was because of this that the old believers[932], ethnically Russian, were ferociously persecuted for two and a half centuries, as well as, later, the Dukhobors[933] and the Molokanes[934], also Russians.

The baptised Jews were numerous in the service of the Russian State; we will not discuss it in this book. Let us quote under Nicholas I, the Count K. Nesselrod, who had a long career at the head of the Ministry of Foreign Affairs; Ludwig Chtiglits, who received the barony in Russia[935]; Maximilian Heine, brother of the poet and military doctor, who ended his career with the rank of state councillor; Governor General Bezak, General of the suite of His Majesty Adelbert, the Colonel of the Horse Guard Meves, the Hirs diplomats, one of whom was Minister under Alexander III. Later, there was the Secretary of State Perets (grandson of the tax-collector Abram Perets[936]), Generals Kaufman-Turkestansky and Khrulyov; The squire Salomon, director of the Alexandrovsky high school; Senators Gredinger, Posen; in the Police Department, Gurovich, Vissarionov, among many others.

Was the conversion to Christianity, especially to Lutheranism, in the eyes of some considered as easy? Are all the tracks open to you at once? Sliosberg observed at one point an "almost massive denial" on the part of young people.[937]

But, of course, seen from the Jewish side, this appeared to be a grave betrayal, "a bonus to the abjuration of his faith... When we think of the number of Jews who resist the temptation to be baptised, one gains a great respect for this unhappy people."[938]

Formerly, it was with candour: we divided people into two categories, "ours" and "others," according to the criterion of faith alone. This state of mind, the Russian State, still reflected it in its dispositions. But, at the dawn

---

[932] Old believers are adepts of the "old faith", the one before the reforms imposed by the Patriarch Nikon in the seventeenth century. They were persecuted.
[933] Doukhobors are "spirit fighters", a religious sect dating back to the seventeenth century, which denies the Church as an institution, the state, and professes a kind of rationalistic spiritualism.
[934] See *supra* (p. 245).
[935] JE, t. 16, p. 116.
[936] *Ibidem*, t. 12, pp. 394-395.
[937] *Sliosberg*, t. 2, p. 94.
[938] *V. Posse*, Evreiskoi zassiliie (The Jewish Violence), Slovo, Saint Petersburg, 1909, 14 (27) March, p. 2.

of the twentieth century, could it not have thought a little and wondered whether such a procedure was morally permissible and practically effective? Could we continue to offer the Jews material welfare at the cost of denying their faith?

And then what advantage could be derived from Christianity? Many of these conversions were for pure convenience. (Some justified themselves by luring themselves: "I can thus be much more useful to my people."[939])

For those who had obtained equal rights in the service of the State, "there no longer existed any restriction of any kind whatsoever which prevented them from gaining access to hereditary nobility" and to receive the highest rewards.

"The Jews were commonly enrolled without difficulty in genealogical records."[940] And even, as we see from the census of 1897, 196 members of the hereditary nobility counted *Hebrew* as their mother tongue (amongst the nobility in their personal capacities and the civil servants, they were 3,371 in the same case[941]). There even was, among the Brodsky, a family of modest artisans, Marshals of the nobility of the province of Ekaterinoslav.

But from the 70s of the nineteenth century onwards, Jews who sought positions in the administration of the State began to encounter obstacles (and this became worse from 1896 onwards); it must be said that few were those who aspired to this kind of routine and poorly paid activity. Moreover, from the 90s, the obstacles also affected the elective functions.

In 1890 a new Zemstvo Ordinance was issued, according to which the Jews were excluded from the self-management of the Zemstvo—in other words, outside the urban areas of the provinces and districts. It was planned to "not allow [the Jews] to participate in the electoral meetings and assemblies of the Zemstvos"[942] (these did not yet exist in the western provinces). The motivation was that "Jews, who usually pursue their particular interests, do not meet the demand for a real, living and social connection with local life."[943] At the same time, to work in the Zemstvo as an independent contractor, to the title of what was called the "outsider element" (element that would introduce into the Zemstvo, several years in advance, the

---

[939] *Sliosberg*, t. 1, p. 198.
[940] JE, t. 7, p.34.
[941] Obschii svod po Imperii rezoultatov razrabotki dannykh pervoi vseobschei perepisi naseleniia, proizvedionnoi 28 ianvaria 1897 g. (General corpus of results for the empire of the data of the first general census of the population carried out on January 28, 1897), t. 2, Saint Petersburg, 1905, pp. 374-386.
[942] JE*, t. 7, p. 763.
[943] *Ibidem**, t. 1, p. 836.

explosive charge of radicalism), was not forbidden to Jews—and there they were many.

The restrictions in the Zemstvos did not affect the Jews of the central Russian provinces because the great majority of them resided in the cities and were more interested in urban administration. But in 1892 there appeared this time a new provision for cities: the Jews lost the right to elect and to be elected delegates to the Dumas and to the municipal offices, as well as to hold any office of responsibility, or conduct there economic and administrative services.

This represented a more than sensible limitation. As delegates, Jews were admitted only in cities of the Pale of Settlement, but here too, subject to a restriction: no more than one-tenth of the number of the municipal duma, and again "on assignment" for the local administration that selected Jewish candidates—an annoying procedure, to say the least. (Particularly for *bourgeois* family men, as Sliosberg rightly points out: what a humiliation for them in relation to their children... how, after that, can they remain loyal to such a government?[944]) "There has been no harder time in the history of Russian Jews in Russia. They were expelled from all positions they had conquered." [945] In another passage, the same author speaks without ambiguity of the bribes received by the officials of the Ministry of the Interior to act in favour of the Jews.[946] (That was to soften somewhat the rigour of the times.)

Yes, the Jews of Russia were undoubtedly bullied, victims of inequality in civil rights. But this is what reminds us of the eminent Cadet V. A. Maklakov, who found himself in the emigration after the revolution: "The 'inequality in rights' of the Jews naturally lost its acuteness in a state where the enormous mass of the population (82%), that on which the prosperity of the country depended, the peasantry—dull, mute, submissive—was also *excluded* from common law, the same for all"[947]—and it stayed in the same situation after the abolition of serfdom; for it also, military service was inescapable, secondary and higher education inaccessible, and it did not obtain that self-administration, that rural Zemstvo which it much need. Another emigrant, D. O. Linsky, a Jew, even bitterly concluded that, in comparison with the levelling up of the soviets, when the entire population of Russia was deprived of all rights, "the inequality in the rights of the

---

[944] *Sliosberg*, t. 3, p. 220.
[945] *Ibidem*, t. 1, p. 259.
[946] *Ibidem*, t. 2, pp. 177–178.
[947] *V. A. Maklakov* (1905-1906), Sb. M. M. Winaver i rousskaia obschestvennost natchala XX veka (Collection M. M. Winaver and Russian civil society in the early twentieth century), Paris, 1937, p. 63.

Jewish population before the revolution appears like an inaccessible ideal."⁹⁴⁸

We have gotten used of saying: the *persecution* of the Jews in Russia. But the word is not fair. It was not a persecution, strictly speaking. It was a whole series of restrictions, of bullying. Vexing, admittedly, painful, even scandalous.

However, the Pale of Settlement, over the years, was becoming more and more permeable.

According to the census of 1897, 315,000 Jews were already residing *outside* its boundaries, that is to say, in sixteen years, a nine-fold increase (and this represented 9% of the total Jewish population of Russia apart from the kingdom of Poland.⁹⁴⁹ Let us compare: there were 115,000 Jews in France, and 200,000 in Great Britain⁹⁵⁰). Let us consider also that the census gave undervalued figures, in view of the fact that in many cities of Russia many craftsmen, many servants serving "authorised" Jews did not have an official existence, being shielded from registration.

Neither the top of the finance nor the educated elite were subject to the restrictions of the "Pale", and both were established freely in the central provinces and in the capitals. It is well known that 14% of the Jewish population practised "liberal professions" ⁹⁵¹ —not necessarily the intellectual type. One thing, however, is certain: in pre-revolutionary Russia, the Jews "occupied a prominent place in these intellectual occupations. The famous Pale of Settlement itself did not in any way prevent a large fraction of the Jews from penetrating more and more into the provinces of central Russia."⁹⁵²

The so-called "artisanal" trades where the Jews were the most numerous were the dentists, the tailors, the nurses, the apothecaries, and a few others, trades of great utility everywhere, where they were always welcome. "In 1905, in Russia, more than 1,300,000 Jews were engaged in artisanal activities,"⁹⁵³

which meant that they could live outside the "Pale". And it must not be forgotten either that "nowhere in the laws it was stipulated, for example, that the craftsman who exercises a trade has no right to engage in

---

[948] *D. O. Linsky*, O natsionalnom samosoznanii ruskogo evreia—Rossia i evrei (About the national consciousness of the Jew of Russia), in RaJ, p. 145.
[949] *Hessen*, t. 2, p. 210; JE, t. 11, pp. 537, 538.
[950] SJE, t. 2, pp. 313-314.
[951] *Larine*, p. 71.
[952] *V. S. Mandel*, Konservativnyie i razrouchitelnyie elementy v evreistve (Conservative elements and destructive elements among Jews), RaJ, p. 202.
[953] *Goldenweiser*, RaJ, p. 148.

commerce at the same time"; moreover, "the notion of 'doing business' is not defined by law": for example, "deposit-selling" with commission, is it trade? Thus, in order to exercise any form of trade (even large-scale trading), to engage in the purchase of real estate, in the development of factories, one had to pass as "artisan" (or "dentist"!) For example, the "artisan" Neimark possessed a factory of sixty workers; typos thus opened their own printing press.[954] And there existed yet another way: several people regroup, and only one pays the fee of the first guild, the others pretending to be his "clerks". Or even, to be "adopted" in a central province by retired Jewish soldiers (the "adopted" father received a pension in return[955]). In Riga, thousands of Jewish families lived on the timber trade until they were expelled due to false attestations.[956] At the dawn of the twentieth century, Jewish settlements were found in all Russian cities of some importance.

J. Teitel testified that "the construction of the Samara-Orenburg railway line resulted in the influx of a large number of Jews to Samara. The supervisors of this railway were Jews—Varchavsky, Gorvitch. For a long time they were also the owners. They occupied the control stations as well as a large number of subordinate jobs. They brought their families from the Pale of Settlement, and thus a very numerous Jewish colony was formed. They also took the export of wheat from the rich province of Samara to foreign countries. It should be noted that they were the first to export eggs from Russia to Western Europe. All these activities were carried out by so-called 'artisans'." And Teitel enumerates three successive governors of the province of Samara as well as a chief of police (who, previously, in 1863, had been "excluded from the University of Saint Petersburg for having participated in student disorders") who "closed their eyes to these so-called artisans." Thus, around 1889, there lived in Samara "more than 300 Jewish families, without a residence permit"[957],—which means that in Samara, in addition to the official figures, there were in fact around 2,000 Jews.

Stories come to us from another end of Russia: at Viazma, "the three pharmacists, the six dentists, a number of doctors, notaries, many shopkeepers, almost all hairdressers, tailors, shoemakers were Jewish. All those who appeared as such were not dentists or tailors, many traded and no one prevented them from doing so. Of its 35,000 inhabitants, Viazma also had about two thousand Jews.[958]

---

[954] *Sliosberg*, t. 2, pp. 51, 197, 188, 193, 195.
[955] *Ibidem*, pp. 22-24.
[956] *Ibidem*, pp. 183 185.
[957] *Teirel*, pp. 36-37, 47.
[958] *Volkov-Mouromrsev*, pp. 98, 101.

In the region of the Army of the Don, where severe restrictions were imposed on Jews in 1880 and where they were forbidden to reside in Cossack villages and suburbs of the cities, there were nevertheless 25,000 keepers of inns and buffets, barbers, watchmakers, tailors. And any delivery of a quantity of goods, no matter the size, depended on them.

The system of restrictions on the rights of the Jews, with the whole range of corrections, reservations and amendments thereto, had been built up stratum after stratum over the years. The provisions aimed at the Jews were scattered in the various collections of laws promulgated at different times, badly harmonised among themselves, badly amalgamated with the common laws of the empire.

The governors complained of it.[959] We must try to penetrate the mysteries of the innumerable derogations, special cases, exceptions of exceptions, which swarmed the legislation on the Jews, to understand what journey of the combatant this represented for the ordinary Jew, and what puzzle for the administration. Such complexity could only engender formalism, with its succession of cruelties; thus, when a head of a family domiciled in a central Russian province lost his right of residence (after his death or as a result of a change of profession), his whole family lost it with him. Families were thus expelled after the death of the head of the family (with the exception of single persons over 70 years of age).

However, complexity did not always play in disfavour of the Jews; it sometimes played to their advantage. Authors write that "it was the police commissioners and their deputies who were responsible for settling the endless wavering in the application of the restrictive measures," which resulted in the use of bribes and to the circumvention of the law[960]—always favourable to the Jews. There were also perfectly workable legal channels. "The contradictory nature of the innumerable laws and provisions on Jews offers the Senate a broad spectrum of interpretations of legislation… In the 90s, most of the provisions appealed by the Jews were annulled" by the Senate. [961] The highest dignitaries often closed their eyes to non-compliance with anti-Jewish restrictions—as G. Sliosberg testified, for example: "Ultimately, Jewish affairs depended on the head of the police department, Pyotr Nikolayevich Dumovo… The latter was always open to the complainants' arguments and I must say, to be honest, that if the

---

[959] S. Dimanstein, Revolioutsionnoie dvijeniie sredi evreiev (The Revolutionary Movement Among the Jews), *op. cit.*, p. 108.
[960] *Goldenweiser*, BJWR-1, p. 114.
[961] JE, t. 14, p. 157.

application of any restrictive regulation were contrary to human charity, [Dournovo] would look into the matter and resolve it favourably."⁹⁶²

"Rather than the new laws, it was the provisions tending to a harder application of the old laws which were felt most painfully by the broad sections of the Jewish population." ⁹⁶³ The process, discreet but irreversible, by which the Jews gradually penetrated into the provinces of central Russia was sometimes stopped by the administration, and some duly orchestrated episodes went down in history.

This was the case in Moscow after the retirement of the all-powerful and almost irremovable Governor General V. A. Dolgorukov, who had regarded with great kindness the arrival of the Jews in the city and their economic activity.

(The key to this attitude obviously resides in the person of the great banker Lazar Solomonovich Poliakov, "with whom Prince Dolgorukov had friendly ties and who, evil tongues affirmed, had opened to him in his bank an unlimited line of credit. That the prince had need of money, there was no doubt about it," for he had yielded all his fortune to his son-in-law, while he himself "loved to live it up, and also had great spendings." Consequently, L. Poliakov "was covered year after year with honours and distinctions." Thanks to this, the Jews of Moscow felt a firm ground beneath their feet: "Every Jew could receive the right of residence in the capital" without actually putting himself "at the service of one of his coreligionists, a merchant of the first Guild."⁹⁶⁴)

G. Sliosberg informs us that "Dolgorukov was accused of yielding too much to the influence of Poliakov." And he explains: Poliakov was the owner of the Moscow mortgage lending, so neither in the province of Moscow nor in any neighbouring province could any other mortgage bank operate (i.e. granting advances on property mortgage-funds). Now, "there was no nobleman possessing land that did not hypothecate his possessions." (Such was the defeat of the Russian nobility at the end of the nineteenth century: and, after that, of what use could it still be for Russia?...) These noblemen found themselves "in a certain dependence on banks"; to obtain large loans, all sought the favours of Lazar Poliakov.⁹⁶⁵

Under the magistracy of Dolgorukov, around the 90s, "there were many recruitments of Jews in the body of merchants of the first guild. This was explained by the reluctance of Muscovite merchants of Christian

---

⁹⁶² *Sliosberg*, t. 2, pp. 175 176.
⁹⁶³ *Hessen*, t. 2, p. 232.
⁹⁶⁴ *Prince B. A. Chetinine*, Khoziaine Moskvy (The Master of Moscow), Istoritcheski vestnik (The Historical Messenger), 1917, t. 148, p. 459.
⁹⁶⁵ *Sliosberg*, t. 2, pp. 44, 45.

denomination to pay the high entrance fees of this first guild. Before the arrival of the Jews, the Muscovite industry worked only for the eastern part of the country, for Siberia, and its goods did not run westward. It was the Jewish merchants and industrialists who provided the link between Moscow and the markets of the western part of the country. (Teitel confirms that the Jews of Moscow were considered the richest and most influential in Russia.) Threatened by the competition, German merchants became indignant and accused Dolgorukov of favouritism towards the Jews.[966]

But the situation changed dramatically in 1891. The new Governor-General of Moscow, the Grand Duke Sergey Alexandrovich [967], an almighty man due to his position and dependent on no one due to his fortune, took the decision to expel all the Jewish craftsmen from Moscow, without any preliminary inquiry as to who was truly a craftsman and who pretended to be a craftsman. Whole neighbourhoods—Zariadie, Marina Roscha—were emptied of their inhabitants.

It is estimated that as many as 20,000 Jews were expelled. They were allowed a maximum of six months to liquidate their property and organise their departure, and those who declared that they did not have the means to ensure their displacement were shipped in prison vans. (At the height of the expulsions and to control how they were executed, an American government commission—Colonel Weber, Dr. Kamster—went to Russia. The astonishing thing is that Sliosberg brought them to Moscow, where they investigated what was happening, how measures were applied to stem the "influx of Jews", where they even visited the Butyrka prison incognito, where they were offered a few pairs of handcuffs, where they were given the photographs of people who had been sent in the vans... and the Russian police did not notice anything! (These were the "Krylov mores"[968]!) They visited again, for many more weeks, other Russian cities. The report of this commission was published in 1892 in the documents of the American Congress... to the greatest shame of Russia and to the liveliest relief of Jewish immigration to the United States.[969] It is because of this harassment that Jewish financial circles, Baron de Rothschild in the lead, refused in 1892 to support Russian borrowing abroad.[970] There had already been attempts in Europe in 1891 to stop the expulsion of the Jews from Moscow.

---

[966] *Ibidem*, pp. 43-44.
[967] Sergey Alexandrovich: grand-duke, brother of Alexander III, governor-general of Moscow. Assassinated in February 1905.
[968] Ivan Andreyevich Krylov (1769–1844): famous Russian publicist and fabulist who denounces in his writings the defects of society and the negligence of the rulers.
[969] *Ibidem*, pp. 31, 42, 50, 60, 63.
[970] *Ibidem*, pp. 7, 174.

The American-Jewish banker Seligman, for example, went to the Vatican to ask the Pope to intercede with Alexander III and exhort him to more moderation.[971] In 1891, "a part of the expelled Jews settled without permission in the suburbs of Moscow." But in the fall of 1892, following the measures taken, an order was made to "expel from Moscow former soldiers of the retired contingent and members of their families not registered in the communities."[972] (It should be noted that in 1893 the large Russian commercial and industrial enterprises intervened to soften these measures.) Then, from 1899, there was almost no new registration of Jews in the first guild of Moscow merchants.[973]

In 1893 a new aggravation of the fate of the Jews arose: the Senate first noticed the existence of a bulletin issued by the Ministry of the Interior, in force since 1880 (the "Charter of Jewish Freedom") which allowed Jews who had already established themselves outside the Pale of Settlement, illegally however, to remain where they were. This bulletin was repealed (except in Courland and Livonia where it was retained). The number of families who had settled over the last twelve years amounted to 70,000! Fortunately, thanks to Dournovo, "life-saving articles were enacted which, in the end, prevented the immense catastrophe that threatened."[974]

In 1893, "certain categories of Jews" were expelled in turn from Yalta, for the summer residence of the Imperial family was not far away, and they were forbidden any new settlement there: "The always increasing influx in the number of Jews in the city of Yalta, the appetite for real estate, threatens this holiday resort of becoming, purely and simply, a Jewish city."[975] (here could have been at play, after all the terrorist attacks in Russia, the security of the Imperial family in its residence in Livadia. Alexander III had every reason to believe—he was only one year away from his death—that he was cordially hated by the Jews. It is not possible to exclude as motive the idea of avenging the persecution of the Jews, as can be deduced by the choice of terrorist targets—Sipiagin, Plehve, Grand Duke Serge.) This did not prevent many Jews from remaining in the Yalta region—judging from what the inhabitants of Alushta wrote in 1909, complaining that the Jews, buyers of vineyards and orchards, "exploit 'to foster their development' the work of the local population," taking advantage of the precarious situation

---

[971] Doneseniie ruskogo posla Izvolskogo iz Vatikana (Report of the Russian Ambassador to the Vatican, Lzvolski), 7 (19) April 1892, Izvestia, 1930, 23 May, p. 2.
[972] SJE, t. 5, p. 474.
[973] JE, t. 11, pp. 336, 338.
[974] *Sliosberg*, t. 2, pp. 180, 182.
[975] JE*, t. 7, p. 594.

of said population and granting loans "at exorbitant rates" which ruin the Tatars, inhabitants of the site.[976]

But there was also another thing in the favour of the tireless struggle against smuggling, the right of residence of the Jews in the Western frontier zone was limited. There was in fact no further expulsion—with the exception of individuals caught in the act of smuggling. (According to memorialists, this smuggling, which consisted in passing the frontier to revolutionaries and their printed works, continued until the First World War.) In 1903–1904, a debate ensued: the Senate provides that the Provisional Regulations of 1882 shall not apply to the frontier zone and that accordingly Jews residing in that area may "freely settle in the rural areas. The Council of the Province of Bessarabia then issued a protest, informing the Senate that 'the entire Jewish population'" in the border area, including those where Jews had illegally settled there, was now seeking to gain access to the countryside where there were already 'more Jews than needed'," and that the border area "now risked becoming for the Jews the 'Promised Area'." The protest passed before the Council of State, which, taking into account the particular case of rural localities, squarely abolished the special regime of the border area, bringing it back to the general regime of the Pale of Settlement.[977]

This softening, however, did not find significant echo in the press or in society. No more than the lifting, in 1887, of the prohibition of the Jews to hire Christian servants. Nor did the 1891 Act introducing into the Penal Code a new article on "responsibility in the event of an open attack on part of the population by another", an article that the circumstances of life in Russia had never required, but which had been sorely lacking during the pogroms of 1881. For greater caution it was now introduced.

And again, let us repeat: the limitations on the rights of the Jews never assumed a racial character in Russia. They applied neither to the Karaites[978], nor to the Jews of the mountains, nor to the Jews of Central Asia, who, scattered and merged with the local population, had always freely chosen their type of activity.

The most diverse authors explain to us, each one more than the other, that the root causes of the restrictions suffered by Jews in Russia are of an economic nature. The Englishman J. Parks, the great defender of these restrictions, nevertheless expresses this reservation: "Before the war [of

---

[976] Novoie Vremia, 1909, 9 (22) Dec., p. 6.
[977] JE, t. 12, pp. 601, 602.
[978] The Karaites or Karaïmes (word meaning "attached" to the letter): a Jewish sect that rejects the orthodox doctrine of the rabbis, admits only the Old Testament and some oral traditions. The Karaites survive in small settlements in Crimea, Odessa, Southern Russia, as well as in Poland and Lithuania.

14–18], some Jews had concentrated considerable wealth in their hands... This had led to fear that abolishing these limitations would allow the Jews to become masters of the country."⁹⁷⁹ Professor V. Leontovitch, a perfectly consistent liberal, notes: "Until recently, we seemed to be unaware that the restrictive measures imposed on Jews came much more from anti-capitalist tendencies than from racial discrimination. The concept of race was of no interest to Russia in those years, except for specialists in ethnology... It is the fear of the strengthening of the capitalist elements, which could aggravate the exploitation of peasants and of all the workers, which was decisive. Many sources prove this."⁹⁸⁰ Let us not forget that the Russian peasantry had just undergone the shock of a sudden mutation: from the transition of feudal relations to market relations, a passage to which it was not at all prepared and which would throw it into an economic maelstrom sometimes more pitiless than serfdom itself.

V. Choulguine writes in this regard as follows: "The limitation of the rights of the Jews in Russia was underpinned by a 'humanistic thought'... It was assumed that the Russian people, taken globally (or at least some of their social strata) was, in a way, immature, effeminate..., that it allowed itself to be easily exploited..., that for this reason it had to be protected by state measures against foreign elements stronger than itself. Northern Russia began to look at the Jews with the eyes of Southern Russia. The Little-Russians had always seen the Jews, whom they knew well in the days of their coexistence with Poland, under the guise of the 'pawnbrokers' who suck the blood of the unfortunate Russian."⁹⁸¹

The restrictions were designed by the government to combat the massive economic pressure that put the foundations of the state at risk. Parks also detects in this vision of things a part of truth; he observes "the disastrous effect which the faculty of exploiting one's neighbour may have," and "the excessive role of innkeepers and usurers in the rural areas of Eastern Europe", even if he perceives the reasons for such a state of affairs "in the peasant's nature more than in the Jews themselves." In his opinion, the vodka trade, as the "main activity of the Jews" in Eastern Europe, gave rise to hatred, and among the peasants even more than among the others. It was he who fed more than one pogrom, leaving a deep and broad scar in the

---

[979] J. Parks, Evrei sredi narodov Obzor pritchin antisemitima (*The Jews among Peoples: An Overview of the Causes of Anti-Semitism*), Paris, YMCA Press, 1932, p. 182.
[980] V. V. Leontovitch, Istoriia liberalizma v Rossii 1762–1914 (History of liberalism in Russia: 1762-1914), transl. of the German, 2ⁿᵈ ed., M., Rousski Pout, 1995, pp. 251, 252. French translation to Fayard Ed., Paris, 1987.
[981] V. V. Choulguine, "Chto nam v nikh ne nravitsa": Ob anti-Semiticism v Rossii ("What we do not like about them": On anti-Semitism in Russia), Paris, 1929, pp. 185, 186.

consciousness of the Ukrainian and Belarusian peoples, as well as in the memory of the Jewish people.[982]

We read in many authors that the Jewish innkeepers lived very hard, without a penny, that they were almost reduced to begging. But was the alcohol market as narrow as that? Many people grew fat with the intemperance of the Russian people—and the landowners of Western Russia, and the distillers, and the drinking-house keepers... and the government! The amount of revenue can be estimated from the time it was entered as national revenue. After the introduction of a state monopoly on spirits in Russia in 1896, with the abolition of all private debits and the sale of beverages by excise duty, the Treasury collected 285 million rubles in the following year—to report to the 98 millions of the direct tax levied on the population. This confirms that not only was the manufacture of spirits "a major source of indirect contributions", but also that the spirits industry's revenues, which until 1896 only paid "4 kopecks of excise duty per degree of alcohol produced," were much higher than the direct revenues of the empire.[983]

But what was at that time the Jewish participation in this sector? In 1886, during the works of the Pahlen Commission, statistics were published on the subject. According to these figures, Jews held 27% (the decimals do not appear here: the numbers have been rounded up everywhere) of all distilleries in European Russia, 53% in the Pale of Settlement (notably 83% in the province of Podolsk, 76% in that of Grodno, 72% in that of Kherson). They held 41% of breweries in European Russia, 71% in the Pale of Settlement (94% in the province of Minsk, 91% in the province of Vilnius, 85% in the province of Grodno). The proportion of manufacturing and sales points in Jewish commerce is 29% in European Russia, 61% in the Pale of Settlement (95% in the province of Grodno, 93% in Mogilev, 91% in the province of Minsk).[984]

It is understandable that the reform which established the state monopoly on spirits was "greeted with horror... by the Jews of the Pale of Settlement."[985]

It is incontestable: the establishment of a State monopoly on spirits dealt a very severe blow to the economic activity of the Jews of Russia. And until

---

[982] *Parks*, pp. 153, 155, 233.
[983] Sbornik materalov ob ekonomitcheskom polojenii evreiev v Rossii (Collection of materials on the economic situation of Jews in Russia), vol. 2, St., Evreiskoie Kolonizatsionnoie Obschestvo (Jewish Colonising Association), 1904, p. 64.
[984] Evreiskaia piteïnaia torgovlia v Rossii. Statistitcheski Vremennik Rossiiskoy Imperii (*The Jewish Trade of Spirits in Russia, Statistical Yearbook of the Russian Empire*), Series III, Book 9, Saint Petersburg, 1886, p. V-X.
[985] *Sliosberg*, t. 2, p. 230.

the First World War (it ended at that time), this monopoly remained the favourite target of general indignation—whereas it merely instituted a rigorous control of the amount of alcohol produced in the country, and its quality. Forgetting that it reached the Christian tenants in the same way (see the statistics above), it is always presented as an anti-Jewish measure: "The introduction at the end of the 90s of the sale of alcohol by the State in the Pale of Settlement has deprived more than 100,000 Jews of their livelihood"; "Power meant... forcing the Jews to leave the rural areas," and since then "this trade has lost for the Jews the importance it once had."[986]

It was indeed the moment—from the end of the nineteenth century—when Jewish emigration from Russia grew remarkably. Is there a link between this emigration and the establishment of the state monopoly on the sale of spirits?

That is difficult to say, but the figure of 100,000 quoted above suggests so. The fact is that Jewish emigration (in America) remained low until 1886 1887; it experienced a brief surge in 1891 1892, but it was only after 1897 that it became massive and continuous.[987]

The "Provisional Regulations" of 1882 had not prevented further infiltration of Jewish spirits into the countryside. Just as, in the 70s, they had found a loophole against the prohibition of selling elsewhere than home by inventing "street" commerce. It had been devised to circumvent the law of May 3rd, 1882 (which also forbade the commerce of vodka by contract issued with a Jew), leasing "on the sly": to set up an inn there, one rented a land by oral and not written contract, in order for the taxes to be covered by the owner, and the proceeds from the sale of drinks went to the Jew.[988] It was through this and other means that the implantation of the Jews in the countryside could continue after the categorical prohibition of 1882. As Sliosberg writes, it was from 1889 that began the "wave of expulsions" of the Jews outside the villages of the Pale of Settlement, which resulted in "a pitiless competition, generating a terrible evil: denunciation" (in other words, Jews began to denounce those among them who lived illegally). But here are the figures put forward by P. N. Miliukov: if in 1881 there were 580,000 Jews living in villages, there were 711,000 Jews in 1897, which means that the rate of new arrivals and births far outweighed those of evictions and deaths. In 1899, a new Committee for Jewish Affairs, the eleventh of the name, with Baron Lexhull von Hildebrandt at its head, was set up to revise the Provisional Regulations. This Committee, wrote Miliukov, rejected the proposal to expel from the

---

[986] Evreiskaya piteinaia torgovlia v Rossii (*Jewish trade of spirits in Russia*), op. cit.
[987] JE, t. 2, pp. 235, 238.
[988] *Cf. Sliosberg*, t. 2, p. 55.

countryside the Jews who illegally established themselves there, and softened the law of 1882.[989]

While "recognising that the peasantry, which is not very developed, has no entrepreneurial spirit and no means of development, must be protected from any contact with Jews," the Committee insisted that "the landowners have no need for the tutelage of the government; the limitation of the right of the owners to manage their property as they see fit depreciates said property and compels the proprietors to employ, in concert with the Jews, all sorts of expedients to circumvent the law"; the lifting of prohibitions on Jews will enable landowners to derive greater benefit from their assets.[990] But the proprietors no longer had the prestige, which might have given weight to this argument in the eyes of the administration.

It was in 1903–1904 that the revision of the Regulations of 1882 was seriously undertaken. Reports came from the provinces (notably from Sviatopolk Mirsky, who was Governor-General and soon to become the Liberal Minister of the Interior), saying that the Regulations had not proved their worth, that it was imperative that the Jews should leave towns and villages where their concentration was too high, and that, thanks to the establishment of a State monopoly on beverages, the threat of Jewish exploitation of the rural population was removed. These proposals were approved by Sipyagin, the minister (who was soon to be shot down by a terrorist), and, in 1908, endorsed by Plehve (soon assassinated in his turn). A list of a hundred and one villages had been drawn up and published, to which fifty-seven others would soon be added, in which the Jews acquired the right to settle and purchase real estate, and to lease it. (In the *Jewish Encyclopædia* dating before the revolution, we read the names of these localities, some of which, already quite important, were to spread rapidly: Yuzovka, Lozovaya, Ienakievo, Krivoy Rog, Sinelnikovo, Slavgorod, Kakhovka, Zhmerynka, Chepetovka, Zdolbuniv, Novye Senjary, among others.) Outside this list and Jewish agricultural settlements, Jews did not get the right to acquire land. However, the Regulations were soon abrogated for certain categories: graduates of higher studies, pharmacists, artisans and former retired soldiers. These people were given the right to reside in the countryside, to engage in commerce and various other trades.[991]

---

[989] P. *Miliukov*, Evreiski vopros v rossii (The Jewish Question in Russia), Schit: Literatourny sbornik (The Shield: Literary Collection) edited by L. Andreev, M. Gorky and F. Sologoub, 3rd ed., M. Rousskoie Obschestvo dlia izoutcheniia evreiskoi jizni (Russian Association for the Study of Jewish Life), 1916, p. 170.
[990] JE, t. 5, pp. 821-822.
[991] *Ibidem*, t. 5, pp. 821–822.

While the sale of spirits and the various kinds of farming—including that of the land—were the main sources of income for Jews, there were others, including notably the ownership of land. Among the Jews, "the aspiration to possess the land was expressed by the acquisition of large areas capable of harbouring several types of activities rather than by the use of small parcels which are to be developed by the owner himself."[992] When the land, which gives life to the peasant, reaches a higher price than that of a purely agricultural property, it was not uncommon for a Jewish entrepreneur to acquire it.

As we have seen, the direct leasing and purchasing of the land by the Jews was not prohibited until 1881, and the purchasers were not deprived of their rights by the new prohibitions. This is how, for example, Trotsky's father, David Bronstein, possessed in the province of Kherson, not far from Elizabethgrad, and held in his possession until the revolution an important business (an "economy" as it was called in the South). He also owned, later on, the "Nadejda" mine in the suburb of Krivoi Rog.[993] On the basis of what he had observed in the exploitation of his father—and, as he heard it, "in all farms it is the same", Trotsky relates that the seasonal workers, who had come by foot from the central provinces to be hired, were very malnourished: never meat nor bacon, oil but very little, vegetables and oatmeal, that's all, and this, during the hard summer work, from dawn to twilight, and even, "one summer, an epidemic of hemeralopia[994] was declared among the workers."[995] For my part, I will argue that in an "economy" of the same type, in Kuban, with my grandfather Scherbak (himself a member of a family of agricultural workers), the day workers were served, during the harvest, meat three times a day.

But a new prohibition fell in 1903: "A provision of the Council of Ministers deprived all Jews of the right to acquire immovable property throughout the empire, outside urban areas, that is to say in rural areas."[996] This limited to a certain extent the industrial activity of the Jews, but, as the *Jewish Encyclopædia* points out, by no means their agricultural activity; in any case, "to use the right to acquire land, the Jews would undoubtedly have delegated fewer cultivators than landlords and tenants. It seems doubtful

---

[992] *Ibidem*, t. 1, p. 422.
[993] Fabritchno-zavodskie predpriatia Rossiskoi Imperii (Factories and Plants of the Russian Empire), 2nd ed., Council of Congresses of Industry and Commerce, 1914, No. 590.
[994] Hemeralopia (in Russian: kourinaïa slepota = chicken blindness) weakening or loss of vision in low light, especially at dusk.
[995] *L. Trotsky*, Moia jizn: Opyt avtobiografii (My Life: autobiographical), t. 1, Berlin, Granit, 1930, pp. 42-43.
[996] JE, t. 7, p. 734.

whether a population as urban as the Jewish population was able to supply a large number of farmers."[997]

In the early years of the twentieth century, the picture was as follows: "About two million hectares which are now owned or leased by Jews in the empire and the Kingdom of Poland... only 113,000... are home to Jewish agricultural settlements."[998]

Although the Provisional Regulations of 1882 prohibited the Jews from buying or leasing out of towns and villages, devious means were also found there, notably for the acquisition of land intended for the sugar industry.

Thus the Jews who possessed large areas of land were opposed to the agrarian reform of Stolypin, which granted land to the peasants on a personal basis. (They were not the only ones: one is astonished at the hostility with which this reform was received by the *press* of those years, and not only by that of the extreme right, but by the perfectly liberal press, not to mention the revolutionary press.) The *Jewish Encyclopædia* argues: "The agrarian reforms that planned to cede land exclusively to those who cultivated it would have harmed the interests of a part of the Jewish population, that which worked in the large farms of Jewish owners."[999] It was not until the Revolution passed that a Jewish author took a look back and, already boiling with proletarian indignation, wrote: "The Jewish landowners possessed under the tsarist regime more than two million hectares of land (mainly around Ukrainian sugar factories, as well as large estates in Crimea and Belarus)", and, moreover, "they owned more than two million hectares of the best land, black earth." Thus, Baron Ginzburg possessed in the district of Dzhankoy 87,000 hectares; the industrialist Brodsky owned tens of thousands of hectares for his sugar mills, and others owned similar estates, so that in total the Jewish capitalists combined 872,000 hectares of arable land.[1000]

After the land ownership came the *trade of wheat* and *cereal products*. (Let us remember that the export of grain "was chiefly carried out by Jews."[1001] "Of the total Jewish population of the USSR, not less than 18%, before the revolution (i.e. more than one million people!] were engaged in the trade of wheat, bosses and members of their families alike, which caused a real animosity of the peasants towards the Jewish population" (because the big buyers did everything to lower the price of the wheat in order to resell it

---

[997] JE, t. 1, p. 423.
[998] *Ibidem.*
[999] *Ibidem.*
[1000] *Larine*, pp. 27, 68, 69, 170.
[1001] SJE, t. 7, p. 337.

for more profit.¹⁰⁰²) In the western provinces and in Ukraine, the Jews bought in bulk other agricultural commodities. (Moreover, how can we not point out that in places like Klintsy, Zlynka, Starodub, Ielenovka, Novozybkov, the old believers, workers and industrious, never let trade go by other hands?) Biekerman believes that the prohibition of Jewish merchants to operate throughout the territory of Russia fostered apathy, immobility, domination by the kulaks. However, "If Russia's trade in wheat has become an integral part of world trade, Russia owes it to the Jews." As we have already seen, "as early as 1878, 60% of wheat exports from the port of Odessa were by Jews. They were the first to develop the wheat trade at Nikolayev," Kherson, Rostov-on-Don, as well as in the provinces of Orel, Kursk, and Chernigov. They were "well represented in the wheat trade in Saint Petersburg." And in the North-West region, out of 1,000 traders of cereal products there were 930 Jews."¹⁰⁰³

However, most of our sources do not shed light on how these Jewish merchants behaved with their trading partners. In fact, they were often very hard and practised procedures that today we would consider illicit; they could, for example, agree among themselves and refuse to buy the crop in order to bring down prices. It is understandable that in the 90s farmers' cooperatives (under the leadership of Count Heiden and Bekhteyev) were set up in the southern provinces for the first time in Russia and a step ahead of Europe. Their mission was to thwart these massive, monopolistic purchases of peasant wheat.

Let us recall another form of commerce in the hands of the Jews: the "export of wood came second after the wheat."¹⁰⁰⁴ From 1813 to 1913, these exports were multiplied by 140! And the Communist Larinus fulminated: "The Jewish proprietors possessed... large forested areas, and they leased a part of it, even in the provinces where the Jews were not normally allowed to reside."¹⁰⁰⁵

The *Jewish Encyclopædia* confirms it: "The Jews acquired the land, especially in the central provinces, chiefly to exploit the forest wealth."¹⁰⁰⁶ However, as they did not have the right to install sawmills in some places, the wood left abroad in the raw state, for a dead loss for the country. (There

---

¹⁰⁰² *Larine*, p. 70.
¹⁰⁰³ *I. M. Dijour*, Evrei v ekonomitcheskojizni Rossii (The Jews in the Economic Life of Russia), BJWR-l *, p. 172.
¹⁰⁰⁴ *Ibidem*, p. 173.
¹⁰⁰⁵ *Larine*, p.69.
¹⁰⁰⁶ JE, t. 1, p. 423.

existed other prohibitions: access for export of timber in the ports of Riga, Revel, Petersburg; the installation of warehouses along the railways).[1007]

Such is the picture. Everything is there. And the tireless dynamism of Jewish commerce, which drives entire states. And the prohibitions of a timorous, sclerotic bureaucracy that only hinders progress. And the ever-increasing irritation these prohibitions provoke among the Jews. And the sale of the Russian forest, exported abroad in its raw state, as a raw material. And the small farmer, the small operator, who, caught in a merciless vise, has neither the relationships nor the skills to invent other forms of trade. And let us not forget the Ministry of Finance, which pours its subsidies on industry and railways and abandons agriculture, whereas the tax burden is carried by the class of the farmers, not the merchants. One wonders: under the conditions of the new economic dynamics that came to replenish the Treasury and was largely due to the Jews, was there anyone to worry about the harm done to the common people, the shock suffered by it, from the break in its way of life, in its very being?

For half a century, Russia has been accused—from the inside as well as from the outside—of having enslaved the Jews economically and having forced them to misery. It was necessary that the years passed, that this abominable Russia disappear from the surface of the earth, it will be necessary to cross the revolutionary turmoil for a Jewish author of the 30s to look at the past, over the bloody wall of the Revolution, and acknowledge: "The tsarist government has not pursued a policy of total eviction of Jews from economic life. Apart from the well-known limitations... in the countryside..., on the whole, the tsarist government tolerated the economic activity of the Jews." The tensions of the national struggle, "the Jews did not feel them in their economic activity. The dominant nation did not want to take the side of a particular ethnic group, it was only trying to play the role of arbiter or mediator."[1008]

Besides, it happened that the government was intruding into the economy on national grounds. It then took measures which, more often than not, were doomed to failure. Thus, "in 1890, a bulletin was diffused under which the Jews lost the right to be directors of corporations that intended to purchase or lease lands."[1009] But it was the childhood of the art of circumventing this law: remaining anonymous. This kind of prohibition in no way impeded the activity of Jewish entrepreneurs. "The role of Jews was especially important in foreign trade where their hegemony was

---

[1007] *Dijour*, SJE-1, p. 173.
[1008] A. *Menes*, Evreiski vopros v Vostotchnoï Evrope (The Jewish Question in Eastern Europe), JW-1, p. 146.
[1009] SJE, t. 7, p. 368.

assured and their geographical location (near borders) and by their contacts abroad, and by their commercial intermediaries skills."[1010]

As regards to the sugar industry, more than a third of the factories were Jewish at the end of the century.[1011] We have seen in previous chapters how the industry had developed under the leadership of Israel Brodsky and his sons Lazar and Leon ("at the beginning of the twentieth century, they controlled directly or indirectly seventeen sugar mills"[1012]). Galperine Moses, "in the early twentieth century had eight factories and three refineries... He also owned 50,000 hectares of sugar beet cropland."[1013]

"Hundreds of thousands of Jewish families lived off the sugar industry, acting as intermediaries, sellers, and so on." When competition appeared, as the price of sugar began to fall, a syndicate of sugar producers in Kiev called for control of production and sale, in order for prices not to fall.[1014] The Brodsky Brothers were the founders of the Refiners' Union in 1903.[1015]

In addition to the grain trade, the wood trade and the sugar industry where they occupied a predominant position, other areas must be cited in which the Jews largely contributed to development: flour milling, fur trade, spinning mills, confection, the tobacco industry, the brewery.[1016] In 1835 they were also present at the major fairs in Nizhny Novgorod.[1017] In Transbaikalia they launched a livestock trade which took off in the 90s, and the same happened in Siberia for the production of coal—Andjero-Soudji hard coal—and the extraction of gold, where they played a major role. After 1892, the Ginzburg "devoted themselves almost exclusively to the extraction of gold." The most prosperous enterprise was the Lena Gold Mining Company, which "was controlled in fact (from 1896 until its death in 1909) by Baron Horace Ginzburg, son of Evzel Ginzburg, founder of the Bank of the same name and president of its branch in Saint Petersburg. (The son of Horace, David, also a baron, remained at the head of the Jewish community of Saint Petersburg until his death in 1910. His sons Alexander and Alfred sat on the board of Lena, the gold mining company.

Another son, Vladimir, married the daughter of the owner of the Kiev sugar factory, L. I. Brodsky.) Horace Ginzburg was also "the founder of... the gold extraction companies from Transbaikalia, Miias, Berezovka, Altai and

---

[1010] JE, t. 13, p. 646.
[1011] *Ibidem*, p. 662.
[1012] RJE, t. 1, p. 171.
[1013] *Ibidem*, p. 264.
[1014] *Sliosberg*, t. 2, p. 231.
[1015] RJE, t. 1, p. 171.
[1016] *Dijour*, BJWR-1, pp. 163, 174.
[1017] JE, t. 11, p. 697.

a few others."[1018] In 1912, a huge scandal about the Lena mines broke out and caused quite a stir throughout the country: the operating conditions were abominable, the workers had been misled... Appropriately, the tsarist government was accused of everything and demonised. No one, in the raging liberal press mentioned the main shareholders, notably the Ginzburg sons.

At the beginning of the twentieth century, Jews represented 35% of the merchant class in Russia.[1019] Choulguine gives us what he observed in the southwest region: "Where have they gone, Russian traders, where is the Russian third estate? ... In time, we had a strong Russian *bourgeoisie*... Where have they gone?" "They were ousted by the Jews, lowered into the social ladder, to the state of *moujiks*."[1020] The Russians in the southwest region have chosen their own fate: it is clear. And at the beginning of the century, the eminent politician V. I. Gourko[1021] observed: "The place of the Russian merchant is more and more frequently taken by a Jew."[1022]

The Jews also gained influence and authority in the booming sector of the cooperative system. More than half of the Mutual Credit and Savings and Loan Companies were in the Pale of Settlement (86% of their members in 1911 were Jewish).[1023]

We have already spoken of the construction and operation of the Russian railways by the Poliakov brothers, Bliokh and Varshavsky. With the exception of the very first lines (the Tsarskoselskaya line and the Nikolaevskaya line), almost all the railways that were later built were made by concessionary companies in which the Jews occupied the command posts; "But, as of the 1890s, the state was the first builder." On the other hand, it is under the leadership of David Margoline that was created in 1883 the great shipping company "on the Dnieper and its tributaries", the main shareholders of which were Jews. In 1911, the company owned a fleet of 78 vessels and accounted for 71% of the traffic on the Dnieper.[1024] Other

---

[1018] SJE, t. 7, p. 369; RJE, t. 1, pp. 315 316; JE, t. 6, p. 527.
[1019] M. *Vernatsky*, Evrei i rousskoie narodnoie khoziaistvo (The Jews and the Russian Economy), p. 30.
[1020] *Choulguine*, pp. 128-129.
[1021] Vladimir Yossifovich Gourko (1863–1917): Deputy Minister of the Interior in 1906, elected member of the Council of the Empire since 1912. Emigrated after the Civil War.
[1022] Vf Gourko, Oustoi narodnogo khoziastva v Rossii: Agrarno-ekonomitcheskie etiudy (The Foundations of the National Economy in Russia: Agrarian and Economic Studies), Saint Petersburg, 1902, p. 199.
[1023] *Dijour*, BJWR-1, p. 176.
[1024] SJE, t. 7, p. 369.

companies operating on the Western Dvina, the Niemen, joined the Mariinsky Canal and the Volga.

There were also about ten oil companies belonging to Jews from Baku. "The biggest were the oil company belonging to the brothers S. and M. Poliak and to Rothschild, and the joint-stock company of the Caspian-Black Sea, behind which was also found the name of Rothschild." These companies were not allowed to extract oil; they specialised in refining and exporting.[1025]

But it was in finance that the economic activity of the Jews was the most brilliant. "Credit is an area where Jews have long felt at home. They have created new ways and have perfected the old. They played a leading role in the hands of a few large capitalists and in the organisation of commercial investment banks. The Jews brought out of their ranks not only the banking aristocracy but also the mass of employees."[1026] The bank of Evzel Ginzburg, founded in 1859 in Saint Petersburg, grew and strengthened thanks to its links with the Mendelssohn in Berlin, the Warburg in Hamburg, the Rothschild in Paris and Vienna. But when the financial crisis of 1892 broke out, and "because of the government's refusal to support its bank with loans," as had happened twice before, E. Ginzburg withdrew from business.[1027] By the 70s, there existed a network of banks founded by the three Poliakov brothers, Jacob, Samuel and Lazar. These are the Azov-Don Commercial Bank (to be later managed by B. Kaminka), the Mortgage Lending of Moscow, the Don Land Bank, the Poliakov Bank, the International Bank and "a few other houses which will later form the Unified Bank."—The Bank of Siberia had A. Soloveitchik at its head, the Commercial Bank of Warsaw was directed by I. Bliokh. In several other large establishments, Jews occupied important posts (Zak, Outine, Khesine, A. Dobryi, Vavelberg, Landau, Epstein, Krongold). "In two large banks only, the Commercial Bank of Moscow and that of the Volga-Kama, there were no Jews either in the leadership or among the staff."[1028] The Poliakov brothers all had the rank of secret counsellor and, as we have said, all three were granted hereditary nobility.[1029]

Thus, at the dawn of the twentieth century, the Pale of Settlement had already completely emptied itself of its substance. It had not prevented the Jews from occupying solid positions in the vital sectors of the country's life, from economy and finance to the intellectual sphere. The "Pale" no longer had any practical utility; its economic and political purpose was

---

[1025] *Dijour*, BJWR-1, pp. 178, 179; JE, t. 13, p. 660; SJE, t. 7, p. 369.
[1026] JE, t. 13, pp. 651, 652.
[1027] JE, t. 6, p. 527.
[1028] *Dijour*, BJWR-1, pp. 174, 175; SJE, t. 6, pp. 670-671.
[1029] JE, t. 12, p. 734; SJE, t. 6, pp. 670-671.

outdated. It had only filled the Jews with anti-government bitterness and resentment; it had thrown oil on the fire of social discontent and had struck the Russian government with the seal of infamy in the eyes of the West.

But let us be clear: this Russian Empire, with the slowness and sclerosis of its bureaucracy, the mentality of its leaders, where and in what way did it fall behind all through the nineteenth century and decades before the revolution? It had been unable to settle a dozen major problems affecting the life of the country. It had not been able to organise local civil self-government, install zemstvos in rural districts, carry out agrarian reform, remedy the state of pernicious state of humiliation of the Church, or communicate with civil society and make its action understood. It had managed neither the boom of mass education nor the development of Ukrainian culture. To this list let us add another point where the delay proved catastrophic: the revision of the real conditions of the Pale of Settlement, the awareness of their influence on all positionings of the State. The Russian authorities have had a hundred years and more to solve the problems of the Jewish population, and they have not been able to do so, neither in the sense of an open assimilation nor by allowing the Jews to remain in voluntary isolation, that which was already theirs a century before.

Meanwhile, during the decades from the 70s to the beginning of the twentieth century, Russian Judaism experienced a rapid development, an undeniable blossoming of its elite, which already felt cramped, not only within the limits of the Pale of Settlement, but in those of the empire.

When analysing the concrete aspects of the inequality in Jewish rights in Russia, the Pale of Settlement and the *numerus clausus*, we must not lose sight of this general picture. For if American Judaism grew in importance, the Jews of Russia at the beginning of the twentieth century still constituted nearly half of the Jewish population of the planet.[1030] This is to be remembered as an important fact in the history of Judaism. And it is still Mr. Biekerman who, looking behind him over the ditch of the revolution, wrote in 1924: "Tsarist Russia was home to more than half the Jewish people. It is natural, consequently, that the Jewish history of the generations that are closest to us is mainly the history of the Jews of Russia." And even though in the nineteenth century "the Jews of the West had been richer, more influential, and more cultured than we were, the vitality of Judaism was nevertheless in Russia. And this vitality grew stronger and stronger at the same time as the Russian Empire flourished… It was only when provinces populated by Jews were united to Russia that this rebirth began. The Jewish population grew rapidly in number, to such an extent that it was

---

[1030] SJE, t. 2, pp. 313-314.

able to leave a very numerous colony overseas; it had amassed and possessed important capital in its hands; a middle class had grown and acquired authority; the standard of living of the lower strata had also grown incessantly. By a variety of efforts, the Jews of Russia had been able to overcome the physical and moral abjection which they had brought from Poland; European culture and education reached Jewish circles... and we went so far in this direction, we have amassed such spiritual wealth that we have been able to afford the luxury of having a literature in three languages..." All this culture, all this wealth, it is in Russia that the Jews of Eastern Europe have received them. Russian Judaism, "by its numbers and by the greenness of the energies it contained, proved to be the backbone of all the Jewish people."[1031]

A more recent author, our contemporary, confirms in 1989 the correctness of this painting brushed by his elder, witness of the time. He wrote: "The public life of the Jews of Russia had reached, at the turn of the two centuries, a degree of maturity and amplitude which many small peoples in Europe might have envied."[1032]

If there is a reproach that cannot be made to the "prison of the people", it is to have denationalised the people, be it the Jews or others. Certain Jewish authors, it is true, deplore the fact that in the 80s "the cultivated Jews of the capital had hardly been involved in the defence of Jewish interests", that only Baron Ginzburg and a few other wealthy Jews with good relations.[1033] "The Jews of Petersburg (30,000 to 40,000 in 1900) lived unconnected with one another, and the Jewish intelligentsia, in its majority, remained aloof, indifferent to the needs and interests of the community as a whole."[1034] Yet it was also the time when "the holy spirit of the Renaissance... hovered over the Pale of Settlement and awakened in the younger generations the forces that had been dormant for many centuries among the Jewish people...

It was a veritable spiritual revolution." Among Jewish girls, "the thirst for instruction showed literarily religious signs." And already, even in Saint Petersburg, "a large number of Jewish students frequented higher education institutions." At the beginning of the twentieth century, "a great

---

[1031] *I. M. Bickerman*, Rossiia i rousskoie evreistvo (Russia and Russian Judaism), RJE, pp. 84-85, 87.
[1032] *E. Finkelstein*, Evrei v SSSR. Pout v XXI vek (The Jews in the USSR. Entry into the 21st Century), Strana i mir: Obschetv. Polititcheski, ekonomitcheski i koultournofilosfski journal (The Country and the World: Socio-political, Economic, Cultural and Philosophical Review), Munich, 1989, no. 1 (49), p. 70.
[1033] *Sliosberg*, t. 1, p. 145.
[1034] *M.A. Krol*, Stranitsy moeï jizni (Pages of my life), t. 1, New York, Union of Russian Jews in New York, 1944, p. 267.

part of the Jewish intelligentsia... felt... that it was its duty to return to its people."[1035]

Thanks to this spiritual awakening at the end of the nineteenth century, very diverse and sometimes contradictory trends emerged in Russian Judaism. Some of them will be called upon to determine to a large extent the destinies of our land throughout the twentieth century.

At the time, the Jews of Russia envisaged at least six possible orientations, however incompatible with each other. Namely:

- the safeguard of their religious identity by isolation, as had been practised for centuries (but this path became more and more unpopular);

- assimilation;

- the struggle for national and cultural autonomy, the active presence of Judaism in Russia as a distinct element;

- emigration;

- adherence to Zionism;

- adherence to the revolution.

Indeed, the proponents of these different tendencies were often united in the work of acculturation of the Jewish masses in three languages—Hebrew, Yiddish and Russian—and in welfare works—in the spirit of the theory of "small gestures" in vogue in Russia in the 80s.

Mutual aid was embodied in Jewish associations, some of which, after the revolution, were able to continue their action in emigration. This was the case with the Society for the Dissemination of Education among the Jews of Russia, which had been founded in 1863. By the mid-90s, this Society was already opening its own schools, with, besides an education in Russian, courses in Hebrew. It convened Pan-Russian conferences on the theme of Jewish popular education.[1036]

In 1891 began the works of a Commission of Jewish History and Ethnography, which in 1908 became the Society of Jewish History and Ethnography. It coordinated the study of Jewish history through Russia and the collection of archives.[1037]

In 1880, the "King of the Railways", Samuel Poliakov, founded the Society of Craft and Agricultural Labour among the Jews (SCAL). The latter

---

[1035] *Krol., op. cit.*, pp. 260-261, 267, 299.
[1036] JE, t. 1, pp. 60-61.
[1037] *Ibidem*, t. 8, p. 466.

collected a good deal of money and "devoted the bulk of its efforts, at the beginning of its efforts, to the transfer of Jewish artisans outside the Pale of Settlement to the central provinces."[1038] We have seen that after the initial authorisation given (in 1865) to this transfer the craftsmen moved only in small numbers. What happened after the pogroms of 1881–1882? We could think: now, they will certainly leave, they have the help the SCAL, plus a subsidy from the government for the displacement, they will not remain there, moping around, confined in this damned Pale where one was condemned to a wretched death, but no: after more than ten years of efforts on the part of the SCAL, only 170 artisans moved! The SCAL decided then to help artisans inside the Pale by purchasing tools, setting up workshops and then creating professional schools.[1039]

Emigration was taken over by the Society for Colonisation by the Jews (SCJ), whose creation followed the opposite course: first abroad, then in Russia.

It was founded in London in 1891 by Baron Moritz von Hirsch, who for this purpose made a donation of 2,000,000 pounds sterling. His idea was the following: to substitute the chaotic emigration of the Jews of Eastern Europe with a well-ordered colonisation, oriented towards the countries requiring cultivators, and thus to bring back at least part of the Jews to the cultivation of the land, to free them from this "anomaly... which arouses the animosity of the European peoples."[1040] "To seek for the Jews who leave Russia 'a new homeland and try to divert them from their usual activity, trade, make them farmers and thereby contribute to the work of rebirth of the Jewish people'."[1041]

This new homeland, it would be Argentina. (Another objective was to divert the wave of Jewish immigration away from the shores of the United States where, owing to the influx of immigrants, the wage decline induced by their competition, there rose the spectre of anti-Semitism.) As it was proposed to populate this land with Jews of Russia, an office of the Society for Colonisation opened in Saint Petersburg in 1892. It "set up 450 information offices and 20 neighbourhood committees. They received the candidates for emigration to help them obtain their exit papers from the territory, they negotiated with the maritime messengers, they procured travellers with tickets at reduced prices, they published brochures" on countries likely to welcome new settlers.[1042]

[1038] *Ibidem*, t. 11, p. 924.
[1039] *Ibidem*, pp. 924-925.
[1040] *Sliosberg*, t. 2, pp. 32, 96–102.
[1041] JE, t. 7, p. 504.
[1042] SJE, t. 2, p. 365.

(Sliosberg denounces in passing the fact that "no person not holding a double title as a banker or a millionaire had access to their direction."[1043])

Since the end of the nineteenth century, the emigration of Jews from Russia had been growing steadily for various reasons, some of which have already been mentioned here. One of the most serious of these was the compulsory conscription: if so many young men (it is Denikin who writes it) chose to mutilate themselves, was it not better to emigrate? Especially when we know that conscription simply did not exist in the United States! (The Jewish authors are silent on this motif, and the *Jewish Encyclopædia* itself, in the article "The Emigration of the Jews of Russia", does not say a single word of it.[1044] It is true that this reason does not explain on its own the emigration boom in the 90s.) Another reason, also of significance: the Provisional Regulations of 1882. The third major shock was the expulsion of Jewish craftsmen from Moscow in 1891.

And also this other, very violent: the establishment of the state monopoly on spirits in Russia in 1896, which deprived all the tenants of drinking places of their income and reduced the revenues of the distillers. (Sliosberg: those who had been expelled from the villages or provinces of the interior were volunteers for emigration.) G. Aronson notes that in the 80s an average of 15,000 Jews emigrated each year, and that they were up to 30,000 in the 90s.[1045]

The attitude of the Russian authorities in the face of this growing emigration—a genuine boon to the State—was benevolent. The Russian Government readily agreed to the establishment of the SCJ in Saint Petersburg, and the measures that it adopted to promote emigration; it did not interfere in any of its actions, authorising the age group of the conscripts to emigrate with their families; it issued free exit visas and granted special rates on trains—on one condition, however: once gone, the emigrants were never to return to Russia again.[1046]

To cross the ocean, it was necessary at the time to pass through England, which meant that in the English port cities there was provisionally a crowd of Jewish emigrants—some of whom remained and settled in Great Britain while others returned there after an attempt to settle in the United States. As early as 1890, English public opinion rebelled against the policy of the Russian government: "The Jewish question is constantly occupying the

---

[1043] *Sliosberg*, t. 2, pp. 29, 98, 100.
[1044] JE, t. 16, pp. 264, 268.
[1045] G. I. Aronson, V borbe za natsionalnye i granjdanskie prava: Obschestvennye telchénia v rousskom evreistve (In the struggle for civil and national rights: Social currents among the Jews of Russia), BJWR-1, p. 212.
[1046] JE, t. 7, p. 507; *Sliosberg*, t. 2, pp. 34–41; SJE, t. 7, p. 366.

columns of the British newspapers... In America, too, the question of the situation of Jews in Russia remains day after day of actuality."[1047] Having assessed the proportions that this migratory flow was likely to take, Great Britain soon closed its doors.[1048]

The immigration to Argentina had also stopped in 1894. The *Jewish Encyclopædia* described this as a "brooding crisis... in the Argentine question."[1049] Sliosberg spoke of the "disenchantment of immigrants in Argentina" (the disgruntled rebelled and sent collective petitions to the administration of Baron Hirsch). The Duma debates highlighted a situation similar to the experience in New Russia: "Immigration to Argentina provides examples that confirm that in many cases people have received land on very advantageous terms, but have abandoned it to engage in other trades more in line with their abilities."[1050]

After this, although its vocation remained in the principle of pushing the Jews to become farming "settlers", the Society for Colonisation renounced this objective. It set itself the task of helping "the excessively disorderly emigration of Jews from Russia", "it was concerned with providing information to the emigrants, defending their interests, being the connection with host countries", and it had to modify its statutes, which had been bequeathed by Baron Hirsch.

Large sums were allocated "to raise the standard of living of Jews in their places of residence"; from 1898 onwards, "action was taken among the population within Russia itself," and in the existing Jewish agricultural colonies the "introduction of more modern tools and methods of cultivation", "the granting of an advantageous credit for the improvement of the soil." However, again, "despite the large sums invested in this sector, agricultural activity remained relatively stagnant." [1051] Conversely, migratory flows outside Russia continued to increase, "in direct connection with the craft crisis and the gradual elimination of small trade and factories"; this flow "reached its peak... in 1906", but was not "able to absorb the annual surplus of the population" of the Jews. It should be noted that "the great mass of emigrants was destined for the United States"—for example, in 1910, they were 73%.[1052] "From 1881 to 1914, 78.6% of

---

[1047] *Sliosberg*, t. 2, pp. 27, 30.
[1048] JE, t. 2, pp. 534 535.
[1049] *Ibidem*, t. 7, p. 504.
[1050] Gosudarslvcnnaia Duma—Vtoroi sozyv (State Duma, 2nd Legislature), Stenogramme, Session 2, Saint Petersburg, 1907, Meeting 24, 9 April 1907, p. 1814.
[1051] JE, t. 7, p. 505, 509; *I. M. Troilsky*, Samodeiatelnost i samopomosch evreiev v Rossii (autonomous activity and mutual assistance of Jews in Russia), BJWR-1, pp. 491, 495.
[1052] JE, t. 16, p. 265.

emigrants from Russia landed in the United States."[1053] From this period, we can thus see what will be the general movement of our century. (Note that at the entrance to the American territory no paper certifying craftsmanship was required, and it followed that during the first six years of the century 63% of Russian immigrants "engaged in industry". This meant that those who left Russia for America were exclusively artisans? This could offer an explanation to the question as to why the artisans did not go to the Central provinces, which were now open to them? But it is also necessary to consider that for many immigrants, and especially for those who had neither resources nor trade, no other answer was possible than that of recognising themselves as part of the "category notoriously well accepted by the Americans."[1054])

One is struck by how few of the emigrants are the individuals belonging to the cultivated stratum, the one allegedly the most persecuted in Russia. These people did not emigrate. From 1899 to 1907, they were barely 1% to do so.[1055]

The Jewish intelligentsia did not in any way tend to emigrate: it was, in its eyes, a way of escaping the problems and fate of Russia at the very moment when opportunities for action were opening up. As late as 1882, the resolution of a Congress of Jewish public figures "called for a definite rejection of the idea of organising an emigration, for this idea contradicts the dignity of the Russian State."[1056] In the last years of the nineteenth century, "the new generation wanted to be actively involved in history… and across the board, from the outside as well as from the inside, it has gone from defensive to offensive… Young Jews now want to write their own history, to affix the seal of their will to their destiny, and also, to a just extent, on the destiny of the country in which they live."[1057]

The religious wing of Russian Judaism also denounced emigration, considering it as a break with the vivifying roots of East European Judaism.

The secular efforts of the new generation were primarily concerned with a vast program of specifically Jewish instruction, culture and literature in Yiddish, the only ones capable of creating a link with the mass of the people. (According to the census of 1897, only 3% of Russian Jews recognised Russian as their mother tongue, while Hebrew seemed forgotten and no one thought it could be reborn.) It was proposed to create

---

[1053] SJE, t. 7, p. 366.
[1054] JE, t. 2, pp. 246 248.
[1055] *Ibidem*, pp. 247-248.
[1056] SJE, t. 7, p. 365.
[1057] V. *Jabotinsky*, Vvedenie (Preface to K. N. Bialik, Pesni i poemy (Songs and poems), Saint Petersburg, ed. Zaltsman, 1914, p. 36.

a network of libraries specially designed for Jews, newspapers in Yiddish (the daily *Der Freynd* appeared in 1903; and it sold like hot cakes in the villages; not belonging to any political party, it nevertheless sought to give political training[1058]). It was in the 90s that took shape "the grandiose metamorphosis of the amorphous Jewish mass into a nation, the Jewish Renaissance."[1059]

One after the other, authors writing in Yiddish became very popular: Mendele Mocher-Sefarim, Scholom-Aleichem, Itzhak-Leibush Peretz. And the poet Bialik, to follow the movement, translated his own poems into Yiddish. In 1908, this trend reached its peak at the Tchernovtsy Conference, which proclaimed Yiddish as the "national language of the Jewish people" and advocated the translation of all printed texts into Yiddish.[1060]

At the same time, considerable efforts were made for Jewish culture in the Russian language. Thus the ten volumes of the *Jewish Library*, of historical and literary content[1061]; the Petersburg magazines born from 1881, *Rassvet* ("The Dawn"), then *Rousski Evrei* ("The Russian Jew"). (They soon stopped appearing: "these publications did not meet the support of the Jewish public itself"[1062]). The magazine *Voskhod* ("The Break of Day") opened its pages to all Jewish authors, translating all the novelties, offering a place of choice for studies on Jewish history,[1063] (May we, Russians, show the same interest in our own history!). For the time being, "the dominant role in the public life of Russian Judaism" was held by the "Jewish Petersburg": "towards the middle of the 90s, [it is in Petersburg that] almost all senior management was formed, the Jewish intellectual aristocracy"; all the talents are in Petersburg.[1064] According to an approximate calculation, only 67,000 Jews spoke Russian fluently in 1897, but it was the cultivated elite. And already "the whole younger generation" in Ukraine in the 90s was raised in Russian, and those who went to study in the high schools completely lost contact with Jewish education.[1065]

[1058] *I. Mark*, Literatoura na idish v Rossii (Literature in Yiddish in Russia), BJWR-1, pp. 537-539.
[1059] *Aronson, op. cit.*, BJWR-1, p. 216.
[1060] *Mark*, LJE-1, pp. 519, 541.
[1061] *G. I. Aronson*, Roussko-evreiskaïa pclchat (The Russian-Jewish Press), BJWR-1, p. 563.
[1062] *Sliosberg*, t. 1, pp. 105, 260.
[1063] *Aronson*, The Russian-Jewish Press, *op. cit.*, pp. 563–568.
[1064] *S. M. Ginzburg*, O roussko-evrciskoï intelligentsii (De l'intelligentsia russo-juive), JW-1. pp. 35-36.
[1065] *I. Ben-Tvi*, Iz istorii rabotchego sionizma v Rossii (About the History of Workers' Zionism in Russia). BJWR-1, p. 272.

There was not, strictly speaking, a slogan of the type: *Assimilation*! We must blend into the Russian element! Nor an appeal to renounce one's nationality. Assimilation was a commonplace phenomenon, but it created a link between Russian Judaism and the future of Russia.[1066] Moreover, Sliosberg refutes the term *assimilation*: "Nothing was more opposed to the truth" than to say that "assimilated persons considered themselves... Russians under the Mosaic Law." On the contrary, "the appetite for Russian culture did not exclude confessing the traditions of Hebrew culture."[1067] However, after the disillusionment of the 80s, "certain Jewish intellectuals, deeply imbued with the idea of assimilation, felt a break in their conception of public life."[1068] Soon, "there soon was only one Jewish organisation left, one party defending assimilation. However... while it had given up arms as a theory, it remained a very real part of the life of the Jews of Russia, at least among those who lived in the big cities."[1069] But it was decided to "break the link between emancipation... and... assimilation"— in other words: to obtain one and not the other, to gain equality but without the loss of Jewishness.[1070] In the 90s, *Voskhod*'s primary objective was to fight for the equal rights of Jews in Russia.[1071]

A "Defence Office" for the Jews of Russia had been formed in Saint Petersburg at the beginning of the century, the members of which were eminent advocates and men of letters. (Before them, Baron Hirsch had been the only one to work as they did: it was to him that all the grievances of the Jews went.) Sliosberg speaks to us in detail about its founders.[1072]

During those years, "the Jewish spirit awoke for the struggle", the Jews were assisted to "a strong thrust of their self-consciousness, public and national"—but a conscience now devoid of any religious form: "The villages deserted by the most fortunate..., the villages abandoned by the young people, gone to join the city..., the galloping urbanisation" undermined the religion "in broad sections of the Jewish population from the 90s", and caused the authority of the rabbis to fall. The scholars of the Talmudic schools themselves were seduced by secularisation.[1073] (That being said, the biographical notes of the *Jewish Encyclopædia* concerning the generation that grew up at the turn of the nineteenth and twentieth

---

[1066] *Ginzburg*, About Russian-Jewish Intelligentsia, *op. cit.*, pp. 37–39.
[1067] *Sliosberg*, t. 2, pp. 301, 302.
[1068] *Hessen*, t. 2, p. 232.
[1069] JE, t. 3, p. 232.
[1070] *I. Mark*, Pamiati I. M. Tcherkover (To the Memory of I. M. Tcherkover), JW-2, New York, 1944, p. 425.
[1071] *Aronson*, The Russian-Jewish Press, *op. cit.*, pp. 564–568.
[1072] *Sliosberg*, L 3, pp. 110–135.
[1073] *Aronson*, The Russian-Jewish Press, *op. cit.*, pp. 213–215.

centuries often include the words "received a traditional religious education".)

On the other hand, as we have pointed out, what developed with unpredictable force and in an unexpected form was *palestinophilia*.

The events in Russia could not but be perceived by the Jews of Russia and by the Russians involved in public life in the light of what was happening at the same time in Europe: contacts were then free and frequent between educated people and the borders were permeable to ideas and events.

European historians point to a "nineteenth-century anti-Semitism... a growing animosity towards Jews in Western Europe, where, however, it seemed that we were making great strides towards its disappearance."[1074] Up to Switzerland where the Jews, in the middle of the century, had not been able to obtain freedom of residence in the townships, the freedom to trade or to exercise handicrafts. In France, it was the blast of the Dreyfus Affair. In Hungary, "the old landed aristocracy... accused the Jews... of having ruined it"; In Austria and in the present-day Czech Republic, at the end of the nineteenth century, an "anti-Semitic movement" was spreading, and "the petty *bourgeoisie*... fought the social-democratic proletariat with anti-Jewish slogans."[1075] In 1898, bloody pogroms took place in Galicia. The rise in all countries of the *bourgeoisie* "increased the influence of the Jews, grouped in large numbers in capitals and industrial centres... In cities such as Vienna and Budapest..., the press, the theatre, the bar, the medical profession, found in their ranks a percentage of Jews much higher than their proportion in the population as a whole. Those years mark the beginning of the great fortunes of certain Jewish merchants and bankers."[1076]

But it was in Germany that the anti-Jewish tendencies manifested themselves with the greatest insistence. Let us first name Richard Wagner (as early as 1869). In the 70s conservative and clerical circles demanded that the rights of German Jews should be restricted and that any new Jewish immigration should be banned. From the end of the 70s, the "intellectual circles themselves," whose spokesman was the Prussian historian Heinrich von Treitschke, said: "The agitators of today have well perceived the mindset of society which regards the Jews as our national misfortune"; "The Jews never succeed in merging with the peoples of Western Europe", and show hatred towards Germanism. Then comes Karl Eugen Duhring,

---

[1074] *Parks*, p. 161.
[1075] Istoria XIX veka v 8-mi t. (Russian translation of the History of the XIX century in 8 volumes, by Lavisse and Rambaud, t. 7), M., 139, pp. 186, 203.
[1076] *Parks*, p. 164.

made famous for his polemic with Marx and Engels[1077]: "The Jewish question is a simple matter of race, and the Jews are a race that is not only foreign but irremediably and ontologically bad." Then comes the philosopher Edward Hartman. In the political sphere, this movement led to the first international anti-Jewish congress of 1882 (in Dresden), which adopted the "Manifesto addressed to the Christian peoples and governments that are dying of Judaism", and demanded the expulsion of Jews from Germany.—But in the early 90s the anti-Jewish parties had regressed and suffered a series of setbacks on the political scene.[1078]

France was also the scene if not of the emergence of an equally aggressive racial theory, at least of a broad anti-Jewish political propaganda: the one broadcast by Edouard Drumont in his *Libre Parole* from 1892. Then came "a real competition between Socialism and anti-Semitism"; "The Socialists did not hesitate to embellish their speeches of outputs against the Jews and to lower themselves right up to anti-Semitic demagogy... A social anti-Semitic fog enveloped the entirety of France."[1079] (Very similar to the propaganda of the populists in Russia in the years 1881–1882.)

And it was then that in 1894 the thunderous Dreyfus Affair broke out. "In 1898, it [anti-Semitism] reached its climax throughout Western Europe—in Germany, France, Great Britain and the United States."[1080]

The Russian press of the years 1870–1890 also issued some anti-Jewish statements, but without the strong theoretical colouring they had in Germany, nor the exacerbated social violence in Austria-Hungary and France. Let us recall the accounts of Vsevolod Krestovsky (*Egyptian Darkness*, among others) and some crude newspaper articles.

It is appropriate to set apart the newspaper *Novoïe Vremia* ("The New Times"), which owed its success to its engaged positions to the "Slav movement" linked to the Russo-Turkish war for the defence of the Balkans. But when "from the theatre of operations were received reports on acts of plunder perpetrated by intendants and suppliers, these suppliers "of Jewish origin" appeared as the incarnation of all Russian Judaism, and *Novoïe Vremia* adopted a frankly anti-Semitic stance." Beginning in the 80s, the newspaper did more than "go into the camp of reactionaries", "it went beyond all the limits of hatred and improbity in the Jewish question. The

---

[1077] Karl Eugen Dühring (1833-1921): German philosopher. His theses, opposed to the economic and social theories of Marx and Engels, were strongly criticised by the latter in the work entitled precisely the Anti-Dühring.
[1078] JE*, t. 2, pp. 696 708.
[1079] *Ibidem*, pp. 676-677.
[1080] R. *Noudelman*, Prizrak brodit po Evrope (A Spectre Haunts Europe), in «22», Tel-Aviv, 1992, no. 84, p. 128.

warning cry 'Beware the Jew!' resounded for the first time in the columns of *Novoïe Vremia*. The paper insisted on the need to take firm measures against the Jews' 'stranglehold' over Russian science, literature and art..." It did not miss an opportunity to denounce the fact of "withdrawing from military service."[1081]

These attacks on Jews, both abroad and in Russia, stirred Vladimir Solovyov, and in 1884 he vigorously criticised them: "The Judaeans have always behaved to us in the manner of the Judaeans, and we, Christians, have not yet learned to behave with Judaism in a Christian way"; "With regard to Judaism, the Christian world *in its mass* has so far shown only an irrational jealousy or a feeble indifference." No, "it is not Christian Europe that is tolerant of Jews, it is the Europe of unbelievers."[1082]

The growing importance of the Jewish question for Russia, Russian society understood it only half a century behind its government. It was only after the Crimean War that "the emerging Russian public opinion began to conceive the existence of a Jewish problem in Russia."[1083] But there needed to elapse a few more decades before it understood the *primacy* of this question. "Providence has brought the greatest part of the Jewish people to our country, and the strongest," wrote Vladimir Solovyov in 1891.[1084]

The year before, with the support of some sympathisers, Solovyov wrote a "Protest" in which it was said that "the sole cause of the so-called Jewish question" was the abandonment of all righteousness and humanity, "a senseless craze for blind national egoism." "To stir up racial and religious hatred, which is so contrary to the spirit of Christianity..., deeply perverts society and can lead to a return to barbarism..." "We must strongly denounce the anti-Semitic movement, "even if only through the instinct of national survival."[1085]

[1081] JE, t. 11, p. 758-759.

[1082] *V. S. Solovyov*, Evreistvo i khristianski vopros (Judaism and the Christian Question), Compl. Works in 10 vols., 2nd ed., St. Petersburg, 1911–1914, vol. 4, pp. 135, 136, 138.

[1083] *Aronson*, The Russian-Jewish Press, *op. cit.*, p. 549.

[1084] Letter from V. Solovyov to F. Hetz, in V. S. Solovyov. Evreiski vopros—Khristianski vopros/Sobranie statei (*The Jewish question—The Christian question—Collection of articles*), Warsaw, Pravda, 1906. p. 34.

[1085] Neopoublikovannyi protest protiv antisemitizma (Protest against anti-Semitism, unpublished [edited by Vladimir Solovyov]), BJWR-1, pp. 574-575. The text of this protest was originally published in the book by F. Hetz, Ob otnoshenii V. Solovyova k evreiskomou voprosou (V. Solovyov's attitude towards the Jewish question) (M., 1920), where it figures under the title "Ob antisemititcheskom dvijenii v petchati: Neizdannaïa statia V. Solovyova" (On the anti-Semitic movement in the press: an unpublished article by V. Solovyov), then it was reprinted in the "free" brochure of Warsaw quoted above.

According to the account given to him by M. Doubnov, Solovyov collected more than a hundred signatures, including those of Tolstoy and Korolenko.[1086]

But the editors of all the newspapers had been ordered not to publish this protest. Solovyov wrote a scalding letter to Tsar Alexander III, but was told that if he persisted, he would be punished with an administrative measure. He gave up.[1087]

Just as in Europe, the multifaceted thrust of Jewish ambitions could not fail to arouse anxiety among the actors of Russian public life here, a fierce opposition there, and there again, on the contrary, sympathy. And, in some, a political calculation. Like the Will of the People in 1881, who understood the profit to be drawn from the Jewish question (at the time, it was in the direction of persecution), the radical and liberal circles of the time, namely the left wing of society, conceived and made theirs for a long time still the idea that the Jewish question could be used as a political map of the struggle against the autocracy: it was necessary to repeat over and over that the only way to obtain equality in rights for the Jews was the definitive overthrow of the power of the tsars. From the Liberals to the Bolsheviks. Passing by the S.-R., all have never ceased to involve the Jews—some with real sympathy—to use them as a convenient asset in the anti-monarchical combat. This asset, the revolutionaries never let it go, they exploited it without the least scruple until 1917.

However, these various tendencies and debates in the newspapers did not affect the attitude of the *people* towards the Jews in *Greater Russia*. Many testimonies confirm this.

Thus J. Teitel, a man who lived for a long time in deep Russia and frequented common people, affirms that "any racial or national hostility is foreign to the common people."[1088] Or, in memoires left by the Viazemsky princes, this episode: there was at Korobovka Hospital, a district of Ousmansky, a somewhat inconsiderate Russian physician, Doctor Smirnov; the peasants did not like him, and his successor, the devoted Doctor Szafran, immediately benefited from the affection and gratitude of all the peasants in the neighbourhood. Another confirmation, inspired by the experience of the prisoners of the years 1880–1890: P. F. Iakoubovitch-Melchine writes: "It would be an ungrateful task to seek, even in the scum

---

[1086] Vladimir Galaktionovich Korolenko (1853–1921) famous Russian writer, great democrat. A political exile, he spent ten years in Eastern Siberia. Denounces police violence and antisemitism. Will be horrified by the terror and despotism of the Bolsheviks.
[1087] *Cf.* BJWR-1*, p. 565.
[1088] *Teitel*, p. 176.

of our people, the least trace of anti-Semitism."[1089] And it was indeed because they sensed this that the Jews of a small town in Belarus addressed a telegram at the beginning of the twentieth century to Madam F. Morozova, the wife of a wealthy merchant, who was in charge of charity: "Give us this much. The synagogue burned down. You know we have the same God." And she sent the sum requested.

Deep down, neither the Russian liberal press nor the Jewish press have ever accused the Russian people of any land-based anti-Semitism. What both of them repeated relentlessly was that anti-Semitism in the popular mass, had been completely fabricated and fuelled by the government. The very formula "Autocracy, Orthodoxy, Nationality" was felt in Jewish circles as a formula directed against the Jews.

In the middle of the twentieth century, we can read from a Jewish writer:

"In tsarist Russia, anti-Semitism had no deep roots among the people... In the broad masses of the people, there was practically no anti-Semitism; moreover, the very question of relations with Judaism did not arise... It was only in certain parts of what was called the Pale of Settlement, and mainly in Ukraine since the time of Polish domination, that, due to certain circumstances on which there is no need to dwell here, a certain tendency towards anti-Semitism manifested itself in the peasantry,"[1090] that is perfectly true. And one could add: Bessarabia.

(One can judge of the antiquity of these feelings and circumstances by reading Karamzin[1091] : the Cossacks who surrounded the False Dmitry[1092]—of the Cossacks of the Don, obviously—treated the Russians of *Jidy* (Jews)[1093], which means that in the western provinces this word was an insult.)

And what about Russian folklore? The Dahl dictionary encompasses Great Russia, and the western provinces, and Ukraine. Editions before the revolution contain a large number of words and expressions formed on the root *jid*-(Judeo-). (Significant detail: in the Soviet edition of 1955, the

---

[1089] JE, t. 10, p. 827.
[1090] S. M. *Schwartz*, Antisemitizm v Sovetskom Soiouze (Anti-Semitism in the Soviet Union), New York, ed. Chekhov, 1952, p. 13.
[1091] Nikolai Mikhailovich Karamzin (1766-1826): Russian writer. His great History of the Russian State made Pushkin say of him that he was the "Christopher Columbus of Ancient Russia."
[1092] The False-Dmitry, said the Usurper: in 1601, this character appeared in Poland pretending to be the son of Ivan IV. He marched on Moscow and occupied the throne from 1905 to 1906. He was killed by conspirator boyars.
[1093] N. M. Karamzin, Istoria Gosudarsva Rossiiskogo (History of the Russian State), 12 vols., 5 ed., Saint Petersburg, Einerling, 1842-1844, t. 11, p. 143.

entire typography of the page containing these words was revised[1094], and the whole lexical "niche" between *jidkii* and *jigalo* has been entirely suppressed.) However, amongst these expressions quoted by Dahl, there are some which are inherited from the Slavonic Church where the word *jid* was by no means pejorative: it was the name of a people. There are also some that come from Polish and post-Polish practice within the Pale of Settlement. Still others were introduced into the language at the time of the Troubles, in the seventeenth century, at a time when, in Greater Russia, there was almost no contact with the Jews. These inheritances are also reflected in the dicta that Dahl mentions in their Russian form—but we can guess under the latter the southern form. (And, what is certain is that they did not leave the bowels of the Ministry of the Interior! ...) And then, let us compare these sayings with others: oh how the people created malicious adages against the Orthodox clergy! Not one, almost, is favourable to it!

A witness of Mariupol[1095] (and he is not the only one, it is a well-known fact) tells us that among them, before the revolution, there was a clear distinction between the two words *evrei* (Hebrew) and *jid* (Jew). The *Evrei* was a law-abiding citizen, whose morals, conduct, and behaviour towards others did not differ in any way from the surrounding environment. While the *Jid* was the *jivoder* (the swindler). And it was not uncommon to hear: "I'm not a *Jid*, I'm an honest *Evrei*, I do not intend to dupe you." (Such words put into the mouths of Jews, we find them in literature, and we have also read them in the pamphlets of the populists.)

This semantic differentiation, we must never lose sight of it when interpreting sayings. All this is the trace of an old national quarrel on the territory of the West and Southwest.

For neither in Central Russia nor in the North and East, not even during the general shock of October 1905, there weren't any anti-Jewish pogroms (if there was indignation, it was against the revolutionary intellectuals in general, against their jubilation and ridicule of the Manifesto of October 17th). But this does not prevent, in the eyes of the whole world, the pre-revolutionary Russia—not the empire, but *Russia*—to bear forever the seal of infamy, that of the pogroms and the Black Hundreds. And it is indelible, encrusted in minds for yet how many centuries to come?

The anti-Jewish pogroms have always and exclusively broken out in South-Western Russia—as it was the case in 1881. And the Kichinev pogrom of 1903 was of the same nature.

[1094] *Dahl*, Toljovyi slovar jivogo velokorousskogo iazyka (*Dictionary of the living Great-Russian language*), t. 1, 1955, p. 541.
[1095] *I. E. Temirov*, Vospominania (Souvenirs), BFRZ, f. 1, A-29, p. 23.

Let us not forget that at the time the population of Bessarabia was largely illiterate, that in Kishinev there were 50,000 Jews, 50,000 Moldovans, 8,000 Russians (in fact, mainly Ukrainians, but the difference was not noted) and a few thousand others. What were the main forces responsible for the pogroms? "The delinquents of the pogroms were mainly Moldovans."[1096]

The Kishinev pogrom began on April 6, the last day of the Jewish Passover and the first day of the Orthodox Passover. (This is not the first time we have observed this tragic link between anti-Jewish pogroms and the Passover of Christians: in 1881, 1882, and 1899 in Nikolaev[1097]—and it fills us with extreme pain and anxiety.)

Let us use the one document that is based on a rigorous investigation carried out right after the events. This is the indictment issued by the local court prosecutor, V. N. Goremykine, who "did not call a single Jew as an accused, for which he was harshly vilified by the reactionary press."[1098] (As we shall see, the court first sat in closed session to "not exacerbate the passions", and the indictment was originally published abroad in the emigrated press organ of Stuttgart *Osvobojdenie* ["Release"].[1099])

The document begins with an account of "the usual clashes between Jews and Christians as happened in recent years at Easter" and "the animosity of the local population towards the Jews." It says that "two weeks before the Passover... rumours circulated in the city, announcing that there would be, during future holidays, aggressions against the Jews." A newspaper, the *Bessarabets* ("the Bessarabian"), had played a role of blaster in publishing "day after day, throughout the last few weeks, incendiary articles, strongly anti-Jewish, which did not go unnoticed among small clerks, pencil-pushers, the entire little people of Bessarabia. Among the last provocative articles in the newspaper was the one about the murder of a Christian child in the village of Doubossary, allegedly carried out by Jews for ritual purposes" (and another rumour ran that a Jew had murdered his Christian servant when she had actually committed suicide[1100]).

And the police of Kishinev, what did it do? "Did not give any particular consideration to the rumours," and despite the fact that "in recent years

---

[1096] SJE, t. 4, p. 327.
[1097] L. *Praisman*, Pogromy i samooborona (Pogroms and self-defense), in "22", 1986-1987, no. 51, p. 176.
[1098] JE, t. 9, p. 507.
[1099] Kichinevski pogrom: Obvinitelnyi akt (*The Kichinev pogrom: the indictment*), Osvobojdenie, Stuttgart, Oct. 19, 1903, no. 9 (33), supplement, pp. 14.
[1100] I. G. *Froumkine*, Iz istorii rousskogo evrcistva: vospominaniia, materialy, dokoumenty (On the history of the Jews of Russia: memoires, materials, documents), BJWR-1, p. 59.

there has been regular fighting between Jews and Christians, the Kishinev police did not take any serious preventive measures," it only reinforced the patrols "for the holidays, in the places where the crowd was going to be the densest", by adding men recruited from the local garrison.[1101] The chief of police gave no clear instruction to his officers.

This is clearly the most unpardonable: repeated brawls every year for the Passover, rumours of such a content—and the police fold their arms. One more sign of the state of decline of the governmental machinery. For there are two things, one: either we let go of the empire (how many wars, how many efforts have been made to unite, for obscure reasons, Moldavia with Russia), or we safeguard the good order which must reign over its entire territory.

On the afternoon of April 6, the streets of the city is invaded by "people in celebration", with "many teenagers" wandering among the crowd, as well as angry people. The boys start throwing stones at nearby Jewish houses, throwing harder and harder, and when the commissioner and his inspectors try to arrest one of them, "they get stones in their turn." Adults then get involved. "The police took no firm measures to stop the disorders" and these led to the sacking of two Jewish shops and a few sheds. In the evening, the disorders subsided, "no assault had been perpetrated against the Jews that day"; the police had arrested sixty people during the day.

However, "on the early morning of April 7, the very agitated Christian population began to assemble in various parts of the city and in the suburbs, in small groups which provoked Jews to clashes of increasing violence." In the same way, from the first hour on the New Market, "more than a hundred Jews had gathered, armed with stakes and pickets, rifles even here and there, who fired a few shots. The Christians had no firearms. The Jews said: 'Yesterday you did not scatter the Russians, today we will defend ourselves.' And some held bottles of vitriol in their hands, which they threw at the Christians they met."

(Pharmacies were traditionally held by Jews.) "Rumours spread throughout the city, reporting that the Christians were being assaulted by the Jews; they swell from mouth to mouth and exasperate the Christian population": one transforms "were beaten" into "were slaughtered", one carries that the Jews have sacked the cathedral and murdered the priest. And now, "in various parts of the town, small groups of fifteen to twenty persons each, chiefly workmen, with teenagers in their lead who throw stones into the

---

[1101] Kichinevski pogrom: Obvinitelnyi akt (The Kichinev pogrom: the indictment), Osvobojdenie, *op. cit.*, p. 1.

window-panes, begin to plunder the shops, the premises, the dwellings of the Jews, smashing everything inside.

These groups are gradually enlarged by the passers-by." Towards two, three o'clock in the morning, "disturbances spread in a more and more extended radius"; "the houses where icons or crosses have been exposed in windows are not affected." "In the sacked premises, everything was totally destroyed, the goods ejected from the shops to be trampled or stolen by individuals who escorted the attackers." They went so far as to "sack the houses of prayer of the Jews, and throw down the sacred scrolls [the Torah] in the street." Drinking places, of course, were sacked; "The wine was poured into the street or drunk on the spot by the bandits."

The inertia of the police, owing to the absence of a proper command, caused these crimes to be perpetrated with impunity, and this did not fail to encourage and excite the evil-doers. The police forces, left to their own devices, far from uniting their efforts, acted according to their instinct... "and the subordinate policemen were mostly mute spectators of the pogrom." However, a phone call was made to the local garrison to call for reinforcements, but "whenever the soldiers went to a certain point, they could not find anybody there," and "in the absence of new instructions, they remained inactive"; "They were scattered in the city in isolated groups, with no clear objective and no coordination with each other"; "They only dispersed the excited crowds." (This garrison was not the most efficient, and, moreover, it was just after Passover: many officers and soldiers were on leave.[1102]) "The inertia of the police... engendered new rumours, saying that the government would have allowed to attack the Jews, since they are enemies of the country"—and the pogrom, unleashed, inebriated, became envenomed. "The Jews, fearing for their possessions and for their lives, lost all composure, fear made them go mad.

Several of them, armed with revolvers, proceeded to counter-attack to defend themselves. Ambushed on street corners, behind fences, on balconies, they began to shoot looters, but awkwardly, without aiming at their targets, so that it did nothing to help them and only aroused in the pogrom troublemakers a terrible explosion of rage. "The crowd of plunderers was seized with rage, and where the shooting had resounded, it came at once to tear everything apart and be violent towards the Jews who were there. "A shot was particularly fatal to the Jews: the man who snatched a young Russian boy, little Ostapov." "From one, two o'clock in

---

[1102] Materialy dlia istorii antievreiskikh pogromov v Rossii (Materials for history 12 vols., 5th ed., Saint Petersburg, Einerling, 1842–1844, 11, pp. 143, S. M. Dubnov and G. I. Krasnyi-Admoni, t. 1, Pg. 1919 (Materials...), p. 340.

the afternoon, the blows of the Jews became more and more violent," and by five o'clock they were accompanied by "a series of murders."

At half-past three in the afternoon, Governor Von Raaben, completely overwhelmed, passed an order to the chief of the garrison, General Bekman, authorising the "use of arms". Bekman immediately had the city canvassed, and the troops, who had "ventured out" walked in good order from that moment on.

"From that moment on, the troops were now able to carry out mass arrests," and energetic measures were taken. At nightfall, the pogrom was under control.

The act stipulates the death toll: "There were 42 deaths, including 38 Jews"; "all the bodies bore traces of blows by blunt objects—clubs, shovels, stones—and some, blows of axes"; "almost all were wounded in the head, some in the chest also. They had no traces of bullets, no evidence of torture or rape either (this was confirmed by doctors' expert opinions and autopsies, as well as by the report of the Medico-Legal Department of the Central Administration of Bessarabia); "there were 456 wounded, including 62 among the Christians...; eight were wounded by bullets... of the 394 Jewish wounded, only five were seriously injured. No trace of abuse... except for a one-eyed man whose healthy eye had been ripped out... three-quarters of the men assaulted were adults; there were three complaints of rape, two of which were prosecuted." Seven soldiers were wounded, including a soldier who "had his face burned with vitriol"; 68 policemen received minor injuries. "There were 1,350 homes ransacked, almost a third of the houses in Kishinev: an enormous figure, the equivalent of a bombing... as for the arrests, "there were 816 on the morning of April 9", and in addition to the investigations into the murders, 664 persons appeared in court.

In some authors, the figures of the victims among the Jews differ from the official statistics, but the gap is not very large. The *Book of the Jews of Russia* estimates that there were 45 Jews killed, 86 seriously wounded, 1,500 houses and shops looted or destroyed.[1103] Biekerman puts forward the figure of 53 dead, but maybe not all Jews.[1104] The recent *Jewish Encyclopædia* (1988) states: "49 people were killed, 586 wounded, more than 1,500 houses and shops looted."[1105]

[1103] *Froumkine*, BJWR-1, p. 59.
[1104] *Biekerman*, RJE, p. 57.
[1105] SJE, t. 4, p. 327.

This is the official description. But we sense what is hiding behind it. We are told: "Only one person, one Jew with one eye" has had the other ripped out.

We learn a little more from Korolenko in his essay *Dom no 13* ("House No. 13").[1106] This poor man was called Meer Weisman: "To my question, wrote Korolenko—did he know who did this?—, he answered with perfect serenity that he did not know, but that 'a kid', the son of his neighbours, had boasted that he had done it with a lead weight attached to a string." We see then that perpetrators and victims knew each other rather well... Korolenko resumed: "It is true that what I advance, I hold of the Jews themselves, but there is no reason not to believe their sayings... Why would they have invented these details? ..."

And, in fact, why would the family of Bentsion Galanter, mortally hit on the head, invent that the murderers had planted nails all over his body? Was not the family of the Nisenson accountant sufficiently tried, why would it add that he had been "rinsed" in a puddle before being massacred? These details are not fiction.

But to those who were far from the events, to the agitators of public opinion, these horrors *were not enough*. What they remembered was not tragedy, misfortune, the dead, but rather: how to exploit them to strike the tsarist power? And they resorted to terrifying exaggerations. To overcome reactions of horror, to try to see clearly in the versions built up in the months and years following, would it not be minimising the tragedy? And to attract many insults?

But to see it clearly is a duty, because we took advantage of the pogrom of Kishinev to blacken Russia and mark her forever of the seal of infamy. Today, all honest historical work on the subject demands a distinction between the horrible truth and the treacherous lies. The conclusion of the indictment is the following: the disorders "have reached the magnitude described only because of the inertia of the police, deprived of an adequate command... The preliminary investigation did not find evidence that the disorders had been premeditated."[1107]

These clues, no further investigation found them either. But so be it: the Office for the Defence of the Jews, which we have already mentioned, (was attended by such eminent persons as Mr. Winaver, Mr. G. Sliosberg, Mr. Bramson, Mr. Koulicher, Mr. A. Braoudo, Mr. S. Pozner, Krohl[1108]), as soon as the news of the pogrom of Kishinev reached it, it excluded from

---

[1106] *V. G. Korolenko*, Dom no 13, Sobr. sotch. (Complete works), t. 9, M. 1995, pp. 406–422.
[1107] The Kichinev pogrom: The indictment, *op. cit.*, pp. 3, 202.
[1108] *Krohl*, Stranitsy... (Pages...), p. 299.

the outset all possible causes apart from that of a conspiracy fomented from above: "Who gave the order of organising the pogrom, who took the direction of the dark forces that perpetrated it?"[1109] "As soon as we learned of the climate in which the killings of Kishinev took place, we did not doubt that this diabolical undertaking had been concocted by the Police Department and carried out at his command." Although, of course, "the wretches kept their project secret," wrote Krohl in the 40s of the 20th century.[1110] "But, as convinced as we are that the killings of Kishinev were premeditated in high places, with the tacit agreement and perhaps at the initiative of Plehve, we can unmask these high-placed assassins and expose them to the light of the world only on one condition: if we have the most indisputable proofs against them.

That is why we decided to send the famous lawyer Zaroudny to Kishinev."[1111]

"He was the most suitable person for the mission we had entrusted to him," "he undertook to reveal the hidden springs of the Kishinev massacre, after which the police, to divert attention, arrested a few dozens thieves and looters."[1112] (Recall that in the aftermath of the pogrom, 816 people were arrested.) Zaroudny gathered information and brought back "material of exceptional importance".

That is to say that "the chief person in charge, the organiser of the pogrom, had been the head of local security, K. Lewendal," a gendarmerie officer who had been appointed to Kishinev shortly before the pogrom. It was "at his command that the police and the troops openly lent a hand to the assassins and the looters."[1113] He would have "totally paralysed the action of the governor."[1114] (It is known, however, that in Russia neither the police nor the troops were under the orders of the Okhrana.)

This said "exceptionally important" material, which denounced the guilty "with absolute certainty," was never published neither at the time or later. Why?

But because, if it had been so, how could Lewendal and his accomplices escape punishment and dishonour? This material is known only by hearsay: a dealer named Pronine and a notary named Pissarjevsky would have been found several times in a certain café and, on Lewendal's instructions,

---

[1109] *Sliosberg*, t. 3, p. 49.
[1110] M. *Krohl*, Kishinevski pogrom 1903 goda i Kishinevski pogromnyi protses (The Kichinev pogrom of 1903 and the trial of the Kichinev pogrom), Mi-2, p. 372.
[1111] *Ibidem*, pp. 372-373.
[1112] *Krohl*, Stranitsy… (Pages…), *op. cit.*, pp. 301, 303.
[1113] *Ibidem*, pp. 301-304.
[1114] *Krohl, op. cit.*, Mi-2, p. 374.

would have planned the pogrom.[1115] And it was after these meetings that all the police and the troops opted for the pogrom. The prosecutor Goremykine examined the charges against Lowendal and declared them unfounded.[1116] (The journalist Kruchevane, whose incendiary articles had really favoured the pogrom, was stabbed in Petersburg two months later by Pinhas Dachevsky who wanted to kill him.[1117])

The authorities, during this time, continued the investigation. The director of the police department, A. A. Lopoukhine (with his liberal sympathies, he was unsuspected in the eyes of the public) was quickly dispatched to Kishinev.

Governor Von Raaden was dismissed, along with several other senior officials from Bessarabia; a new governor was appointed, Prince S. Urusov (soon to be a prominent K. D., and would sign the appeal to the rebellion called "Vyborg's Appeal"). A bulletin from the Minister of the Interior, Plehve, was published in *The Messenger of the Government* of April 29: in it he stated his indignation at the inaction of the authorities of Kishinev; he called on all provincial governors, city governors and police chiefs to vigorously halt all violence by taking all possible measures.[1118]

The Orthodox Church also expressed itself. The Holy Synod issued a bulletin inviting the clergy to take measures to extirpate feelings of hostility towards the Jews. Some of the hierarchs, notably Father John of Kronstadt, who were very much listened to and revered by the faithful, appealed to the Christian people, expressing their disapproval, their exhortations, their appeals for appeasement. "They have substituted for the Christian holiday a sanguinary and satanic orgy."[1119] And Bishop Antony (Krapovitsky) declared: "The punishment of God will befall the wretches who have spilled blood related to that of the God-Man, to His pure Mother, the apostles and the prophets... so that you know how much the Divine Spirit cherishes the Jewish people, still rejected today, and know what is His wrath against those who would want to offend Him."[1120] A text on the subject was distributed to the people. (The long exhortations and explanations of the Church, however, were not unrelated to an archaic state

---

[1115] Ibidem.
[1116] Report to the Prosecutor No. 1392 of 20 Nov. 1903; Report to the prosecutor No. 1437 of 1 Dec. 1903, in Materialy... [Materials...], *op. cit.*, pp. 319, 322–323.
[1117] RJE, t. 1, p. 417.
[1118] In Materialy... [Materials...], *op. cit.*, pp. 333-335; Pravitelstvennyi vestnik (Government Messenger). Saint Petersburg, no. 97, 1903, 29 April (12 May).
[1119] *J. de Cronstadt*: My thoughts about the violence perpetrated by Christians against the Jews in Kishinev, in Materialy... [Materials...], *op. cit.*, pp. 354, 356.
[1120] Homily of Bishop Antoine of 30 April 1903, in Materialy... [Materials...], *op. cit.*, pp. 354, 356.

of mind, frozen for centuries and to be surpassed by the formidable evolutions in progress.)

In the first days of May, a month after the events, an information campaign but also one of intoxication about the pogrom broke out in the Russian press as well as in the European and American ones. In Petersburg, fanatical articles spoke of assassinations of mothers and infants, of rape—sometimes of underage girls, sometimes of women under the eyes of their husbands or of their father and mother; there was talk of "torn tongues; a man was ripped open, a woman's head was pierced with nails driven in by the nostrils."[1121] Less than a week had elapsed when these horrifying details appeared in the papers of the West.

Western public opinion gave it full credence. The influential Jews in England relied on these fabrications and included them word for word in their public protest.[1122] Should we repeat: *"No evidence of abuse or rape was observed on the bodies."* Due to a new wave of newspaper articles, forensic pathologists were asked to submit supplementary reports. The doctor of the City Health Service, named Frenkel (who had examined the bodies in the Jewish cemetery), and another named Tchorba (who had received the dead and wounded at the hospital in the Kishinev Zemstvo between 5 P.M., the second day after the Passover, and noon, the third day, and then at the Jewish hospital), and the doctor Vassiliev (who had carried out an autopsy of thirty-five corpses)—all attested the absence of traces of torture or violence on the bodies described in the newspapers.[1123] It was later learned at the trial that doctor Dorochevsky—the one who, it was thought, had supplied these frightening reports—had seen nothing of these atrocities, and declined any responsibility for the publication of the tabloids.[1124] As for the prosecutor at the Criminal Chamber of Odessa, he had, in reply to a question from Lopoukhine regarding the rapes, "secretly conducted his own investigation": the accounts of the families of the victims themselves did not confirm any case of rape; the concrete cases, in the expertise, are positively excluded.[1125] But who paid attention to the examinations and conclusions of doctors? Who cares about the prosecutor's specific research? All these documents may remain, turning yellow, in cabinets files!

[1121] Sankt-Peterburgskie vedomosti (*News from Saint Petersburg*), 24 April (7 May 1903), p. 5.
[1122] Baltimore Sun, 16 May 1903, p. 2; The Jewish Chronicle, 15 May 1903, p. 2; Protest by the Board of Deputies and the Anglo-Jewish Association, Times, 18 May 1903, p. 10.
[1123] In Materialy… [Materials…], *op. cit.*, pp. 174-175.
[1124] *Ibidem*, p. 279.
[1125] *Ibidem*, pp. 172-173.

All that the witnesses had not confirmed, all that Korolenko had not related, the authorities did not have the presence of mind to refute it. And all these *details* spread throughout the world, and took the form of a *fact* in public opinion, which they were to remain throughout the twentieth century, and which they will probably still be throughout the whole of the twenty-first century—cold, frozen, stowed forever in the name of Russia.

However, Russia, for many years now, but with increasing acuteness, knew a mad, deadly distortion between "civil society" and the government. It was a struggle to the death: for the liberal and radical circles, and even more so for the revolutionaries, any incident (true or false) discrediting the government was a blessing, and for them everything was permitted—any exaggeration, any distortion, any make-up of facts; the important thing was to humiliate power as severely as possible. For the Russian radicals, a pogrom of this gravity was a *chance* in their fight!

The government resolved to forbid all publication in the newspapers concerning the pogrom, but it was a blunder, for the rumours were re-echoed with greater force by the European and American press; All the rantings escalated with even more impunity—exactly as if there had never been any police report.

And here it was, the great offensive launched against the government of the tsar. The Bureau for the Defence of the Jews sent telegrams to all the capitals: organise protest meetings everywhere![1126] A member of the Bureau wrote: "We have communicated the details of the atrocities... in Germany, France, England, the United States... The impression that our information caused was shattering; in Paris, Berlin, London and New York, there were protest meetings in which the speakers painted a frightening picture of the crimes committed by the tsarist government."[1127] Here he is, they thought, the Russian bear as it has been since the dawn of time! "These atrocities shocked the world. And now, without any restraint, the police and the soldiers have by all means *assisted the assassins and the plunderers* in perpetrating their inhuman acts."[1128] The "cursed autocracy" has marked itself with an indelible stigma! In meetings, they stigmatised the new plan of tsarism, "premeditated by it". In the synagogues of London, they accused... the Holy Synod of having committed this killing due to religious inspiration. Some of the hierarchs of the Catholic Church also declared their disapproval. But it was by far the European and American press that showed themselves as being the most virulent (notably the press tycoon William Hearst): "We accuse the tsarist power of being responsible for the

---

[1126] *Krohl, op. cit.,* RW-2, pp. 376-377.
[1127] *Krohl,* Stranitsy... (Pages...), *op. cit.,* p. 302.
[1128] *Krohl, op. cit.,* RW-2, pp. 371-372.

massacre of Kishinev. We declare that his guilt in this holocaust is total. It is before his door and in front of any other that the victims of this violence are exposed. "May the God of Justice descend here below to finish with Russia as He has finished with Sodom and Gomorrah... and let him evacuate this pestilential focus from the face of the earth." "The killing of Kishinev surpasses in insolent cruelty all that has ever been recorded in any civilised nation"[1129]... (including, one must believe, the extermination of the Jews in medieval Europe?).

Alas, Jews more or less circumspect, more or less stunned, joined in the same assessment of the events. And not less than thirty years after the events, the respectable jurist G. Sliosberg retains the same details in publications of emigration—(even though he himself never went to Kishinev, then or later): the nails planted in the head of the victim (he goes so far as attributing this information to the account of Korolenko!), and the rapes, and the presence of "several thousand soldiers" (the modest garrison of Kishinev had never seen as many!) who "seemed to be there to protect the perpetrators of the pogrom."[1130]

But Russia, in the field of communication, was inexperienced, unable to justify itself coherently seeing it was still unaware of the methods used for this.

Meanwhile, the so-called "cold premeditation" of the pogrom was not supported by any solid proof—none that was commensurate with the raging campaign. And although lawyer Zaroudny had already "closed his investigation and... firmly established that the chief organiser and the sponsor of the pogrom was none other than the chief of the local Okhrana, Baron Lewendal"[1131]—even in this variant, the character of Lewendal did not reach the government sufficiently, it was necessary to draw a little more to reach the central power.

But here we are!—six weeks after the pogrom, in order to further stir up general indignation, and to dishonour the key figure of power, one "discovered" (no one knows by whom, but very appropriately) an "ultra-secret letter" from the Minister of Interior Plehve to the governor of Kishinev, Von Raaben (not a bulletin addressed to all the governors of the Pale of Settlement, no, but a letter addressed to him alone ten days before the pogrom), in which the minister, in rather evasive terms, gave advice: if serious disturbances occur in the province of Bessarabia, not to repress them by arms, but to use only persuasion. And now an individual, very

---

[1129] "Remember Kichineff" (editorial), *The Jewish Chronicle*, 15 May 1903, p. 21; 22 May 1903, p. 10; *Baltimore Sun*, 16 May 1903, p. 4.
[1130] *Sliosberg*, vol. 3, pp. 48 49, 61, 64.
[1131] *Ibidem*.

timely there too, transmitted the text of this letter to an English correspondent in Saint Petersburg, D. D. Braham, and the latter hastened to publish it in London in the *Times* of 18 May 1903.[1132]

A priori: what is the weight of a single publication in a single newspaper, which nothing corroborates—neither on the spot nor later? But it weighs as much as you want! Enormously, even! And in this case, the publication of the *Times* was supported by the protest of prominent British Jews, with Montefiore at their head (from an internationally-known family).[1133]

Thanks to the climate that reigned throughout the world, this letter was a colossal success: the sanguinary intentions against the Jews of the universally abhorred tsarism, which had not yet been proved, were suddenly "attested with supporting documents." Articles and meetings had a new upsurge throughout the world. On the third day after the publication, the *New York Times* pointed out that "three days already that the letter was disclosed—and no denial occurred", and the British press has already declared it to be authentic. "What can we say about the level of civilisation of a country, of which a minister can give his signature to such exactions?" [1134] The Russian government, in its awkwardness and incomprehension of the gravity of the matter, found nothing better to do than to negligently abandon a laconic denial signed by the head of the Police Department, A. Lopoukhine, and only on the ninth day after the scandalous publication of the *Times*,[1135] but instead of investigating the falsification, he simply settled on expelling Braham from the territory.

One can argue with certainty that this was indeed a forgery, for several reasons. Not only because Braham never exhibited any proof of the authenticity of the letter. Not only because Lopoukhine, the declared enemy of Plehve, had himself denied this text. Not only because Prince Urusov, the great Jewish sympathiser who had succeeded Von Raaben and controlled the archives of the governorate, found no "letter of Plehve." Not only because poor Von Raaben, dismissed, his life and career broken, never, in his desperate efforts to restore his reputation, complained of having received instructions "from above"—which would have immediately restored his career and made him the idol of liberal society. The main reason lies in the fact that the State archives in Russia had nothing in common with the rigged archives of the Soviet era when any document was concocted upon request or others burned in secret. No, in the Russian archives everything was preserved, inviolably and forever. Immediately

---

[1132] *Times*, 18 May 1903, p. 10.
[1133] "Protest by the Board of Deputies and the Anglo-Jewish Association", *Times*, 18 May 1903, p. 10.
[1134] *New York Times*, 19 May 1903, p. 10; 21 May 1903, p. 8.
[1135] *Times*, 27 May 1903, p. 7.

after the February Revolution, an extraordinary commission of inquiry of the Provisional Government, and, still more zealously, the "Special Commission for the Study of the History of the Pogroms," with investigators as serious as S. Dubnov, Krasny-Admoni, did not find the document in Petersburg or Kishinev, nor its record it upon entrance or exit; they found only the *translation* into English of Braham's English text (as well as papers containing "indications of severe punishment and dismissal... sanctioning any illegal action by agents responsible for the Jewish question").[1136]

After 1917, what was still to be feared? But not a single witness, not a single memorialist, was able to tell the story of where this immortal telegram had fallen, or to boast of having acted as an intermediary. And Braham himself—neither at the time, nor later—didn't say a single word about it.

But this did not prevent the constitutional-Democratic newspaper *Retch* ("The Word") from writing with confidence, on 19 March 1917: "The bloodbath of Kishinev, the counter-revolutionary pogroms of 1905 were organised, as was definitively established, by the Police Department." And, in August 1917, at the Moscow State Conference, the President of the Special Commission of Inquiry publicly declared that he would "soon present the police department's documents concerning the organisation of anti-Jewish pogroms"—but neither soon nor later, neither the Commission, nor, subsequently, the Bolsheviks exhibited any document of this kind. Thus the lie encrusted itself, practically up to now! ... (In my *November 16*, one of the characters evokes the pogrom of Kishinev, and in 1986 the German publisher adds an explanatory note in this regard stating: "Anti-Jewish Pogrom, carefully prepared, which lasted two days.

The Minister of the Interior Plehve had conjured the governor of Bessarabia, in the event of a pogrom, not to use firearms."[1137]) In the recent *Jewish Encyclopædia* (1996) we read this statement: "In April 1903, the new Minister of the Interior, Plehve, organised with his agents a pogrom in Kishinev."[1138]

(Paradoxically, we read in the previous tome: "The text of Plehve's telegram published in the *Times* of London... is held by most scholars as being a fake"[1139]). And here: the false story of the Kishinev pogrom made

---

[1136] P. P. *Zavarsine*, Rabota taino politsii (The Work of Your Secret Police), Paris, 1924, pp. 68-69.
[1137] November sechzehn, München-Zürich, Piper, 1986, p. 1149. French Trans., ed. Fayard, Paris, 1985.
[1138] SJE, t. 7, p. 347.
[1139] *Ibidem*, t. 6, p. 533.

much more noise than the real, cruel and authentic one. Will the point be made one day? Or will it take yet another hundred years?

The incompetence of the tsarist government, the decrepitude of its power, had manifested itself on various occasions, in Transcaucasia, for example, during the killing spree between the Armenians and Azeris, but the government was declared guilty only in the affair of Kishinev.

"The Jews," wrote D. Pasmanik, "have never imputed the pogrom to the people, they have always accused the power and the administration exclusively... No facts could ever shake this opinion, a furthermore perfectly superficial opinion."[1140] And Biekerman emphasised that it was a matter of public knowledge that pogroms were for the government a form of struggle against the revolution. More circumspect minds reasoned thus: if in the recent pogroms no technical preparation by the power is attested, "the state of mind which reigns in Saint Petersburg is such that any virulent judeophobe will find among the authorities, from the minister to the last sergeant of town, a benevolent attitude towards him." Yet the Kishinev trial, which took place in the autumn of 1903, showed exactly the opposite.

For the liberal and radical opposition, this trial was to be transformed into a battle against the autocracy. Were sent as "civil parties" eminent lawyers, Jews and Christians—Mr. Karabchevsky, O. Gruzenberg, S. Kalmanovitch, A. Zaroudny, N. Sokolov. The "brilliant left-wing advocate" P. Pereverzev and a few others joined as *defenders* of the accused "so that they would not be afraid to tell the court... who had prompted them to start the carnage"[1141]—to clarify: to say that it was the power that had armed them. The "civil parties" demanded that further investigation be carried out and that the "real culprits" should be placed on the stand. The authorities did not publish the transcripts so as not to exacerbate the passions in the city of Kishinev, nor those already white-hot of world opinion. Things were all the easier: the squad of activists who surrounded the "civil parties" made their own reports and sent them through the world, via Romania, for publication. This, however, did not modify the course of the trial.

The killers' faces were scrutinized, but the culprits were undoubtedly the authorities—guilty only, it is true, of not having intervened in a timely manner.

At that point, the group of lawyers split a collective statement stating that "if the court refuses to bring to justice and punish the main culprits of the

---

[1140] *D. S. Pasmanik*, Rousskaïa revolioutisiia i evreistvo (Bolchevisme i ioudaïsme) (The Russian Revolution and Judaism [The Bolshevism and Judaism]), Paris, 1923, p. 142.
[1141] *Krohl*, Stranitsy... (Pages...) *op. cit.*, p. 303.

pogrom"—that is, not some ordinary Governor Von Raaben (he no longer interested anyone), but indeed Minister Plehve himself and the central government of Russia—"they [the defenders] will have nothing more to do in this trial." For they "encountered such hostility on the part of the court that it gave them no possibility... to defend freely and in conscience the interests of their clients, as well as those of justice."[1142] This new tactic of the lawyers, which constituted a purely political approach, proved to be quite fertile and promising; it made a great impression on the whole world. "The action of lawyers has been approved by all the best minds in Russia."[1143]

The trial before the Criminal Division of Odessa was now proceeding in order. The prognostications of Western newspapers that "the trial of Kishinev will only be a masquerade, a parody of justice,"[1144] were not confirmed in any way. The accused, in view of their number, had to be divided into several groups according to the gravity of the charge. As mentioned above, there were no Jews among the accused.[1145] The chief of the gendarmerie of the province had already announced in April that out of 816 people arrested, 250 had been dismissed for inconsistency of the charges against them, 446 had immediately been the subject of judicial decisions (as evidenced in the *Times*), and "persons convicted by the court have been sentenced to the heaviest penalties"; about 100 were seriously charged, including 36 accused of murder and rape (in November, they will be 37). In December, the same chief of the gendarmerie announced the results of the trial: deprivation of rights, property, and penal colony (seven years or five years), deprivation of rights and disciplinary battalion (one year and one and a half years). In all, 25 convictions and 12 acquittals.[1146] The real culprits of real crimes had been condemned, the ones we have described. The condemnations, however, were not tender—"the drama of Kishinev ends on a usual contradiction in Russia: in Kishinev, criminals seem to be subjected to a rigorous judicial repression," the *American Jewish Yearbook* stated, astonished.[1147]

In the spring of 1904, the Cassation proceedings in Petersburg were made public.[1148] And in 1905 the Kishinev pogrom was once again examined in the Senate; Winaver took the floor to prove nothing new.

[1142] *Krohl, op. cit.*, JW2*, pp. 379-380.
[1143] *Sliosberg*, t. 3, p. 69.
[1144] *Times*, 10 November 1903, p. 4.
[1145] JE, t. 9, p. 507.
[1146] Materialy... (Materials...), *op. cit.*, p. 147; *Times*, 18 May 1903, p. 8; Materialy..., *op. cit.*, p. 294.
[1147] *The American Jewish Year Book*, 5664 (1903–1904), Philadelphia, 1903, p. 22.
[1148] *Froumkine*, BJWR-1, pp. 60, 61.

In reality, the affair of the Kishinev pogrom had inflicted a hard lesson on the tsarist government by revealing to it that a State that tolerates such infamy is a scandalously impotent State. But the lesson would have been equally clear without poisonous falsifications or false additions. Why did the simple truth about Kichinev's pogrom seem insufficient? Presumably because this truth would have reflected the true nature of the government— a sclerotic organisation, guilty of bullying the Jews, but which remained unsteady and incoherent. However, with the aid of lies, it was represented as a wise persecutor, infinitely sure of himself, and evil. Such an *enemy* could only deserve annihilation.

The Russian government, which for a long time already had been largely surpassed on the international stage, did not understand, either on the spot nor afterwards, what a shocking defeat it had just wiped out there. This pogrom soiled a stinking stain on *all* of Russian history, all the ideas that the world had of Russia *as a whole;* the sinister gleam of fire projected by it announced and precipitated the upheavals which were soon to shake the country.

Chapter 9

During the Revolution of 1905

The Kishinev pogrom produced a devastating and indelible effect on the Jewish community in Russia. Jabotinsky: Kishinev traces "the boundary between two epochs, two psychologies." The Jews of Russia have not only experienced deep sorrow, but, more profoundly so, "something which had almost made one forget the pain—and that was shame."[1149] "If the carnage of Kishinev played a major role in the realisation of our situation, it was because we then realised that the Jews were cowards."[1150]

We have already mentioned the failure of the police and the awkwardness of the authorities—it was therefore natural that the Jews had asked themselves the question: should we continue to rely on the protection of public authorities?

Why not create our own armed militias and defend ourselves weapons in hand? They were incited by a group of prominent public men and writers—Doubnov, Ahad Haam, Rovnitsky, Ben-Ami, Bialik: "Brothers... cease weeping and begging for mercy. Do not expect any help from your enemies. Only rely on your own arms!"[1151]

These calls "produced on Jewish youth the effect of an electric shock."[1152] And in the overheated atmosphere that began to reign after the Kishinev pogrom, "armed groups of self-defence" quickly saw the light at various locations in the Pale of Settlement. They were generally financed "by the Jewish community"[1153], and the illegal introduction of weapons from

---

[1149] V. Jabotinsky, Vvedenie (Preface to Kh. N. Bialik, Pesni i poemy (Songs and Poems), Saint Petersburg, Zalzman ed., 1914, pp. 42 43.

[1150] V. Jabotinsky, V traournye dni (Days of Mourning), Felietony, Saint Petersburg, Tipografia "Guerold", 1913, p. 25.

[1151] M. Krohl, Kishinovsky pogrom 1903 goda Kishinëvskiy pogromnyi protsess (The Kishinev pogrom of 1903), BJWR-2, New York, 1944, p. 377.

[1152] Ibidem.

[1153] S. Dimanstein, Revoloutsionnoïe dvijenie sredi ievreyev (The revolution-Saint Petersburg, 1905: Istoria rcvoloutsionnovo dvijenia v otdelnykh otcherkakh (History of the Revolutionary Movement—abbreviated: "1905") / pod redaktskiei M. N. Pokrovskovo, vol. 3, vyp. 1, M. L., 1927, p. 150.

abroad did not pose a problem for the Jews. It was not unusual for these weapons to fall into the hands of very young people.

Official reports do not indicate the existence of armed groups among the Christian population. The government struggled as best it could against the bombs of terrorists. When armed militias began to develop, it saw in them—it is only natural—totally illegal demonstrations, the premises of the civil war, and it banned them by the means and information it had at its disposal. (Also today, the whole world condemns and prohibits "illegal paramilitary formations.") A highly operational armed group was formed in Gomel under the direction of the local committee of the Bund. On March 1st, 1903, the latter had organised "festivities" for the anniversary of the "execution of Alexander II."[1154]

In this city, where Christians and Jews were nearly equal in number[1155], and the socialist Jews were more than determined, the establishment of armed groups of self-defence was particularly strong. This was to be noted during the events of August 29th and September 1st 1903—the Gomel pogrom.

According to the findings of the official investigation, the responsibility for the Gomel pogrom is shared: Christians and Jews mutually attacked each other.

Let us take a closer look at the official documents of the time, in this case the indictment of the Gomel affair, based on the police reports drawn up on the spot. (Police reports, which date back to the early twentieth century in Russia, have repeatedly proven their accuracy and their irreproachable precision—and this up to the hustle and bustle of the days of February 1917, up to the moment where the police stations of Petrograd were vested by the insurgents, burnt down—since then, this stream of minutely-recorded information was cut off, and remained so for us.)

At the Gomel trial, the indictment states: "The Jewish population... began to procure weapons and to organise self-defence circles in the event of trouble directed at the Jews... Some residents of Gomel had the opportunity to attend Jewish youth training sessions outside the city and which gathered up to a hundred people practising shooting guns."[1156]

[1154] *N. A. Buchbinder*, Ivrevskoye rabotchee dvijenie v Gomele (1890-1905) (The Jewish Workers' Movement in Gomel [1890–1905]), Krasnaya lelopis: Istoritcheskii journal, Pg., 1922, nos. 2-3, pp. 659.
[1155] *Ibidem*, p. 38.
[1156] Kievskaya soudebnaya palata: Delo o gomelskom pogrom (Kiev courthouse: the Gomel pogrom case), Pravo, Saint Petersburg, 1904, no. 44, pp. 3041, 3042.

"The generalisation of the possession of weapons, on the one hand, the awareness of one's numerical superiority and cohesion, on the other hand, have emboldened the Jewish population to the extent that, among its youth, they spoke not only of self-defence, but of indispensable revenge for the Kishinev pogrom." Thus hatred expressed in one place is reflected in another, distant—and against the innocent.

"For some time past, the attitude of the Jews of Gomel has become not only contemptuous, but frankly provocative; the attacks—both verbal and physical—on peasants and workers have become commonplace, and the Jews display their contempt in all sorts of ways even against the Russians belonging to higher social strata, for example, by forcing soldiers to change sidewalk." On August 29th, 1903, everything started with a banal incident in a market: an altercation between the herring merchant Malitskaya and her client Chalykov; she spat in his face, the dispute turned into a brawl, "immediately several Jews rushed upon Chalykov, threw him to the ground, and began to strike him with everything they could put their hands on. A dozen peasants wanted to defend Chalykov, but the Jews immediately emitted whistles previously agreed upon, causing a considerable influx of other Jews... No doubt these whistles were a call for help... thus they immediately mobilised the entire Jewish population of the city"; "on foot, by car, armed as they could, the Jews flocked to the market everywhere. Very soon, the Street of the Market, the market itself and all the adjacent streets were swarming with people; The Jews were armed with stones, sticks, hammers, specially-made clubs or even simply iron bars. Everywhere shouts were heard: 'Let's go, Jews! To the market! It is the pogrom of the Russians!' And all this mass went into small groups to pursue the peasants to strike them"—and the latter were numerous, on a market day. "Leaving there their purchases, the peasants—when they had time—jumped on their chariots and hastened to leave the city... Witnesses say that when they caught Russians, the Jews beat them without mercy, they beat old people, women and even children. For example, a little girl was pulled out of a chariot and dragged by her hair on the roadway." "A peasant by the name of Silkov had placed himself at some distance to enjoy the spectacle while nibbling a piece of bread. At that moment, a Jew who ran behind him struck his throat with a mortal knife wound, then disappeared among the crowd." Other episodes are listed. An officer was only saved thanks to the intervention of Rabbi Maiants and the owner of the neighbouring house, Rudzievsky. Upon arriving at the scene, the police were welcomed "on the Jews' side, by a hail of stones and by revolver shots... which started not only from the crowd but also from the balconies of neighbouring buildings"; "the violence against the Christian population continued almost until the evening, and it was only with the arrival of a detachment from the army that the mobs of Jews were dispersed"; "the

Jews struck the Russians, and especially the peasants, who... were incapable of any resistance, either because of their small number compared to that of the Jews or because of their lack of defences... That day, all the victims were Russians... many wounded, people beaten to a pulp."[1157] The indictment concludes with regard to the events of August 29th that they "undeniably had the character of an 'anti-Russian pogrom'."[1158]

These facts caused "deep indignation among the Christian population", which reinforced "the euphoric mood" of the Jews, their "enthusiasm"...: "We are no longer in Kishinev!" On September 1st, after the midday siren, the railway workers were abnormally noisy as they left the workshops, shouts and exclamations were heard, and the chief of police ordered to block the bridge leading to the city. Then the workers spread to the neighbouring streets and "stones flew to the windows of houses inhabited by Jews," while "in the city were beginning to form large gatherings of Jews" who "threw from a distance pieces of wood and stones onto the crowd of workers"; "two paving stones thrown by the Jewish crowd" struck a police commissioner in the back who fell unconscious. The Russian crowd began to yell: "the kikes have killed the commissary!" and undertook to sack Jewish houses and shops. The intervention of the troop, which separated the adversaries and deployed itself in the face of both, prevented the shedding of blood. On the Jews' side, stones were thrown, and revolver shots were fired at the soldiers "with a shower of insults." The commander asked Rabbi Maiants and Doctor Zalkind to intervene with the Jews, but "their appeals for calm were of no effect and the crowd continued its agitation"; it was only possible to draw it back by pointing the bayonets. The main success of the army was to prevent "the breakers from reaching the city centre, where were found the shops and houses of the wealthy Jews." Then the pogrom moved to the outskirts of the city. The chief of the police still tried to exhort the crowd, but they cried out: "You are with the Jews, you have betrayed us! The salvos drawn by the troops upon the Russians as well as on the Jews curbed the pogrom, but two hours later it resumed in the suburbs—again shootings on the crowd, several dead and wounded, and then the pogrom ceased. However, the indictment refers to the presence in the city centre of "groups of Jews who conducted themselves in a very provocative manner and opposed the army and the police... As on 29 August, all were armed... many brandished revolvers and daggers", "going as far as firing shots or throwing stones on the troops charged to protect their property"; "they attacked the Russians who ventured alone in the streets, including the soldiers": a peasant and a beggar were killed. During that day, three middle-class Jews succumbed to

---
[1157] *Ibidem*, pp. 3041-3043.
[1158] *Ibidem*, p. 3041.

"deadly wounds". Towards the evening the disorders ceased. Five Jews and four Christians had been killed. "Nearly 250 commercial or residential premises belonging to Jews had been affected by the pogrom." On the Jewish side, "the overwhelming majority of active participants in the events consisted exclusively of... young people," but many "more mature" people, as well as children, had handed them stones, boards, and logs."[1159]

No description of these events can be found by any Jewish writer.

"The Gomel pogrom had not taken its organisers off guard. It had been prepared for a long time, the formation of self-defence had been put in place soon after the events of Kishinev."[1160] Only a few months after Kishinev, the Jews could no longer despise themselves for the resigned attitude with which they were accused of, among others, by the poet Bialik. And, as always happens with armed groups of this type, the boundary between defence and attack became blurred. The first was fed by the Kishinev pogrom, the second of the revolutionary spirit of the organisers.

(Activism of Jewish youth had already manifested itself before. Thus, in 1899, the "Chklov affair" was revealed: in this city where there were nine Jews for a Russian, disarmed Russian soldiers—they were demobilised—were severely beaten by Jews. After examining this episode, the Senate considered it to be a manifestation of ethnic and religious hatred of Jews towards Russians under the same article of the Penal Code as that had been applied to the trial of those responsible for the Kishinev pogrom.)

This activism must not be accounted for solely by the Bund. "At the head of this process [of creating, at a steady pace, organisations of self-defence] are found the Zionists and the parties close to Zionism—the Zionist-Socialists and the 'Poalei Zion'." Thus, it is how in Gomel, in 1903, "the majority of the detachments were organised by the 'Poalei Zion' party."[1161] (Which contradicts Buchbinder, fervent admirer of the Bund—I do not really know whom to believe.)

When the news of Gomel's pogrom reached Saint Petersburg, the Jewish Defence Office dispatched two lawyers—still Zaroudny and N. D. Sokolov—to proceed to a private investigation as soon as possible. Zaroudny once again gathered "irrefutable proofs" that the pogrom had been organised by the Department of Security,[1162] but here also, they were

---

[1159] *Ibidem*, pp. 3043-3046.
[1160] Buchbinder, op. cit., *p. 69.*
[1161] L. *Praisman,* Pogromy i samooborona (The pogroms and self-defence), "22": Obchtchestvenno-polititcheskii literatoumyi newspaper Ivreiskoi intelligentsii iz SSSR v Izraele, Tel Aviv, 1986–1987, no. 51, p. 178.
[1162] From the minouvehikh dnei: Zapiski ruskovo ievreia (Things of the past: memories of a Russian Jew), V 3-kh t. Paris, 1933 1934. t. 3, pp. 78 79.

not made public. (Thirty years later, even Sliosberg, who participated in the trials of Gomel, followed suit in his Memoirs in three volumes, asserting, without any shred of evidence—which seems incomprehensible on the part of a lawyer—, mistaking the dates—and those errors that can be attributed to age, he found no one to correct them—, that the Gomel pogrom had been deliberately organised by the police. He excludes also all offensive action on the part of the self-defence detachments of the Bund and of the Poalei Zion. (He speaks of it incoherently and confusedly, for example: "The young people of the self-defence groups quickly put an end to the misbehaviour and drove out the peasants", "the young Jews gathered promptly and, on more than one occasion, they were able to repel the rioters,"[1163] just like that, without using any weapons? ...) The official investigation was proceeding seriously, step by step—and during that time Russia was plunging into the Japanese war. And it was not until October 1904 that Gomel's trial took place—in a white-hot political atmosphere.

Forty-four Christians and 36 Jews appeared before the court; Nearly a thousand people were called to the witness stand.[1164] The Defence Office was represented by several lawyers: Sliosberg, Kupernik, Mandelstam, Kalmanovich, Ratner, Krohl. From their point of view, it was unjust that even a single Jew should be included in the bench of the accused: for the entire Jewish community in Russia "it was like a warning against recourse to self-defence."[1165] From the government's point of view, this was not "self-defence".

But the lawyers of the Jewish defendants did not deal with the details, nor the Jewish property that had really been sacked—they focused only on one thing: to uncover the "political motives" of the pogrom, for example, to point out that Jewish youth, in the midst of the fray, was shouting: "Down with the autocracy!" In fact, shortly afterwards, they decided to abandon their clients and leave the courtroom collectively in order to send an even stronger message: to repeat the precedent of the Kishinev trial.[1166]

This method, as skilful as it was revolutionary, was entirely in the air of the time in December 1904: these liberal advocates wanted to explode the judicial system itself!

After their departure, "the trial quickly came to an end" insofar as it was now possible to examine the facts. Some of the Jews were acquitted, the others were sentenced to penalties not exceeding five months; "The

---

[1163] *Ibidem*, p. 77.
[1164] Delo o gomelskom pogrom (Kiev courthouse: the Gomel pogrom case), *op. cit.*, p. 3040.
[1165] JE, t. 6, p. 666.
[1166] *Sliosberg*, t. 3, pp. 78-87.

condemnations which befell the Christians were equal to those of the Jews."[1167] In the end, there were about as many convictions on one side as on the other.[1168]

By plunging into the Japanese war, by adopting a rigid and insightful stance in the conflict over Korea, neither the Emperor Nicholas II nor the high dignitaries around him realised how much, on the international plane, Russia was vulnerable to the west and especially to the "traditionally friendly" America.

Nor did they take into account the rise of Western financiers, who were already influencing the policy of the great powers, increasingly dependent on credit. In the nineteenth century things did not happen this way yet, and the Russian government, always slow to react, did not know how to perceive these changes.

However, after the Kishinev pogrom, Western opinion had become firmly established in an attitude of repulsion towards Russia, considered as an old scarecrow, an Asiatic and despotic country where obscurantism reigns, where the people are exploited, where the revolutionaries are treated without pity, subjected to inhuman sufferings and deprivations, and now they are massacring the Jews "by the thousands", and behind all this there is the hand of the government! (As we have seen, the government was unable to rectify this distorted version of the facts in time, with energy and efficiency.) So, in the West, people began to consider it appropriate, even worthy of consideration, to hope that the revolution would break out in Russia as soon as possible: it would be a good thing for the whole world— and for the Jews of Russia in particular.

And, above all, the incompetence, the incapacity, the unpreparedness to conduct far-off military operations against a country that at that time seemed small and weak, in the context of an agitated, openly hostile public opinion, that longed for the defeat of its own country.

The sympathy of the United States for Japan expressed itself abundantly in the American press. It "hailed every Japanese victory and did not hide its desire to see Russia undergo a rapid and decisive setback."[1169] Witte mentions twice in his Memoirs that President Theodore Roosevelt was on

---

[1167] JE, t. 6, p. 667.
[1168] *I. G. Froumkine*, Iz istorii ruskovo ievreïstva—(Sb.) Kniga o rousskom cvrcïve: Ot 1860 godov do Revolutsii 1917 g. (Aspects of the History of Russian Jews), in BJWR-1, p. 61.
[1169] *F. R. Dulles, The Road to Tehran: The Story of Russia and America*, 1781 1943, Princeton, NJ, Princeton University Press, 1944, pp. 88 89.

the side of Japan and supported it.[1170] And Roosevelt himself: "As soon as this war broke out I brought to Germany's and France's attention, with the utmost courtesy and discretion, that in case of an anti-Japanese agreement" with Russia "I would immediately take the side of Japan and would do everything in the future to serve its interests."[1171] It may be supposed that Roosevelt's intentions were not unknown to Japan.

And it was there that the very powerful banker Jakob Schiff appeared—one of the greatest of the Jews, he who could realise his ideals thanks to his exceptional position in the economic sphere."[1172] "From his earliest years Schiff took care of business affairs"; he emigrated from Germany to New York and soon became head of the Bank Kuhn, Loeb & Co. In 1912, "he is in America the king of rail, owner of twenty-two thousand miles of railroads"; "he also has a reputation as an energetic and generous philanthropist; he is particularly sensitive to the needs of the Jewish community."[1173] Schiff was particularly keen on the fate of the Russian Jews—hence his hostility towards Russia until 1917.

According to the *Encyclopædia Judaica* (in English), "Schiff made a remarkable contribution to the allocation of credits to his own government and to that of other countries, particularly pointing out a loan of 200 million dollars to Japan during the conflict opposing it to Russia in 1904 1905.

Outraged by the anti-Semitic policy of the tsarist regime in Russia, he eagerly supported the Japanese war effort. He constantly refused to participate in lending to Russia and used his influence to deter other institutions from doing so, while granting financial aid to the self-defence groups of Russian Jews."[1174] But while it is true that this money allowed the Bund and the Poalei Zion to supply themselves with weapons, it is no less likely that they also benefited from other revolutionary organisations in Russia (including the S.-R. who, at the time, practised terrorism). There is evidence that Schiff, in an interview with an official of the Ministry of Finance of Russia, G. A. Vilenkine, who was also one of his distant relatives, "acknowledged that he contributed to the financing of the revolutionary movement in Russia" and that "things had gone too far"[1175] to put an end to it.

[1170] S. I. *Witte*, Vospominania. Tsarstvovanie Nikolaïa (Memoirs, The Reign of Nicholas II). In 2 vols., Berlin, Slovo, 1922, t. 1, pp. 376, 393.
[1171] T. *Dennett*, Roosevelt and the Russo-Japanese War, Doubleday, Page and Company, 1925 (reprinted: Gloucester, Mass., Peter Smith, 1959), p. 2.
[1172] *Sliosberg*, t. 3, p. 155.
[1173] JE, t. 16, p. 41.
[1174] *Encyclopædia Judaica*, vol. 14, Jerusalem, Keter Publishing House, Ltd., 1971, p. 961.
[1175] A. *Davydov*, Vospominania, 1881-1955 (Memoirs, 1881–1955), Paris, 1982.

However, in Russia, Baron G. O. Ginzburg continued to intervene in favour of equal rights for the Jews. To this end, in 1903 he visited Witte at the head of a Jewish delegation. The latter (who had already dealt with the Jewish question when he was secretary-general of the government) replied to them then: that the Jews should be granted equal rights only gradually, but "in order for the question to be raised, the Jews must adopt 'a completely different behaviour'," that is to say, to refrain from interfering in the political life of the country. "It is not your business, leave it to those who are Russian by blood and civil status, it is not for you to give us lessons, you should rather take care of yourself."

Ginzburg, Sliosberg, and Koulicher agreed with this opinion, other participants did not, particularly Winaver, who objected: "The time has come to grant equal rights to all the subjects [of the empire]… The Jews must support with all their strength those of the Russians who fight for it, and thus against the power in place."[1176]

From the Japanese war, from the beginning of 1904, the Russian government sought financial support from the West, and in order to obtain it, was willing to promise an extension of the rights of the Jews. At Plehve's request, high personalities came into contact with Baron Ginzburg on this subject, and Sliosberg was sent abroad to survey the opinion of the greatest Jewish financiers. As a matter of principle, Schiff "declined all bargaining over the number and nature of the rights granted to the Jews." He could "enter into financial relations only with a government that recognises to all its citizens the equality of civic and political rights… 'One can only maintain financial relations with civilized countries'." In Paris, Baron de Rothschild also refused:

"I am not prepared to mount any financial operation whatsoever, even if the Russian government brings improvements to the fate of the Jews."[1177]

Witte succeeded in obtaining a large loan without the help of Jewish financial circles. Meanwhile, in 1903 1904, the Russian government had undertaken to lift certain provisions limiting the rights of the Jews (we have already mentioned them in part). The first step in this direction, and the most important, had been, during Plehve's lifetime, and by way of derogation of the 1882 Regulations, the lifting of the prohibition on Jews settling in 101 densely populated localities which were not considered cities despite significant industrial and commercial activity, particularly in the grain trade.[1178] Secondly, the decision to promote a group of Jews to

---

[1176] *Witte*, Memoirs, *op. cit.*, t. 2, pp. 286, 287.
[1177] *Sliosberg*, t. 3, pp. 97, 100-101.
[1178] JE, t. 5, p. 863.

the rank of avowed attorneys, which had not been done since 1889.[1179] After the assassination of Plehve and the era of "confidence" inaugurated by the short-lived minister of the Interior Sviatopolk-Mirsky, this process continued. Thus, for Jews with higher education, the lifting of restrictive measures taken in 1882 took place, including the right to settle in areas previously prohibited to them, such as those of the Army of the Don, of Kuban, of Terek. The ban on residence in the border strip of 50 versts was also lifted; they re-established the right (abolished under Alexander II after 1874) to reside throughout the whole territory of the empire for "the brass of the army of Jewish origin... with exemplary service records."[1180] On the occasion of the birth of the heir to the throne, in 1904, amnesty was decreed on the fines, which had befallen the Jews who had evaded their military obligations.

But all these concessions came too late. In the node of the Japanese war that surrounded Russia, they were henceforth not accepted, as we have seen, neither by Western Jewish financiers, nor by the majority of Jewish politicians in Russia, nor, with strong reason, by Jewish youth. And in response to statements made by Sviatopolk-Mirsky when he took office—promising relief in both the Pale of Settlement and the choice of an activity—a declaration of "more than six thousand people" (The signatures had been collected by the Jewish Democratic Group): "We consider all efforts to satisfy and appease the Jewish population by partial improvements in their condition as futile. We consider as null and void any policy of gradually lifting the prohibitions weighing on us... We are waiting for equal rights... we make of it a matter of honour and justice."[1181]

It had become easier to weigh on a government entangled in war.

It goes without saying that, in a context in which cultivated Russian society had only contempt for power, it was difficult to expect Jewish youth to manifest massively its patriotic enthusiasm. According to the data provided by General Kushropkin, then Minister of War, then commander-in-chief of the eastern front, "in 1904 the number of insubordinates among the Jewish conscripts doubled compared with the year 1903; more than 20,000 of them have evaded their military obligations without good cause. Out of 1,000 conscripts, more than 300 were missing, while among the Russian conscripts this number fell to only 2 per 1,000. As for the Jewish reservists, they deserted en masse on the way to the area of military operations."[1182]

[1179] *Sliosberg*, t. 2, p. 190.
[1180] JE, t. 5, pp. 671, 864.
[1181] *Frumkin*, op. cit., BJWR-1, pp. 64, 109,110.
[1182] A. N. *Kouropatkine*, Zadatchi russko armii (The Problems of the Russian Army), Saint Petersburg, 1910, t. 3, pp. 344-345.

An American statistic suggests indirectly that from the beginning of the Japanese war there was a wave of mass emigration of Jews of military service age. During the two years of war, the figures for Jewish immigration to the United States increased very sharply for people of working age (14–44 years) and men: the former were 29,000 more than what they were expected, (compared to other immigrant categories); the second, 28,000 more (compared to women). After the war, the usual proportions were found.[1183] (*The Kievian* newspaper reported at the time that "from 20,000 to 30,000 Jewish soldiers and reservists... have gone into hiding or fled abroad."[1184] In the article "Military service in Russia" of the *Jewish Encyclopædia*, we can see a comparative picture of insubordination among Jews and Christians, according to official figures, the proportion of the former compared with the latter is 30 to one in 1902 and 34 to one in 1903. The *Jewish Encyclopædia* indicates that these figures can also be explained by emigration, deaths not taken into account, or miscalculations, but the inexplicable absence in this table of statistical data for 1904 and 1905, leaves no possibility of obtaining a precise idea of the extent of the insubordination during the war.[1185]

As for the Jewish fighters, the *Jewish Encyclopædia* says that there were between 20,000 and 30,000 during the war, not to mention the 3,000 Jews serving as doctors; and it points out that even the newspaper *Novoïe Vremia*, although hostile to the Jews, recognised their courageous behaviour in combat.[1186] These statements are corroborated by the testimony of General Denikin "In the Russian army, the Jewish soldiers, resourceful and conscientious, adapted well, even in times of peace. But in times of war all differences were self-effacing, and individual courage and intelligence were also recognised."[1187] A historical fact: the heroism of Iossif Troumpeldor who, having lost a hand, asked to remain in the ranks. In fact, he was not the only one to distinguish himself.[1188]

At the end of this war lost by Russia, President Theodore Roosevelt agreed to mediate the talks with Japan (Portsmouth, USA). Witte, who led the Russian delegation, evokes "this delegation of Jewish big shots who came to see me twice in America to talk to me about the Jewish question." These

---

[1183] JE, t. 2, pp. 239-240.
[1184] Kievlianine, 16 Dec. 1905— V. V. Choulguine, "Chto nam v nikh ne nravitsa..." Ob Antisemilizm v Rossii ("What we do not like about them..." On Anti-Semitism in Russia), Paris, 1929, annexes, p. 308.
[1185] JE, t. 5, pp. 705-707.
[1186] *Ibidem*, t. 3, pp. 168-169.
[1187] A. I. Denikine, Pout rousskovo ofitsera (*The Routine of a Russian Officer*), New York, ed. Imeni Chekhov, 1953, p. 285.
[1188] JE, t. 3, p. 169.

were Jakob Schiff, the eminent lawyer Louis Marshall and Oscar Strauss, among others.

The position of Russia had become rather uncomfortable, which imposed a more conciliatory tone on the Russian minister than in 1903. Witte's arguments "raised violent objections on the part of Schiff."[1189] Fifteen years later, Kraus, one of the members of this delegation, who in 1920 became president of the B'nai B'rith Lodge, said: "If the tsar does not give his people the freedoms to which it is entitled, the revolution will be able to establish a republic that will allow access to these freedoms."[1190]

During the same weeks, a new danger began to undermine Russian-American relations. On his way back to Witte, T. Roosevelt asked him to inform the Emperor that the trade agreement which had long bound (1832) his country to Russia would suffer if it applied confessional restrictions to American businessmen going to its territory.[1191] This protest, which, of course, was a matter of principle, concerned, in practice, a significant number of Russian Jews who had immigrated to the United States and had become American citizens.

They returned to Russia—often to engage in revolutionary activities—henceforth as merchants who were not subject to any professional or geographical limitation. This landmine could only explode a few years later.

For several years Stuttgart had published the *Osvoboj-denie*[1192] magazine, and the great mass of cultivated Russians scarcely concealed its sympathies for the illegal organisation Union for Liberation. In the autumn of 1904, a "banqueting campaign" was held in all the major cities of Russia, where impassioned and premonitory toasts were called for the overthrow of the "regime". Participants from abroad also spoke in public (such as Tan Bogoraz). "Political unrest had penetrated all layers of the Jewish community." The latter was engulfed in this bubbling, without distinction of classes or parties.

Thus "many Jewish public men, even of patriotic sensibility, were part of the Union for Liberation."[1193] Like all Russian liberals, they proved to be "defeatists" during the Japanese war. Like them, they applauded the

---

[1189] *Witte, op. cit.*, t. 1, pp. 394–395.
[1190] *B'nai B'rith News*, May 1920, vol. XII, no. 9.
[1191] *Witte, op. cit.*, p. 401.
[1192] Organ of the Union for Liberation, organisation of the liberal opposition, which became the Constitutional-Democratic Party (or KD, or Cadet) in 1905.
[1193] G. I. Aronson, V borbe za grajdanskie i natsionalnye prava: Obchtchestvennye tetchenia v rousskom evreïstve (The struggle for civil and national rights: The movements of opinion within the Jewish community of Russia), BJWR-1, pp. 221–222.

"executions" of the ministers Bogolepov, Sipiagin, Plehve. And this entire "progressive" Russia pushed even the Jews in this direction, unable to admit that a Jew could be more on the right than a left-wing democrat, but feeling that he should, more naturally yet, be a socialist. A Conservative Jew? Ugh! Even in an academic institution such as the Jewish Historical-Ethnographic Commission, "in these tumultuous years there was no time to serenely engage in scientific research…" it was necessary "to make History".[1194] "The radical and revolutionary movements within the Russian Jewish community have always been based on the idea that the problem of equal rights… the fundamental historical question of the Jews of Russia, would be solved only when one would cut once for all the head of the Medusa and all the serpents that spring from it."[1195]

During these years in Saint Petersburg, the Jewish Defence Office developed its activities with the aim of "fighting anti-Semitic literature and disseminating appropriate information on the legal situation of Jews in order to influence mainly the opinion of liberal Russian circles." (Sliosberg points out that these activities were largely subsidised by the international EKO[1196].[1197]) But it was not so much Russian society that it was a question of influencing. The Bureau did not open branches in Russia, not even in Moscow, Kiev, or Odessa: on the one hand, Zionist propaganda absorbed all the energy of the most cultivated Jews; on the other, "Bund propaganda mobilised the greater part of the educated Jewish youth." (Sliosberg insisting that the Bund be condemned, Winaver objected that he should not quarrel with the Bund: "it disposes of energy and propaganda power."[1198] However, the Bureau soon maintained a strong relationship, built on reciprocal information and mutual aid, with the American Jewish Committee (chaired by J. Schiff, then Louis Marshall), the English Jewish Committee (Claude Montefiore, Lucine Woolf), the Alliance in Paris and the Support Committee of the German Jews (*Hilfsverein der deutschen Juden*: James Simon, Paul Nathan[1199]).

Here is the testimony of M. Krohl: "The heart of our group was the 'Press Office'[whose mission was to disseminate] through the Russian and foreign press serious information about the situation of the Jews in Russia." It was A. I. Braudo who undertook this task. "He accomplished it perfectly. Under the conditions of the Russia of that time, this kind of work required

---

[1194] M. L. Vichnitser, Iz peterbourgskikh vospominanii (Memories of Petersburg), BJWR-1, p. 41.
[1195] S. Ivanovich, Ievrei i sovetskaya diktatoura (The Jews and the Soviet Dictatorship), pp. 41-42.
[1196] Jewish mutual aid committee.
[1197] *Sliosberg*, t. 3, pp. 132, 248, 249.
[1198] *Ibidem*, pp. 138, 168.
[1199] *Ibidem*, pp. 142-147, 152, 157.

a great deal of prudence," was to be carried out "in the greatest secrecy. Even the members of the Defence Office did not know by what means or by what channels he had succeeded in organising such and such a press campaign... A large number of articles published in the Russian or foreign press of the time, often with great repercussions, had been communicated to the newspapers or magazines either personally by Braudo, or through his intermediary."[1200]

"Providing serious information" to launch "this or that press campaign"— it is a bit chilling, especially in light of what happened in the 20th century. In today's language, it is called "skilful manipulation of the media."

In March 1905 the Defence Bureau convened in Vilnius the Constituent Congress of the "Union for the Equal Rights for the Jewish People in Russia,"[1201] but it quickly proceeded to its self-dissolution and joined the direction of the Union for the integrality of rights (the expression "integrality", because it was stronger than that of "equal rights", had been proposed by Winaver. Today, we evoke it under a hybrid form such as the "Union for Achieving Integral Equality of Rights"[1202]).

It was wanted that this new Union bring together all Jewish parties and groups.[1203] But the Bund denounced this congress as a *bourgeois*. However, many Zionists could not remain in their splendid isolation. The prodromes of the Russian revolution led to a split in their ranks. And some of these fractions did not resist the temptation to participate in the great things that unfolded before their eyes! But in so doing, they exerted an influence on the strictly civic orientation of the congress agenda. The idea was making its way not only to fight for civic rights but also, with the same energy, for national rights.[1204]

Sliosberg fought against the influence of the Zionists "who wanted to withdraw the Jews from the number of citizens of Russia" and whose demands "were often formulated only for demagogic reasons." For the Jewish community in Russia "has in no way been limited in the expression of its national life...

Was it appropriate to raise the question of national autonomy of the Jews when none of the nationalities living in Russia possessed it, whereas the Russian people themselves, in their orthodox part, were far from being free in the expression of their religious and national life?" But, "at that time,

---

[1200] *M. Krohl*, Stranitsy moiei jisni (Pages of my life), t. 1, New York, 1944, pp. 299, 300.
[1201] JE, t. 14, p. 515.
[1202] RJE, t. 3, M., 1997, p. 65.
[1203] JE, t. 14, p. 515.
[1204] *Aronson*, The Struggle..., *op. cit.*, p. 222.

demagogy assumed a very special significance in the Jewish backstreet."[1205]

Thus, in place of the notion, clear in the eyes of everyone, of "equality of rights", which certainly had not yet happened, but seemed no longer to lag behind political developments, the slogan was issued for *the integrality of rights* of the Jews. What was meant by this was that, in addition to equal rights, "national autonomy" was also recognised. "It must be said that those who formulated these requirements did not have a very clear idea of their content. The creation of Jewish schools was not limited by any law. The study of the Russian language was required... insofar as it was not a question of *Heders*.[1206]

But other more civilised countries also imposed the use of the State language in relations with the administration as well as in school.[1207] Thus, there was no "national autonomy" for the Jews in the United States. But the "obtentionists" ("Union for the obtention...") demanded "national and cultural self-determination" on the territory of Russia, as well as a substantial autonomy for the Jewish communities (and, in the same breath: the secularisation of these, to tear them away from the religious influence of Judaism—which suited both the Zionists and the Socialists). Later, this was called "national-personal autonomy". (Accompanied by the requirement that the Jewish cultural and social institutions be financed by the State but without it interfering in their functioning.) And how can we imagine the "self-management" of a nation scattered territorially? The Second Congress of the Union, in November 1905, took the decision to convene a Jewish National Assembly of Russia.[1208]

All these ideas, including the "national-personal autonomy" of the Jews of Russia, were expressed and continued in various forms until 1917. However, the Union for the Integrality of Rights proved ephemeral. At the end of 1906, the Jewish People's Anti-Zionist Group seceded (Winaver, Sliosberg, Koulicher, Sternberg) on the grounds that it refused the idea of a Jewish National Assembly; shortly afterwards it was the turn of the Jewish People's Party (S. Doubnov—religious and cultural nationalism, notably the right to use the Jewish language in public life throughout the country, but with what means, how?); then the Jewish Democratic Group (Bramson, Landau), close to the Labour Party.[1209] The Union for the integrality of rights was also accused of having rallied to the KD and, consequently, was "no longer being able to represent the Jewish population

---

[1205] *Sliosberg*, t. 3, pp. 170–171.
[1206] Jewish elementary schools.
[1207] *Ibidem*, p. 170.
[1208] JE, t. 14, p. 516.
[1209] *Ibidem*, t. 7, pp. 437-440.

of Russia"; the Zionists regarded the "secularists" as "partisans of assimilation", and the socialists as *bourgeois*.[1210] In short, at the beginning of 1907, the Union ceased to exist.[1211]

The Zionists were increasingly drawn into the revolutionary whirlpool, and in November 1906, at their All-Russian Congress in Helsinfors, it was declared "indispensable not only to turn to the daily needs and demands of the Jews of Russia, but also to engage fully in their political and social struggle"[1212]; Jabotinsky insisted that the Zionist program should include the requirement of the establishment in Russia of the sovereignty of the people; D. Pasmanik objected that "such a demand can only be made by those who are ready to stand on the barricades."[1213] At the end of its work, the Congress brought its "sanction to the rallying of the Zionists to the Liberation Movement".[1214] But the latter was just about to lose momentum after the failure of Vyborg's manifesto.[1215]

The author of this program, Jabotinsky, put forward the following arguments: the goal set by Zionism can only be reached in several decades, but by fighting for their full rights, Jews will understand better what Zionism is.[1216]

However, he said: "We leave the first ranks to the representatives of the majority nation. We cannot pretend to play a *leading* role: we are *aligning* ourselves.[1217] In other words: Palestine is one thing; in the meantime, let us fight in Russia. Three years earlier, Plehve had told Herzl that he feared precisely this kind of drift of Zionism.

Sliosberg is far from minimising the role of the Zionists: "After the Congress of Helsinfors, they decided to take control of all public activities of the Jews" by trying to "impose their influence at the local level". (In the first Duma, of the 12 Jewish deputies, five were Zionists.) But he also notes that this profusion of parties was "the business of small circles of

---

[1210] *Sliosberg*, t. 3, pp. 257–258.
[1211] JE, t. 14. p. 517.
[1212] *Aronson*, The Struggle..., *op. cit.*, p. 224.
[1213] D. S. *Pasmanik*, Chevo je my dobivaïemsia? (What do we really want?), Rossia i Ievrei, Sb 1 (Russia and the Jews, book 1—later: RJ) / Otetchestvennoïe obedinenie rousskikh ievreyev za granitsei, Paris, YMCA Press, 1978, p. 211.
[1214] *Aronson*, The Struggle..., *op. cit.*, p. 224.
[1215] After the dissolution of the first Duma, about two hundred deputies met at Vyborg, and expressed their opposition to the government in the form of a manifesto, which did not meet with any public echo.
[1216] G. *Svet*, Rousskie evrei v sionizme i v stroitelstve Palestiny i Izrailia (Russian Jews in Zionism and the Construction of Palestine and Israel), BJWR-1, pp. 263-264.
[1217] V. *Jabotinsky*, Ievreiskaya kramola (The Jewish Conspiracy), Felietony, p. 43.

intellectuals", not of the Jewish masses, and their propaganda "only caused to confuse the issues."[1218]

True, all this scattering did not contribute to the clarification of the debate: it was no longer very clear what the Russian Jews were fighting, for what rights—equal or integral?—or on which plan—civic or national?

And, let us not forget: "All these groups composed only of intellectuals...did not understand Orthodox Jews, who eventually understood the need to organise to combat the growing anti-religious influence exerting itself on Jewish youth." And it was thus that "was born what was later to develop in 'T'Agoudat Israel'." "This movement was concerned that "Jewish revolutionary elements are recruited among the Jewish youth who have moved away from religion," whereas "the majority of the Jews are religious and, while demanding recognition of their rights and the lifting of the prohibitions against them, remain loyal subjects of the Emperor and are far from any idea of overthrowing the existing regime."[1219]

When one studies the history of Russian Jews at the beginning of the twentieth century, there are few references to Orthodox Jews. Sliosberg once said, raising the ire of the Bund: "With the *melameds*[1220] behind me, I rely on a greater number of Jews than the Bund leaders, for there are more *melameds* among the Jews than the workers."[1221] In fact, the secularisation of Jewish society in no way affected the existence of traditional communities in the Pale of Settlement. For them, all the ancestral questions concerning the organisation of their lives, the religious instruction, the rabbinate, remained topical. During the temporary lull of 1909, the reform of the traditional Jewish community was discussed with great seriousness at the Kovno Congress. "The work of the Congress proved to be very fruitful, and few Jewish assemblies could have equalled it by the seriousness and wisdom of the resolutions adopted there."[1222]

"Orthodox Judaism has always been in conflict—not always open, but rather latent—with the Jewish intelligentsia. It was clear that in condemning the movement for the liberation of the Jews it hoped to win the government's favour."[1223] But it was too late: on the eve of the 1905 revolution, we have seen that the autocratic regime had lost control of the country. As for traditional Judaism, it had already lost a whole

---

[1218] *Sliosberg*, t. 3, pp. 253, 255, 262.
[1219] *Ibidem*, pp. 225-256.
[1220] Teachers teaching in *heders*.
[1221] *Ibidem*, p. 258.
[1222] *Ibidem*, p. 263.
[1223] *Ibidem*, p. 265.

generation—moreover it was not the first—who had gone towards Zionism, secular liberalism, rarely enlightened conservatism, but also, and with the heaviest consequences, towards the revolutionary movement.

The new generation of revolutionaries had emerged at the turn of the century. Its leaders, Grigory Gershuni and Mikhail Gotz, had decided to revive the terrorist methods of The Will of the People. "Gershuni took upon himself the heavy responsibility of creating in Russia a new revolutionary party called to succeed with dignity to the Will of the People," and "thanks to his talents as organiser as well as to those of other revolutionaries entirely devoted to the cause, this party was born at the end of the year 1901." "At the same time... was also constituted its armed faction. Its creator and its inspirer was none other than the very same Gershuni."[1224] Among the S.-R.[1225], the Jews "immediately played a leading role." Amongst them were "An-ski Rappoport, K. Jitlovsky, Ossip Minor, I. Roubanovitch" and—still him!—Mark Natanson. The armed faction included among its members "Abraham Gotz, Dora Brilliant, L. Zilberberg", not to mention the famous Azef. It is among the S.-R. That M. Trilisser was also formed—he who later would become famous in the Cheka. "Among the grassroots activists of the S.-R. party, there were also quite a few Jews," even though, adds Schub, "they never represented a tiny minority." According to him, it is even "the most Russian" of the revolutionary parties.[1226] For security reasons, the seat of the party was transferred abroad (for example, the Bund was absent), in Geneva, at M. Gotz and O. Minor's place.

As for Gershuni, this indomitable "tiger", after succeeding in deceiving Zubatov's[1227] vigilance, he began to criss-cross Russia, like B. Savinkov, fomenting terrorist actions and checking their proper execution. It was thus that he was present at the Place Saint-Isaac during the assassination of Sipiagin[1228]; he was at Ufa when Governor Bogdanovitch was killed[1229]; and at Kharkov when it was Governor Obolensky's turn; on the Nevsky prospect during the failed attack on Pobedonostsev[1230]. The execution was always entrusted to "Christians" such as P. Karpovitch, S. Balmachov, E. Sozonov, etc. (The bombs used for the assassination of Plehve, Grand Duke Sergey Aleksandrovich, and planned attacks on Grand Duke Vladimir

---

[1224] *Krohl*, Stanitsy... (Pages...), *op. cit.*, pp. 283-284.
[1225] Social Revolutionaries.
[1226] *D. Schub*, Evrei rousskoï revolutsii (*The Jews in the Russian Revolution*), JW-2, p. 138.
[1227] Chief of the Russian secret police at the beginning of the twentieth century.
[1228] Minister of the Interior assassinated in 1902.
[1229] SJE, t. 2, p. 111.
[1230] Politician with revolutionary ideas, very influential with the emperors Alexander and Nicolas II (1827–1907).

Alexandrovich and Interior Ministers Boulygin and Durnovo were made by Maximilian Schweitzer, who in 1905 was himself victim of the machine he was making.[1231]) Arrested by chance, Gershuni was condemned to death, reprieved by the Emperor without having asked for it; in 1907 he found an ingenious means of escaping from the prison of Akatuysk, hiding in a cabbage-barrel, and then gained by way of Vladivostok, America and Europe; the Russian government demanded his extradition from Italy, but the European liberal opinion was unanimous in refusing it and Clemenceau also used his influence: he was also, as we know, a "tiger". Soon after, Gershuni died of a sarcoma in the lung. Among other leading S.-R. terrorists, we must also mention Abraham Gotz, who played an active part in the attacks on Dournovo, Akimov, Shuvalov, Trepov[1232], and played a role in the assassination of Mine and Rieman. (But, he had the misfortune of living much longer than his elder brother, who died prematurely—and the Bolsheviks later gave him a hard time.) To play with History, precautions were less taken than the previous revolutionary generation. Less well known than others, Pinhas (Pyotr) Rutenberg is not less worthy of interest. In 1905 he trained groups of fighters in Saint Petersburg and supplied them with weapons. Inspired by Gapon[1233], he was at his side on 9 January 1905; But it was also he who, in 1906, "by order of the S.-R. party, organises and supervises his assassination" (later he will author a book entitled *Gapon's Assassination*[1234]). In 1919, he immigrated to Palestine where he distinguished himself in the electrification of the country. There, he shows that he is capable of building; but in his early years, in Russia, he certainly does not work as an engineer, he destroys! One loses the trace of the "student of Zion", irresponsible instigator of the mutiny of Sveaborg, who, however, escaped the slaughter that ensued.

Apart from the S.-R., each year brought with it new social-democratic fighters, theorists, and talkers. Some had short-lived notoriety in narrow circles, such as Alekandra Sokolovskaya, whom History retained only because she was Trotsky's first wife and the mother of his two daughters. Others have been unjustly forgotten: Zinovy Litvine-Sedoi, the chief of staff of the detachments of the Krasnaya Presnia district during the armed insurrection in Moscow; Zinovy Dosser, a member of the "troika" who led this insurrection. Among its leaders, we can cite again "Marat"—V. L.

[1231] RJE, t. 3, pp. 378–379.
[1232] P. Dournovo (1845-1915), Minister of the Interior in 1905–1906; P. Shuvalov (1830-1906), Russian diplomat and politician; D. Trepov (1855–1906), Deputy Minister of the Interior, one of the leaders of the repression of the revolution of 1905–1907.
[1233] G. Gapon (1870-1906), priest and agent of the secret police, one of the persons responsible for the massacre of demonstrators in Saint Petersburg, 9 January 1905.
[1234] RJE, t. 2, p. 517.

Chanzer, Lev Kafenhausen, Lubotsky-Zagorsky (who for nearly a century gave his pseudonym[1235] to the monastery of The Trinity Saint Sergius) and Martin Mandelstam-Liadov, member of the executive Commission of the RSDLP[1236] for the organisation of the armed insurrection.[1237] Others—like F. Dan or O. Nakhamkis—were to play an important role later in 1917.

Despite Bakunin's aversion for the Jews, there are many of them among the leaders and theorists of anarchism. But "other Russian anarchists, such as Kropotkin, had no hostility towards the Jews and tried to win them over to their cause." [1238] Among these leaders are Yakov Novomirsky, Alexander Gue, Lev Tcherny, V. Gordine.[1239] One of them, I. Grossman-Rochin, evokes with the greatest respect the figure of Aron Eline, of Bialystok: "a famous terrorist", but not only "a specialist in gory operations" "never does he fall... into 'systematic activism'."[1240] "The least patient among the mass of Jews... are looking for a faster way to achieve socialism. And this recourse, this 'ambulance', they find in anarchism."[1241] It is the Jews of Kiev and Southern Russia who have been most attracted to anarchism, and in the documents relating to the Bogrov affair[1242] there is often mention of smaller-scale anarchists, forgotten by history.

We have already observed, but it is worth recalling, that it was not only because of the inequalities of which they were the victims that many Jews were rushing into the revolution. "The participation of the Jews in the revolutionary movement which had gained the whole of Russia is only partly explained by their situation of inequality... The Jews merely shared the general feeling of hostility towards the autocracy.[1243] Should we be surprised? Young people from the intelligentsia, both Russian and Jewish, heard in their families, all year long, only "crimes perpetrated by the power", of the "government composed of assassins", and they precipitated

---

[1235] Zagorsk.
[1236] Russian Social-Democratic Labour Party.
[1237] RJE, t. 1, pp. 436, 468; t. 2, pp. 13, 218.
[1238] SJE, t. 1, p. 124.
[1239] A. Vetlouguine, Avanturisly Grajdanskoy voïny (Adventurers of the Civil War), Paris, Imprimerie Zemgor, 1921, pp. 65 67, 85.
[1240] I. Grossman-Rochin, Doumy o bylom (Reflections on the Past) (Iz istorii Belostotskovo, anarkhitcheskovo, "tchemosnamenskovo" dvijenia), Byloïe, M., 1924, nos. 27, 28, p. 179.
[1241] Ben-Khoïrin, Anarkhism i ievreïskaïa massa (Anarchism and the Jewish masses) (St. Petersburg) Soblazn sotsializma: Revolutsia v Rossi i ievrci / Sost. A. Serebrennikov, Paris, M., YMCA Press, Rousskii Pout, 1995, p. 453.
[1242] See *infra*, Chapter 10.
[1243] SJE, t. 7, p. 398.

the revolutionary action with all the energy of their fury. Bogrov like the others.

In 1905, the Jewish historian S. Doubnov accused all Jewish revolutionaries of "national treason." In his article entitled "Slavery in the Revolution," he wrote: "This entire numerous army of young Jews, who occupy the most prominent positions in the Social Democratic Party and who run for positions of command, has formally cut off all ties with the Jewish community... You build nothing new, you are only the valets of the revolution, or its commissionaires."[1244]

But as time passed, the approval of the adults to their revolutionary progeny grew. This phenomenon was intensified among the "fathers" of the new generation and was on the whole more marked among the Jews than among the Russians. Meier Bomach, member of the Duma, declared ten years later (1916):

"We do not regret that the Jews participated in the struggle for liberation... They were fighting for your freedom."[1245] And six months later, in the conflagration of the new revolution, in March 1917, the celebrated lawyer O. O. Gruzenberg held these passionate but not unfounded remarks before the leaders of the Provisional Government and the Soviet of deputies of workers and soldiers: "We generously offered to the revolution a huge 'percentage' of our people—almost all its flower, almost all its youth... And, when in 1905 the people rose up, countless Jewish fighters came to swell their ranks, carried by an irresistible impulse."[1246] Others will say the same thing: "Historical circumstances made the Jewish masses of Russia unable to not participate in the most active way in the revolution."[1247] "For the Jews, the solution of the Jewish question in Russia was the triumph of progressive ideas in this country."[1248]

The revolutionary effervescence that had seized Russia was undoubtedly stirred up by that which reigned among the Jews.

However, youth alone, trained in intellectual or manual labour, could not make the revolution. One of the top priorities was to win over to the revolutionary cause, and to lead the industrial workers, and especially those of Saint Petersburg, to battle. However, as noted by the director of the police department at the time, "at the initial stage of its development, the

---

[1244] *Dimanstein*, "1905*", *op. cit.*, t. 3, v. 1, p. 174.
[1245] Mejdounarodnoïe finansovoïe polojenie tsarskoi Rossii vo vremia mirovoï voïny (The financial situation of tsarist Russia during the World War), Krasnyi Arkhiv, 1934, t. 64, p. 28.
[1246] Retch, 1917, 25 March, p. 6.
[1247] *Dimanstein*, "1905", *op. cit.*, p. 175.
[1248] JE, t. 7, p. 370.

workers' movement... was foreign to political aspirations." And even on the eve of January 9th, "during an extraordinary meeting which they had organised on December 27th, the workers chased a Jew who tried to make political propaganda and distribute leaflets, and three Jewish women who sought to propagate political ideas were apprehended."[1249]

In order to train the workers of Saint Petersburg, Gapon's pseudo-religious propaganda took place.

On 9 January, even before the troops opened fire, it was the young Simon Rechtzammer (the son of the director of the Warehouse and Grain Storage Company) who took the lead of the only barricade erected that day (On the fourth street of Saint-Basil's island), with the destruction of the telegraph and telephone lines and the attack on the police station. Moreover, the workers of this quarter were employed two days later "to copiously beat the intellectuals."[1250]

We know that the Russian revolutionaries who immigrated to Europe welcomed the news of the shooting of Petersburg with a mixture of indignation and enthusiasm: it's about time!! Now it's going to blow!! As for the propagation of this enthusiasm—and of the insurrection—in the Pale of Settlement, it was the tireless Bund who harnessed himself, whose hymn (An-ski said of it that it was "The *Marseillaise* of the Jewish Workers") included the following words:

> Enough of loving our enemies, we want to hate them!! ...
> ... it is ready the pyre! We will find enough logs
> For its holy flames to engulf the planet!![1251]

(Let us note in passing that *The International* was translated into Russian by Arkadi Kotz as early as 1912.[1252] Several generations were religiously imbued with his words: *Stand up! The damned of the earth!* and *of the past let us make a clean slate...*)

The Bund immediately issued a proclamation ("about two hundred thousand copies"): "The revolution has begun. It burned in the capital, its

---

[1249] Doklad direktora departamenta politsii Lopoukhina ministrou vnoutrennykh del o sobytiakh 9-vo ianvaria (Report of the Director of the Police Department, Lopoukhine, to the Minister of the Interior on the events of 9 January), Krasnaya Ictopis, 1922, no. 1, p. 333.
[1250] V Nevsky, Ianvarskie dni v Peterbourgue v 1905 godou (The Days of January in Petersburg in 1905), *ibidem*, pp. 51, 53.
[1251] Soblazn Sotsializma, p. 329.
[1252] RJE, t. 2, p. 70.

flames covering the whole country... To arms! Storm the armouries and seize all the weapons... Let all the streets become battlefields!"[1253]

According to the *Red Chronicle* of the Soviet regime's beginnings, "the events of 9 January in Saint Petersburg echoed a great deal in the Jewish workers' movement: they were followed by mass demonstrations of the Jewish proletariat throughout the Pale of Settlement. At their head was the Bund. To ensure the massive nature of these demonstrations, detachments of the Bund went to workshops, factories, and even to the workers' homes to call for the cessation of work; they employed force to empty the boilers of their steam, to tear off the transmission belts; they threatened the owners of companies, here and there shots were fired, at Vitebsk one of them received a jet of sulphuric acid. It was not "a spontaneous mass demonstration, but an action carefully prepared and organised." N. Buchbinder regrets, however, that "almost everywhere the strikes were followed only by the Jewish workers... In a whole series of towns the Russian workers put up a strong resistance to the attempts to stop factories and plants." There were week-long strikes in Vilnius, Minsk, Gomel, Riga, of two weeks in Libava. The police had to intervene, naturally, and in several cities the Bund constituted "armed detachments to combat police terror."[1254] In Krinki (the province of Grodno), the strikers gunned the police, interrupted telegraphic communications, and for two days all the power was in the hands of the strike committee. "The fact that workers, and among them a majority of Jews, had thus been able to hold power from the beginning of 1905, was very significant of what this revolution was, and gave rise to many hopes."

It is no less true that the Bund's important participation in these actions "might lead one to believe that discontent was above all the result of the Jews, while the other nationalities were not that revolutionary."[1255]

The strength of the revolutionaries manifested itself through the actions, carried out in broad daylight, of armed detachments of "self-defence" which had been illustrated during the Gomel pogrom and which had since then grown considerably stronger. "Self-defence was most often in close contact with the armed detachments of political organisations... It can be said that the whole Pale of Settlement was covered by a whole network of armed self-defence groups which played an important military role—only a professional army could face them."[1256]—At the height of the revolution, they were joined by Zionist groups of various tendencies: "the particularly

---

[1253] *Dimanstein*, "1905", *op. cit.*, p. 144.
[1254] *N. Buchbinder,* 9 ianvaria i icvskoye rabotchee dvijenie (On 9 January and Jewish Labour Movement), Krasnaya Letopis, 1922, no. 1, pp. 81, 87.
[1255] *Dimanstein*, "1905", *op. cit.*, pp. 145, 147.
[1256] *Ibidem*, pp. 150-151.

active participation of the Poalei Zion", as well as "armed detachments of the ZS [Zionist Socialists]", But also from SERP. So that "in the armed operations that occurred during the revolution, these socialists belonging to different currents of Zionism found themselves at our side,"[1257] remembers S. Dimanstein, later a prominent Bolshevik leader.

The Bund was to continue its military operations throughout this changing and uncertain year of 1905. Special mention should be made to the April events in Jitomir. According to the *Jewish Encyclopædia*, it was a pogrom against the Jews, moreover "fomented by the police."[1258] As for Dimanstein, who boasts of having "actively participated in the 1905 revolution on the territory of the so-called Pale of Settlement," he wrote: "It was not a pogrom, but a fight against the troops of the counter-revolution."[1259] The *Jewish Encyclopædia* indicates that up to twenty Jews were killed[1260]; the new one: "almost fifty (according to other sources, about thirty-five)."[1261] According to the latter, "disorders began after provocateurs had declared that Jews had fired shots on the portrait of the tsar outside the city."[1262] While *The Messenger of the Government* gives as a fact that, two weeks before the pogrom, "a crowd of nearly three hundred people gathered outside the city... to practice shooting with revolvers... by aiming for the portrait of His Majesty the Emperor." After this, several brawls broke out between the Jews and the Christians within the city—still according to *The Messenger of the Government*, the aggressors were mostly Jews.[1263] According to the new *Jewish Encyclopædia*, on the day of the event, "the Jewish detachments of self-defence heroically resisted the rioters." From a neighbouring village, a group of young armed Jews came to their rescue, when, on the way, "they were stopped by Ukrainian peasants" at Troyanovo. "They tried to take refuge among the Jewish inhabitants of the village, but these did not let them in" and, a characteristic fact, "indicated to the peasants where two of them had been hiding"; "ten members of the detachment were killed."[1264]

At the time, a particularly effective manœuvre had already been devised: "The funerals of the victims who fell for the revolution constituted one of the most effective means of propaganda capable of inflating the masses", which had for consequence that "the fighters were aware that their death would be used for the profit of the revolution, that it would arouse a desire

---

[1257] *Ibidem*, pp. 123-124.
[1258] SJE, t. 2, p. 513.
[1259] *Dimanstein*, "1905", *op. cit.*, p. 144.
[1260] JE, t. 7, p. 602.
[1261] SJE, t. 2, p. 513.
[1262] *Ibidem*, t. 6, p. 566.
[1263] Pravo, 5 May 1905, pp. 1483-1484.
[1264] SJE, t. 2, p. 513; *Dimanstein*, "1905", *op. cit.*, pp. 151-152.

for vengeance among the thousands of people who were going to attend their funeral," and that on these occasions "it was relatively easier to organise manifestations. The liberal circles considered it their duty to ensure that the police did not intervene during a funeral." Thus "the funeral became one of the components of revolutionary propaganda in 1905."[1265]

In the summer of that year, "the police terror was massive, but there were also many acts of revenge on the part of the workers who threw bombs on patrols of soldiers or Cossacks, murdered policemen, whether officers or not; these cases were far from being isolated", because it was "a step backwards or forwards for the revolution in the Jewish sector." [1266] Example: the Cossacks killed a Bund militant in Gomel; eight thousand people attend his funeral, revolutionary speeches are given—and the revolution advances, always advances! And when the time came to protest against the convening of the "Boulyguine"[1267] consultative Duma, the campaign "moved from the Stock Exchange in the Jewish quarter to the synagogues… where speakers of the Party intervened during the service… under the protection of armed detachments that sealed off the exits… During these assemblies, it was frequent that resolutions prepared in advance were adopted without discussion"—the unfortunate faithfuls come to pray, did they have a choice? Go and talk to these fellows! There is no question of "stopping the revolutionary process at this stage…"[1268]

The project of convocation of this consultative Duma, which was not followed up on due to the events of 1905, started from the assumption that they did not possess it for the designation of municipal self-government bodies, it had been originally planned to not grant the Jews the right to vote. But the revolutionary momentum was growing, the Jewish municipal councillors appointed by the provincial authorities resigned demonstratively here and there, and the Duma Elections Act of August 1905 already provided for the granting of voting rights to the Jews. But the revolution continued its course, and public opinion rejected this consultative Duma, which was therefore not united.

The tension remained high throughout this unhappy year 1905; the government was overtaken by the events. In the fall, strikes, notably in the railways, were being prepared everywhere in Russia. And, of course, the Pale of Settlement was not spared. In the region of the Northwest, during early October, was seen "a rapid rise… of the revolutionary energy of the masses", "a new campaign of meetings takes place in the synagogues"

[1265] *Dimanstein*, "1905", *op. cit.*, p. 153.
[1266] *Ibidem*, p. 164.
[1267] A. Boulyguine (1851-1919). Minister of the Interior in 1905.
[1268] *Ibidem*, pp. 165-166.

(always in the same way, with men posted at exits to intimidate the faithful), "we prepare ourselves feverishly for the general strike." In Vilnius, during a meeting authorised by the governor, "some shot the immense portrait of the Emperor that was there, and some smashed it with chairs"; An hour later, it was on the governor in person that one drew— here it was, the frenzy of 1905! But in Gomel, for example, the Social Democrats could not agree with the Bund and "they acted in disorder"; as for the social revolutionists, they "joined" the Zionist Socialists; and then "bombs are thrown at the Cossacks, who retaliate by shooting and knocking on all those who fall under their hand, without distinction of nationality,"[1269]—a very pretty revolutionary outburst! They were rubbing their hands!

It is not surprising that "in many places... we could observe well-to-do and religious Jews actively fighting the revolution. They worked with the police to track down Jewish revolutionaries, to break up demonstrations, strikes, and so on." Not that it was pleasing to them to find themselves on the side of power.

But, not having detached themselves from God, they refused to witness the *destruction* of life. Still less did they accept the revolutionary law: they venerated *their* Law. While in Bialystok and other places the young revolutionaries assimilated the "Union of the Jews" to the "Black Hundreds" because of its religious orientation.[1270]

According to Dimanstein, the situation after the general strike in October could be summarised as follows: "The Bund, the ZS and other Jewish workers' parties called for insurrection," but "there a certain weariness could be perceived."[1271] Later, like the Bolsheviks, the Bund boycotted early in the 1906[1272] the elections to the first Duma, still caressing the hopes of a revolutionary explosion. This expectation having been disappointed, it resigned itself to bring its positions closer to those of the Mensheviks; in 1907, at the fifth Congress of the RSDLP, of the 305 deputies, 55 were members of the Bund. And it even became a "supporter of extreme Yiddishism."[1273]

It is in this amped atmosphere, very uncertain for the power in place, that Witte persuaded Nicholas II to promulgate the Manifesto of 17 October 1905.

[1269] *Ibidem*, pp. 167-168.
[1270] *Ibidem*, pp. 173-175.
[1271] *Ibidem*, pp. 177-178.
[1272] JE, t. 5, pp. 99, 100.
[1273] SJE, t. 1, p. 560.

(More exactly, Witte wanted to publish it in the form of a simple government press release, but it is Nicholas II himself who insisted that the promulgation of the Manifesto, made in the name of the tsar, should assume a solemn character: he thought he would thus touch the hearts of his subjects.) A. D. Obolensky, who drew up the initial draft, reported that among the three main points of the Manifesto there was a special one devoted to the rights and freedoms of the Jews—but Witte (doubtlessly at the pressing request of the Emperor) modified its formulation by addressing in a general way the respect for individuals and the liberty of conscience, expression, and assembly."[1274] The question of the equal rights of the Jews was therefore no longer mentioned. "It was only in the speech published at the same time than the Manifesto... that Witte spoke of the need to "equalise all Russian subjects before the law irrespective of their confession and nationality."[1275]

But: we must make concessions only at the right time and in a position of strength—and this was no longer the case. Liberal and revolutionary opinion laughed at the Manifesto, seeing it only as a capitulation, and rejected it. The Emperor, like Witte, was deeply affected, but also certain representatives of the Jewish intelligentsia: "For what the best of the Russians had been waiting for decades was finally realised... In fact, the Emperor willingly surrendered the autocratic regime and pledged to hand over the legislative power to the representatives of the people... One would have thought that this change would fill everyone with joy"—but the news was welcomed with the same revolutionary intransigence: the struggle continues![1276] In the streets, the national flag, the portraits of the Emperor and the coat of arms of the State were torn off.

The account of Witte's interview with the Petersburg press on 18 October, following the promulgation of the Manifesto, is rich in information. Witte obviously expected manifestations of gratitude and relied on the friendly support of the press to calm the spirits, he even openly solicited it. He obtained only scathing replies, first from the director of the *Stock Exchange News*, S. M. Propper, then from Notovitch, Khodski, Arabajine, and Annensky; all demanded with one voice: proclaim immediately political amnesty! "This requirement is categorical!" General Trepov must be dismissed from his post as governor-general of Saint Petersburg. This is the unanimous decision of the press." *The unanimous decision of the press!* And to withdraw the Cossacks and the army from the capital: "We shall not publish any more newspapers as long as the troops are there!" The army

---

[1274] Manifest 17 oktiabria (Dokoumenry) (The Manifesto of 17 October [documents]), Krasnyi arkhiv, 1925, t. 11-12, pp. 73, 89.
[1275] SJE, t. 7, p. 349.
[1276] *Sliosberg*, t. 3, p. 175.

is the *cause* of the disorder... The security of the city must be entrusted to the "popular militia"! (That is to say, to the detachments of revolutionaries, which meant creating in Petersburg the conditions for a butchery, as it would soon be in Odessa, or, in the future, to set up in Petersburg the conditions favourable to the future revolution of February.) And Witte implored: "Let me breathe a little!", "Help me, give me a few weeks!"; he even passed among them, shaking hands with each one.[1277] (For his part, he will remember later: Propper's demands "meant for me that the press had lost its head.") Despite this, the government had intelligence and courage to refuse the establishment of anarchy and nothing serious happened in the capital.

(In his Memoirs, Witte relates that Propper "had arrived in Russia from abroad, a penniless Jew with no mastery of the Russian language... He had made his mark in the press and had become the head of the *Stock Exchange News*, running through the antechambers of influential figures... When I was Minister of Finance, [Propper] begged for official announcements, various advantages, and eventually obtained from me the title of commercial advisor."

However, at this meeting, he formulated, not without a certain insolence, "demands, even declarations" like this one: "We have no confidence in the government."[1278])

In the course of the same month of October, *The Kievian* published an account of an officer returning to Moscow just at that moment, after a year and a half of captivity in Japan, who was initially moved to tears by the generosity of the Emperor's Manifesto, which opened up favourable prospects for the country. At the mere sight of this officer in battle dress, the welcome which the Muscovite crowd received from him was expressed in these terms: "Spook! Suck-up! The tsar's lackey!" During a large meeting in the Theatre Plaza, "the orator called for struggle and destruction"; another speaker began his speech by shouting: "Down with the autocracy!" "His accent betrayed his Jewish origins, but the Russian public listened to him, and no one found anything to reply to him." Nods of agreement met the insults uttered against the tsar and his family; Cossacks, policemen and soldiers, all without exception—no mercy! And all the Muscovite newspapers called for armed struggle."[1279]

In Petersburg, as is well known, a "Soviet of the Workers' Deputies" was formed on 13 October, headed by the incomparable Parvus and Trotsky,

---

[1277] Manifest 17 oktiabria (The Manifesto of 17 October), *op. cit.*, pp. 99-105.
[1278] *Witte*, Memoirs, *op. cit.*, t. 2, pp. 52-54.
[1279] Kievlianin, 1905, no. 305: *Choulguine*, annexes, *op. cit.*, pp. 271-274.

and with the straw man Khroustalëv-Nossarëv as a bonus. This Soviet aimed for the complete annihilation of the government.

The events of October had even greater and more tragic consequences in Kiev and Odessa: two great pogroms against the Jews, which must now be examined. They were the subject of detailed reports of *Senate committees of inquiry*—these were the most rigorous investigative procedures in Imperial Russia, the Senate representing the highest and most authoritative judicial institution and of the greatest independence.

It is Senator Tourau who drafted the report on the Kiev pogrom.[1280] He writes that the causes of this "are related to the troubles that have won the whole of Russia in recent years", and he supports this assertion by a detailed description of what preceded it and the course of the facts themselves.

Let us remind that after the events of 9 January in Saint Petersburg, after months of social unrest, after the infamous defeat against Japan, the imperial government found nothing better to do to calm the minds than to proclaim on the 27th of August, the complete administrative autonomy of the higher education institutions and the territory on which they were located. This measure had no other result than to turn up the revolutionary heat.

It is thus, writes Senator Tourau, that "individuals having nothing to do with the scientific activity of these institutions were free to access them," and they did so "for the purpose of political propaganda." At the University and Polytechnic of Kiev "a series of meetings were organised by the students, to which participated an external audience," and they were called "popular meetings"; a more numerous day-to-day public went there: at the end of September, up to "several thousand people." During these meetings, red flags were displayed, "passionate speeches were given about the deficiencies of the political regime in place, on the necessity of fighting the government"; "funds were raised for the purchase of weapons", "leaflets were distributed and brochures on revolutionary propaganda were sold." In mid-October, "the university as well as the Polytechnic Institute had gradually been transformed into arenas for open and unbridled anti-government propaganda. Revolutionary militants who were, until recently, prosecuted by the authorities for organising clandestine meetings in private places, now felt invulnerable," they "hatched and discussed plans to bring down the existing political system." But even this did not seem sufficient

---

[1280] Vseppodaneïchiï ottchët o proizvedennom senatorom Tourau izsledovanii pritchin besporiadkov, byvehikh v gor. Kicvc (Report of Senator Tourau on the causes of the disorders in the city of Kiev), Materialy k istorii rousskoi kontr-revolutsii, t. 1. Pogromy po olitsialnym dokoumentam, Saint Petersburg, 1908, pp. 203-296.

and the revolutionary action began its expansion: by attracting the "pupils of secondary schools", in other words, high school pupils, and by moving the field of revolutionary activity: (A Jewish student takes the floor to denounce the Kishinev pogrom, immediately leaflets are spread out in the room and cries are heard: "Down with the police! Down with the autocracy!"); in some cases at a meeting of the Society of Art and Literature (windows are broken, "we break chairs and staircase ramps to throw them on peacekeepers"). And there was no authority to prevent this: the universities, autonomous, now had *their own law*.

The description of these events, supported by the statements of more than five hundred witnesses, alternates throughout this report with remarks on the Jews who stand out in the background of this revolutionary crowd. "During the years of the Russian revolution of 1905 1907, the revolutionary activity of the Jews increased considerably". No doubt the novelty of the thing made it seem obvious. "The Jewish youth," the report says, "dominated by numbers both at the 9 September meeting at the Polytechnic Institute and during the occupation of the premises of the Arts and Literary Society"; and, also, on 23 September in the University Hall where "up to 5,000 students and persons outside the university were gathered, with more than 500 women among them." On October 3rd, at the Polytechnic Institute, "nearly 5,000 people gathered... with a Jewish majority of women." The preponderant role of the Jews is mentioned again and again: at the meetings of 5–9 October; at the university meeting on 12 October, in which "participated employees of the railway administration, students, individuals of indeterminate professions" as well as "masses of Jews of both sexes"; on 13 October at the university where "nearly 10,000 people from diverse backgrounds gathered" and speeches were delivered by S-R. and Bund militants. (The *Jewish Encyclopædia* confirms the fact that even beyond Kiev, during demonstrations celebrating new freedoms, "most of the protesters in the Pale of Settlement were Jews." However, it calls "lies" the information according to which, in Ekaterinoslav, "they were collecting silver for the Emperor's coffin in the street," and in Kiev they "lacerated the portraits of the Emperor in the premises of the Municipal Duma."[1281] Yet this last fact is precisely confirmed by the Tourau report.)

In Kiev, in October, the revolutionary movement was gaining momentum. Alexander Schlichter (future Bolshevik leader, specialist in flour requisitions and "Agriculture Commissioner" in Ukraine just before the great organised famine) fomented a south-western railway strike, paralysing the trains to Poltava, Kursk, Voronezh, and Moscow. Threats were made to force the workers of the Kiev mechanical construction factory to go on strike on 12 October. At the university, "exceptional

---

[1281] SJE, t. 6, p. 567.

collections 'for armaments' took place: the participants threw gold coins, bank notes, silverware, a lady even offered her earrings." "Flying detachments" were formed with the mission of interrupting by force the work in high schools, the factories, the transports, the commerce, and to "prepare the armed resistance to the forces of order." The whole movement "had to take to the streets." On the 14th of October, the newspapers ceased to appear, with the exception of *The Kievian*, aligned on the right; only the telegrammes relating to the liberation movement were allowed to pass. The "flying detachments" prevented the trams from rolling, breaking their windows (some passengers were wounded). At the first appearance of the agitators everything was closed, everything stopped; the post office closed its doors after a bomb threat; streams of students and pupils were converging towards the university at the call of Schlichter, as well as "young Jews of various professions".

It was then that the authorities took the first steps. It was forbidden to meet in the streets and in public squares, and the cordoning off by the army of the university and the Polytechnic took place in order for only the students to be allowed in, "arrest... of a few individuals for contempt of the police and the army", of some S.-R. and Social Democrats, of the lawyer Ratner, who "had actively participated in popular meetings" (Schlichter, him, had taken off). The trams began to circulate again, the shops re-opened their doors, and in Kiev the days of 16 and 17 October went by peacefully.

It was in this context (which was that of many other places in Russia) that the Emperor, relying on the gratitude of the population, launched on 17 October the Manifesto establishing the liberties and a parliamentary system of government. The news reached Kiev by telegram on the night of the 18th, and in the morning the text of the Manifesto was sold or distributed in the streets of the city (as for the newspaper *The Kievian*, "Jewish student youth rushed to buy it and immediately tear it ostensibly into pieces"). The authorities ordered *ipso facto* the release of both those who had been arrested in the last days and those who had previously been "charged with assault on the security of the State", with the exception, however, of those who had used explosives. Both the police and the army had deserted the streets, "important rallies" were formed, at first calmly. "In the vicinity of the university there was a large crowd of students, high school pupils and "a significant number of young Jews of both sexes".

Giving way to their demands, the rector "had the portal of the main building opened." Immediately "the great hall was invaded by a part of the crowd which destroyed the portraits of the Emperor, tore up the red hangings" to make flags and banners, and some "noisily invited the public to kneel before Schlichter by virtue of victim of arbitrariness." If "those who were near him actually fell on their knees," another part of the public "considered that all that had just taken place was offensive to their national sentiments." Then the crowd went to the Municipal Duma, and at its head Schlichter pranced around on a horse, displaying a red band, and at every halt harangued the crowd, claiming that "the struggle against the government was not over." Meanwhile, in the Nicholas Park, "the Jews had thrown a rope around the statue of the Emperor [Nicholas I] and tried to overthrow it from its pedestal"; "At another place, Jews wearing red bands began to insult four soldiers who passed by, spitting on them"; the crowd threw stones on a patrol of soldiers, wounded six, and two demonstrators were hit by the firing of a riposte. However, the interim mayor was visited by a group of peaceful citizens who "asked for the opening of the meeting room of the municipal council" so that the grateful protesters could "express their feelings about the Manifesto. Their request was met" and a peaceful rally was held "under the presidency of the municipal councillor Scheftel." But a new wave, many thousands of people wearing red badges and ribbons, flocked in; "it was made up of students, people of different social classes, age, sex and condition, but the Jews were especially noted for it"; one party burst into the meeting room, the others occupied the square in front of the Duma. "In a moment all the national flags which had decorated the Duma on the occasion of the Manifesto were torn out and replaced by red and black banners. At that moment a new procession approached, carrying at arm's length the lawyer Ratner who had just gotten out of prison; he called the crowd to release all the other prisoners; on the balcony of the Duma, Schlichter publicly embraced him. For his part, the latter "exhorted the population to go on a general strike... and pronounced insulting words addressed to the person of the Sovereign. In the meantime, the crowd had torn the Emperor's portraits hung in the assembly hall of the Duma, and broken the emblems of imperial power which had been placed on the balcony for the festivities." "There is no doubt that these acts were perpetrated by both Russians and Jews"; a "Russian worker" had even begun to break the crown, some demanded that it should be put back in its place, "but a few moments later it was again thrown to the ground, this time by a Jew who then broke in half of the letter 'N'"; "Another young man, Jewish in appearance," then attacked the jewels of the diadem. All the furniture of the Duma was shattered, the administrative documents torn. Schlichter directed the operations: in the corridors, "money was collected for unknown purposes". Excitement in front of the Duma, however, only increased; perched on the roof of stationary trams, orators delivered fiery speeches; but it was Ratner and Schlichter who were the most successful from the balcony of the Duma. "An apprentice of Jewish nationality began shouting from the balcony: 'Down with the autocracy!'; another Jew, properly dressed: 'Same to the swine!'"; "Another Jew, who had cut the tsar's head from the picture, reproducing him, introduced his own by the orifice thus formed, and began to yell at the balcony: 'I am the tsar!'"; "the building of the Duma passed completely into the hands of revolutionary socialist extremists as well as the Jewish youth who had sympathised with them, losing all control of itself."

I dare say that something stupid and evil has revealed itself in this frantic jubilation: the inability to remain within certain limits. What, then, prompted these Jews, in the midst of the delirious plebs, to trample so brutally what the people still venerated? Aware of the precarious situation of their people and their families, on 18 and 19 October they could not, in dozens of cities, refrain from embarking in such events with such passion, to the point of becoming its soul and sometimes its main actors?

Let us continue reading the Tourau report: "Respect for the national sentiment and the symbols venerated by the people was forgotten. As if a part of the population... did not shy away from any means of expressing its contempt..."; "the indignities carried out to the portraits of the Emperor excited an immense popular emotion. Cries came from the crowd gathered in front of the Duma: 'Who has dethroned the tsar?', others wept." "Without being a prophet, one could foresee that such offences would not be forgiven to the Jews," "voices rose to express astonishment at the inaction of the authorities; here and there, in the crowd... they began to shout: 'We must break some kikes!'" Near the Duma, the police and an infantry company stood idly by. At that moment, a squadron of dragoons appeared briefly, greeted by shots from the windows and the balcony of the Duma; they began to bombard the infantry company with stones and bottles, to blast it from all sides: the Duma, the Stock Exchange, the crowd of demonstrators. Several soldiers were wounded; the captain gave orders to open fire. There were seven dead and one hundred and thirty wounded. The crowd dispersed. But on the evening of the 18th of October, "the news of the degradations committed on the Emperor's portraits, the crown, the emblems of the monarchy, the national flag, circled the city, and spread into the suburbs. Small groups of passers-by, mostly workers, craftsmen, merchants, who commented on the events with animation put the full responsibility for them on the Jews, who always stood out clearly from the other demonstrators." "In the Podol district, the workers' crowd decided to seize all the 'democrats'... who had fomented the disturbances and placed them in a state of arrest 'pending the orders of His Majesty the Emperor'." In the evening, "a first group of demonstrators gathered in the Alexander Plaza, brandishing the portrait of the Emperor and singing the national anthem. The crowd grew rapidly and, as many Jews returned from the Krechtchatik with red insignia in the buttonhole, they were taken for the perpetrators of the disorders perpetrated in the Duma and became the target of aggressions; some were beaten." This was already the beginning of the pogrom against the Jews.

Now, to understand both the unpardonable inaction of the authorities during the sacking of the Duma and the destruction of the national emblems, but also their even more unpardonable inaction during the pogrom itself, one has to take a look at what was happening *within* the organs of power. At first glance, one might think it was the result of a combination of circumstances. But their accumulation has been such in Kiev (as well as in other places) that one cannot fail to discern the mismanagement of the imperial administration of the last years, the consequences of which were fatal.

As for the governor of Kiev, he was simply absent. Vice-Governor Rafalski had just taken office, had not had time to find his bearings, and lacked confidence in the exercise of *temporary* responsibilities. Above him, Governor General Kleigels, who had authority over a vast region, had, from the beginning of October, taken steps to be released from his duties—for health reasons. (His real motivations remain unknown, and it is not excluded that his decision was dictated by the bubbling revolution of September, which he did not know how to control.) In any case, he, too, considered himself as *temporary*, while in October the directives of the Ministry of the Interior continued to rain on him—10 October: take the most energetic measures "to prevent disorder in the street and to put an end to it by all means in case they occur"; 12: "repress street demonstrations, do not hesitate to use armed force"; 13: "do not tolerate any rally or gathering in the streets and, if necessary, disperse them by force". On 14 October, as we have seen, the unrest in Kiev has crossed a dangerous limit.

Kleigels brought together his close collaborators, including the Kiev chief of police, Colonel Tsikhotski, and the deputy head of security (again, the leader was absent), Kouliabka, a man as agitated as he was ineffective, the very one who, by stupidity, was about to expose Stolypin to the blows of his assassin.[1282]

From the panicked report of the latter stemmed the possibility not only of demonstrations of armed people in the streets of Kiev, but also of an armed insurrection. Kleigels, therefore, renounced reliance on the police, put in place the provisions for "recourse to the armed forces to assist the civil authorities"—and, on 14 October, handed over "his full powers to the military command", more precisely to the commander—on a *temporary* basis once again (the commander himself is absent, but it must be said that the situation is anything but worrying!)—from the Kiev military region, the general Karass. The responsibility for security in the city was entrusted to General Drake. (Is it not comical enough: which of the surnames that have just been enumerated makes it possible to suppose that the action is

---

[1282] See *infra*, Chapter 10.

taking place in Russia?) General Karass "found himself in a particularly difficult situation" insofar as he did not know the "data of the situation nor of the staff of the administration and of the police"; "By giving him his powers, General Kleigels did not consider it necessary to facilitate the work of his successor; he confined himself to respecting forms, and at once ceased to deal with anything."

It is now time to talk about the chief of police, Tsikhotski. As early as 1902, an administrative inspection had revealed that he concealed the practice of extortion of the Jews in exchange for the right of residence. It was also discovered that he lived "above his means", that he had bought—as well as for his son-in-law—properties worth 100,000 rubles. It was considered that he should be brought to justice when Kleigels was appointed Governor-General; very quickly (and, of course, not without having received a large bribe), the latter intervened so that Tsikhotski was kept at his post and even obtained a promotion and the title of general. Regarding the promotion, it did not work, but there were no penalties either, although General Trepov had been working towards this end from Petersburg. Tsikhotski was informed at the beginning of October that Kleigels had asked to leave his post at the end of the month—his morale fell even lower, he saw himself already condemned. And on the night of the 18th of October, at the same time as the Imperial Manifesto, the official confirmation of the retirement of Kleigels came from Saint Petersburg.

Tsikhotski now had nothing to lose. (Another detail: even though the situation was so troubled, Kleigels left his post *even before* the arrival of his successor, who was none other than the pearl of the Imperial administration, General Sukhomlinov, the future Minister of Defence who scuttled the preparations for the war against Germany; as for the functions of Governor-General, they were *temporarily* assumed by the aforesaid General Karass.) And it was thus that "there was no rapid termination of the confusion that had settled within the police after the handing over of power to the army, but that it only increased to manifest itself with the greatest acuity during the disorders."

The fact that Kleigels had "renounced his 'full powers'… and that these had been handed over for an indefinite period to the military authorities of the city of Kiev is mainly at the origin of the uncertain mutual relations which later established themselves between civil authorities and military authorities"; "the extent and limits of the powers [of the army] were not known to anybody" and this vagueness "lead to a general disorganisation of services."

This manifested itself from the beginning of the pogrom against the Jews. "Many police officers were convinced that the power had been fully handed over to the military command and that only the army was competent to act and to repress the disorders"; that is why they "did not feel concerned by the disorders which took place in their presence. As for the army, referring to an article of the provisions on the use of the armed forces to assist the civil authorities, it was awaiting indications from the police, considering with reason that it was not its responsibility to fulfil the missions of the latter": these provisions "stipulated precisely" that the civil authorities "present at the scene of the disorders should guide the joint action of the police and the army with a view to their repression." It was also up to the civil authorities to determine when to use force. Moreover, "Kleigels had not considered it useful to inform the military command about the situation in the city, nor had he told it what he knew about the revolutionary movement in Kiev. And this is what made units of the army begin to scour the city aimlessly."

So, the pogrom against the Jews began in the evening of 18 October. "At its initial stage, the pogrom undoubtedly assumed the character of retaliation against the offence to national sentiment. The assaults against the Jews passed in the street, the destruction of shops and the merchandise they contained were accompanied by words such as: 'Here it is, your liberty! Here it is, your Constitution and your revolution! This, this is for the portraits of the tsar and the crown!'" The next morning, 19 October, a large crowd came from the Duma to the Cathedral of Saint Sophia, bearing the empty frames of the Tsar's portraits and the broken emblems of the imperial power. It stopped at the university to have the damaged portraits restored; a mass was celebrated and "the Metropolitan Flavian exhorted the people not to indulge in excesses and return home". "But while the people who formed the heart of the patriotic demonstration... maintained an exemplary order, individuals who joined them along the way allowed themselves to be subjected to all kinds of violence against the Jewish passers-by, as well as high school pupils or students in uniform." They were then joined by "the workers, the homeless of the flea market, the bums"; "groups of rioters sacked the houses and shops of the Jews, threw into the street their goods and merchandise, which were partly destroyed on the spot, partly plundered"; "the servants, the guardians of buildings, the little shopkeepers apparently saw nothing wrong with taking advantage of the property of others"; "others, on the contrary, remained isolated to all interested goals until the last day of the disorders," "they tore from the hands of their companions the objects that they had stolen and, without paying attention to their value, destroyed them on the spot." The rioters did not touch the shops of the Karaites nor the "houses where they were presented portraits of the Emperor." "But, on the whole, only a few hours after it had begun, the pogrom took the form of a pitiless rampage. On the 18th, it continued long into the night, then stopped on its own, to resume on the morning of the 19th, and to cease only on the evening of the 20th.

(There were no fires, except one in the Podol district.) On the 19th, "luxury shops belonging to Jews were sacked as far as the city centre on the Krechtchatik. The heavy metal curtains and the locks were forced after half an hour of hard work"; "Expensive textiles, velvet cloths were thrown into the street and spread out in the mud, in the rain, like rags of no value. In front of the shop of the jeweller Markisch, on the Krechtchatik, the pavement was littered with precious objects"—and the same for fashion shops, the dry goods stores; the pavement was fraught with account books, invoices. In Lipki (the chic neighbourhood) "the private mansions of Jews were sacked,—that of Baron Ginzburg, of Halperine, of Alexander and Leon Brodksy, of Landau, and many more. All the luxurious decoration of these houses was destroyed, the furniture broken and thrown into the street"; likewise, "a model secondary school for the Jews, the Brodsky school, was ravaged," "there was nothing left of the marble staircases and the wrought iron ramps." In all, it was "nearly fifteen hundred apartments and commercial premises belonging to Jews were plundered." Starting from the fact that "nearly two-thirds of the city's trade was in the hands of Jews," Tourau assessed losses—including the richest mansions—to "several million rubles." It had been planned to ransack not only Jewish houses, but also those of prominent liberal personalities. On the 19th, Bishop Plato "led a procession through the streets of Podol where the pogrom had been particularly violent, urging the people to put an end to the abuses.

Imploring the crowd to spare the lives and property of the Jews, the bishop knelt several times before it... A broken man came out of the crowd and shouted threateningly: 'You too, you're for the Jews?'"

We have already seen the carelessness that prevailed among the authorities. "General Drake did not take appropriate measures to ensure the proper organisation of security." The troops "should not have been scattered in small detachments," "there were too many patrols," and "the men often stayed idle."

And here we are: "What struck everyone during the pogrom was the obvious inaction, close to complacency, which was shown by both the army and the police. The latter was virtually absent, and the troops moved slowly, merely replying to the shots fired from certain houses, while on either side of the street the shops and apartments of the Jews were sacked with impunity." A prosecutor asked a patrol of Cossacks to intervene to protect stores that were looted nearby; "the Cossacks replied that they would not go, that it was not their sector."

More serious still: a whole series of witnesses had "the impression that the police and the army had been dispatched not to disperse the breakers but to protect them." Here the soldiers declared that they had "been ordered to ensure that there were no clashes and that the Russians were not attacked." Elsewhere they said that if they had "taken an oath to God and to the tsar," it was not to protect "those who had lacerated and jeered at the portraits of the tsar." As for the officers, "they considered themselves powerless to prevent disorders, and felt themselves entitled to use force only in cases where the violence was directed against their men." Example: of a house "ran out a Jew covered with blood, pursued by the crowd. An infantry company was right there, but it paid no attention to what was going on and quietly went up the street." Elsewhere, "the plunderers were massacring two Jews with table legs; a detachment of cavalry stationed ten paces away contemplated placidly the scene." It is not surprising that the man in the street could have understood things like this: "The tsar graciously granted us the right to beat the kikes for six days"; and the soldiers: "You see, is all this conceivable without the approval of the authorities?" For their part, the police officers, "when they were demanded to put an end to the disorders, objected that they could do nothing to the extent that the full powers had been transferred to the military command." But there was also a large crowd of thugs that took flight "due to a police commissioner who brandished his revolver, assisted by only one peacekeeper", and "police officer Ostromenski, with three patrolmen and some soldiers, succeeded in preventing acts of looting in his neighbourhood without even resorting to force."

The looters did not have firearms, while the young Jews, they, had some. However, unlike what happened in Gomel, here the Jews had not organised their self-defence, even though "shots were fired from many houses" by members of self-defence groups who included in their ranks "both Jews and Russians who had taken their part"; "It is undeniable that in some cases these shots were directed against the troops and constituted acts of retaliation for the shots fired on the crowd during the demonstrations" of the previous days; "Sometimes Jews fired on the patriotic parades organised in response to the revolutionary demonstrations that had taken place before." But these shots "had deplorable consequences. Without producing any effect on the rioters, they gave the troops a pretext to apply their instructions to the letter"; "as soon as shots came from a house, the troops who were there, without even inquiring whether they were directed against them or against the rioters, sent a salvo into its windows, after which the crowd" rushed in and ransacked it. "We saw cases where we were firing at a house solely because someone had claimed that shots had gone"; "it also happened that the looters climbed the stairs of a house and fired shots towards the street to provoke the troops' retaliation" and then engage in plundering.

And things got worse. "Some of the policemen and soldiers did not disdain the goods thrown into the street by the vandals, picked them up and hid them in their pockets or under their hoods." And, although these cases "were exceptional and punctual", one still saw a police officer dismantling the door of a shop himself, and a corporal imitating him. (The false rumours of looting by the army began to circulate when General Evert ordered in his area to confiscate goods taken by the looters and stolen goods and to transport them to the warehouses of the army for subsequent restitution to their owners on presentation of a receipt, thus saving property worth several tens of thousands of rubles.)

It is hardly surprising that this scoundrel of Tsikhotski, seeing his career broken, not only did not take any action concerning the action of the police (having learned of the beginning of the pogrom on the evening of the 18th, he did not communicate by telegram any information to the neighbourhood police stations before late in the evening on the 19th), not only did he not transmit any information to the generals of military security, but he himself, passing through the city, had "considered what was going on with calm and indifference", contenting himself to say to the plunderers: "Move along, gentlemen" (and those few, encouraged one another: "Do not be afraid, he's joking!"); and when, from the balcony of the Duma, they began to shout: "Pound the kikes, plunder, break!" And the crowd then carried the chief of police in triumph, the latter "addressed greetings in response to the cheering of the demonstrators." It was not until the 20th, after General Karass had sent him a severe warning (as to the Director of the Governor-General's Chancery, he declared that Tsikhovsky would not escape the penal colony), that he ordered the police to take all measures to put an end to the pogrom. Senator Tourau effectively had to bring him to justice.

Another security official, disgruntled with his career, General Bessonov, "was in the midst of the crowd of rioters and was peacefully parleying with them: 'We have the right to demolish, but it is not right to steal.' The crowd shouted: 'Hurray!'" At another moment he behaved "as an indifferent witness to the plunder. And when one of the breakers shouted: 'Slam the kikes!'

[Bessonov] reacted with an approving laugh." He reportedly told a doctor that "if he had wanted to, he could have put an end to the pogrom in half an hour, but the Jews' participation in the revolutionary movement had been too great, they had to pay the price." After the pogrom, summoned by the military authorities to explain himself, he denied having spoken favourably of the pogrom and declared, on the contrary, to have exhorted people to return to calm: "Have mercy on us, do not force the troops to use their weapons… to shed Russian blood, our own blood!"

Delegations went one after the other to General Karass, some requesting that some of them take troops out of the city, others for the use of force, and others for taking measures to protect their property. However, throughout the day of the 19th, the police did nothing and the military executed orders badly.

On 20 October, Karass ordered "to encircle and apprehend the hooligans." Many arrests were made; once, the army opened fire on the rioters, killing five and wounding several others. By the evening of the 20th, the pogrom was definitely over, but late in the evening "the rumour that the Jews murdered Russians sowed dismay among the population"; retaliation was feared.

During the pogrom, according to police estimates (but a number of victims were taken by the crowd), there were a total of 47 deaths, including 12 Jews, and 205 wounded, one-third of them Jews.

Tourau concludes his report by explaining that "the root cause of the Kiev pogrom lies in the traditional enmity between the population of Little Russia and the Jewish population, motivated by differences of opinion. As for its immediate cause, it resides in the outrage of national sentiment caused by the revolutionary manifestations to which the Jewish youth had taken an active part." The working class "imputed to the Jews only" the responsibility for the "blasphemies uttered against what was most sacred to them. They could not understand, after the grace granted by the Emperor, the very existence of the revolutionary movement, and explained it by the desire of the Jews to obtain 'their own liberties'." "The flip side of the war in which Jewish youth had always openly expressed its deepest satisfaction, its refusal to fulfil its military obligations, its participation in the revolutionary movement, acts of violence and the killings of agents of the State, its insulting attitude towards the armed forces... all this incontestably provoked exasperation towards the Jews among the working class," and "this is why in Kiev there have been several cases where many Russians gave open shelter to unfortunate Jews who fled from the violence, but categorically refused Jewish youth."

As for the newspaper *The Kievian*, it wrote[1283]: "Poor Jews! Where is the fault of these thousands of families? ... For their misfortune, these poor Jews could not control their brainless youngsters... But brainless youngsters, there are also some among us, the Russians, and we could not control them either!"

The revolutionary youth scoured the countryside, but it was the peaceful adult Jews who had to pay the piper. Thus, on both sides, we have dug a

---

[1283] Kievlianin, 1905, nos. 290, 297, 311, 317, 358, in *Choulguine*, annexes, *op. cit.*, pp. 286-302.

bottomless abyss. As for the Odessa pogrom, we have a similar and equally detailed report, that of Senator Kozminski.[1284]

In Odessa, where a lively revolutionary sentiment had always existed, the tremors had started since January; the blast took place on the 13th of June (independently, therefore, of the arrival of the *Potemkin* battleship in the harbour of Odessa on the 14th). The entire day of the 14th of June passed in turmoil, especially among the young, but this time also among the workers, whose "numerous crowds began to impose by force the cessation of work in plants and factories." A crowd "of about three hundred people attempted to break into a [tea] parlour... Several shots were fired at the head of the local police station, who was preventing the crowd from entering, but the latter was dispersed" by a salvo shot by a detachment of policemen. "However, the crowd soon re-formed," and proceeded to the police station; some shots were fired from the Doks house: "from the windows and the balcony, several shots were fired at the police officers." Another group "erected a barricade with building materials in the street, and then began shooting at a police detachment." In another street, a crowd of the same kind "overturned several tramway wagons with horses". "A fairly large group of Jews broke into a tin factory, threw tobacco in the eyes [of a police officer]..., scattered at the appearance of a police detachment while opening fire with revolvers; among them four Jews [their names follow] were arrested on the spot"; at a crossroads, "a gathering of Jews was formed, [two of them] fired revolver shots at a mounted guard"; "in general, throughout the day of 14 June, almost all the streets of the city were the scene of clashes between Jews and the security forces, during which they used firearms and projectiles," wounding several police officers. "A dozen Jews were also wounded," which the crowd took to hide them. As he tried to escape, a certain Tsipkine threw a bomb, causing his own death as well as that of police officer Pavlovski.

It was at this time that the *Potemkin* entered the Odessa harbour! A crowd of nearly five thousand people assembled, "many men and women gave speeches calling the people for an uprising against the government"; among the students who got aboard the battleship were Konstantin Feldman (who urged to support the movement in town by cannonading it, but "the majority of the crew opposed it").

[1284] Vseppodanischi ottehel senatora Kuzminskovo o pritchinakh bezporiadkov, proiskhodivehikh v r. Odcssc v oktiabre 1905 g., Io poriadke deïstvi m mestnykh vlaslei (Report by Senator Kouzminski on the causes of the disorders in the city of Odessa in October 1905 and on the actions carried out by the local authorities), Kievskii i odcsskii pogromy v ottehetakh senatorov Tourau i Kouzminskovo. SPb., Letopissets, (1907), pp. 111-220.

And the authorities in all this? The governor of Odessa—in other words, the head of the police—Neudhart, was already completely distraught on the day of the arrival of the *Potemkin*; he felt (as in Kiev) that "the civil authorities were unable to restore order, and that is why he had handed over all subsequent decisions aimed at the cessation of disorder to the military command, that is to say, the commander of the Odessa garrison, General Kakhanov. (Did there exist a superior authority to that one in Odessa? Yes, of course, and it was Governor General Karangozov, who, as the reader will have guessed, was acting on a *temporary* basis, and felt hardly at ease.) General Kakhanov found nothing better than to have the port sealed by the army and to enclose the thousands of "unsafe elements" who had gathered there to cut them off—not yet contaminated—from the city.

On 15 June, the uprising in Odessa and the *Potemkin* mutiny collapsed into one movement: the inhabitants of the city, "among whom many students and workers" boarded the battleship, exhorting "the crew to common actions". The crowd in the harbour rushed to "plunder the goods that were stored there", beginning with the boxes of wine; then stormed the warehouses to which it set fire (more than 8 million rubles of losses). The fire threatened the quarantine port where foreign vessels were anchored and import goods were stored.

Kakhanov still could not resolve to put an end to the disorder by force, fearing that the *Potemkin* would reply by bombarding the city. The situation remained equally explosive on the 15th. The next day the *Potemkin* drew five salvos on the town, three of them blank, and called on the commander of the armed forces to board the ship to demand the withdrawal "of the troops from the city and the release of all political prisoners." On the same day, 16 June, at the funeral of the only sailor killed, "scarcely had the procession entered the town than it was joined by all kinds of individuals who soon formed a crowd of several thousand persons, principally young Jews," and on the grave an orator, "after shouting 'Down with the autocracy!', called on his comrades to act with more determination, without fear of the police."

But that very day, and for a long time, the state of siege was proclaimed in the city. The *Potemkin* had to take off to escape the squadron that had come to capture it. And although the four days it had been anchored in the port Odessa "and the many contacts which had been established between the people and it substantially raised the morale of the revolutionaries" and "gave rise to the hope of a possible future support of the armed forces", despite of that the summer was going to end calmly, perhaps even no upset would have occurred in Odessa if, on the 27th of August, had been promulgated the incomparable law on the autonomy of higher education institutions! Immediately, "a 'soviet coalition' was formed by the students," which, "by its determination and audacity, succeeded in bringing under its influence not only the student community but also the teaching force" (professors feared "unpleasant confrontations with the students, such as the boycott of classes, the expulsion of such and such professor from the amphi, etc.").

Large gatherings took place at the university, "fund-raising to arm the workers and the proletariat, for the military insurrection, for the purchase of weapons with a view to forming militias and self-defence groups", "discussions were held about the course of action to be taken at the time of the insurrection."

At these meetings the "faculty of professors" took an active part, "sometimes with the rector Zantchevski at its head," who promised to "make available to the students all the means at their disposal to facilitate their participation in the liberation movement."

On 17 September, the first meeting at the university took place "in the presence of an outside public so numerous that it had to be split into two groups"; The S.-R. Teper "and two Jewish students made speeches calling on the public to lead the struggle to free the country from political oppression and a deleterious autocracy." On 30 September, the state of siege was lifted in Odessa and henceforth rushed to these meetings "students of all educational establishments, some of whom were not more than fourteen years old"; the Jews "were the principal orators, calling for open insurrection and armed struggle."

On 12 and 13 October, before all other *secondary* schools, "the pupils of two business schools, that of the Emperor Nicholas I and that of Feig, ceased to attend classes, being the most sensitive to revolutionary propaganda"; on the 14th, it was decided to halt the work in all the other secondary schools, and business schools and the students went to all the high schools of the city to force the pupils to go on course strikes. The rumour went around that in front of the Berezina high school, three students and three high school students had been wounded with swords by police officers. Certainly, "the investigation would establish with certainty that none of the young people had been affected and that the pupils had not yet had time to leave the school." But this kind of incident, what a boon to raise the revolutionary pressure! On the same day, the courses ceased at the university, forty-eight hours after the start of the school year; the striking students burst into the municipal Duma shouting: "Death to Neudhart!" and demanding that they stop paying salaries to the police.

After the episode of the *Potemkin*, Neudhart had regained power in his hands, but until the middle of October he did not make any measure against the revolutionary meetings—besides, could he do very much when the autonomy of universities had been established? On the 15th he received orders from the Ministry of the Interior to prohibit the entrance of outsiders to the university, and on the following day he surrounded the latter by the army, while ordering the cartridges to be taken out from the armouries, until then sold over-the-counter. "The closure of the university to the outside world provoked great agitation among Jewish students and Jewish youth," an immense crowd set out, closing the shops on its way (the American armoury was plundered), overturning streetcars and omnibuses, sawing trees to make barricades, cutting off telegraph and telephone wires for the same purpose, dismantling the gates of the parks. Neudhart asked Kakhanov to have the town occupied by the troops.

Then, "the barricades behind which the demonstrators had gathered—mostly Jews, among them women and adolescents—, they began to fire on the troops; shots were fired from the roofs of houses, balconies, and windows"; the army opened fire in its turn, the demonstrators were scattered and the barricades dismantled. "It is impossible to accurately estimate the number of deaths and injuries that occurred on that day, as the health team—consisting mainly of Jewish students in red-white blouses with a red cross—hurried to take the wounded and the dead to the university infirmary"—thus in an autonomous and inaccessible zone—, "at the Jewish hospital or at the emergency stations near the barricades, as well as in almost all pharmacies." (They had stopped delivering medicine even before the events.) According to the governor of the city, there were nine deaths, nearly 80 wounded, including some policemen.

"Among the participants in the disorders were apprehended that day 214 people, of whom 197 Jews, a large number of women, and 13 children aged 12 to 14 years." And all this, still twenty-four hours before the incendiary effect of the Manifesto was felt.

One might think that by exposing the role of the Jews so frequently in revolutionary movements, the Senate's report was biased. But it must be borne in mind that in Odessa the Jews represented one-third of the population, and, as we have seen, a very significant proportion of the student population; it must also be borne in mind that the Jews had taken an active part in the Russian revolutionary movement, especially in the Pale of Settlement. In addition, Senator Kouzminski's report provides evidence of its objectivity in many places.

On 16 October, "when they arrived at the police station, the people arrested were victims of assault by the police and soldiers"; however, "neither the governor of the city nor the police officials responded in due course… and no investigation was carried out"; it was not until later that more than twenty of those who had been in this precinct declared that "those arrested had been systematically beaten; first they were pushed down a staircase leading to the basement... many of them fell to the ground and it was then that policemen and soldiers, arranged in a row, beat them with the back of their sabres, rubber truncheons, or simply their feet and fists"; the women were not spared. (It is true that, on the same evening, municipal councillors and justices of the peace went to the scene and gathered complaints from the victims. As for the senator, he identified several culprits during his inquiry in November and had them brought to justice.)

"On the 17th of October, the whole town was occupied by the army, patrols were criss-crossing the streets, and public order was not troubled all day.

However, the Municipal Duma had met to discuss emergency measures, including how to replace the state police with an urban militia. On the same day, the Bund's local committee decided to organise a solemn funeral for the victims who had fallen the day before on the barricades, but Neudhart, understanding that such a demonstration would cause, as always, a new revolutionary explosion, "gave the order to remove in secret, of the Jewish hospital" where they were, the five corpses and "to bury them before the scheduled date", which was done on the night of 18. (The next day the organisers demanded that the corpses be unearthed and brought back to the hospital. Due to the developments of events, the bodies were embalmed there and remained in that state for a long time.) And it was at this time that the news of the Imperial Manifesto spread, pushing Odessa towards new storms.

Let us quote first of all the testimony of members of a Jewish self-defence detachment: "During the pogrom, there was a certain coordination centre that worked quite well... Universities played an enormous role in the preparation of the events of October... the soviet coalition of the Odessa University included" a Bolshevik, a Menshevik, an S.-R., a representative of the Bund, Zionist Socialists, the Armenian communities, Georgian and Polish ones as well.

"Student detachments were formed even before the pogrom"; during "immense meetings at the university", money was collected to buy weapons, "of course not only to defend ourselves, but with a view to a possible insurrection." "The soviet coalition also raised funds to arm the students"; "when the pogrom broke out, there were two hundred revolvers at the university," and "a professor...

procured another hundred and fifty others." A "dictator" was appointed at the head of each detachment "without taking into account his political stance", and "it happened that a detachment composed mainly of members of the Bund was commanded by a Zionist-Socialist, or vice versa"; "on Wednesday [19 October], a large quantity of weapons were distributed in a pro-Zionist synagogue"; "the detachments were made up of Jewish and

Russian students, Jewish workers, young Jews of all parties, and a very small number of Russian workers."[1285]

A few years later, Jabotinsky wrote that during the pogroms of the year 1905 "the new Jewish soul had already reached its maturity."[1286] And in the still rose-tinted atmosphere of the February Revolution, a major Russian newspaper gave the following description: "When, during the Neudhart pogroms in 1905, the young militiamen of self-defence travelled through Odessa, weapons in their fists, they aroused emotion and admiration, we were heavy-hearted, we were touched and full of compassion..."[1287]

And this is what one of our contemporaries wrote: "The courage shown by Gomel's fighters inflames tens of thousands of hearts. In Kiev, 1,500 people are engaged in self-defence detachments, in Odessa several thousands."[1288] But in Odessa, the number of combatants as well as their state of mind—and, in response, the brutality of the police forces—gave a much different turn to events than they had experienced in Kiev.

Let us go back to the Kuzminski report. After the proclamation of the Manifesto, on the morning of the 18th, General Kaoulbars, commanding the military district of Odessa, in order "to give the population the possibility of enjoying without restrictions the freedom in all its forms granted by the Manifesto," ordered the troops not to appear in the streets, "so as not to disturb the joyous humour of the population." However, "this joyous mood did not last." On all sides "groups of Jews and students began to flock towards the city centre," brandishing red flags and shouting: "Down with the autocracy!", while speakers called for revolution. On the façade of the Duma, two of the words forming the inscription in metal letters "God save the Tsar" were broken; the Council Chamber was invaded, "a large portrait of His Majesty the Emperor was torn to shreds," the national flag which floated on the Duma was replaced by a red flag. The headdresses of three ecclesiastics, who were in a cab at a funeral, were stolen; later, the funeral procession they conducted was repeatedly stopped, "religious songs interrupted by cheers." "There was a headless scarecrow bearing the inscription 'Here is the Autocracy', and a dead cat was showed off while collecting money 'to demolish the tsar' or 'for Nicholas's death'." "The young people, especially the Jews, who were obviously aware of their superiority, taught the Russians that their freedom had not been freely granted to them, that it had been torn from the government by the Jews...

[1285] Odesskii pogrom i samooborona (The Odessa pogrom and self-defence), Paris, Zapadnyi Tsentralnyi Komitet Samooborony Poalei Zion, 1906, pp. 50-52.
[1286] V. *Jabotinsky*, Vvedenic (Preface), in K. N. Bialik. Pesni i poemy, *op. cit.*, p. 44.
[1287] D. *Aizman*, Iskouchenie (Temptation), Rousskaïa volia, 29 April 1917, pp. 2-3.
[1288] *Praisman,* in "22", *op. cit.,* p. 179.

They declared openly to the Russians: 'Now we are going to govern you'," but also:

"We have given you God, we will give you a tsar." A large crowd of Jews waving red flags long pursued two peacekeepers, one of them managed to escape by the roofs, while on the other, a man named Goubiy, the crowd "armed with revolvers, axes, stakes, and iron bars, found him in an attic, and hurt him so badly that he died during his transport to the hospital; the concierge of the building found two of his fingers cut by axe." Later, three police officers were beaten and wounded, and the revolvers of five peacekeepers were confiscated.

The prisoners were then freed in one, two, and three police stations (where on the 16th there had been beatings, but the detainees had already been released on the orders of Neudhart; in one of these precincts, the liberation of the prisoners was negotiated in exchange for Goubiy's corpse; sometimes there was nobody behind bars. As for the rector of the university, he actively participated in all this, transmitting to the prosecutor the demands of "a crowd of five thousand people", while "the students went so far as to threaten to hang the police officers". Neudhart solicited the advice of the mayor of the city, Kryjanovsky, and a professor at the university, Shtchepkin, but they only demanded that he "disarm the police on the spot and make it invisible," otherwise, added Shchepkin, "the victims of popular revenge cannot be saved, and the police will be legitimately disarmed by force." (Interrogated later by the senator, he denied having spoken so violently, but one can doubt his sincerity in view of the fact that on the same day he had distributed 150 revolvers to the students and that, during the inquiry, he refused to say where he had procured them.) After this interview, Neudhart ordered (without even warning the chief of police) to withdraw all the peacekeepers "in such a way that from that moment the whole of the city was deprived of any visible police presence"—which could have been understood if the measure had been intended to protect the life of the agents, but at the same time, the streets had been deserted by the army, which, for the moment, was pure stupidity. (But we remember that in Petersburg this was precisely what the press owners demanded from Witte, and it had been difficult for him to resist them.)

"After the police left, two types of armed groups appeared: the student militia and the Jewish self-defence detachments. The first was set up by the 'soviet coalition' which had procured arms." Now, "the municipal militia, made up of armed students and other individuals, placed themselves on guard" instead of policemen. This was done with the assent of General Baron Kaulbars and the governor of the city, Neudhart, while the police chief, Golovin, offered his resignation in protest and was replaced by his deputy, von Hobsberg. A provisional committee was set up at the Municipal Duma; in one of his first statements, he expressed his gratitude to the students of the university "for their way of ensuring the security of the city with energy, intelligence, and devotion".

The committee itself assumed rather vague functions. (During the month of November the press took an interest in one of the members of this committee, also a member of the Duma of the Empire, O. I. Pergament, and in the second Duma somebody had to recall that he proclaimed himself President "of the Republic of the Danube and the Black Sea," or "President of the Republic of South Russia,"[1289] in the intoxication of those days, this was not unlikely.) And what could happen after the streets had been deserted, during these feverish days, by both the army and the police, and that the power had passed into the hands of an inexperienced student militia and groups of self-defence?

"The militia arrested persons who seemed suspicious to it and sent them to the university for examination"; here a student "walked at the head of a group of Jews of about sixty persons who fired revolver shots at random"; "the student militia and Jewish self-defence groups themselves perpetrated acts of violence directed against the army and peaceful elements of the Russian population, using firearms and killing innocent people."

The confrontation "was inevitable, given the crystallisation of two antagonistic camps among the population." On the evening of the 18th, "a crowd of demonstrators waving red flags, and composed predominantly of Jews, tried to impose a stoppage of work at the factory at Guen... The workers refused to comply with this demand; after which the same crowd, crossing Russian workmen in the street, demanded that they should uncover themselves before the red flags. As the latter refused,"—well here it is, the proletariat!—from the crowd "shots were fired; the workers, though unarmed, succeeded in dispersing it," and pursued it until it was joined by another crowd of armed Jews, up to a thousand people, who began to fire on the workmen...; four of them were killed. This is how "brawls and armed clashes between Russians and Jews were unleashed at various points in the city; Russian workers and individuals without any definite occupation, also known as *hooligans*, began to chase the Jews and to beat them up, and then move on with the rampage and destruction of houses, apartments and shops belonging to Jews." It was then that a police commissioner called "an infantry company which put an end to the clashes."

[1289] Gossudarstvennaya Duma—Vtoroy Sozyv (The Duma of Elai—second convocation), Slenogralitcheskiï ollchel, p. 2033.

On the following day, 19 October, "towards 10, 11 in the morning, there were seen forming in the streets... crowds of Russian workers and persons of various professions carrying icons, portraits of His Majesty the Emperor, as well as the national flag, and singing religious hymns. These patriotic demonstrations composed exclusively of Russians were formed simultaneously at several locations in the city, but their starting point was in the port from where set off a first manifestation of workmen, especially numerous." There exists "reasons to assert that the anger provoked by the offensive attitude of the Jews over the whole of the previous day, their arrogance and their contempt for the national sentiment shared by the Russian population had to, in one way or another, lead to a reaction of protest." Neudhart was not ignorant of the fact that a demonstration was being prepared and he authorised it, and it passed under the windows of the commander of the military district and the governor of the city, and then proceeded to the cathedral. "As it went on, the crowd was swollen by the addition of passers-by, including a large number of hooligans, tramps, women and adolescents." (But it is appropriate here to draw a parallel between the story of a member of the Poalei Zion: "The pogrom of Odessa was not the work of hooligans... During these days the police did not allow entrance to the city to the tramps of the port,"; "it was the small artisans and the small merchants who gave free rein to their exasperation, the workers and apprentices of various workshops, plants, or factories", "Russian workers lacking political consciousness"; "I went to Odessa only to see a pogrom organised by provocation, but, alas, I did not find it!" And he explains it as hatred between nationalities.[1290])

"Not far from the Cathedral Square..., several shots were fired towards the crowd of protesters, one of them killed a little boy who was carrying an icon"; "the infantry company who arrived on the spot was also greeted by gunfire."

They fired from the windows of the editorial office of the newspaper *Yuzhnoye Obozrenie,* and "during the entire route of the procession gunshots came from windows, balconies, roofs"; "moreover, explosive devices were launched in several places on the demonstrators", "six people were killed" by one of them; in the centre of Odessa, "at the corner of Deribassov and Richelieu, three bombs were thrown on a squadron of Cossacks." "There were many deaths and wounded among the demonstrators," "not without reason the Russians blamed the Jews, and it is why shouts merged quickly from the crowd: 'Beat up the kikes!', 'Death to the heebs!',", and "at various points in the city the crowd rushed to the Jewish shops to plunder them"; "these isolated acts were rapidly transformed into a generalised pogrom: all the shops, houses and

---

[1290] Odesskiï pogrom... (The pogrom of Odessa), Poalei Zion. pp. 64–65.

apartments of the Jews on the path of the demonstration were completely devastated, all their property destroyed, and what had escaped the vandals was stolen by the cohorts of hooligans and beggars who had followed the lead of the protesters"; "it was not uncommon for scenes of looting to unfold under the eyes of demonstrators carrying icons and singing religious hymns." On the evening of the 19th, "the hatred of the antagonist camps reached its peak: each one hit and tortured mercilessly, sometimes with exceptional cruelty, and without distinction of sex or age, those who fell into their hands." According to the testimony of a doctor at the university clinic, "hooligans threw children from the first or second floor onto the road; one of them grabbed a child by the feet and smashed his skull against the wall. For their part, the Jews did not spare the Russians, killing those they could at the first opportunity; during the day they did not show themselves in the streets, but fired on the passers-by from the doors, from the windows, etc., but in the evening they met in numerous groups," going as far as "besieging police stations." "The Jews were particularly cruel with police officers when they managed to catch them." (Here is now the point of view of the Poalei Zion: "The press spread a legend that self-defence had taken a huge crowd of hooligans and locked them up in the university premises. Numbers in the order of 800 to 900 individuals were cited; it is in fact necessary to divide this number by ten. It was only at the beginning of the pogrom that the vandals were brought to the university, after which things took a completely different turn."[1291] There are also descriptions of the Odessa pogrom in the November 1905 issues of the newspaper *The Kievian*.[1292])

And what about the police, in all this? In accordance with Neudhart's stupid dispositions, "on 19 October... as on the following days, the police were totally absent from the streets of Odessa": a few patrols, and only occasionally.

"The vagueness that reigned in the relations between civil authorities and military authorities, which ran counter to the legal provisions," had the consequence that "the police officers did not have a very clear idea of their obligations"; even more, "all the police officers, considering that the responsibility for the political upheavals was incumbent on the Jews" and that "these were revolutionaries, felt the greatest sympathy for the pogrom which was unfolding before their eyes and judged even superfluous to conceal themselves." Worse: "In many cases, police officers themselves incited hooligans to ransack and loot Jewish houses, apartments, and shops"; and at the height of it: "in civilian clothes, without their insignia", they themselves "took part in these rampages," "directed the crowd," and

---

[1291] *Ibidem*, p. 53.
[1292] The Kievlianin, 14 Nov. 1905, in *Choulguine*, annexes, *op. cit.*, pp. 303-308.

there were even "cases where police officers fired on the ground or in the air to make the military believe that these shots came from the windows of houses belonging to Jews."

And it was the police who did that! Senator Kouzminski brought to trial forty-two policemen, twenty-three of whom were officers.

And the army—"scattered over the immense territory of the city" and supposed to "act autonomously"? "The military also did not pay any attention to the pogroms, since they were not aware of their exact obligations and were not given any indication by the police officers", they "did not know against whom or according to what order they should use armed force; on the other hand, the soldiers could assume that the pogrom had been organised with the approval of the police." Consequently, "the army took no action against the vandals." Worse still, "there is evidence that soldiers and Cossacks also took part in the looting of shops and houses." "Some witnesses affirmed that soldiers and Cossacks massacred innocent people for no reason."

Again, these are innocent people who have paid for others.

"On 20 and 21 October, far from subsiding, the pogrom gained frightening momentum"; "the plunder and destruction of Jewish property, the acts of violence and the killings were openly perpetrated, and with complete impunity, day and night." (Point of view of the Poalei Zion: on the evening of the 20th, "the university was closed by the army" while "inside it, we had barricaded ourselves in the event of an assault by the troops. Detachments of self-defence no longer went into town." In the latter, on the other hand, "self-defence had organised itself spontaneously", "powerful detachments of townspeople", "equipped with weapons of opportunity: hatchets, cutlasses, limes", "defended themselves with determination and anger equal to those they were victims of, and succeeded in protecting their perimeter almost completely."[1293]

On the 20th, a group of municipal councillors headed by the new mayor (the former Kryjanovsky, who noted his powerlessness in the face of what was happening in the university, where even weapons were being gathered, and had resigned on the 18th) went to General Kaulbars, "urging him to take all the power in his hands to the extent that the military command… alone is capable of saving the city." The latter explained to them that "before the declaration of the state of siege, the military command had no right to interfere in the decisions of the civil administration and had no other obligation" than to assist it when it requested it. "Not to mention that the firing of the troops and the bombs thrown at them made it extremely

---

[1293] Odesskiï pogrom… (The pogrom of Odessa), Poalei Zion, pp. 53–54.

difficult to restore order." He finally agreed to intervene.—On the 21st of October he gave orders to take the most energetic measures against the buildings from which shots were fired and bombs were thrown. On the 22nd: "order to take down on the spot all those who guilty of attacks on buildings, businesses or persons." As early as the 21st, calm began to return to different parts of the city; from the 22nd, "the police ensured the surveillance of the streets" with the reinforcement of the army; "the streetcars began to circulate again and in the evening, one could consider that the order was restored in the city."

The number of victims was difficult to define and varies from one source to another. The Kuzminski report states that "according to information provided by the police, the number of people killed amounts to more than 500 persons, including more than 400 Jews; as to the number of injuries recorded by the police, it is 289..., of which 237 Jews. According to the data collected from the cemetery guardians, 86 funerals were celebrated in the Christian cemetery, 298 in the Jewish cemetery." In the hospitals were admitted "608 wounded, including 392 Jews." (However, many had to be those who refrained from going to hospitals, fearing that they would later be prosecuted.)—The *Jewish Encyclopædia* reports 400 deaths among the Jews.[1294]—According to the Poalei Zion: based on the list published by the rabbinate of Odessa, "302 Jews were killed, including 55 members of self-defence detachments, as well as 15 Christians who were members of these same detachments"; "among the other deaths, 45 could not be identified; 179 men and 23 women were identified."

"Many deaths among the vandals; no one counted them, nor cared to know their number; in any event, it is said that there were not less than a hundred."[1295] As for the Soviet work already quoted, it did not hesitate to put forward the following figures: "more than 500 dead and 900 wounded among the Jews."[1296]

One should also mention, by way of illustration, the hot reactions of the foreign press. In the *Berliner Tageblatt*, even before the 21st of October, one could read: "Thousands and thousands of Jews are massacred in the south of Russia; more than a thousand Jewish girls and children were raped and strangled."[1297]

On the other hand, it is without exaggeration that Kuzmininski summarises the events: "By its magnitude and its violence, this pogrom surpassed all those who preceded it."—He considers that the main person in charge is

---

[1294] SJE, t. 6, p. 122.
[1295] Odesskiï pogrom... (Le pogrom d'Odessa), Poalei Zion, pp. 63-64.
[1296] *Dimanstein*, in "1905", t. 3, v. 1, p. 172.
[1297] *Choutguine*, Annexes, p. 292.

the governor of the city, Neudhart. The latter made an "unworthy concession" by yielding to Professor Chtchepkin's demands, by withdrawing the police from the city and handing it over to a student militia that did not yet exist. On the 18th, "he did not take any measure... to disperse the revolutionary crowd that had gathered in the streets", he tolerated that power would go to "the ramifications of Jews and revolutionaries" (did he not understand that reprisals in the form of a pogrom would follow?). His negligence could have been explained if he had handed power over to the army, but that did not happen "during the entire period of the troubles." This did not, however, prevent him from broadcasting during the events fairly ambiguous statements and later, during the investigation, to lie to try to justify himself. Having established "the evidence of criminal acts committed in the exercise of his functions," Senator Kouzminski had Neudhart brought to justice.

With respect to the military command, the senator had no power to do so.

But he indicates that it was criminal on behalf of Kaulbars to yield on 18 October to the demands of the Municipal Duma and to withdraw the army from the streets of the city. On the 21st, Kaulbars also uses equivocal arguments in addressing the police officers gathered at the governor's house: "Let us call things by name. It must be acknowledged that in our heart we all approve of this pogrom. But, in the exercise of our functions, we must not let the persecution we may feel for the Jews transpire. It is our duty to maintain order and to prevent pogroms and murders."

The senator concluded his report by stating that "the troubles and disorders of October were provoked by causes of undeniably revolutionary character and found their culmination in an anti-Jewish pogrom solely because it was precisely the representatives of that nationality which had taken a preponderant part in the revolutionary movement." But could we not add that it is also due to the long-standing laxity of the authorities over the excesses of which the revolutionaries were guilty?

But as "the conviction that the events of October were the sole cause of Neudhart's actions...", "his provocations", immediately after the end of the disorders "several commissions were formed in Odessa, including the University, the Municipal Duma and the Council of the Bar Association"; they were actively engaged in collecting documents proving that "the pogrom was the result of a provocation." But after examining the evidence, the senator "discovered... no evidence" and the investigation "did not reveal any facts demonstrating the participation of even a single police officer to the organisation of the patriotic manifestation." The senator's report also highlights other aspects of the year 1905 and the general era.

On 21 October, "as rumours spread throughout the city that bombs were being made and weapons were being stored in large quantities within the university compound," the military district commander proposed to have the buildings inspected by a Committee composed of officers and professors. The rector told him that "such an intrusion would violate the autonomy of the university". Since the day it was proclaimed in August, the university was run by a commission composed of "twelve professors of extremist orientation".

(Shchepkin, for example, declared at a meeting on October 7th: "When the hour strikes and you knock on our door, we will join you on your *Potemkin!*"), But this commission itself was made under the control of the student "soviet coalition" who dictated its orders to the rector. After the rejection of Kaulbars' request, the "inspection" was carried out by a commission composed of professors and three municipal councillors, and, of course, "nothing suspicious" was discovered.—"Facts of the same nature were also be observed in the Municipal Duma. There, it was the municipal employees who manifested claims to exercise influence and authority"; their committee presented to the Duma, composed of elected representatives, demands "of an essentially political character"; on the 17th, the day of the Manifesto, they concocted a resolution: "At last the Autocracy has fallen into the precipice!"—as the senator writes, "it is not excluded that at the outset of the troubles there might have been inclinations to take the whole of power."

(After that, it was the revolutionary wave of December, the comminatory tone of the Soviet of Workers' Deputies—"we demand" the general strike—the interruption of electric lighting in Odessa, the paralysis of commerce, transport, the activity of the port, bombs were flying again, "the destruction in sets of the new patriotic-oriented newspaper *Rousskaïa retch*[1298], "the collection [under threat] of money to finance the revolution", the cohorts of disaffected high school students and the population frightened "under the yoke of the revolutionary movement.")

This spirit of 1905 (the spirit of the whole "liberation movement"), which had manifested itself so violently in Odessa, also broke out in these "constitutional days"[1299] in many other cities of Russia; both in and outside the Pale of Settlement, the pogroms "broke out everywhere... on the very day when was received the news of the Proclamation" from the Manifesto.

Within the Pale of Settlement, pogroms were held in Kremenchug, Chemigov, Vinnitsa, Kishinev, Balta, Ekaterinoslav, Elizabethgrad, Oman, and many other towns and villages; the property of the Jews was most often

---

[1298] "The Russian Word"
[1299] Because of the proclamation of the Manifesto modifying the Russian regime.

destroyed but not looted. "Where the police and the army took energetic measures, the pogroms remained very limited and lasted only a short time. Thus at Kamenets-Podolsk, thanks to the effective and rapid action of the police and the army, all attempts to provoke a pogrom were stifled in the bud." "In Chersonese and Nikolayev, the pogrom was stopped from the beginning."[1300]

(And, in a south-western town, the pogrom did not take place for the good reason that adult Jews administered a punishment to the young people who had organised an anti-government demonstration after the proclamation of the Imperial Manifesto of 17 October."[1301])

Where, in the Pale of Settlement, there was no single pogrom, it was in the northwest region where the Jews were most numerous, and it might have seemed incomprehensible if the pogroms had been organised by the authorities and "generally proceeded according to the same scenario."[1302]

"Twenty-four pogroms took place outside the Pale of Settlement, but they were directed against all the progressive elements of society,"[1303] and not exclusively against the Jews—this circumstance puts in evidence what pushed people to organise pogroms: the shock effect provoked by the Manifesto and a spontaneous impulse to defend the throne against those who wanted to put down the tsar. Pogroms of this type broke out in Rostov-on-the-Don, Tula, Kursk, Kaluga, Voronezh, Riazan, Yaroslav, Viazma, Simferopol, "the Tatars participated actively in the pogroms at Kazan and Feodossia."[1304] In Tver, the building of the Council of the Zemstvo was sacked; at Tomsk the crowd set fire to the theatre where a meeting of the Left took place; two hundred persons perished in the disaster! In Saratov, there were disturbances, but no casualties (the local governor was none other than Stolypin[1305]).

On the nature of all these pogroms and the number of their victims, the opinions diverge strongly according to the authors. The estimates that are made today are sometimes very fanciful. For example, in a 1987 publication: "in the course of the pogroms we count a thousand killed and tens of thousands of wounded and maimed"—and, as echoed by the press

---

[1300] Report of Senator Kouzminski, pp. 176–178.
[1301] Report of Senator Tourau, p. 262.
[1302] SJE, t. 6, p. 566.
[1303] *Ibidem*.
[1304] JE, t. 12, pp. 620-622.
[1305] *I. L. Teitel,* Iz moiii jizni za 40 let (Memories of 40 years of my life), Paris, 1925, pp. 184-186.

at the time: "Thousands of women were raped, very often under the eyes of their mothers and children."[1306]

Conversely, G. Sliosberg, a contemporary of the events and with all the information, wrote: "Fortunately, these hundreds of pogroms did not bring about significant violence on the person of the Jews, and in the overwhelming majority of cases the pogroms were not accompanied by murders."[1307] As for the women and the elderly, the rebuttal comes from the Bolshevik fighter Dimanstein, who declared with pride: "Jews who were killed or wounded were for the most part some of the best elements of self-defence, they were young and combative and preferred to die rather than surrender."[1308]

As for the origins of the pogroms, the Jewish community and then the Russian public opinion in 1881 were under the tenacious hold of a hypnosis: undoubtedly and undeniably, the pogroms were manipulated by the government!

Petersburg guided by the Police Department! After the events of 1905, the whole press also presented things as such. And Sliosberg himself, in the midst of this hypnosis, abounds in this sense: "For three days, the wave of pogroms has swept over the Pale of Settlement [we have just seen that this area was not touched in full and that, conversely, other regions of Russia were—A. S.], and according to a perfectly identical scenario, were planned in advance."[1309]

And this strange absence, in so many, many authors, if only one would attempt to explain things differently! (Many years later, I. Frumkin acknowledged at least: the pogroms of 1905 were "not only anti-Jewish, but also counter-revolutionary."[1310] And no one even asks the question: and if the root causes were the same and should be sought in political events, the state of mind of the population? Are not the same concerns expressed in this way? Let us recall that the crowd had here and there demonstrated against the strikers before the proclamation of the Manifesto. Let us also recall that a general strike of the railways took place in October and that the communications had been interrupted throughout the country—and, in spite of this, so many pogroms broke out at the same time? It should also be noted that the authorities ordered investigations in a whole series of towns and that sanctions were imposed on police officers convicted of breaches of duty. Let us recall that during the same period the peasants

---

[1306] *Praisman*, in "22", 1986/87, no. 51, p. 183.
[1307] *Sliosberg*, t. 3, p. 180.
[1308] *Dimanstein*, t. 3, p.172.
[1309] *Sliosberg*, t. 3, p. 177.
[1310] *Frumkin*, BJWR-1, p. 71.

organised pogroms against the landowners all over the place, and that they all proceeded in the same way. Without doubt, we are not going to say that these pogroms were also contrived by the Police Department and that they did not reflect the same uneasiness among all the peasants.

It seems that one proof—only one—of the existence of a scheme exists, but it does not point in the direction of power either. The Minister of the Interior R. N. Dournovo discovered in 1906 that an official in charge of special missions, M. S. Komissarov, had used the premises of the Police Department to secretly print leaflets calling for the fight against Jews and revolutionaries.[1311] It should be emphasised, however, that this was not an initiative of the Department, but a conspiracy by an adventurer, a former gendarmerie officer, who was subsequently entrusted with "special missions" by the Bolsheviks, to the Cheka, to the GPU, and was sent to the Balkans to infiltrate what remained of the Wrangel army[1312].

The falsified versions of events have nonetheless solidly embedded themselves in consciences, especially in the distant regions of the West, where Russia has always been perceived through a thick fog, while anti-Russian propaganda was heard distinctly. Lenin had every interest in inventing the fable according to which tsarism "endeavoured to direct against the Jews the hatred which the workers and peasants, overwhelmed by misery, devoted to the nobles and capitalists"; and his henchman, Lourie-Larine, tried to explain this by class struggle: only the rich Jews would have been targeted—whereas the facts prove the contrary: it was precisely they who enjoyed the protection of the police.[1313]

But, even today, it is everywhere the same version of the facts—let us take the example of the *Encyclopædia Judaica*: "From the beginning, these pogroms were *inspired* by government circles. The local authorities received *instruction* to give freedom of action to the thugs and to protect them against Jewish detachments of self-defence."[1314] Let us take again the *Jewish Encyclopædia* published in Israel in the Russian language: "By *organising* the pogroms, the Russian authorities sought to…"; "the government *wanted* to physically eliminate as many Jews as possible"[1315] [emphasis in italics added everywhere by me—A. S.]. All these events, therefore, would not have been the effect of the criminal laxity of the local

---

[1311] Retch, 1906, 5 May.
[1312] One of the main components of the White Army.
[1313] *I. Larme,* Ievrei i antisemitizm v SSSR (The Jews and Anti-Semitism in the USSR), M.-L. 1929, pp. 36, 292.
[1314] Encyclopædia Judaica, vol. 13, p. 698.
[1315] SJE, t. 6, p. 568.

authorities, but the fruit of a machination carefully guarded by the central government?

However, Leo Tolstoy himself, who at the time was particularly upset with the government and did not miss an opportunity to speak ill of it, said at the time: "I do not believe that the police push the people [to the pogroms]. This has been said for Kishinev as well as for Baku... It is the brutal manifestation of the popular will... The people see the violence of the revolutionary youth and resist it."[1316]

At the tribune of the Duma, Chulguine proposed an explanation similar to that of Tolstoy: "The posse justice is very widespread in Russia as in other countries... What happens in America is rich in lessons regarding this...: posse justice is called lynching... But what has recently happened in Russia is even more terrible—it is the form of posse justice called pogrom! When the power went on strike, when the most inadmissible attacks on the national sentiment and the most sacred values for the people remained completely unpunished, then, under the influence of an unreasoned anger, it began to do justice to itself.

It goes without saying that in such circumstances the people are incapable of differentiating between the guilty and the innocent and, in any case, what has happened to us—it has rejected all the fault on the Jews. Of these, few guilty have suffered, for they have been clever enough to escape abroad; it is the innocent who have massively paid for them."[1317] (Cadet leader F. Rodichev, for his part, had the following formula: "Anti-Semitism is the patriotism of disoriented people"—let us say: where there are Jews.)

The tsar had been too weak to defend his power by the law, and the government proved its pusillanimity; then the petty *bourgeois*, the petty traders and even the workers, those of the railways, the factories, the very people who had organised the general strike, revolted, stood up in a spontaneous way to defend their most sacred values, wounded by the contortions of those who denigrated them. Uncontrollable, abandoned, desperate, this mass gave free rein to its rage in the barbaric violence of the pogroms.

And in the case of a contemporary Jewish writer who is also lacking in sagacity when he persists in asserting that "undoubtedly, tsarist power played a major role in the organisation of anti-Jewish pogroms", we find in a nearby paragraph: "We are absolutely convinced that the Police Department was not sufficiently organised to implement simultaneous

---

[1316] D. P. Makovitsky, 1905-1906 v Iasnoi Poliane (1905 1906 in Yasnaya Poliana), Golos minovehevo. M., 1923, no. 3, p. 26.
[1317] Second Duma, shorthand for the debates, 12 March 1907, p. 376.

pogroms in six hundred and sixty different places that same week." The responsibility for these pogroms "is not solely and not so much for the administration, but rather for the Russian and Ukrainian population in the Pale of Settlement."[1318]

On the latter point, I agree as well. But subject to a reservation, and it is of size: the Jewish youth of this time also carries a heavy share of responsibility in what happened. Here manifested itself a tragic characteristic of the Russian-Ukrainian character (without attempting to distinguish which of the Russians or Ukrainians participated in the pogroms): under the influence of anger, we yield blindly to the need to "blow off some steam" without distinguishing between good and bad; after which, we are not able to take the time—patiently, methodically, for years, if necessary—to repair the damage. The spiritual weakness of our two peoples is revealed in this sudden outburst of vindictive brutality after a long somnolence.

We find the same impotence on the side of the patriots, who hesitate between indifference and semi-approval, unable to make their voice heard clearly and firmly, to guide opinion, to rely on cultural organisations. (Let us note in passing that at the famous meeting at Witte's, there were also representatives of the press of the right, but they did not say a word, they even acquiesced sometimes to Propper's impertinences.)

Another secular sin of the Russian Empire tragically had its effects felt during this period: the Orthodox Church had long since been crushed by the State, deprived of all influence over society, and had no ascendancy over the popular masses (an authority which it had disposed of in ancient Russia and during the time of the Troubles, and which would soon be lacking very much during the civil war!). The highest hierarchs were able to exhort the good Christian people, for months and years, and yet they could not even prevent the crowd from sporting crucifixes and icons at the head of the pogroms.

It was also said that the pogroms of October 1905 had been organised by The Union of the Russian People. This is not true: it did not appear until November 1905, in instinctive reaction to the humiliation felt by the people. Its programme at the time had indeed global anti-Jewish orientations: "The destructive, anti-governmental action of the Jewish masses, solidarity in their hatred for everything Russian and indifferent to the means to be used."[1319]

[1318] *Praisman*, in "22", 1986-87, no. 51, pp. 183, 186, 187.
[1319] Novoie vremia, 1905, 20 Nov. (3 Dec), pp. 2, 3.

In December, its militants called on the Semienovski regiment to crush the armed insurrection in Moscow. Yet the Union of the Russian People, which was ultimately made legendary by rumours and fears, was in reality only a shabby little party lacking in means whose only *raison d'être* was to lend its support to the autocratic monarch, which, early as the spring of 1906, had become a constitutional monarch. As for the government, it felt embarrassed to have support for such a party. So that the latter, strong of its two or three thousand local soviets composed of illiterates and incompetents, found itself in opposition to the government of the constitutional monarchy, and especially to Stolypin.—From the tribune of the Duma, Purishkevich[1320] interrogated in these terms the deputies, "since the appearance of the monarchist organisations, have you seen many pogroms in the Pale of Settlement?... Not one, because the monarchists organisations struggled and struggled against Jewish predominance by economic measures, cultural measures, and not by punches."[1321]—These measures were they so cultural, one might ask, but no pogrom is actually known to have been caused by the Union of the Russian People, and those which preceded were indeed the result of a spontaneous popular explosion.

A few years later, the Union of the Russian People—which, from the start, was merely a masquerade—disappeared in the mist of general indifference. (One can judge of the vagueness that surrounded this party by the astonishing characteristic that is given in the *Jewish Encyclopædia*: the anti-Semitism of the Union of the Russian People "is very characteristic of nobility and great capital"![1322])

There is another mark of infamy, all the more indelible as its outlines are vague: "the Black Hundreds."

Where does that name come from? Difficult to say: according to some, this is how the Poles would have designated out of spite the Russian monks who resisted victoriously the assault of the Trinity Lavra of Saint Sergius in 1608-1609. Through obscure historical channels, it reached the twentieth century and was then used as a very convenient label to stigmatise the popular patriotic movement that had spontaneously formed. It was precisely its character, both imprecise and insulting, that made it a success. (Thus, for example, the four KDs who became emboldened to the point of entering into negotiations with Stolypin were denounced as "KD-Black-Hundreds". In 1909, the *Milestones* Collection was accused of "propagating in a masked form the ideology of the Black Hundreds.") And the "expression" became commonplace for a century, although the Slavic

---

[1320] V. Purishkevich (1870–1920), one of the leaders of the Russian extreme right.
[1321] Stenographic Record of the Third Duma, 1911, p. 3118.
[1322] JE, t. 14, p. 519.

populations, totally dismayed and discouraged, were never counted by hundreds but by millions.

In 1908 1912, the *Jewish Encyclopædia* published in Russia, in its honour, did not interfere in giving a definition of the "Black Hundreds": the Jewish intellectual elite of Russia had in its ranks sufficient minds that were balanced, penetrating, and sensible. But during the same period before the First World War, the *Brockhaus-Efron Encyclopædia* proposed a definition in one of its supplements: "The 'Black Hundreds' has been for a few years the common name given to the dregs of society focused on pogroms against Jews and intellectuals." Further, the article broadens the statement: "This phenomenon is not specifically Russian; it appeared on the stage of history... in different countries and at different times."[1323] And it is true that, in the press after the February revolution, I found the expression "the Swedish Black Hundreds!"...

A wise contemporary Jewish author rightly points out that "the phenomenon which has been designated by the term 'Black Hundreds' has not been sufficiently studied."[1324]

But this kind of scruple is totally foreign to the famous *Encyclopædia Britannica* whose authority extends to the entire planet: "The Black Hundreds or Union of the Russian People or organisation of reactionary and anti-Semitic groups in Russia, constituted during the revolution of 1905. Unofficially encouraged by authorities, the Black Hundreds recruited their troops for the most part from the landowners, the rich peasants, the bureaucrats, the police, and the clergy; they supported the Orthodox Church, autocracy and Russian nationalism. Particularly active between 1906 and 1911..."[1325]

One remains stunned before so much science! And this is what is being read to all cultivated humanity: "recruited their troops for the most part from the landowners, the rich peasants, the bureaucrats, the police, and the clergy!" It was thus those people who smashed the windows of the Jewish shops with their sticks! And they were "particularly active" after 1905... when the calm had returned!

True, in 1905–1907 there were actions against landowners, there were even

more pogroms against the Jews. It was always the same ignorant and brutal crowd that ransacked and looted houses and property, massacring people

---

[1323] Entsiklopcditcheskii slovar, Spb., Brockhaus i Efron. Dopoln, t. 2 (4/d), 1907, p. 869.
[1324] Boris Orlov, Rossia bez evrcev (Russia without the Jews), "22", 1988, no. 60, p. 151.
[1325] Encyclopædia Britannica. 15th ed., 1981, vol. II, p. 62, cl. 2.

(including children), and even cattle; but these massacres never led to condemnation on the part of the progressive intelligentsia, while the deputy in the Duma Herzenstein, in a speech in which he took with passion and reason the defence of small peasant farms, alerting parliamentarians of the danger of an extension of the fires of rural estates, exclaimed: "The illuminations of the month of May last year are not enough for you, when in the region of Saratov one hundred and fifty properties were destroyed practically in a single day?"[1326]

These illuminations were never forgiven. It was, of course, a blunder on his part, from which it should not be inferred that he was glad of such a situation.

Would he have used this word, however, about the pogroms against the Jews of the preceding autumn?

It was not until the Great, the real revolution, that the violence against the noble landlords was heard, they "were no less barbaric and unacceptable than the pogroms against the Jews… There is, however, in the left-wing circles a tendency to consider… as positive the destruction of the old political and social system."[1327]

Yes, there was another frightening similarity between these two forms of pogroms: the sanguinary crowd had the feeling of being *in its right*. The last pogroms against the Jews took place in 1906 in Sedlets, in Poland—which is beyond our scope—and in Bialystok during the summer. (Soon after, the police stifled a pogrom in preparation in Odessa after the dissolution of the first Duma.)

In Bialystok was constituted the most powerful of the anarchist groups in Russia. Here, "important bands of anarchists had made their appearance; they perpetrated terrorist acts against owners, police officers, Cossacks, military personnel."[1328] The memories left by some of them make it possible to represent the atmosphere of the city very clearly in 1905–1906: repeated attacks by the anarchists who had settled in the Street de Souraje, where the police did not dare go any more. "It was very common for policemen on duty to be assassinated in broad daylight; This is why we saw fewer and fewer of them…"

Here is the anarchist Nissel Farber: "he threw a bomb at the police station," wounding two peacekeepers, a secretary, killing "two *bourgeois* who were there by chance," and, lack of luck, perished himself in the explosion. Here is Guelinker (a.k.a. Aron Eline): he also launched a bomb, which seriously

---

[1326] Proceedings of the First Duma, May 19th 1906, p. 524.
[1327] *I. O. Levine*, Evrei v revolutsii (The Jews in the Revolution), RaJ, p. 135.
[1328] *Dimanstein*, t. 3, p. 163.

wounded the deputy of the chief of police, a commissioner, two inspectors and three agents. Here is another anarchist whose bomb "wounds an officer and three soldiers," hurts him as well, in fact, "and, unfortunately, kills a militant of the Bund." Here again it is a commissioner and a peacekeeper who are killed, there are two gendarmes, and again the same "Guelinker kills a concierge."

(Apart from the attacks, the "expropriation of consumer products" was also practised—food had to be eaten.) "The authorities lived in fear of an 'uprising' of the anarchists in the Street de Souraje," the police had taken the habit of "expecting such an uprising for today, tomorrow or the day after tomorrow."

"The majority... of the anarchists... were leaning towards a resolute armed action in order to maintain, as much as possible, an atmosphere of class war."

To this end, terror was also extended to the Jewish "*bourgeois*". The same Farber attacked the head of a workshop, a certain Kagan, "at the exit of the synagogue... he wounded him seriously with a knife in the neck"; another little patron, Lifchitz, suffered the same fate; also "the wealthy Weinreich was attacked in the synagogue," but the revolver was of poor quality and jammed three times." There was a demand for a series of "significant 'gratuitous' actions against the *bourgeois*: "the *bourgeois* must feel himself in danger of death at every moment of his existence." There was even the idea of "disposing all along [the main street of Bialystok] infernal machines to blow up the entire upper class" at once. But "how to transmit the *anarchist* 'message'?" Two currents emerged in Bialystok: the "gratuitous" terrorists and the "communards" who considered terrorism to be a "dull" and mediocre method, but tended towards the armed insurrection "in the name of communism without State": "To invest in the city, to arm the masses, to resist several attacks by the army and then to drive them out of the city," and, "at the same time, to invest in plants, factories and shops." It was in these terms that, "during meetings of fifteen to twenty thousand people, our speakers called for an armed uprising." Alas, "the working masses of Bialystok having withdrawn from the revolutionary vanguard that they themselves had suckled from," it was imperative to "overcome... the passivity of the masses." The anarchists of Bialystok thus prepared an insurrection in 1906. Its course and its consequences are known as the "pogrom of Bialystok".[1329]

It all began with the assassination of the chief of police, which took place precisely in this "Street de Souraje where the Jewish anarchist organisation

---

[1329] Iz istorii anarkhitcheskovo dvijenia v Bialystoka (Aspects of the history of the anarchist movement in Bialystok), Soblazn sotsializma, pp. 417-432.

was concentrated"; then someone shot or threw a bomb on a religious procession.

After that, a commission of inquiry was dispatched by the State Duma, but alas, alas, three times alas, it failed to determine "whether it was a shot or some sort of whistling: witnesses were unable to say." [1330] This, the communist Dimanstein wrote very clearly, twenty years later, that "a firecracker was thrown at an Orthodox procession as a provocation."[1331]

Nor can one exclude the participation of the Bund who, during the "best" months of the 1905 revolution, had burned with a desire to move to armed action, but in vain, and was withering away to the point of having to consider renewing allegiance to the Social democrats. But it is of course the anarchists of Bialystok themselves who manifested themselves with the most brilliance.

Their leader, Judas Grossman-Rochinin, recounted after 1917 what this nest of anarchists was: above all, they were afraid of "yielding to a wait-and-see approach and to common sense". Having failed in organising two or three strikes because of the lack of support from the population, they decided in June 1906 to "take charge of the city" and expropriate the tools of production. "We considered that there was no reason to withdraw from Bialystok without having given a last class struggle, that it would have come down to capitulating in front of a complex problem of a superior type"; if "we do not move to the ultimate stage of the struggle, the masses will lose confidence [in us]." However, men and weapons were lacking to take the city, and Grossman ran to Warsaw to seek help from the armed fraction of the PPS (the Polish Socialists). And there he heard a newsagent shouting: "Bloody pogrom in Bialystok!... thousands of victims!"... Everything became clear: the reaction had preceded us!"[1332]

And it is there, in the passage "to the ultimate stage of the struggle", that is doubtlessly found the explanation for the "pogrom". The revolutionary impetus of the Bialystok anarchists was expressed subsequently. At the trial, in the pleadings of the lawyer Gillerson who "called for the overthrow of the government and the political and social system existing in Russia", and which, for precisely this reason, was himself prosecuted. As for the Duma commission, it considered that "the conditions of a pogrom had also been created by various elements of society who imagined that fighting the Jews was tantamount to fighting the liberation movement."[1333]

[1330] JE, t. 5, pp. 171-172.
[1331] *Dimanslein*, t. 3, p. 180.
[1332] *Grossman-Rochtchine*, Byloïe, 1924, nos. 27-28. pp. 180-182.
[1333] JE, t. 5, pp. 171-174.

But after that "firecracker thrown by the provocation" which the Duma Committee had not been able to detect, what had been the course of events?

According to the commission's findings, "the systematic execution of innocent Jews, including women and children, was carried out under the pretext of repressing the revolutionaries." There were "more than seventy dead and about eighty wounded" among the Jews. Conversely, "the indictment tended to explain the pogrom by the revolutionary activity of the Jews, which had provoked the anger of the rest of the population." The Duma Committee rejected this version of the facts: "There was no racial, religious, or economic antagonism in Bialystok between Jews and Christians."[1334]

And here is what is written today: "This time the pogrom was purely military. The soldiers were transformed into rioters," and chased the revolutionaries. At the same time, these soldiers were said to be afraid of the detachments of Jewish anarchists in the Street de Souraje, because "the war in Japan... had taught [Russian soldiers] to beware of gunshots"—such were the words pronounced in the Municipal Duma by a Jewish councillor.[1335] Against the Jewish detachments of self-defence are given the infantry and the cavalry, but, on the other side, there are bombs and firearms.

In this period of strong social unrest, the Duma committee concluded to a "strafing of the population", but twenty years later, we can read in a Soviet book (in any case, the "old regime" will not come back, will not be able to justify itself, and so we can go ahead!): "They massacred entire families with the use of nails, they pierced their eyes, cut tongues, smashed the skulls of children, etc."[1336] And a luxury book edited abroad, sensationalist book, denunciatory, a richly illustrated folio, printed on coated paper, entitled *The Last Autocrat* (decreeing in advance that Nicholas II would indeed be the "last"), proposed the following version: the pogrom "had been the object of such a staging that it seemed possible to describe the program of the first day in the Berlin newspapers; thus, two hours before the beginning of the Bialystok pogrom, the Berliners could be informed of the event."[1337] (But if something appeared in the Berlin press, was it not merely an echo of Grossman-Rochin's shenanigans?) Moreover, it would have been rather absurd on the part of the Russian government to provoke pogroms against the Jews even as the Russian ministers were lobbying among Western financiers in the hope of obtaining loans. Let us remember

---

[1334] *Ibidem*, pp. 170. 172.
[1335] *Praisman*, pp. 185-186.
[1336] *Dimanstein*, t. 3, p. 180.
[1337] Der Leizte russischc Allcinherrscher, Berlin, Eberhard Frowein Verlag (1913), p. 340.

that Witte had great difficulty in obtaining from the Rothschilds, who were ill-disposed towards Russia because of the situation of the Jews and the pogroms, "as well as other important Jewish establishments,"[1338] with the exception of the Berliner banker Mendelssohn. As early as December 1905, the Russian ambassador to London, Benkendorf, warned his minister: "The Rothschilds are repeating everywhere... That Russia's credit is now at its lowest level, but that it will be restored immediately if the Jewish question is settled."[1339]

At the beginning of 1906, Witte disseminated a government communiqué saying that "finding a radical solution to the Jewish problem is a matter of conscience for the Russian people, and this will be done by the Duma, but even before the Duma unites itself, the most stringent provisions will be repealed insofar as they are no longer justified in the present situation."[1340] He begged the most eminent representatives of the Jewish community of Saint Petersburg to go as a delegation to the tsar, and he promised them the most kind welcome. This proposal was discussed at the Congress of the Union for the Integrality of Rights—and after the fiery speech of I. B. Bak (editor of the *Retch* newspaper) it was decided to reject it and to send a less important delegation to Witte, not to provide answers, but to make accusations: to tell him "clearly and unambiguously" that the wave of pogroms was organised "at the initiative and with the support of the government."[1341]

After two years of revolutionary earthquake, the leaders of the Jewish community in Russia who had taken the upper hand did not for a moment contemplate accepting a progressive settlement regarding the question of equal rights. They felt that they were carried by the wave of victory and had no need to go to the tsar in the position of beggars and loyal subjects. They were proud of the audacity displayed by the Jewish revolutionary youth. (One must position oneself in the context of the time when the old imperial army was believed to be immovable, to perceive the significance of the episode during which, in front of the regiment of Rostov grenadiers standing at attention, his commander, Colonel Simanski, had been *arrested* by a volunteer Jew!) After all, perhaps these revolutionaries had not been guilty of "national treason," as Doubnov had accused them, perhaps they

---

[1338] A. *Popov*, Zaem 1906 g. V Donesseniakh ruskovo posla v Parije (The loan of 1906 through the despatches of the Russian ambassador to Paris), Krasnyy arkhiv, 1925, t. 11/12, p. 432.

[1339] K peregovoram Kokovtseva o zaïme v 1905-1906 gg. (The Kokovtsev Talks for Borrowing), Krasnyy arkhiv, 1925, t. 10, p. 7.

[1340] Perepiska N.A. Romanova i P.A. Solypina (Correspondence between N. A. Romanov and P. A. Stolypin). Krasnyi Arkhiv, 1924, t. 5, p. 106.

[1341] *Sliosberg*, t. 3, pp. 185-188.

were the ones who were in the truth?—After 1905, only the fortunate and prudent Jews were left to doubt it.

What was the record of the year 1905 for the entire Jewish community in Russia? On the one hand, "the revolution of 1905 had overall positive results... it brought to the Jews political equality even when they did not even enjoy civil equality... Never as after the "Liberation Movement" did the Jewish question benefit from a more favourable climate in public opinion."[1342] But, on the other hand, the strong participation of the Jews in the revolution contributed to the fact that they were henceforth all identified with it. At the tribune of the Duma in 1907 V. Chouglin proposed to vote a resolution to find that "... the western half of Russia, from Bessarabia to Warsaw, is full of hatred towards the Jews whom they consider the responsible for all their misfortunes..."[1343]

This is indirectly confirmed by the increase in Jewish emigration from Russia. If, in 1904 1905, there was still an increase in emigration among mature men, the whole age pyramid is concerned from 1906 onwards. The phenomenon is therefore not due to the pogroms of 1881–1882, but indeed those of 1905 1906. From now on, for the United States alone, the number of immigrants rose to 125,000 people in 1905 1906 and to 115,000 in 1906-1907.[1344]

But at the same time, writes B. I. Goldman, "in the short years of agitation, higher education institutions did not rigorously apply the *numerus clausus* to the Jews, a relatively large number of Jewish professional executives, and as they were more skilful than the Russians in placing themselves on the market, without always being distinguished by a great moral rigour in their activity, some began to speak of a "hold of the Jews" on the intellectual professions.[1345]

And "in the 'Project for Universities' prepared in 1906 by the Ministry of Public Instruction, no mention was made to the *numerus clausus*." In 1905 there were 2,247 (9.2%) Jewish students in Russia; in 1906, 3,702 (11.6%); In 1907, 4,266 (12%).[1346]

In the program of reforms announced on August 25th, 1906 by the Government, the latter undertook to re-examine, among the limitations to which the Jews were subjected, those which could be immediately lifted

---

[1342] G. A. *Landau*, Revolutsionnye idei v ievreïskoi obchtchcstvennosti (Revolutionary ideas in Jewish opinion). RaJ, p. 116.
[1343] Stenographic Record of Debates at the Second Duma, 6 March 1907, p. 151.
[1344] JE, t. 2, pp. 235 236; SJE, t. 6, p. 568.
[1345] B. I. *Goldman* (B. Gorev), Icvrci v proizvedcniakh rousskikh pissatelei (The Jews in Russian Literature), Pd. Svobodnoïe slovo, 1917, p. 28.
[1346] SJE, t. 7, p. 348.

"insofar as they merely provoke dissatisfaction and are obviously obsolete."

However, at the same time, the Russian government could no longer be affected by the revolution (which was prolonged for another two years by a wave of terrorism hardly contained by Stolypin) and by the very visible participation of the Jews in this revolution.

To these subjects of discontent was added the humiliating defeat against Japan, and the ruling circles of Saint Petersburg yielded to the temptation of a simplistic explanation: Russia is fundamentally sound, and the whole revolution, from beginning to end, is a dark plot hatched by the Jews, an episode of the Judeo-Masonic plot. Explain everything by one and the same cause: the Jews! Russia would long have been at the zenith of glory and universal power if there were no Jews!

And, clinging to this short but convenient explanation, the high spheres only brought the hour of their fall even closer.

The superstitious belief in the historical force of conspiracies (even if they exist, individual or collective) leaves completely aside the main cause of failures suffered by individuals as well as by states: human weaknesses.

It is our Russian weaknesses that have determined the course of our sad history—the absurdity of the religious schism caused by Nikon[1347], the senseless violence of Peter the Great and the incredible series of counter-shocks that ensued, wasting our strength for causes that are not ours, the inveterate sufficiency of the nobility and bureaucratic petrification throughout the nineteenth century. It is not by the effect of a plot hatched from the outside that we have abandoned our peasants to their misery. It was not a plot that led the great and cruel Petersburg to stifle the sweet Ukrainian culture. It was not because of a conspiracy that four ministries were unable to agree on the assignment of a particular case to one or the other of them, they spent years in exhausting squabbles mobilising all levels of the hierarchy. It is not the result of a plot if our emperors, one after the other, have proved incapable of understanding the evolution of the world and defining the true priorities. If we had preserved the purity and strength, which were formerly infused into us by Saint Sergius of Radonezh, we should not fear any plot in the world.

No, it can not be said in any case that it was the Jews who "organised" the revolutions of 1905 or 1917, just as one cannot say that it was this nation

---

[1347] Patriarch of the Russian Church, who in the seventeenth century wished to impose by force a reform of liturgical texts and ritual, which gave rise to the schism of the "old believers".

as a whole that fomented them. In the same way, it was not the Russians or the Ukrainians, taken together as nations, who organised the pogroms.

It would be easy for us all to take a retrospective look at this revolution and condemn our "renegades." Some were "non-Jewish Jews,"[1348] others were "internationalists, not Russians." But every nation must answer for its members in that it has helped to train them.

On the side of the Jewish revolutionary youth (but also of those who had formed it) as well as those of the Jews who "constituted an important revolutionary force,"[1349] it seems that the wise advice Jeremiah addressed to the Jews deported to Babylon was forgotten: "Seek peace for the city where I have deported you; pray to Yahweh in its favour, for its peace depends on yours." (Jeremiah 29 7.)

While the Jews of Russia, who rallied the revolution, only dreamed of bringing down this same city without thinking of the consequences.

In the long and chaotic human history, the role played by the Jewish people—few but energetic—is undeniable and considerable. This also applies to the history of Russia. But for all of us, this role remains a historical enigma.

For the Jews as well.

This strange mission brought them everything but happiness.

[1348] See, for example, *Paul Johnson*, A History of the Jews, Harper Collins, 1987, p. 448.
[1349] SJE, t. 7, p. 349.

Chapter 10

The Period of the Duma

The Manifesto of 17 October marked the beginning of a qualitatively new period in Russian history, which was later consolidated by a year of Stolypin's government: the period of the Duma or of limited Autocracy, during which the previous principles of government—the absolute power of the tsar, the opacity of the ministries, the immutability of the hierarchy— were rapidly and sensibly restricted. This period was very difficult for all the *higher spheres,* and only men with a solid character and an active temperament could enrol with dignity in the new era. But public opinion also found it difficult to get accustomed to the new electoral practices, to the publicity of the debates in the Duma (and even more to the responsibility of the latter); and, in its left wing, the enraged Leninists as well as the enraged of the Bund simply boycotted the elections to the first Duma: we have nothing to do with your parliaments, we will achieve our ends by bombs, blood, convulsions! And so "the attitude of the Bund towards the Jewish deputies of the Duma was violently hostile."[1350]

But the Jews of Russia, led by the Union for the integrity of rights, were not mistaken and, expressing their sympathy for the new institution, "participated very actively in the elections, voting most often for the representatives of the [Cadet] party who had placed the equality of rights for the Jews on its agenda." Some revolutionaries who had regained their spirits shared the same dispositions. Thus Isaac Gurvitch, who had emigrated in 1889—an active supporter of the Marxist left, was the co-founder of the American Social-Democratic Party—, returned to Russia in 1905, where he was elected to the Duma Electoral College.[1351]—There were no limitations on the Jews in the elections, and twelve of them sat in the first Duma; it was true that most of them came from the Pale of Settlement, while the Jewish leaders of the capital, who did not have the property qualifications, could not be elected: only Winaver, L.

[1350] JE, t. 5, p. 100.
[1351] RJE, t. 1, p. 392.

Bramson[1352], and the converted Jew M. Herzenstein (to whom Prince P. Dolgorukov had given his place).

As the number of Jews in the Duma was significant, the Zionist deputies proposed forming an "independent Jewish group" abiding by "the discipline of a real political party", but the non-Zionist deputies rejected this idea, contenting itself "to meet from time to time to discuss matters of direct concern to Jewish interests," [1353] agreeing however, to comply already to "a genuine discipline in the sense of strictly abiding by the decisions of a college composed of members of the Duma and those of the Committee for the integrality of rights"[1354] (the "Political Bureau").

At the same time a solid alliance was formed between the Jews and the Cadet party. "It was not uncommon for the local chapters of the Union [for the integrality of rights] and the constitutional-democratic party to be composed of the same people."[1355] (Some teased Winaver by calling him the "Mosaic Cadet".) "In the Pale of Settlement, the overwhelming majority of the [Cadet] party members were Jews; in the interior provinces, they represented in number the second nationality... As Witte wrote, 'almost all Jews who graduated from higher education joined the party of People's Freedom [that is, The Cadets]... which promised them immediate access to equal rights.' This party owes much of its influence on the Jews who provided it with both intellectual and material support."[1356] The Jews "introduced coherence and rigour... into the Russian 'Liberation Movement' of 1905."[1357]

However, A. Tyrkova, an important figure in the Cadet party, notes in his memoirs that "the chief founders and leaders of the Cadet party were not Jews.

There were not, among the latter, any personality sufficiently prominent to drive the Russian liberals behind it, as the Jew Disraeli had done for the English Conservatives in the middle of the nineteenth century... The people that mattered most within the Cadet party were Russians. This does not mean that I deny the influence of these Jews who have joined our masses. They could not fail to act upon us, if only by their inexhaustible energy. Their very presence, their activity, did not allow us to forget them, to forget their situation, to forget that they had to be helped." And, further

---

[1352] JE, t. 7, p. 370.
[1353] JE, t. 7, p. 371.
[1354] G. B. Sliosberg, t. 3, p. 200.
[1355] SJE, p. 349.
[1356] *Ibidem*, pp. 398-399.
[1357] V. V. *Choulguine*, "Chto nam v nikh ne nravitsa...", Ob Antisemitism v Rossii ("What we do not like about them..." On anti-Semitism in Russia), Paris, 1929, p. 207.

on: "Reflecting on all these networks of influence of the Jews [within the Cadet party], one cannot overlook the case of Miliukov. From the beginning, he became their favourite, surrounded by a circle of admirers, more precisely feminine admirers... who cradled him in muted melodies, cajoled him, covered him without restraint of praise so excessive that they were comical."[1358]

V. A. Obolensky, also a member of the party, describes a Cadet club during the time of the First Duma at the corner of Sergevskaya and Potmekinskaya streets. The elite of the secularised Jewish society and the elite of the Russian politicised intelligentsia were mingled: "There were always a lot of people, and the public, composed mostly of wealthy Jewish Petersburgers, was very elegant: the ladies wore silk robes, shiny brooches and rings, the gentlemen had the airs of well-nourished and self-satisfied *bourgeois*. Despite our democratic convictions, we were somewhat shocked by the atmosphere that prevailed in this 'Cadet club'. One can imagine the embarrassment experienced by the peasants who came to attend the meetings of our parliamentary group. A 'party of gentlemen', that is what they said to each other when they ceased to attend our meetings."[1359]

At the local level, cooperation between the Union for the integrity of rights and the Cadet Party was manifested not only in the presence of "as many Jewish candidates as possible", but also in the fact that "the local factions of the Union [for the integrity of rights] was instructed to support [non-Jews] who promised to contribute to the emancipation of the Jews."[1360] As explained in 1907 the cadet newspaper Retch, in reply to questions repeatedly asked by other newspapers: "*Retch* has, in its time, formulated very precisely the conditions of the agreement with the Jewish group... The latter has the right to challenge the electoral college and to oppose nominations to the Duma."[1361]

During the parliamentary debates, the Duma, following the logic of the Imperial Manifesto, raised the question of equal rights for Jews within the general framework of granting the same rights to all citizens. "The State Duma has promised to prepare a 'law on the full equalisation of the rights of all citizens and the abrogation of any limitations or privileges associated with membership to a social class, nationality, religion or sex'."[1362] After

---

[1358] *A. Tyrkova-Williams*, Na poutiakh k svobode (The Paths to Freedom), New York, ed. Chekov, 1952, pp. 303-304.
[1359] *V. A. Obolensky*, Moïa jizn. Moi sovremenniki (My life, My contemporaries), Paris, YMCA Press. 1988, p. 335.
[1360] SJE, t. 7, p. 349.
[1361] Retch (The Word), 1907, 7 (19) January, p. 2.
[1362] JE, t. 7, p. 371.

adopting the main guidelines of this law, the Duma lost itself in debates for another month, multiplying "thunderous declarations followed by no effect"[1363], to be ultimately dissolved. And the law on civil equality, especially for the Jews, remained pending.

Like most Cadets, the Jewish deputies of the First Duma signed Vyborg's appeal, which meant that it was now impossible for them to stand for elections; Winaver's career particularly suffered from it. (In the First Duma, he had made violent remarks, although he would later advise the Jews not to put themselves too much in the spotlight to prevent a recurrence of what had happened in the revolution of 1905.)

"The participation of the Jews in the elections of the second Duma was even more marked than during the first election campaign... The Jewish populations of the Pale of Settlement showed the strongest interest in this election. The political debate reached all levels of society." Nevertheless, as the *Jewish Encyclopædia* published before the Revolution indicates, there was also an important anti-Jewish propaganda carried out by right-wing monarchist circles, particularly active in the western provinces; "the peasants were persuaded that all progressive parties were fighting for the equal rights of the Jews to the detriment of the interests of the ethnic population"[1364]; that "behind the masquerade of the popular representation, the country was governed by a Judeo-Masonic union of spoliators of the people and traitors to the fatherland"; that the peasant should be alarmed at the "unprecedented number of new masters unknown to the elders of the village, and whom he henceforth had to nourish with his labour"; that the Constitution "promised to replace the Tatar yoke by that, injurious, of the international *Kahal*." And a list of the existing rights to be abrogated was drawn up: not only were Jews not to be elected to the Duma, but they all had to be relegated to the Pale of Settlement; prohibiting them from selling wheat, grain and timber, working in banks or commercial establishments; confiscating their properties; prohibiting them from changing their names; to serve as publisher or editor of news organisation; to reduce the Pale of Settlement itself by excluding the fertile regions, to not grant land to the Jews within the province of Yakutsk; in general, to regard them as foreigners, to substitute for them military service by a tax, etc. "The result of this anti-Semitic propaganda, spread both orally and in writing, was the collapse of progressive candidates in the second Duma throughout the Pale

---

[1363] V. A. *Maklakov*, 1905-1906 gody (1905-1906)—M. Winaver i ruskaya obchtchestvennost nachala XX veka (M. Winaver and the Russian public opinion at the beginning of the twentieth century), Paris, 1937, p. 94.
[1364] JE, t. 7, p. 372.

of Settlement."[1365] There were only four Jewish deputies in the second Duma (including three Cadets).[1366]

But even before these elections, the government addressed the issue of equal rights for Jews. Six months after taking office as Prime Minister in December 1906, Stolypin had the government adopt a resolution (the so-called "Journal of the Council of Ministers") on the continuation of the lifting of restrictions imposed on Jews, and this in essential areas, thus orienting itself towards integral equality. "They considered to eliminate: the prohibition of Jews from residing in rural areas within the Pale of Settlement; the prohibition of residing in rural areas throughout the Empire for persons enjoying the right of universal residence"; "the prohibition of including Jews in the directory of joint stock companies holding land."[1367]

But the Emperor replied in a letter dated 10 December: "Despite the most convincing arguments in favour of adopting these measures... an inner voice dictates with increasing insistence not to take this decision upon myself."[1368]

As if he did not understand—or rather forgot—that the resolution proposed in the *Journal* was the direct and inescapable consequence of the Manifesto he had signed himself a year earlier...

Even in the most closed bureaucratic world, there are always officials with eyes and hands. And if the rumour of a decision taken by the Council of Ministers had already spread to the public opinion? And here we are: we will know that the ministers want to emancipate the Jews while the sovereign, he, stood in its way...

On the same day, 10 December, Stolypin hastened to write to the Emperor a letter full of anxiety, repeating all his arguments one by one, and especially: "The dismissal of the *Journal* is for the moment not known by anyone," it is therefore still possible to conceal the equivocations of the monarch. "Your Majesty, we have no right to put you in this position and shelter ourselves behind you." Stolypin would have liked the advantages accorded to the Jews to appear as a favour granted by the tsar. But since this was not the case, he now proposed to adopt another resolution: the Emperor made no objections on the merits, but did not want the law to be promulgated over the head of the Duma; it must be done by the Duma.

[1365] JE, t. 2, pp. 749-751.
[1366] JE, t. 7, p. 373.
[1367] SJE, t. 7, p. 351.
[1368] Perepiska N. A. Romanova and P. A. Solypina (Correspondence between N. A. Romanov and P. A. Stolypin), Krasnyi Arkhiv, 1924, vol. 5, p. 105; See also SJE, t. 7, p. 351.

Secretary of State S. E. Kryjanovski said that the emperor then adopted a resolution which went along in this direction: that the representatives of the people take responsibility both for raising this issue as well as resolving it. But, no one knows why, this resolution received little publicity, and "on the side of the Duma, absolutely nothing happened."[1369]

Widely to the left, penetrated by progressive ideas and so vehement towards the government, the second Duma was free! Yet, in the second Duma, there was still less talk of the deprivation of rights suffered by the Jews than in the first."[1370] The law on equal rights for Jews was not even discussed, so, what can be said about its adoption…

Why then did the second Duma not take advantage of the opportunities offered to it? Why did it not seize them? It had three entire months to do it. And why did the debates, the clashes, relate only to secondary, tangential issues? The equality of the Jews—still partial, but already well advanced—was abandoned.

Why, indeed, why? As for the "Extra-Parliamentary Extraordinary Commission", it did not even discuss the plan to repeal the restrictions imposed on Jews, but circumvented the problem by focusing on *integral* equality "as quickly as possible."[1371]

Difficult to explain this other than by a political calculation: the aim being to fight the Autocracy, the interest was to raise more and more the pressure on the Jewish question, and to certainly not resolve it: ammunition was thus kept in reserve. These brave knights of liberty reasoned in these terms: to avoid that the lifting of restrictions imposed on the Jews would diminish their ardour in battle.

For these knights without fear and without reproach, the most important, was indeed the fight against the power.

All this was beginning to be seen and understood. Berdyaev, for example, addressed the whole spectrum of Russian radicalism with the following reproaches: "You are very sensitive to the Jewish question, you are fighting for their rights. But do you feel the 'Jew', do you feel the soul of the Jewish people?… No, your fight in favour for the Jews does not want to know the Jews."[1372]

Then, in the third Duma, the Cadets no longer had the majority; they "did not take any more initiatives on the Jewish question, fearing that they

---

[1369] *S. E. Kryjanorski*, Vospominania (Memoirs), Berlin, Petropolis, pp. 94-95.
[1370] SJE, t. 7, p. 351.
[1371] JE, t. 7, p. 373.
[1372] *Nikolai Berdyaev*, Filosofia neravenstva (The Philosophy of Inequality), Paris, YMCA Press, 1970, p. 72.

would be defeated... This caused great discontent among the Jewish masses, and the Jewish press did not deprive itself of attacking the party of the People's Freedom."[1373] Although "the Jews had participated in the electoral campaign with the greatest ardour and the number of Jewish voters exceeded that of the Christians in all the cities of the Pale of Settlement," they were beaten by the opposing party, and in the third Duma there were only two Jewish deputies: Nisselovitch and Friedman.[1374] (The latter succeeded to remain up to the fourth Duma.)—Beginning in 1915, the Council of State included among its members a Jew, G. E. Weinstein, of Odessa. (Just before the revolution, there was also Solomon Samoylovich Krym, a Karaim.[1375])

As for the Octobrists[1376] whose party had become a majority in the third Duma, on the one hand they ceded, not without hesitation, to the pressure of public opinion which demanded equal rights for the Jews, which led to the criticism of Russian nationalist deputies: "We thought that the Octobrists remained attached to the defence of national interests"—and now, without warning, they had relegated to the background both the question of "the granting of equal rights to the Russians of Finland" (which meant that this equality did not exist in this "Russian colony"...) and that of the annexation by Russia of the Kholm region in Poland, with all Russians that inhabit it—but "they have prepared a bill to abolish the Pale of Settlement."[1377] On the other hand, they were attributed statements "of manifestly anti-Semitic character": thus the third Duma, on the initiative of Guchkov, issued in 1906 "the wish... that Jewish doctors not be admitted to work in the army health services"[1378]; likewise, "it was proposed to replace the military service of the Jews by a tax."[1379] (In the years preceding the war, the project of dispensing the Jews from military service was still largely and seriously debated; and I. V. Hessen published a book on this subject entitled *The War and the Jews*.) In short, neither the second, third, nor fourth Dumas took it upon themselves to pass the law on the integral equality of rights for the Jews. And every time it was necessary to ratify the law on equality of rights for *peasants* (promulgated by Stolypin

---

[1373] *Sliosberg*, t. 3, p. 247.

[1374] JE, t. 7, pp. 373-374.

[1375] A. A. Goldenweiser, Pravovoe polojenie ievreyev v Rossii (The legal position of Jews in Russia), [Sb.] Kniga o ruskom evreïstve Ot 1860 godov do Revolutsii 1917 g. (Aspects of the History of Russian Jews), in BJWR-1, p. 132; RJE, L 1, p. 212, t. 2, p. 99.

[1376] Dissenting Cadet Party, founded by Guchkov, demanding the strict application of 30 October Manifesto.

[1377] Third Duma, Stenographic Record of Debates, 1911, p. 2958.

[1378] JE, t. 7, p. 375.

[1379] SJE, t. 7, p. 353.

as of 5 October 1906), it was blocked by the same Dumas, under the pressure of the left, on the grounds that the peasants could not be granted equal rights before they were granted to the Jews (and the Poles)!

And thus the pressure exerted upon this execrated tsarist government was not relieved, but doubled, quintupled. And not only did this pressure exerted on the government not be relieved, not only were these laws not voted upon by the Duma, but it would last until the February Revolution.

While Stolypin, after his unfortunate attempt in December 1906, quietly took administrative measures to partially lift the restrictions imposed on the Jews.

An editorialist from *Novoie Vremia*, Menshikov, condemned this method: "Under Stolypin, the Pale of Settlement has become a fiction."[1380] The Jews "are defeating the Russian power by gradually withdrawing all its capacity to intervene... The government behaves as if it were a Jew."[1381]

Such is the fate of the middle way.

The general outcry of the parties of the left against a policy of progressive measures, this tactical refusal for a smooth evolution towards equal rights, was strongly supported by the Russian press. Since the end of 1905, it was no longer subject to prior censorship. But it was not only a press that had become free, it was a press that considered itself a full-fledged actor in the political arena, a press, as we have seen, that could formulate demands, such as that of *withdrawing the police from the streets of the city*! Witte said it had lost its reason.

In the case of the Duma, the way in which Russia, even in its most remote provinces, was informed of what was going on there and what was said there, depended entirely on journalists. The shorthand accounts of the debates appeared late and with very low circulation, so there was no other source of information than the daily press, and it was based on what they read that the people formed an opinion. However, the newspapers systematically distorted the debates in the Duma, largely opening their columns to the deputies of the left and showering them with praise, while to the deputies of the right they allowed only a bare minimum.

A. Tyrkova says that in the second Duma, "the accredited journalists formed their own press office," which "depended on the distribution of places" among the correspondents. The members of this office "refused to give his card of accreditation" to the correspondent of the Journal the *Kolokol* (favourite newspaper of the priests of the countryside). Tyrkova

---

[1380] Novoie Vremia, 1911, 8 (21) Sept., p. 4.
[1381] *Ibidem*, 10 (23) Sept., p. 4.

intervened, noting that "these readers should not be deprived of the possibility of being informed about the debates in the Duma by a newspaper in which they had more confidence than those of the opposition"; but "my colleagues, among whom the Jews were the most numerous..., got carried away, began shouting, explaining that no one was reading the *Kolokol*, that that newspaper was of no use."[1382]

For the Russian nationalist circles, responsibility for this conduct of the press was simply and solely the responsibility of the Jews. They wanted to prove that almost all journalists accredited to the Duma were Jews. And they published "whistle-blowing" lists listing the names of these correspondents.

More revealing is this comical episode of parliamentary life: one day, answering to the attacks of which he was the object, Purishkevich pointed, in the middle of his speech, the box of the press, located near the tribune and delimited by a circular barrier, and said: "But see this *Pale of Settlement of the Jews!*"—Everyone turned involuntarily to the representatives of the press, and it was a general burst of laughter that even the Left could not repress. This "Pale of Settlement of the Duma" became an adopted wording.

Among the prominent Jewish publishers, we have already spoken of S. M. Propper, owner of the *Stock Exchange News* and unfailing sympathiser of the "revolutionary democracy". Sliosberg evokes more warmly the one who founded and funded to a large extent the cadet newspaper *Retch*, I. B. Bak: "A very obliging man, very cultured, with a radically liberal orientation." It was his passionate intervention at the Congress of the Jewish mutual aid committees at the beginning of 1906 that prevented a conciliation with the tsar. "There was no Jewish organisation devoted to cultural action or beneficence, of which I. Bak was not a member"; he was particularly distinguished by his work in the Jewish Committee for Liberation.[1383] As for the *Retch* newspaper and its editor-in-chief I. V. Hessen, they were far from limiting themselves to Jewish questions alone, and their orientation was more generally liberal (Hessen subsequently proved it in emigration with the *Roul* and the Archives of the Russian Revolution). The very serious *Russkie Vedomosti* published Jewish authors of various tendencies, both V. Jabotinsky and the future inventor of war communism, Lourie-Larine. S. Melgounov noted that the publication in this body of articles favorable to the Jews was explained "not only by the desire to defend the oppressed, but also by the composition of the

---

[1382] *Tyrkova-Williams*, pp. 340-342.
[1383] *Sliosberg*, t. 3, pp. 186-187.

newspaper's managing team."[1384] "There were Jews even among the collaborators of the *Novoie Vremia* of Suvorin"; the *Jewish Encyclopædia* quotes the names of five of them.[1385]

The newspaper *Russkie Vedomosti* was long dominated by the figure of G. B. Iollos, called there by Guerzenstein who had been working there since the 80s. Both were deputies to the First Duma. Their lives suffered cruelly from the atmosphere of violence engendered by political assassinations— these being the very essence of the revolution—a "rehearsal" of 1905-06. According to the Israeli *Jewish Encyclopædia*, the responsibility for their assassination would rest with the Union of the Russian People.[1386] For the Russian *Jewish Encyclopædia*, if the latter bore responsibility for the assassination of Guerzenstein (1906), Iollos, him, was killed (1907) by "Black Hundreds Terrorists."[1387]

Jewish publishers and journalists did not restrict their activities to the capital or to highly intellectual publications, but they also intervened in the popular press, such as the *Kopeika*, a favourite reading of the concierges— a quarter of a million copies in circulation, it "played a major role in the fight against anti-Semitic denigration campaigns." (It had been created and was led by M. B. Gorodetski.[1388]) The very influential *Kievskaya Mysl* (to the left of the Cadets) had as editor-in-chief Iona Kugel (they were four brothers, all journalists), and D. Zaslavski, a wicked rascal, and, what seems to us very moving, Leo Trotsky! The biggest newspaper of Saratov was edited by Averbakh-senior (brother-in-law of Sverdlov). In Odessa appeared for some time the *Novorossiysky Telegraf*, with strong right-wing convictions, but measures of economic suffocation were taken against it— successfully.

The Russian press also had "migrant" stars. Thus L. I. Goldstein, an inspired journalist who wrote in the most diverse newspapers for thirty-five years, including the *Syn Otetchestva*, and it was also he who founded and directed the *Rossia*, a clearly patriotic newspaper. The latter was closed because of a particularly virulent chronicle directed against the Imperial family: "These Obmanovy gentlemen". The press was to celebrate Goldstein's jubilee in the spring of 1917.[1389]—As well as the discreet Garvei-Altus, who had a moment of glory for his chronicle "The Leap of

---

[1384] S. P. *Melgunov*, Vospominania i dnevniki. Vyp. I (Memoirs and Journal, 1), Paris, 1964, p. 88.
[1385] SJE, t. 7, p. 517.
[1386] Nationalist mass organisation founded in October 1905 by Dr. Dubrovin and Vladimir Purishkevich.
[1387] *Ibidem*, p. 351; RJE, t. 1, pp. 290, 510.
[1388] RJE, t. 1, p. 361.
[1389] Novoie Vremia, 1917, 21 April (4 May); as well as other newspapers.

the Passionate Panther", in which he poured a torrent of calumnies on the Minister of the Interior, N. A. Maklakov.

(But all this was nothing compared to the unheard-of insolence of the "humouristic leaflets" of the years 1905-1907 which covered in muck, in unimaginable terms, all the spheres of power and of the State. The chameleon Zinovi Grjebine: in 1905 he published a satirical leaflet, the *Joupel*; in 1914–1915 he directed the right-minded *Otetchestvo*, and in 1920 he set up a Russian publishing house in Berlin in collaboration with the editions of the Soviet State.[1390])

But if the press reflected all sorts of currents of thought, from liberalism to socialism, and, as far as the Jewish thematic was concerned, from Zionism to Autonomism, it was a position deemed incompatible with journalistic respectability: which consisted in adopting a comprehensive attitude towards power. In the 70s, Dostoyevsky had already noted on several occasions that "the Russian press is out of control." This was even to be seen on the occasion of the meeting of 8 March 1881, with Alexander III, newly enthroned emperor, and often afterwards: the journalists acted as self-proclaimed representatives of society.

The following statement was attributed to Napoleon: "Three opposition papers are more dangerous than one hundred thousand enemy soldiers." This sentence applies largely to the Russo-Japanese war. The Russian press was openly defeatist throughout the conflict and in each of its battles. Even worse, it did not conceal its sympathies for terrorism and revolution.

This press, totally out of control in 1905, was considered during the period of the Duma, if we are to believe Witte, as essentially "Jewish" or "semi-Jewish"[1391]; or, to be more precise, as a press dominated by left-wing or radical Jews who occupied key positions. In November 1905, D. I. Pikhno, editor-in-chief for twenty-five years of the Russian newspaper *The Kievian* and a connoisseur of the press of his time, wrote: "The Jews... have bet heavily on the card of the revolution... Those, among the Russians, who think seriously, have understood that in such moments, the press represents a force and that this force is not in their hands, but in that of their adversaries; that they speak on their behalf throughout Russia and have forced people to read them because there is nothing else to read; and as one cannot launch a publication in one day, [the opinion] has been drowned beneath this mass of lies, incapable of finding itself there."[1392]

[1390] RJE, t. 1, p. 373.
[1391] S. I. *Witte*, Vopominania. TsarsLvoanie Nikolaïa II (Memoirs, The reign of Nicholas II) in 2 vols., Berlin, Slovo, 1922, t. 2, p. 54.
[1392] The Kievian, 1905, 17 Nov. in *Choulguine*, Annexes, pp. 285-286.

L. Tikhomirov did not see the national dimension of this phenomenon, but he made in 1910 the following remarks about the Russian press: "They play on the nerves... They cannot stand contradiction... They do not want courtesy, fair play... They have no ideal, they do not know what that is." As for the public formed by this press, it "wants aggressiveness, brutality, it does not respect knowledge and lets itself be deceived by ignorance."[1393]

At the other end of the political spectrum, here is the judgement that the Bolshevik M. Lemke passed on the Russian press: "In our day, ideas are not cheap and information is sensational, self-assured and authoritative ignorance fills the columns of the newspapers."

More specifically, in the cultural sphere, Andrei Bely—who was anything but a right-wing man or "chauvinist"—wrote these bitter lines in 1909: "Our national culture is dominated by people who are foreign to it... See the names of those who write in Russian newspapers and magazines, literary critics, musical critics: they are practically nothing but Jews; there are among them people who have talent and sensibility, and some, few in number, understand our national culture perhaps better than the Russians themselves; but they are the exception. The mass of Jewish critics is totally foreign to Russian art, it expresses itself in a jargon resembling Esperanto, and carries on a reign of terror among those who try to deepen and enrich the Russian language."[1394]

At the same time, V. Jabotinsky, a perspicacious Zionist, complained of "progressive newspapers financed by Jewish funds and stuffed with Jewish collaborators," and warned: "When the Jews rushed en masse into Russian politics, we predicted that nothing good would come of it, neither for Russian policy nor for the Jews."[1395]

The Russian press played a decisive role in the assault of the Cadets and the intelligentsia against the government before the revolution; the deputy in the Duma A. I. Chingariov expresses well the state of mind that reigned there: "This government only has to sink! To a power *like this* we cannot even throw the smallest bit of rope!" In this regard, it may be recalled that the First Duma observed a minute of silence in memory of the victims of the Bialystok pogrom (refusing to admit, as we have seen, that it was an armed confrontation between anarchists and the army); the second Duma also paid tribute to Iollos, murdered by a terrorist; but when Purishkevich

---

[1393] Iz dncvnika L. Tikhomirova (*Excerpts from the diary of L. Tikhomirov*). Krasny Arkhiv, 1936, t. 74, pp. 177-179.

[1394] Boris Bougayev (Andrei Bely), Chtempelevennaïa kultura (*The Obliterated Culture*), Viesy, 1909, no. 9, pp. 75-77.

[1395] Vl. *Jabotinsky*, Dezertiry i khoziaieva (Deserters and Masters), Felietony, Spb, 1913, pp. 75-76.

offered to observe a minute of silence in memory of the officers and soldiers who had died in the course of their duty, he was removed from the sitting and the parliamentarians were so manic that they thought it unthinkable to pity those who ensured security in the country, that elementary security which they all needed.

A. Koulicher drew up a fair assessment of this period, but too late, in 1923, in emigration: "Before the revolution there were, among the Jews of Russia, individuals and groups of individuals, the activity could be characterised... precisely by the lack of sense of responsibility in the face of the confusion that reigned in the minds of the Jews... [through] the propagation of a 'revolutionary spirit' as vague as it was superficial... All their political action consisted in being more to the left than the others. Confined to the role of irresponsible critics, never going to the end of things, they considered that their mission consisted of always saying: 'It is not enough!'... These people were 'democrats'... But there was also a particular category of democrats—moreover, they referred to themselves as the 'Jewish Democratic Group'—who attached this adjective to any substantive, inventing an unsustainable talmud of democracy... With the only end to demonstrate that the others were not yet sufficiently democrats... They maintained an atmosphere of irresponsibility around them, of contentless maximalism, of insatiable demand. All of which had fatal consequences when the revolution came." [1396] The destructive influence of this press is undoubtedly one of the weaknesses, of great vulnerability, of Russian public life in the years 1914-1917.

But what became of the "reptilian press", the one that laid down in front of the authorities, the press of the Russian nationalists? The *Russkoye Znamya* of Dubrovin—it was said that things fell from your hands so much he was rude and bad. (Let us note, in passing, that it was forbidden to circulate it in the army at the request of certain generals.) The *Zemshchina* was hardly better—I do not know, I have not read any of these papers. As for the *Moskovskiye Vedomosti*, out of breath, they no longer had readers after 1905.

But where were the strong minds and sharp pens of the conservatives, those who were concerned about the fate of the Russians? Why were there no good newspapers to counterbalance the devastating whirlwind?

It must be said that, in view of the agile thought and writing of the liberal and radical press, so accountable for its dynamism to its Jewish collaborators, the Russian nationalists could only align slow, rather soft, spirits who were not at all prepared to fight this kind of battle (but what is

---

[1396] A. *Koulicher*, Ob otvetstvennosti i bezotvetstvennosti (responsibility and irresponsibility). Ievsreiskaya tribouna, Paris, 1923, no. 7 (160), 6 April, p. 4.

there to say about this state of affairs today!). There were only a few literary types exasperated by the left press, but totally devoid of talent. Moreover, right-wing publications were facing serious financial difficulties. While the newspapers financed by "Jewish money"—as Jabotinsky used to say—offered very good wages, hence the profusion of wordsmiths; and, above all, all these journals without exception were interesting. Finally, the left-wing press and the Duma demanded the closure of the "subsidised newspapers", that is to say, supported in secret and rather weakly by the government.

State Secretary S. E. Kryjanovski acknowledged that the government was providing financial support to more than 30 newspapers in various parts of Russia, but without success, both because the right lacked educated people, prepared for journalistic activity, and because the power itself did not know how to do it either. More gifted than others was I. I. Gourland, a Jew of the Ministry of the Interior, a unique case—who, under the pseudonym of "Vassiliev", wrote pamphlets sent in sealed envelopes to prominent public figures.

Thus the government had only one organ which merely enumerated the news in a dry and bureaucratic tone, the *Pravitelstvenny Vestnik*. But to create something strong, brilliant, convincing, to openly go to the conquest of public opinion even in Russia—let us not even talk about Europe!—that, the imperial government either did not understand the necessity of it, or was incapable of doing so, the enterprise being beyond its means or intelligence.

The *Novoie Vremia* of Suvorin long maintained a pro-governmental orientation; it was a very lively, brilliant and energetic newspaper (but, it must be said, equally changing—sometimes favourable to the alliance with Germany, sometimes violently hostile to it), and, alas, not always knowing how to make the difference between national revival and attacks on the Jews. (Its founder, old Suvorin, sharing his property among his three sons before dying, gave them as a condition to never yielding any of their shares to Jews.) Witte ranked *Novoie Vremia* among the newspapers which, in 1905, "had an interest to be of the left…, then turned right to become now ultra-reactionaries. This very interesting and influential journal offers a striking example of this orientation." Although very commercial, "it still counts among the best."[1397] It provided a great deal of information and was widely disseminated—perhaps the most dynamic of the Russian newspapers and, certainly, the most intelligent of the organs of the right. And the leaders of the right? And the deputies of the right in the Duma?

[1397] *Witte*, t. 2, p. 55.

Most often they acted without taking into account the real relationship between their strengths and their weaknesses, showing themselves both brutal and ineffective, seeing no other means of "defending the integrity of the Russian State" than calling for more bans on Jews. In 1911, the deputy Balachov developed a programme that went against the current and the times: *reinforcing* the Pale of Settlement, removing Jews from publishing, justice, and the Russian school. Deputy Zamyslovski protested that within the universities, the Jews, the S.-R.s, the Social Democrats enjoyed a "secret sympathy"—as if one could overcome by decree a "secret sympathy"—In 1913 the Congress of the Union of the nobility demanded (as had already been done in 1908 under the third Duma) that more Jews be taken into the army, but that they be symmetrically excluded from public functions, the territorial and municipal administration, and justice.

In the spring of 1911, Purishkevich, striving with others against an already weakened Stolypin, proposed to the Duma these extreme measures: "Formally forbid the Jews to take any official duty in any administration... especially in the periphery of the Empire... The Jews convicted of having tried to occupy these functions will have to answer before justice."[1398]

Thus the right reproached Stolypin for making concessions to the Jews.

When he had taken office in the spring of 1906, Stolypin had had to consider the Manifesto of 17 October as a *fait accompli*, even if it had to be slightly amended. That the Emperor had hastily signed it without sufficient reflection—it no longer mattered, it had to be applied, the State had to be rebuilt in the midst of difficulties, in accordance with the Manifesto and in spite of the hesitations of the tsar himself. And this implied equal rights for the Jews.

Of course, the restrictions imposed on the Jews continued, not only in Russia. In Poland, which was considered—as well as Finland—to be oppressed, these limitations were even more brutal. Jabotinsky writes: "The yoke that weighs heavily on Jews in Finland is beyond measure even with what is known of Russia or Romania... The first Finnish man, if he surprises a Jew out of a city, has the right to arrest the criminal and take him to the police station. Most trades are forbidden to Jews. Jewish marriages are subject to compulsory and humiliating formalities... It is very difficult to obtain permission to build a synagogue... The Jews are deprived of all political rights." Elsewhere in Austrian Galicia, "the Poles do not hide that they see in the Jews only a material used to strengthen their political power in this region... There have been cases where high school students were excluded from their establishment 'for cause of Zionism', one hinders in a thousand and one ways the functioning of Jewish schools,

---

[1398] Stenographic Record of the Debates in the Third Duma, 1911, p. 2911.

manifests hatred towards their jargon (Yiddish), and the Jewish Socialist Party itself is boycotted by the Polish Social-Democrats."[1399] Even in Austria, although a country of Central Europe, hatred towards the Jews was still alive, and many restrictions remained in force, such as the Karlsbad baths: sometimes they were simply closed to the Jews, sometimes they could only go there in the summer, and the "winter Jews" could only access it under strict control.[1400]

But the system of limitations in Russia itself fully justified the grievances expressed in the *Jewish Encyclopædia* as a whole: "The position of the Jews is highly uncertain, inasmuch as it depends on how the law is interpreted by those responsible for applying it, even at the lowest level of the hierarchy, or even simply their goodwill... This blur... is due to... the extreme difficulty of achieving uniform interpretation and application of the laws limiting the rights of the Jews... Their many provisions have been supplemented and modified by numerous decrees signed by the emperor on the proposal of various ministries... and which, moreover, were not always reported in the General Code of Laws"; "Even if he has an express authorisation issued by the competent authority, the Jew is not certain that his rights are intangible"; "A refusal emanating from a junior official, an anonymous letter sent by a competitor, or an approach made in the open by a more powerful rival seeking the expropriation of a Jew, suffice to condemn him to vagrancy."[1401]

Stolypin understood very well the absurdity of such a state of affairs, and the irresistible movement that then pushed for a status of equality for the Jews, a status that already existed to a large extent in Russia.

The number of Jews established outside the Pale of Settlement increased steadily from year to year. After 1903, the Jews had access to an additional 101 places of residence, and the number of these was still significantly increased under Stolypin, which implemented a measure which the tsar had not taken in 1906 and which the Duma had rejected in 1907. The former *Jewish Encyclopædia* indicates that the number of these additional places of residence amounted to 291 in 1910-1912 [1402]; As for the new *Encyclopædia*, it puts the number to 299 for the year 1911.[1403]

The old *Encyclopædia* reminds us that from the summer of 1905 onwards, in the wake of revolutionary events, "the governing bodies [of educational establishments] did not take into account the *numerus clausus* for three

---

[1399] *Vl. Jabotinsky*, Homo homini lupus, Felietony, pp. 111-113.
[1400] JE, t. 9, p. 314.
[1401] JE, t. 13, pp. 622-625.
[1402] JE, t. 5, p. 822.
[1403] SJE, t. 5, p, 315.

years."[1404] From August 1909 onwards, the latter was reduced from what it was before in the higher and secondary schools (now 5% in the capitals, 10% outside the Pale of Settlement, 15% within it[1405]), but subject to compliance.

However, since the proportion of Jewish students was 11% at the University of Saint Petersburg and 24% at that of Odessa[1406], this measure was felt to be a new restriction. A restrictive measure was adopted in 1911: the *numerus clausus* was extended to the outside world[1407] (for boys only, and in girls' institutions the real percentage was 13.5% in 1911). At the same time, artistic, commercial, technical and vocational schools accepted Jews without restrictions. "After secondary and higher education, the Jews rushed into vocational education" which they had neglected until then. Although in 1883 "Jews in all municipal and regional vocational schools" accounted for only 2% of the workforce, 12% of boys and 17% of girls in 1898.[1408] In addition, "Jewish youth filled private higher education institutions"; thus, in 1912, the Kiev Institute of Commerce had 1,875 Jewish students, and the Psycho-Neurological Institute, "thousands".

Beginning in 1914, any private educational institution could provide courses in the language of its choice.[1409]

It is true that compulsory education for all was part of the logic of the time. Stolypin's main task was to carry out the agrarian reform, thus creating a solid class of peasant-owners. His companion in arms, Minister of Agriculture A. V. Krivoshein, who was also in favour of abolishing the Pale of Settlement, insisted at the same time that be limited "the right of anonymous companies with shares" to proceed with the purchase of land, to the extent that it was likely to result in the formation of a "significant Jewish land capital"; indeed, "the penetration into the rural world of Jewish speculative capital risked jeopardising the success of the agrarian reform" (at the same time he expressed the fear that this would lead to the emergence of anti-Semitism unknown until then in the countryside of Greater Russia[1410]). Neither Stolypin nor Krivoshein could allow that the

---

[1404] JE, t. 13, p. 55.
[1405] SJE, t. 7, p. 352.
[1406] S. V. *Pozner*, Ievrei v obschechei chkole… (The Jews in the Public School…), SPb, Razoum, 1914, p. 54.
[1407] SJE, t. 6, p. 854; t. 7, p. 352.
[1408] JE, t. 13, pp. 55-58.
[1409] *I. M. Troitsky*, Ievrei vrusskoï chkole (The Jews and the Russian School), in BJWR-1, pp. 358, 360.
[1410] *K. A. Krivoshein*, A. V. Krivoshein (1857-1921) Evo znatchenie v istorii Rossii natchal XX veka (A. V. Krivoshein: his role in the history of Russia at the beginning of the twentieth century), Paris, 1973, pp. 290, 292.

peasants remain in misery due to the fact of not owning land. In 1906, Jewish agricultural settlements were also deprived of the right to acquire land belonging to the State, which was now reserved for peasants.[1411]

The economist M. Bernadski cited the following figures for the pre-war period: 2.4% of Jews worked in agriculture, 4.7% were liberal professionals, 11.5% were domestic servants, 31% worked in commerce (Jews accounted for 35% of merchants in Russia), 36% in industry; 18% of the Jews were settled in the Pale of Settlement.[1412] In comparing the latter figure to the 2.4% mentioned above, the number of Jews residing in rural areas and occupied in agriculture had not increased significantly, while according to Bernadski, "it was in the interest of the *Russians* that Jewish forces and resources were investing themselves in all areas of production", any limitation imposed on them "represented a colossal waste of the productive forces of the country." He pointed out that in 1912, for example, the Society of producers and manufacturers of an industrial district in Moscow had approached the President of the Council of Ministers so that the Jews would not be prevented from playing their role of intermediary link with Russian industrial production centres.[1413]

B. A. Kamenka, chairman of the Board of Directors of Azov Bank and the Don, turned to the financing of the mining and metallurgical industry and sponsored eleven important enterprises in the Donets and Urals region.[1414]—There was no restriction on the participation of Jews in joint-stock companies in the industry, but "the limitations imposed on joint-stock companies wishing to acquire property triggered an outcry in all financial and industrial circles." And the measures taken by Krivoshein were to be abrogated.[1415]

V. Choulguine made the following comparison: "The 'Russian power' seemed very ingenuous in the face of the perfectly targeted offensive of the Jews. The Russian power reminded one of the flood of a long and peaceful river: an endless expanse plunged into a soft sleepiness; there is water, oh my God there is, but it is only sleeping water. Now this same river, a few versts farther away, enclosed by strong dikes, is transformed into an

---

[1411] JE, t. 7, p. 757.
[1412] *M. Bernadski*, Ievrci I ruskoye narodnoïe khoziaïstvo (*The Jews and the Russian economy*), in Chtchit literatourny sbornik/pod red. L. Andreeva, M. Gorkovo and E Sologouba. 3-e izd., Dop., M. Rousskoye Obchtchestvo dlia izoutchenia ievreiskoi jisni, 1916. pp. 28, 30; SJE, t. 7, p. 386.
[1413] *Bernadski*, Chtchit, pp. 30, 31.
[1414] RJE, t. 1, p. 536.
[1415] *Krivoshein*, pp. 292-293.

impetuous torrent, whose bubbling waters precipitate itself madly into turbines."[1416]

It is the same rhetoric that is heard on the side of liberal economic thought: "Russia, so poor... in highly skilled workforce..., seems to want to further increase its ignorance and its intellectual lagging in relation to the West."

Denying the Jews access to the levers of production "amounts to a deliberate refusal to use... their productive forces."[1417]

Stolypin saw very well that this was wasteful. But the different sectors of the Russian economy were developing too unevenly. And he regarded the restrictions imposed on Jews as a kind of customs tax that could only be temporary, until the Russians consolidated their forces in public life as well as in the sphere of the economy, these protective measures secreted an unhealthy greenhouse climate for them. Finally (but after how many years?), the government began to implement the measures for the development of the peasant world, from which were to result a true and genuine *equality of rights* between social classes and nationalities; a development which would have made the Russians' fear of the Jews disappear and which would have put a definitive end to all the restrictions of which the latter were still victims.

Stolypin was considering using Jewish capital to stimulate Russia's economy by welcoming their many joint-stock companies, enterprises, concessions and natural resource businesses. At the same time, he understood that private banks, dynamic and powerful, often preferred to agree among themselves rather than compete, but he intended to counterbalance this phenomenon by "nationalising credit", that is, the strengthening of the role of the State Bank and the creation of a fund to help entrepreneurial peasants who could not obtain credit elsewhere.

But Stolypin was making another political calculation: he thought that obtaining equal rights would take some of the Jews away from the revolutionary movement. (Among other arguments, he also put forward: at the local level, bribery was widely used to circumvent the law, which had the effect of spreading corruption within the State apparatus.)

Among the Jews, those who did not give in to fanaticism realised that, despite the continued restrictions, in spite of the increasingly virulent (but impotent) attacks on right-wing circles, those years offered more and more favourable conditions to the Jews and were necessarily leading to equal rights.

[1416] *Choulguine*, p. 74.
[1417] *Bernadski*, pp. 27. 28.

Just a few years later, thrown into emigration by the "great revolution", two renowned Jewish figures meditated on pre-revolutionary Russia: Self-taught out of poverty at the cost of the greatest efforts, he had passed his bachelor's degree as an external candidate at the age of thirty and obtained his university degree at thirty-five; he had actively participated in the Liberation Movement and had always regarded Zionism as an illusory dream—his name was Iosif Menassievich Bikerman. From the height of his fifty-five years of age he wrote: "Despite the regulations of May [1882] and other provisions of the same type, despite the Pale of Settlement and *numerus clausus*, despite Kishinev and Bialystok, I was a free man and I felt as such, a man who had before him a wide range of possibilities to work in all kinds of fields, who could enrich himself both materially and spiritually, who could fight to improve his situation and conserve his strength to continue the fight. The restrictions... were always diminishing under the pressure of the times and under ours, and during the war a wide breach was opened in the last bastion of our inequality. It was necessary to wait another five or fifteen years before obtaining complete equality before the law; we could wait."[1418]

Belonging to the same generation as Bikerman, he shared very different convictions and his life was also very different: a convinced Zionist, a doctor (he taught for a time at the Faculty of Medicine in Geneva), an essayist and a politician, Daniil Samoylovich Pasmanik, an immigrant as well, wrote at the same time as Bikerman the following lines: "Under the tsarist regime, the Jews lived infinitely better and, whatever may be said of them, their conditions of life before the war—both materially as well as others—were excellent. We were then deprived of political rights, but we could develop intense activity in the sphere of our national and cultural values, while the chronic misery that had been our lot disappeared progressively."[1419]—"The chronic economic slump of the Jewish masses diminished day by day, leaving room for material ease, despite the senseless deportations of several tens of thousands of Jews out of the Front areas. The statistics of the mutual credit societies... are the best proof of the economic progress enjoyed by the Jews of Russia during the decade preceding the coup. And so it was in the field of culture. Despite the police regime—it was absolute freedom in comparison with the present Bolshevik regime—Jewish cultural institutions of all kinds prospered. Everything was

---

[1418] *I. M. Bikerman*, Rossia i ruskoye Ivreisstvo (Russia and its Jewish Community), in Rossia i ievrei (*The Conservative and Destructive Elements among the Jews*), in RaJ, p. 33.
[1419] *D. S. Pasmanik*, Ruskaya revolutsia i ievreisstvo (Bolshevik i iudaism) (The Russian Revolution and the Jews [Bolshevism and Judaism]), Paris. 1923, pp. 195-196.

bursting with activity: organisations were booming, creation was also very alive and vast prospects were now open."[1420]

In a little more than a century, under the Russian crown, the Jewish community had grown from 820,000 (including the Kingdom of Poland) to more than five million representatives, even though more than one and a half million chose to emigrate,[1421]—an increase of a factor of eight between 1800 and 1914. Over the last 90 years, the number of Jews had multiplied by 3.5 (going from 1.5 million to 5,250,000), whereas during the same period the total population of the Empire (including the new territories) had multiplied by only 2.5.

However, the Jews were still subject to restrictions, which fuelled anti-Russian propaganda in the United States. Stolypin thought he could overcome it by *explaining* it, inviting members of Congress and American journalists to come and see, in Russia itself. But in the autumn of 1911, the situation became so severe that it led to the denunciation of a trade agreement with the United States dating back eighty years. Stolypin did not yet know what the effect of a passionate speech of the future peacemaker, Wilson, might be, nor what the unanimity of the American Congress could mean. He did not live enough to know.

Stolypin, who imprinted its direction, gave its light and name to the decade before the First World War,—all the while he was the object of furious attacks on the part of both the Cadets and the extreme right, when deputies of all ranks dragged him in the mud because of the law on the Zemstvo reform in the western provinces—was assassinated in September 1911.

The first head of the Russian government to have honestly raised and attempted to resolve, in spite of the Emperor's resistance, the question of equality for the Jews, fell—irony of History!—under the blows of a Jew. Such is the fate of the middle way...

Seven times attempts had been made to kill Stolypin, and it was revolutionary groups more or less numerous that had fermented the attacks—in vain. Here, it was an isolated individual who pulled it off.

At a very young age, Bogrov did not have sufficient intellectual maturity to understand the political importance of Stolypin's role. But from his childhood he had witnessed the daily and humiliating consequences of the inequality of the Jews, and his family, his milieu, his own experience cultivated his hatred for imperial power. In the Jewish circles of Kiev, which seemed ideologically mobile, no one was grateful to Stolypin for his attempts to lift the restrictions imposed on the Jews, and even if this feeling

---

[1420] *D. S. Pasmanik*, Tchevo je my dobivaïemsia? (But what do we want?), RaJ, p. 218.
[1421] SJE, t. 7, pp. 384-385.

had touched some of the better off, it was counterbalanced by the memory of the energetic way in which he had repressed the revolution of 1905-1906, as well as by the discontent with his efforts to "nationalise credit" in order to openly compete with private capital.

The Jewish circles in Kiev (but also in Petersburg where the future murderer had also stayed) were under the magnetic influence of a *field* of absolute radicalism, which led young Bogrov not only to feel entitled, but to consider it his duty to kill Stolypin.

This *field* was so powerful that it allowed the following combination: Bogrov-senior rose in society, he is a capitalist who prospers in the existing system; Bogrov-junior works at destroying this system and his father, after the attack, publicly declares that he is proud of him.

In fact, Bogrov was not so isolated: he was discreetly applauded in the circles which once manifested their unwavering fidelity to the regime.

This gunshot that put an end to the hope that Russia ever recovered its health could have been equally fired at the tsar himself. But Bogrov had decided that it was impossible, for (as he declared himself) "it might have led to persecution against the Jews," to have "damaging consequences on their legal position." While the Prime Minister would simply not have such effects, he thought. But he was deceived heavily when he imagined that his act would serve to improve the lot of the Jews of Russia.

And Menshikov himself, who had first reproached Stolypin with the concessions he had made to the Jews, now lamented his disappearance: our great man, our best political leader for a century and a half—assassinated! And the assassin is a Jew! A Jew who did not hesitate to shoot the Prime Minister of Russia!? "The gunshot of Kiev... must be considered as a warning signal... the situation is very serious... we must not cry revenge, but finally decide to resist!"[1422]

And what happened then in "Kiev the reactionary" where the Jews were so numerous? In the first hours after the attack, they were massively seized with panic and began to leave the city. Moreover, "the Jews were struck with terror not only in Kiev, but in the most remote corners of the Pale of Settlement and of the rest of Russia."[1423] The Club of Russian Nationalists expressed its intention to circulate a petition to drive out all the Jews of Kiev (which remained at the stage of intentions). There was not the start of a beginning of pogrom. The President of the youth organisation "The Two-Headed Eagle", Galkin, called for destroying the offices of the local security and for busting some Jew: he was immediately neutralised. The

---

[1422] Novoie Vremia, 1911, 10 (23) Sept., p. 4.
[1423] *Sliosberg*, t. 3, p. 249.

new Prime Minister, Kokovtsov, urgently recalled all Cossack regiments (they were manœuvring away from the city) and sent a very firm telegram to all the governors: to prevent pogroms by any means, including force. The troops were concentrated in greater numbers than during the revolution. (Sliosberg: if pogroms had broken out in 1911, "Kiev would have been the scene of a carnage comparable to the horrors of the time of Bogdan Khmelnitsky."[1424])

No, nowhere in Russia there was the slightest pogrom. (Despite this, there has been much written, and insistently, that the tsarist power had never dreamed of anything but one thing: to organise an anti-Jewish pogrom.)

Of course, the prevention of public disorder is one of the primary duties of the State, and when this mission is fulfilled, it does not have to expect recognition. But that under such extreme circumstances—the assassination of the head of government—, that it was possible to avoid pogroms, the threat of which caused panic among the Jews, it nevertheless merited a small mention, if only in passing. Well, no, we did not hear anything like *that* and no one spoke about *it*.

Difficult to believe, but the Kiev Jewish community did not publicly express condemnation nor regret regarding this assassination. On the contrary.

After the execution of Bogrov, many Jewish students were ostensibly in mourning. However, all this, the Russians noted it. Thus, in December 1912, Rozanov wrote: "After [Stolypin's assassination] something broke in my relationship [to the Jews]: would a Russian ever have dared to kill Rothschild or any other of *'their* great men'?"[1425]

If we look at it from a historical point of view, two important arguments prevent the act committed by Bogrov from being considered on behalf of the "powers of internationalism". The first and most important: it was not the case.

Not only the book written by his brother[1426], but different neutral sources suggest that Bogrov really believed that he could work this way to improve the lot of the Jews. And the second: to return to certain uncomfortable episodes in history, to examine them attentively to deplore them, is to assume one's responsibilities; but to deny them and wash one's hands, that's just low.

[1424] *Ibidem.*
[1425] Perepiska V. V. Rozanova and M. O. Gerschenzona (The correspondence of V. V. Rozanov and M. O. Gerschenzon), Novy mir. 1991, no. 3, p. 232.
[1426] *Vladimir Bogrov*, Drnitri Bogrov I oubiestvo Stolypina... (Dmitri Bogrov and the assassination of Stolypin...), Berlin, 1931.

Yet this is what happened almost immediately. In October 1911, the Duma was arrested by the Octobrists on the murky circumstances of the assassination of Stolypin. This provoked an immediate protest from the deputy Nisselovitch: why, when formulating their interpellation, did the Octobrists *not conceal* the fact that the murderer of Stolypin was Jewish? It was there, he declared, antisemitism!

I shall have to endure this incomparable argument myself. Seventy years later, I was the object of a heavy accusation on the part of the Jewish community in the United States: why, in my turn, *did I not conceal*, why did I say that the assassin of Stolypin was a Jew[1427]? It does not matter if I have endeavoured to make a description as complete as possible. It does not matter what the fact of being Jew represented in the motivations of his act. No, *non-dissimulation* betrayed my anti-Semitism!!

At the time, Guchkov replied with dignity: "I think that there is much more anti-Semitism in Bogrov's very act. I would suggest to the Deputy Nisselovitch that he should address his passionate words not to us but to his fellow coreligionists. Let him use all the force of his eloquence to convince them to keep away from two profane professions: that of spy in the service of the secret police and that of terrorist. He would thus render a much greater service to the members of his community!"[1428]

But what can one ask of the Jewish memory when Russian history itself has allowed this murder to be effaced from its memory as an event without great significance, as a smear as marginal as it is negligible. It was only in the 80s that I started to pull it out of oblivion—for seventy years, to mention it was considered inappropriate. As the years go by, more events and meanings come to our eyes.

More than once I have meditated on the whims of History: on *the unpredictability of the consequences* it raises on our path—I speak of the consequences of our actions. The Germany of William II opened the way for Lenin to destroy Russia, and twenty-eight years later it found itself divided for half a century.—Poland contributed to the strengthening of the Bolsheviks in the year 1919, which was so difficult for them, and it harvested 1939, 1944, 1956, 1980.—With what eagerness Finland helped Russian revolutionaries, she who could not bear, who did not suffer from the particular freedoms at her disposal—but within Russia—and, in return, she suffered forty years of political humiliation ("Finlandisation").—In

---

[1427] In *The Red Wheel*, First Knot, *August Fourteen*, ed. Fayard / Seuil.
[1428] A. *Guchkov*, Retch v Gosudarstvennoi Doume 15 Oct. 1911 (Address to the Duma of 15 Oct. 1911)—A. I. Goutchkov v Tretieï Gosoudarstvennoï Doume (1907-1912), Sbornik retchei (Collection of speeches delivered by A. Guchkov to The Third Duma), Spb, 1912, p. 163.

1914, England wanted to put down the power of Germany, its competitor on the world stage, and it lost its position of great power, and it was the whole of Europe that had been destroyed. In Petrograd, the Cossacks remained neutral both in February and in October; a year later, they underwent their genocide (and many of the victims were these *same* Cossacks).—In the first days of July 1917, the S.-R. of the left approached the Bolsheviks, then formed a semblance of a "coalition", a broad platform; a year later they were crushed as no autocracy could have had the means to do so.

These distant consequences, none of us are capable of foreseeing them, ever. The only way to guard against such errors is to always be guided by the compass of divine morality. Or, as the people say: "Do not dig a pit for others, you will fall into it yourself."

Similarly, if the assassination of Stolypin had cruel consequences for Russia, the Jews neither derived any benefit from it. Everyone can see things in his own way, but I see here the giant footsteps of History, and I am struck by the unpredictable character of its results.

Bogrov killed Stolypin, thus thinking of protecting the Jews from oppression. Stolypin would in any case have been removed from office by the Emperor, but he would surely have been recalled again in 1914-16 because of the dizzying deficiency in men able to govern; and under his government we would not have had such a lamentable end neither in the war nor in the revolution. (Assuming that with him in power we would have engaged in this war.)

First footstep of History: Stolypin is killed, Russia works its last nerves in war and lies under the heel of the Bolsheviks. Second footstep: however fierce they are, the Bolsheviks reveal themselves as being more lame than the imperial government, abandoning half of Russia to the Germans a quarter of a century later, including Kiev.

Third footstep: the Nazis invest in Kiev without any difficulty and annihilate its Jewish community. Again the city of Kiev, once again a month of September, but thirty years after Bogrov's revolver shot.

And still in Kiev, still in 1911, six months before the assassination of Stolypin, had started what would become the Beilis affair[1429]. There is good reason to believe that under Stolypin, justice would not have been degraded as such. One clue: one knows that once, examining the archives of the Department of Security, Stolypin came across a note entitled "The Secret of the Jews" (which anticipated the "Protocols"[1430]), in which was

---
[1429] See *infra*, following pages.
[1430] The famous forgery of the Protocols of the Elders of Zion.

discussed the "International Jewish plot". Here is the judgement he made: "There may be logic, but also bias... The government cannot use under any circumstance this kind of method."[1431] As a result, "the official ideology of the tsarist government never relied on the 'Protocols'."[1432]

Thousands and thousands of pages have been written about the Beilis trial. Anyone who would like to study closely all the meanders of the investigation, of the public opinion, of the trial itself, would have to devote at least several years to it. This would go beyond the limits of this work. Twenty years after the event, under the Soviet regime, the daily reports of the police on the progress of the trial were published[1433]; they can be commended to the attention of amateurs. It goes without saying that the *verbatim* record of the entire proceedings was also published. Not to mention the articles published in the press.

Andrei Yushchinsky, a 12-year-old boy, pupil of a religious institution in Kiev, is the victim of a savage and unusual murder: there are forty-seven punctures on his body, which indicate a certain knowledge of anatomy— they were made to the temple, to the veins and arteries of the neck, to the liver, to the kidneys, to the lungs, to the heart, with the clear intention of emptying him of his blood as long as he was still alive, and in addition— according to the traces left by the blood flow—in a standing position (tied and gagged, of course). It can only be the work of a very clever criminal who certainly did not act alone.

The body was discovered only a week later in a cave on the territory of the factory of Zaitsev. But the murder was not committed there.

The first accusations do not refer to ritual motives, but the latter soon appears: the connection is made with the beginning of Jewish Passover and the construction of a new synagogue on the grounds of Zaitsev (a Jew). Four months after the murder, this version of the accusation leads to the arrest of Menahem Mendel Beilis, 37, employed at the Zaitsev factory. He is arrested without any real charges against him. How did all this happen?

The investigation into the murder was carried out by the criminal police of Kiev, a worthy colleague, obviously, of the Security section of Kiev, which

---

[1431] *Sliosberg**, t. 2, pp. 283-284.
[1432] R. *Nudelman*, Doklad na seminare: Sovetskii antisemitizm—pritchiny i prognozy (Presentation at the seminar: Soviet antisemitism—causes and prognoses), in "22", review of the Jewish intelligentsia of the USSR in Israel, Tel Aviv, 1978, no. 3, p. 145.
[1433] Protsess Beilisa v otsenke Departamenta politsii (The Beilis trial seen by the Police Department), Krasny Arkhiv, 1931, t. 44, pp. 85-125.

had gotten tangled up in the Bogrov affair[1434] and thus caused the loss of Stolypin.

The work was entrusted to two nobodies in all respects similar to Kouliabko, Bogrov's "curator", Michtchouk, and Krassovsky, assisted by dangerous incompetents (they cleaned the snow in front of the cave to facilitate the passage of the corpulent commissioner of police, thus destroying any potential indications of the presence of the murderers). But worse still, rivalry settled between the investigators—it was to whom the merit of the discovery of the guilty person would be attributed, by whom the best version would be proposed—and they did not hesitate to get in each other's way, to sow confusion in the investigation, to put pressure on the witnesses, to stop the competitor's indicators; Krassovksy went so far as to put makeup on the suspect before introducing him to a witness! This parody of inquiry was conducted as if it were a trivial story, without the importance of the event even crossing their minds.

When the trial finally opened, two and a half years later, Michtchouk had run off to Finland to escape the charge of falsification of material evidence, a significant collaborator of Krassovsky had also disappeared, and as for the latter, dismissed of his duties, he had switched sides and was now working for Beilis's lawyers.

For nearly two years, we went from one false version to another; for a long time the accusation was directed to the family of the victim, until the latter was completely put out of the question. It became clearer and clearer that the prosecution was moving towards a formal accusation against Beilis and towards his trial.

He was therefore accused of murder—even though the charges against him were doubtful—because he was a Jew. But how was it possible in the twentieth century to inflate a trial to the point of making it a threat to an entire people?

Beyond the person of Beilis, the trial turned in fact into an accusation against the Jewish people as a whole—and, since then, the atmosphere around the investigation and then the trial became superheated, the affair took on an international dimension, gained the whole of Europe, and then America. (Until then, trials for ritual murders had taken place rather in the Catholic milieu: Grodno (1816), Velij (1825), Vilnius, the Blondes case (1900), the Koutais affair (1878) took place in Georgia, Doubossar (1903) in Moldavia, while in Russia strictly speaking, there was only the Saratov affair in 1856. Sliosberg, however, does not fail to point out that the Saratov affair also had also a Catholic origin, while in Beilis's case it was observed

---

[1434] See *supra*, chapter 9.

that the band of thieves who had been suspected at one time was composed of Poles, that the ritual crime expert appointed at the trial was a Catholic, and that the attorney Tchaplinski was also Polish.[1435])

The findings of the investigation were so questionable that they were only retained by the Kiev indictment chambre by three votes to two. While the monarchist right had sparked an extensive press campaign, Purishkevich expressed himself in the Duma in April 1911: "We do not accuse the Jews as a whole, we cry for the truth" about this strange and mysterious crime. "Is there a Jewish sect that advocates ritual murders...? If there are such fanatics, let them be stigmatised"; as for us, "we are fighting against many sects in Russia," our own[1436], but at the same time he declared that, according to him, the affair would be stifled in the Duma by fear of the press. Indeed, at the opening of the trial, the right-wing nationalist Chulguine declared himself opposed to it being held and to the "miserable baggage" of the judicial authorities in the columns of the patriotic *Kievian* (for which he was accused by the extreme Right to be sold to the Jews). But, in view of the exceptionally monstrous character of the crime, no one dared to go back to the accusation in order to resume the investigation from scratch.

On the other side, the liberal-radicals also launched a public campaign relayed by the press, and not only the Russian press, but that of the whole world. The tension had reached a point of no return. Sustained by the partiality of the accusation, it only escalated, and the witnesses themselves were soon attacked. According to V. Rozanov, every sense of measure had been lost, especially in the Jewish press: "The iron fist of the Jew... falls on venerable professors, on members of the Duma, on writers..."[1437]

However, the ultimate attempts to get the investigation back on track had failed. The stable near the Zaitsev factory, which was initially neglected by Krassovsky and then assumed to have been the scene of the crime, burned down two days before the date fixed for its examination by hasty investigators. A brazen journalist, Brazul-Brouchkovsky, conducted his own investigation assisted by the same Krassovsky, now released from his official duties. (It must be remembered that Bonch-Bruevich[1438] published a pamphlet accusing Brazoul of venality.[1439]) They put forward a version

---

[1435] *Sliosberg*, t. 3, pp. 23-24, 37.
[1436] Stenographic Record of the Debates at the Third Duma, 1911, pp. 3119-3120.
[1437] V. V. *Rozanov*, Oboniatelnoye i osiazatelnoye otnochenie ievreyev krovi (The Olfactory and Tactile Relationship of the Jews to Blood), Stockholm, 1934, p. 110.
[1438] Vladimir Bonch-Bruevich (1873-1955), sociologist, publisher, publicist very attached to Lenin, collaborator of Pravda, specialist in religious matters.
[1439] N. V. *Krylenko*, Za piat let. 1918-1922: Obvinitelnye retchi. (Five years, 1918-1922: Indictments...), M., 1923, p. 359.

of the facts according to which the murder was allegedly committed by Vera Cheberyak, whose children frequented Andrei Yushchinsky, herself flirting with the criminal underworld. During their long months of inquiry, the two Cheberyak sons died under obscure circumstances; Vera accused Krassovsky of poisoning them, who in turn accused her of killing her own children. Ultimately, their version was that Yushchinsky had been killed by Cheberyak in person with the intention of simulating a ritual murder. She said that the lawyer Margoline had offered her 40,000 rubles to endorse the crime, which he denied at the trial even though he was subject at the same moment to administrative penalties for indelicacy.

Trying to disentangle the innumerable details of this judicial imbroglio would only make the understanding even more difficult. (It should also be mentioned that the "metis" of the revolution and the secret police were also involved. In this connection, mention should be made of the equivocal role and strange behaviour during the trial of Lieutenant-Colonel Gendarmerie Pavel Ivanov—the very one who, in defiance of all laws, helped Bogrov, already condemned to death, to write a new version of the reasons which would have prompted him to kill Stolypin, a version in which the full weight of responsibility fell on the organs of Security to which Ivanov did not belong.) The trial was about to open in a stormy atmosphere. It lasted a month: September-October 1913. It was incredibly heavy: 213 witnesses summoned to the bar (185) presented themselves, still slowed down by the procedural artifices raised by the parties involved; the prosecutor Vipper was not up to the standard of the group of brilliant lawyers—Gruzenberg, Karabtchevski, Maklakov, Zaroudny—who did not fail to demand that the blunders he uttered be recorded in the minutes, for example: the course of this trial is hampered by "Jewish gold"; "they [the Jews in general] seem to laugh at us, see, we have committed a crime, but no one will dare to hold us accountable."[1440] (Not surprisingly, during the trial, Vipper received threatening letters—on some were drawn a slipknot—and not just him, but the civil parties, the expert of the prosecution, probably also the defence lawyers; the dean of the jury also feared for his life.) There was a lot of turmoil around the trial, selling passes for access to hearings, all of Kiev's educated people were boiling. The man in the street, him, remained indifferent.

A detailed medical examination was carried out. Several professors spread their differences as to whether or not Yushchinsky had remained alive until the last wound, and how acute were the sufferings he had endured. But it was the theological-scientific expertise that was at the centre of the trial: it focused on the very principle of the possibility of ritual murders perpetrated

---

[1440] *Ibidem*, pp. 356, 364.

by Jews, and it was on this that the whole world focused its attention.[1441] The defence appealed to recognised authorities in the field of Hebraism, such as Rabbi Maze, a specialist in the Talmud. The expert appointed by the Orthodox Church, Professor I. Troitsky of the Theological Academy of Petersburg, concluded his intervention by rejecting the accusation of an act of cold blood attributable to the Jews; he pointed out that the Orthodox Church had never made such accusations, that these were peculiar to the Catholic world. (Bikerman later recalled that in Imperial Russia the police officers themselves cut short "almost every year" rumours about the Christian blood shed during the Jewish Passover, "otherwise we would have had a 'case of ritual murder' not once every few decades, but every year."[1442] The main expert cited by the prosecution was the Catholic priest Pranaitis. To extend the public debate, the prosecutors demanded that previous ritual murder cases be examined, but the defence succeeded in rejecting the motion. These discussions on whether the murder was ritual or not ritual only further increased the emotion that the trial had created through the whole world.

But it was necessary that a judgment should be pronounced—on this accused, and not another—and this mission went to a dull jury composed of peasants painfully supplemented by two civil servants and two petty *bourgeois*; all were exhausted by a month of trials, they fell asleep during the reading of the materials of the case, requested that the trial be shortened, four of them solicited permission to return home before its conclusion and some needed medical assistance.

Nevertheless, these jurors judged on the evidence: the accusations against Beilis were unfounded, not proved. And Beilis was acquitted. And that was the end of it. No new search for the culprits was undertaken, and this strange and tragic murder remained unexplained.

Instead—and this was in the tradition of Russian weakness—it was imagined (not without ostentation) to erect a chapel on the very spot where the corpse of young Yushchinsky had been discovered, but this project provoked many protests, because it was judged reactionary. And Rasputin dissuaded the tsar from following up on it.[1443]

This trial, heavy and ill-conducted, with a white-hot public opinion for a whole year, in Russia as in the rest of the world, was rightly considered a battle of Tsou-Shima.[1444] It was reported in the European press that the

---

[1441] Retch, 1913, 26 Oct. (8 Nov.), p. 3.
[1442] *Bikerman*, RaJ, p. 29.
[1443] Sliosberg, t. 3, p. 47.
[1444] An allusion to the terrible naval reverse suffered by Russia in its war against Japan (27-28 May 1905).

Russian government had attacked the Jewish people, but that it was not the latter that had lost the war, it was the Russian State itself.

As for the Jews, with all their passion, they were never to forgive this affront of the Russian monarchy. The *fact* that the law had finally triumphed did nothing to change their feelings.

It would be instructive, however, to compare the Beilis trial with another that took place at the same time (1913-15) in Atlanta, USA; a trial which then made great noise: the Jew Leo Frank, also accused of the murder of a child (a girl raped and murdered), and again with very uncertain charges. He was condemned to be hung, and during the proceedings of cassation an armed crowd snatched him from his prison and hanged him.[1445] On the *individual* level, the comparison is in favour of Russia. But the Leo Frank affair had but little echo in public opinion, and did not become an object of reproach.

There is an epilogue in the Beilis case.

"Threatened with revenge by extreme right-wing groups, Beilis left Russia and went to Palestine with his family. In 1920 he moved to the United States.

He died of natural causes, at the age of sixty, in the vicinity of New York.[1446]

Justice Minister Shcheglovitov (according to some sources, he had "given instructions for the case to be elucidated as a ritual murder"[1447]) was shot by the Bolsheviks.

In 1919 the trial of Vera Cheberyak took place. It did not proceed according to the abhorred procedures of tsarism—no question of popular jury!—and lasted only about forty minutes in the premises of the Cheka of Kiev. A member of the latter, who was arrested in the same year by the Whites, noted in his testimony that "Vera Cheberyak was interrogated exclusively by Jewish Chekists, beginning with Sorine" [the head of the Blumstein Cheka]. Commander Faierman "subjected her to humiliating treatment, ripped off her clothes and struck her with the barrel of his revolver... She said: 'You can do whatever you want with me, but what I said, I will not

---

[1445] V. *Lazaris*, Smert Leo Franka (Death of Leo Frank), in "22", 1984, no. 36, pp. 155-159.
[1446] SJE, t. 1, pp. 317, 318.
[1447] *Ibidem*, p. 317.

come back on it... What I said at the Beilis trial, nobody pushed me to say it, nobody bribed me...'" She was shot on the spot.[1448]

In 1919, Vipper, now a Soviet official, was discovered in Kaluga and tried by the Moscow Revolutionary Tribunal. The Bolshevik prosecutor Krylenko pronounced the following words: "Whereas he presents a real danger to the Republic... that there be one Vipper less among us!" (This macabre joke suggested that R. Vipper, a professor of medieval history, was still alive.) However, the Tribunal merely sent Vipper "to a concentration camp... until the communist regime be definitively consolidated."[1449] After that, we lose his track.

Beilis was acquitted by peasants, those Ukrainian peasants accused of having participated in the pogroms against the Jews at the turn of the century, and who were soon to know the collectivisation and organised famine of 1932-33—a famine that journalists have ignored and that has not been included in the liabilities of this regime.

Here is yet another of these footsteps of History...

[1448] Chekist o Tcheka (A Chekist speaks of the Cheka). Na tchoujoï storone: Istoriko literatournye sborniki / pod red. S. P. Melgounova, t. 9. Berlin: Vataga; Prague: Plamia, 1925, pp. 118, 135.
[1449] *Krylenko*, pp. 367-368.

Chapter 11

Jews and Russians before the First World War: The Growing Awareness

In Russia—for another ten years it escaped its ruin—the best minds among the Russians and the Jews had had time to look back and evaluate from different points of view the essence of our common life, to seriously consider the question of culture and national destiny.

The Jewish people made its way through an ever-changing present by dragging behind it the tail of a comet of three thousand years of diaspora, without ever losing consciousness of being "a nation without language nor territory, but with its own laws" (Salomon Lourie), preserving its difference and its specificity by the force of its religious and national tension—in the name of a superior, meta-historical Providence. Have the Jews of the nineteenth and twentieth centuries sought to identify with the peoples who surrounded them, to blend into them? It was certainly the Jews of Russia who, longer than their other co-religionists, had remained in the core of isolation, concentrated on their religious life and conscience. But, from the end of the nineteenth century, it was precisely this Jewish community in Russia that began to grow stronger, to flourish, and now "the whole history of the Jewish community in the modern age was placed under the sign of Russian Jewry", which also manifested "a sharp sense of the movement of History."[1450]

For their part, the Russian thinkers were perplexed by the particularism of the Jews. And for them, in the nineteenth century, the question was how to *overcome* it. Vladimir Solovyov, who expressed deep sympathy for the Jews, proposed to do so by the love of the Russians towards the Jews.

Before him, Dostoyevsky had noticed the disproportionate fury provoked by his remarks, certainly offensive but very scarce, about the Jewish people: "This fury is a striking testimony to the way the Jews themselves regard the Russians... and that, in the motives of our differences with the Jews, it is perhaps not only the Russian people who bears all the

---

[1450] B. T. *Dinour*, Religiozno-natsionalny oblik ruskovo ievreistava (The religious and national aspects of the Jews of Russia), in BJWR-1, pp. 319, 322.

responsibility, but that these motives, obviously, have accumulated on both sides, and it cannot be said on which side there is the most."[1451]

From this same end of the nineteenth century, Teitel reports the following observation: "The Jews are in their majority materialists. Strong in them is the aspiration to acquire material goods. But what contempt for these material goods whenever it comes to the inner 'I', to national dignity! Why, in fact, the mass of Jewish youth—who has completely turned away from religious practice, which often does not even speak its mother tongue— why did this mass, if only for the sake of form, not convert to Orthodoxy, which would have opened to it wide the doors of all the universities and would have given it access to all the goods of the earth?" Even the thirst for knowledge was not enough, while "science, superior knowledge was held by them in higher esteem than fortune." What held them back was the concern not to abandon their coreligionists in need. (He also adds that going to Europe to study was not a good solution either: "Jewish students felt very uncomfortable in the West... The German Jew considered them undesirable, insecure people, noisy, disorderly,"; and this attitude was not only that of the German Jews, "the French and Swiss Jews were no exception."[1452]

As for D. Pasmanik, he also mentioned this category of Jews converted under duress, who felt only more resentment towards the power and could only oppose it. (From 1905, conversion was facilitated: it was no longer necessary to go to orthodoxy, it was enough to become a Christian, and Protestantism was more acceptable to many Jews. In 1905 was also repealed the prohibition to return to Judaism.[1453])

Another writer bitterly concluded, in 1924, that in the last decades preceding the revolution it was not only "the Russian government... which definitely ranked the Jewish people among the enemies of the country", but "even worse, it was a lot of Jewish politicians who ranked themselves among these enemies, radicalising their position and ceasing to differentiate between the 'government' and the fatherland, that is, Russia... The indifference of the Jewish masses and their leaders to the destiny of Great Russia was a fatal political error."[1454]

[1451] *F. M. Dostoyevsky*, Dnevnik pisatelia za 1877, 1880 i 1581 gody (Journal of a writer, March 1877, chapter 2), M., L., 1929, 1877, Mart, gl 2, p. 78.
[1452] *I. L. Teitel*, Iz moiii jizni za 40 let (Memories of 40 years of my life), Paris, I. Povolotski i ko., 1925, pp. 227-228.
[1453] JE, t. 11, p. 894.
[1454] *V. S. Mandel*, Konservativnye i pazrouchitelnye elementy v ievreïstve (Conservative and destructive elements among Jews), in RaJ, pp. 201, 203.

Of course, like any social process, this—and, moreover, in a context as diverse and mobile as the Jewish milieu—did not take place linearly, it was split; in the hearts of many educated Jews, it provoked rifts. On the one hand, "belonging to the Jewish people confers a specific position in the whole of the Russian milieu." [1455] But to observe immediately a "remarkable ambivalence: the traditional sentimental attachment of many Jews to the surrounding Russian world, their rootedness in this world, and at the same time an intellectual rejection, a refusal across the board. Affection for an abhorred world."[1456]

This approach so painfully ambivalent could not fail to lead to equally painfully ambivalent results. And when I. V. Hessen, in an intervention in the second Duma in March 1907, after having denied that the revolution was still in its phase of rising violence, thus denying right-wing parties the right to arise as defenders of the culture against anarchy, exclaimed: "We who are teachers, doctors, lawyers, statisticians, literary men, would we be the enemies of culture? Who will believe you, gentlemen?"—They shouted from the benches of the right: "You are the enemies of Russian culture, not of Jewish culture!"[1457]

Enemies, of course not, why go so far, but—as the Russian party pointed out—are you really, unreservedly, our friends? The rapprochement was made difficult precisely by this: how could these brilliant advocates, professors and doctors not have in their heart of hearts primarily Jewish sympathies? Could they feel, entirely and unreservedly, Russian by spirit? Hence the problem was even more complicated. Were they able to take to heart the interests of the Russian State in their full scope and depth?

During this same singular period, we see on the one hand that the Jewish middle classes make a very clear choice to give secular education to their children in the Russian language, and on the other there is the development of publications in Yiddish—and comes into use the term "Yiddishism": that the Jews remain Jewish, that they do not assimilate.

There was still a path to assimilation, doubtlessly marginal, but not negligible: that of mixed marriages. And also a current of superficial assimilation consisting in adapting artificial pseudonyms to the Russian way.

[1455] D. O. Linsky, O natsionalnom samosoznanii ruskovo ievreia (The national consciousness of the Russian Jew), RaJ, p. 142.
[1456] G. A. Landau, Revolioutsionnye idei v ievreïskoi obctchestvennosti (Revolutionary Ideas in Jewish Society), RaJ, p. 115.
[1457] Stenographic Record of the Debates of the Second Duma, 13 March 1907, p. 522.

(And who did this most often?! The great sugar producers of Kiev "Dobry"[1458], "Babushkin"[1459], prosecuted during the war for agreement with the enemy. The editor "Iasny"[1460] that even the newspaper of constitutional-democrat orientation *Retch* called an "avid speculator", an "unscrupulous shark."[1461] Or the future Bolshevik D. Goldenbach, who regarded "all of Russia as a country without worth" but disguised himself as "Riazanov" to bother the readers with his Marxist theoretician ratiocinations until his *arrest* in 1937.) And it was precisely during these decades, and especially in Russia, that Zionism developed. The Zionists were ironical about those who wanted to assimilate, who imagined that the fate of the Jews of Russia was indissolubly linked to the destiny of Russia itself.

And then, we must turn first to Vl. Jabotinsky, a brilliant and original essayist, who was brought, in the years preceding the revolution, to express not only his rejection of Russia but also his despair. Jabotinsky considered that Russia was nothing more than a halt for the Jews on their historical journey and that it was necessary to hit the road—to Palestine.

Passion ignited his words: it is not with the Russian people that we are in contact, we learn to know it through its culture, "mainly through its writers..., through the highest, the purest manifestations of the Russian spirit,"—and this appreciation, we transpose it to the whole of the Russian world. "Many of us, born of the Jewish intelligentsia, love the Russian culture with a maddening and degrading love... with the degrading love of swine keepers for a queen." As for the Jewish world, we discover it through the baseness and ugliness of everyday life.[1462]

He is merciless towards those who seek to assimilate. "Many of the servile habits that developed in our psychology as our intelligentsia became russified," "have ruined the hope or the desire to keep Jewishness intact, and lead to its disappearance." The average Jewish intellectual forgets himself: it is better not to pronounce the word "Jew", "the times are no longer about that"; we are afraid to write: "we the Jews", but we write: "we the Russians" and even: "we the Russkoffs". "The Jew can occupy a prominent place in Russian society, but he will always remain a second class Russian," and this, all the more so because he retains a specific 'inclination of the soul'."—We are witnessing an epidemic of baptisms for interest, sometimes for stakes far more petty than obtaining a diploma.

[1458] Literally "good", "generous".
[1459] Formed from "babushka"—"grandmother", "granny".
[1460] Literally "clear", "bright".
[1461] *P. G.* —Marodiory knigi 3 (The Marauders of the Book), in Retch, 1917, 6 May, s.
[1462] *Vl. Jabotinsky*, [Sb] Felietony. SPb.: Tipografia Gerold, 1913, pp. 9–11.

"The thirty pennies for equal rights..." When abjuring our faith, strip yourself also of our nationality.[1463]

The situation of the Jews in Russia—and not at any time, but precisely after the years 1905 1906—seemed to him desperately gloomy: "The objective reality, that is, the fact of living abroad, has turned itself against our people today, and we are weak and helpless."—"Already in the past we knew we were surrounded by enemies"; "this prison" (Russia), "a pack of dogs"; "the body lying, covered with the wounds of the Jewish people of Russia, tracked, surrounded by enemies and defenceless"; "six million human beings swarming in a deep pit..., a slow torture, a pogrom that does not end"; and even, according to him, "newspapers financed by Jewish funds" do not defend the Jews "in these times of unprecedented persecution." At the end of 1911, he wrote: "For several years now the Jews of Russia have been crammed on the bench of the accused", despite the fact we are not revolutionaries, that "we have not sold Russia to the Japanese" and that we are not Azefs[1464] or Bogrovs[1465]"; and in connection with Bogrov: "This unfortunate young man—he was what he was—, at the hour of such an admirable death[!], was booed by a dozen brutes from the cesspool of the Kievian Black Hundreds, come to ensure that the execution had indeed taken place."[1466]

And, returning again and again to the Jewish community itself: "Today we are culturally deprived, as at the bottom of a slum, of an obscure impasse."—"What we suffer above all is contempt for ourselves; what we need above all is to respect ourselves... The study of Jewishness must become for us the central discipline... Jewish culture is now the only plank of salvation for us."[1467]

All of this, we can, yes, we can understand it, share it. (And we, Russians, can do it, especially today, at the end of the twentieth century.) It does not condemn those who, in the past, have campaigned for assimilation: in the course of History "there are times when assimilation is undeniably desirable, when it represents a necessary stage of progress." This was the case after the sixties of the nineteenth century, when the Jewish intelligentsia was still in its embryonic state, beginning to adapt to the surrounding environment, to a culture that had reached maturity. At that time, assimilation did not mean "denying the Jewish people, but on the contrary, taking the first step on the road to autonomous national activity,

---

[1463] *Vl. Jabotinsky*, [Sb] Felietony, pp. 16, 62 63, 176–180, 253–254.
[1464] Azef Evno (1569-1918), terrorist, double agent (of the S.-R. and the Okhrana), unmasked by A. Bourtsev.
[1465] The assassin of Stolypin; *Cf. supra*, chapter 10.
[1466] *Ibidem*, pp. 26, 30, 75, 172, 173, 195, 199, 200, 205.
[1467] *Ibidem*, pp. 15, 17, 69.

taking a first step towards renewal and rebirth of the nation." It was necessary to "assimilate what was foreign to us in order to be able to develop with new energy what was our own." But half a century later, many radical transformations took place both inside and outside the Jewish world. The desire to appropriate universal knowledge has become widespread as never before. And it is then, now, that must be inculcated to the younger generations the *Jewish* principles. It is now that there is a threat of an irremediable dilution in the foreign environment:

"There is no day that passes in which our sons do not leave us" and "do not become strangers to us"; "enlightened by the Enlightenment, our children serve all the peoples of the Earth, except ours; no one is there to work for the Jewish cause." "The world around us is too magnificent, too spacious and too rich"—we cannot admit that it diverts Jewish youth from "the ugliness of the daily existence of the Jews... The deepening of national values of Jewishness must become the main axis... of Jewish education."—"Only the bond of solidarity allows a nation to hold" (we ourselves would need it!—A. S.), while denial slows down the struggle for the right of the Jews: one imagines that there is a way out, and "we leave... lately... in compact masses, with lightness and cynicism."[1468]

Then, letting himself be carried away: "The royal spirit [of Israel] in all its power, its tragic history in all its grandiose magnificence..." "Who are we to justify ourselves before them? Who are they to demand accountability?"[1469]

The latter formula, we can also respect it fully. But under the condition of reciprocity. Especially since it is not up to any nation or religion to *judge* another.

The calls to return to Jewish *roots* did not remain unheeded in those years.

In Saint Petersburg, before the revolution, "we could note in the circles of the Russo-Jewish intelligentsia a very great interest in Jewish history."[1470] In 1908, the Jewish Historical-Ethnographic Commission expanded into a Jewish Historical-Ethnographic Society,[1471] headed by M. Winaver. It worked actively and efficiently to collect the archives on the history and ethnography of the Jews of Russia and Poland—nothing comparable was established by Jewish historical science in the West. The magazine *The Jewish Past*, led by S. Dubnov, then was created.[1472] At the same time began the publication of the *Jewish Encyclopædia* in sixteen volumes

---

[1468] *Ibidem*, pp. 18-24, 175, 177.
[1469] *Ibidem*, pp. 14, 200.
[1470] Pamiati, M. L. Vichnitsera, BJWR-1. p. 8.
[1471] JE, t. 8, p. 466.
[1472] JE, t. 7, pp. 449 450.

(which we use extensively in this study), and the *History of the Jewish People* in fifteen volumes. It is true that in the last volume of the *Jewish Encyclopædia*, its editors complain that "the elite of the Jewish intelligentsia has shown its indifference to the cultural issues raised by this *Encyclopædia*," devoting itself exclusively to the struggle for the equality—all formal—of rights for the Jews.[1473]

Meanwhile, on the contrary, in other minds and other Jewish hearts there was a growing conviction that the future of the Jews of Russia was indissolubly linked to that of Russia. Although "scattered over an immense territory and among a foreign world..., the Russian Jewish community had and was conscious of being a unique whole. Because unique was the environment that surrounded us..., unique its culture... This unique culture, we absorbed it throughout the whole country."[1474]

"The Jews of Russia have always been able to align their own interests to those of all the Russian people. And this did not come from any nobility of character or a sense of gratitude, but from a perception of historical realities."

Open controversy with Jabotinsky: "Russia is not, for the millions of Jews who populate it, a step among others on the historical path of the wandering Jew...

The contribution of Russian Jews to the international Jewish community has been and will be the most significant. There is no salvation for us without Russia, as there is no salvation for Russia without us."[1475]

This interdependence is affirmed even more categorically by the deputy of the second and third Dumas, O. I. Pergament: "No improvement of the internal situation of Russia 'is possible without the simultaneous enfranchisement of the Jews from the yoke of inequality'."[1476]

And there, one cannot ignore the exceptional personality of the jurist G. B. Sliosberg: among the Jews he was one of those who, for decades, had the closest relations with the Russian State, sometimes as Deputy to the Principal Secretary of the Senate, sometimes as a consultant to the Ministry of the Interior, but to whom many Jews reproached his habit of *asking* the authorities for rights for the Jews, when the time had come *demand* them. He writes in his memoirs: "From childhood, I have become accustomed to

---

[1473] JE, t. 16, p. 276.
[1474] I. M. Bikerman, Rossia i rousskoye ievreisstvo (Russia and the Jewish Community of Russia), RaJ. p. 86.
[1475] St. Ivanovich, Ievrei i sovetskaya dikiatoura (The Jews and the Soviet Dictatorship), in JW, pp. 55-56.
[1476] JE, t. 12, pp. 372 373.

consider myself above all as a Jew. But from the beginning of my conscious life I also felt like a son of Russia... Being a good Jew does not mean that one is not a good Russian citizen."[1477]—"In our work, we were not obliged to overcome the obstacles encountered at every step by the Jews of Poland because of the Polish authorities... In the Russian political and administrative system, we Jews did not represent a foreign element, insofar as, in Russia, cohabited many nationalities. The cultural interests of Russia did not conflict in any way with the cultural interests of the Jewish community. These two cultures were somewhat complementary."[1478] He even added this somewhat humorous remark: the legislation on Jews was so confusing and contradictory that in the 90s, "it was necessary to create a specific jurisprudence for the Jews using purely Talmudic methods."[1479]

And again, in a higher register: "The easing of the national yoke which has been felt in recent years, shortly before Russia entered a tragic period in its history, bore in the hearts of all Russian Jews the hope that the Russian Jewish consciousness would gradually take a creative path, that of reconciling the Jewish and Russian aspects in the synthesis of a higher unity."[1480]

And can we forget that, among the seven authors of the incomparable *Milestones*[1481], three were Jews: M. O. Gershenzon, A. S. Izgoev-Lande, and S. L. Frank?

But there was reciprocity: in the decades preceding the revolution, the Jews benefited from the massive and unanimous support of progressive circles.

Perhaps the amplitude of this support is due to a context of bullying and pogroms, but it has never been so complete in any other country (and perhaps never in all the past centuries). Our intelligentsia was so generous, so freedom-loving, that it ostracised anti-Semitism from society and humanity; moreover, the one who did not give his frank and massive support to the struggle for equal rights of the Jews, who did not make it a priority, was considered a "despicable anti-Semite". With its ever-awakening moral consciousness and extreme sensitivity, the Russian intelligentsia sought to understand and assimilate the Jewish view of priorities affecting the whole of political life: is deemed progressive all that is a reaction against the persecution of the Jews, all the rest is reactionary. Not only did Russian society firmly defend the Jews against the

---

[1477] *Sliosberg*, t. 1, pp. 3 4.
[1478] *Sliosberg*, t. 2, p. 302.
[1479] *Sliosberg*, t. 1, p. 302.
[1480] *Linsky*, RaJ, p. 144.
[1481] *Vekhi*: resounding collection of articles (1909) in which a group of intellectuals disillusioned from Marxism invited the intelligentsia to reconcile with the power.

government, but it forbade itself and forbade anyone to show any trace of a shadow of criticism of the conduct of each Jew in particular: and if this bore anti-Semitism within me? (The generation formed at that time retained these principles for decades.)

V. A. Maklakov evokes in his memoirs a significant episode that occurred during the congress of the Zemstvos in 1905, when the wave of pogroms against the Jews and intellectuals had just swept through and began to rise in strength the pogroms directed against landowners. "E. V. de Roberti proposed not to extend the amnesty [demanded by the congress] to the crimes related to violence against children and women." He was immediately suspected of wanting to introduce a "class" amendment, that is to say, to concern himself with the families of the noble victims of pogroms. "E. de Roberti hastened... to reassure everybody: 'I had absolutely no plan in regard to the property of the noblemen... Five or twenty properties burned down, this has no importance. I have in view the mass of immovable property and houses belonging to Jews, which were burned and pillaged by the Black Hundreds'."[1482]

During the terror of 1905 1907, Gerzenstein (who had been ironic about the property fires of the noblemen) and Iollos were considered as martyrs, but no one among the thousands of other innocent victims, were considered so. In *The Last Autocrat*, a satirical publication that the Russian liberals published abroad, they succeeded in placing the following legend under the portrait of the general whom the terrorist Hirsch Lekkert had attempted in vain to assassinate: "*Because of him*"[I emphasise—A. S.], the tsar "had executed... the Jew Lekkert."[1483]

It was not just the parties of the opposition, it was the whole mass of middle-class civil servants who were trembling at the idea of sounding like "non-progressives". It was necessary to enjoy a good personal fortune, or possess remarkable freedom of mind, to resist with courage the pressure of general opinion. As for the world of the bar, of art, of science, ostracism immediately struck anyone who moved away from this magnetic field.

Only Leo Tolstoy, who enjoyed a unique position in society, could afford to say that, *for him*, the Jewish question was in the 81st place.

The *Jewish Encyclopædia* complained that the pogroms of October 1905 "provoked in the progressive intelligentsia a protestation that was not

---

[1482] *V. A. Maklakov*, Vlast i obchtchestvennost na zakate staroï Rossii (Vospominania sovremennika) [The power and opinion during the twilight of ancient Russia (Memoirs of a Contemporary)], Paris: Prilojenie k "Illioustrirovannoï Rossii" II n 1936, p. 466.
[1483] Der Letzte russische Alleinherscher (The Last Autocrat: Study on the Life and Reign of the Emperor of Russia Nicholas II), Berlin, Ebcrhard Frowein Verlag [1913], p. 58.

specific [i.e., exclusively Jewish-centred], but general, oriented towards all manifestations of the 'counter-revolution' in all its forms."[1484]

Moreover, Russian society would have ceased to be itself if it had not brought everything to a single burning question: tsarism, still tsarism, always tsarism!

But the consequence was this: "After the days of October [the pogroms of 1905], concrete aid to the Jewish victims was brought only by the Jews of Russia and other countries."[1485] And Berdyaev added: "Are you capable of feeling the soul of the Jewish people?... No, you are fighting... in favour of an abstract humanity."[1486]

This is confirmed by Sliosberg: "In politically evolved circles," the Jewish question "was not political in the broad sense of the term. Society was attentive to manifestations of the reaction in all its forms."[1487]

In order to correct this misjudgement of Russian society, a collection of articles entitled *Shchit* [The Shield] was published in 1915: it took on globally and exclusively the defence of the Jews, but without the participation of the latter as writers, these were either Russian or Ukrainian, and a beautiful skewer of celebrities of the time was assembled there—nearly forty names.[1488] The whole collection was based on a single theme: "Jews in Russia"; it is univocal in its conclusions and its formulations denote in some places a certain spirit of sacrifice.

A few samples— *L. Andreev*: "The prospect of an approaching solution to the Jewish problem brings about a feeling of 'joy close to fervour', the feeling of being freed from a pain that has accompanied me all my life," which was like "a hump on the back"; "I breathed poisonous air..."— *M. Gorky*: "The great European thinkers consider that the psychic structure of the Jew is culturally higher, more beautiful than that of the Russian." (He then rejoiced at the development in Russia of the sect of the Sabbatists and that of the "New Israel".)— *P. Maliantovitch*: "The arbitrariness to which the Jews are subjected is a reproach which, like a stain, covers the name of the Russian people... The best among the Russians feel it as a shame that pursues you all your life. We are barbarians among the civilised peoples of humanity... we are deprived of the precious right to be proud of our people... The struggle for the equal rights of the Jews represents for the Russian man... a national cause of prime importance... The arbitrariness

---

[1484] JE, t. 12, p. 621.
[1485] JE, t. 12, p. 621.
[1486] *Nikolai Berdyaev*, Filosofia neravenstva (Philosophy of Inequality), 2nd ed., Paris, YMCA Press, 1970, p. 72.
[1487] *Sliosberg*, t. 1, p. 260.
[1488] Shchit (the Shield), 1916.

subjected to the Jews condemns the Russians to failure in their attempts to attain their own happiness." If we do not worry about the liberation of the Jews, "we will never be able to solve our own problems."—*K. Arseniev*: "If we remove everything that hinders the Jews, we will see 'an increase in the intellectual forces of Russia'."— *A. Kalmykova*: "On the one hand, our 'close spiritual relationship with the Jewish world in the domain of the highest spiritual values'; on the other, 'the Jews may be the object of contempt, of hatred'."— *L. Andreev*: "It is we, the Russians, who are the *Jews of Europe*; our *border*, it is precisely the *Pale of Settlement*."— *D. Merezhkovsky*:

"What do the Jews expect of us? Our moral indignation? But this indignation is so strong and so simple... that we only have to scream with the Jews. This is what we do."—By the effect of I am not sure which misunderstanding, Berdyaev is not one of the authors of the *Shield*. But he said of himself that he had broken with his milieu from his earliest youth and that he preferred to frequent the Jews.

All the authors of the *Shield* define anti-Semitism as an ignoble feeling, as "a disease of consciousness, obstinate and contagious" (D. Ovsianikov-Kulikovsky, Academician). But at the same time, several authors note that "the methods and processes... of anti-Semites [Russians] are of foreign origin" (P. Milyukov). "The latest cry of anti-Semitic ideology is a product of the German industry of the spirit... The 'Aryan' theory... has been taken up by our nationalist press... Menshikov [1489] [copies] the ideas of Gobineau" (F. Kokochkin). The doctrine of the superiority of the Aryans in relation to the Semites is "of German manufacture" (see Ivanov).

But for us, with our hump on our backs, what does it change? Invited by the "Progressive Circle" at the end of 1916, Gorky "devoted the two hours of his lecture to rolling the Russian people in the mud and raising the Jews to the skies," as noted by the Progressive deputy Mansyrev, one of the founders of the "Circle".[1490]

A contemporary Jewish writer analyses this phenomenon objectively and lucidly: "We assisted to a profound transformation of the minds of the cultivated Russians who, unfortunately, took to heart the Jewish problem much more greatly than might have been expected... Compassion for the Jews was transformed into an imperative almost as categorical as the formula 'God, the Tsar, the Fatherland'"; as for the Jews, "they took

---

[1489] Menshikov Michel (1859–1918), began a career as a sailor (until 1892), then became a journalist at the *New Times*, supported Stolypin. After October, takes refuge in Valdai. Arrested in August 1918 by the Bolsheviks, he was executed without trial.

[1490] *Kn. S. P. Mansyrev*, Moi vospominania (My memories)//[Sb.] Fevralskaïa revolioutsia / sost. S. A. Alexeyev. M. L., 1926, p. 259.

advantage of this profession of faith according to their degree of cynicism."[1491] At the same time, Rozanov spoke of "the avid desire of the Jews to seize everything."[1492]

In the 20s, V. Choulguine summed it up as follows: "At that time [a quarter of a century before the revolution], the Jews had taken control of the political life of the country... The brain of the nation (if we except the government and the circles close to it) found itself in the hands of the Jews and was accustomed to think according to their directives." "Despite all the 'restrictions' on their rights, the Jews had taken possession of the soul of the Russian people."[1493]

But was it the Jews who had seized the Russian soul or did the Russians simply not know what to do with it?

Still in *the Shield*, Merezhkovsky tried to explain that philo-Semitism had arisen in reaction to anti-Semitism, that the blind valourisation of a foreign nationality was asserted, that the absolutisation of the "no" led to that of the "yes".[1494] And Professor Baudouin de Courtenay acknowledged that "many, even among the 'political friends' of the Jews, experience repulsion and acknowledge it in private. Here, of course, there is nothing to do. Sympathy and antipathy... are not commanded." We must nevertheless rely "not on affects, but on reason."[1495]

The confusion that reigned in the minds of those days was brought to light with greater significance and reach by P. B. Struve, who devoted his entire life to breaking down the obstacles erected on the path that would lead him from Marxism to the rule of law, and, along the way, also obstacles of other kinds.

The occasion was a polemic—fallen into a deep oblivion, but of great historical importance—which broke out in the liberal *Slovo* newspaper in March 1909 and immediately won the entirety of the Russian press.

Everything had begun with the "Chirikov affair", an episode whose importance was inflated to the extreme: an explosion of rage in a small literary circle accusing Chirikov—author of a play entitled *The Jews*, and well disposed towards them—to be anti-Semitic. (And this because at a

---

[1491] A. *Voronel*, in "22": Obchtchestvenno-polititcheski i literatourny newspaper Ivreiskoi intelligentsii iz SSSR v Izrailie, Tel Aviv, 1986, no. 50, pp. 156–157.
[1492] Perepiska V. V. Rozanova and M. O. Gerchenzona (Correspondence of V. Rozanov and M. Gerchenzon), Novy Mir, 1991, no. 3, p. 239.
[1493] *V. V. Choulguine*, "Chto nam v nikh ne nravitsa...": Ob antisemitzme v Rossii ("What we do not like about them..." On anti-Semitism in Russia), Paris, 1929, pp. 58, 75.
[1494] Shchit (the Shield), p. 164.
[1495] *Ibidem*, p. 145.

dinner of writers he had let himself go on to say that most of the literary critics of Saint Petersburg were Jews, but were they able to understand the reality of Russian life?) This affair shook many things in Russian society. (The journalist Lioubosh wrote about it: "It is the two kopeck candle that set fire to Moscow.") Considering that he had not sufficiently expressed himself on the Chrikov affair in a first article, Jabotinsky published a text entitled "Asemitism" in the *Slovo* newspaper on 9 March 1909. He stated in it his fears and his indignation at the fact that the majority of the progressive press wanted to silence this matter. That even a great liberal newspaper (he was referring to the *Russian News*) had not published a word for twenty-five years on "the atrocious persecutions suffered by the Jewish people… Since then the law of silence has been regarded as the latest trend by progressive philo-Semites." It was precisely here that evil resided: in passing over the Jewish question. (We can only agree with this!) When Chirikov and Arabajine "assure us that there is nothing anti-Semitic in their remarks, they are both perfectly right." Because of this tradition of silence, "one can be accused of anti-Semitism for having only pronounced the word 'Jew' or made the most innocent remark about some particularity of the Jews… The problem is that the Jews have become a veritable taboo that forbids the most trivial criticism, and that it is them that are the big losers in the affair." (Here again, we can only agree!) "There is a feeling that the word 'Jew' itself has become an indecent term." "There is here an echo of a general state of mind that makes its way among the middle strata of the progressive Russian intelligentsia… We can not yet provide tangible proofs of it, we can only have a presentiment about this state of mind"—, but it is precisely this that torments him: no proofs, just an intuition—and the Jews will not see the storm coming, they will be caught unprepared. For the moment, "we see only a small cloud forming in the sky and we can hear a distant, but already menacing roll." It is not anti-Semitism, it is only "Asemitism", but that also is not admissible, neutrality cannot be justified: after the pogrom of Kishinev and while the reactionary press peddles "the inflamed tow of hatred", the silence of the progressive newspapers about "one of the most tragic questions of Russian life" is unacceptable.[1496]

In the editorial of the same issue of *Slovo*, were formulated the following reservations about Jabotinsky's article: "The accusations made by the author against the progressive press correspond, in our opinion, to the reality of things.

We understand the sentiments that have inspired the author with his bitter remarks, but to impute to the Russian intelligentsia the intention, so to speak deliberately, of sweeping the Jewish question under the rug, is unfair.

[1496] Vl. Jabotinsky, Asemitizm (Asemitism), in Slovo, SPb., 1909, 9 (22) March, p. 2; See also: [Sb.] Felietony, pp. 77 83.

The Russian reality has so many unresolved problems that we cannot devote much space to each one of them... Yet, if many of these problems are resolved, this will have very important effects, including for the Jews who are citizens of our common homeland."[1497]

And if the editorialist of the *Slovo* had then asked Jabotinsky why he did not defend one or the other of those fools who uttered "the most innocent remark about some particularity of the Jews"? Was Jewish opinion interested only in them, did they take their part? Or was it enough to observe how the Russian intelligentsia got rid of these "anti-Semites"? No, the Jews were no less responsible than the others for this "taboo".

Another article in the same paper helped launch the discussion: "The agreement, not the fusion", of V. Golubev. Indeed, the Chirikov affair "is far from being an isolated case", "at the present time... the national question... is also of concern to our intelligentsia". In the recent past, especially in the year of the revolution[1498], our intelligentsia has "sinned very much" by cosmopolitanism. But "the struggles that have been fought within our community and between the nationalities that populate the Russian State have not disappeared without leaving traces." Like the other nationalities, in those years, "the Russians had to look at their own national question...; when nationalities deprived of sovereignty began to self-determine, the Russians felt the need to do so as well." Even the history of Russia, "we Russian intellectuals, we know it perhaps less well than European history." "Universal ideals... have always been more important to us than the edification of our own country." But, even according to Vladimir Solovyov, who is however very far removed from nationalism, "before being a bearer of universal ideals, it is essential to raise oneself to a certain national level. And the feeling of raising oneself seems to have begun to make its way into our intelligentsia." Until now, "we have been silent on our own peculiarities." Remembering them in our memory does not constitute a manifestation of anti-Semitism and oppression of other nationalities: between nationalities there must be "harmony and not fusion".[1499]

The editorial team of the newspaper may have taken all these precautions because it was preparing to publish the following day, 10 March, an article by P. B. Struve, "The intelligentsia and the national face", which had coincidentally arrived at the same time than that of Jabotinsky and also dealing with the Chirikov case.

[1497] Slovo, 1909, 9 (22) March, p. 1.
[1498] of 1905.
[1499] *V. Golubev*, Soglachenie, a ne stianie, Slovo, 1909, 9 (22) March, p. 1.

Struve wrote: "This incident," which will "soon be forgotten", "has shown that something has moved in the minds, has awakened and will no longer be calmed. And we will have to rely on that." "The Russian intelligentsia hides its national face, it is an attitude that imposes nothing, which is sterile."—"Nationality is something much more obvious [than race, colour of skin] and, at the same time, something subtle. It is the attraction and repulsion of the mind and, to become aware of them, it is not necessary to resort to anthropometry or to genealogy. They live and palpitate in the depths of the soul." One can and must fight to make these attractions/repulsions not be brought into law, "but 'political' equity does not require from us 'national' indifference." These attractions and repulsions belong to us, they are our goods", "the organic feeling of our national belonging… And I do not see the slightest reason… to renounce this property in the name of anyone or anything."

Yes, insists Struve, it is essential to draw a border between the legal, the political domains and the realm where these sentiments live. "Especially with regard to the Jewish question, it is both very easy and very difficult."—"The Jewish question is formally a question of law", and, for this reason, it is easy and natural to help solve it: to grant the Jews equal rights—yes, of course! But at the same time it is "very difficult because the force of rejection towards the Jews in different strata of Russian society is considerable, and it requires great moral force and a very rational mind to, despite this repulsion, resolve definitively this question of right." However, "even though there is a great force of rejection towards the Jews among large segments of the Russian population, of all the 'foreigners' the Jews are those who are closest to us, those who are the most closely linked to us. It is a historico-cultural paradox, but it is so. The Russian intelligentsia has always regarded the Jews as Russians, and it is neither fortuitous nor the effect of a 'misunderstanding'. The deliberate initiative of rejecting Russian culture and asserting Jewish 'national' singularity does not belong to the Russian intelligentsia, but to this movement known as Zionism…

I do not feel any sympathy for Zionism, but I understand that the problem of 'Jewish' nationality does indeed exist," and even poses itself more and more. (It is significant that he places "national" and "Jewish" in quotation marks: he still cannot believe that the Jews think of themselves as others.) "There does not exist in Russia other 'foreigners' who play a role as important in Russian culture… And here is another difficulty: they play this role while remaining Jews." One cannot, for example, deny the role of the Germans in Russian culture and science; but by immersing themselves in Russian culture, the Germans completely blend into it. "With the Jews, that's another matter!"

And he concludes: "We must not deceive [our national feeling] or hide our faces... I have a right, like any Russian, to these feelings... The better it is understood... the less there will be misunderstandings in the future."[1500]

Yes... Oh, if we had woken up, as much as we are, a few decades earlier! (The Jews, they, had awakened long before the Russians.)

But the very next day, it was a whirlwind: as if all the newspapers had waited for that! From the liberal *Hacha Gazeta* ("Is this the right *moment* to talk about this?") and the right-wing newspaper *Novoie Vremia* to the organ of the Democratic constitutional party *Retch* where Milyukov could not help exclaiming: Jabotinsky "has succeeded in breaking the wall of silence, and all the frightening and threatening things that the progressive press and the intelligentsia had sought to hide from the Jews now appear in their true dimension." But, later on, argumentative and cold as usual, Milyukov goes on to the verdict. It begins with an important warning: *Where does it lead? Who benefits from it?* The "national face" which, moreover, "we must not hide", is a step towards the worst of fanaticism! (Thus, the "national face" *must* be hidden.) Thus "the slippery slope of æsthetic nationalism will precipitate the intelligentsia towards its degeneration, towards a true tribal chauvinism" engendered "in the putrid atmosphere of the reaction reigning over today's society."[1501]

But P. B. Struve, with an almost juvenile agility in spite of his forty years, retaliates as soon as 12 March in the columns of the *Slovo* to the "professorial speech" of Milyukov. And, above all, to this sleight of hand: "Where does it lead?" ("Who benefits from it?" "Who will draw the chestnuts from the fire?"—this is how people will be silenced—whatever they say—for a hundred years or more. There is a falsifying process that denotes a total inability to understand that a speech can be honest and have weight in itself.)—"Our point of view is not refuted on the merits", but confronted on the polemic mode to "a projection": "Where does it lead?"[1502] (A few days later, he wrote again in the *Slovo*: "It is an old process to discredit both an idea that one does not share and the one who formulates it, insinuating perfidiously that the people of *Novoie Vremia* or *Russkoye Znamya* will find it quite to their liking. This procedure is, in our opinion, utterly unworthy of a progressive press."[1503]) Then, as to the substance: "National questions are, nowadays, associated with powerful, sometimes violent feelings. To the extent that they express in everyone the

---

[1500] P. *Struve*, Intelligentsia i natsionalnoïe litso, Slovo, 1909, 10 (23) March, p. 2.
[1501] P. *Milyukov*, Natsionalizm protiv natsionalizma (Nationalism Against Nationalism), Retch, 1909, 11 (24) March, p. 2.
[1502] P. *Struve*, Polemitcheskie zigzagui i nesvoïevremennaya pravda (polemical zigzags and undesired truth), Slovo, 1909, 12 (25) March, p. 1.
[1503] Slovo, 1909, 17 (30) March, p. 1.

consciousness of their national identity, these feelings are fully legitimate and... to stifle them is... a great villainy." That is it: if they are repressed, they will reappear in a denatured form. As for this "'Asemitism' which would be the worst thing, it is in fact a much more favourable ground for a legal solution of the Jewish question than the endless struggle between 'anti-Semitism' and 'philo-Semitism'. There is no non-Russian nationality that needs... all Russians to love it without reservation. Even less that they pretend to love it. In truth, 'Asemitism', combined with a clear and lucid conception of certain moral and political principles and certain political constraints, is much more necessary and useful to our Jewish compatriots than a sentimental and soft 'philo-Semitism'", especially if this one is simulated.—And "it is good that the Jews see the 'national face'" of Russian constitutionalism and democratic society. And "it is of no use to them to speak under the delusion that this face belongs only to anti-Semitic fanaticism." This is not "the head of the Medusa, but the honest and human face of the *Russian nation*, without which the *Russian State* would not stand up." [1504] —And again these lines of *Slovo*'s editorial team: "Harmony... implies recognition and respect for all the specificities of each [nationality]."[1505]

Heated debates continued in the newspapers. "Within a few days a whole literature was formed on the subject." We assisted "In the Progressive Press... to something unthinkable even a short time ago: there is a debate on the question of Great-Russian nationalism!"[1506] But the discussion only reached this level in the *Slovo*; the other papers concentrated on the question of "attractions and repulsions".[1507] The intelligentsia turned its anger towards its hero of the day before.

Jabotinsky also gave voice, and even twice... "The bear came out of his lair," he lashed out, addressed to P. Struve, a man who was however so calm and well-balanced. Jabotinsky, on the other hand, felt offended; he described his article, as well as that of Milyukov, as "a famous batch": "their languorous declamation is impregnated with hypocrisy, insincerity, cowardice and opportunism, which is why it is so incorrigibly worthless"; and to ironise in quoting Milyukov: thus "the holy and pure Russian intelligentsia of old" "felt feelings of 'repulsion' at the encounter of the Jews?... Bizarre, no?" He criticised "the 'holy and pure' climate of this marvellous country", and the zoological species of *Yursus judaeophagus*

[1504] P. *Struve*, Slovo, 1909, 12 (25) March, p. 1.
[1505] V. *Golubev*, K polemike o natsionalizme (On the controversy regarding nationalism), *ibidem*, p. 2.
[1506] M. *Slavinski*, Ruskie, velikorossy i rossiane (*The Russians, the Great Russians, and the citizens of Russia*), *ibidem*, 14 (27) March, p. 2.
[1507] Slovo*, 1909, 17 (30) March, p. 1.

intellectualis." (The conciliatory Winaver also took for his rank: "the Jewish footman of the Russian palace").

Jabotinsky fulminated at the idea that the Jews should wait "until was resolved the central political problem" (i.e. the tsar's deposition): "We thank you for having such a flattering opinion on our disposition to behave like a dog with his master", "on the celerity of faithful Israel". He even concluded by stating that "never before the exploitation of a people by another had ever been revealed with such ingenuous cynicism."[1508]

It must be admitted that this excessive virulence hardly contributed to the victory of his cause. Moreover, the near future was going to show that it was precisely the deposition of the tsar which would open the Jews to even more possibilities than they sought to obtain, and cut the grass under the foot of Zionism in Russia; so much and so well that Jabotinsky was also deceived on the merits.

Much later and with the retreat of time, another witness of that era, then a member of the Bund, recalled that "in the years 1907–1914, some liberal intellectuals were affected by the epidemic, if not of open anti-Semitism, at least 'Asemitism' that struck Russia then; on the other hand, having gotten over the extremist tendencies that had arisen during the first Russian revolution, they were tempted to hold the Jews accountable, whose participation in the revolution had been blatant." In the years leading up to the war, "the rise of Russian nationalism was present... in certain circles where, at first sight, the Jewish problem was, only a short time before, perceived as a Russian problem."[1509]

In 1912, Jabotinsky himself, this time in a more balanced tone, reported this judicious observation of a prominent Jewish journalist: as soon as the Jews are interested in some cultural activity, immediately the latter becomes foreign to the Russian public, who is no longer attracted to it. A kind of invisible *rejection*. It is true, that a national demarcation cannot be avoided; it will be necessary to organise life in Russia "without external additions which, in so large a quantity, perhaps cannot be tolerated [by the Russians]."[1510]

To consider all that has been presented above, the most accurate conclusion is to say that within the Russian intelligentsia were developing simultaneously (as history offers many examples) two processes that, with regard to the Jewish problem, were distinguished by a question of

---
[1508] *Vl. Jabotinsky*, Medved iz berlogui—Sb. Felietony, pp. 87–90.
[1509] *G. I. Aronson*, V borbe za grajdanskie i natsionalnye prava Obchtchestvennye tetchenia v rousskom ievreïstve (The fight for civil and national rights currents of opinion in the Jewish community of Russia), BJWR-1, pp. 229, 572.
[1510] *Vl. Jabotinsky*—[Sb.] Felietony, pp. 245–247.

temperament, not by a degree of sympathy. But the one represented by Struve was too weak, uncertain, and was stifled. Whilst the one who had trumpeted his philo-Semitism in the collection *The Shield* enjoyed a wide publicity and prevailed among public opinion. There is only to regret that Jabotinsky did not recognise Struve's point of view at its fair value.

As for the 1909 debate in the *Slovo* columns, it was not limited to the Jewish question, but turned into a discussion of Russian national consciousness, which, after the eighty years of silence that followed, remains today still vivacious and instructive,—P. Struve wrote: "Just as we must not Russify those who do not want it, so we must not dissolve ourselves in Russian multinationalism."[1511]—V. Golubev protested against the "monopolisation of patriotism and nationalism by reactionary groups": "We have lost sight of the fact that the victories won by the Japanese have had a disastrous effect on the popular conscience and national sentiment. Our defeat not only humiliated our bureaucrats," as public opinion hoped, "but, indirectly, the nation as well." (Oh no, not "indirectly": quite directly!) "Russian nationality... has vanished."[1512]

Nor is it a joke that the flourishing of the word "Russian" itself, which has been transformed into "authentically Russian". The progressive intelligentsia has let these two notions go, abandoning them to the people of the right. "Patriotism, we could only conceive it in quotation marks." But "we must compete with reactionary patriotism with a popular patriotism... We have frozen in our refusal of the patriotism of the Black Hundreds, and if we have opposed something of it, it is not another conception of patriotism, but of universal ideals."[1513] And yet, all our cosmopolitanism has not allowed us, until today, to fraternise with the Polish society...[1514]

A. Pogodin was able to say that after V. Solovyov's violent indictment of Danilevsky's book, *Russia and Europe*, after Gradovsky's articles, were "the first manifestations of this consciousness which, like the instinct of self-preservation, awakens among the peoples when danger threatens them."

(Coincidentally—at the very moment when this polemic took place, Russia had to endure its national humiliation: it was forced to recognise with pitiable resignation the annexation by Austria of Bosnia and Herzegovina,

---

[1511] *P. Struve*, Slovo, 1909, 10 (23) March, p. 2.
[1512] *V. Golubev, ibidem*, 12 (25) March, p. 2.
[1513] *V. Golubev*, O monopolii na patriotizm (On the monopoly of patriotism), *ibidem*, 14 (27) March, p. 2.
[1514] *V. Golubev*, Ot samuvajenia k ouvajeniou (From self-respect to respect), *ibidem*, 25 March (7 April), p. 1.

which was equivalent to a "diplomatic Tsou-Shina".) "Fatality leads us to raise this question, which was formerly entirely foreign to the Russian intelligentsia, but which life itself imposes on us with a brutality that forbids all evasion."[1515]

In conclusion, the *Slovo* wrote: "A fortuitous incident triggered quite a journalistic storm." This means that "Russian society needs national awareness". In the past, "it had turned away not only from a false anti-national policy... but also from genuine nationalism without which a policy cannot really be built." A people capable of creation "cannot but have its own face."[1516]

"Minine [1517] was certainly a nationalist." A constructive nationalist, possessing the sense of the State, is peculiar to *living* nations, and that is what we need now.[1518] "Just as three hundred years ago, history tells us to reply," to say, "in the dark hours of trial... if we have the right, like any people worthy of the name, to exist by ourselves."[1519]

And yet—even if, apparently, the year 1909 was rather peaceful—one felt that the Storm was in the air! However, certain things were not lost sight of (M. Slavinski): "Attempts to Russify or, more exactly, to impose the Russian-Russian model on Russia... have had a disastrous effect on living national peculiarities, not only of all the non-sovereign peoples of the Empire, but also and above all of the people of Great-Russia... The cultural forces of the people of Great Russia proved insufficient for this." "For the nationality of Great Russia, only the development of the interior, a normal circulation of blood, is good."[1520] (Alas! even today, the lesson has not been assimilated). "Necessary is the struggle against physiological nationalism, [when] a stronger people tries to impose on others who are less so a way of life that is foreign to them."[1521] But an empire as this could not have been constituted solely by physical force, there was also a "moral force". And if we possess this force, then the equality of rights of other peoples (Jews as well as Poles) does not threaten us in any way.[1522]

In the nineteenth century already, and *a fortiori* at the beginning of the twentieth century, the Russian intelligentsia felt that it was at a high level

---

[1515] A. Pogodin, K voprosou o natsionalizme (On the national question), *ibidem*, 15 (28) March, p. 1.
[1516] Slovo, 1909, 17 (30) March, p. 1.
[1517] Hero of the Russian resistance to the Polish invasion in the early seventeenth century.
[1518] A. Pogodin, *ibidem*, 15 (28) March, p. 1.
[1519] Slovo, 1909, 17 (30) March, p. 1.
[1520] M. Slavinski, Slovo, 1909, 14 (27) March, p. 2.
[1521] A. Pogodin, *ibidem*, 15 (28) March, p. 1.
[1522] Slovo, 1909, 17 (30) March, p. 1.

of global consciousness, universality, cosmopolitanism or internationality (at the time, little difference was made between all these notions). In many fields, it had almost entirely denied what was Russian, national. (From the top of the tribune of the Duma, one practised at the pun: "patriot-Iscariot.") As for the Jewish intelligentsia, it did not deny its national identity. Even the most extreme of Jewish socialists struggled to reconcile their ideology with national sentiment. At the same time, there was no voice among the Jews—from Dubnov to Jabotinsky, passing by Winaver—to say that the Russian intelligentsia, who supported their persecuted brothers with all their souls, might not give up *his own* national feeling. Equity would have required it. But no one perceived this disparity: under the notion of *equality of rights*, the Jews understood *something more*.

Thus, the Russian intelligentsia, solitary, took the road to the future. The Jews did not obtain equal rights under the tsars, but—and probably partly for this very reason—they obtained the hand and the fidelity of the Russian intelligentsia. The power of their development, their energy, their talent *penetrated* the consciousness of Russian society. The idea we had of our perspectives, of our interests, the impetus we gave to the search for solutions to our problems, all this, we incorporated it to the idea that they were getting of it themselves. We have adopted their vision of our history and how to get out of it.

Understanding this is much more important than calculating the percentage of Jews who tried to destabilise Russia (all of whom we did), who made the revolution or participated in Bolshevik power.

Chapter 12

During the War (1914–1916)

The First World War was undoubtedly the greatest of the follies of the twentieth century. With no real motives or purposes, three major European powers—Germany, Russia, Austria-Hungary—clashed in a deadly battle which resulted in the first two not recovering for the duration of the century, and the third disintegrating. As for the two allies of Russia, seemingly victors, they held out for another quarter of a century, and then lost their power of domination forever.

Henceforth, the whole of Europe ceased to fulfil its proud mission of guiding humanity, becoming an object of jealousy and incapable of keeping in its weakened hands its colonial possessions.

None of the three emperors, and even less Nicholas II and his entourage, had realised in *what* war they were plunging, they could imagine neither its scale nor its violence. Apart from Stolypin and after him, Durnovo, the authorities had not understood the warning addressed to Russia between 1904 and 1906.

Let us consider this same war with the eyes of the Jews. In these three neighbouring empires lived three-quarters of the Jews of the planet (and 90% of the Jews of Europe[1523]) who were on top of that living in the area of future military operations, of the province of Kovno (then Livonia) up to Austrian Galicia (then Romania). And the war placed them before an interrogation as pressing as it was painful: could all, living on the front steps of these three empires, preserve their imperial patriotism under these conditions? For if, for the armies that were advancing, behind the front was the enemy, for the Jews established in these regions, behind the front lived neighbours and coreligionists. They could not want this war: could their mindset shift brutally towards patriotism? As for the ordinary Jews, those of the Pale of Settlement, they had even less reason to support the Russian army. We have seen that a century before, the Jews of western Russia had helped the Russians against Napoleon. But, in 1914, it was quite different: *in the name of what* would they help the Russian army? On behalf of the

---

[1523] SJE, t. 2, 1982, pp. 313-314.

Pale of Settlement? On the contrary, did the war not give rise to the hope of a liberation? With the arrival of the Austrians and the Germans, a new Pale of Settlement was not going to be established, the *numerus clausus* would not be maintained in the educational establishments!

It is precisely in the western part of the Pale of Settlement that the Bund retained influence, and Lenin tells us that its members "are in their majority Germanophiles and rejoice at the defeat of Russia."[1524] We also learn that during the war, the Jewish autonomist movement *Vorwarts* adopted an openly pro-German position. Nowadays, a Jewish writer notes finely that, "if one reflects on the meaning of the formula 'God, the Tsar, the Fatherland...', it is impossible to imagine a Jew, a loyal subject of the Empire, who could have taken this formula seriously," in other words, in the first degree.[1525]

But, in the capitals, things were different. Despite their positions of 1904-1905, the influential Jewish circles, like the Russian liberals, offered their support to the autocratic regime when the conflict broke out; they proposed a pact. "The patriotic fervour which swept Russia did not leave the Jews aside."[1526] "It was the time when, seeing the Russian patriotism of the Jews, Purishkevich[1527] embraced the rabbis."[1528] As for the press (not *Novoie Vremia*, but the liberal press, "half-Jewish" according to Witte, the same one who expressed and oriented the jolts of public opinion and who, in 1905, literally *demanded* the capitulation of power), it was, from the first days of the war, moved by patriotic enthusiasm. "Over the head of little Serbia, the sword is raised against Great Russia, the guarantor of the inalienable right of millions of people to work and to life!" At an extraordinary meeting of the Duma, "the representatives of the different nationalities and different parties were all, on this historic day, inhabited by the same thought, a single emotion made all the voices tremble... That no one lay a hand on Saint Russia!... We are ready for all sacrifices to defend the honour and dignity of Russia, one and indivisible...

'God, the Tsar, the people'—and victory is assured... We, Jews, defend our country because we are deeply attached to it."

Even if, behind this, there was a well-founded calculation, the expectation of a gesture of recognition in return—the attainment of equal rights, even

---

[1524] V. I. Lenin, Complete Works in 55 volumes [in Russian], 1958–1965, t. 49, p. 64.
[1525] A. Voronel, "22", Tel Aviv, 1986, no. 50, p. 155.
[1526] SJE, t. 7, p. 356.
[1527] Vladimir Purishkevich (1870–1920), monarchist, opponent of Rasputin, the assassination of whom he participated in. Arrested in 1917, then given amnesty, he participated in the White movement and died of typhus in Novorossiysh.
[1528] D. S. Pasmanik, Rousskaya revoliutsia i ievreisstvo (Bolchevizm i Ioudaizm) (The Russian Revolution and the Jews [Bolshevism and Judaism]), Paris, 1923, p. 143.

if it was only once the war was over—, the government had to, by accepting this unexpected ally, decide to assume—or promise to assume—its share of obligations.

And, in fact, did the achievement of equal rights necessarily have to come through the revolution? Moreover, the crushing of the insurrection by Stolypin "had led to a decline in interest in politics in Russian as well as Jewish circles,"[1529]—which, at the very least, meant that there was a move away from the revolution. As Chulguine[1530] declared: "Combating the Jews and the Germans simultaneously was above the forces of power in Russia, it was necessary to conclude a pact with somebody."[1531] This new alliance with the Jews had to be formalised: it was necessary to produce at least a document containing promises, as had been done for the Poles. But only Stolypin would have had the intelligence and the courage to do so. Without him, there was no one to understand the situation and take the appropriate decisions. (And, from the spring of 1915, even more serious mistakes were made.)

The liberal circles, including the elite of the Jewish community, also had in view another consideration that they took for a certainty. From the year 1907 (again, without urgent necessity), Nicholas II had allowed himself to be dragged into a military alliance with England (thus putting around his neck the rope of the subsequent confrontation with Germany). And, now, all the progressive circles in Russia were making the following analysis: the alliance with the democratic powers and the common victory with them would inevitably lead to a global democratisation of Russia at the end of the war and, consequently, the definitive establishment of equal rights for the Jews. There was, therefore, a sense for the Jews of Russia, and not only for those who lived in Petersburg and Moscow, to aspire to the victory of Russia in this war.

But these considerations were counterbalanced by the precipitated, massive *expulsion* of the Jews from the area of the front, ordered by the General Staff at the time of the great retreat of 1915. That the latter had the power to do so was the result of ill-considered decisions taken at the beginning of the war. In July 1914, in the heat of the action, in the agitation which reigned in the face of the imminence of conflict, the Emperor had signed without reflection, as a document of secondary importance, the provisional

---

[1529] SJE, t. 7, p, 356.

[1530] Basile Choulguine (1878–1976), leader of the right wing of the Duma with whom he breaks at the time of the Beilis affair. Participates in the Progressive Bloc. Collects with Guchkov the abdication of Nicholas II. Immigrated to Yugoslavia until 1944, he was captured there and spent twelve years in camps. Dies almost centenary.

[1531] V. V. *Choulguine,* "Chto nam v nikh ne nravitsa..." Ob Antisemitism v rossii ("What we do not like about them..." On anti-Semitism in Russia), Paris. 1929, p. 67.

Regulation of the field service which gave the General Staff unlimited power over all the neighbouring regions of the front, with a very wide territorial extension, and this, without any consultation with the Council of Ministers. At the time, no one had attached any importance to this document, because all were convinced that the Supreme Command would always be assured by the Emperor and that there could be no conflict with the Cabinet. But, as early as July 1914, the Emperor was persuaded not to assume the Supreme Command of the armies. As a wise man, the latter proposed the post to his favourite, the fine speaker Sukhomlinov, then Minister of Defence, who naturally declined this honour. It was the great prince Nicholas Nicolaevich who was appointed, and the latter did not consider it possible to begin by upsetting the composition of the General Staff, at the head of which was General Yanushkevich. But, at the same time, the provisional regulations were not altered, so that the administration of a third of Russia was in the hands of Yanushkevich, an insignificant man who was not even a military officer by profession.

From the very beginning of the war, orders were given locally for the expulsion of the Jews from the army areas.[1532] In August 1914, the newspapers read: "The rights of the Jews... Telegraphic instruction to all the governors of provinces and cities to stop the acts of mass or individual expulsion of Jews."

But, from the beginning of 1915, as testified the doctor D. Pasmanik, a medic on the front during the war, "suddenly, throughout the area of the front and in all circles close to power, spread the rumour that the Jews were doing espionage."[1533]

During the summer of 1915, Yanukhovich—precisely him—tried to mask the retreat of the Russian armies, which at that time seemed appalling, by ordering the *mass* deportation of the Jews from the front area, arbitrary deportation, without any examination of individual cases. It was so easy: to blame all the defeats on the Jews!

These accusations may not have come about without the help of the German General Staff, which issued a proclamation calling on the Jews of Russia to rise up against their government. But opinion, supported by many sources, prevails that in this case it was Polish influence that was at work. As Sliosberg wrote, just before the war, there had been a brutal explosion of antiSemitism, "a campaign against Jewish domination in industry and commerce...

[1532] SJE, t. 7, p. 356.
[1533] *Pasmanik, op. cit.*, p. 144.

When war broke out, it was at its zenith... and the Poles endeavoured by all means to tarnish the image of the Jewish populations in the eyes of the Supreme Command by spreading all sorts of nonsense and legends about Jewish espionage."[1534]—Immediately after the promises made by Nikolai Nikolaevich in the Appeal to the Poles of 14 August, the latter founded in Warsaw the "Central Committee of the Bourgeoisie", which did not include a single Jew, whereas in Poland the Jews represented 14% of the population. In September, there was a pogrom against the Jews in Souvalki.[1535]—Then, during the retreat of 1915, "the agitation which reigned in the midst of the army facilitated the spread of the calumnies made up by the Poles."[1536] Pasmanik asserts that he is "in a position to prove that the first rumours about the treason of the Jews were propagated by the Poles", a part of which "was actively assisting the Germans.

Seeking to avert suspicion, they hastened to spread the rumour that the Jews were engaged in espionage."[1537] In connection with this expulsion of the Jews, several sources emphasised the fact that Yanukhevich himself was a "Pole converted to Orthodoxy".[1538]

He may have undergone this influence, but we consider these explanations insufficient and in no way justifying the attitude of the Russian General Staff.

Of course, the Jews in the front area could not break their ties with the neighbouring villages, interrupt the "Jewish post", and turn into the enemies of their co-religionists. Moreover, in the eyes of the Jews in the Pale of Settlement, the Germans appeared as a European nation of high culture, much different from the Russians and the Poles (the black shadow of Auschwitz had not yet covered the earth or crossed the Jewish conscience...). At that time, the *Times* correspondent, Steven Graham, reported that as soon as the smoke of a German ship appeared on the horizon, the Jewish population of Libava "forgot the Russian language" and began to speak German. If they had to leave, the Jews preferred to go to the German side.—The hostility displayed by the Russian army, and then their deportation, could only provoke their bitterness and cause some of them to collaborate openly with the Germans.

[1534] G. B. *Sliosberg, op. cit.*, t. 3, pp. 316-317.
[1535] I G. Froumkine, Iz istorii ruskovo ievreistava, [Sb.] Kniga o ruskom evreïstve: Ot 1860 godov do Revolutsii 1917 g. (Aspects of the History of Russian Jews), in BJWR, pp. 85-86.
[1536] *Sliosberg, op. cit.*, t. 3, p. 324.
[1537] *Pasmanik, op. cit.*, p. 144.
[1538] For example: SJE, t. 7, p. 357.

In addition to the accusations against the Jews living in these areas, the Jews were accused of cowardice and desertion. Father Georges Chavelsky, chaplain of the Russian Army, was attached to the Staff, but often went to the front and was well informed of all that was going on there; he wrote in his memoirs: "From the first days of the war, it was repeated with insistence that the Jewish soldiers were cowards and deserters, and local Jews spies and traitors. There were many examples of Jews who had gone to the enemy or fled; or Jewish civilians who had given information to the enemy, or, in the course of their offensives, had delivered to them Russian soldiers and officers who had lingered on the spot, etc., etc. The more time passed, the more our situation deteriorated, the more the hatred and the exasperation against the Jews increased. rumours were spreading from the front to the rear... they created a climate that was becoming dangerous for all Jews in Russia."[1539]—Second Lieutenant M. Lemke, a Socialist who was then in Staff, recorded, in the newspaper he was secretly keeping, reports from the southwest Front, in December 1915; he noted in particular: "There is a disturbing increase in the number of Jewish and Polish defectors, not only in the advanced positions but also in the rear of the front."[1540]—In November 1915, one even heard during a meeting of the Progressive Bloc bureau the following remarks, noted by Milyukov: "Which people gave proof of its absence of patriotism?—The Jews."[1541]

In Germany and Austria-Hungary, the Jews could occupy high-level positions in the administration without having to abjure their religion, and this was also true in the army. While in Russia, a Jew could not become an officer if he did not convert to orthodoxy, and Jews with higher levels of education were most often completing their military service as simple soldiers. One can understand that they did not rush in to serve in such an army. (In spite of this, Jews were decorated with the cross of Saint-George.) Captain G. S. Doumbadze recalled a Jew, a law student, who received this decoration four times, but refused to enter the School of Officers in order not to have to convert, which would have caused his father to die of grief. Later he was executed by the Bolsheviks.[1542])

[1539] *Father Georgui Chavelsky*, Vospominania poslednevo protopresvitera ruskoï armii i flota (Memoirs of the last chaplain of the Russian Army and Russian Hood) v. 2-kh t, t. 1, New York, ed. Chekhov, 1954, p. 271.
[1540] *Mikhail Lemke*, 250 dnei v tsarskoy Stavke (25 sentences 1915—ioulia 1916) (250 days in the General Staff (25 Sept. 1915-July 1916), PG GIZ, 1920, p. 353.
[1541] Progressivny blok v 1915 1916 gg (The Progressive Bloc in 1915 1916), Krasny arkhiv: Istoritcheskiï Journal Tsentrarkhiva RSFSR, M. GIZ, 1922–1941, vol. 52, 1932, p. 179.
[1542] *G. S. Doumbadze* (Vospominania), Biblioteka-fond "Rousskoie Zaroubejie", f/l, A-9, p. 5.

For all that, it would be unreliable and implausible to conclude that all these accusations were mere fabrications. Chavelsky writes: "The question is too vast and complex... but I cannot help saying that at that time there was no lack of motives for accusing the Jews... In times of peace, it was tolerated that they be assigned to civilian tasks; during the war... the Jews filled the combat units... During the offensives, they were often in the rear; when the army retreated, they were at the front. More than once they spread panic in their units... It cannot be denied that the cases of espionage, of going over to the enemy were not rare... We couldn't avoid finding suspicious that the Jews were also perfectly informed of what was happening on the front. The 'Jewish telephone' sometimes worked better and faster than all the countryside's telephones... It was not uncommon for the news of the front to be known in the small hamlet of Baranovichi, situated near the General Staff, even before they reach the Supreme Commander and his Chief of Staff."[1543] (Lemke points out the Jewish origins of Chavelsky himself.[1544])

A rabbi from Moscow went to the Staff to try to persuade Chavelsky that "the Jews are like the others: there are some courageous, there are some cowards; there are those who are loyal to their country, there are also the bastards, the traitors," and he cited examples taken from other wars. "Although it was very painful for me, I had to tell him everything I knew about the conduct of Jews during this war," "but we were not able to reach an agreement."[1545]

Here is yet the testimony of a contemporary. Abraham Zisman, an engineer, then assigned to the Evacuation Commission, recalled half a century later: "To my great shame, I must say that [the Jews who were near the front] behaved very despicably, giving the German army all the help they could."[1546]

There were also charges of a strictly economic nature against the Jews who supplied the Russian army. Lemke thus copied the order to the General Staff signed by the Emperor on the very day of his taking office as Supreme Commander (this order had therefore been prepared by Yanushkevich): Jewish suppliers abused the orders for bandages, horses, bread given to them by the army; they receive from the military authorities documents certifying "that they have been entrusted with the task of making purchases for the needs of the army... but without any indication of quantity or place." Then "the Jews have certified copies of these documents made and

---

[1543] Father Chavelsky, op. cit., t. 1, p. 272.
[1544] *Lemke, op. cit., p. 37.*
[1545] Father Chavelsky, op. cit., t. 1, pp. 272–273.
[1546] Novaya Zaria, San Francisco, 1960, 7 May, p. 3.

distributed to their accomplices", thus acquiring the possibility of making purchases all over the Empire. "Thanks to the solidarity between them and their considerable financial resources, they control vast areas where are bought mainly horses and bread," which artificially raises prices and makes more difficult the work of the officials responsible of supplies.[1547]

But all these facts cannot justify the conduct of Yanushkevich and the General Staff. Without making an effort to separate the good wheat from the chaff, the Russian High Command launched an operation, as massive as it was inept, for the expulsion of the Jews.

Particularly striking was the attitude towards the Jews of Galicia who lived in Austro-Hungarian territory. "From the beginning of the First World War, tens of thousands of Jews fled from Galicia to Hungary, Bohemia, and Vienna.

Those who remained suffered greatly during the period of the Russian occupation of this region."[1548] "Bullying, beatings, and even pogroms, frequently organised by the Cossack units, became the daily lot of the Jews of Galicia."[1549] This is what Father Chavelsky writes: "In Galicia, hatred towards the Jews was still fuelled by the vexations inflicted under the Austrian domination of the Russian populations [in fact, Ukrainian and Ruthenian] by the powerful Jews"[1550] (in other words, these same populations were now participating in Cossack arbitrariness).

"In the province of Kovno all the Jews were deported without exception: the sick, the wounded soldiers, the families of the soldiers who were at the front."[1551] "Hostages were required under the pretext of preventing acts of espionage," and facts of this kind "became commonplace."[1552]

This deportation of the Jews appears in a stronger light than in 1915—contrary to what would happen in 1941—there was no mass evacuation of urban populations. The army was withdrawing, the civilian population remained there, nobody was driven out—but the Jews and they alone were driven out, all without exception and in the shortest possible time: not to mention the moral wound that this represented for each one, this brought about the ruin, the loss of one's house, one's property. Was it not, in another form, always the same pogrom of great magnitude, but this time

---

[1547] *Lemke*, op. cit., p. 325.
[1548] SJE, t. 2, p. 24.
[1549] SJE, t. 7, p. 356.
[1550] Father Chavelsky, op. cit., *p. 271.*
[1551] SJE, t. 7, p. 357.
[1552] *Sliosberg, op. cit.,* t. 3, p. 325.

provoked by the authorities and not by the populace? How can we not understand the Jewish misfortune?

To this we must add that Yanushkevich, like the high-ranking officers who were under his command, acted without any logical reflection, in disorder, precipitation, incoherence, which could only add to the confusion. There exists no chronicle nor account of all these military decisions. Only echoes scattered in the press of the time, and also in "The Archives of the Russian Revolution" by I. V. Hessen, a series of documents[1553] collected at random, without follow-up; and then, as with Lemke, copies of documents made by individuals. This scattered data nevertheless allow us to form an opinion on what happened.

Some of the provisions foresee expelling Jews from the area of military operations "in the direction of the enemy" (which would mean: in the direction of the Austrians, across the front line?), to send back to Galicia the Jews originating from there; other directives foresee deporting them to the rear of the front, sometimes at a short distance, sometimes on the left bank of the Dnieper, sometimes even "beyond the Volga". Sometimes it is "cleansing the Jews of a zone of five versts from the front", sometimes we speak of a zone of fifty versts.

The evacuation timeframes are sometimes five days, with authorisation to take away one's property, sometimes twenty-four hours, probably without this authorisation; as for the resisters, they will be taken under escort. Or even: no evacuation, but in the event of a retreat, take hostages among the significant Jews, especially the rabbis, in case Jews denounce either Russians or Poles who are well disposed in regard to Russia; in the event of execution of these by the Germans, carry out the execution of the hostages (but how can we know, verify that there were executions in German-occupied territory? It was truly an incredible system!). Other instruction: we do not take hostages, we just designate them among the Jewish population inhabiting our territories—they will bear responsibility for espionage in favour of the enemy committed by other Jews. Or even: avoid at all costs that the Jews be aware of the location of the trenches dug in the rear of the front (so that they cannot communicate it to the Austrians through their co-religionists,—it was known that Romanian Jews could easily cross the border); or even, on the contrary: oblige precisely civilian Jews to dig the trenches. Or even (order given by the commander of the military region of Kazan, General Sandetski, known for his despotic behaviour): assemble all the Jewish soldiers in marching battalions and

---

[1553] Dokoumenty o presledovanii ievreev (Documents on the persecution of the Jews), Arkhiv Rousskoi Revolutsii (Archives of the Russian Revolution), izdavayemy I.V. Gessenom, Berlin: Slovo, 1922-1937, t. 19, 1928, pp. 245-284.

send them to the front. Or, conversely: discontent provoked by the presence of Jews in the combat units; their military ineptitude.

There is a feeling that in their campaign against the Jews, Yanushkevich and the General Staff were losing their minds: what exactly did they want?

During these particularly difficult weeks of fighting, when the Russian troops retreated, exhausted and short of ammunition, a flyer containing a "list of questions" was sent to the heads of units and instructed them to assemble information on "the moral, military, physical qualities of Jewish soldiers", as well as their relations with local Jewish populations. And the possibility was considered of completely excluding Jews from the army after the war.

We also do not know the exact number of displaced persons. In *The Book of the Jewish Russian World*, we read that in April 1915, 40,000 Jews were expulsed from the province of Courland, and in May 120,000 of them were expelled from Kovno.[1554] In another place, the same book gives an overall figure for the whole period, amounting to 250,000[1555] *including* Jewish refugees, which means that the deportees would hardly have accounted for more than half of this digit. After the revolution, the newspaper *Novoie Vremia* published information according to which the evacuation of all the inhabitants of Galicia dispersed on the territory of Russia 25,000 persons, including nearly a thousand Jews.[1556] (These are numbers that, for the moment, are too weak to be probable.) On 10-11 May 1915, the order was issued to put an end to the deportations, and these ceased. Jabotinsky drew the conclusion of the expulsion of the Jews from the zone of the front in 1915 by speaking of a "catastrophe probably unprecedented since the reign of Ferdinand and Isabella" in Spain in the fifteenth century.[1557] But is there not also something of a move of History in the fact that this massive deportation—itself, and the indignant reactions it provoked—would make a concrete contribution to the much desired suppression of the Pale of Settlement?

Leonid Andreyev had rightly observed: "This famous 'barbarity' of which we are accused of... rests entirely and exclusively on our Jewish question and its bloody outbursts."[1558]

[1554] A. A. *Goldenweiser*, Pravovoïc polojenie ievreyev v Rossii (The legal situation of Jews in Russia), BJWR-1, p. 135.
[1555] G. I. *Aronson*, V borbe za grajdanskie i nalsionainyc prava Obchtchestvennye tetchenia v rousskom evreïstve (The struggle for civil and national rights: the movements of opinion within the Jewish community of Russia), BJWR-1, p. 232.
[1556] *Novoie Vremia*, 1917, 13 April, p. 3.
[1557] *Sliosberg, op. cit.*, t. 1, Introduction by V. Jabotinsky, p. xi.
[1558] L. *Andreyev*, Pervaya stoupen (First Step), Shchit (the Shield), 1916, p. 5.

These deportations of Jews were resonant on a planetary scale. From Petersburg, during the war, Jews defending human rights transmitted information about the situation of their co-religionists to Europe; "Among them, Alexander Isayevich Braudo distinguished himself by his tireless activity."[1559] A. G. Shlyapnikov relates that Gorky had sent him documents on the persecution of Jews in Russia; he brought them to the United States. All this information spread widely and rapidly in Europe and America, raising a powerful wave of indignation.

And if the best among the representatives of the Jewish community and the Jewish intelligentsia feared that "the victory of Germany... would only reinforce anti-Semitism... and, for that reason alone, there could be no question of sympathies towards the Germans or hopes for their victory,"[1560] a Russian military intelligence officer in Denmark reported in December 1915 that the success of anti-Russian propaganda "is also facilitated by Jews who openly declare that they do not wish the victory of Russia and its consequence: the autonomy promised to Poland, for they know that the latter would take energetic measures with a view to the expulsion of Jews from within its borders"[1561]; In other words, it was Polish anti-Semitism that was to be feared, not German antiSemitism: the fate which awaited the Jews in a Poland which had become independent would perhaps be even worse than that which they underwent in Russia.

The British and French Governments were somewhat embarrassed to openly condemn the attitude of their ally. But at that time, the United States was increasingly engaged in the international arena. And in the still neutral America of 1915, "sympathies were divided...; some of the Jews who came from Germany were sympathetic to the latter, even though they did not manifest it in an active manner."[1562] Their dispositions were maintained by the Jews from Russia and Galicia, who, as the Socialist Ziv testified, wished for (it could no longer be otherwise) the defeat of Russia, and even more so by the "professional revolutionists" Russian-Jews who had settled in the United States.[1563] To this was added the anti-Russian tendencies in the American public: very recently, in 1911, the dramatic break-up of an eighty-year-old US-Russian economic agreement took place. The

---

[1559] *Sliosberg, op. cit.*, t. 3, pp. 343-344.
[1560] *Ibidem*, p. 344.
[1561] *Lemke, op. cit.*, p. 310.
[1562] *Sliosberg, op. cit.*, t. 3, p. 345.
[1563] G. A. Ziv, Trotsky: Kharakteiistika. Po litchym vospominaniam (Trotsky: a characteristic, personal memories), New York. Narodopravstvo, 1921, 30 June, pp. 60 63.

Americans regarded the official Russia as a country that was "corrupt, reactionary, and ignorant".[1564]

This quickly translated into tangible effects. As early as August 1915, we read in the reports that Milyukov was holding meetings of the Progressive Bloc: "The Americans pose as a condition [of aid to Russia] the possibility for American Jews to have free access to Russian territory,"[1565]—always the same source of conflict as in 1911 with T. Roosevelt.—And when a Russian parliamentary delegation went to London and Paris in early 1916 to apply for financial aid, it was faced to a categorical refusal. The episode is told in detail by Shingaryov[1566], in the report he presented on 20 June 1916 to the Military and Maritime Commission of the Duma after the return of the delegation. In England, Lord Rothschild replied to this request: "You are affecting our credit in the United States." In France, Baron Rothschild declared: "In America, the Jews are very numerous and active, they exert a great influence, in such a manner that the American public is very hostile to you." (Then "Rothschild expressed himself even more brutally", and Shingaryov demanded that his words not be included in the record.) This financial pressure from the Americans, the rapporteur concludes, is a continuation of a policy that has led them to break our trade agreement in 1911 (but, of course, to that was added the massive deportations of Jews undertaken in the meantime). Jakob Schiff, who had spoken so harshly of Russia in 1905, now declared to a French parliamentarian sent to America: "We will give credit to England and France when we have the assurance that Russia will do something for the Jews; the money you borrow from us goes to Russia, and we do not want that."[1567]—Milyukov evoked the protests at the Duma tribune of "millions and millions of American Jews... who have met a very wide echo in American opinion. I have in my hands many American newspapers that prove it... Meetings ending with scenes of hysteria, crying jags at the evocation of the situation of the Jews in Russia. I have a copy of the provision made by President Wilson, establishing a 'Jewish Day' throughout the United States to collect aid for the victims." And "when we ask for money to American bankers, they reply: Pardon, how is that?

We agree to lend money to England and France, but on condition that Russia does not see the colour of it... The famous banker Jakob Schiff,

---

[1564] *German Bernsrein*, Retch, 1917, 30 June, pp. 1–2.
[1565] Progressivny blok v 1915-1917 gg., Krasny arkhiv, 1932, vol. 50 51, p. 136.
[1566] Andrei Shingaryov(1869 1918), one of the leaders of the Cadet party, was a member of the first Provisional Government in 1917. Arrested by the Bolsheviks and massacred in his prison.
[1567] Mejdunarodnoïe polojenie tsarskoi Rossii vo vremia mirovoï voïny (The international situation of tsarist Russia during the world war), Krasny arkhiv, 1934, vol. 64, pp. 5–14.

who rules the financial world in New York, categorically refuses any idea of a loan to Russia..."[1568]

The *Encyclopædia Judaica*, written in English, confirms that Schiff, "using his influence to prevent other financial institutions lending to Russia..., pursued this policy throughout the First World War"[1569] and put pressure on other banks to do the same.

For all these upheavals provoked by the deportations, both in Russia and abroad, it was the Council of Ministers who had to pay for the broken pots even though the Staff did not consult it and gave no attention to its protests. I have already quoted a few snippets of the passionate debates that were agitating the Cabinet on this subject. [1570] Here are a few others. Krivoshein[1571] was in favour of temporarily granting the Jews the right to settle in all the cities of Russia:

"This favour granted to the Jews will be useful not only from a political point of view, but also from an economic point of view... Up to now, our policy in this field made one think of this sleeping miser on his gold, which does not benefit from it and does not allow others to do so." But Roukhlov replied: this proposal "constitutes a fundamental and irreversible modification of legislation which has been introduced throughout History with the aim of protecting the Russian heritage from the control of the Jews, and the Russian people of the deleterious influence of the neighbouring of the Jews... You specify that this favour will be granted only for the duration of the war..., but we must not be in denial": after the war, "not one government will be found" to "send the Jews back to the Pale of Settlement... The Russians are dying in the trenches and meanwhile the Jews will settle in the heart of Russia, benefit from the misfortunes endured by the people, of general ruin. What will be the reaction of the army and the Russian people?"—And again, during the following meeting: "The Russian population endures unimaginable hardships and suffering, both on the front and in the interior of the country, while Jewish bankers buy from

---

[1568] Doklad P. N. Milioukova v Voïenno-morskoï komissii Gosoud. Doumy 19 iounia 1916g., Krasny arkhiv, 1933, t. 58, pp. 13 14.
[1569] *Encyclopædia Judaica*, Jerusalem, 1971, vol. 14, p. 961.
[1570] A. Solzhenitsyn, Krasnoye Koleso (The Red Wheel), t. 3, M. Voïenizdat, 1993, pp. 259-263, (French translation: March seventeen, t. 1, Paris: Fayard).
[1571] Close collaborator of Stolypin, Minister of Agriculture (1906–1915), dies in emigration (1857-1921).

their co-religionists the right to use Russia's misfortune to exploit tomorrow this exsanguinated people."[1572]

But the ministers acknowledged that there was no other way out. This measure was to be "applied with exceptional speed"—"in order to meet the financial needs of the war."[1573] All of them, with the exception of Roukhlov, signed their name at the bottom of the bulletin authorising the Jews to settle freely (with the possibility of acquiring real estate) throughout the Empire, with the exception of the capitals, agricultural areas, provinces inhabited by the Cossacks and the Yalta region.[1574] In the autumn of 1915 was also repealed the system of the annual passport, which had hitherto been compulsory for the Jews who were now entitled to a permanent passport. (These measures were followed by a partial lifting of the *numerus clausus* in educational establishments and the authorisation to occupy the functions of litigator within the limits of the representation quotas.[1575]) The opposition that these decisions met in the public opinion was broken under the pressure of the war.

Thus, after a century and a quarter of existence, the Pale of Settlement of the Jews disappeared forever. And to add insult to injury, as Sliosberg notes, "this measure, so important in its content…, amounting to the abolition of the Pale of Settlement, this measure for which had fought in vain for decades the Russian Jews and the liberal circles of Russia, went unnoticed!"[1576] Unnoticed because of the magnitude assumed by the war. Streams of refugees and immigrants were then overwhelming Russia.

The Refugee Committee, set up by the government, also provided displaced Jews with funds to help settlements.[1577] Until the February revolution, "the Conference on Refugees continued its work and allocated considerable sums to the various national committees," including the Jewish Committee.[1578] It goes without saying that were added to this the funds contributed by many Jewish organisations that had embarked on this task with energy and efficiency. Among them was the Union of Jewish Craftsmen (UJC), created in 1880, well-established and already extending

---

[1572] Tiajëlye dni. Sekretnye zasedania soveta ministrov. 16 ioulia sentiabria 1915 (The difficult days, the secret meetings of the Council of Ministers, 16 July September 1915). Sost. A. N. Yakhontov, Archives of the Russian Revolution, 1926, vol. 18, pp. 47 48, 57.
[1573] *Ibidem*, p. 12.
[1574] SJE, t. 7, pp. 358–359.
[1575] *Ibidem*, p. 359.
[1576] *Sliosberg*, t. 3, p. 341.
[1577] *I. L Teitel*, Iz moiii jizni za 40 let (Memories of 40 years of my life), Paris: I. Povolotski i ko., 1925, p. 210.
[1578] *Sliosberg*, t. 3, p. 342.

its action beyond the Pale of Settlement. The UJC had developed a cooperation with the World Relief Committee and the "Joint" ("Committee for the distribution of funds for aid to war-affected Jews").

All of them provided massive aid to the Jewish populations of Russia; "The 'Joint' had rescued hundreds of thousands of Jews in Russia and Austria-Hungary."[1579] In Poland, the UJC helped Jewish candidates for emigration or settled as farmers—because "during the war, Jews who lived in small villages had been driven, not without coercion by the German occupier, to the work of the land."[1580] There was also the Jewish Prophylactic Society (JPS), founded in 1912; it had given itself for mission not only to direct medical aid to the Jews, but also the creation of sanatoriums, dispensaries, the development of sanitary hygiene in general, the prevention of diseases, "the struggle against the physical deterioration of Jewish populations" (Nowhere in Russia there existed yet organisations of this kind). Now, in 1915, these detachments were organising for Jewish emigrants, all along their route and at their place of destination, supply centres, flying medical teams, countryside hospitals, shelters and pædiatric consultations.[1581]— Also in 1915, appeared the Jewish Association for the Assistance of War Victims (JAAWV); benefiting of support from the Committee for Refugees and the so generously endowed by the State "Zemgor" (association of the "Union of Zemstvos" and the "Union of Cities"), as well as credit from America, the JAAWV set up a vast network of missionaries to help the Jews during their journey and their new place of residence, with rolling kitchens, canteens, clothing distribution points, (employment agencies, vocational training centres), childcare establishments, schools. What an admirable organisation!—let us remember that approximately 250,000 refugees and displaced persons were taken care of; according to official figures, the number of these was already reaching 215,000 in August 1916.[1582]—and there was also the "Political Bureau" near the Jewish Deputies of the fourth Duma, which resulted from an agreement between the Jewish Popular Group, the Jewish People's Party, the Jewish Democratic Group and the Zionists; during the war, it deployed "considerable activity".[1583]

In spite of all the difficulties, "the war gave a strong impulse to the spirit of initiative of the Jews, whipped their will to take charge."[1584] During

---

[1579] SJE, t. 2, p. 345.

[1580] D. Lvovitch, L. Bramson i Soiouz ORT (L. Bramson and the UJC), JW-2, New York, 1944, p. 29.

[1581] I. M. Troitsky, Samodeiatetnost i camopomochtch evreiev v Rossii (The spirit of initiative and mutual help among the Jews of Russia), BJWR-1, pp. 479-480, 485-489.

[1582] Aronson, BJWR-1, p. 232; I. Troitsky, ibidem, p. 497.

[1583] Aronson, op. cit., p. 232.

[1584] I. Troitsky, op. cit., p. 484.

these years "the considerable forces hidden hitherto in the depths of the Jewish consciousness matured and revealed to the open... immense reserves of initiative in the most varied fields of political and social action."[1585]—In addition to the resources allocated by the mutual aid committees, the JAAWV benefited from the millions paid to it by the government. At no time did the Special Conference on Refugees "reject our suggestion" on the amount of aid: 25 million in a year and a half, which is infinitely more than what the Jews had collected (the government paid here the wrongs of the General Staff); as for the sums coming from the West, the Committee could retain them[1586] for future use.

It is thus that with all these movements of the Jewish population—refugees, displaced persons, but also a good number of volunteers—the war significantly altered the distribution of Jews in Russia; important settlements were established in towns far from the front, mainly Nizhny Novgorod, Voronezh, Penza, Samara, Saratov, but also in the capitals. Although the abolition of the Pale of Settlement did not concern Saint Petersburg and Moscow, these two cities were now practically open. Often, they would go there to join relatives or protectors who had settled there long ago. In the course of memoirs left by contemporaries, one discovers for example a dentist of Petersburg named Flakke: ten-room apartment, footman, servant, cook—well-off Jews were not uncommon, and, in the middle of the war, while there was a shortage of housing in Petrograd, they opened up opportunities for Jews from elsewhere. Many of them changed their place of residence during those years: families, groups of families that left no trace in history, except sometimes in family chronicles of a private nature, such as those of the parents of David Azbel: "Aunt Ida... left the coldness and somnolence of Chernigov at the beginning of the First World War to come and settle in Moscow."[1587] The new arrivals were often of a very modest condition, but some of them came to influential positions, such as Poznanski, a clerk in the Petrograd Military Censorship Commission, who had the upper hand "over all secret affairs".[1588]

Meanwhile, the General Staff mechanically poured out its torrents of directives, sometimes respected, sometimes neglected: to exclude Jews under the banner of all activities outside armed service: secretary, baker, nurse, telephonist, telegrapher. Thus, "in order to prevent the anti-government propaganda supposed to be carried out by Jewish doctors and nurses, they should be assigned not to hospitals or country infirmaries, but

---

[1585] *Aronson, op. cit.,* p. 230.
[1586] *Sliosberg, op. cit.,* t. 3, pp. 329–331.
[1587] *D. Azbel,* Do, vo vremia i posle (Before, during and after), Vremya i my, New York, Jerusalem, Paris. 1989, no. 104, pp. 192,193.
[1588] *Lemke, op. cit.,* p. 468.

'to places not conducive to propaganda activities such as, for example, the advanced positions, the transport of the wounded on the battlefield'."[1589] In another directive: expel the Jews out of the Union of Zemstvos, the Union of Cities and the Red Cross, where they concentrate in great numbers to escape armed service (as did also, we note in passage, tens of thousands of Russians), use their advantageous position for propaganda purposes (as did any liberal, radical, or socialist who respected themselves) and, above all, spread rumours about "the incompetence of the high command" (which corresponded to a large extent to reality[1590]). Other bulletins warned against the danger of keeping the Jews in positions that brought them into contact with sensitive information: in the services of the Union of Zemstvos of the western front in April 1916, "all the important branches of the administration (including those under the defence secrecy) are in the hands of Jews", and the names of those responsible for the registration and classification of confidential documents are cited, as well as that of the Director of the Department of Public Information, who, "by his functions, has free access to various services of the army at the rear of the front or in the regions".[1591]

However, there is no evidence that the ranting of the General Staff on the necessity of chasing the Jews from the Zemgor had any tangible results. Always well informed, Lemke observes that "the directives of the military authorities on the exclusion of the Jews" from the Zemgor "were not welcomed". A bulletin was published stating that "all persons of Jewish confession who are dismissed by order of the authorities shall be reimbursed for two months with salary and travel allowances and with the possibility of being recruited prioritarily in the establishments of the Zemgor at the rear of the front."[1592] (The Zemgor was the darling of the influential Russian press. It is thus that it unanimously declined to reveal its sources of financing: in 25 months of war, on 1 September 1916, 464 million rubles granted by the government—equipment and supplies were delivered directly from state warehouses—compared with only nine million collected by Zemstvos, towns, collects.[1593] If the press refused to publish these figures, it is because it would have emptied of its meaning the opposition between the philanthropic and charitable action of the Zemgor and that of a stupid, insignificant, and lame government.)

[1589] SJE, t. 7, p. 357.
[1590] *Archives of the Russian Revolution*, 1928, t. XIX, pp. 274, 275.
[1591] *Lemke, op. cit.*, p. 792.
[1592] *Ibidem*, p. 792.
[1593] S. *Oldenburg*, Tsarstvovanie Imperatora Nikolai II (the reign of Emperor Nicholas II), t. 2, Munich, 1949, p. 192.

Economic circumstances and geographical conditions meant that among the army's suppliers, there were many Jews. A letter of complaint expressing the anger of the "Orthodox-Russian circles of Kiev..., driven by their duty as patriots", points to Salomon Frankfurt, who occupied a particularly high position, that of "delegate of the Ministry of Agriculture to the supply of the army in bacon" (it must be said that complaints about the disorganisation caused by these requisitions were heard all the way to the Duma). Also in Kiev, an obscure "agronomist of a Zemstvo of the region", Zelman Kopel, was immortalised by History because of having ordered an excessive requisition just before Christmas 1916, he deprived of sugar a whole district during the holidays (In this case, a complaint was also lodged against the local administration of the Zemstvos[1594]).

In November 1916, the deputy N. Markov, stigmatising in the Duma "the marauders of the rear and trappers" of State property and National Defence, designated, as usual, the Jews in particular: in Kiev, once again, it was Cheftel, a member of the Municipal Council, who blocked the warehouses and let rot more than 2,500 tons of flour, fish, and other products that the town kept in reserve, while at the same time, "the friends of these gentlemen sold their own fish at grossly inflated prices"; it was V. I. Demchenko, elected from Kiev to the Duma, who hid "masses of Jews, rich Jews" (and he enumerates them) "to make them escape military service"; it was also, in Saratov, "the engineer Levy" who supplied "through the intermediary of the commissioner Frenkel" goods to the Military-Industrial Committee at inflated prices.[1595] But it should be noted that the military-industrial committees set up by Guchkov [1596] were behaving in exactly the same way with the Treasury. So...

In a report of the Petrograd Security Department dated October 1916, we can read: "In Petrograd, trade is exclusively in the hands of Jews who know perfectly the tastes, aspirations, and opinions of the man in the street"; but this report also refers to the widespread opinion on the right according to which, among the people, "the freedom enjoyed by Jews since the beginning of the war" arouses more and more discontent; "it is true, there still exists officially some Russian firms, but they are in fact controlled by Jews: it is impossible to buy or to order anything without the intervention

---

[1594] Iz zapisnooi knijki arkhivista, Soob. Mr. Paozerskovo (Notebooks of an Archivist, Comm. by M. Paozerski), Krasny Arckhiv, 1926, t. 18, pp. 211-212.
[1595] Gosudarstvennaya Duma—Tchetvërty sozyv (Fourth Duma of the Empire), transcript of the proceedings, 22 Nov. 1916, pp. 366–368.
[1596] Alexander Guchkov (1882-1936), founder and leader of the Octobrist party, president of the third Duma (March 1910 March 1911), president of the All-Russia War Industry Committee, became Minister of War and Navy in the first temporary government. Emigrated in 1918. He died in Paris.

of a Jew."[1597] (Bolshevik publications, such as Kaiourov's book[1598] at that time in Petrograd, did not fail to disguise reality by alleging that in May 1915, during the sacking of German firms and shops in Moscow, the crowd also attacked the Jewish establishments—which is false, and it was even the opposite that happened: during the anti-German riot, the Jews, because of the resemblance of their surnames, protected themselves by hanging on the front of their shop the placard: "This shop is Jewish"—and they were not touched, and Jewish trade was not to suffer in all the years of war.)

However, at the top of the monarchy—in Rasputin's morbid entourage—, a small group of rather shady individuals played an important role. They not only outraged the right-wing circles—it is how, in May 1916, the French ambassador to Petrograd, Maurice Paleologue, noted in his diary: "A bunch of Jewish financiers and dirty speculators, Rubinstein, Manus, etc., have concluded an agreement with him [Rasputin] and compensate him handsomely for services rendered. On their instructions, he sends notes to ministers, to banks or to various influential personalities."[1599]

Indeed, if in the past it was Baron Ginzburg who intervened openly in favour of the Jews, this action was henceforth conducted secretly by the upstarts who had clustered around Rasputin. There was the banker D. L. Rubinstein (he was the director of a commercial bank in Petrograd, but confidently made his way to the entourage of the throne: he managed the fortunes of Grand Duke Andrei Vladimirovich, made the acquaintance of Rasputin through A. Vyrubova[1600] then was decorated with the order of Saint Vladimir, he was given the title of State Counsellor, and therefore of the "Your Excellency".) But also the industrialist I. P. Manus (director of the Petrograd wagon factory, member of the Putilov factory board, the board of two banks and the Russian Transport Company, also a State Councillor).

Rubinstein attached to Rasputin a permanent "secretary", Aron Simanovich, a rich jeweller, diamond dealer, illiterate but very skilful and

---

[1597] Politicschkoye polojenie Rossii nakanoune Fevralskoi revoloutsii (*Political situation in Russia on the eve of the February Revolution*), Krasny arkhiv, 1926, t. 17, pp. 17, 23.
[1598] V. *Kairorov*, Petrogradskie rabotchie v gody imperialistitcheskoy vonny (Workers of Petrograd during the years of the imperialist war), M., 1930.
[1599] *Maurice Paleologue*, Tsraskaia Rossia nakanoune revolioutsii (Imperial Russia on the eve of the revolution), M., Pd., GIZ, 1923, p. 136.
[1600] Anna Vyrubova (1884-1964), maid of honour of the Empress of which she was for a long time the best friend, fanatic admirer of Rasputin, permanent intermediary between the imperial couple and the starets. She was arrested in 1917, freed and re-arrested, and managed to escape to Finland where she would live for more than 45 years, completely forgotten about.

enterprising (but what did Rasputin need of a "secretary", he who possessed nothing?...)

This Simanovich ("the best among the Jew", would have scribbled the "starets" on his portrait) published in immigration a little book boasting about the role he had played at that time. We find in it all sorts of gossip without interest, of fabrications (he speaks of the "hundreds of thousands of Jews executed and massacred by order of the Grand Duke Nikolai Nikolaevich"[1601]); but, through this scum and those surges of boastfulness, one can glimpse real facts, quite concrete.

For example, the "dentists affair"—for most Jews—which had broken out in 1913: "a veritable dentist's diploma factory had been elaborated" which flooded Moscow, [1602] —their detention gave the right to permanent residence and dispensed of military service. There were about 300 of them (according to Simanovich: 200). The false dentists were condemned to one year in prison, but, on the intervention of Rasputin, they were pardoned.

"During the war... the Jews sought protection from Rasputin against the police or the military authorities," and Simanovitch proudly confides that "many Jewish young men implored his help to escape the army," which, in time of war, gave them the possibility of entering the University; "There was often no legal way"—but Simanovich claims that it was always possible to find a solution. Rasputin "had become the friend and benefactor of the Jews, and unreservedly supported my efforts to improve their condition."[1603]

By mentioning the circle of these new favourites, one cannot fail to mention the unparalleled adventurer Manassevich-Manoulov. He was, in turn, an official of the Ministry of the Interior and an agent of the Russian secret police in Paris, which did not prevent him from selling abroad secret documents from the Police Department; he had conducted secret negotiations with Gapon; when Stürmer[1604] was appointed Prime Minister, he was entrusted with "exceptional 'secret missions'."[1605]

[1601] *A. Simanovich*, Rasputin i ievrei. Vospominania litchnovo sekretaria Grigoria Rasputin (Rasputin and the Jews, Memoirs of the personal secretary of Grigory Rasputin), [Sb.] Sviatoï tchërt. Taïna Grigoria Raspoutina: Vospom., Dokoumenty, Materialy sledstv. Komissii. M. Knijnaya Palata, 1991, pp. 106-107.
[1602] *Sliosberg, op. cit.*, t. 3, p. 347.
[1603] *Simanovitch*, pp. 89, 100, 102, 108.
[1604] Rasputin's *protégé*, became President of the Council of Ministers (2 February 23 November 1916), with his duties as Minister of the Interior (16 March 17 July) and Foreign Affairs (20 July - 23 November). After February, he was arrested and imprisoned at the Pierre-et-Paul fortress where he died on 2 September 1917.
[1605] *S. Melgunov*, Legenda o separatnom mire. Kanoun revolioutsii (The Legend of the Separated Peace, The Eve of the Revolution), Paris, 1957, pp. 263, 395, 397.

Rubinstein barged into public life by buying out the newspaper *Novoie Vremia* (see chapter 8), hitherto hostile to the Jews. (Irony of history: in 1876, Suvorin had bought this paper with the money of the banker of Warsaw Kroneberg, and at the beginning, well oriented towards the Jews, he opened its columns to them. But, at the beginning of the war between Russia and Turkey, *Novoie Vremia* suddenly changed course, "went to the side of the reaction," and, "as far as the Jewish question was concerned, no longer put a stop to hatred and bad faith."[1606]) In 1915, Prime Minister Goremykin[1607] and the Minister of the Interior Khvostov, Junior[1608] in vain prevented Rubinstein's buyback of the newspaper,[1609] he achieved his aims a little later,—but we were already too close to the revolution, all that did not serve much. (Another newspaper on the right, the *Grajdanin* was also partially bought by Manus).

S. Melgounov nicknamed the "quintet" the small group which treated his affairs in the "antechamber"[1610] of the tsar—through Rasputin. Given the power of the latter, it was no small matter: dubious characters were in the immediate vicinity of the throne and could exert a dangerous influence on the affairs of the whole of Russia. Britain's ambassador, Buchanan, believed that Rubinstein was linked to the German intelligence services.[1611] This possibility cannot be ruled out.

The rapid penetration of German espionage into Russia, and its links with the speculators of the rear, forced General Alekseyev[1612] to solicit from the emperor, during the summer of 1916, the authorisation to carry out investigations beyond the area of competence of the General Staff,—and thus was constituted the "Commission of Inquiry of General Batiushin". Its first target was the banker Rubinstein, suspected of "speculative operations with German capital", financial manipulation for the benefit of the enemy, depreciation of the ruble, overpayment of foreign agents for orders placed by the General Stewardship, and speculative operations on wheat in the

---

[1606] JE, t. 11, pp. 758, 759.

[1607] Ivan Goremykin (1839–1917), Prime Minister first in April July 1906, then from January 1914 to January 1916.

[1608] Alexis Khvostov, Junior (1872–1918), leader of the rights in the fourth Duma, Minister of the Interior in 1915–1916. Shot by the Bolsheviks.

[1609] Pismo ministra vnoutrennikh del A. N. Khvostova Predsedateliou soveta ministrov I. L. Goremykinou ot 16 dek. 1915 (Letter from the Minister of the Interior A. N. Khvostov to the President of the Council of Ministers I. L. Goremykin, dated 16 December 1915), Delo naroda, 1917, 21 March, p. 2.

[1610] *Melgunov, op. cit.,* p. 289.

[1611] *Ibidem,* p. 402.

[1612] Mikhail Alekseyev (1857 1918), then Chief of Staff of the Supreme Commander. Will advise the tsar to abdicate. Supreme Commander until 3 June 1917. After October, organiser of the first White army, in the Don.

region of the Volga. On the decision of the Minister of Justice, Rubinstein was arrested on 10 July 1916 and charged with high treason.[1613]

It was from the empress in person that Rubinstein received the strongest support. Two months after his arrest, she asked the Emperor "to send him discreetly to Siberia, not to keep him here, so as not to annoy the Jews"—"speak of Rubinstein" with Protopopov[1614]. Two weeks later, Rasputin sent a telegram to the emperor saying that Protopopov "implores that no one come to disturb him", including counter-espionage...; "he spoke to me of the detainee with gentleness, as a true Christian."—Another three weeks later, the Empress: "About Rubinstein, he is dying. Send immediately a telegram [to the northwest Front]... for him to be transferred from Pskov under the authority of the Minister of the Interior"—that is, of that good and gentle Christian of Protopopov! And, the following day: "I hope you sent the telegram for Rubinstein, he's dying." And the next day: "Have you arranged for Rubinstein to be handed over to the Minister of the Interior? If he stays in Pskov, he will die,—please, my sweet friend!"[1615]

On 6 December, Rubinstein was released—ten days before the assassination of Rasputin, who had just enough time to render him a last service. Immediately afterwards, the Minister Makarov[1616], whom the Empress detested, was dismissed. (Shortly thereafter, he will be executed by the Bolsheviks.)—It is true that with the liberation of Rubinstein, the investigation of his case was not finished; he was arrested again, but during the redeeming revolution of February, along with other prisoners who languished in the tsarist gaols, he was freed of the Petrograd prison by the crowd and left ungrateful Russia, as had the time to do so Manassevich, Manus, and Simanovich. (This Rubinstein, we will still have the opportunity to meet him again.) For us who live in the 90s of the twentieth century,[1617] this orgy of plundering of State property appears as an experimental model on a very small scale... But what we find in one case

---

[1613] *V. N. Semennikor*, Politika Romanovykh nakanoune revolioutsii. Ot Antanty—k Guermanii (Politics of the Romanovs on the Eve of the Revolution: From the Agreement to Germany), M., L., GIZ, 1926, pp. 117, 118, 125.

[1614] Last tsarist Minister of the Interior. Accused of intelligence with Germany (perpetrated in Sweden during the summer of 1916 on the occasion of a trip to England of a delegation of the Duma). Imprisoned by the Provisional Government. Executed by the Bolsheviks.

[1615] Pisma imperatritsy Aleksandry Fëdorovny k Imperatorou Nikolaiou II / Per. S angi. V. D. Nabokoa (Letters of the Empress Alexandra Fecorovna to the Emperor Nicholas II/trad. from English by V. D. Nabokov), Berlin Slovo, 1922, pp. 202, 204, 211, 223, 225, 227.

[1616] Minister of Justice from 20 July 1916 to 2 January 1917. Executed by the Cheka in September 1918.

[1617] Time when the writing of this present volume was completed, and allusion to the state of Yeltsinian Russia.

or another, it is a government both pretentious and lame that leaves Russia abandoned to its destiny.

Educated by the Rubinstein case, the General Staff had the accounts of several banks checked. At the same time, an investigation was opened against the sugar producers of Kiev—Hepner, Tsekhanovski, Babushkin, and Dobry. They had obtained permission to export sugar to Persia; they had made massive shipments, but very little merchandise had been reported by the customs and had reached the Persian market; the rest of the sugar had "disappeared", but, according to some information, it had passed through Turkey—allied to Germany—and had been sold on the spot. At the same time, the price of sugar had suddenly risen in the regions of the South-West, where Russia's sugar industry was concentrated. The sugar deal was conducted in an atmosphere of rigour and intransigence, but the Batiushin commission did not carry out its investigation and forwarded the file to an investigative judge of Kiev, who began by expanding the accused, and then they found support alongside the throne.

As for the Batiushin Commission itself, its composition left much to be desired. Its ineffectiveness in investigating the Rubinstein case was highlighted by Senator Zavadski.[1618] In his memoirs, General Lukomski, a member of the Staff, recounts that one of the chief jurists of the commission, Colonel Rezanov, an indisputably competent man, was also found to be quite fond of menus, good restaurants, boozy dinners; another, Orlov, proved to be a renegade who worked in the secret police after 1917, then went to the Whites and, in emigration, would be marked by his provocative conduct. There were probably other shady figures on the committee who did not refuse bribes and had capitalised on the release of the detainees. Through a series of indiscriminate acts, the commission drew the attention of the Military Justice of Petrograd and senior officials of the Ministry of Justice.

However, there was not only the Staff to deal with the problem of speculators, in relation to the activities "of the Jews in general". On 9 January 1916, Acting Director of the Police Department, Kafafov, signed a classified defence directive, which was addressed to all provincial and city governors and all gendarmerie commands. But the "intelligence service" of public opinion soon discovered the secret, and a month later, on 10 February, when all business ceased, Chkheidze[1619] read out this document from the tribune of the Duma. And what could be read there was

---

[1618] S. V. *Zavadski*, Na velikom izlome (The Great Fracture), Archives of the Russian Revolution, 1923, t. 8, pp. 1922.

[1619] Menshevik leader, deputy to the third and fourth Dumas; In February 1917, president of the Petrograd Soviet. Emigrated in 1921, committed suicide in 1926.

not only that "the Jews make revolutionary propaganda", but that "in addition to their criminal activity of propaganda... they have set themselves two important objectives: to artificially raise the price of essential commodities and withdraw from circulation common currency"—they thus seek "to make the population lose confidence in the Russian currency", to spread the rumour that "the Russian government is bankrupt, that there is not enough metal to make coins." The purpose of all this, according to the bulletin, was "to obtain the abolition of the Pale of Settlement, because the Jews think that the present period is the most favourable to achieve their ends by maintaining the trouble in the country." The Department did not accompany these considerations with any concrete measure: it was simply "for information".[1620]

Here is the reaction of Milyukov: "The method of Rostopchin[1621] is used with the Jews—they are presented to an overexcited crowd, saying: they are the guilty, they are yours, do what you want with them."[1622]

During the same days, the police encircled the Moscow Stock Exchange, carried out identity checks among the operators and discovered seventy Jews in an illegal situation; a roundup of the same type took place in Odessa. And this also penetrated the Duma Chamber, causing a real cataclysm—what the Council of Ministers feared so much a year ago was happening: "In the current period, we can not tolerate within the Duma a debate on the Jewish question, a debate which could take on a dangerous form and serve as a pretext for the aggravation of conflicts between nationalities."[1623] But the debate really took place and lasted several months.

The most lively and passionate reaction to the bulletin of the Department was that of Shingaryov[1624]—he had no equal to communicate to his listeners all the indignation which aroused in his heart: "there is not an ignominy, not a turpitude which the State has not been guilty towards the Jew, it which is a Christian state... spreading calumny over a whole people without any foundation... Russian society will be able to cure its evils only when you will withdraw that thorn, this evil that gangrenes the life of the country—the persecution of nationalities... Yes, we hurt for our

---

[1620] Archives of the Russian Revolution, 1925, vol. 19, pp. 267–268.
[1621] Governor of Moscow at the beginning of the nineteenth century. It was long believed that he had set fire to the city when the French armed there in 1812. Father of the Countess of Segur.
[1622] Stenographic record of the debates of the Fourth Duma. 10 February 1916, p. 1312.
[1623] Archives of the Russian Revolution, 1926, t. 18, p. 49.
[1624] Andrei Shingaryov(1869 1918), Zemstvo doctor, leader of the Cadet party, will be Minister of Agriculture in the first Provisional Government, and Finance in the second. Slaughtered in his hospital bed on 18 January 1918.

government, we are ashamed of our State! The Russian army found itself without ammunition in Galicia—"and the Jews would be responsible for it?" "As for the rise in prices, there are many complex reasons for this... Why, in this case, does the bulletin mention only the Jews, why does it not speak of the Russians and even others?"

Indeed, prices had soared all over Russia. And the same goes for the disappearance of coins. "And it is in a bulletin of the Department of Police that one can read all this!"[1625]

Nothing to object.

Easy to write a bulletin in the back of an office, but very unpleasant to respond to a raging Parliament. Yet this was what its author, Kafafov, had to resolve. He defended himself: the bulletin did not contain any directive, it was not addressed to the population, but to local authorities, for information and not for action; it aroused passions only after being sold by "timorous" civil servants and made public from the rostrum. How strange, continued Kafafov: we are not talking here of other confidential bulletins which have also, probably, been leaked; thus, as early as May 1915, he had himself initialled one of this order:

"There is a rise in hatred towards Jews in certain categories of the population of the Empire", and the Department "demands that the most energetic measures be taken in order to prevent any demonstration going in this direction", any act of violence of the population directed against the Jews, "to take the most vigorous measures to stifle in the bud the propaganda that begins to develop in certain places, to prevent it from leading to outbreaks of pogroms." And even, a month earlier, at the beginning of February, this directive sent to Poltava: reinforce surveillance so as to "be able to prevent in time any attempt to pogrom against the Jews."[1626]

And to complain: how is it that that bulletins such as *these* do not interest public opinion, that, those, they are allowed to pass in the utmost silence?

In his heated speech, Shingaryov immediately warned the Duma against the danger of "engaging in debates on the boundless ocean of the Jewish question."

But that was what happened because of the publicity reserved for this bulletin. Moreover, Shingaryov himself pushed clumsily in this direction, abandoning the ground for the defence of the Jews to declare that the real

---

[1625] Stenographic Record of the Debates of the Fourth Duma, 8 March 1916, pp. 3037–3040.
[1626] *Ibidem*, pp. 3137-3141.

traitors were the Russians: Sukhomlinov[1627], Myasoedov, and General Grigoriev, who had shamefully capitulated at Kovno.[1628]

This provoked a reaction. Markov[1629] objected that he had no right to speak of Sukhomlinov, the latter being for the moment only accused. (The Progressive Bloc was successful in the Sukhomlinov affair, but at the end of the Provisional Government, it itself had to admit that time had been wasted, that there had been no treason there.) Myasoedov had already been convicted and executed (but some facts may suggest that it was also a fabricated affair); Markov limited himself to adding that "he had been hanged in the company of six Jewish spies" (what I did not know: Myasoedov had been judged alone) and that, here is one to six, that was the report.[1630]

Among certain proposals contained in the programme that the Progressive Bloc had succeeded in putting together in August 1915, "the autonomy of Poland" seemed somewhat fantastical insofar as it was entirely in the hands of the Germans; "the equality of rights for peasants" did not have to be demanded of the government, because Stolypin had made it happen and it was precisely the Duma which did not endorse it, positing precisely as a condition the simultaneous equality of the Jews; so much so that "the gradual introduction of a process of reducing the limitations of rights imposed on Jews"—even though the evasiveness of this formulation was obvious—nevertheless became the main proposal of the programme of the Bloc. The latter included Jewish deputies [1631] and the Yiddish press reported: "The Jewish community wishes the Progressive Bloc a good wind!"

And now, after two years of an exhausting war, heavy losses on the front and a feverish agitation in the rear, the extreme right waved its admonitions:

"You have understood that you must explain yourself before the people over your silence about the military superiority of the Germans, your silence about the fight against the soaring prices, and your excessive zeal to want to grant equal rights to the Jews!" That is what you are demanding

---

[1627] Minister of War ineffective from 1909 to 1915, arrested on 3 May 1916, released in November through Rasputin.
[1628] *Ibidem*, pp. 3036-3037.
[1629] Nikolai Markov (1876–1945), called at the Duma "Markov-II" to distinguish him from homonyms. Leader of the extreme right. In November 1918, he went to Finland, then to Berlin and Paris where he directed a monarchist revue, The Two Headed Eagle. He moved to Germany in 1936, where he directed an anti-Semitic publication in Russian. Died in Wiesbaden.
[1630] *Ibidem*, p. 5064.
[1631] SJE, t. 7, p. 359.

"of the government, at the present moment, in the midst of war,—and if it does not meet these demands you blow it off and recognise only one government, the one that will give equality to the Jews!" But "we are surely not going to give equality now, just now that everyone is white-hot against the Jews; in doing so, you only raise public opinion against these unfortunates."[1632]

Deputy Friedman refutes the claim that the people are at the height of exasperation: "In the tragic context of the oppression of the Jews, however, there is a glimmer of hope, and I do not want to ignore it: it is the attitude of the Russian populations of the interior provinces towards the Jewish refugees who arrive there." These Jewish refugees "receive help and hospitality". It is "the pledge of our future, our fusion with the Russian people." But he insists that the responsibility for all the misfortunes of the Jews rests with the government, and he lays his accusations at the highest level: "There was never a pogrom when the government did not want it." Through the members of the Duma, "I am addressing the 170 million inhabitants of Russia…: they want to use your hands to lift the knife on the Jewish people of Russia!"[1633]

To this was replied: do the deputies of the Duma only know what is thought of in the country? "The country does not write in Jewish newspapers, the country suffers, works… it is bogged down in the trenches, it is there, the country, and not in the Jewish newspapers where work John Does obeying mysterious guidelines." It was even said, "That the press is controlled by the government is an evil, but there is an even greater evil: that the press is controlled by the enemies of the Russian State!"[1634]

As Shingaryov had sensed, the liberal majority of the Duma was, now, no longer interested in prolonging the debate on the Jewish question. But the process was on and nothing could stop it. And it was a never-ending series of speeches that came in the middle of the other cases to be dealt with for four months until the end of the fall session.

The right accused the Progressive Bloc: no, the Duma was not going to tackle the problem of rising prices! "You are not going to fight with the banks, the unions, against strikes in the industry, because that would be tantamount to fighting against the Jews." Meanwhile, the Reformist Municipality of Petrograd "gave the town supply to two Israelites, Levenson and Lesman: the first the meat supply, the second the food

---

[1632] Stenographic Record of the Debates of the Fourth Duma, February 1916, p. 1456 and 28-29 February 1916, p. 2471.
[1633] *Ibidem*, pp. 1413-1414, 1421, 1422.
[1634] *Ibidem*, pp. 1453-1454, 2477.

shops—although he had illegally sold flour to Finland. Other examples of suppliers artificially inflating prices are given.[1635]

(None of the deputies took it upon himself to defend these speculators.) After that, it is impossible that the question not come up for discussion, so current during these years of war, of the *numerus clausus*! As we have seen, it had been re-established after the revolution of 1905, but was gradually mitigated by the common practice of day school in high schools and the authorisation given to Jews who had completed their medical studies abroad to pass the State diploma in Russia; other measures were taken in this direction—but not the abrogation pure and simple—in 1915, when the Pale of Settlement was abolished. P. N. Ignatiev, Minister of Public Instruction in 1915–1916, also reduced the *numerus clausus* in higher education institutions.

And in the spring of 1916, the walls of the Duma echoed the debate on this issue at length. The statistics of the Ministry of Education are examined, and Professor Levachev, deputy of Odessa, states that the provisions of the Council of Ministers (authorising the derogatory admission of children of Jews called up for military service) have been arbitrarily extended by the Ministry of Education to the children of Zemgor employees, evacuation agencies, hospitals, as well as persons declaring themselves [deceitfully] dependent on a parent called up for military service. Thus, of the 586 students admitted in 1915 in the first year of medicine at the University of Odessa, "391 are Jews", that is to say two thirds, and that "only one third remain for the other nationalities." At the University of Rostov-on-Don: 81% of Jewish students at the Faculty of Law, 56% at the Faculty of Medicine, and 54% at the Faculty of Sciences.[1636]

Gurevich replies to Levachev: this is proof that the *numerus clausus* is useless! "What is the use of the *numerus clausus*, when even this year, when the Jews benefited from a higher than normal arrangement, there was enough room to welcome all Christians who wanted to enter the university?" What do you want—empty classrooms? Little Germany has a large number of Jewish teachers, yet it does not die of it![1637]

Markov's objection: "Universities are empty [because Russian students are at war, and they send [to the universities] masses of Jews." "Escaping military service," the Jews "have overwhelmed the University of Petrograd and, thanks to that, will swell the ranks of the Russian intelligentsia… This phenomenon…

[1635] *Ibidem*, p. 4518.
[1636] *Ibidem*, pp. 3360-3363.
[1637] *Ibidem*, p. 3392.

is detrimental to the Russian people, even destructive," because every people "is subject to the power of its intelligentsia." "The Russians must protect their elites, their intelligentsia, their officials, their government; the latter must be Russian."[1638]

Six months later, in the autumn of 1916, Friedman harped on about this by asking the Duma the following question: "Thus it would be better for our universities to remain empty... it would be better for Russia to find itself without an intellectual elite rather than admit Jews in too great numbers?"[1639]

On the one hand, Gurevitch was obviously right: why should the classrooms have been left empty? Let each one do what he has to do. But, in asking the question in these terms, did he not comfort the suspicions and bitterness of the right: therefore, we do not work *together*? One group to make war, the other to study?

(My father, for example—he interrupted his studies at Moscow University and joined the army as a volunteer. It seemed at the time that there was no alternative: to not go to the front would have been dishonourable. Who, among these young Russian volunteers, and even among the professors who remained in the universities, understood that the future of the country was not only played on the battlefields? No one understood it neither in Russia, nor in Europe.) In the spring of 1916, the debate on the Jewish question was suspended on the grounds that it provoked undesirable agitation in public opinion. But the problem of nationalities was put back on the agenda by an amendment to the law on township Zemstvos. The creation of this new administrative structure was discussed during the winter of 1916-17 during the last months of the existence of the Duma. And then one fine day, when the main speakers had gone for refreshments or had returned to their penates, and that there was little left for the sitting than half of the well-behaved deputies, a peasant of Viatka, named Tarassov, managed to sneak into the tribune. Timidly, he spoke, striving to make the members of the house understand the problem of the amendment: it provides that "everyone is admitted, and the Jews, that is, and the Germans, all those who will come to our township. And to those, what will be their rights?

These people who are going to be registered [in our township]... but they are going to take places, and the peasants, no one takes care of them... If it is a Jew who runs the township administration and his wife who is secretary, then the peasants, them, what are their rights?... What is going to happen, where will the peasants be?... And when our valiant warriors

---

[1638] *Ibidem*, pp. 1456, 3421, 5065.
[1639] *Ibidem*, p. 90.

return, what will they be entitled to? To stay in the back; but during the war, it was on the front line that they were, the peasants... Do not make amendments that contradict the practical reality of the peasant life, do not give the right to the Jews and the Germans to participate in the elections of the township zemstvos, for they are peoples who will bring nothing useful; on the contrary, they will greatly harm and there will be disorders across the country. We peasants, we are not going to submit to these nationalities."[1640]

But in the meantime, the campaign for equal rights for Jews was in full swing. It now enjoyed the support of organisations that had not previously been concerned with the issue, such as the Gvozdev Central Workers' Group[1641], which represented the interests of the Russian proletariat. In the spring of 1916, the Workers' Group claimed to be informed that "the reaction [implied: the government and administration of the Ministry of the Interior] is openly preparing a pogrom against the Jews throughout Russia". And Kozma Gvozdev repeated this nonsense at the Congress of Military-Industrial Committees.—In March 1916, in a letter to Rodzianko[1642], the Workers' Group protested against the suspension of the debate on the Jewish question in the Duma; And the same Group accused the Duma itself of complacency towards the anti-Semites: "The attitude of the majority at the meeting of 10 March is *de facto* to give its direct support and to reinforce the policy of anti-Jewish pogroms led by the power...

By its support of the militant anti-Semitism of the ruling circles, the majority in the Duma is a serious blow to the work of national defence."[1643] (They had not agreed, they had not realised that in the Duma it was precisely the left who needed to end the debate.)—The workers also benefited from the support of "Jewish groups" who, according to a report by the Security Department in October 1916, "have overwhelmed the capital and, without belonging to any party, are pursuing a policy violently hostile to the power."[1644]

[1640] *Ibidem*, pp. 1069-1071.
[1641] Also said Kouzma Gvozdiov (born in 1883), a worker, a Menshevik leader, a defender, president of the Central Workers' Group; After February, member of the Central Executive Committee of the Petrograd Soviet, Minister of Labour of the Fourth Provisional Government. In camp or in prison from 1930 onwards.
[1642] President of the Duma from 1911 to 1917.
[1643] K istorii gvosdevchtchiny (Contribution to the history of the Gvozdev movement), Krasny arkhiv. 1934, t. 67, p. 52.
[1644] Politikchkoye polojenie Rossii nakanoune Fevralskoi revolioutsii (Political situation in Russia on the eve of the February Revolution), Krasny arkhiv, 1926, t. 17, p. 14.

And the power in all this? Without direct evidence, it can be assumed that within the ministerial teams that succeeded each other in 1916, the decision to proclaim equal rights for the Jews was seriously considered. This had been mentioned more than once by Protopopov, who had already succeeded, it seems, in turning Nicholas II in this direction. (Protopopov also had an interest in going quickly to cut short the campaign that the left had set in motion against him.)—And General Globachev, who was the last to direct the Department of Security before the revolution, writes in his memoirs, in the words of Dobrovolsky, who was also the last Minister of Justice of the monarchy: "The bill on equal rights for the Jews was already ready [in the months that preceded the revolution] and, in all likelihood, the law would have been promulgated for the 1917 Easter celebrations."[1645]

But in 1917, the Easter celebrations were to take place under a completely different system. The ardent aspirations of our radicals and liberals would then have come true.

"Everything for victory!"—Yes, but "not with that power!" Public opinion, both among the Russians and among the Jews, as well as the press, all were entirely directed towards Victory, were the first to claim it,—only, *not with this government! Not with this tsar!* All were still persuaded of the correctness of the simple and brilliant reasoning they had held at the beginning of the war: before it ends (because afterwards it would be more difficult) and by winning a victory over victory on the Germans, to throw down the tsar and change the political regime.

And that is when the equal rights for the Jews would come.

We have examined in many ways the circumstances in which took place one hundred and twenty years of common life between Russians and Jews within the same State. Among the difficulties, some have found a solution over time, others emerged and increased in the course of the years prior to the spring of 1917. But the evolving nature of the processes in motion visibly taking over and promised a constructive future.

And it was at that moment that a blast disintegrated the political and social system of Russia—and thus the fruits of evolution, but also the military resistance to the enemy, paid for with so much blood, and finally the prospects for a future of fulfilment: it was the revolution of February.

[1645] K. I. *Globatchev*, Pravda o russkoï revolutionsii: Vospominania byvchevo Nachalnika Petrogradskovo Okhrannovo Otdelenia. Dekabr 1922 (The truth about the Russian revolution: memoirs of the former head of the Petrograd Security Department, December 1922), Khranenie Koloumbiïskovo ouniversiteta, machinopis, p. 41.

Other titles

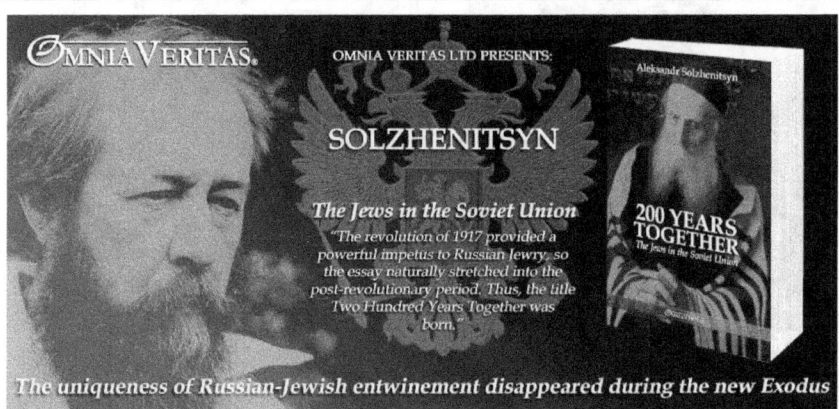

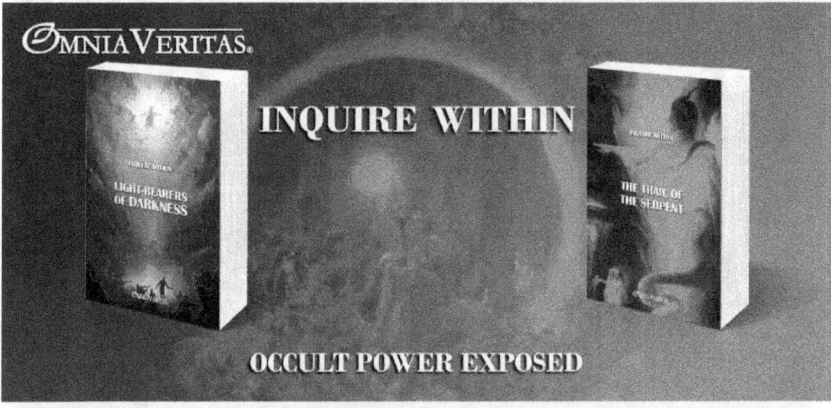

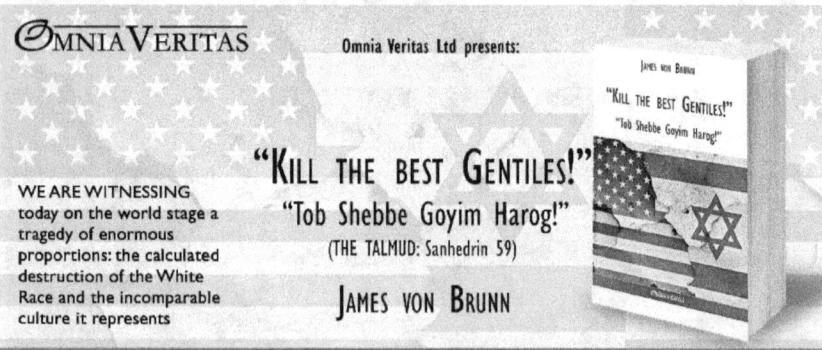

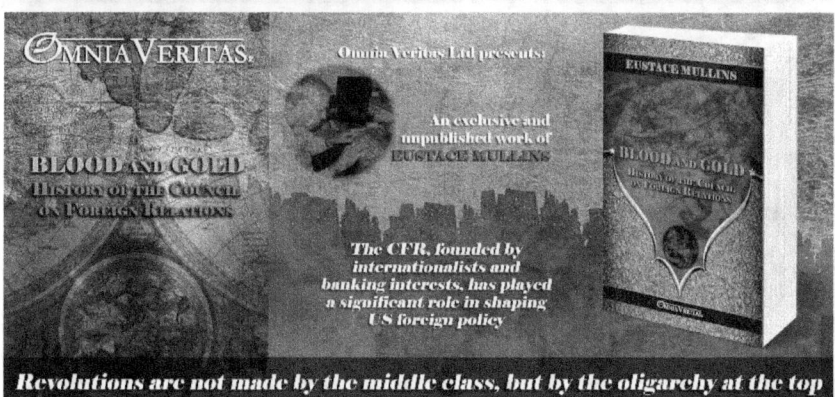

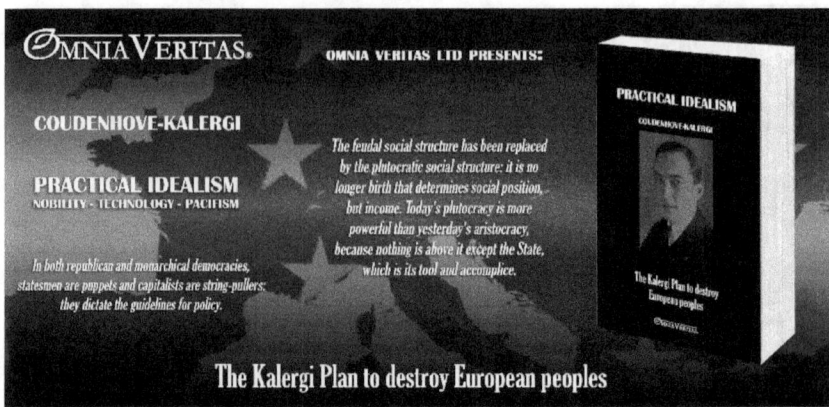

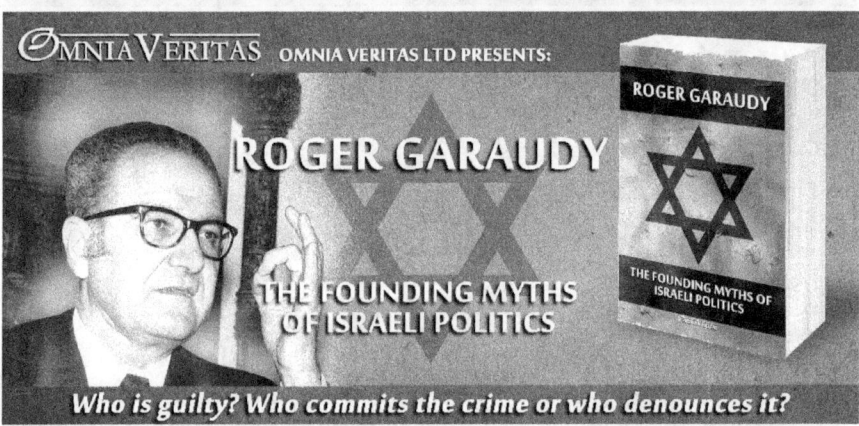
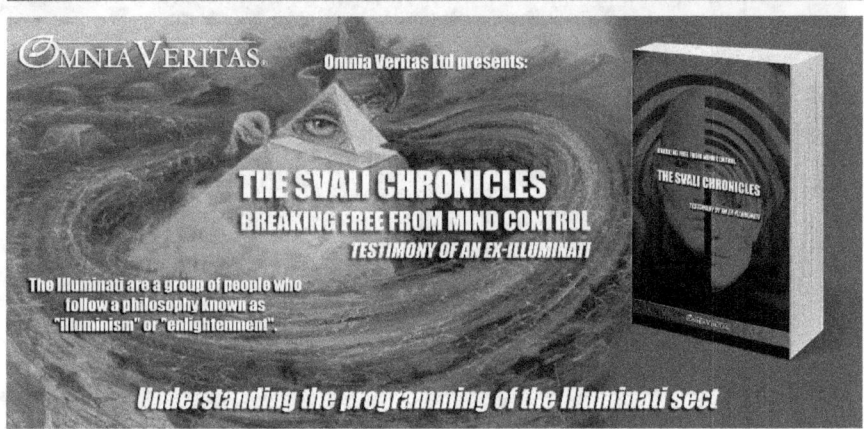

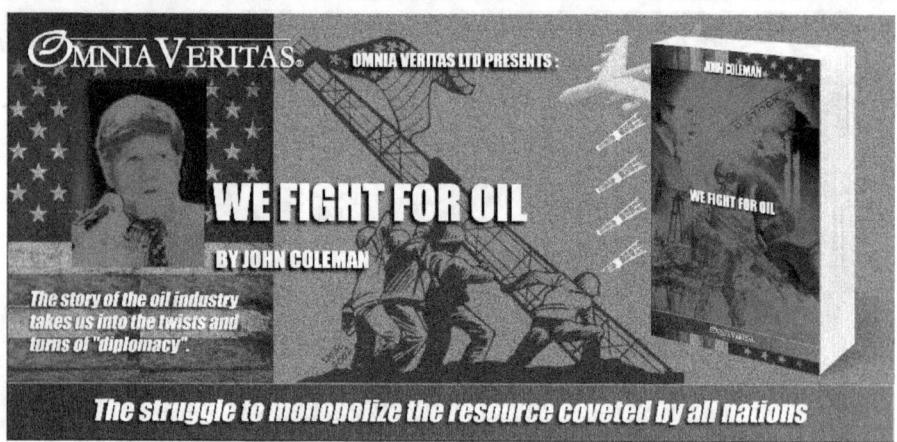

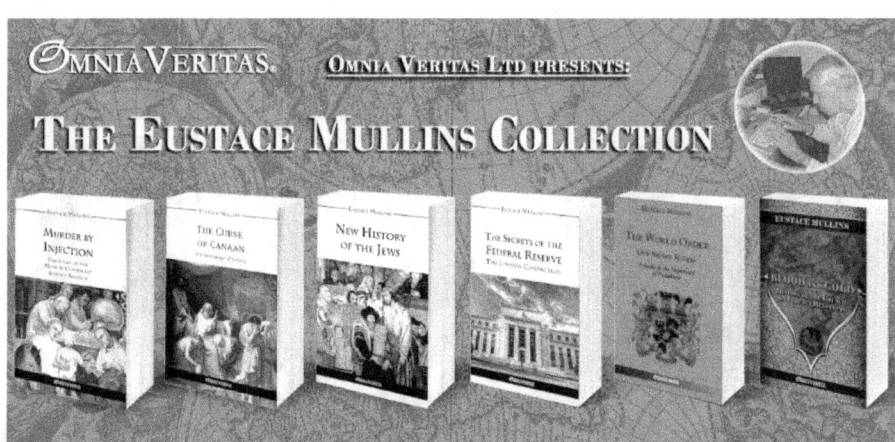

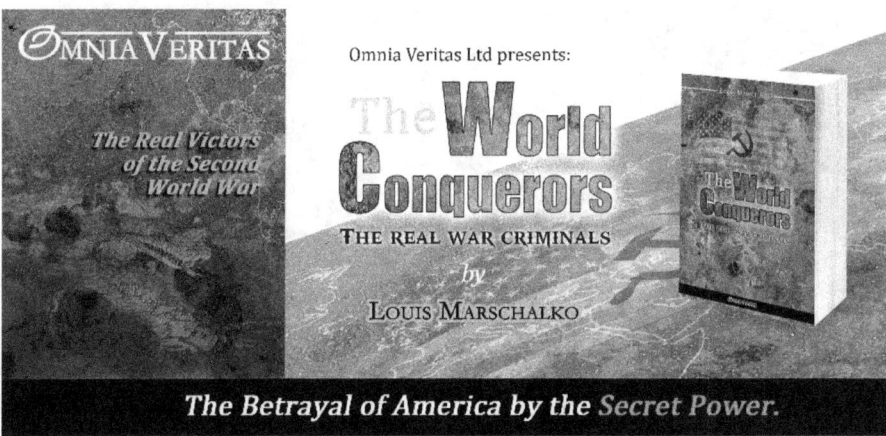

www.ingramcontent.com/pod-product-compliance
Lightning Source LLC
Chambersburg PA
CBHW050323230426
43663CB00010B/1717